For Mena –

Eat well and live your dreams !

[signature]
+ Christmastide 2013

[signature] Savannah

Essentials of

SOUTHERN COOKING

TECHNIQUES AND FLAVORS OF A CLASSIC
AMERICAN CUISINE

DAMON LEE FOWLER

LYONS PRESS
Guilford, Connecticut
An imprint of Globe Pequot Press

Lyons Press is an imprint of Globe Pequot Press.

Recipes in this book were previously published in *Damon Lee Fowler's New Southern Kitchen* and *Damon Lee Fowler's New Southern Baking*.

Editor: Amy Lyons
Project editor: Ellen Urban
Text design and layout: Nancy Freeborn

Photography by Damon Lee Fowler: 27, 42, 51, 63, 67, 71, 85, 89, 95, 143, 145, 156, 197, 201, 208, 211, 215, 230, 240, 243, 261, 279, 387, 391. Photography by Ron Manville with styling by Sarah-Jane Bedwell: viii, 45, 54, 114, 127, 153, 175, 179, 195, 199, 214, 219, 237, 239, 247, 257, 307, 317, 346, 351, 395, 397. Photo Courtesy of John Carrington: 124. Photography Licensed by Shutterstock.com: iii, 6, 14-15, 17, 19, 21, 25, 29, 33, 35, 36, 39, 47, 49, 57, 60, 77. 82, 87, 101, 102, 106, 120, 123, 129, 135, 149, 158, 161, 163, 165, 189, 222, 225, 227, 228, 231, 233, 235, 245, 249, 250, 259, 264, 269, 271, 273, 274, 299, 301, 302, 308, 313, 323, 324, 327, 331, 333, 341, 342, 343, 345, 355, 362, 371, 378, 383, 385, 388, 402, 404, 407.

Library of Congress Cataloging-in-Publication data is available on file.

ISBN 978-0-7627-9222-1

Printed in the United States of America

10 9 8 7 6 5 4 3 2 1

For my parents.

And as always, for Tim.

In memory of the incomparable Marcella Hazan

ABOUT THE AUTHOR

Damon Lee Fowler is a culinary historian, food writer, and the author of a number of cookbooks, including *Classical Southern Cooking, Fried Chicken: The World's Best Recipes, Savannah Chef's Table,* and *The Savannah Cookbook.* His work has appeared in a number of national publications, including *Bon Appétit, Food & Wine,* and *Relish.* He lives, eats, and writes in Savannah, Georgia, where he is the featured food writer for the *Savannah Morning News.*

CONTENTS

PREFACE

On a cold, bleak December night that perfectly mirrored our feelings, my scattered family converged on Charleston to be with my younger brother as he faced surgery for cancer. We were all bone-tired, worried, and, needless to say, food was the last thing on our minds.

Everyone else was at a hotel, but I, unable to face what lay ahead in such an impersonal atmosphere, had called my friend and mentor Nathalie Dupree. She immediately insisted that I come and stay at the cozy Queen Street single house that she and her husband, Jack Bass, are suffered to share by Minou, the fat, lazy cat who really owns the place. They had dinner obligations and had gone out, but Nathalie promised that supper would be waiting even though she knew I didn't feel like eating.

Sure enough, her wonderfully crowded, sun-yellow kitchen was filled with the rich aroma of a still-warm casserole of shrimp and grits. The room's bright color reminded me so much of my grandmother's kitchen from my early childhood that just sitting down at the small table by the fireplace was a comfort. With the happy jumble of a cook's kitchen added in (there were at least six pepper mills, an enormous bottle of bourbon stuffed to its neck with vanilla beans, and a china butter dish scattered amid stacks of blue enameled iron and weathered copper cookware), not to mention the unmistakable essence of a beloved friend and mentor, it was exactly where I needed to be.

As the distinctive flavor of the season's last fresh shrimp, simply seasoned and folded into rich, creamy cheese grits, met my tongue, my appetite revived and some of the dull ache of uncertainty eased. It was not the same as having Nathalie take my hand and tell me that everything would be all right, but it was close.

My life as a writing cook has been touched by many people, and I treasure all those friendships, especially the many other Southern writers who have undertaken to champion our regional cuisine in cookbooks and other publications. But Nathalie has been the big sister I never had, a constant touchstone in my life, the colleague and friend I turn to in joy and in trouble. We don't always agree; in fact, part of what I treasure about her friendship is that she loves it when we do disagree, because that means we're going to have a great time arguing and will probably both come away from it all the wiser, even (and especially) when we never find common ground. I cannot imagine my life without her, and whatever merit my work might have owes a good deal to her.

When I think back on that moment in her kitchen, and reflect on a lifetime of writing about moments like it, I realize that there's something in the times we share over food that stays with us. I remember another evening in that same kitchen, when Nathalie whipped up a batch of apples in caramel cream for a friend who had been cheated out of dessert at a banquet. I remember sitting down with my mother to a steaming bowl of vegetable soup and hot corn bread after a long, tiring drive. I remember sharing dreams, laughter, and tears over an all-the-way chili dog with fellow author Ronni Lundy. These moments leave their mark even when the food itself is not memorable: I still fondly recall laughing with Southern writer John Shelton Reed and his wife, Dale, over a much-anticipated meal that had turned out to be so pretentious and deeply unsatisfying that it left us wishing we'd just settled for a pizza at the place where we stopped for iced tea on the way.

What I hope to have accomplished on the pages that follow is that they will inspire you to go into your own kitchen and make not just memories, but good ones that will stay with you and with those for whom you cook. Keep in mind that they will probably not remember how you set the table; they will almost certainly not recall how clever or inventive you have been; what they will remember is how it tasted—and how much care you took in making a meal for them, even when you aren't actually sitting with them.

After all, physical hunger is only a small part of what we hope to satisfy when we gather around the table.

Damon Lee Fowler
Savannah ~ June 2013

INTRODUCTION

A Southern Kitchen

The American South is a land famous for its sharp contrasts, glaring contradictions, and great eccentrics. To begin to understand it, you must first understand that Southerners don't see those facts as handicaps, but as points of pride. When Southern humorist Florence King observed, "Build a fence around the South and you'd have one big madhouse," it wasn't a criticism: The greatest compliment one Southerner can pay another is to call them eccentric. We might put on a show of being affronted, but somewhere deep inside, we're thinking, Why, thank you!

Possibly the only other place on earth with as many sharp contrasts, glaring contradictions, and great eccentrics is Italy, which is probably why this Southern boy immediately felt at home when he first went there as an impressionable young architecture student. Southerners get along in Italy because we relate to Italians on a gut level: We understand *domani mattina*; we know it doesn't really mean "tomorrow morning." At any rate, it didn't take any time for me fall in love with the country, its people, and, most of all, its cooking.

Given all that, it will not, perhaps, seem at all improbable that one of my earliest and greatest mentors when I started writing about Southern cooking was an Italian. After I came home I literally stumbled onto Marcella Hazan's groundbreaking books *The Classic Italian Cook Book* and *More Classic Italian Cooking*. They very quickly became my kitchen bibles, and ever since, Marcella has been a quiet, guiding hand in my life as a cook, at first only from the pages of those books, but later as a real mentor and friend. While I wouldn't call that friendship intimate, and my direct study with her consisted of a single afternoon in my own kitchen more than twenty years ago, her culinary voice has been with me in my kitchen for the whole of my adult life—sharing equal footing with (and at times even overriding) those of my mother and maternal grandmother.

Through all those years, one of the things that I've come to realize is that her voice resonated not because it was different from Mama's and MaMa's but, once one got past accents, because it was essentially the same. There's a common culinary language of shared ingredients, techniques, and flavors, but it goes much deeper than that. The key to grasping it can be found in Marcella's arresting opening to *The Classic Italian Cook Book*: "The first useful thing to know about Italian cooking is that, as such, it actually doesn't exist."

She goes on to explain that the Italian peninsula is a study in contrasts. From its chilly Alpine north, through its fertile central plains, to the warm, rocky landscape of its southern tip, the terrain and climate change drastically. More significantly, until Garibaldi's unification in the nineteenth century, Italy had not been under a single government since the fall of the Roman Empire. For more than a thousand years it was divided into a patchwork of fiercely independent, and often hostile, city-states. In short, while it's not a very large country, the Italy we know today was forged from a confederation of many smaller countries, each with its own culture, language, and cooking. There are places in Italy where factory pasta and pizza did not exist until very recent times. The thing we loosely call "Italian cooking" is therefore not a single cuisine, but a collection of many.

All that is why Italy resonates with Southerners: The particulars are a little different, and the time line is compressed into centuries rather than millennia, but the same exact things can be said of the South. After a lifetime of living with, cooking, and eating this elusive thing we call "Southern cooking," and more than twenty-five years of writing about it, the one thing I can say of it with any certainty is that "as such, it actually doesn't exist."

The South is also a study in contrasts, amplified by its sheer size, which is more than five times that of the Italian peninsula. Until the Civil War ended arguments over the nature of our central government, the Southern region was composed of a loose confederation of more than a dozen states that more or less saw themselves as independent. Though bound together by common economic interests and therefore never as hostile toward one another as were those Italian city-states, each had its own culture, dialect, and cooking styles. And that's without factoring in the social divisions and harsh undercurrents of racial and ethnic tensions that were the ugly fallout of more than two centuries of legal slavery and another century of legal segregation.

The startling contrasts of climate and terrain that divide Italy also divide the South, not just across the states but also within them. Except for Texas and Louisiana, which are cases all to themselves, and the interior states (Tennessee, Kentucky, West Virginia, and Arkansas), which have their own divisions, each state from Maryland to Mississippi has rugged mountains, fertile central plains, and balmy coastline. The part of the South where I was born and raised was the rolling, red-clay hills of upstate Georgia and South Carolina; the part of the South where I have lived the lion's share of my adult life is the capital of Georgia's moss-draped, marsh-laced Lowcountry, a place of black, sandy soil as flat and regular as a tabletop. Though the distance between them is barely three hundred miles, their climatic, terrestrial, and cultural differences could not be sharper if they were separated by the Atlantic Ocean.

In short, the South is a complicated patchwork; to suppose that it could be united in a single cuisine would be simplistic if not downright naive. It cannot be summed up (as has so often been attempted) in a glass of sweet tea, bunful of pulled pork, and platter of fried chicken any more than one could sum Italian cooking with a glass of Chianti, slice of pizza, and platter of marinara-topped spaghetti.

But just as there's a great deal of common ground among the many cuisines of Italy, things that make its thousands of regional wines, cheese-topped flatbreads, and platters of pasta recognizably Italian, there's a great deal of common ground in the regional cuisines of the South, things that make sweet tea, barbecued pig, and fried chicken recognizably Southern to the extent that they've become stereotypical icons and unifying elements on our table.

Most of that common ground lies in the fact that all the cuisines under the Southern cooking blanket, from the exuberant Cajun cookery of the Louisiana Bayou, to the forthright, humble fare of Appalachia, to the refined, seafood-enriched, rice-based cuisine of the Carolina and Georgia Lowcountry, have come out of home kitchens. These foundations were not created in a moment, and despite the posturing of some professionals, have nothing to do with restaurant cooking, but have evolved organically over the centuries, sustained and nourished by simple techniques and remembered flavors that have passed from generation to generation—mother to daughter, father to son.

The other key factor is that the South has traditionally been an agrarian economy, so its cuisines have remained close to the land, even when radical, massive urbanization in the last quarter of the twentieth century swept across its pastoral landscape like Sherman's army. The farm-to-table movement that has become the fashion among our professional chefs is nothing new to Southern home cooks. The farmers' markets that have sprouted in the South's urban centers, once again making local, freshly harvested produce readily accessible to those without the luxury of a garden plot or so much as a gardening relative, are not a new idea, but a welcome return to an old one.

All that is why, until recently, these cuisines have remained singular and territorial, and why they remain grounded in the face of a flood of new ideas and ingredients unleashed by our age of mass media and by new immigrants to the South. As the cooking continues to evolve and territorial lines soften and blur, even (and especially) in a professional setting, the things that adapt and endure are those that remain close to the land and rooted to the ageless patterns that have been a part of our home kitchens for more than three centuries.

That is where I see the closest kinship between the cooking of Italy and the South. Both these complex collections of cuisines resonate with so many people because they are firmly rooted to the land and grounded by the home kitchens from which they have sprung. This cooking comes from people who have a comfortable sense of who they are and what they are about in the kitchen. We have no interest in being fashionable, trendy, or clever. Even better, we have no interest in "reinventing" anything. When we embrace a new ingredient, technique, or dish, it's because it rings true to the traditions passed down by our ancestors.

I wish I could say that I came to that place of comfort on my own, but I didn't. It took Marcella and Italian cooking to give me that. I'd thought that the keen self-awareness and comfortable sense of identity that had drawn me to Italian cooking had done so because it was generally lacking in Southerners. But as it turns out, they were mainly lacking in just one Southerner—me. The more I learned of the patterns of Italian kitchens, the more I began to respect and revere the patterns of my own culinary heritage. That is why Italian cooking is a common theme here on these pages and throughout these recipes: It's what brought me home to my Southern kitchen.

One of the proudest moments in my life was the afternoon that I picked up the telephone to hear Marcella's voice saying, "I am so proud of you." She was not talking about my mastery of the fluffy egg pasta that I teach in my cooking classes or the pesto alla Genovese or spaghetti alla carbonara that are as routine in my home kitchen as shrimp and grits. I would hope that she's proud of what she has taught me about her native cooking, and that I do her justice whenever I teach an Italian dish. But in that moment, her pride was for what she had taught me about embracing and celebrating my own heritage.

There will be those who read this and see absolutely no connection between Italy and the South, who will perhaps think that I'm merely playing an angle or have become more eccentric than even a Southerner ought to be. It doesn't matter. All cookbooks are personal: Each of us who undertakes to share what we know about cooking carries with us a legion of voices and teachers who have shaped our kitchen patterns, but in the end the experience we bring to the pot is singular and unique. What follows here is what I know of this complicated jigsaw puzzle that we call Southern cooking. And what I know of it has been inextricably woven with what I know of Italian cooking. You don't have to agree or disagree with that fact, but what I do hope is that you'll take what I've shared here into your own kitchen, cook it, savor it, and let a little of my Southern kitchen become a part of yours.

A SOUTHERN PANTRY

Pantry is such a snug, old-fashioned word, conjuring for most of us images of neat rows of amber, red, gold, and green homemade conserves sparkling like jewels; barrels of flour and cornmeal; fragrant hams hanging from the ceiling; and strings of dried beans, okra, and herb bundles draped like Christmas garland. Nowadays, it exists only in our imaginations: Most of us today have never actually seen such a wonder. Indeed, our "pantry" may not be a room at all, but little more than one or two cabinet shelves. Yet that old-fashioned image, however archaic, remains firmly fixed in most of our minds, and actually, when we begin sorting through them, we realize that our one or two shelves still hold essentials that have not changed in four centuries.

Giving Your Pantry a Southern Accent

No matter how much or how little things change, the one thing that historians, students of social patterns, and home cooks will all agree on is that the language of Southern cooking—like the languid spoken language that rolls off a Southern tongue—is derivative. It's a language of flavors gleaned from Africa, Native America, England, France, Spain, and Asia, and its accent varies subtly from region to region and often even from community to community. The comforting thing for us is that despite its far-flung origins, none of that flavor vocabulary is exotic or hard to come by. Just as you can turn your accent into a Southern one by slowing it down and subtly changing its inflection, adding a few idioms here and there along with a touch of attitude, turning the average pantry into a Southern one is a matter of adding a little attitude and a few key elements. What follows are a few of those key elements that you'll absolutely need. This is by no means comprehensive; some essentials are so particular to a recipe or technique that they're discussed with the recipe in which they are used.

The attitude you'll just have to develop yourself.

Flavor Bases, Prepared Condiments, and Conserves

Broth

Good broth is the foundation on which virtually every great cuisine in the world is built. When I was an architecture student, our design professors didn't spend much time on the foundations of buildings. Occasionally, one who could think of nothing else to criticize would make a point of a structure that looked insubstantial, but for the most part, the attitude was "leave all that stuff to the engineers." Far too many good cooks are willing to do the same with their cooking, never thinking much about the broth they use. Yet, just as the most beautiful building has no substance without a solid foundation, so it is with cooking. Bad broth will undermine the best soup or stew and weaken it.

That is not to say that good cooking doesn't allow for shortcuts. There are times when having a process already completed, particularly a time-consuming one such as puff pastry, can be a blessing, if not an outright lifesaver. But too many good cooks take for granted that commercially prepared broth is one shortcut that is always safe. I remember reading a survey of packaged chicken broth in which the author chastised cranks like me, asserting that there wasn't a cook left in the country who routinely made his or her own and we all should stop pretending otherwise. Well, at the risk of sounding like my Baptist-preacher father, "everyone is doing it" is an excuse, not a justification.

All that said, we don't live in an ideal world where every cook in the country can always have a stockpot on the back of the stove. For many recipes, there's nothing wrong with using packaged broth. Some frozen ones may even be as good as most people would make themselves, and for some of us, storing quantities of homemade broth is not always feasible. Most cooks (me included) occasionally resort to a can. The gourmet-food police aren't going to come break down your door and carry you away. With care and good judgment on your part, the results will be just fine.

But it doesn't follow that packaged broth is always desirable, and there are times when homemade broth is the difference between a good dish and a great one. From all the fuss, you'd think that broth making was difficult. But it's just about the easiest task in the kitchen, and its rewards are large.

Doctoring Store-Bought Broth

Here are a few tips on getting the most from it when you resort to purchased broth. First, look at the label before buying: The first ingredient (after water) should be chicken or beef, or, if water isn't listed, chicken or beef stock. If salt comes first or if the meat is followed by the words "bouillon powder," pass it by. You'd be as well off to use a bouillon cube. Also avoid broth containing monosodium glutamate (MSG). Not only is it a cheap way of boosting the flavor of a weak broth, it often lends a harsh aftertaste, and many people are sensitive to it.

Some of the recipes for this book indicate that canned broth can be used if it is diluted half and half with water even if the label says to use it full strength. There are two reasons for this: First, the broth is not the starring ingredient, it's there to underpin and boost the other flavors; second, there is often additional cooking involved in which the broth will be reduced and concentrated. If you don't dilute it, the result will taste tinny and often be too salty, even, oddly enough, when you've used a low-sodium broth.

Where the broth itself will be more pronounced in the finished recipe, canned broth will need more help than merely diluting it, and the recipe will call for doctored broth. Here's how to do that: For each 15- to 16-ounce can of broth, add an equal amount of water; 1 small yellow onion, thinly sliced; 1 clove garlic, mashed and peeled; 1 small carrot, peeled and thickly sliced; the leafy top from 1 rib celery; 1 large sprig parsley; and 1 quarter-sized slice ginger. Bring the broth to a boil over medium heat and simmer for at least 20 minutes. Depending on how you plan to use it, and whether you have them on hand, you may also add a sprig of parsley and thyme, the trimmings from a leek, half the peel of a medium tomato (if the broth is beef), or an extra carrot (if the broth is chicken).

Chicken Consommé

Consommé is broth that's enhanced and reduced until it's rich enough to jelly when chilled. The strained broth is simmered, often with fresh meat and other flavorings added, until it's concentrated and is then clarified. It's often served chilled and jellied. It can be a much more involved process than this, but for the recipe in this book that requires it, simply strain and degrease the broth and then simmer until it is reduced by 20-25 percent.

basic (beef, chicken, or pork) broth

When you do choose to make your own broth, here is the basic recipe for a truly good one. Use it to make any kind of broth you may need, chicken, beef, veal, or pork, varying the ingredients where noted depending on which meat is used. Happily, broth is at its best when made from scraps and trimmings, which are very inexpensive and even, at times, available from the butcher for the asking. You can freeze your own trimmings until you have enough for the stockpot, but make sure they are well wrapped and use them within 3 months: Freezer-burned scraps will result in a broth that tastes freezer-burned. When using fatty scraps, don't trim off the fat because it will help flavor the broth. The fat itself will be easily removed when the broth has been strained and chilled.

5 pounds meat scraps and bones (chicken, beef, veal, or pork, or a mixture of all)

2 large yellow onions, 1 peeled and thinly sliced, 1 peeled but left whole and stuck with 4 whole cloves (for veal, pork, or beef, use 3 onions, 2 sliced)

1 large carrot, peeled and thickly sliced (2 for chicken broth)

1 large rib celery, including the leafy top (2 for chicken broth)

1 large leek, split, thoroughly washed, and sliced, including the green top

3 to 4 large cloves garlic, lightly crushed and peeled but left whole

1 quarter-sized slice fresh ginger root (2 for chicken broth)

1 large sprig parsley with at least 3 inches of leafy stalk, or use leftover parsley stems

2 large sprigs fresh thyme (at least 3 inches long), or leftover thyme stems, or 1 teaspoon dried thyme tied in cheesecloth or placed in a stainless steel tea ball

2 bay leaves

8 whole black peppercorns

5 quarts water

Salt

1. Put all the ingredients into an 8–10 quart stockpot, adding a small handful of salt. Loosely cover and bring slowly to a simmer over low heat, about 30 to 45 minutes.

2. Adjust the heat so that the liquid simmers very slowly, the bubbles not quite breaking the surface. With the lid askew, let it simmer for a minimum of 2 hours, 3 or 4 will only improve it. For concentrated broth, leave the lid off. (You can interrupt the simmer at any point after the first hour, cool, cover, and refrigerate and finish it later.)

3. Turn off the heat and let the broth settle for 30 minutes. Strain it through a wire mesh strainer and let it cool completely. Cover and refrigerate until it's chilled and the fat on the surface is congealed. Lift off and discard the fat. The broth will keep for up to a week in the refrigerator and for up to 6 months if frozen in small portions.

Brown Beef or Pork Broth: For added depth of color in beef or pork broth, brown the bones and scraps before using them. Position a rack in the upper third of the oven and preheat to 450°F. Spread the bones and scraps on a rimmed baking sheet or roasting pan, lightly drizzle them with a tablespoon or so of peanut oil, and toss until they are coated. Roast until well-browned but not scorched, about 30 minutes. You may also brown the sliced onion, carrot, and celery in 1 tablespoon of peanut oil or butter over medium-high heat before adding the other ingredients to the stockpot. Be careful not to scorch them or the broth will have a sharp, acrid aftertaste.

Makes about 4 quarts

additions to broth

Many scraps, vegetables, and aromatic flavorings can be employed in the stockpot, though some of them fight one another or may not be compatible with all meat bases. Here are a few notes on additions that are useful.

Leftover roast or stew bones: These can be wiped clean, frozen, and saved to boost flavor, but be careful of the seasonings used in the roast; either wipe them away or make sure that they will not dominate the broth.

Tomatoes: Some traditional Southern cooks also add the parings from a large fresh tomato to beef, veal, or pork broth, which deepens the color and gives a rosy tint to veal broth. But add them sparingly and with caution; they can easily overpower everything else.

Onion parings: Substituting the fleshy parings of onions for all or part of the vegetable is a good way of using scraps, but don't use the dry, papery skin.

Salt pork: For a strong beef or pork broth, a ¼-inch-thick slice of lean salt pork or country ham (about 2 by 4 inches) will add a fine underpinning and will make it especially useful in seasoning stews and slow-cooked vegetables. Don't use it in chicken or veal broth, however. It would overpower them.

Periodically, additions to broth turn up in printed recipes that I cannot recommend. Here are the worst offenders and why you should avoid them.

The dry, papery skin of onions or garlic: Though these deepen the color, they lend a harsh, almost artificial flavor as if the broth was made with powdered dried onion or garlic.

Turmeric in chicken broth: Though turmeric gives chicken broth a lovely yellow color, it has a distinct taste that will make the broth less versatile. Good chicken scraps will lend a fine golden color on their own, but if you want a deeper yellow broth, add an extra carrot or a cup of carrot parings and scraps.

More herbs: Added herbs, particularly strongly flavored ones such as tarragon, rosemary, sage, or oregano may fight with other ingredients when you use the broth in a soup or other recipe. If additional herb flavoring is wanted, those herbs are added in the individual recipe, not to the broth.

ham broth

The rich aroma and subtle flavor of salt-cured pork is a characterizing element of so much good Southern cooking, but modern health concerns have made many traditional cooks begin to avoid it. Ham broth is one way to get those traditional flavors without the fat. However, as is true of Basic Broth (page 10), you should not trim away the fat from the scraps: It must be present during the cooking to give the broth its full depth of flavor. Once finished, chill the broth and lift the congealed fat from the top. Its flavor will have been infused into the liquids.

1 leftover ham bone, with some meat still attached, or 1½ pounds ham hocks

2 large yellow onions, 1 peeled and thinly sliced, 1 peeled but left whole and stuck with 4 whole cloves

1 medium rib celery, thickly sliced

1 medium carrot, peeled and thickly sliced

8 to 10 whole black peppercorns

1 whole pod hot pepper such as cayenne, Serrano, or jalapeño

1 large bay leaf

4 quarts water

Salt

1. Put all the ingredients except the salt into a 6–8 quart stockpot. Bring slowly to a simmer over medium heat, uncovered, about 30 minutes. As soon as bubbles begin breaking the surface, reduce the heat to low and simmer slowly for at least 1½ hours; 3 or 4 hours will be even better if you have the time.

2. Turn off the heat. Taste and add salt if it is needed, then let the broth cool. Strain it and refrigerate until the fat on top has solidified. Skim off the fat and discard it or save it to use for sautéing. The fat will keep in the refrigerator for several weeks, up to 3 months if frozen in a well-sealed container. The broth will keep for up to a week, refrigerated, or as long as 3 months frozen in small batches.

Makes about 3½ quarts

shellfish (or fish) stock for seafood soups, stews, and sauces

Many Southern recipes for fish, shellfish, and seafood soups are founded on the distinctive flavor and rosy-orange color that can only come from the shells of shrimp, crabs, and crawfish. Buying shellfish still in their shells may mean more work for the cook, but the work is not much and the rewards are large; the fish is tastier when cooked in its shell, and the shells can be put to good use in the stockpot. You can of course substitute water where shellfish stock is called for, but the finished product will be missing an undertone that would make it exceptional. Bones, shells, scraps, and heads can be frozen if you can't use them right away, but they are all more perishable than the flesh of the fish and should be used within a couple of weeks if possible.

4 cups shrimp, crawfish, or crab shells, including the heads, if possible, or about 2 pounds fish bones and heads

3 quarts water

1 medium onion, thickly sliced

3 to 4 cloves garlic, peeled but left whole

2 leafy celery tops

2 large sprigs parsley

1 teaspoon peppercorns

1 whole fresh or dried pod hot red pepper such as cayenne, Serrano, or jalapeño

Salt, optional

1. Put all the ingredients except the salt in a 6–8 quart stockpot. Bring it to almost a boil over medium-high heat. It boils over easily, so don't let your attention stray. As soon as foam forms on top, reduce the heat to medium-low and simmer, uncovered, for 1 hour.

2. Raise the heat to medium-high and reduce the liquid to about ⅔ its original volume, skimming off any foam that rises to keep it from boiling over. Turn off the heat, allow the broth to settle. If you need the broth to be seasoned, add salt to taste, then strain it, discard the solids, and let it cool. Refrigerate or freeze the broth promptly. It will keep for 3 or 4 days in the refrigerator, up to 3 months in the freezer.

Makes about 2 quarts (8 cups)

HERBS IN THE SOUTHERN KITCHEN

There is a popular myth that traditional Southern cooking, while it employs many spices, makes spare use of herbs. It is, therefore, presumed that Southern cooks are only just now discovering the benefits of herbs in cooking. Nothing could be further from the truth. Without a wide variety of herbs, both fresh and dried, traditional Southern cooks would be lost. Cooks of the classical Southern age (before the War Between the States) from Mary Randolph, author of the first known Southern cookbook, to Annabella Hill, the last of the antebellum authors, made wide use of herbs in their cooking. Both ladies mention as many as 14 culinary herbs and were free with such supposedly "unknown" ones as sweet basil, garlic, marjoram, rosemary, and thyme. Bay leaves, sage, and mint have always been essential to traditional Southern cooking. It's true that sometime in the mid-twentieth century, for reasons lost in time, many Southern cooks hadn't a single herb on hand other than a box of rubbed sage, but it's more accurate to say that these cooks are today renewing their acquaintance with herbs, not discovering them for the first time.

Both dried and fresh herbs are used in Southern kitchens, and contrary to the posturing of some chefs, neither is necessarily superior to the other. There are times when the more concentrated flavors of dried herbs are preferred; others when we want the bright herbal subtlety of fresh ones. Sometimes they can be used interchangeably, but not always. Wherever herbs are called for in this book, the recipe will indicate whether you should use dried or fresh. Actually, they should all be "fresh." Even dried herbs should still have good color and a pungent fragrance.

bouquet garni

This flavoring bundle of herbs with the fancy French name is essential for flavoring soups, stews, and stocks not only in France, but in every Western cuisine. You can buy fancy dried bouquet garni for a premium, and you can substitute dried herbs, but it won't have the lovely subtlety of a fresh one. But while they're best made with fresh herbs, you don't have to use the prime leaves: The stems have exactly the same flavor, so take advantage of the stems that are leftover from using the herb in another recipe.

1 leafy celery top

1 large sprig parsley, or 2–3 leftover parsley stems

1 large sprig thyme, or 2–3 leftover thyme stems

1 large sprig (or 2–3 leftover stems) marjoram, oregano, rosemary, sage, or savory

2 bay leaves, preferably fresh

1. Lay a 6-inch square of cheesecloth on a work surface and gather the herbs on it into a bundle with the bay leaves on either side. Fold the cheesecloth around them.

2. Tie the bundle with a kitchen twine, lacing it up as you would the ribbons of a ballet slipper.

For 1 bouquet garni

BOURBON IN THE KITCHEN

We will not revisit the reason that Leah Chase gave me the nickname "Dr. Jack Daniels"—which I have not been able to shake off, except to say that it has appropriately stuck. In my entire adult life as a cook, there has never been a time when I did not have bourbon or another distilled corn whiskey in my pantry. It's an integral and indispensable element of flavor in my cooking that I would be hard pressed to do without. Bourbon is used in the South in exactly the same way brandy, cognac, and grappa are used in other cuisines, but it runs deeper than that. There is a smoothness, a suave subtlety to bourbon that other wood-aged spirits lack. In fact, when a recipe calls for brandy or cognac, bourbon is always what I use.

When choosing a cooking whiskey, pick one that you would enjoy drinking but don't waste a premium sipping whiskey on the kitchen pots. I once walked into Nathalie Dupree's kitchen to find that she had stuffed an enormous bottle of premium single-barrel whiskey full of vanilla beans. Nathalie doesn't drink at all and the whiskey was a gift, so the prodigal extravagance of that extract was lost on her. Yes, it was a lovely extract, but a lesser-quality whiskey would have produced one that was just as lovely.

Government regulations specify that bourbon is any whiskey distilled from mash that's more than half corn; they don't proscribe a territory. But bourbon was born in Kentucky, in the county whose name it bears, and for most Southerners, real bourbon comes from a confined area around Bourbon County. There are other perfectly good Southern whiskies, such as Tennessee's Jack Daniels, that will make little or no difference in the pot. Here are a few key label distinctions you'll need to know when shopping for them. Straight means it's distilled from mash that's at least 51 percent corn. Sour mash is from a blend of old mash (to help fermentation) and new mash. Blended (which is most of them) means that it's a mixture of several batches, and single-barrel is from a single, premium batch.

homemade bourbon vanilla

Making your own vanilla extract may seem a little extreme, particularly since good-quality extracts are available to us, and commercial extracts can certainly be used in any recipe in this book. Once you taste the rich depth of flavor that bourbon lends to vanilla and understand the distinctive difference that so simple a preparation can make, you're sure to think the small effort required is well worth it. If you bake often, you can make this in larger batches: Just allow 1 vanilla bean for every ¼ cup of whiskey.

4 whole imported vanilla beans

1 cup bourbon

1. Split the vanilla beans in half lengthwise, then cut each half into quarters. Put the beans into a clean jar or bottle with a tight fitting lid. Add the bourbon, tightly put on the lid, and give the jar a good shake.

2. Put it in a cool, dark cupboard that you use frequently. At least once a day for 2 weeks, give the jar a gentle shake. After 2 weeks, you no longer need to agitate the jar. Keep it in a cool place away from direct light.

3. Every time you use the vanilla, replace what you take out with an equal amount of bourbon. It will replenish itself for at least a year or two before the fragrance and flavor begin to fade. I've kept one batch going for as long as 5 years. When the flavor begins to fade, stop replenishing and use up the extract. Then start a new batch with fresh beans, or strain the old extract, measure it, and use it as a base for your next batch.

Makes 1 cup

PEACH CONSERVES

Peaches are among the earliest fruits imported into the South by Europeans, and arguably the most enduring. They are so completely woven into Southern food that it is difficult to imagine our cooking without this fragrant member of the plum family. Peach ice cream is almost an icon of summer, and spicy cobblers, made from fresh, canned, frozen, and dried fruit, are a favorite all year-round. Peaches are also a favorite for preserving in jam, marmalade, pickles, and chutney. Here are two particularly lovely conserves that are essential elements of some of the recipes in this book.

peach-orange marmalade

This sumptuous preserve is heaven on biscuits, toast, or a slice of pound cake, but it is also a wonderful foil for meat, game, and poultry. It is the defining condiment for Grilled Duck Breasts with Warm Peach-Orange Marmalade (page 174) and is also delicious with roasted turkey or game such as wild duck or venison.

1 lemon

1 medium to large orange

2 pounds peaches

3 cups sugar

1. Halve the lemon and juice it through a strainer into a glass or stainless bowl that will hold at least 5 cups. Remove the zest from the orange in julienne, either with a bar zester, or remove it with a vegetable peeler in strips and cut it into julienne with a sharp chef's knife. Add the zest to the bowl with the juice, then cut the orange in half and juice it through a strainer into the bowl.

2. Peel, split, pit, and thinly slice the peaches, then cut the slices into ½-inch chips. As you finish them, put them in the bowl with the lemon juice and toss until coated. When all the peaches are chipped, sprinkle the sugar over them and gently stir until it's well mixed. Set aside in a cool place for at least 1 hour, but for no more than 2, stirring occasionally to keep the sugar well distributed.

3. Transfer the peaches to a 3–4 quart heavy-bottomed stainless steel or enameled saucepan and bring it to a simmer over medium-high heat, stirring frequently. Reduce the heat to medium-low and simmer, stirring occasionally, until it's thick and the peaches are very tender and translucent, about 1 hour.

4. Let it sit for a few minutes and skim off and discard any foam that settles on top. While it's still hot, spoon it into clean, sterilized half-pint canning jars and seal with new lids. Process in a water bath for 10 minutes (see page 22). Allow them to cool completely, and make sure the lids have sealed before storing in a cool, dark cupboard or pantry.

Makes 4 to 5 half-pints

peach chutney

Before mangoes were imported and grown commercially in Florida and California, they were rarely available to the average Southern cook for making chutney, so over the years, other fruits and vegetables have been popularly substituted for them, peaches in particular, which have a similar texture to mangoes. In Georgia, where peaches seem almost to be our birthright, it's only natural that our state fruit would become the one most commonly found in the chutney jar.

Any peach will work in this recipe, as will mangoes if you have them available to you. The choice of fruit is yours to make, though you should be aware that each choice affects the color and flavor. Yellow peaches and mangoes make a richer, more golden chutney than white peaches, but white ones add fine aroma and a subtly floral element to the flavor. Golden raisins will make the chutney a little sweeter and will help it hold its lovely golden-peach color. Currants will darken it but will lend a more complex flavor.

1 large lemon

2 pounds firm, slightly under-ripe peaches

1 cup currants or golden raisins (see notes above)

1 cup chopped yellow onion (about 1 medium onion)

1 large, or 2 small, cloves garlic, lightly crushed, peeled and minced

1 tablespoon finely minced fresh ginger

1 or 2 green or red chile peppers (depending on their heat and your taste)

3 cups cider vinegar

2 cups sugar

2 bay leaves

1 tablespoon yellow or white mustard seeds

1 teaspoon salt

1. Grate the zest from the lemon into a 2-quart glass or stainless steel bowl. Cut the lemon in half and juice it through a strainer into the bowl. Peel, halve, pit, and thinly slice the peaches, then cut the slices into ½-inch chips. Add them to the bowl with the lemon juice and zest as you go, tossing well to coat them. When all the peaches are sliced, add the currants, onion, garlic, ginger, and hot pepper. Gently toss until well mixed.

2. Stir the vinegar and sugar together in a 3–4-quart heavy-bottomed stainless steel or enameled saucepan or stockpot until the sugar is mostly dissolved. Add the bay leaves, mustard seeds, and salt. Bring to a boil over medium-high heat, stirring until the sugar is completely dissolved. Add the remaining ingredients, bring it back to a boil, then reduce the heat to medium-low and simmer, stirring occasionally, until it's thick and the peaches and onions are tender, about an hour. Turn off the heat.

3. Remove and discard the bay leaves. Immediately ladle the chutney into sterilized half-pint jars, and seal with new lids. Process the jars in a water bath for 10 minutes (see page 22 for the method). Allow the jars to cool completely, and make sure the lids have sealed before storing them in a cool, dark cupboard or pantry.

Makes 6 to 7 half-pints

pepper vinegar

This tart and spicy condiment is commonplace in Southern kitchens and, in the Deep South, can be found on many tables both at home and in public diners, right alongside the salt and pepper. It's used to flavor soups and stews, add spice to salad dressings, and as a condiment for vegetables, especially greens.

6 ounces whole fresh red or green cayenne or other hot peppers

About 1 cup cider vinegar (see step 1)

1. Pack the peppers into a sterilized pint jar. Bring the vinegar to a boil and pour it over them, filling the jar to within ¼ inch of the top. The peppers must be completely submerged, so heat a little more vinegar if you don't have enough.

2. Seal the jar with a new canning lid and ring seal. Refrigerate and let stand for at least 2 weeks (a month is better) before using. Or, for more prolonged storage, process it in a boiling water bath for 10 minutes (see page 22), and then store in a cool, dark cupboard.

Makes 1 pint

canning conserves for prolonged storage

Any preserve or relish, such as the previous three recipes, can be canned for prolonged storage. Canning is a simple vacuum-sealing process and isn't difficult, but if you've never done it, take the time to become familiar with a few key fundamentals.

THE EQUIPMENT

First, it's important to use the right jars for home canning. Used commercial jelly and pickle jars are not designed for home use and aren't suitable for this process. Use only jars specifically made for home canning. The jars can be used over and over again, and the rings can be used until they show signs of rust, but never re-use the sealing lids. The sealing compound may be damaged in a way you can't see. New jars are usually packed with lids, and replacements are available wherever jars are sold. Old-fashioned glass clamp jars with rubber rings are charming but aren't suitable for canning.

There are two types of canning processors available, pressure and water-bath canners. The latter is more versatile and can be used for things other than canning, and is the type used here. The pot is a deep enameled or stainless steel kettle fitted with a rack that is not only useful for removing the jars from the hot water bath, but it keeps them from bouncing on the bottom of the pot and knocking into one other during processing. The pot must be deep enough for the jars to be submerged in water by at least an inch.

Aside from the proper jars, lids, and processor, it's helpful to have a large pair of tongs for handling the jars, a stainless wide-mouthed canning funnel for filling them, a magnetic lid lifter, and plenty of clean cotton or linen kitchen towels.

THE PROCESS

Everything that touches prepared conserve must be sterile to prevent spoilage after the jar is sealed. Sterilize jars by boiling them in water to cover for 10 minutes; boil the lids for 1 minute in a stainless pan, then turn off the heat and let them remain in the water until you are ready to use them. Don't touch anything that will touch the conserve with your bare hands after it has been sterilized.

Use a wide-mouthed funnel and stainless-steel tongs, ladles, spoons, or forks for filling the jars with conserve. For whole pickles and fruit preserves, leave no less than ½ inch of head room at the top of the jar, and cover it with the pickling or preserving syrup by at least ¼ inch, leaving an overall headroom of ¼ inch (pack them tightly so they don't float, but not so tightly that they won't be surrounded by the pickling solution or preserving syrup). For jams, marmalades and so forth, leave ¼-inch of headroom. Once the jars are filled, use a magnetic lid lifter to remove the lid from its hot water bath and place the lids without touching the inside of it. Screw on the rings until just lightly tightened. Don't tighten the rings too much, or the air will not be able to escape, preventing a proper seal.

To process them, put enough water in the pot to cover the jars by at least an inch and bring it to a boil. Put the jars into the rack and lower them into the water. Cover and let it come back to a boil. Boil 10 minutes for pickles and solid conserves like chutney, 5 minutes for jelly.

When the jars first come out of the bath, they're very hot and fragile and must not touch each other or any cool surface. Spread out clean, double-folded cotton or linen towels. Take the jars out of the bath with the rack and then move them to the towels using jar tongs, never allowing them to touch one another. As the jars cool, the vacuum formed in the top will pull the dome of the lid inward, making a "popping" sound as it seals. Let the jars sit for 24 hours before storing them; any that don't seal should be refrigerated and used as soon as possible.

STORING HOME-CANNED CONSERVES

All unprocessed conserves must be refrigerated and will keep for up to 2 months if packed in a sterile jar. Processed conserves should be stored in a cool, dark cupboard or pantry. I try to use canned goods within a year, though most will last a lot longer. Do not eat any conserve with a bulging lid: Put on a pair of disposable food service gloves (botulism can be absorbed through your skin) and throw it out. Regardless of whether the lid is bulging, if you are ever in doubt about any conserve, don't eat it; throw it out. It's better to lose the little bit of work and material than to end up being poisoned.

crystallized citrus peel

It's easy to imagine the cook who first decided not to waste the fragrant lemon and orange parings that were leftover after the fruit had been peeled and prepared for the table, fiddling around with honey or sugar syrup until the tart, brightly colored peelings were plump and sweet. This ancient confection is still one of the most delicious candies ever devised, the nearest thing to perfection in the confectioner's art until chocolate came along to coat it with a dark layer of silk and send it over the top.

Crystallized citrus peel is not only delicious as candy, it's indispensable in holiday baking, particularly in making fruit cake (page 326). Unhappily, commercially candied peel, mostly made with high-fructose syrup, is not worth looking at, let alone eating. Our only alternative is to make it at home. It isn't difficult or time-consuming and is an excellent way to use leftover citrus peelings that would otherwise be thrown out. Traditional recipes called for blanching the peel in three or four changes of water to remove all the bitterness, but doing so with modern hybrid fruit removes an important element of the flavor. I find that doing it just twice is usually enough.

To use leftover rinds from juice, or the breakfast table, cut each half into quarters and scoop out any remaining pulp and membrane. Wash well under cold water and store them in an air-tight container, such as a plastic storage bag, refrigerated, for up to 3 days, until you have enough rinds for a batch. If you are taking the rinds from whole fruit, cut them into quarters and pull out the sections with their outer membranes. The fruit can be used in fruit salad, or sectioned and served as is.

1 pound whole orange, grapefruit, or lemon rinds, scraped clean of any pulp and connective membrane, but with the white pith left intact

1½ pounds (3 cups) sugar

1. If you aren't sure the fruit hasn't been coated with colored wax, scrub the rinds under warm water and pat dry, otherwise rinse them well under cold running water and pat dry.

2. Put enough water into a heavy-bottomed stainless steel or enameled pot or preserve kettle to completely cover the rinds. Bring it to a boil over medium-high heat and add the rinds. Let the water return to a boil and cook briskly for 5 minutes. Drain, refresh the rinds under cold running water, and then cover them with cold water. Return the pot to the heat and bring the water to a boil. Allow to boil for 3 to 5 minutes and drain thoroughly. When the rind is cool enough to handle, cut it into ¼-inch wide strips. Return it to the pot and sprinkle 1 cup of the sugar over it. Place the pot over medium-low heat and bring it to a simmer, stirring frequently. A syrup will form as the sugar melts into the moisture remaining in the rinds. Cook, stirring occasionally, until most of this syrup is absorbed by the rinds, about 10 minutes. Turn off the heat.

3. Spread the peel on a wire cooling rack set over a baking sheet to catch drips, and let it dry at room temperature until it is firm and only a little sticky, about 8 hours. You may also do this in an oven set on the "warm" setting; it should take 2 to 4 hours. Check it frequently after the first hour to make sure the candy does not dry too much.

4. Spread the remaining 2 cups of sugar on a wax paper or parchment lined cookie sheet and roll the rinds in it until they are coated. Wipe the rack clean and return them to it until they are dry to the touch. Store the candy in an airtight tin or plastic container. If it gets sticky and wet, roll it in more sugar.

Makes about 2 pounds

THE SOUTHERN DAIRY

Dairy products found in a Southern kitchen are mostly universal and do not need an introduction, but one or two are so important that they do need a little explaining. Many of the recipes call for whole milk. Don't substitute low-fat or skimmed milk unless the recipe specifies that you can. It's not my purpose or place to give you a health lecture, although removing fat from milk also removes some of the nutrients, and whole foods are usually more digestible. Our primarily concern here is taste and how the milk reacts in cooking. Skimmed or low-fat milk won't react in the same way as whole milk.

Buttermilk and yogurt: True buttermilk is the naturally soured liquid left over from making butter. Whole milk or cream is agitated until the fats separate and solidify. Modern commercial buttermilk, on the other hand, is not a by-product; it's whole or skimmed milk soured with added enzymes. Most of it also contains thickeners and/ or emulsifiers to make it thick and creamy. These additives can have an affect on how the milk reacts in cooking, but in most cases it's negligible. When using commercial buttermilk, taste it first to see if you will need to hold back on salt in the recipe. If you can get real buttermilk from a local dairy, it's far better. When I can't get that, I substitute plain, all-natural yogurt thinned to buttermilk consistency with regular milk.

Regardless of which you use, choose a whole milk product. The label will read "whole milk" or "made with whole milk." The reason for this is that for the best flavor and texture the fat must still be in the milk when it's processed into buttermilk or yogurt. When it's removed before the milk is soured, the flavor of the finished product is always sharper and never as full. If fat is a concern, use buttermilk or all-natural yogurt that isn't homogenized; the fat rises to the top and can be removed before you use it.

Sour cream and crème fraîche: Commercial sour cream will work in a recipe in which the cream is not heated or cooked, but will not answer when the cream is to be heated. It's usually no more than 24% and often as little as 16% milk fat. Far superior to it is crème fraîche, which was the sour cream of our ancestors, the kind intended in historical recipes. It has a mild, nutty tang that makes it an ideal topping or binder for cold salads and sweets and, more important, will heat without curdling. It's expensive, but happily easy to make. You'll need cream that is at least 36% milk fat (most commercial heavy cream is), but if you can get minimally treated cream that's 40–45%, that's even better.

crème fraîche

2 tablespoons all-natural whole milk
Greek yogurt or regular whole milk yogurt

2 cups 36% minimum milk fat heavy cream

1. If using Greek yogurt, it won't need straining. Skip to step 2. If using plain yogurt, put it in a wire mesh sieve lined with a double layer of cheesecloth and spoon the yogurt into it. Let stand in the sink for 30 minutes to drain off the whey.

2. Scrape the yogurt into a glass or ceramic bowl and slowly (and lightly) whisk in the cream. You don't want to whip it, just evenly mix the two together. Cover with a towel or cheesecloth and let stand at room temperature until the cream is clotted and thick, about 4 to 6 hours, if the weather is warm, or as long as 8 hours if it is fairly cool.

3. Scrape it into a clean glass pint canning jar, cover tightly and refrigerate until needed. It should keep for about two weeks.

Cheese: Cheese is an essential element of all Southern cooking. The most common is cheddar: choose a well-aged Canadian, English, or Vermont cheddar or English Farmhouse cheese. Parmesan is another essential that has a long tradition in the South, having been imported at least since the beginning of the eighteenth century. Use real Parmigiano-Reggiano: This is no time to be cheap. There are several other traditional cheeses called for throughout this book, including regionally made blue, goat, and specialty artisan cheeses. They're discussed with the recipes that call for them.

Makes 1 pint

FAT AND CURED PORK

Fats, especially the kinds traditionally used in a Southern kitchen, have become culinary bad boys these days, and yet without fat in our diet, even those that have been deemed "bad," we could not survive. Not only are fats as essential to our health as water, without them, we could hardly cook at all. Even boiling and steaming require the natural fats within the food so that the food reacts properly to the heat. The fat may be removed at the end of a process—as in a broth or in the making of buttermilk or yogurt, but its presence during the process deeply affects the flavor.

That said, the circumstances of our lives have changed drastically in the last century. We no longer do the kind of heavy work that our ancestors did and so no longer need the amounts of fat that many old recipes contained. Many cooks have abandoned some of the old fats and flavoring salt pork altogether; the drippings jar by the stove has been replaced with a bottle of olive oil. This is reflected in many of the recipes of this book. However, I still use those culinary bad-boys all the time in my cooking. What I, and many other Southern cooks, have preferred to do rather than abandon them is to rethink the way we use them. Used sensibly, they can actually be good tools for cooks who want to cut the amount of overall fat in their cooking.

The advantage that bacon drippings, salt pork fat, lard, and butter have over other supposedly "more healthy" fats is flavor: They're loaded with it. Consequently, they can and should be used in much smaller quantities than a mildly flavored fat such as canola oil. Conversely, it's easy to get carried away using a flavorless fat, since it doesn't have a dominant taste. It's less easy to overuse butter or drippings, since they will inevitably taste heavy and greasy when too much goes into the pot. In short, a pat of butter, a small spoonful of drippings, a dollop of pure lard add a lot more than just fat to the mix and therefore go a lot further. They add richness, a sense of luxury on the palate. They feel and taste indulgent. Here are a few essential notes on the use of these products in the new Southern kitchen, but first a word on the pantry's "newcomer."

Olive Oil

After my first cookbook on historical Southern cooking had been out for a few years, a learned colleague collared me at a culinary meeting and asked skeptically, "Just what is it with you and olive oil in Southern cooking?"

She echoes an old and widely held misconception that olive oil is essentially a new product in

Southern kitchens. Recent history would seem to bear this out, but a mere glance at historical cookbooks tells another story. It was so important that early colonists in Carolina and Georgia tried to grow olives for oil; while the experiment failed, shipping records and advertisements tell us that these same colonists still found it essential enough to import in substantial quantities. It was expensive, but cookbooks suggest that it was an integral part of Southern cookery and medicine—at least, for the upper classes that could afford cookbooks. Naturally, poorer families used this oil sparingly, if at all.

Until the twentieth century, olive oil was pretty much the only salad oil available; it was often referred to as such in recipes—"a spoonful of salad oil" or, not infrequently, "sweet oil." Because of its expense, it tended to be reserved mainly for salads and medicinal ointments and tonics, but it does make an occasional appearance in other recipes, usually for sauces, fish, and shellfish. It was also used for basting roasted pork, probably because it withstood the intense heat of a hearth fire better than butter.

When other, less expensive oils began to appear at the end of the nineteenth century, the use of olive oil declined in the South for a time. The waning demand made good quality olive oil difficult to come by. That doesn't mean it disappeared; it didn't. But today, good olive oil is more commonplace in our region than good lard, and it is widely available to almost all households. Southern cooks have begun to integrate olive oil into real Southern food, using it in distinctly Southern (as opposed to Mediterranean) ways. Aside from salads, it's substituted for bacon drippings or lard (my mother's olive oil biscuits, page 262, for example), and used in flavoring marinades, for sautéing, for basting roasts, and for moistening many cooked vegetables and all kinds of fish and shellfish.

However you use it, use the best-quality olive oil that you can afford, and learn to trust your own palate in this regard. But don't let economy be the only thing that makes the decision for you. Think of it this way: The better the flavor, the less you will tend to use, so good oil tends to be the better investment in the long run.

There are excellent books on olive oil available, so there is no point to going on at length about it in these pages. Here is a brief explanation of the terms and grades that you will need to know about when shopping for it. Extra virgin is the oil extracted from the first cold pressing, virgin is from the second cold pressing. Pure olive oil is from later pressings in which heat and/or chemicals may have been applied to help extract the oils. Cold-pressing means that heat has not been used to extract the oil, but the term is not exact and does not mean that no heat has been applied at all. Extra virgin and virgin oils have the most flavor and color because they contain more of the essence of the fruit. Predictably, oils from later pressings have less flavor and color.

When I want to really taste the oil, even in cooking, I use extra virgin olive oil. Much like drippings and butter, if the oil is full-flavored, I use far less in the long run. When the flavor is not as important, or when extra virgin oil would either be too strong or might too easily burn (as in frying), I use plain olive oil, or peanut, corn, or canola oil. Many cooks use extra virgin oil mainly for salads and for dressing pasta, and pure oil for their other cooking, because heat changes the flavor of olive oil. Well, it changes the flavor of just about everything: That's not always a bad thing.

Oil, like any other organic substance, will eventually spoil and go rancid. Extra virgin olive oil is especially susceptible to this because of the olive solids that it contains. So, first, make sure you are buying good oil: It should have a clean, fresh smell and taste distinctly of olives. Old oil will smell heavy and greasy and will leave behind an unpleasant acrid taste on the tongue. Light and heat accelerate the deterioration. If the market stores olive oil on the top shelf where it is fully exposed to the store's lighting system, it may already be compromised, even if it's bottled in dark colored glass. Once you get it home, store it in an airtight container in a cool, dark cupboard. If you use it infrequently, you may even want to store it in the refrigerator. Some claim that this will do damage to the flavor, but it will not do as much damage as heat.

Salt-Cured Pork, Bacon, Drippings, and Other Cured Pork Products

Ever since man first learned to herd pigs, they've been preserving pork in salt. Southern cooking is infamous for its prodigal use of cured pork and its rendered fat, but these things are indispensable to most of the world's most ancient cuisines, including those of China, France, and Italy. One of the most striking of the many parallels between Southern cooking and all three of those classic cuisines is the way that salt-cured pork is used in them. Here are the basic types that are called for in this book.

Bacon: In the old cookbooks, "bacon" meant any cut of pork that was salt-cured but not smoked, but today American bacon is by definition a particular cut (the belly) and is almost always smoked with an aromatic hardwood. To avoid confusion, when a recipe calls for bacon in this book, it means smoked American-style bacon. Good bacon is universally available; I prefer the market-cut variety that often still has its rind because it's usually a drier cure and has better flavor. But if you find your choices are limited, smoked Italian pancetta (pancetta afumicata) makes a good substitute.

Dry- and brine-cured salt pork: This type of cured pork is usually from the side of the animal. Dry-salt curing means it's rubbed with salt and air-aged; sometimes salt pork is brined and then air dried. Unlike bacon it never contains sugar and is never smoked. It is preferred when one wants the savory underpinning of salted pork without the added weight of smoke flavoring or sugar. The cure is identical to Italian pancetta, which is an ideal substitute if salt pork is not available where you live.

Country ham: Despite what often appears in your market's deli case, "ham" is not an idea or curing method; there was a time when it didn't even mean cured meat. A ham is the haunch or back thigh of an animal, and cured ham is the hind leg of a hog. It can be cured in heavy brine (as in most supermarket hams) or by rubbing it with dry salt and spice and hanging to dry-cure. It may or may not contain sugar, and may or may not be smoked, though most American hams are. Southern country hams are usually both air-cured and smoked. Sometimes they're rubbed with ash for both flavor and protection against insects. Yet the flavor of smoke in country ham is more subtle than breakfast bacon. It's used when one wants

a richer, more distinctive flavor, but not a smoky aftertaste. Any good quality dry-cured ham (such as prosciutto) makes an excellent substitute.

Salt pork substitutes: Though pork's reputation has improved in recent times and is no longer being quite so vilified, you may still have reasons, whether health-related, religious, or philosophical, for avoiding it in your cooking. There are many reasonable and delicious substitutes, including a touch of anchovy, a splash of Asian fish sauce, and a well-scraped leftover rind from Parmigiano-Reggiano. Acceptable substitutes are suggested in the recipes. Use all your senses when using them. Anchovies, for example, should be kept very subtle—a little will lend that subtle underpinning that you're after, and even a smidgen too much will be overpoweringly fishy.

Some suggested substitutes are too laughable to even think about, but there's one I find so unsatisfactory that it warrants mention here: imitation ham made with turkey or soy protein. Most have too much synthetic smoke flavoring, which lends a harsh, bitter aftertaste, and none come anywhere near the subtlety of real salt-cured pork.

Lard and drippings: Lard is pure, rendered pork fat, the finest of which is leaf fat from the saddle and belly of the hog. Buy it from a butcher, where it is stored in a refrigerated case. Check the label to make sure it does not contain preservatives, and if the container is not sealed, open it. Fresh lard is creamy-white with a mild, faintly oily, but fresh, clean smell. Avoid any that is dark and smells oily and heavy. You may also render your own lard to ensure freshness and quality, using the instructions that follow. Drippings are the fat rendered from any meat, but the ones most frequently used in Southern cooking are from bacon and country ham. Once, drippings were kept in a container near the stove to be spooned out as needed, but today we use them less often and they spoil easily, so store drippings, well-sealed, in the refrigerator. They will keep for a couple of months.

Rendering lard: Wash and pat dry 4 pounds of fresh pork fat (preferably leaf fat from the saddle around the kidneys). Cut it into small dice or put it through a meat grinder (if you have one, or see if the butcher will do this for you). Put it in a deep, heavy-bottomed pot such as a cast iron Dutch oven over low heat. Let it cook until the fat is dissolved and the solids sink to the bottom. When the solids turn brown, turn off the heat and lift them out with a skimmer and drain them well on absorbent paper. These are the cracklings, which can be used in place of shortening as a flavorful addition to Southern corn bread and certain kinds of Italian and French country loaves. Let the lard cool enough to handle and strain it into a clean container with a tight-fitting lid.

PREPPING VEGETABLES

One last thing before we move on to the recipes. Flavoring vegetables, including celery, garlic, leeks, onions, and tomatoes, are frequently called for in the recipes that follow. Most cookbook authors and cooking teachers take for granted that every cook knows exactly how to tackle an onion, a clove of garlic, or a fresh, unpeeled tomato. So did I, until I began to pay attention to how my cooking students struggled with them or vigorously took notes as I peeled and chopped. It took me a while to realize that many readers and students did not grow up—as I did—with a grandmother in the kitchen. Vague instructions, or worse, no instructions, leave such cooks feeling helpless, intimidated, and inadequate. There's no reason to feel this way. As I tell my students, not knowing isn't a crime; not asking is. The cookbook standard "1 onion, peeled and chopped" or just "1 chopped onion" may be fine for anyone who already knows how, but if you don't, that onion looks like some many layered monster that is just lying in wait to humiliate its abuser.

Let's take that mystery away right here. These vegetables require some basic but particular preparation, but repeating the method every time they are needed would double the pages of the book. To omit them altogether would be irresponsible. Here is what you need to know about the peeling, trimming, and cutting of those ubiquitous basics.

Celery

A head of celery is a cluster of ribs or stalks, each with its own leafy top. The challenge in preparing celery is getting rid of the dirt that collects between these ribs and the tough, fibrous "strings" that run like vertical conduits through it.

Break off as many outer ribs as you will need. Scrub each under cold running water with a vegetable brush or your fingers until all the dirt is gone. Drain, then take the upper part of the rib and break it back toward the outer side at the joint where the leafy top attaches to the main rib. Pull the top gently downward: this will pull away the toughest strings. Discard the strings but save the leafy top for use in the stockpot or for a Bouquet Garni (page 15). If there are still tough strings and you want to be sure to get rid of all of them, peel them away with a vegetable peeler. This last step is not really necessary, particularly if the celery is chopped. Cut the rib into halves or thirds, cut each piece vertically into small sticks, then gather the sticks into a small bundle and slice across

them, making dice as small as you need for the individual recipe.

Garlic

Contrary to popular belief, garlic has always been an element of many of the South's regional cuisines. A head or bulb of garlic is a cluster of smaller bulbs, called variously cloves, buttons, fingers, and toes. There are several ways of preparing it for the pot, depending on what you want from it. The more garlic is mangled, the stronger the flavor will be. That is because crushing releases the strongly flavored acids that give garlic its characteristic pungency. Here's how to get what you need from them.

Peeling garlic and leaving it whole, for subtle flavor: Break the clove from the root which holds the head together, trim the root end, and then rub and pull the papery skin off, making sure not to crush it. The clove is then put whole into the pot and removed at the end of the cooking, when it has gently infused a subtle, almost meaty flavor—as when making broth or slow-simmering certain vegetables without salt pork.

Peeling and chopping garlic, for a distinct flavor: Remove the skin by lightly crushing the clove with the flat side of a knife blade to loosen it, then slip it off. Chop the clove as fine as needed for the recipe, using a good sharp knife.

Crushing garlic, for a riotous, strong garlic flavor: Give the clove a sharp, determined whack with the flat side of the knife or a mallet. Remove the skin and discard it, then chop the garlic if it is required by the recipe. Crushing the clove releases the strong acids more immediately, lending the least subtlety and most intense flavor.

Many students ask why I don't mince with a garlic press. Simple: Presses don't mince, they puree, and pureed garlic is very strongly flavored. Unless the recipe calls for puree, you should not use a press to process the garlic.

Onions

No one should feel intimidated by onions after seeing the way even professional chefs sometimes struggle with them. The job is not difficult and needn't cause a flood of tears once you know a trick or two.

Trimming and peeling onions: Cut off the root tendrils, cutting through the outer, papery layer at the same time but leaving all the other layers of the onion still attached. Cut off the dried sprout end. If you must have full rings, cut a vertical slit in through the paper skin and the first fleshy layer of the onion and peel the outer layers away. The remaining onion can then be cut crosswise into rings. If you need strips or chopped onion, stand the onion on the sprout end (which you've flattened by cutting off the dried sprout), cut it in half vertically and pull away the outer skin.

Cutting the peeled onion into strips or dice: Lay half of the onion cut-side-down on a cutting board. Following the vertical grooves and lines in the onion, cut through to the center, gradually angling the knife with each cut, but being careful not to cut through the root end. For strips, cut off the root end and separate the cut onion into strips; to chop or dice it, leave the root attached and cut crosswise from the stem end with a sharp knife, making the dice as small or large as needed for the individual recipe.

Leeks

This member of the onion family looks a lot like a scallion on steroids. The challenge is to clean all of the dirt that's buried within its multiple leaves. The outer leaves are loose and have a crease down the center like a folded piece of paper. First, peel off the first couple of tough, outer layers and trim off the tough dark green tops and most of the root. Lay the leek flat on a work surface. If the leek will be sliced or chopped, lay your hand on top of it and holding the knife parallel to the cutting board, cut it in half from the root end. Wash each half under cold running water, holding it root end up and bending back the outer layers to rub away the dirt between them. Chop or slice it in exactly the same way as an onion.

If the vegetable is to be used whole, slip the knife along the leaves at the crease, cutting only through the outer few. Bend them back and keep slicing through leaves until there is no longer a layer of dirt between them. Turn the vegetable over and repeat this step with the other side. Hold it under cold running water, root up, and gently folding back the cut outer leaves, rub until all the dirt is gone.

Tomatoes

Tomatoes are so much a part of Southern cooking that most Southerners could not imagine being without them. Whether they are straight off the vine, eaten out of hand like an apple, or distilled into a complex Sauce Creole, their presence is as ubiquitous in the Southern kitchen as it is in an Italian one. The problem they present the cook is how to get rid of the tough peeling and small, slippery seeds. Depending on how the tomatoes

are to be used, there are several methods that can be employed.

Peeling tomatoes with a vegetable peeler: When the tomatoes are eaten raw, or mustn't be cooked at all before they are put into a recipe, it is easiest to peel them with a vegetable peeler. There are serrated vegetable peelers that make this job a snap. Simply cut out the stem scar and core, and skin the tomato by cutting with the peeler in a sawing back and forth motion.

Peeling tomatoes with a paring knife: This is an easy way to remove the peeling from thick salad or sandwich slices. Core and slice the tomato first, then slip a paring knife just under the peeling of each slice and cut it away with a gentle sawing motion. The seeds can be poked out of the seed cavities if necessary.

Peeling tomatoes by blanching: This is the easiest way to remove the peeling when the tomatoes will undergo further cooking. Put them in a heat-proof bowl and completely cover them with boiling water. Leave them for 1 minute, then drain and refresh the tomatoes under cold running water (this will help loosen the peel by causing the warmed inner flesh to contract away from the peel). Core each tomato and slip off the peeling.

To seed tomatoes: Fit a wire mesh strainer over a glass or stainless steel bowl; cut the peeled tomato in half crosswise, and scoop the seeds into the strainer. Discard the seeds and use the tomatoes and their collected juices (if needed) as directed by the recipe.

Now we are ready to do some serious cooking.

CHAPTER ONE

TO BEGIN WITH

There was a time when appetizers, hors d'oeuvres, and other such dainty pre-dinner fare were as foreign to a Southern palate as sashimi. The exception was the Creole canapé, which pretty much proved the rule. Southerners have not, historically, been a nation of grazers, and our appetites rarely need teasing to be stirred up: We are always hungry when it's time for dinner. Food for parties and receptions was more elegant than our everyday fare, of course, but it was still substantial and filling. Until late in the nineteenth century, it was rarely the kind of dainty, palate-teasing nibble that we now associate with party tables. By the 1920s, however, when Mrs. Dull included a whole chapter of canapés in her iconic *Southern Cooking*, the appetizer had become a permanent fixture down South, whether it accompanied a glass of sweet tea or a pickled-okra-garnished martini on the porch, or led the way at dinner in the dining room. All the same, Southerners still like small bites to have substance, and many of the dishes found here could serve as the main course for a brunch, luncheon, or supper.

roasted pecans

Few Southern hosts are without a tin of roasted pecans on standby in the pantry—or, at the very least, a pound or two of raw shelled pecans in the freezer that can be popped into the oven at a moment's notice. A perfectly roasted pecan is a lot more than a careful balance of caramelized butter, salt, and the unique earthy, sweet flavor of this native nut. Distilled in it is the crossroad of cultures that makes up this place we call the South—a tangle of poverty and refinement, of austerity and luxury—even of underlying social tensions that we try our best to pretend aren't there. Whenever I have that taste in my mouth, all the best memories of my childhood flood my consciousness, reminding me of everything that is good about being a Southerner.

What follows is an example of how recipes never remain static. Roasted pecans have been included in several of my books, but each one is different from its predecessor, because I've never stopped trying to improve on them, and because each attempt has sparked conversations with other Southern cooks who are sure they know better.

1 pound shelled whole pecans

2 tablespoons unsalted butter

Salt

1. Position a rack in the center of the oven and preheat to 275°F. Put the pecans in a rimmed pan such as a 9 x 13-inch sheet cake pan and shake the pan to level them. Cut the butter into teaspoon-size bits and scatter it over the pecans.

2. Put the pecans into the center of the oven and roast until the butter is melted, about 5 minutes. Take them out and toss until the pecans are glossy and well coated, then return them to the oven and roast 45 minutes longer, or until they're just a shade darker than when they were raw. The pecans continue to cook after they come out of the oven, so don't let them get too dark. To test them for doneness, cool a pecan slightly and break it in half. The center should be distinctly beige but not dark tan.

3. While the pecans are hot, salt them generously and toss until they are well coated. Serve warm or at room temperature. Once the pecans are completely cooled, store them in an airtight tin box or plastic container.

Rosemary Roasted Pecans: Sprinkle 2 tablespoons of chopped fresh rosemary (do not use dried) over the pecans along with the salt in step 3. Toss until the herb is evenly distributed. These are best served warm, but are still very good at room temperature.

Makes about 3½ cups, serving 4–6 as an hors d'oeuvre

bourbon spiced pecans

Spiced pecans, slightly sweet and tingling with cayenne, are a traditional holiday favorite popular throughout the South. Sometimes they include curry powder; sometimes the cayenne shines alone. Here, a splash of bourbon adds a subtle depth to the flavor and counters the bitter edge that the curry spices can sometimes lend. The secret to doing it well is to use a restrained hand with the seasonings.

1 pound shelled whole pecans

2 tablespoons unsalted butter

2 tablespoons bourbon

2 tablespoons sugar

1½ teaspoons mild curry powder

Ground cayenne pepper

Salt

1. Position a rack in the center of the oven and preheat to 275°F. Put the pecans into a rimmed pan such as a 9 × 13-inch sheet cake pan and shake the pan to level them. Cut the butter into teaspoon-size bits and scatter it over the pecans.

2. Put the pan into the center of the oven and roast until the butter is melted, about 5 minutes. Take them out and toss until the pecans are glossy and well coated with butter. Return them to the oven and toast for 20 minutes.

3. Sprinkle the pecans with the bourbon, sugar, curry powder, a small pinch or so of cayenne, and a generous pinch of salt. Toss until the nuts are uniformly coated and toast 20 minutes more, stirring occasionally. As with the previous recipe, they should only be a little darker than they were raw. Do not overcook or the spices will be bitter. Taste and adjust the salt and cayenne, stopping just shy of where you'd like it to be, as the flavors will develop as the nuts cool. Toast 2–3 minutes more. Cool completely before serving.

Makes about 3½ cups, serving 4–6 as an hors d'oeuvre

pecan-crusted goat cheese with warm peach chutney

Chef John Malik in Greenville, South Carolina, has a short fuse for the over-the-top fusion cooking that has unhappily been embraced by some of his Southern colleagues. When I suggested there ought to be a way to serve goat cheese that did not taste as if it had been routed through France or Southern California, this recipe spilled right out of his mouth and is as deeply Southern as his drawl.

½ **cup finely chopped pecans**

8-ounce log goat cheese, well chilled

½ **cup homemade (see page 20) or commercial peach chutney**

Dry Toast Points (recipe follows), a crusty French baguette cut into rounds, or crackers

1. Position a rack in the upper third of the oven and preheat to 375°F. Spread the pecans on a plate or shallow bowl such as a soup plate. Unwrap the cheese: If you are serving this as a cocktail hors d'oeuvre, place the log whole on top of the pecans; if you want to serve it on individual plates as a first course, cut crosswise into four equal rounds. Gradually and carefully roll the cheese in the pecans, pressing the nuts gently but firmly into the entire surface until the cheese is completely coated.

Note: This can be made ahead through step 1. Wrap the cheese (separately, if you have more than one) in plastic wrap and refrigerate until you are ready to bake it.

2. Place the coated cheese on an ungreased baking sheet and put it into the upper third of the oven. Bake until the cheese is warmed through

and softened and the pecans are lightly browned, about 10 minutes. Do not overcook or the cheese will melt altogether.

3. Transfer the cheese to a serving plate or individual salad plates. Heat the chutney over low heat (or at medium power in the microwave). When it is just beginning to bubble, remove it from the heat and spoon it evenly over or to one side of the cheese. Serve at once with toast points, baguette rounds, or crackers passed separately.

Serves 6–8 as an hors d'oeuvre, 4 as a first course

DRY TOAST POINTS

More elegant and also more neutral than salted crackers, dry toast points are an easy way to give a homemade character to pâtés, spreads, or cheese platters.

1 loaf firm, home-style sandwich bread, preferably thin-cut

1. Position a rack in the center of the oven and preheat to 250°F. Cut the crusts from the bread, then stack 5–6 slices at a time and cut them on the diagonal into four equal triangles.

2. Spread the bread on a large baking sheet in one layer. Bake in the center of the oven until the toasts are completely dry, crisp, and a pale tan color, about 30 minutes. Allow to cool completely and store in an airtight tin.

Makes about 100

southern caviar with corn bread madeleines (or mini hoecakes)

There is an almost ubiquitous black-eyed pea salad that has become popular under the names "Southern," "Texas," or just "Redneck" caviar. It's delicious, but that isn't what I'm talking about here. I mean the real thing, sturgeon roe, harvested from Southern waters off the coasts of Carolina and Georgia, and served up with real Southern flair.

It's natural that Southerners would pair local caviar with corn bread. The complement of flavors and textures is perfect, but the better the quality of the caviar, the more subtle the corn bread should be. Ordinary lumpfish or whitefish roe can stand up to more spice, and you might add a pinch of cayenne to the batter and even crumble in a slice of cooked bacon, but fine caviar would be overwhelmed by either of them. Baking it in mini madeleine pans makes an elegant presentation, but if you don't have them, use mini muffin pans or just lightly grease a cookie sheet and drop the batter by teaspoons onto it.

1 cup fine stone-ground cornmeal

½ teaspoon salt

¼ teaspoon freshly ground black pepper

1 teaspoon baking powder

2 tablespoons minced scallions or other green onions (green part only)

Grated zest from 1 lemon

1 large egg

¾ cup buttermilk or ½ cup plain whole-milk yogurt mixed with ¼ cup milk

2 tablespoons melted bacon drippings, unsalted butter, or extra-virgin olive oil

4 ounces Georgia or Carolina caviar (see notes above)

1 cup sour cream

2–3 lemons, each cut into wedges

1. Position a rack in center of the oven and preheat to 400°F. Whisk together the meal, salt, pepper, and baking powder in a mixing bowl. Stir in the onions and lemon zest. Whisk together the egg, buttermilk or yogurt, and fat in a separate bowl. Make a well in the center of the meal and pour in the liquids. Quickly stir the ingredients together, using as few strokes as possible. The batter can be a little lumpy.

2. Lightly grease two mini madeleine pans or a large baking sheet with drippings or butter. Drop the batter into the wells by the level teaspoon— so that they're almost level full—or drop by teaspoonfuls onto the greased cookie sheets, spacing ½ inch apart. Bake in the center of the oven until golden-brown, about 10 minutes. They can be made a couple of days ahead, cooled, and stored in airtight containers; spread them on a rimmed baking sheet and reheat at 250°F before serving.

3. While the bread bakes (or reheats), place the caviar, sour cream, and lemon in separate chilled bowls. As soon as the bread is done, transfer it to a napkin-lined basket. Arrange the bread, caviar, sour cream, and lemon on a tray and serve at once, while the corn bread is still piping hot.

Makes about 60 mini madeleines or hoecakes, serving 10–20

classic pimiento cheese

If my childhood summers could be condensed into a single taste, that taste would be pimiento cheese—a simple and yet sublime duet of cheddar and pimiento peppers, held together with just enough mayonnaise to make it spreadable. Making it with my grandmother is one of my earliest and best culinary memories, my very small hands the perfect size for working part of the cheese to a paste with the mayonnaise before the rest was folded into it. In my entire life as a cook I cannot remember a summer without a ready supply in my refrigerator. Sometimes called the "house pâté" of the South (and not always as a compliment), pimiento cheese was, throughout the twentieth century, essential stock in the refrigerator of any Southern cook who aspired to be known as a good one. The oldest recipe I've found is a sketchy outline in Martha McCulloch-Williams's Dishes & Beverages of the Old South, published in 1913, but its very offhand treatment gives away that it was by then already commonplace. By 1928 it was so taken for granted that Mrs. Dull mentioned it in Southern Cooking but didn't bother to give a recipe.

In an effort to dress this simple spread up, it has suffered more abuse (and by Southerners who ought to know better) than just about anything in all of Southern cooking. Decently aged cheddar, quality pimientos, and good mayonnaise (that is, homemade) need nothing more than restraint. There's no place here for olives (even pimiento-stuffed), sun-dried tomatoes, roasted bell peppers (which are not at all the same as pimientos), Thai chili sauce, or—heaven help us—jam and chutney.

To make the perfect summer sandwich, just spread pimiento cheese generously on thick-sliced white, wheat, or rye bread and dig in. When the weather cools, brush it with butter and grill it until the bread is toasted golden-brown and the cheese is melted. To dress it up for afternoon tea or reception finger sandwiches, use thin-sliced bread, trim off the crusts, and cut them into small triangles or fingers. Don't feel bound by two slices of bread: You can pipe it from a pastry bag fitted with an open star tip into 3-inch lengths of washed, dried, and strung celery (or just spoon it in and rake the top with a fork); or let it soften to room temperature and serve as a spread with crackers. Or simply wait until no one's looking and eat it straight from the bowl with a spoon.

8 ounces (1 small block, about 2 generous cups grated) extra-sharp cheddar

2 ounces (½ cup grated) Parmigiano-Reggiano cheese

About 5–6 tablespoons mayonnaise, preferably Homemade Mayonnaise (page 230)

1 (4-ounce) jar diced pimientos, drained but liquid reserved, roughly chopped

Ground cayenne pepper

1. Finely grate half the cheddar and all of the Parmigiano through the finest holes of a box grater, or with a rotary cheese grater, a Microplane grater, or the fine shredding disk in the food processor. Mix together lightly.

2. Knead in 4 tablespoons of the mayonnaise until the cheese is creamy and very smooth. This can be done in a food processor fitted with a steel blade, but be careful not to overprocess it or the mayonnaise could break and make the pimiento cheese oily.

3. Coarsely grate the remaining cheese. Work it, the pimientos, and a tablespoon of reserved pimiento liquid into the creamed cheese until it is almost smooth but still a bit lumpy. Add the remaining mayonnaise by tablespoonfuls until it is just spreadable (it should be very thick and taste of cheese, not mayonnaise). Season with cayenne or hot sauce to taste, and mix well.

Makes about 2½ cups

spicy cheese straws

This venerable Southern classic is a standard for any hostess worth her iced tea. These crisp morsels often intimidate novices until they understand that they're just a savory butter shortbread—one of the simplest of all cookies. Mixing by hand is a little laborious, but happily the food processor makes short work of it. The best cheese for these is an old, super-sharp cheddar, the kind that will practically take the roof off your mouth. My grandfather used to buy wheels of aged cheddar for the grocery and age them in a protected corner of the meat locker for at least another year before he'd sell them. If you can't get such wonders, mixing in a bit of Parmigiano-Reggiano gives it just the right kick. Orange cheddar lends the most traditional color to these spicy little tidbits, and is the only kind that a traditional Southern cook would use. Dairies and home cheesemakers have been coloring cheddar with annatto for at least two centuries, but if you've got a snob thing against it, white cheddar will, of course, work just as well.

12 ounces (¾ pound) well-aged, extra-sharp cheddar

4 ounces (¼ pound) Parmigiano-Reggiano (no substitutes)

¼ pound (½ cup or 1 stick) unsalted butter, softened

1 generous teaspoon ground cayenne pepper, or more, to taste

½ teaspoon salt

10 ounces (about 2 cups) Southern soft wheat flour or all-purpose flour

1. Grate the cheeses with a rotary cheese grater, the fine holes of a box grater, or the fine shredding disk in the food processor. In a food processor fitted with a steel blade or with a mixer, cream the cheeses and butter until fluffy and smooth.

2. Add the cayenne, salt, and flour, processing or working the dough until it's smooth. Gather it into a ball, wrap well in plastic wrap, and chill for at least half an hour or up to 1 hour, but don't let it get completely hard. If you make it ahead to bake later, let it soften at room temperature for about half an hour, so that it's still cool but pliable.

3. Position a rack in the center of the oven and preheat to 325°F. Put the dough in a cookie press fitted with the star die and press it out into narrow 2½-inch straws on an ungreased baking sheet, leaving about ½ inch clear between. If you don't have a press, lightly flour a work surface and roll the dough out ¼ inch thick. Cut it with a sharp knife or a zigzag pastry wheel into ½ x 2½-inch strips, laying them on the buttered baking sheet as you go. Or for a more decorative straw without the cookie press, roll them out a little thicker than ⅛ inch, cut them as directed above, and gently twist each straw into a spiral.

4. Bake for about 18–20 minutes, being careful not to let the straws brown on top. The bottoms should be golden, but the tops and sides should not color. Cool on the pan before transferring them to an airtight storage container.

Makes about 10 dozen

blue cheese straws

Clemson University, where I studied architecture some of the time and subjected dozens of my class-mates and professors to my early attempts at cooking and baking for the rest of it, is the birthplace of one of the Southeast's oldest regional cheeses—a creamy, richly blue-veined cow's-milk cheese known simply as Clemson Blue. Once aged in old tunnels dug by the Confederate army for reasons that are now lost to time and legend, today it is cured in modern cellars—an environment that is, perhaps, a little less romantic, but far more dependable, since artificial lakes and booming land development have forever changed the climate of that formerly pastoral and once much cooler region.

This variation on the classic cheese straw pays tribute to my alma mater's prize dairy product, but any high-quality blue will do—Maytag, Danish blue, Roquefort, or Gorgonzola. Since blue cheese has a powerful, dominating flavor that's too strong to use by itself, here it's toned down by mixing in an equal amount of white cheddar.

½ **pound (8 ounces) extra-sharp white cheddar**

½ **pound (8 ounces) well-aged blue cheese**

¼ **pound (½ cup or 1 stick) unsalted butter, softened**

½ **teaspoon ground cayenne pepper, or more, to taste**

1 **teaspoon freshly ground black pepper**

½ **teaspoon salt**

10 **ounces (about 2 cups) Southern soft wheat flour or all-purpose flour**

1. Finely grate the cheddar with a rotary cheese grater, a box grater, or the shredding disk of a food processor. Crumble the blue cheese into the bowl of a food processor fitted with a steel blade or into the bowl of a mixer. Add the cheddar and butter and cream them together until fluffy and smooth.

2. Add the cayenne, black pepper, salt, and flour and work it into a uniform dough. Gather it into a ball, wrap well in plastic wrap or waxed paper, and chill for at least half an hour to 1 hour. Don't let it get hard; if you are making it ahead to bake later, allow enough time for it to soften at room temperature until it is pliable but still cool.

3. Position a rack in the center of the oven and preheat to 325°F. Put the dough in a cookie press fitted with the star die and press it out into 2½-inch straws on an ungreased cookie sheet, leaving about ½ inch clear between. You may also roll the dough out and cut it into strips or spiral twists: See step 3 of Spicy Cheese Straws, page 44.

4. Bake about 18–20 minutes, until lightly browned on the bottom and pale gold on top. Cool the straws on the pan before transferring them to an airtight storage container.

Makes about 10 dozen

asparagus shortcake

The name of this lovely dish is usually met by a startled, slightly puzzled look, since today, most of us expect "shortcake" to be sweet. But savory short-cakes—fresh, hot biscuits split and filled with savory vegetable or meat sauces—are an old idea that has been around Southern kitchens for generations. This one combines asparagus with two of its natural complements—ham and leeks. It's an especially lovely way to freshen asparagus that has been in the grocer's refrigerator longer than you might like.

1 pound asparagus, washed, trimmed, and peeled as directed on page 188

1 medium leek

4 Old-Fashioned Southern Shortcakes (page 399)

2 tablespoons unsalted butter

4 ounces country ham, cut into julienne

1 cup heavy cream

Whole nutmeg in a grater

Whole white pepper in a mill

1 medium or 2 small scallions or other green onions, trimmed and thinly sliced

1. Cut the asparagus into 1-inch lengths, setting aside eight of the tips for garnish. Trim the leek and split it lengthwise. Holding it root-end up, wash the leek thoroughly under cold running water, bending back the layers to make sure that all the grit and dirt are washed away. Pat it dry and thinly slice it.

2. Position a rack in the center of the oven and preheat to 250°F. Put the shortcakes on a cookie sheet and put them in the oven while you make the filling. Put the leek and butter in large skillet or sauté pan. Turn on the heat to medium-high and sauté, tossing often, until softened but not colored, about 3 minutes. Add the asparagus and ham and sauté until the ham loses its raw red color and the asparagus is just shy of crisp-tender, about 2 minutes longer.

3. Add the cream; season liberally with nutmeg and white pepper. Bring the cream to a boil and cook, shaking the pan or stirring frequently to prevent sticking, until the cream is lightly thick-ened, about 3 minutes longer. Add the onions and toss half a minute longer. Taste and adjust the seasoning, give it one last stir, and turn off the heat.

4. Split the shortcakes crosswise and place the bottom halves on warm serving plates. Spoon the filling equally over them and cover it with the shortcake tops. Garnish each serving with two of the reserved asparagus tips and serve at once.

Serves 4

pork tenderloin biscuits with chutney butter

In the days before modern meatpacking, the first cold snap of autumn made Southern pigs nervous. Pork is more perishable than most other meats, and cold weather was the only time pigs could be safely butchered. From butchering the meat, through making the sausage, and starting the curing process for the hams and bacon, hog-killing days were a busy time, but not so busy that one couldn't take a moment to indulge in a fat biscuit stuffed with fresh pork tenderloin, sliced, seasoned with salt, pepper, and sometimes rubbed sage, then floured and pan-fried. Chutney, applesauce, or a slice of fried apple might be added, but more often than not the meat did not need anything more to make it one of the most satisfying breakfasts known to man.

This is a slightly dressier version, but it's actually less trouble. Instead of being sliced and pan-fried the tenderloin roasts in one piece, with almost no attention required of the cook. Then it is thinly sliced and piled onto biscuits slathered with a simple but heady mixture of chutney and butter. The sandwiches will tend to drip butter when you bite into them, but they are worth it, so be sure to pass absorbent napkins when you serve them.

1 pork tenderloin (about 12 ounces)

Extra-virgin olive oil

Salt and whole black pepper in a mill

1 tablespoon crumbled dried sage

1 batch Southern Breakfast Biscuits (page 260, not made ahead but where indicated in the recipe)

Chutney Butter (recipe follows)

1. Position a rack in the upper third of the oven and preheat to 500°F. Trim the excess fat and silver skin from the tenderloin, wipe it with a paper towel, and rub it with olive oil. Generously sprinkle all sides with salt, a liberal grinding of pepper, and the sage. Lightly rub the bottom of a small roasting pan with olive oil and put in the tenderloin.

2. Put the pan in the upper third of the oven and immediately reduce the heat to 450°F. Roast 10 minutes, or until the outside is seared and lightly browned. Drizzle a little more oil over it, pour about ¼ cup water into the pan, and reduce the heat to 375°F. Roast, basting occasionally, until the pork reaches an internal temperature of 130–135°F, about 15–20 minutes longer. If the liquid dries up completely, add a few spoonfuls of water, but don't add so much that the roast is swimming in it.

3. Remove the pork from the oven and raise the oven temperature to 500°F. Transfer the pork to a platter, loosely tent it with foil, and let it stand while you make the biscuits according the recipe on page 260. While they bake, slice the tenderloin across the grain as thinly as you can.

4. While the biscuits are still warm, split them and spread both sides generously with Chutney Butter. Place about two slices of pork on the bottom half of each biscuit, cover with the top half, and serve immediately. Make sure each person is supplied with an absorbent napkin; the one drawback of these biscuits is that they do tend to drip as the butter melts.

Makes 12 biscuits, serving 6–8

chutney butter

This savory-sweet butter is also delicious with ham (particularly country ham), lamb, and turkey, and it's spectacular spooned into a steaming-hot, freshly roasted sweet potato: Just split the potato down the center, wrap a napkin around it and pucker it, then spoon in a tablespoon of Chutney Butter. You'd have to die to get any closer to heaven.

¼ **pound (½ cup or 1 stick) unsalted butter, softened**

¼ **cup your favorite chutney**

Salt and cayenne pepper

1. With a mixer or fork, whip the butter until fluffy. Mix in the chutney until the butter is smooth; taste and add a pinch or so of salt as needed. If the chutney wasn't very spicy, add a pinch or so of cayenne—not enough to make it hot, just to brighten the flavor. Whip until the butter is smooth and fluffy and the seasonings are incorporated.

2. Allow it to stand at room temperature for 15–20 minutes. Taste and correct the seasonings. The butter can be served right away or stored, well covered, in the refrigerator. Allow it to return to room temperature; just before serving, give it a light whip until it is fluffy.

Makes about ¾ cup

mushrooms with sausage-bourbon filling

Stuffed mushrooms come and go in popularity, but never seem to go out of style in Savannah. Anytime they appear on a buffet table, they disappear just as quickly. The secret to really good ones is to choose mushrooms that are very fresh and to fill them with compatible flavors. White (sometimes called "button") mushrooms or champignons are too mild for most fillings and are too easily overwhelmed. Brown ("crimini") mushrooms are better suited to stronger flavors. The process is a little time consuming, but not difficult, particularly if you do not get carried away with too many ingredients.

Stuffed mushrooms are traditionally served at parties as finger food, but these also make a fine first course or side dish for almost any poultry, pork, or veal dish that does not already contain mushrooms.

24 medium crimini (sometimes labeled golden-brown or baby portobello) mushrooms

½ pound bulk breakfast sausage

1 medium yellow onion, trimmed, split lengthwise, peeled, and minced

2 large or 3 medium cloves garlic, lightly crushed, peeled, and minced

1 tablespoon fresh sage or ½ teaspoon dried sage (omit if sausage contains sage)

¼ cup bourbon

½ cup heavy cream (minimum 36% milk fat)

1 cup dry bread crumbs

Salt and whole black pepper in a mill

Whole nutmeg in a grater

1. Wipe the mushrooms with a dry cloth and snap off the stems. Lightly butter a baking pan that will comfortably hold the mushrooms and put the caps on it, stem-side up. Chop the stems and set them aside.

2. Crumble the sausage into a skillet or sauté pan set over medium-high heat. Sauté, crumbling the meat with a fork or spatula, until it has lost its raw red color. Add the onion and continue sautéing until golden, about 5–8 minutes. Add the garlic and optional sage and sauté until fragrant, about a minute longer. Add the chopped stems and sauté for a minute more. Slowly pour in the bourbon and let it completely evaporate. Add the cream, bring it to a boil, and turn off the heat.

3. Off the heat, stir in the bread crumbs, then taste and season as needed with salt, a few grindings of pepper, and a generous grating of nutmeg. Fill the stem cavity of the mushroom caps with this mixture, mounding it up until all the filling is used. You can make the mushrooms a couple of hours ahead to this point; cover and refrigerate until you're ready to bake them.

4. Position a rack in the upper third of the oven and preheat to 375°F. Bake the mushrooms until the caps are tender and the top of the filling is lightly browned, about 10 minutes. Serve hot, but if they are to be eaten as finger food, let them cool enough to be picked up with the fingers.

Serves 6 as a first course, 8–10 as an hors d'oeuvre

scalloped oysters

The constancy of scalloped oysters is a great comfort; they weave a continuous thread in the tapestry of Southern cooking that is little changed since the early recipes recorded by Mary Randolph (1824) and Sarah Rutledge (1847). Now, as then, they're considered an essential on many Southern holiday tables. Most modern cooks use crushed cracker crumbs instead of the bread crumbs of older recipes, and have abandoned the individual scallop shells from which the dish gets its name. I prefer the individual shells because they cook more evenly than a casserole, are much easier to serve, and are not much more trouble than dumping everything in a casserole.

1 pint shucked fresh oysters

¼ pound (1 stick) unsalted butter

2 cups finely crushed cracker crumbs

2 lemons

Nutmeg in a grater

Whole white pepper in a mill

Cayenne pepper

¼ cup finely chopped parsley

6 small scallop shells

1. Pour the oysters into a wire mesh sieve set over a bowl to catch their liquor. Save the liquor: It freezes well and can be used for stock in fish soup or gumbo.

2. Melt the butter in a large skillet over medium heat. Turn off the heat and stir in the cracker crumbs, mixing until they're thoroughly coated. Grate in the zest from the lemons, then season with liberal gratings of nutmeg, white pepper, and a couple of pinches of cayenne—all to taste. Add the parsley and stir until it is evenly mixed.

3. Spread a 1/2-inch-thick layer of rock salt on a rimmed baking sheet or line it with crumpled foil. Press the scallop shells into the salt or foil until they're stable. Sprinkle the oysters with lemon juice, then stir them together with half the crumbs. Divide this evenly among the shells and sprinkle generously with the remaining crumbs.

4. Position a rack 6 inches below the heat source and preheat the broiler for 15 minutes. Broil the oysters until the crumbs are lightly browned. Serve at once with lemon wedges.

Serves 6

broiled oysters on the half shell

Barbecue has been called man's most primal form of cooking, and it may well be, but broiling oysters in their shells over a hot bed of coals is surely as ancient. It cannot have been lost on early humans that oysters that had been heated were much easier to open and eat. The method survives today all along the Georgia and Carolina coast, where oyster "roasts" are a popular winter entertainment. Despite the name, the oysters are really broiled in the old sense of the word, over outdoor pits of hardwood coals not unlike those used for barbecue.

Modern broiling, under the flame rather than over it, is a wholly different way of cooking that evolved in the twentieth century with gas and electric ranges. The first recipes for it were exquisitely simple: The oysters were opened, blanketed with a piece of bacon, and run under the flame until the bacon was crisp. There's nothing easier or better. This recipe stays close to that simplicity and near-perfect combination of flavors, but with a lighter hand on the fat . . . if you happen to worry about such things.

24 live oysters in shell

¼ cup finely minced thick-cut bacon (about 2 slices)

¼ cup finely minced green onion tops (green part only)

Grated zest of 1 lemon

½ cup cracker crumbs

Whole black pepper in a mill

1 lemon, cut into 8 wedges

1. Position a rack 4–6 inches from the heat source and preheat the broiler for at least 15 minutes. Shuck the oysters and cut them loose from the shell, but leave them in the deep halves. Discard the shallow top shells. Spread a ½-inch-thick layer of rock salt on a rimmed baking sheet or line it with crumpled foil. Press the oysters in the shells into the salt or foil until they are level and stable.

2. Mix together the bacon, onion, lemon zest, and crumbs. Liberally grind pepper over it and toss until well blended. Sprinkle the bacon-crumb mixture evenly over each oyster.

3. Broil the oysters until the bacon-crumb topping is golden-brown and the gills are lightly curled, about 4 minutes. Serve at once, garnished with lemon wedges.

Serves 4–6 as a first course

lucy-mama's oysters

"Lucy-Mama" was the somewhat incongruous pet name of my good friend and fellow cookbook author Ruth Adams Bronz's grandmother. An imperious Louisiana dowager, she never quite got over the scandalous fact that all her grandchildren were born in Texas. ("You don't have to say you're from Texas, dear," she'd correct them, "just say your people are from Louisiana.") Ruth added to the scandal by leaving the South altogether and settling in the far northeast corner of Massachusetts. There she hosts a sumptuous Thanksgiving dinner every year for up to thirty people, the menu for which embraces every corner of the globe and changes annually—except for her grandmother's scalloped oysters. The one time she tried to omit them, it moved her guests to near mutiny. Once you taste them, you will understand why. The recipe is exactly as Ruth learned to make it from Lucy-Mama, with one exception: Instead of baking the oysters in one large dish, she divides them among individual scallop shells.

1 quart shucked oysters and their liquor

30 saltine crackers

½ cup (4 ounces or 1 stick) unsalted butter, divided

½ cup chopped parsley

¾ cup chopped scallions, both white and green parts

1 cup heavy cream

1 tablespoon Worcestershire sauce

2 teaspoons Tabasco sauce

Salt and whole black pepper in a mill

1. Position a rack in the center of the oven and preheat to 425°F. Butter eight individual scallop shells or a 10-inch pie plate or 2-quart gratin. If using scallop shells, spread a ½-inch-thick layer of rock salt on a rimmed baking sheet or line it with crumpled foil. Strain the oysters, reserving their liquor. Crush the saltines to medium crumbs.

2. Melt two-thirds of the butter in a large skillet over medium heat until foamy. Add two-thirds of the saltine crumbs and stir until they're evenly coated. Add the parsley and scallions and toss (the crumbs should be quite dry and just beginning to brown). Add the oyster liquid and cream and simmer, stirring often, until reduced by one-fourth, watching carefully. Stir in the oysters, Worcestershire, and Tabasco; season well with salt and pepper to taste.

3. Divide the oysters among the shells or pour into the prepared baking dish. Wipe out the skillet, add the remaining butter, and melt it over medium-low heat. Turn off the heat, add the remaining crumbs, and toss until coated. Sprinkle the crumbs over the oysters. If you've used scallop shells, press them into the salt or foil on the prepared baking sheet. Bake until bubbly, about 10 minutes.

Serves 8

seviche of gulf scallops

Seviche—pickled raw or fried fish—is another interesting parallel between the South and the Mediterranean. Both variations are quite old: There is a recipe for seviche in the first known Southern cookbook, and the method has been known to and used by most coastal cooks since at least the early nineteenth century. Probably their proliferation around the Gulf rim and on the eastern coast of Florida can be credited to constant cross-trade with the Caribbean and Spain. But history lesson aside, they have remained steadily popular and are a delicious summer hors d'oeuvres or light main course.

This version takes advantage of the small, sweet bay scallops that are never mentioned in older recipes. But you can substitute larger sea scallops or firm, saltwater fish if you prefer them—or if they are what you have on hand.

1 pound small bay scallops, or 1 pound sea scallops cut into ½-inch chunks (or 1 pound very fresh, white-fleshed saltwater fish such as flounder, grouper, pompano, yellowtail, or snapper, cut into ½-inch chunks)

⅔ cup freshly squeezed lime juice

FINISHING DRESSING I: RAW CREOLE SAUCE

1 cup fresh, ripe tomatoes, peeled with a vegetable peeler, cored, seeded, and chopped (about 1 large or 2 medium)

½ cup finely chopped scallions (about 2) or Vidalia or other sweet onions

1 medium green chile pepper (such as jalapeño), stemmed, split lengthwise, seeds and membranes removed, and finely minced

1 large or 2 small cloves garlic, lightly crushed, peeled, and finely minced

¼ cup reserved lime juice

Salt

FINISHING DRESSING II: LIME MAYONNAISE

½ cup Homemade Mayonnaise (page 230, made with lemon or lime juice) or commercial mayonnaise

Grated zest of 1 lime

2 tablespoons reserved lime juice

½ cup finely chopped scallions (about 2) or Vidalia or other sweet onions

Salt and whole white pepper in a mill

FOR SERVING:

4–8 lettuce leaves or 2 ripe avocados, split lengthwise, pitted, and peeled

¼ cup chopped fresh chives, green onion tops, or cilantro

1. Rinse the scallops under cold running water, drain well, and pat dry with paper towels or a clean cloth. Put them in a glass or stainless bowl and add the lime juice. Toss until they're well coated, cover tightly, and refrigerate, stirring once or twice, for at least 8 hours. Drain off but reserve the lime juice, and finish the dish in either of the following ways.

2. To finish with Raw Creole Sauce: Stir together the tomatoes, onions, chile pepper, and garlic. Add ¼ cup of the reserved lime juice and a large

pinch of salt. Mix thoroughly and taste the sauce. Adjust the seasonings, adding a little more lime juice and salt to suit your taste. Pour this over the scallops and toss gently until evenly mixed. Cover and refrigerate for 30 minutes. Taste and adjust for lime juice and salt, then discard any remaining juice. Keep chilled until ready to serve. Skip to step 4.

3. To finish with Lime Mayonnaise: Stir the mayonnaise and zest together in a glass or stainless-steel bowl. Fold in 2 tablespoons of the reserved lime juice; it should be the consistency of thick cream. Add the onion, a small pinch of

salt, several grindings of white pepper, and the scallops. Toss gently until well mixed, cover, and refrigerate for up to 2 hours. Taste and adjust the lime juice, salt, and pepper. Discard any remaining juice.

4. Serving the seviche: Put 1–2 lettuce leaves or an avocado half onto each of four chilled salad plates. Divide the scallops evenly among them, sprinkle the chives, green onion tops, or cilantro over them, and serve at once.

Serves 4

shrimp butter

Closely related to potted shrimps, an old English conserve of cooked shrimp pounded to a paste, mixed with spices, and stored under a thick layer of clarified butter, shrimp butter or paste has been a staple on Lowcountry tables ever since the first English landed here. It is delicious served as a spread at tea or cocktail time, and when chilled and sliced it can also do duty as a first course or a savory accompaniment for breakfast grits, either served cold or gently warmed by sautéing in a lightly buttered pan.

Salt

1½ pounds shrimp

¼ pound (1 stick) unsalted butter, softened

2 tablespoons finely minced shallot or yellow onion

1 small clove garlic, lightly crushed, peeled, and minced

Ground cayenne pepper

2 dozen Dry Toast Points (page 40), Melba toast rounds, or crackers

1. Put 3 quarts of water in a 4-quart pot and turn on the heat to medium-high. When the water begins boiling, add a small handful of salt, let the salt dissolve, and add the shrimp. Immediately cover the pot, turn off the heat, and count 2 minutes. The residual heat will be enough to cook the shrimp. As soon as they turn bright pink and curl, they're ready. Immediately drain and rinse under cold running water to arrest the cooking.

2. Peel the shrimp and put them into the work bowl of a food processor fitted with a steel blade. Add the butter, onion, garlic, and a small pinch each of salt and cayenne pepper. Process until the shrimp are a smooth paste. Taste and adjust the seasonings, being stingy with the cayenne (it should brighten here, not set the dish on fire).

3. You may pack the paste into a lightly buttered 3-cup mold or small loaf pan and chill it until it is set, or simply pile it into a crystal or china serving bowl. Serve chilled or at room temperature with Dry Toast Points or plain crackers.

Makes about 2 cups, serving 6 as a first course, 8–12 as an appetizer

CHAPTER TWO

EGGS

FOR BREAKFAST, BEFORE, AND BETWEEN

Eggs are so obliging: They take well to virtually every form of cooking, are quick and filling, and fit in at any meal. Most cultures with domesticated birds in the yard have taken advantage of them, but Southerners seem more partial to them than almost anyone else: Our repertory of egg cookery is some of the most varied in the world. If these neat little ovals were suddenly to go missing from our larders, we could probably get along without them, but it wouldn't be easy. Hard-cooked, they're almost as essential in the salad bowl as oil and vinegar, and their emptied whites are unsurpassed as a carrier for savory fillings. Poached, they enhance everything from the traditional pot of greens to elegantly layered brunch dishes. Scrambled, fried, or rolled into fluffy omelets, they make the perfect quick meal at any time of the day from the crack of dawn till midnight. The recipes that follow are arranged according to the cooking method used rather than the occasion because, in Southern tables, eggs are welcome at any time.

hard-cooked eggs

There are three common failures in hard-cooking eggs: rubbery whites, a dusky-green coating like tarnished copper on the surface of the yolk, and whites that stick like glue to the shell and tear apart when they're peeled. The first two result from taking "hard-boiled" too literally: They're a sure sign that the eggs are overcooked, and at a rolling boil. Eggs must never boil hard, and just like a prime steak, they toughen when overcooked. Surprisingly, the third problem arises because the eggs are very fresh. For most preparations, freshness is paramount, and for poaching,

omelets, meringues, and baked goods, new-laid eggs are essential. For hard-cooking, the eggs should be a couple of weeks old. As the egg white matures, it loses moisture, lessening the tendency for the membranes to cling to the shell.

You may cook as few as two or as many as a dozen eggs this way. If you need more than a dozen, cook them in batches to ensure consistent results.

1. Using a clean pushpin or needle, gently prick each egg at the large end to help prevent the shell from cracking as its contents warm. Put the eggs in a heavy-bottomed pan that will hold them in one layer and add enough cold water to cover them by at least ½ inch. Bring the water just to a full boil over medium-high heat.

2. Cover the pan with a tight-fitting lid and remove it from the heat. Let it stand 10 minutes, drain, and rinse the eggs under cold running water. Lightly tap the eggs on all sides to crack the shells, cover with cold water, and let stand for another minute before peeling them. Begin at the large end, where there's usually an air pocket that will help you get the shell loose. Use them as soon as possible after peeling them, preferably before they're refrigerated, but if that's not an option put them in a glass or stainless steel container, cover tightly, and refrigerate for up to 2 days.

asparagus-stuffed eggs

This is a lighter, and only slightly more difficult, variation on the classic deviled egg. They look like the conventional article, but the first bite is downright transcendental. There's no special secret; asparagus and eggs were simply made for each other.

If the asparagus you are using is especially large, you may not have a full twenty-four tips. In that case, cut the tips in half lengthwise and use only a half to garnish each egg. If the stem portion is especially large, you can also roughly chop the upper portion so that the texture in the stuffing mixture will be less chunky, but don't puree all of it: The mixture needs the solid bits of asparagus. Otherwise, the stuffing will just be mushy and dull.

12 Hard-Cooked Eggs (page 60)

1 pound asparagus, trimmed, peeled, and cooked as for Basic Asparagus (page 190)

3 tablespoons freshly squeezed lemon juice

3 tablespoons unsalted butter, softened

Salt and cayenne pepper

2 tablespoons thinly sliced green onion tops or chives

1. Peel the eggs and halve them lengthwise. Scoop the yolks into the bowl of a food processor fitted with a steel blade. Set the whites, cut-side up, on a deviled egg plate or platter or plate. Thickly slice the bottom half of the asparagus stalks and set them aside. Cut off the tips and set aside twenty-four of them to use as garnish (see notes above). Thinly slice the remaining asparagus and set it aside.

2. Add the thick-sliced parts of the asparagus stalks, lemon juice, and butter to the yolks. Cover and process until the asparagus is pureed and the mixture is fluffy and smooth. Taste and season as needed with salt and cayenne.

3. Transfer it to a ceramic or glass mixing bowl and fold in the thin-sliced asparagus. Taste and correct the seasonings, adding more salt and cayenne if needed. Spoon the filling into the cups of the egg whites, mounding it on top. Garnish with the asparagus tips and sliced green onion tops. If you've made them more than an hour ahead of time, cover and refrigerate, but let them sit at room temperature for half an hour before serving.

Makes 24 stuffed eggs, serving 8 as a first course, 24 as an hors d'oeuvre

classic southern deviled eggs

If you really want to win the heart of almost anyone born and raised south of the Mason-Dixon line, forget exotic dress (or undress), potent elixirs, and voodoo incantations: All you need is a plate of simple, honest deviled eggs. The star of these lovely hors d'oeuvres has risen and fallen everywhere but here in the South, where they never go out of style, and remain a quintessential element for every picnic and reception. Even in our laid-back times when special-ized serving dishes have become anachronistic, the one piece of tableware that new brides down South can bank on getting is a deviled egg plate. No matter how sophisticated the party's guests profess to be, the deviled eggs will be the first thing to disappear from the table, leaving latecomers to hover around the empty plate with looks of wistful disappointment.

This is more outline than a recipe: no two cooks really make them the same way—not even mother and daughter. The daughter may insist she's faithfully followed Mama to the letter, but differences always creep in. But that's the beauty; even if six Southerners all brought deviled eggs to the same potluck party, there would still be plenty of variety on the table. In other words, feel free to let evolution take its natural course: If you find you prefer a softer filling, add more mayonnaise or a splash of cream; if you like the eggs to have more bite, up the mustard or cayenne, or dust the tops with pepper. If you want to fancy them up, top each with a slice of pimiento-stuffed olive, a caper, a sliver of country ham or lox, a small cooked shrimp, or a dollop of caviar or salmon roe. Or fold in ¼ cup of chopped ham, smoked salmon, sweet or sour pick-les, olives, or capers—or whatever else (within reason) you like.

Just remember: Simpler is easier and always seems to please the crowd the most.

12 Hard-Cooked Eggs (page 60)

½ cup mayonnaise, preferably Homemade Mayonnaise (page 230)

1 tablespoon prepared mustard (your choice)

Salt and ground cayenne

Sweet paprika

About 2 tablespoons minced chives or parsley, or whole sprigs of dill, optional

1. Peel the eggs and halve them lengthwise. Scoop the yolks into a ceramic or glass mixing bowl. Set the whites, cut-side up, on a deviled egg plate or platter. Roughly mash the yolks with a fork to the texture of coarse meal, then blend in the mayon-naise and mustard. Season to taste with salt and cayenne and beat until smooth. (You may do this step in the food processor: Put the yolks in the work bowl that has been fitted with the metal blade. Pulse until they're the texture of coarse meal, then add the mayonnaise, mustard, salt, and cayenne; process until smooth.)

2. Spoon or pipe the filling into the egg whites, mounding it up a little. (If you want to seal your stature with the Southern Belle crowd, pipe it, using a pastry bag fitted with a star tip.) Lightly dust the top with paprika. You may further garnish them with chives, parsley, or dill sprigs. They can be made several hours ahead; cover with something that will not touch the tops of the eggs and refrigerate until you are ready to serve them.

Makes 24 stuffed eggs, serving 8 as a first course, 10–12 as an hors d'oeuvre

Curried Deviled Eggs: Another picnic favorite, these are simply Classic Southern Deviled Eggs with a teaspoon or more of mild curry powder mixed into the filling.

Crab-Stuffed Deviled Eggs: Omit the mayonnaise, mustard, and salt from Classic Southern Deviled Eggs and substitute the following:

¼ **cup Dijon-style mustard**

Juice of 1 lemon

1–2 pinches ground cayenne pepper

4 medium or 3 large scallions or other green onions, trimmed and thinly sliced

1 pound (2 cups) cooked crabmeat, picked over to remove any bits of shell and cartilage

2 tablespoons capers, roughly chopped

Prepare the yolk filling as directed in the recipe for Classic Southern Deviled Eggs, using the yolks, mustard, lemon juice, and cayenne. Fold in the scallions, crab, and capers, and spoon the filling (you won't be able to pipe this one) into the egg whites.

poached eggs

Many cooks are intimidated by the prospect of poaching eggs, particularly in quantity, which I suppose is why there are so many different egg-poaching devices around. But actually, it is very easy to do without any of these contraptions. I've poached as many as two dozen eggs in front of a class of students. All you need is a lidded pan, a slotted spoon, a little (though not much) time and patience, and a few pointers.

+ Make sure the eggs are very fresh, and take them from the refrigerator 30 minutes before you plan to cook them so that they'll be at room temperature.

+ Choose a saucepan or deep sauté pan that will hold at least 2 inches of water.

+ Break each egg into a shallow bowl first. This will catch any bad eggs or broken yolks before they make it into the pan, but it also helps the egg hold together when it hits the water.

+ The water should be bubbling but not boiling hard. If you're poaching more than four eggs at once, when all the eggs in the pan are set—which will be a matter of seconds—remove it from the heat, cover, and let the residual heat finish the cooking. This will ensure tender whites and soft, runny, but thick yolks.

+ Do not make a vortex in the center of the pan by stirring the water in a circular motion. This doesn't help the egg hold its shape; in fact, it only makes the white throw off more tendrils or streamers, especially if the eggs aren't very fresh.

+ A splash (and only a splash) of white wine vinegar will help the egg hold its shape, but too much will give it a harsh vinegary undertone.

+ Don't crowd the pan. Leave about ½ inch of space around each egg so they will cook evenly and be easier to remove from the pan.

1. Put at least 1½ and up to 2 inches of water in a deep, lidded saucepan or lidded nonstick deep sauté pan. You need enough water for the eggs to float, but if they have too far to travel before they settle, they are likely to throw off a lot of streamers and "angel wings" (thin sheets of white). Turn on the heat to high, bring the water to a boil, then reduce the heat to medium. When the boil has settled to a steady bubble, one at a time break each egg into a shallow bowl and slip it into the pan. Continue until the pan is filled but not crowded, allowing about ½ inch between each egg.

2. When all the eggs are in the pan, let them simmer until the whites are set and the yolk is still quite soft, about 1½–2 minutes altogether. If you're doing eight eggs at a time, cover the pan and turn off the heat. Let this stand undisturbed for 3 minutes for a medium soft poach. Remove the eggs with a slotted spoon, allowing them to drain thoroughly, and trim off any loose tendrils of white. Serve warm, passing salt, pepper, and softened butter separately, or in one of the following recipes.

poached eggs with crab sauce

This is ideal brunch food: easy on the cook, impressive looking at the table, and wonderfully good to eat. It's especially good for cooks with little or no help in the kitchen: Though it can't be made ahead, when all the elements are prepped it can be ready in 10 minutes or less. Make the toast ahead, have the water already simmering for the eggs, and poach them while the sauce is going through its final simmer.

The crab sauce is also delicious spooned over omelets, broiled fish, or simply toast points as a first course, and makes a terrific sauce for egg pasta such as fettuccine. And it doubles easily: Simply multiply everything except the butter by two but only increase the butter by half.

8 ounces (1 cup) lump crabmeat

2 tablespoons unsalted butter

2 tablespoons minced shallots or yellow onions

Salt and cayenne pepper

1 tablespoon tomato paste

1 cup heavy cream

8 hoecakes (page 258), or 4 Southern Breakfast Biscuits (page 260), split and toasted; or 8 triangles or rounds of bread, toasted

8 poached eggs (page 64)

1. Pick over the crabmeat, removing any shell or cartilage. Warm the butter and shallots in a skillet or sauté pan over medium-high heat. Sauté, tossing often, until the shallots are pale gold. Add the crab and toss until it is hot through. Taste and season as needed with salt and cayenne. Stir in the tomato paste until the crab is evenly coated.

2. Add the cream and gently stir until it has an even, pink color. Bring to a boil and cook, stirring occasionally, until lightly thickened, about 2–3 minutes. Turn off the heat.

3. Place two toasts or hoecakes, or one split biscuit, on each of four warm serving plates. Lay an egg on each piece of bread and spoon a little of the sauce over each. Serve at once.

Serves 4

eggs savannah

Think of this as Eggs Benedict with a Southern attitude. It begins with structure of that universal brunch standard: A poached egg nestles on top of a sliver of sautéed ham and bit of toasted bread and is topped off with a drizzle of savory sauce. But the elements under and over that egg are those of a hearty, traditional Southern breakfast: cornmeal hoecakes, fine old country ham, pan-grilled tomatoes, and red-eye gravy.

8 hoecakes (page 258)

1 tablespoon ham or bacon drippings or unsalted butter

8 thin slices country ham

2 ripe medium tomatoes, cored, peeled with a vegetable peeler, and sliced into 8 even slices

Whole black pepper in a mill

8 poached eggs (page 64)

¼ cup strong coffee or tea

¾ cup water

2 tablespoons cold unsalted butter, cut into bits

1. Preheat the oven to 200°F. Put the hoecakes on a sheet pan and warm them in the oven, about 10 minutes. Divide them (two per serving) among four warm plates. Put the drippings in a skillet that will hold all the ham in one layer and turn on the heat to medium-high. When the fat is melted and hot, slip in the ham and sauté it quickly for about half a minute per side; do not overcook. Lay the ham over the hoecakes.

2. Add the sliced tomatoes to the hot pan and cook, turning once, until they are beginning to color and wilt slightly, about 4 minutes per side. Lay them over the ham. Sprinkle them with a few liberal grindings of pepper and top them with a poached egg.

3. Pour the coffee or tea and water into the pan and bring it to a boil, stirring and scraping to release any cooking residue that may have stuck to the pan. Boil rapidly until the gravy has reduced by a little more than half and is the consistency of a thin glaze. Turn off the heat and swirl in the butter. Spoon the gravy evenly over the eggs and serve at once.

Serves 4

shrimp omelet

An exquisitely simple but elegant dish frequently found on Lowcountry breakfast tables is Shrimp and Eggs, which is nothing more than leftover boiled shrimp and fresh eggs scrambled together. But breakfast, in Savannah, may as often close the day as begin it, and shrimp with eggs is a favorite way to end a formal evening. To appreciate it, you must have the context: The party's over, but intimate friends are lingering, not quite ready to head home. The edges have softened: Evening pumps and jackets have come off; black ties are loosened; discarded earrings glitter in empty ashtrays and bonbon dishes. Someone opens the last of the champagne, and someone else takes the last of the shrimp from the buffet and mixes them with eggs. Perhaps a few cold biscuits will be split and toasted. Everyone takes a plate and a glass, and, with stocking feet up and hair down, happily settles in for the best part of the night.

4 ounces (headless weight, about 12) medium shrimp, cooked as directed in step 1 of Shrimp Butter (page 58)

4 large eggs

Salt and cayenne pepper

3 tablespoons unsalted butter

1. If the shrimp are not already peeled, peel them, removing the tail fins, and cut them in half crosswise. Break the eggs into a glass or stainless bowl. Season them with a large pinch of salt and a small pinch of cayenne, and lightly beat them with a fork.

2. Put the butter in a large nonstick or well-seasoned, heavy-bottomed 9-inch omelet pan and turn on the heat to medium-high. When the butter is very hot and the foaming subsides, add the eggs. Let them sit for about 5 seconds until a film forms on the bottom, then begin vigorously swirling the pan until soft but still-moist curds form.

3. Scatter the shrimp across the center of the omelet and, tipping the pan over a plate, let the omelet roll over on itself onto the plate. You can also roll the omelet with the aid of a spatula if that's easier for you: Push the eggs gently to one side of the pan so that the side of the omelet curls, then flip it over on top of itself. If you like the omelet a little more set, roll it back into the pan, turn off the heat, and let it sit half a minute longer. Serve at once.

Serves 2

CHAPTER THREE

GRITS AND RICE

Almost everyone will agree that grits are one of the true universal icons of the Southern table, as deeply Southern as a magnolia. If you are not a Southerner, then, it may shock you to learn that we don't all eat grits. There are places in our region where this hot cereal is almost unheard of (well, except for the few lonely packets of instant grits in the hot cereal aisle of the supermarket), and I'm not referring to ethnic communities in the South's larger cities, or the enclaves of retired snowbirds who live part-time in South Florida.

Efforts to explain this inevitably fall short. I was once at a conference where one social historian boldly drew a "grits line" across the center of the country, claiming that grits were only found south of that line; later that day, another tried to turn the line into a confining loop that hugged the Atlantic to the east and Gulf of Mexico to the south, cutting off the tip of Florida and half of Texas, and excluding Arkansas to the west and most of Kentucky to the north. They very nearly caused a riot, because neither of these misguided souls was even remotely right. There is not, and never has been, any such thing as a neat Maginot Line embroidering a "grits" region. Even if it were possible to draw a "grits map" of the South (something I, for one, would never attempt), it would have no neat borders, but would look more like someone had slung a pot of grits at it and let them splatter.

But that is neither here nor there: What you need to know is, where grits are eaten down South, they are deeply loved and staunchly defended—and as Southern as it gets.

breakfast grits

This is actually the basic method for preparing grits for any occasion and for any of the recipes that follow. Exact proportions of grits to water are a little tricky; a lot depends on the humidity of the day, the amount of moisture in the grits before they are cooked, and, sometimes, I think, the way you are holding your mouth. The usual proportion is four parts water to one part grits, but this can and does vary, especially with whole corn grits, so keep a teakettle of water simmering close at hand in case the grits need more water. Never add cold water to cooking grits; they just get confused and seem to take that much longer before they get tender.

One is always learning: I have been cooking grits since I was four years old and it was only lately that I learned the secret to really creamy grits from friend and fellow cookbook author Kathy Starr. She never adds salt while the grits are cooking, claiming that salt prevents them from properly absorbing moisture and releasing enough starch to give them that fine, creamy texture. Who cares if there's anything scientific about it? Kathy has cooked more grits than most of us have even seen. Just trust her on this one and hold back the salt until they're done.

The best pot for cooking grits is one that has a porcelain-enamel or stainless-steel interior and a heavy bottom. An ideal alternative to such a pot is a ceramic-lined slow cooker. This type of cooker is especially fine for cooking grits in large quantities. The longer grits cook (even the quick-cooking variety) the better, so choose a pot that will allow a slow, steady simmer.

4 cups water

1 cup raw grits (either whole corn or hominy grits)

Salt

1. Bring the water to a boil in a stainless-steel or enameled pot. Slowly stir in the grits, pouring them in a thin, steady stream. Bring the liquid back to a boil, stirring constantly. Meanwhile, bring a teakettle full of water to a boil, reduce the heat under it to low, and have it simmering.

2. Reduce the heat under the grits to the slowest simmer you can manage and set the lid askew over the pot. Cook, stirring frequently at first and then occasionally as it begins to thicken, until the grits absorb all the moisture and are thick and creamy, about an hour. If they get too thick, or if the water is absorbed before the grits are tender, replenish the moisture as needed with the simmering water. Season well with salt, simmer for a few minutes to absorb the flavoring, then taste and adjust the salt. Serve hot.

Serves 4

hominy and whole corn grits

Actually, it would be nice if earnest social historians would spend less time worrying about where and how grits are eaten and more time discussing what they are. (And don't worry me with the fact that I am not using singular pronouns and verbs: Grits can be either singular or plural, so let it go.) Grits are a cereal made of coarsely ground corn—historically, hominy, the ancient staple of many Native American diets. Hominy is simply whole corn kernels treated with lye, which not only removes the tough outer skin and chaff, but changes the corn's structure so that when ground into meal it will hold together when shaped into tortillas. It also adds nutrients that are not present in the untreated grain, which is why Native Americans never got pellagra. Most nationally marketed brands are actually hominy grits—unfortunately, of uneven quality.

Partly because of that uneven quality in commercial hominy grits, there's been a fad for grits made from the whole grain—and with the fad has come a lot of snob posturing about their superiority. But there's nothing wrong with hominy grits, and there are even times when they're preferable to those fashionable grits made from whole corn. Anyway, unless the grits are well prepared, it won't matter what kind they are. This chapter tells you how to do it right.

gussied grits

Although home cooks have long made use of leftover grits in casseroles or even in the frying pan, and would sometimes serve company what my grandmother would have called "gussied up" grits, few of those old-style cooks would recognize some of the stuff that is being served in these nouvelle Southern establishments around the country. Sometimes it's enough to make traditionalists like me lie down with a bottle of bourbon, particularly when I see the unwieldy lists of odd ingredients and notice how many extra pots and steps they require.

That isn't to say that some of those new dishes aren't ingenious and absolutely delicious—but many of them are impractical for home cooks to manage. The recipes that follow are a few simple home-style preparations that don't require a battery of equipment and a specialty grocery in your pantry. Feel free to experiment with them and make them your own, but do try to remember that this is basic soul food.

A word on milk in grits: In the last couple of decades, people have taken to cooking their grits in milk and cream. There may be times when this is appropriate, but I don't care for it, especially if the grits are served plain or are topped with seafood. It makes the texture creamier, yes (well, hello), but it also muddies the flavor, making them heavy and wearying after just a few bites, and makes scorching far more likely.

CHEESE GRITS

Before adding the salt to Breakfast Grits in step 2, stir in 1 cup sharp cheddar, gruyère, or Parmigiano-Reggiano cheese (or a combination). Stir until the cheese is melted, taste, and then add salt as needed. Allow the grits to simmer for a minute so that the seasoning is absorbed. You may make cheese grits ahead and reheat them by baking: Pour them into a 2-quart casserole and sprinkle another ¼ cup grated cheese over the top. Cover and refrigerate it if you are making it more than an hour ahead, then bake at 350°F in the center of the oven until hot and bubbly, about 30 minutes.

fried grits

Despite their plebeian-sounding name, these little cakes of golden-fried grits are an elegant way to recycle leftovers, and make a spectacular carrier for creamed seafood, chicken, or ham. Grits are full of natural gelatin, and, when cold, set up into a jellied cake that can then be sliced and broiled, baked, or, in this case, fried. Since they're seldom served on their own, but usually as a carrier for other food, they are simply seasoned, usually with nothing more than salt. But if you like, you may up the flavor by stirring in a couple of tablespoons of minced onion, ham, herbs, or cheese while the grits are hot.

Have whatever topping you plan to serve over the grits completely ready before you fry the cakes, so that they can be served as soon as they are taken from the pan.

2 cups hot Breakfast Grits (page 70)

¼ cup all-purpose flour

1 large egg, lightly beaten

1 cup cracker crumbs or matzo meal

Lard or peanut or vegetable oil for frying

1. Rinse a 9 × 9-inch glass casserole or two tumblers with cool water. Pour the hot grits into the casserole or tumblers, cool, and then refrigerate until the grits are chilled. Unmold the grits onto a cutting board and, using a sharp knife dipped in cool water, cut them into 3-inch squares or into round cakes about ½ inch thick.

2. Lightly roll the grits cakes in the flour, then dip them in the egg, allowing the excess egg to flow back into the bowl. Roll the cakes in the cracker crumbs or matzo meal and lay them on a clean, dry platter. Allow them to sit for at least 10, and up to 30, minutes.

3. Put enough lard or oil in a large, heavy-bottomed skillet or sauté pan to cover the bottom by ½ inch. Turn on the heat to medium-high. When the fat is hot, but not quite smoking (about 375°F), put in enough grits cakes to fill the pan without crowding. Fry, turning once, until golden on all sides and hot through, about 2–3 minutes per side.

4. Lift them from the fat with a slotted spatula, holding it over the pan to allow all the fat to drain. Blot briefly on absorbent paper (butcher paper, brown grocery bags, or paper towels) and immediately transfer to plates. Serve at once.

Serves 4

baked grits and greens

Every March 17, Savannah is host to what is said to be the third largest St. Patrick's Day celebration in the country. For three days the whole town, from the fountains in the Southside's suburban malls all the way to (and including) the Savannah River, is awash with green. Pre-parade breakfasts and brunches are commonplace, and a frequent centerpiece of these meals is, of course, grits . . . garishly dyed as green as the river. It looks as frightening as it sounds. Here are green grits that come by the color more naturally, and in a combination that is a lot more traditional, not to mention appealing.

1 pound fresh spinach or swiss chard greens; or 1 (10-ounce) package frozen whole-leaf spinach, thawed, squeezed dry, and roughly chopped

2 tablespoons unsalted butter

4 medium green onions such as scallions, washed, trimmed, and thinly sliced

1 recipe Breakfast Grits (page 70)

½ cup heavy cream (minimum 36% milk fat)

1½ cups freshly grated extra-sharp white cheddar or Parmigiano-Reggiano, or equal portions of both, divided

Salt and whole white pepper in a mill

2 large eggs, well beaten

1. Position a rack in the center of the oven and preheat to 350°F. If using frozen spinach, skip to step 2. Wash the greens in a basin of cold water, changing the water if necessary, until all the dirt is removed. Drain, but not thoroughly—there should still be plenty of water clinging to the leaves—and put the greens in a deep, lidded frying pan or Dutch oven. Cover and cook over medium-high heat until they're just wilted, about 3 minutes. Immediately drain and refresh the greens under cold running water, draining well. Gently squeeze dry and roughly chop them.

2. Wipe out the pan in which the greens cooked and put in the butter. Warm it over medium heat; when it's almost melted, add the green onions and sauté until wilted, about 2 minutes. Add the greens and heat them through, about 2 minutes more. Turn off the heat.

3. In a large mixing bowl, stir together the grits and cream. Mix in the greens and 1 cup of the cheese. Taste and add salt, if needed, and a few liberal grindings of pepper. Thoroughly mix in the eggs. Lightly butter a 9-inch square or 10-inch round casserole and pour in the grits and greens, leveling the top with a spatula. Sprinkle with the remaining cheese, and bake in the center of the oven, until set and lightly browned, about 35–40 minutes. Serve hot.

Serves 6–8

spoonbread

This classic soft, soufflé-like bread is so closely connected with Virginia that it's often called "Virginia Spoonbread" in regional cookbooks. Many a native of that state is ready and willing to fight for their claim to its invention, and since the oldest printed recipes known to us did come from Mary Randolph's *The Virginia House-Wife* (1824), who's to say it wasn't? The picturesque name, probably derived from the fact that it's more of a soufflé than a bread, came late in the nineteenth century; Mrs. Randolph called it Batter Bread and baked it in small, individual servings rather like popovers or muffins, which would not have needed a spoon. Through time, cooks have preferred square tins, pottery pudding dishes, china teacups, and individual ramekins. Each of these gives slightly differing results, but the batter usually varies only in detail. Late in the nineteenth century, baking powder found its way into spoonbread, but while many modern recipes still call for it, it's completely unnecessary and doesn't belong.

3 cups whole milk or 2 cups whole milk
and 1 cup light cream

1 cup fine cornmeal

3 tablespoons butter

1 teaspoon salt

3 large eggs, separated

1. Position a rack in the center of the oven and preheat to 350°F. Scald the milk in a heavy-bottomed pan over medium-low heat, stirring frequently. Gradually whisk in the meal in a thin, steady stream, pouring it either from your fist or from a spouted measuring cup. Cook, stirring frequently, until it's a thick mush, about 3–5 minutes. Off the heat, beat in the butter and salt and set it aside to cool slightly.

2. Lightly butter a 2-quart soufflé dish, round casserole, or other baking dish that's at least 2 inches deep. Separate the eggs, putting the whites in a clean copper, stainless-steel, or glass bowl. Lightly beat the yolks and mix them into the mush.

3. Using a clean whisk or mixer, beat the whites until they form firm but not dry peaks. Add them gradually to the mush and gently but thoroughly fold them in. Pour the batter into the prepared dish and bake it in the center of the oven until risen and golden-brown on the top, about 45 minutes. It should be set, but still soft, like a soufflé. Serve at once from the baking dish.

Serves 4

awendaw, or hominy spoonbread

This elegant, enigmatically named dish is simply spoonbread with grits. Food historian John Martin Taylor places its origins in the Carolina Lowcountry. The name is certainly regional, deriving from a Native American name for an ancient fishing village near Charleston, South Carolina, and one of the first known recipes for it is found in Sarah Rutledge's bible of Lowcountry cookery, *The Carolina Housewife* (1847). Regardless of its pedigree, the technique is the same as spoonbread. The rise is not quite as spectacular since the eggs are not separated, but it puffs handsomely and should be served straight from the oven. Best of all, it's homey and cozy, perfect for family suppers yet elegant enough for a "best company" dinner.

2 cups hot Breakfast Grits (page 70)

2 tablespoons unsalted butter

4 large eggs

2 cups whole milk

1 cup stone-ground white cornmeal

1 teaspoon salt

1. Position a rack in the center of the oven and preheat to 375°F. Lightly butter a 2-quart soufflé dish or deep casserole. While the grits are still quite hot, mix in the butter until it's melted. Let it cool slightly and then beat in the eggs and then the milk. Gradually stir in the cornmeal and salt.

2. Pour the batter into the prepared dish and bake it in the center of the oven until it is set and lightly browned on top, about 45 to 50 minutes. Serve at once.

Serves 8

carolina-style rice

Until mechanized harvesting and a hurricane brought on a collapse of the industry in the 1920s, Carolina Gold Rice was a staple money crop of the Carolina and Georgia tidewater regions. Today rice culture has moved west, to Louisiana and Texas, but nearly a century after the end of Carolina Gold's reign in the Carolina and Georgia Lowcountry, rice is still a staple throughout the region. And the cookery, informed by that of the West African rice-growing slaves who built the culture, is like nowhere else in the country.

To prepare rice as Lowcountry cooks do, with fluffy, separate grains that almost rattle the plate when they land on it, use the best-quality long-grain rice you can find, always wash it before cooking to remove the excess starch (even if it's labeled "pre-washed"), and never stir it once the water begins to boil. When it is done, it's fluffed by picking it with a fork.

1 cup raw, long-grain rice (my own everyday rice preference is an imported basmati)

Salt

1. Put the rice in a 3-quart pot and fill the pot to within an inch of the rim with water. Pick up a handful of rice with both hands and rub it between your fingers until the water is milky. Drain it over a wire mesh sieve to catch any run-away grains and repeat this at least twice more, or until the water is nearly clear. Drain well and add 2 cups cold water and a healthy pinch of salt. Lightly stir to dissolve the salt and bring the pot to a boil over medium-high heat. Just before it's boiling, give it a stir to make sure that the rice isn't sticking, and put the spoon away.

2. Reduce the heat to low and set the lid askew (I actually leave it uncovered). Let the rice simmer for 12 minutes, or until clear, dry steam holes have formed on the surface and most, if not all, of the water is absorbed. Gently fold the top rice under with a fork, "fluffing" not stirring it.

3. Tightly cover the pot, let it cook a minute more to build the steam, and then turn off the heat. Let stand for 12 minutes. You may hold it like this for up to an hour without harm. When you are ready to serve, fluff again by picking it with the fork and turn it out into a serving bowl.

Serves 4

about pilaus

Pilau (spelled variously perlow, perloo, and occasionally pilaf) is one of the great rice dishes of the Lowcountry region of Carolina and Georgia. Pilau is really more of a technique than a specific recipe, and there are hundreds of variations, including the famed euphoniously named Hoppin' John, which is really just a pilau made of peas and rice.

It's a technique that is, unfortunately, all too often misunderstood. I've heard it compared to Italy's risotto, another rice dish that's more of a technique than a specific recipe. But there, the resemblance ends. The two have absolutely nothing in common. Risotti are made with fat, short-grain rice; the cooking liquid is gradually stirred in. In fact, the cook almost never stops stirring. Pilaus are made with long-grain rice that's usually coated with a little fat to keep the grains from releasing starch into the cooking liquid, which is added all at once. Significantly, the rice is never stirred after the liquid is added.

As you would expect, the results from these two techniques are completely different. In a well-made risotto, the rice is al dente and held together by a creamy, enrobing sauce that's created by the constant stirring, which releases the surface starch of the rice. A well-made pilau consists of tender and yet distinctly separate grains of rice that easily stand alone. There is no creamy sauce: In fact, not only is the rice coated with fat to keep it separate, it's thoroughly washed before it is cooked to remove as much of the surface starch as possible.

shrimp pilau

Because the famed Carolina Gold Rice with which these dishes were originally made was grown right next to salt marshes teeming with brown inlet shrimp, shrimp pilau seems an especially appropriate way of illustrating the technique. Most old recipes called for the shrimp to cook in the rice for the entire time. While this does infuse more flavor into the rice, it makes the shrimp tough. For maximum flavor while preserving the texture of the shrimp, modern cooks use broth made from shrimp shells for flavor and add the shrimp at the end.

1¼ pounds (headless weight) shrimp

4 ounces (about 4 slices) extra-thick-sliced bacon or pancetta, diced

1 medium onion, trimmed, split lengthwise, peeled, and chopped

1 medium green bell pepper, stem, seeds, and membranes removed, chopped

1 large rib celery, strung and diced small

1 large clove garlic, lightly crushed, peeled, and minced

1 bay leaf

1 tablespoon chopped parsley

1 cup raw rice, washed and drained (see Carolina-Style Rice, page 77, for the method)

2 cups chopped ripe tomatoes, blanched, peeled, and seeded (page 35), or chopped canned tomatoes with their juices

1 cup Shellfish Broth (page 13)

1 pod cayenne or other hot pepper, left whole

Salt and whole black pepper in a mill

10–12 fresh basil leaves

1. Peel the shrimp, completely removing the tails. Put the bacon in a deep skillet or flameproof casserole over medium heat. Fry until the fat is rendered and the bacon is browned. Spoon off all but 2 tablespoons of fat, add the onion, pepper, and celery, and sauté, tossing occasionally, until softened but not browned, about 5 minutes. Add the garlic, bay leaf, and parsley and toss until fragrant, about half a minute.

2. Add the rice and stir until it's evenly coated with fat and beginning to toast, about a minute. Add the tomatoes, broth, and hot pepper, and season well with salt and pepper. Stir once, let it come back to a boil, and reduce the heat to the lowest possible setting. Cover tightly and simmer 12 minutes, or until the liquid is absorbed.

3. Carefully fold the top grains of rice under to the bottom. Don't stir—fold. Spread the shrimp over the rice, cover tightly, and steam for a minute more. Turn off the heat and let sit, tightly covered, until the rice is tender and the shrimp are pink and cooked through, about 8–10 minutes. Scatter the basil over it and fluff with a fork, tossing to mix in the shrimp, and serve at once.

Serves 4

shrimp and rice croquettes

Rice croquettes (or fritters as they're sometimes called) point straight back to the West African slaves who did so much to shape Lowcountry cooking along the South Carolina and Georgia coast. Rice fritters may be sweet, as in calas or the jam-filled croquettes of South Carolina (see page 81), or savory—filled with ham, chicken, shrimp, or other seafood. Except for calas, such fritters have all but disappeared from modern Southern tables, but old cookbooks suggest that they were once more widely enjoyed. Sweet fritters are ideal as a brunch sweet bread or as a dessert after any meal. Savory fritters such as this one are a fine main course for a brunch or luncheon, but can also be served as an elegant and unusual hot hors d'oeuvre.

2 cups hot, cooked Carolina-Style Rice (page 77)

1 tablespoon unsalted butter

½ cup soft white bread crumbs

Salt, ground cayenne, and whole black pepper in a mill

1 lemon

2 large eggs, lightly beaten

2 tablespoons minced scallions or other green onions, or yellow onions

½ pound (headless weight) raw shrimp, peeled, deveined, and chopped

1 cup fine cracker crumbs or dry bread crumbs

Lard or peanut or canola oil, for frying

1. While the rice is hot, mix the butter into it and stir in the soft crumbs. Season well with salt, cayenne, and a generous grinding of black pepper, making it spicier than you'd normally do. Grate in the zest from the lemon, then halve it and, using a sieve to catch the seeds, squeeze in a teaspoon or so of its juice. Mix well. Spread it on a platter until it is somewhat cooled, then stir in the eggs, scallion, and shrimp. Spread it once again, cover it with plastic wrap, and refrigerate until chilled and set, about 2 hours.

2. Moisten your hands and scoop up the mixture by rounded tablespoonfuls. Roll one into a ball in your hands and then roll it in the dry crumbs until it is coated. Put the fritters on a clean, dry platter and refrigerate until you are ready to fry them.

3. Put enough lard or oil to come halfway up the sides of a deep skillet or enameled iron Dutch oven. Warm it over medium-high heat until it is hot but not quite smoking (375°F). Add enough fritters to fill the pan without crowding and fry, turning once if necessary, until uniformly golden and cooked through, about 3 minutes. Drain thoroughly, blot briefly on absorbent paper, then transfer the fritters to a wire cooling rack set over a rimmed baking sheet. Repeat with the remaining fritters. Serve piping hot.

Cheese Rice Fritters: Omit the shrimp and lemon and stir in 1 cup grated sharp cheddar or gruyère and 2 tablespoons grated Parmigiano-Reggiano.

Serves 4

carolina jam croquettes

First cousin to New Orleans calas, jam-filled rice croquettes are an old-fashioned—indeed, almost archaic—Lowcountry treat, but they're delicious and deserve to be returned to modern tables, not just in the Lowcountry, but everywhere.

2 cups whole milk or half-and-half

½ cup sugar

1 cup raw long-grain rice

Whole nutmeg in a grater

1 lemon

¼ cup all-purpose flour

2 large eggs

½ cup raspberry, blackberry, strawberry, or damson plum jam or preserves

1 cup fine cracker crumbs or dry bread crumbs

Lard or peanut or canola oil, for frying

Superfine or confectioners' sugar, for dusting the croquettes

1. Put the milk in a 2-quart saucepan and bring to a simmer over medium heat, stirring often to prevent scorching. Add the sugar, stirring until it is dissolved, and then add the rice. Bring back to a simmer, reduce the heat to low, loosely cover, and simmer, fluffing occasionally with a fork to be sure it isn't scorching, until the rice is very soft, about 20 minutes. Turn off the heat.

2. Add a generous grating of nutmeg. Grate in the zest from the lemon, then cut the lemon in half and, through a wire mesh strainer, squeeze in the juice from one of the halves. Sprinkle the flour over all and stir until evenly mixed. Spread it on platter to cool. When it is almost room temperature, turn it into a bowl and stir in the eggs, then spread it on the platter once again, cover with plastic wrap, and refrigerate until chilled and set, about 2 hours.

3. Moisten your hands; scoop a tablespoon of rice into one hand and make an indentation in it with your thumb. Fill it with ½ teaspoon jam and cover with another tablespoon of rice. Seal the edges together and gently roll it into a ball. Lightly roll it in the crumbs and put it on a clean, dry plate. Repeat with the remainder of the rice and jam. Refrigerate, uncovered, until you're ready to fry.

4. Put enough lard or oil in a deep skillet or enameled iron Dutch oven to come halfway up the sides. Warm it over medium-high heat until it is hot but not quite smoking (375°F). Add enough fritters to fill the pan without crowding and fry, turning once if necessary, until uniformly golden and cooked through, about 3 minutes. Drain thoroughly, blot briefly on absorbent paper, then transfer the fritters to a wire cooling rack set over a rimmed baking sheet. Repeat with the remaining fritters. Dust generously with confectioners' sugar and serve piping hot.

Serves 4

CHAPTER FOUR

THE SOUTHERN SOUP KETTLE

A simmering soup is surely one of the most satisfying, reassuring, and soul-nurturing things in any kitchen. In a Southern one, there was a time when what was in the soup pot would, like Italy's minestrone, identify where you were more accurately than terrain or local dialect. If it held crawfish, filé, and thyme, you were in Louisiana; if it contained okra and shrimp, or blue crab and its orange roe, you were in the Carolina-Georgia Lowcountry; if there were peanuts and oysters, you were in Virginia. Today a Creole crawfish bisque may turn up in Nashville, and velvety Carolina she-crab soup or seafood gumbo can and often does turn up anywhere from New York to Texas.

But it isn't only a cross-mixing within the South that has challenged these traditions; other cuisines have made their imprint. A country okra-thickened vegetable soup may have a spoonful of Genoese pesto mixed in; a stir of the gumbo pot may turn up squid or mussels; lemongrass and Asian fish sauce may perfume a bowl of chicken and rice soup. As regional identities blur, many purists argue that we're in danger of losing our roots. But they forget that no cuisine is static, and without a lively blending of traditions in the first place, there would have been no Southern cooking. Besides, as these cuisines evolve and incorporate new ingredients, somehow those things get used in a way that's peculiarly Southern, and take on the regional character of the soup they embellish. When I set out to develop these recipes, my only requisite was that they had to satisfy that thing at the back of my palate that perked up and said, *Yes, that tastes of home.*

butterbean soup

Butterbeans are a variety of limas (but don't try to tell that to most Southerners, who want to think they're different vegetables). They have a rich texture and fine buttery flavor (hence the name). They make any dish that includes them taste rich without being heavy. This soup has no milk, cream, or ham, and very little butter, yet it tastes like pure indulgence. As if that isn't enough to recommend it, the whole thing can be made a day ahead, and is actually better the next day.

Butterbeans stand up well to freezing, and this soup can be made with frozen butterbeans or Fordhook limas. It's an especially warming and welcome thing to serve in the winter when the frozen variety is all that will be available to you.

1 pound fresh (or frozen, thawed) green butterbeans or Fordhook Limas

2 tablespoons unsalted butter

1 medium yellow onion, trimmed, split lengthwise, peeled, and chopped fine

2 medium ribs celery, including the leafy top, washed, strung, and chopped fine

2 cups Chicken Broth (page 10) or 1 cup canned broth mixed with 1 cup water (even if the label reads "use full strength")

Zest from ½ lemon, removed with a vegetable peeler in large pieces

1 large sprig fresh sage, or 5-6 whole dried sage leaves, tied in a cheesecloth or tea ball

Salt and whole white pepper in a mill

¼ cup thinly sliced green onion tops

1. Put the butterbeans in a large, heavy-bottomed pot with enough water to cover them by an inch. Bring it to a boil over medium-high heat, skimming off any scum that rises to the top, then reduce the heat to low. Simmer until the beans are tender and the liquid is somewhat reduced (barely covering the beans), about 20–30 minutes. Turn off the heat and transfer the beans and their cooking liquid to a glass or stainless bowl.

2. Wipe out the pot and put in the butter, onion, and celery. Turn the heat to medium and sauté, tossing frequently, until the vegetables are translucent, about 5 minutes.

3. Add the broth, butterbeans and their cooking liquid, lemon zest, sage, a large pinch of salt, and several grindings of white pepper. Bring the liquid to a boil and reduce the heat to medium-low. Simmer until the flavors are thoroughly blended and the vegetables are very tender. Remove and discard the lemon zest and sage. Puree a cup of the beans and stir them back into the soup, taste and adjust the seasonings, and heat for 2 minutes more. Serve hot, sprinkling thinly sliced green onion over each portion.

Notes: Any variety of fresh or frozen green lima beans such as Fordhooks, Southern butterbeans, or tiny, elegant butter peas works well in this recipe. Don't use the large yellow variety of limas or speckled butterbeans—the kind that turn a dark coppery brown when cooked—both have a far too assertive flavor.

Serves 4

asparagus and leek soup

Traditional Southern asparagus soup is usually very rich with cream, and is only at its best with the freshest asparagus possible. This one contains no cream, so its flavor is lighter and fresher; it is also, oddly enough, more forgiving of asparagus that is not as fresh as you might like. This is partly thanks to leeks, whose bright herbal flavor restores much of the spring freshness to asparagus that has been left too long in refrigerated storage, and partly to the concentrated flavor achieved by simmering the asparagus trimmings in the broth.

There are two ways to finish it, both delicious: It can be served as a traditional puree, or you can omit the puree, serving it as a clear soup. Both ways have their charms. The former tastes buttery and rich with all the silky texture of a cream-based soup, while the latter allows all the flavors to mingle and yet remain distinct and light.

1 pound asparagus

2 medium leeks

1 medium yellow onion, trimmed, split lengthwise, peeled, and thinly sliced

6 cups Chicken Broth (page 10)
or 6 cups Doctored Canned Broth (page 9)

2 tablespoons unsalted butter

Salt and whole white pepper in a mill

Whole nutmeg in a grater

2 medium green onions, thinly sliced

1. Wash the asparagus under cold running water. Cut off and discard about ½ inch of the stems' cut ends and peel the tough lower half, reserving all the trimmings and peelings. Put the asparagus in a separate bowl of cold water. Split the leeks lengthwise and rinse under cold running water with the root end pointing upward, bending back the leaves to remove any dirt that you find in between. Pull away the outer tough, dark green leaves. Cut off the dark green tops and separate them from the light green, tender inner leaves. Thickly slice the leek trimmings and add them to the other trimmings.

2. Put the asparagus and leek trimmings, onion, and broth in a large saucepan and bring it to a boil over medium-high heat. Reduce the heat to low, skim away the scum as it rises, and simmer at least 30 minutes—longer won't hurt it. Turn off the heat.

3. Strain the broth, discarding the solids. Return the broth to the pan and bring it back to a simmer over medium heat. Meanwhile, thinly slice the leeks crosswise and cut the asparagus into 1-inch pieces. Select six of the tips, roughly chop them, and set them aside for garnish. Put the leeks and butter in a sauté pan or skillet and turn on the heat to medium-low. Sweat the leeks until they are bright green and crisp-tender, about 5–8 minutes. Add the asparagus and raise the heat to medium. Sauté, tossing constantly, until the asparagus is bright green and hot through, but still quite crisp, about 2 minutes.

4. Transfer the leeks and asparagus to the broth, add a small pinch or so of salt, a few liberal grindings of white pepper, and a generous grating of nutmeg. Bring the liquid back to a simmer and cook until the vegetables are just tender, about 4–6 minutes more. Taste and adjust the seasonings, then turn off the heat. The soup may be served as is at this point, with the green onion tops and chopped raw asparagus tips scattered over each serving Or, you may opt for a more sumptuous, creamy version as follows.

5. Take up 1 cup of the solids with a slotted spoon and set them aside. Puree the soup in batches with a food mill or in a blender or food processor fitted with a steel blade. Return it to the pot and stir in the reserved solids. Reheat the soup over medium heat, stirring frequently to prevent scorching, or chill and serve the soup cold. Either way, garnish each serving with a sprinkling of green onion tops and chopped raw asparagus tips.

Serves 6

white bean soup

If this were a French or Italian recipe, it would carry the picturesque suffix *a la papa* or *di babbo* and would seem a lot more exotic than it is. Both phrases only mean "in the manner of Daddy," which loses a little something in the translation. What follows is, more or less, my father's way of making bean soup, which is more of an idea than a recipe. My father has been an occasional and highly experimental cook for as long as I can remember: His bean soup is rarely the same twice, depending on his whim, the kind of beans that are in the pot, and what happens to be in the refrigerator at the time. As varied as those soups may have been, one thing is constant: His love for beans keeps his instincts from betraying him. This recipe is built on taste memories of his best efforts—all of which were simple and sturdy but warming and very satisfying to eat.

1 pound dried great northern or white kidney (cannellini) beans

Salt

3 tablespoons unsalted butter

1 medium onion, trimmed, split lengthwise, peeled, and chopped

1 large carrot, peeled and chopped

1 large clove garlic, mashed, peeled, and minced

4 cups Chicken or Meat Broth (page 10)

Whole black pepper in a mill

1 tablespoon chopped fresh sage
or 1 teaspoon crumbled dried sage

1. Put the beans in a colander and rinse thoroughly under cold running water. Drain and transfer them to a glass bowl; cover them with cold water by about 2 inches. Let them soak 8 hours or overnight, adding more water if the beans absorb enough to be uncovered.

2. Put the beans and their soaking liquid in a pot and add enough water to cover them by 1 inch. Bring it to a boil over medium-high heat, skimming off any foam that rises to the surface, then reduce the heat to medium-low, loosely cover, and cook until the beans are tender, about 1–2 hours, depending on the beans. Add several generous pinches of salt, stir carefully to keep from breaking up the beans, and simmer for about 10 minutes longer. Turn off the heat.

3. Put the butter, onion, and carrot in a large, heavy pot and set it over medium heat. Sauté, tossing frequently, until the onion is translucent but not browned, about 5 minutes. Add the garlic and sauté, tossing constantly, until fragrant, about half a minute more. Add the broth and bring to a boil.

4. Drain the beans, reserving the cooking liquid, and add them to the broth. Stir well, and thin the soup to the consistency you prefer with the reserved cooking liquid. (If you are making the soup ahead, save any remaining cooking liquid in case the soup needs to be diluted later on.) Season well with salt and a liberal grinding of pepper, and add the sage. Bring it to a boil, reduce the heat to medium-low, and simmer, stirring occasionally, until the onion and carrot are meltingly tender and the beans have absorbed all the

flavors, about 20–30 minutes more. Taste and adjust the seasonings, simmer for a minute or so to allow them to blend, and turn off the heat.

Note: The soup can be made up to 2 days ahead. Completely cool it before storing, covered, in the refrigerator. Gently reheat it over medium heat and simmer for 5 minutes before serving. Often the soup will have thickened considerably; but it will be thicker cold than when reheated, so wait until it is heated to thin it with a little broth, water, or the liquid reserved from precooking the beans.

Serves 4 as a main course, 8 as a first course

corn and okra soup

Corn and okra are essential background for any good Southern vegetable soup, but here they move from supporting cast to shine all on their own. This soup is exceptional when all the ingredients are very fresh, but if you can't get really fresh, sweet corn, a good-quality frozen corn may be substituted. There is no substitute for fresh, young okra: Frozen okra loses its texture and, unless it has been properly frozen, much of its flavor. So even though the okra is to be cut up, choose the pods as if you were going to use them whole: Select only small crisp ones with no brown edges down the ridges.

¾ **pound fresh young okra**

2 **tablespoons butter, bacon drippings, or extra-virgin olive oil**

1 **medium onion, split lengthwise, peeled, and chopped**

1 **tablespoon chopped fresh sage or 1 teaspoon crumbled dried sage**

5 **cups Basic Broth (page 10, made from either beef or chicken) or 2½ cups canned broth and 2½ cups water (even if the label reads "use full strength")**

1 **whole pod cayenne or other hot pepper**

2 **cups sweet corn kernels, freshly cut from the cob (about 4 large ears), or 2 cups good-quality frozen corn kernels such as Shoepeg**

Salt, ground cayenne pepper, or hot sauce

1. Wash the okra under cold running water, rubbing it gently to remove the outer fuzz on each pod. Trim off the stem caps and thinly slice the pods into thin rounds. Set aside.

2. Put the butter or drippings and onion into a large saucepan over medium heat. Sauté, tossing frequently, until the onion is pale gold, about 6–8 minutes. Add the okra and sage and sauté, tossing constantly, until bright green. The mixture will become sticky as the okra throws off its juices. Add the broth and pod of cayenne and bring to a boil. Reduce the heat to low and cook, stirring occasionally, until the okra is tender, about 10–15 minutes, depending on size and freshness.

3. Stir in the corn and raise the heat to medium-high. Return to a simmer, then reduce the heat once more and simmer until the corn is tender, about 10–15 minutes longer, depending on how young and fresh the corn is. Taste and adjust the seasonings, adding salt and a pinch of cayenne or a dash or so of hot sauce if needed. Simmer a minute or so more to blend the flavors, then turn off the heat. Serve hot.

Note: The soup can be made up to 2 days ahead. Reheat gently over medium-low heat and simmer for 5 minutes before serving.

Serves 6

cucumber buttermilk soup

For a long time in many parts of the South, nearly every community of any size had at least one restaurant owned and operated by a Greek family. The main fare was solidly Southern, but alongside the fried chicken, fish, smothered steak, macaroni pie, and slow-cooked vegetables, one would inevitably find Greek salad, moussaka, and baklava. It was only a matter of time before suggestions of Greek cookery found their way into home kitchens. This soup is probably one such suggestion, but its pedigree is neither here nor there: What counts is that it is as easy to make as it is delicious.

2 large, firm cucumbers

2 large or 4 small scallions or other green onions, or ½ medium Vidalia Sweet onion

2 cups whole-milk buttermilk or plain whole-milk yogurt

Salt and whole white pepper in a mill

1. Lightly peel the cucumbers with a vegetable peeler, leaving a blush of green on them. Cut them in half lengthwise. Scoop out and discard the seeds. Cut the cucumbers into thin slices (a little less than ¼ inch thick), then cut ½ cup of them into small dice and set this aside. Thinly slice 2 tablespoons of the green tops of the scallions and set them aside, then thickly slice the remaining scallions.

2. Put the sliced cucumber, scallions, and buttermilk or yogurt into a blender or food processor fitted with a steel blade. Puree on high speed until perfectly smooth. Taste and season with salt and several liberal grindings of pepper. Pulse to mix the seasonings, taste and adjust them, and pulse once more.

3. Pour the soup into a glass bowl or tureen, and stir in the reserved diced cucumber. You may serve the soup at once or refrigerate it for several hours or overnight to allow the flavors to further develop. Allow it to sit at room temperature for 30 minutes before serving. Garnish each serving with a sprinkling of the reserved green onion tops.

Cucumber-Watercress Soup: This lovely variation combines two classic Southern chilled soups into one. Don't bother to dice any of the cucumber, omit the white pepper, and add ¼ (packed) cup of watercress leaves to the blender with all of the cucumber in step 2. Garnish with thinly sliced cucumber and finely julienned watercress leaves.

Serves 4

ruth's three-mushroom consommé

In most of the South, mushroom soup is usually rich with cream, but chef and cookbook author Ruth Adams Bronz understands that when the rest of the menu is rich, something full-flavored but not quite so heavy is called for. The first time I made this with Ruth, we were preparing Thanksgiving dinner for thirty-two people. The menu included Lucy-Mama's Oysters (page 55), and she wanted to precede them with something that could hold its own without dulling everyone's palate with richness. She achieved that with the concentrated flavors of a homemade consommé base and dried porcini mushrooms.

1 ounce dried porcini mushrooms

½ pound crimini mushrooms

½ pound shiitake mushrooms

1 medium yellow onion, thinly sliced

3 tablespoons butter, divided

2 large cloves garlic, lightly crushed, peeled, and chopped fine

6 cups Chicken Consommé (page 9)

1 bouquet garni, made of 2 bay leaves and 2 sprigs each parsley and thyme

1 cup Madeira or dry red wine

1 bunch green onions

1. Put the dried mushrooms in a heatproof bowl and pour 1 cup boiling water over them. Soak for 30 minutes, then lift out the mushrooms, dipping them to loosen any dirt clinging to them, and set aside. Strain the soaking liquid through a coffee filter or undyed paper towel and set it aside. Wipe the fresh mushrooms with a clean, dry cloth. Trim off the excess stem from the criminis, and remove the shiitake stems altogether. Set the stem trimmings aside and thinly slice the mushrooms.

2. Put the sliced yellow onion, mushroom stems, and 2 tablespoons of the butter in a large saucepan over medium heat. Sauté, stirring often, until the onion is wilted and translucent. Add the garlic and sauté until fragrant, about 1 minute more. Raise the heat to medium-high. Add the reserved mushroom soaking liquid, broth, and bouquet garni. Bring to a boil, reduce the heat to low, and simmer 30 minutes. Turn off the heat.

3. Strain the broth through a sieve into a large bowl, pressing on the solids to extract all their juice. Wipe out the pot. Add the remaining butter and turn on the heat to medium-high. When it is melted and frothy, add the fresh mushrooms and reconstituted porcini. Sauté until the fresh mushrooms are beginning to color, about 4 minutes. Pour the strained broth over them and bring it to a boil. Add the wine and bring it back to a simmer. Cook until the mushrooms are tender, about 10 minutes. Turn off the heat.

Note: The soup may be made ahead up to this point. Cool, then cover and refrigerate. The next day, skim off the fat and reheat the soup over medium heat.

4. Thinly slice the green tops of the green onions. Ladle the soup into individual soup plates or bowls, sprinkle with the green onions, and serve at once.

Serves 8

sweet potato bisque (or vichyssoise)

This is not merely a French leek and potato soup with a different kind of potato thrown into the pot. In it, the many elements that have shaped Southern food are distilled together: the earthy-sweet flavor of native sweet potatoes handsomely melding with leeks and broth in a Northern European way, with ginger and thyme lacing the brew and hinting of France, the West Indies, Africa, and the Far East all at once. Delicious either hot or cold, it makes a fine first course virtually any time of the year.

3 medium or 2 large leeks

1 medium yellow onion, trimmed, split, peeled, and thinly sliced

2 tablespoons unsalted butter

1½ pounds orange-fleshed sweet potatoes, peeled and sliced ¼ inch thick

4 cups Chicken Broth (page 10), or 2 cups canned broth and 2 cups water (even if the label reads "use full strength"), or 4 cups water

3 quarter-size slices fresh ginger

2 large healthy sprigs fresh thyme (or 1 teaspoon dried thyme in a tea ball or tied in a double layer of cheesecloth)

Salt, ground cayenne, and whole white pepper in a mill

2 cups whole milk or half-and-half

1 large sprig fresh sage, plus 6 leaves, thinly sliced, for garnish

¼ cup sliced Toasted Pecans (page 232)

¼ cup heavy cream

1. Trim the root and dark outer leaves from the leeks and split them in half lengthwise. Rinse under cold running water with the root pointing upward, folding back the layers to remove the dirt in between. Pat dry and thinly slice the white part and most of the pale inner greens. Set aside ¼ cup of the sliced greens for garnish.

2. Bring the leeks, onion, and butter to a simmer in a 4-quart saucepan over medium heat. Simmer 10 minutes. Layer the sweet potatoes on top, cover, and let them warm through, about 2–3 minutes. Add the broth, ginger, and thyme, and season with salt, cayenne, and a generous grinding of white pepper. Raise the heat and bring to a boil, then reduce the heat to a simmer and cook until the potatoes are very soft, about 20 minutes.

3. Turn off the heat and let the soup settle. Remove and discard the ginger and thyme. Puree in batches in a blender or food processor. You may make the soup several hours ahead to this point. Cover and refrigerate the puree if you're making it more than a couple of hours ahead or planning to serve it cold.

4. When you are ready to finish the soup, if serving warm return it to the pot and bring it gently to a simmer over medium-low heat. Slowly whisk in the milk and bring it back to a simmer, then simmer 3–4 minutes. Taste and correct the seasonings. To serve it cold, whisk in the milk cold, taste and adjust the seasonings, and allow it to sit at room temperature for a few minutes to take the blunt chill off it. Hot or cold, garnish each serving with a light sprinkling of leek greens, sage, pecans, and a drizzle of cream.

Serves 6

summer (or winter) squash bisque

Freshly gathered yellow summer squash taste cleanly of sunshine and warm earth, buttery-sweet and reminiscent of fresh corn. Leeks, onion, and a touch of fresh herbs are all they need to round out their flavor. Hot or cold, this wonderful soup makes a delicious beginning for any summer meal when it is made with those delicate squash. But it is equally delicious made with sturdier winter squash such as acorn, butternut, or pumpkin.

1½ pounds yellow summer squash (crooknecks, pattypan, or yellow zucchini), or winter squash such as acorn, butternut, or kabocha

1 medium leek

1 small yellow onion, split, peeled and thinly sliced

2 tablespoons unsalted butter

2 cups Chicken Broth (page 10) or Doctored Canned Broth (page 9), or 1 cup canned broth mixed with 1 cup water (even if the label says "use full strength")

1 bouquet garni made with 1 large sprig each celery, fresh sage, and thyme

Salt and whole white pepper in a mill

2 cups whole milk

½ cup heavy cream

2 tablespoons thinly sliced fresh chives or green onion tops

1. Wash the squash thoroughly under cold running water, gently scrubbing to remove any grit that is clinging. Pat dry, then trim off the blossom and stem ends. (If you are using winter squash, peel, split in half, and remove and discard the seeds.) Slice the squash crosswise about ¼ inch thick. Trim the root and remove the first few layers of dark outer leaves from the leek, split lengthwise, and rinse under cold running water, root-end up, folding back the layers to remove any dirt between them. Pat dry and thinly slice the white and inner pale green parts.

2. Warm the leek, onion, and butter into a large, heavy-bottomed saucepan over medium-high heat. Sauté, tossing often, until translucent, about 4 minutes. Add the squash and toss until they're hot through, about a minute more. Add the broth and bouquet garni and season with salt and a grinding of white pepper. Bring to a boil, loosely cover, and reduce the heat to low. Simmer until the squash are tender, about 20 minutes. Turn off the heat.

3. Remove and discard the bouquet garni. Puree the soup in batches in a blender or food processor. The soup can be made several hours or a day ahead to this point. Cool, cover, and refrigerate if you're making it more than 2 hours ahead or serving it cold.

4. When you are ready to finish the soup, to serve it hot, return it to the pot, bring it to a simmer over medium heat, and stir in the milk. Return it to a simmer, taste and adjust the seasonings, and simmer 3–5 minutes longer. To serve it cold, stir in the milk cold, taste and adjust the seasonings, and let it sit at room temperature for 30 minutes before serving. (*Note:* Winter Squash Bisque should always be served hot.)

5. To serve hot, drizzle a tablespoon of cream into each serving, and top with pepper and chives or onions. To serve cold, whip the cream until it holds soft peaks. Put a dollop on each serving and sprinkle each with white pepper and chives or green onions.

Serves 6

tomato velvet

Tomato-basil soups are quite popular down South but all too often fall short of wonderful. Their failing is that the cook has indifferently used canned tomatoes and actually cooked the basil in the soup. The whole point of this soup is the perfect union of basil's brightness and the natural fresh sweetness of ripe tomatoes. Canned tomatoes not only lack that quality, they often have citric acid added as a preservative, which lends a sharp taste and can cause the milk to curdle. As for the basil, it's one herb that should rarely see heat. Cooking compromises its flavor, often giving it a bitter, sharp edge. That's why it's added only at the very end. Wait until you need it to slice it or it will darken and can sometimes turn bitter.

I like this soup best chilled, but it's also delicious warm or cold.

2 pounds fresh ripe tomatoes

1 medium Vidalia or other sweet onion, split, peeled, and thinly sliced

1 tablespoon unsalted butter

½ cup water

1 whole small hot pepper, such as cayenne, serrano, or jalapeño

1 large sprig parsley

Salt

1½ cups whole milk

½ cup heavy cream

2 tablespoons each thinly sliced chives (or green onion tops) and fresh basil

Whole white pepper in a mill

1. Blanch, core, and peel the tomatoes as directed on page 35. Working over a wire mesh sieve set in a large bowl, halve them crosswise and scoop out the seeds into the sieve. Roughly chop the pulp and add it to their collected juices.

2. Sweat the onion in the butter in a large, heavy-bottomed saucepan over medium-low heat, stirring often, until the onion is translucent and soft, but not colored, about 10 minutes. Add the tomatoes and their juices, water, whole pepper pod, parsley, and salt to taste. Bring to a boil, reduce the heat to low, and simmer until the tomatoes break down and the onion is tender, about 30 minutes. Turn off the heat.

3. Remove and discard the hot pepper and parsley, and puree the soup in batches in a blender or food processor. It can be made several hours ahead to this point. Cool, cover, and refrigerate it if you're making it more than 4 hours ahead or plan to serve it cold.

4. If serving warm, bring the soup back to a simmer in a heavy-bottomed pan over medium-low heat, then stir in the milk, return it to a simmer, and let it simmer 3–4 minutes, stirring often. Taste and adjust the seasoning and simmer a minute longer. If you're serving it cold, stir in the milk, taste and adjust the seasoning, and let it sit at room temperature to lose the deep chill.

5. Hot or cold, drizzle each serving with a spoonful of cream (or for cold soup whip the cream until it holds soft peaks and top each serving with a dollop). Sprinkle lightly with herbs and white pepper and serve.

Serves 6

savannah crab soup with tomatoes

This really is more of a stew than a soup—thick, hearty, and warming. In most of the South, a fish stew is milk- or cream-based; one may almost take that for granted. But occasionally, lovely tomato-based exceptions do turn up: the conch chowders of Florida, for example, or "Muddle," the great fish stew of North Carolina's Outer Banks. This lovely Lowcountry soup from my adopted hometown is another one.

4 pounds ripe tomatoes, or 4 cups Italian canned tomatoes, seeded and chopped, with their juices

1 medium yellow onion, split lengthwise, peeled, and chopped

2 medium ribs celery, strung and chopped

2 tablespoons extra-virgin olive oil

2 large or 3 small cloves garlic, lightly crushed, peeled, and minced

4 cups Fish or Shrimp Broth (page 13)

1 large or 2 small bay leaves

1 tablespoon chopped fresh thyme, or 1 teaspoon crumbled dried thyme

1 tablespoon chopped fresh marjoram, or 1 teaspoon crumbled dried marjoram

1 large sprig parsley

2 small hot peppers, left whole

Salt

2 lemons, 1 whole and 1 thinly sliced

1 pound (2 cups) cooked crabmeat, carefully picked over to remove any bits of shell

1 tablespoon chopped parsley

1. If you are using canned tomatoes, then skip to step 2. If using fresh tomatoes, blanch, core, and peel them as directed on page 35. Over a wire sieve set into a large bowl, halve them crosswise and scoop out the seeds. Roughly chop them and add them to their collected juices. Discard the seeds.

2. Put the onion, celery, and olive oil in a large heavy-bottomed saucepan over medium-high heat and sauté, tossing frequently, until the onion is translucent, about 4 minutes. Add the garlic and sauté until fragrant, about half a minute longer. Add the stock, tomatoes, bay leaf, thyme, marjoram, parsley sprig, and hot pepper pods (left whole); season with salt. Using a vegetable peeler, cut a 1 × 3-inch piece of zest from a lemon and add it to the soup, then halve the lemon. Bring the soup to a boil, reduce the heat, and simmer slowly until the vegetables are tender and the tomatoes have almost dissolved, about an hour.

Note: The soup can be made to this point up to 2 days ahead. Turn off the heat, let cool, transfer to a storage container, cover, and refrigerate until you are ready to serve it. Bring it back to a simmer over medium-low heat before proceeding.

3. Stir in the crab and bring the soup back to a simmer. Squeeze in the juice of half a lemon. Taste and adjust the salt and lemon juice, and simmer another minute. Turn off the heat. Remove and discard the hot peppers, parsley sprig, and lemon zest. Serve at once, garnishing each serving with a slice of lemon and a sprinkling of parsley.

Serves 6 as a main course, 8 as a first course

cream of crab soup

One of the hallmark standards of Carolina Lowcountry cookery is She-Crab Soup, a variation on cream of crab that Charleston chef William Deas created in the early twentieth century simply by dressing it up with the coral-orange roe from female crabs. Unhappily, his elegant variation has become more famous than is good for it, turning up in practically every anthology of Southern cooking and on restaurant menus all over the South. I say unfortunately because, while some of these interpretations remain faithful to Mr. Deas's original, only a few actually have roe in them, and most of them, having been subjected to "reinventing," bear little resemblance to the original and are as awful as they are popular.

But the main problem with many adaptations is less bad execution than the fact that the essential ingredient (crab roe) is only available at certain times of the year, in only a few places, and is strictly regulated. Meanwhile, the simple, elegant soup that inspired Mr. Deas is delicious without depending on having roe-bearing female crab in the pot. Sometimes appearing in old manuscripts as crab stew, it was and still is a standard on supper tables throughout the Lowcountry, but can be dressed up for company simply by adding a splash of sherry and garnish.

16 ounces (1 pound or 2 tightly packed cups) cooked crabmeat

3 tablespoons unsalted butter

½ cup finely minced or grated shallots or yellow onion

2 tablespoons all-purpose flour

4 cups whole milk

2 cups heavy cream

Salt

Ground cayenne pepper

Dry mustard

About 1 large blade mace, a large pinch powdered mace, or whole nutmeg in a grater

¼ cup dry sherry, optional

8 very thin slices lemon, optional

2 tablespoons finely minced parsley, optional

1. Pick through the crabmeat and remove any bits of shell. Put the butter and shallots in a heavy-bottomed saucepan over medium-low heat. Simmer until the shallots are soft but not colored, about 5 minutes. Stir in the flour and simmer, stirring constantly, about 2 minutes.

2. Gradually whisk in the milk and cream. Season well with salt and a small pinch each of cayenne and mustard, add the mace or nutmeg to taste, and heat, stirring constantly, until lightly thickened, about 5–8 minutes.

3. Stir in the crabmeat and let it heat through, stirring frequently, about 5 minutes more. Taste and adjust the seasonings, then simmer 1 minute. Off the heat, stir in the sherry (if using) and immediately ladle the soup into heated bowls or soup plates. For a more elegant presentation, you may float a thin slice of lemon on each serving and sprinkle on a little minced parsley.

Serves 8 as a first course, 4 as a main dish

oyster bisque

This sumptuous soup was once enjoyed all along the eastern seaboard, and recipes turn up in eighteenth- and nineteenth-century cookbooks from Maryland to Savannah. Historical versions seem wildly extravagant to us now, because they inevitably called for twice as many oysters as ended up in the tureen, but in those days oyster beds were so abundant that no one thought twice about using half of the shellfish just to flavor the broth. Today no one would waste good oysters like that. We use the extra liquor that our ancestors discarded. The real secret is that the oysters that do end up in the bowl are chopped fine, thus lending every spoonful a good portion of rich oyster flavor.

2 pints shucked oysters, with their liquor

1 small yellow onion, trimmed, split lengthwise, and minced

2 large ribs celery, strung and minced

1 blade mace or whole nutmeg in a grater

Salt and whole black pepper in a pepper mill

Ground cayenne

4 cups whole milk

2 cups heavy cream

2 tablespoons unsalted butter

3 tablespoons all-purpose flour

2 teaspoons Worcestershire sauce

8 thin slices lemon

2 tablespoons chopped fresh parsley

8 tablespoons medium-dry (Amontillado) sherry or (Sercial) Madeira

1 cup Buttered Croutons (page 101)

1. Pick over the oysters for bits of shell. Strain their liquor into a large saucepan and add the onion, celery, mace or a generous grating of nutmeg, a little salt, a generous grinding of pepper, and a pinch of cayenne. Bring it to a simmer over medium heat and cook until the onion and celery are softened, about 8–10 minutes. Add the oysters and cook, stirring occasionally, just until the gills begin to curl, about 2–4 minutes. Lift out the oysters and vegetables with a slotted spoon and transfer them to a colander set over a bowl. Strain their broth and return it to the pot. When the oysters are cool enough to handle, mince them fine. Some cooks leave half the oysters whole, and I prefer it that way. Add any broth that has drained from them to the liquid in the pot.

2. Bring the broth back to a simmer over medium heat. Add the milk and cream and let it come back to a simmer, stirring frequently to prevent scorching. Melt the butter in a small pan over medium heat and stir in the flour. Cook, stirring often, until bubbly and smooth, about 2 minutes. Gradually whisk in 2 cups of the broth and milk and cook, stirring constantly, until it is quite thick. Gradually stir this into the remaining broth and milk, bring it to a simmer, stirring constantly, and cook until thick, about 5 minutes.

3. Add the minced oysters, vegetables, and Worcestershire; taste and adjust the seasonings, then let it heat through. If you've left some oysters whole, add them last and let them just warm through. Serve at once, with a slice of lemon and sprinkling of parsley over each serving, passing sherry or Madeira and croutons separately.

Serves 8

lowcountry shrimp bisque

This beautiful bisque is typical of the simple elegance that has graced the tables of Charleston, Beaufort, and Savannah for more than two centuries. Though rich, it's subtle and delicate. Classic bisques are thickened with egg yolks, but this one employs an old-fashioned bread crumb liaison—more stable than eggs but with the same silken texture. Any white bread crumbs will work, but egg breads such as brioche or French Rolls (page 286) lend the most elegant finish.

4 cups (1 quart) water

2 pounds whole small to medium shrimp (with heads still attached), or 1 pound if headed

3 tablespoons unsalted butter

¼ cup (about 1 medium) finely minced shallot or yellow onion

2 tablespoons finely minced white "heart" celery (an inner rib of the stalk)

3 cups half-and-half

Salt and ground cayenne pepper

¼ cup soft white bread crumbs

6 tablespoons dry sherry

1 lemon, thinly sliced

Ground cayenne or paprika, for garnish

1. Have a basin of ice water ready. Bring the water to a boil in a heavy-bottomed 3-quart pot over high heat. Add the shrimp, cover, and count 2 minutes or until the shrimp just turn pink and curl. Lift them out of the cooking liquid with a frying skimmer and plunge them in the ice water to arrest their cooking. Drain, head (if using whole), shell, and devein the shrimp, then cover and refrigerate. Return their shells (and heads) to the cooking liquid and bring it back to a boil over medium-high heat, watching carefully—it will foam up and boil over. Cook until it is reduced to 3 cups. Turn off the heat. Strain the stock, discarding the solids, and let it cool. You may make the broth up to a day ahead.

2. Wipe out the pot and put in the butter, shallot, and celery. Sauté over medium heat, tossing often, until the vegetables are softened but not colored, about 8 minutes. Add the stock, bring to a simmer, then add the half-and-half. Season with salt and a small pinch of cayenne, and return the soup to a simmer, stirring often to prevent scorching. Add the crumbs, return to a simmer, and lower the heat to medium-low. Simmer, stirring often, until the crumbs dissolve completely and the soup is thickened, about 20 minutes.

Note: The bisque can be made ahead up to this point. Let it cool and store it, well covered, in the refrigerator. Bring it back to a simmer over medium-low heat before proceeding. The soup may thicken even more after it is cooled and reheated, so if it's too thick, add a little half-and-half.

3. Stir in the shrimp and cook until they are just heated through and have absorbed some of the flavors, about 2 minutes longer. Taste, adjust the seasonings, simmer half a minute more, then turn off the heat. You may stir the sherry into the soup or put a spoonful into each soup plate just before ladling the soup in. Serve at once, garnishing each serving with a slice of lemon and light sprinkling of cayenne or paprika.

Serves 4

buttered croutons

Cut 1-inch slices of day-old firm bread such as Classical Southern Wheat Bread into 1-inch cubes. Preheat the oven to 300°F. For each cup of cubed bread, put 2 tablespoons butter in a rimmed sheet pan. Bake until the butter melts, then add the bread and toss to coat. Bake, stirring occasionally, until golden brown and crisp, about half an hour.

georgia chicken and sausage gumbo

Along the short stretch of coastline where Georgia connects with the Atlantic Ocean, there was once a flourishing rice culture rivaling that of South Carolina. In fact, there are supposed to have been times when more Carolina Gold was exported from Georgia than Carolina. Certainly the influence of the Lowcountry rice kitchen extended deep into Georgia's marshy coastline. Here gumbo retains distinct traces of West African traditions: Okra is an essential; you can't call it gumbo if okra isn't in the pot; a few spoonfuls of rice are inevitable; and chicken will almost always be present, even when the pot is full of seafood. In fact, all you need to do to make this into a Georgia seafood gumbo is stir in a pint each of small peeled inlet shrimp, picked lump crabmeat, and shucked oysters.

Notice the primary herb is bay leaf. This is no accident. Bay laurel flourishes on the barrier islands, and great trees of it survive in many old gardens and cemeteries. It has long been an essential in the region's cookery.

In recent years many Georgia cooks have begun to add a well-browned Creole roux to the pot, but I find that heavy and cloying, and still prefer the older version.

4 pounds ripe tomatoes or 4 cups canned whole Italian tomatoes, chopped, with their juices

1 pound mild smoked pork sausage, sliced ¼ inch thick

1 chicken (3–3½ pounds), cut up for frying as directed on page 167 (not skinned)

2 large yellow onions, split, peeled, and chopped

2 large or 3 medium green sweet bell peppers, cored, seeded, and chopped

2 large stalks celery, strung and chopped

4 large cloves garlic, lightly crushed, peeled, and minced

3–4 bay leaves, depending on their size

1 pound young okra, washed under cold running water, stemmed, and sliced crosswise ¼ inch thick

Salt and cayenne pepper

About 4–5 cups hot Carolina-Style Rice (page 77)

1. If you're using canned tomatoes, skip to step 2. Blanch, core, and peel the tomatoes as directed on page 35. Over a wire sieve set into a large bowl, halve them crosswise (lengthwise if using plum tomatoes), and scoop out the seeds. Roughly chop the tomatoes and add them to the collected juices in the bowl. Discard the seeds.

2. Put the sausage in a large (at least 7-quart) heavy-bottomed Dutch oven (preferably enameled iron). Over medium heat, lightly brown the sausage on all sides. Remove it with a slotted spoon, leaving the rendered fat in the pot, and drain on absorbent paper. Add and brown the chicken a few pieces at a time (about 3 minutes per side).

3. Spoon off all but 2 tablespoons of the fat. Add the onions, peppers, and celery to the pot and sauté, tossing often, until softened and just beginning to color, about 5–8 minutes. Add the garlic and sauté until fragrant, about half a minute longer.

4. Add the sausage, chicken, tomatoes and their juices, bay leaves, okra, a couple of large pinches of salt, and a large pinch or so of cayenne (go easy on both; you can adjust the seasonings later). Bring the gumbo to a boil, reduce the heat to low, loosely cover, and simmer, stirring occasionally, for at least 1 hour—2 is better. Turn off the heat. Let it settle until the fat floats to the top and spoon it off. Remove all the chicken and let it cool enough to handle. Skin and bone it, discarding both skin and bones, and cut the meat into small bite-size bits. Return the chicken to the pot.

Note: You may make the gumbo to this point up to 2 days ahead. Cool it completely and, if the pot is not enamel-lined, transfer it to a storage container. Cover and refrigerate. Remove any fat that congeals on the top before proceeding.

5. To serve, remove and discard the bay leaves and reheat gently over medium-low heat. Taste and adjust the seasonings, simmer half a minute more, and serve with rice.

Serves 8–10

shrimp and green tomato gumbo

Here are most of the traditional ingredients of a good seafood gumbo, but with a twist: Green tomatoes replace the usual ripe ones. Also, unlike most gumbos, it does not need to simmer for hours on the back of the stove. It goes together quickly—less than an hour from start to finish—including all the peeling, chopping, and simmering. The result is tart, clean-flavored, and refreshing. However, it does benefit greatly from being made a day ahead so that the flavors can blend and develop.

¾ pound young, firm okra

1½ pounds green tomatoes (about 3 large or 4 medium)

1 medium leek

2 tablespoons bacon drippings or olive oil

1 large or 2 medium yellow onions, split, trimmed, peeled, and chopped

1 large or 2 small cloves garlic, lightly crushed, peeled, and minced

1 or 2 small green hot peppers (to taste), stem, seeds, and membranes removed, minced

6 cups Shrimp Broth (page 13), Chicken Broth (page 10), or Doctored Canned Broth (page 9), or 3 cups canned broth mixed with 3 cups water (even if the label says "use full strength")

1 bouquet garni, made from a leafy celery top, 2 bay leaves, 2 large sprigs thyme, 2 large sprigs parsley

Salt and white pepper in a mill

½ pound (headless weight) shrimp, peeled

½ pound crabmeat, picked over to remove any bits of shell

2 lemons, 1 halved and 1 cut into thin slices

2 small, thin scallions or other green onions, thinly sliced

1. Rinse the okra under cold running water, gently rubbing to remove the fuzz, and drain. Trim off the stem caps and slice crosswise about ¼ inch thick. Core the tomatoes and cut them into ½-inch dice. Split the leek lengthwise and rinse under cold running water, root-end up, folding back the layers to remove any dirt between them. Thinly slice both the white and tender green parts.

2. Warm the leek, drippings, and onion in a heavy-bottomed 3- to 4-quart saucepan over medium-high heat. Sauté, tossing, until the vegetables are translucent and softened, but not colored, about 4 minutes. Add the garlic and hot pepper and sauté until fragrant, about half a minute. Add the tomatoes, toss until heated through, and add the okra. Toss until the okra is bright green, then add the broth and bouquet garni; season lightly with salt and a grinding of white pepper. Bring to a boil, reduce the heat to low, and simmer until the vegetables are tender, about 30 minutes.

Note: The gumbo can be made to this point several hours or days ahead. Cool, transfer to a storage container, cover, and refrigerate. Bring it back to a simmer over medium heat before proceeding.

3. Add the shrimp and crab, bring the soup back to a simmer, and simmer until the shrimp curl and turn pink, about 3–5 minutes. Turn off the heat. Remove and discard the bouquet garni. Add the juice from half a lemon, then taste and adjust the lemon juice, salt, and pepper. Serve hot, garnishing each serving with a slice of lemon and sprinkling of scallions.

Serves 4 as a main course, 6 as first course

the gumbo family

Gumbo is so closely associated with the Creole and Cajun cookery of Louisiana that many people take for granted that it comes from that region. But like fried chicken and barbecue, it is truly a universal Southern dish—or, I should say, culinary idea. There are as many versions of gumbo as there are cooks, and there's no single ingredient—not even the okra for which it is named—that can be called essential. Only barbecue is as regionally varied and passionately defended within those regional boundaries.

The history of this stew is lost in legend, the traces of African, Native, and European influences so tangled up in the pot that its true origins are impossible to trace. On the southern Atlantic coast where I live, the distinct fragrance of West Africa dominates; inland and to the north, the stew is so anglicized that no African would recognize it; when okra disappears altogether and filé powder is stirred into the pot, not only does one feel and taste New Orleans, one can hear the distinct whisper of Native American cooks. Once, a pot of gumbo was more reliable than a road map: One taste told you exactly where you were. Today that's no longer true, but the distinctions are still marked enough for most cooks to be very territorial. Taste a gumbo in Brunswick, Georgia, then go west to New Orleans—or for that matter only a few miles inland to Waycross or north to Savannah—and describe it, and you can bank on it: The most polite response you will get is "Humph! That's not gumbo!"

CHAPTER FIVE

FISH AND SHELLFISH

Some of the most vivid memories of my early childhood involve the murky smell of lake water, the squish of clay mud between my toes, and the flash of silvery fish scales catching the sunlight as a hooked brim or bass erupted with a great splash from the water's still surface. From the time I could stand on my own feet and hold a pole without dropping it, my father tried to coax me into loving to fish as much as he did. To his disappointment, I could never get past the fact that the poor fish was being tricked with food.

Fishing, you see, is a big deal in the South.

Between the great arc of the Gulf rim, Florida peninsula, and Atlantic seaboard, the South has more than half the coastline of the lower forty-eight states, and most of its wetlands. Add in the lion's share of the nation's major estuaries, and you'll begin to understand this obsession with a fishing pole. I've heard it said that the South's national sport is college football, but that's not a sport down here; it's a religion. The national sport is fishing.

Given all that, one would expect Southerners to excel at cooking the catch, and we do. Some of America's oldest and most varied fish and shellfish cookery comes from our region. Yet visitors who come South often don't think so. The standard lament is that they came down here looking forward to eating a lot of fresh fish only to be disappointed by what they believe is a limited repertory. "All you people know how to do with a fish is fry it!" they complain, and it's easy to see how they could come to this conclusion. We do love fried fish, and it's a specialty of many restaurants and fish camps across the region.

But that doesn't mean frying is the only thing we know how to do. It just means that many of us prefer to leave the frying to professional cooks, not only because it circumvents the smell at home but because restaurant equipment keeps the fat filtered and hot, and makes it much easier to do the frying well. While many fish restaurants are branching out and offering things that aren't batter-fried, the best place to experience the true variety of Southern fish and shellfish cookery is in private homes, where the catch is broiled, baked, roasted, grilled, and poached. My response to the complainers, therefore, is simply to suggest that instead of whining, you should be nicer to the people you meet and maybe they'll invite you home to dinner.

These recipes reflect the lighter hand that's the hallmark of the South's home fish cookery. Much of what you'll find here looks fresh and new—as if it's from the cutting-edge kitchens of the South's most innovative new chefs—but they're home classics that have been around for a long time. What marks them is their simplicity: Though many are elegant, they're not complicated and require no special skills. None of them is fried—by design—and only a few have quantities of cream, butter, or bacon. What they do have is plenty of flavor.

baked catfish with potatoes and onions

Catfish are an odd, almost primeval-looking bottom-feeding fish that have become one of the icons of the Southern table that Southern food snobs protest are nothing more than a cliché. But clichés usually have a reason for being, and the fact is, if there's freshwater catfish in the pan, it's almost a sure thing that a Southerner is standing over it. Catfish stew is our chowder, and whole catfish, skinned, rolled in cornmeal, and crisp-fried with hush puppies is our answer to fish-and-chips. This is another traditional way of cooking this fish that may not be as well known, but it's equally satisfying. Sage, potatoes, and onions are a fragrant foil for its earthy flavor. This is also another good example of how closely the cooking of the South parallels that of Italy. Ligurians often cook similarly strong-flavored fish in exactly the same way. Substitute olive oil for the butter and any Ligurian would feel right at home.

2 pounds small, waxy boiling potatoes

2 ounces (4 tablespoons or ½ stick) unsalted butter, softened, divided

2 medium onions, trimmed, split, peeled, and sliced as thinly as possible

Salt and whole white peppercorns in a pepper mill

2 tablespoons chopped fresh sage or 2 teaspoons crumbled dried sage, divided

2 tablespoons chopped fresh parsley, divided

4 catfish fillets (about 8 ounces each)

1. Position a rack in the center of the oven and preheat to 400°F. Scrub the potatoes under cold running water. Put at least 1 inch of water into a large pot and fit it with a steamer insert. Bring to a boil over medium-high heat, add the potatoes to the steamer insert, cover, and reduce the heat to medium. Steam until the potatoes are almost cooked through—about 10 minutes. A knife should insert easily but meet a little resistance in the middle. Remove the potatoes and let them cool enough to handle, then peel and slice ¼ inch thick.

2. Lightly butter a 9 x 13-inch bake-and-serve dish and put in the potatoes and 2 tablespoons of the butter. Toss gently to coat the potatoes, then spread them flat in a single layer. Separate the onions into rings and scatter half of them over the potatoes. Season generously with salt, a liberal grinding of white pepper, and sprinkle on half the sage and parsley. Put the dish into the oven and bake until the onions wilt and begin to brown, about 15 minutes.

3. Remove it from the oven and lay the fish over the potatoes in a single layer. Season well with salt and a generous grinding of white pepper. Scatter the remaining onions, sage, and parsley over the top. Dot with the remaining butter and bake until the fish is just cooked through and the onions are lightly browned, about 20 minutes more. Serve hot from the baking dish.

Serves 4

pecan-crusted catfish

Fish crusted with finely chopped pecans has become popular in many upscale Southern restaurants. The combination is an especially happy one with catfish, and it has become a standard in many Southern home kitchens. Usually, the fish is either sautéed or fried, but I find it is easier to manage, and less heavy tasting, when it's baked instead.

½ cup fine cracker crumbs

½ cup finely chopped pecans

3 large lemons, 1 whole, 2 cut into wedges for serving

1 rounded tablespoon chopped fresh sage or 2 teaspoons crumbled dried sage, divided

Whole black pepper in a pepper mill

¼ cup all-purpose flour

2 large eggs

4 medium catfish fillets (about 6 ounces each)

Salt

3 tablespoons unsalted butter, melted

1. Mix together the crumbs and pecans in a wide, shallow bowl. Grate in the zest from the whole lemon and then cut the lemon in half. Add the sage, season generously with black pepper, and toss until well mixed. Spread the flour on a plate. Break the eggs in another wide, shallow bowl, squeeze in the juice from one of the lemon halves, and beat until well mixed. Thoroughly butter a rimmed baking sheet.

2. Sprinkle the fillets with salt, and one at a time, lightly roll them in the flour, shake off the excess, and then dip them in the eggs until coated, letting the excess flow back into the bowl. Roll them in the crumbs and lay them in the prepared baking pan. Let rest at least 15 minutes.

3. Position a rack in the upper level of the oven and preheat to 450°F. Brush the fish well with the melted butter and bake on the upper rack of the oven until cooked through and nicely browned, about 10–15 minutes, depending on the thickness of the fish. Transfer to a warm platter or individual serving plates, scatter the lemon wedges among them, and serve at once.

Serves 4

pan-broiled rainbow trout with sage, onions, and wine

The savory marriage of smoked bacon and sage composes one of the great flavor combinations in Southern cooking, and it is traditional with freshwater fish. This is a robust treatment for a robust fish. Ideally, it should be made only with trout that have been caught shortly before being cooked. But if you don't live where you can get such wonders, any distinctive small, whole fish such as bream, carp, bass, herring, whiting, or catfish can be cooked by this method.

4 small whole rainbow trout (about 8 ounces each), cleaned, scaled, and gutted

Salt and whole black pepper in a pepper mill

Ground cayenne pepper

1 medium onion, trimmed, split, peeled, and sliced as thinly as possible

16–20 whole fresh sage leaves, plus small sprigs for garnish

4 large sprigs thyme, plus small sprigs, for garnish

8 pieces thin-sliced bacon, preferably hickory-smoked

2 lemons, 1 whole and 1 cut into wedges, for serving

1 cup dry white wine

1. Rinse the fish under cold running water and pat dry. Season the belly cavities well with salt, pepper, and cayenne. Insert several slices of onion, 2 or 3 sage leaves, and a large sprig of thyme into each. Wrap each fish with 2 slices of bacon, securing them with toothpicks, then tuck a couple of sage leaves under the bacon. Remove the zest from the whole lemon with a bar zester or a vegetable peeler and cut it into julienne with a sharp knife. Halve the lemon.

2. Warm a large, heavy-bottomed, well-seasoned iron or nonstick skillet over a medium-high heat. When it's hot, add the fish and cook until the bottom side of the bacon is browned, about 3 minutes. Turn carefully and cook until the second side is browned, about 3 minutes longer. Reduce the heat to medium and continue cooking, turning once more, until the fish is cooked through and the bacon is brown, about 4–6 minutes longer. Remove the fish to a warm platter.

3. Spoon off all but a tablespoon of the fat remaining in the pan. Add the remaining onion and sauté until it's wilted and beginning to brown, about 3–4 minutes. Add the wine and bring it to a boil, stirring and scraping the pan to loosen any of the browned bits of cooking residue. Add the lemon zest and the juice from one of the lemon halves. Bring it back to a boil and cook until the wine is reduced by half. Turn off the heat. Refresh the sauce with a squeeze from the other lemon half. Stir, taste and adjust the seasoning, and pour it over the fish. Scatter the lemon wedges, sprigs of sage, and small sprigs of thyme among them and serve at once.

Serves 4

trout poached with white wine, rosemary, and ginger

Adapted from a very old recipe in a seventeenth-century cookbook that belonged to Martha Washington, this has become a standard in my repertory. Rosemary and ginger are made for strongly flavored, oily fish such as trout and mackerel, but are also superb with milder fish such as grouper, pompano, salmon, or swordfish.

6 freshwater or sea trout steaks or fillets (about 4 ounces each)

Dry white wine

6 tablespoons unsalted butter, divided

Salt

2 large sprigs rosemary, plus additional sprigs for garnish

2 quarter-size slices ginger

3 lemons, 1 cut in half and 2 cut into 6 wedges each

1. Put the fish into a deep lidded skillet or sauté pan that will hold them snugly, but in one layer. Add enough wine to completely cover them and then remove the fish. Add 1 tablespoon of the butter, a healthy pinch of salt, the large sprigs of rosemary, and the ginger. Bring to a boil over medium heat, and let it boil briskly for 2 minutes.

2. Return the fish to the pan, raise the heat to medium-high, and bring to a simmer. Reduce the heat to low and cover. If you're using steaks, poach until they're just cooked through, about 4 minutes. For fillets, simmer 1 minute, turn off the heat, and let stand, covered, for 6 minutes.

3. Remove the fish to a warm platter and cover. Raise the heat to medium-high, bring the cooking liquid to a boil, and boil until it is reduced and syrupy. Off the heat, freshen it with a squeeze of lemon juice, then whisk in the remaining butter in bits. Pour a little of the sauce over the fish, then put the remainder into a warm sauceboat. Garnish with the sprigs of rosemary and lemon wedges and serve at once, passing the sauce separately.

Serves 6

crab-stuffed flounder fillets

A very old specialty along the Carolina and Georgia coast is whole flounder split open, partially boned, and stuffed with deviled crab. The crabmeat adds sweetness and character to the mild-flavored fish. But since fresh, whole flounder are not universally available outside those areas, many cooks roll more readily available fillets around the savory filling instead.

4 flounder fillets (6 ounces each)

12 ounces (about 1½ tightly packed cups) crabmeat

8 tablespoons (½ cup or 1 stick) unsalted butter, divided

½ cup finely chopped shallots or yellow onions

½ cup finely chopped green or red bell peppers

2 large cloves garlic, lightly crushed, peeled, and minced

1 cup soft, stale bread crumbs

Salt and whole black pepper in a pepper mill

Ground cayenne

Worcestershire sauce

Paprika

About ½ cup dry vermouth or white wine

1. Rinse the fish under cold water and pat dry. Pick through the crabmeat for lingering bits of shell. Position a rack in the center of the oven and preheat to 375°F.

2. Warm 2 tablespoons of the butter with the shallots and bell peppers in a medium sauté pan or skillet over medium heat. Sauté, tossing often, until the onion is translucent, about 4 minutes. Add the garlic and sauté until fragrant, about half a minute. Turn off the heat.

3. Add the crumbs and crabmeat and toss until mixed. Season liberally with salt, pepper, cayenne and a few dashes of Worcestershire, to taste. Toss well. Lay the flounder skin-side down on a work surface. Sprinkle lightly with salt. Mold the crabmeat into four equal lumps and put one on each fillet, then roll each fillet around the filling.

4. Generously butter an oval or square casserole that will hold the fillets snugly in one layer. Put in the fillets, seam-side down, and dot generously with the remaining butter. Dust lightly with paprika and pour the vermouth around the edges. Bake 15 minutes. Baste well, dust with more paprika, and bake, basting occasionally, until the fish is cooked through and the stuffing hot, about 15 minutes longer. Serve with the pan juices spooned over each serving.

Serves 4

flounder in lemon-pecan brown butter

The South's native pecans pair well with fish, and here they're mated with flounder—the mild, delicate white-fleshed flatfish that flourishes in the southern Atlantic and Gulf of Mexico. Flounder is not, perhaps, as sweet as its flashier cousin, sole, but when paired with pecans and capers, it certainly holds its own. Capers have been imported into the South ever since the English colonies stabilized in the late seventeenth century, and have always been a staple with seafood in all the South's port cities from Louisiana to Baltimore. They were so important to local cooks that one often finds recipes for preserving nasturtium buds as a substitute.

4 flounder fillets (8 ounces each), skinned

Salt and whole white pepper in a mill

4 tablespoons (¼ cup) clarified butter

½ cup unbleached all purpose flour

6 tablespoons (¾ stick) unsalted butter

½ cup pecans, cut into slivers at their natural grooves

3 tablespoons nonpareil capers, drained

2 tablespoons chopped flat-leaf parsley

2 lemons, zest removed from 1 with a bar zester or peeler and cut into fine julienne, and 1 thinly sliced for garnish

1. Rinse the fish under cold running water and pat dry. Season liberally on all sides with salt and white pepper. Heat the clarified butter in a wide, shallow skillet or sauté pan over medium heat. When its hot bubbling subsides, quickly roll the fillets in the flour, shake off the excess, and slip them into the pan. Sauté, turning once, until golden-brown and just cooked through, about 2–3 minutes per side. Take care not to overcook them. Remove to a warm platter or serving plates.

2. Put the unsalted butter in the pan and return it to the heat, stirring and scraping to loosen any cooking residue. When it is fully melted, add the pecans and sauté, tossing frequently, until the butter and pecans are a uniform golden-brown. Add the capers and let them heat through, then remove the pan from the heat and add the parsley, lemon zest, and the juice from half the zested lemon. Taste and adjust the salt and lemon juice as needed, then pour the sauce evenly over the fish. Garnish with sliced lemon and serve at once.

Serves 4

baked grouper with orange-ginger sherry butter

Grouper is a mild, sweet-fleshed fish that flourishes in the waters of the Gulf of Mexico and the Atlantic coast of Florida, Georgia, and Carolina. It's popular throughout Florida and all around the Gulf rim—more popular than is good for it. Overfishing has forced many states to begin regulating the catch, and grouper is becoming correspondingly expensive. When you can get it, its delicate flavor begs for simple treatment, and since the flesh of grouper is firm and compact, it is often grilled. Unfortunately, the grill, while certainly simple, is not the best place for a respectable grouper to find itself. Smoke can overpower the sweetness and give the fish an acrid sharpness that there's not enough lemon juice in the world to cover up. I prefer to pan-fry, oven-broil, or bake it, as is done here, in a fragrant bath of orange juice, lemon juice, and sherry.

2 pounds grouper fillets (four 8-ounce fillets)

4 small or 2 large scallions or other green onions, thinly sliced, white and green parts separated

Salt and whole white pepper in a pepper mill

1 lemon

½ medium orange

½ cup dry sherry

1 tablespoon finely minced fresh ginger

5 tablespoons cold unsalted butter, cut into teaspoon-size bits

1. Position a rack in the center of the oven and preheat to 450°F. Rinse the fish under cold running water and pat dry. Butter a 9 x 13-inch glass or ceramic casserole and lay the fish in it in one layer. Sprinkle the scallions over it, reserving 2 tablespoons of the greens. Season well with salt and white pepper. Remove the zest from the lemon and orange with a bar zester or vegetable peeler and cut it into julienne with a sharp knife. Sprinkle it over the fish.

2. Separately juice the lemon and orange through a strainer set over a glass or stainless-steel bowl. You should have equal parts orange and lemon juice—about 2 tablespoons of each. Stir them together and then stir in the sherry and ginger and pour it over the fish. Bake in the center of the oven, basting several times, until just cooked through (it will flake slightly and be opaque in the center), about 15–18 minutes, depending on the thickness.

3. Remove the fish to a warm platter. Pour the pan juices into a small saucepan and bring them to a boil over medium-high heat. Cook until reduced by half, turn off the heat, and whisk in the butter by bits. Spoon a little of the sauce over the fish and pour the remainder into a sauceboat. Sprinkle with the reserved green onions and serve at once, passing the sauce separately.

Serves 4

broiled snapper with bacon

When I was in college, I dated, for a time, a lovely, intense English major who rented rooms in the home of an austere widow. The lady guarded her tenants like an old mother hen and took no nonsense from gentlemen callers, but we suspected a generous heart lurking somewhere beneath her crusty exterior and, though it took us time, we found it. We also found a marvelous cook. Both ladies have long since passed from my life—I can't even recall the landlady's name—but I can never forget the lovely aroma that filler her house as she showed me how a sensible Southern cook broils a piece of snapper.

4 strips thin-sliced bacon, preferably applewood-smoked

4 red snapper fillets (about 6 ounces each)

Butter or extra-virgin olive oil

2 lemons, 1 halved and 1 cut into wedges

Whole black pepper in a pepper mill

1. Position a rack 6 inches below the broiling element of the oven and preheat the broiler for at least 15 minutes before you are ready to cook. Bring a pan of water to a rolling boil and drop in the bacon. Let it boil 1 minute, then drain and pat dry. Rinse the fish under cold running water and pat dry. Butter a large, rimmed baking sheet and put the fish on it in one layer. Squeeze over it the juice from 1 of the lemon halves. Season with a generous grinding of pepper and lay a strip of bacon down the center of each fillet.

2. Broil 6 inches below the heat source until the bacon is browned and crisp and the fish is just cooked through, about 4–6 minutes, depending on the thickness of the fillets. The fish should no longer be pink or translucent at the center, but opaque and white all the way through. Transfer the fillets to a serving platter, scatter lemon wedges among them, and serve at once.

Serves 4

deviled crab

Crab cakes are standard fare on many Southern restaurant menus and are a signature of modern Southern cooking. They're so popular that it seems petty to quibble over them. But as good as they can be, crab cakes have two major drawbacks: They require too much breading and egg to hold together, and they're troublesome to cook. That's why I prefer Deviled Crab: They can be tossed together in minutes and require almost no attention once they go into the oven.

"Deviled," of course, has nothing to do with satanic incantations; it only means the cook has used a lot of hot spice. In the South that usually means either mustard or cayenne pepper, or both, but when seasoning crab, too much of either is a mistake. This sweet, delicate meat is easily overwhelmed, so use a little restraint.

1 pound (1 pint) fresh crabmeat (meat from about 12 steamed crabs), 8 back shells reserved

2 tablespoons extra-virgin olive oil, divided

½ medium yellow onion, peeled and minced

1 medium green bell pepper, stem, core, seeds, and membranes removed, minced

1 large or 2 medium cloves garlic, lightly crushed, peeled, and finely minced

1 small fresh or dried hot red chile pepper such as cayenne, seeded and minced

Juice of ½ lemon (about 1 tablespoon)

1 tablespoon Dijon mustard

½ cup soft bread crumbs (about 1 thick slice white bread, crust removed)

Salt

¼ cup dry bread crumbs

1. Position a rack in the center of the oven and preheat to 400°F. Pick over the crab for any lingering bits of cartilage and shell. Put 1 tablespoon of the olive oil with the onion and bell pepper in a skillet or sauté pan over medium-high heat and sauté, tossing often, until the onion is beginning to color, about 5 minutes. Add the garlic and hot pepper and toss until fragrant, about half a minute more. Turn off the heat, add the crab, and toss lightly. Sprinkle in the lemon juice and fold in the mustard. Add the soft crumbs, toss, then taste and season with salt as needed.

2. Cover the bottom of a rimmed baking sheet with about ½-inch of rock salt or crumpled foil. (Or omit the salt or foil and use four small ramekins or gratin dishes.) Divide the crab among the shells (or dishes), mounding it a little on top, and set the shells into the salt or foil, filling side up. If using dishes, just put them directly onto the baking sheet.

3. Wipe out the pan, add the remaining oil, and warm over medium heat. Stir in the dry crumbs, mixing until the oil is evenly absorbed. Sprinkle them evenly over the crab and bake in the center of the oven until the crumbs are nicely browned and the filling is hot, about 15–20 minutes.

Serves 4

lowcountry crab au gratin

Cream and sherry bring out the best in crabmeat, and are the essential base of any good she-crab soup. It's a luxurious combination in all senses of the word, as elegant on the palate as it is on the plate. Here that simple triad is allowed to take center stage and shine, with just enough onion, spice, and sharp cheese in the backup band to act as counterpoint.

1 pound fresh crabmeat

2 medium green onions, minced, or ¼ cup minced yellow onion

2 tablespoons unsalted butter, divided

2 teaspoons all-purpose flour

1 cup heavy cream (minimum 36% milk fat)

¼ cup dry sherry, such as Amontillado

2 tablespoons freshly grated Parmigiano-Reggiano cheese

Salt and whole white peppercorns in a pepper mill

Whole nutmeg in a grater

¼ cup dry bread crumbs or cracker crumbs

½ cup (about 2 ounces) grated sharp white cheddar or gruyère cheese

1. Pick over the crab and remove any bits of shell or cartilage. Put the onions and 1 tablespoon of the butter into a heavy-bottomed saucepan over medium heat. Sauté, tossing often, until translucent, about 4 minutes. Sprinkle the flour into the pan and stir until smooth. Cook 1 minute and slowly stir in the cream. Bring to a simmer, stirring constantly, and reduce the heat to low. Simmer, stirring frequently, until lightly thickened, about 3 minutes. Stir in the sherry, bring it back to a simmer, and turn off the heat.

2. Position a rack in the upper third of the oven and preheat to 400°F. Lightly butter a 2-quart casserole or four individual gratin dishes or 12-ounce ramekins. Stir the crab and Parmigiano into the cream sauce. Season with salt, a liberal grinding of white pepper, and a light grating of nutmeg. Taste and adjust the seasonings, and transfer to the casserole or divide among the ramekins.

3. Melt the remaining butter in a small skillet over low heat. Turn off the heat and stir in the crumbs. Toss until the butter is evenly absorbed. Sprinkle the cheddar or gruyère over the casserole or individual gratins or ramekins, dust it with the crumbs, and bake until the filling is bubbly and the cheese is melted, about 15 minutes. Serve hot.

Serves 4

seafood ragout a la henry's, with peppers and white wine

For decades Henry's restaurant, in the old Market District of Charleston, was one of the few places outside private dining rooms where you could count on dining well in the city. Tables blanketed with linen and sparkling with heavy silver dotted black-and-white tile floors. Seasoned waiters, immaculate in white jackets and black ties, gave equally immaculate service. One of my best memories of Henry's was a delicate seafood ragout, brought to the table bubbly and fragrant in a gratin dish and then dexterously scooped onto a cake of fried grits with an enormous silver spoon. Sadly, old Henry's is no more, and the cook who made that ragout is long dead. This is as close as I could get to the memory.

2 tablespoons extra-virgin olive oil or unsalted butter

1 small yellow onion, trimmed, split lengthwise, peeled, and chopped

1 small or ½ large red bell pepper, stem, core, seeds, and membranes removed, chopped

1 large or 2 small cloves garlic, lightly crushed, peeled, and minced

1 rounded tablespoon chopped fresh marjoram or 2 teaspoons dried marjoram

2 bay leaves

Salt, ground cayenne pepper, and whole white pepper in a pepper mill

1 tablespoon flour

½ cup wine

1½ cups Shellfish Stock (page 13), made from shrimp shells and oyster liquor

½ pound (1 cup) lump crabmeat, picked over for any lingering bits of shell

½ pound dry-packed bay scallops

½ pound (headless weight) medium shrimp, peeled, shells reserved for the stock

1 dozen freshly shucked oysters, well drained (liquor reserved for the stock)

1 recipe Fried Grits (page 73), or Breakfast Grits (page 70), or Carolina-Style Rice (page 77)

1. Warm the oil, onion, and pepper in a large, heavy-bottomed lidded skillet or flameproof casserole over medium-high heat, and sauté, tossing often, until the onion is translucent, about 4 minutes. Add the garlic, marjoram, and bay leaves and toss until fragrant, about half a minute longer. Season lightly with salt and cayenne and generously with white pepper, and sprinkle in the flour. Toss until the flour is smoothly mixed with the vegetables.

2. Slowly stir in the wine and bring to a boil, stirring constantly. Stir in the stock and return it to a boil. Reduce the heat to a medium-low, loosely cover, and simmer until the vegetables are tender and the sauce is thick, about 15 minutes. The sauce should be very thick, since the shellfish will dilute it with their juices as they cook.

3. Add the crab and simmer for 3–4 minutes to allow it to absorb the flavors, then add the scallops and shrimp. Cover the pan and simmer until the scallops are opaque and the shrimp have curled and turned pink, about 2 minutes longer. Add the oysters and simmer until their gills curl, about 1 minute longer, and turn off the heat. Taste and adjust the seasonings. Remove and discard the bay leaves and serve at once over Fried Grits, Breakfast Grits, or Carolina-Style Rice.

Serves 4

crawfish or shrimp étouffée

The explosive popularity of the cuisines of Louisiana over the last thirty years has made crawfish étouffée one of the best known of all Southern dishes—almost too well known. Restaurants from Boston to San Diego feature it, and it has become a standard of home cooks who have never been within three states of the Louisiana border. With this popularity has come reinvention and complication: Many versions have become so elaborate that one needs three sous-chefs and a lay-reader to get through the recipe.

Maybe it's the French that inspires such unnecessary and even unfortunate elaborations. The word *étouffée* is often used as a noun, and by people who ought to know better. It is not an object, but a process: Étouffer is a verb meaning "to smother," and it's an apt description for what happens. Had the dish developed in any other than a Creole or Cajun kitchen, it might as easily have been called "smothered mudbugs," which would not, perhaps, have quite the same cachet, but it would more accurately place étouffée where it belongs, with other homey fare such as smothered pork chops and country-fried steak.

Stock made from the shells and heads of the shellfish really makes a difference. If you already have Shellfish Stock (page 13) on hand, you can use it as directed in the recipe and freeze the shells and heads for the next time you make stock (but use them within 6 weeks). If you don't have stock on hand and have the time, by all means use the reserved shells and heads from the shellfish to make a stock before proceeding with the recipe.

2 tablespoons olive or peanut oil

¼ cup all-purpose flour

1 medium yellow onion, trimmed, split lengthwise, peeled, and chopped

1 medium green bell pepper, stem, core, seeds, and membranes removed, chopped

1 large rib celery, trimmed, strung, and chopped

1 large or 2 small cloves garlic, lightly crushed, peeled, and minced

1 teaspoon dried thyme (do not use fresh)

1 bay leaf

Salt, ground cayenne pepper, and whole black pepper in a pepper mill

2 cups Shellfish Stock (page 13)

2 pounds whole cooked crawfish or 1½ pounds (headless weight) medium raw shrimp, heads and shells reserved for stock (see headnote above)

2 cups Carolina-Style Rice (page 77)

¼ cup thinly sliced scallions or other green onions (green tops only)

1. Make a roux: Put the oil and flour in a large, heavy-bottomed skillet over medium-high heat. Cook, stirring constantly with a long-handled spoon, until the flour is toasted a rich red-brown—about the color of milk chocolate. Do not allow it to scorch: It should smell pleasantly toasty, like a crusty loaf of bread.

2. Add the onion, pepper, and celery, stirring vigorously until they're coated. Toss until the onion is translucent and the pepper is bright green, about 2 minutes. Add the garlic, thyme, and bay leaf, and lightly season with salt, cayenne, and a grinding of pepper. Toss until fragrant, about half a minute, and slowly stir in the stock. Bring to a boil, reduce the heat to medium, and simmer, stirring occasionally, until the sauce is thick and the vegetables tender, about 20 minutes.

3. If you're using shrimp, skip to step 4. If you're using crawfish, add the peeled tails and simmer until heated through, about 2 minutes. If the sauce is too thick, thin it with a few spoonfuls of stock. Turn off the heat, remove and discard the bay leaf, and skip to step 5.

4. If you're using shrimp, simmer until the sauce is a little thicker than you want at the end; the shrimp throw off moisture as they cook and dilute it. Add them to it and simmer, stirring often, until they turn pink and curl, about 2–3 minutes. Do not overcook. Turn off the heat and remove and discard the bay leaf.

5. Mold each serving of rice in a custard cup or teacup rinsed with cold water. Invert the cup over a serving plate and lift it away. Spoon the étouffée around the rice, sprinkle with scallions, and serve at once.

Serves 4

oysters in leek and bourbon cream

Oysters and cream have been a duo on Southern tables for hundreds of years. This is not without reason: When oysters are simmered in cream and ladled over crisp toast points or fluffy biscuits, they lift an ordinary meal into a new dimension. They once were a standard at any Charleston or Savannah ball or reception; the supper table was not considered complete without them. Here, the combination is enhanced by the bright herbal accent of leeks and the suave undertone of bourbon. Don't be tempted to splash in more of the latter. It is here to underpin the flavor, not to turn the thing into a cocktail.

1 pint shucked oysters

2 medium (or 1 large) leeks

2 tablespoons unsalted butter

1 large or 2 medium cloves garlic, lightly crushed, peeled, and minced

2 quarter-size slices fresh ginger, minced

1 tablespoon bourbon

1 cup heavy cream

3 small (2-inch-diameter) hoecakes (page 258)

Salt and whole white pepper in a pepper mill

1 tablespoon chopped fresh parsley

1. Pour the oysters into a sieve set over a stainless-steel or glass bowl. Drain at least 10 minutes. (Save their liquor and freeze it; it's an ideal substitute for fish stock.) Remove any tough and yellowed leaves from the leeks, trim the roots, and split them in half lengthwise. Holding them root-end up, wash thoroughly under cold running water, bending back the leaves to get all the dirt from between the layers. Thinly slice the white and most of the tender green parts.

2. Melt the butter in a large sauté pan over medium-high heat. Add the leeks and sauté, tossing often, until they are wilted, about 3–4 minutes. Add the garlic and ginger and toss until fragrant, about half a minute more. Add the bourbon and let it evaporate, then pour in the cream. Bring to a boil and cook until the sauce is thick, about 2–3 minutes. It should be somewhat thicker than a cream sauce, since the oysters will dilute it as they throw off moisture when they cook. Turn off the heat. You may prepare it to this point several hours in advance. Cover and refrigerate the oysters and sauce in separate containers.

3. Half an hour before you are ready to serve the oysters, preheat the oven to 150°F (or the "warm" setting). Put the hoecakes on a baking sheet in a single layer and warm them in the oven while you finish the oysters. Bring the sauce to a simmer over medium heat. Add the oysters, a small pinch of salt (go easy, especially if the oysters are salty), and a liberal grinding of white pepper. Bring to a simmer and cook until the oysters plump and their gills curl, 1–2 minutes. Do not overcook. Turn off the heat, and taste and adjust the seasonings.

4. Put two hoecakes per serving onto warmed individual serving plates. Spoon the oysters and sauce over them, sprinkle with parsley, and serve at once.

Serves 4

sherried shrimp

This lovely recipe is one of the most exquisitely simple recipes for shrimp in all of Southern cooking. It comes from the household receipt book of Elizabeth Malone Smart, a Savannah dowager of the old school whose granddaughter, Connie Hartridge, is mistress of the historic Battersby-Hartridge House on Savannah's Lafayette Square. Its elegant simplicity is deceptive: Its success depends entirely on the quality of the few ingredients and on the carefulness with which the cook handles them.

1 large clove garlic, lightly crushed and peeled, but left whole

8 tablespoons (½ cup or 1 stick) unsalted butter

48 large shrimp (about 1½ pounds), peeled

Salt and ground cayenne pepper/

½ cup dry sherry

3 tablespoons chopped flat-leaf parsley

3 cups Carolina-Style Rice (page 77), or crusty bread

1. Sauté the garlic in the butter in a large sauté pan over medium heat until it's golden, about 2 minutes, then remove and discard it. Add the shrimp and sauté, tossing almost constantly, until they are curled and pink, about 2–3 minutes, depending on size. Season well with salt and cayenne (our local inlet shrimp often don't need added salt), and remove them with a slotted spoon to a warm platter.

2. Add the sherry to the pan and bring to a boil, stirring and scraping the bottom of the pan; let it boil half a minute. Stir in the parsley and pour it over the shrimp. Serve at once, over rice or with plenty of crusty bread to sop up the sauce.

Serves 4

lowcountry breakfast shrimp

Otherwise known as "shrimp and grits," this traditional breakfast dish has also, in recent years, become a staple dinner appetizer in any nouvelle Southern restaurant worth its herb garnish. Breakfast shrimp is not so much a recipe as it is an idea. There are dozens of variations, from simple bowls of boiled shrimp and grits passed separately to those elaborate, complexly flavored nouvelle concoctions. The best is still the simplest: Freshly caught shrimp are peeled, sautéed in copious quantities of butter, and poured over a snowy bed of slow-cooked grits. If the shrimp are freshly caught and sweet, I wouldn't make it any other way. This version, while not quite as simple, is no less true to tradition, and is kind to shrimp that have been frozen.

1¼ pounds (headless weight) medium shrimp

¼ pound thick-cut bacon, cut into ½-inch dice

1 medium yellow onion, trimmed, split, peeled, and cut into ½-inch dice

1 large clove garlic, lightly crushed, peeled, and minced

2 tablespoons all-purpose flour

Salt and ground cayenne pepper

2 cups hot Breakfast Grits (page 70)

1. Peel the shrimp, reserving the shells; cover and set aside (refrigerate them if you are not finishing the dish immediately). Put the shells and 2 cups water in a stainless-steel or enameled pot. Turn on the heat to medium-high and bring to a boil, being careful not to let it boil over (because the shells contain protein, they create a lot of foam at first). Reduce the heat to medium and simmer until the liquid is reduced to 1 cup. Turn off the heat and strain the broth into a stainless-steel or glass bowl. Discard the shells. If you are not proceeding with the recipe right away, cool, cover, and refrigerate the broth.

2. When you are ready to finish the shrimp, sauté the bacon in a large sauté pan or skillet over medium heat, tossing occasionally, until browned but not crisp. Spoon off all but 2 tablespoons of fat and add the onion. Raise the heat to medium-high and sauté, tossing often, until it's pale gold, about 4–5 minutes. Add the garlic and sauté until fragrant, about half a minute. Sprinkle the flour into the pan and cook, stirring constantly, until lightly browned, about 2 minutes more.

3. Add the shrimp and sauté, tossing constantly, until they begin to turn pink, about a minute. Season lightly with salt and cayenne. Slowly stir in the shrimp broth and bring it to a boil. Simmer, stirring occasionally, until the gravy is lightly thickened and the shrimp are just cooked through, about 2 minutes. If the gravy is too thin when the shrimp are done, lift the shrimp from the pan with a slotted spoon and boil until it's lightly thickened, then return the shrimp to the pan and turn off the heat. Taste and adjust the seasonings; serve at once over hot grits.

Serves 4

sautéed shrimp with tomatoes and okra

Here is an example of how the same ingredients can be very different, depending on how they are treated by the cook. Shrimp, tomatoes, peppers, and okra are all essential elements of a good seafood gumbo, but instead of a slow simmer, here they are treated to a lightning-quick sauté. The flavors are lighter, fresher, and more direct. This is how Lowcountry cooks like to do shrimp and tomatoes when both are in season. The flavor of ripe, fresh tomatoes is essential, so don't substitute the canned variety.

2 pounds (about 3 large or 4 medium) ripe tomatoes

1 pound very small, fresh okra, each pod no more than 3 inches long

2 tablespoons bacon drippings, or unsalted butter, or extra-virgin olive oil

1 large yellow onion, trimmed, split, peeled, and cut into large dice

1 large green bell pepper, stem, core, seeds, and membranes removed, cut into large dice

1 small fresh green or red hot chile pepper, such as a jalapeño or cayenne, stem, seeds, and membranes removed, minced

2 large or 3 small cloves garlic, lightly crushed, peeled, and finely chopped

Salt

2 pounds (headless weight) shrimp, peeled and deveined

8 large or 12 small fresh basil leaves

2 cups hot Carolina-Style Rice (page 77)

1. Blanch, peel, and seed the tomatoes as directed on page 35. Cut them into quarters. Lightly rub the okra under cold running water. Trim the stems, but don't remove the caps altogether.

2. Warm the fat in a large, lidded skillet or sauté pan over medium-high heat. When it's hot, add the onion and both peppers and sauté, tossing constantly, until the onion is translucent, about 4 minutes. Add the garlic and sauté until fragrant, about half a minute. Lift the tomatoes from their juices and add them. Sauté until they begin to break down, about 2 minutes. Add the okra and toss until it is bright green, about 1 minute.

3. Add the reserved tomato juices and season liberally with a couple of pinches of salt. Cover tightly and steam 4 minutes, or until the okra is crisp-tender and the tomato juice is thickened. Uncover, add the shrimp, and cook, tossing, until they are pink and curled, about 2 minutes more. Turn off the heat. Cut or tear the basil into very small bits and stir it into the pan. Taste and adjust the salt and basil, adding more as needed, then serve at once over Carolina-Style Rice.

Serves 4

shrimp stew with bacon and tomatoes

We think of shrimp as summer food, since that's their peak season, but along the coast of Carolina, Georgia, and the Gulf of Mexico, local shrimp are in season until at least November and sometimes through to Christmas. This stew is a heartier way of enjoying them in cooler weather.

1½ pounds large shrimp

4 ounces (about 2 slices) extra-thick-cut bacon, cut into ¼-inch dice

½ cup minced shallots

2 large cloves garlic, minced

1 large anchovy fillet, rinsed, patted dry, and minced, or 1 tablespoon anchovy paste

1 small hot pepper, stemmed, seeded, and minced, or ¼ teaspoon crushed pepper flakes

1 tablespoon chopped fresh rosemary or 2 teaspoons Herbes de Provence

1 bay leaf (omit if using Herbes de Provence)

2 tablespoons minced parsley, divided

½ cup dry white vermouth

2 cups (about 1½ pounds) peeled and diced fresh tomatoes, or canned whole tomatoes, seeded and diced (do not use canned diced tomatoes)

Salt

1 tablespoon unsalted butter

1. Peel the shrimp, reserving their shells, cover, and refrigerate. Put the shells in a heavy-bottomed enamel or stainless-steel saucepan with 4 cups of water. Bring to a boil over medium heat, skimming the foam as it rises, and reduce the heat to a gentle simmer. Simmer until the liquid is reduced to 1 cup. Turn off the heat and strain the broth, discarding the shells.

2. Sauté the bacon over medium heat in a large, deep-sided, lidded skillet or braising pan until golden-brown. Add the shallots and sauté until translucent, about 3–4 minutes. Add the garlic, anchovy, hot pepper, and rosemary and bay leaf (or herbes de Provence), and 1 tablespoon of the parsley. Sauté until fragrant, about half a minute more, and add the vermouth. Bring to a boil, stirring and scraping the pan, and boil until the vapors no longer sting.

3. Add the broth (made from shells) and tomatoes; season to taste with salt. Bring to a boil and reduce the heat to a steady simmer. Cook until the sauce is thick, about 30 minutes. The stew can be made ahead to this point. Cool, cover, and refrigerate if you're making it more than an hour ahead. Reheat gently over medium-low heat before proceeding.

4. Raise the heat to medium, add the shrimp, and bring to a simmer. Cover, lower the heat, and cook slowly, stirring occasionally, until the shrimp are just curled and pink, about 5–7 minutes. Turn off the heat, swirl in the butter, sprinkle with the remaining tablespoon of parsley, and serve hot.

Serves 4

CHAPTER SIX

BEEF, VEAL, LAMB, AND PORK

My maternal grandfather spent the first half of his life on a succession of farms in the Carolina hill country. The second half, the part I remember, was spent as a butcher and manager of a country store. Though entirely self-taught, he knew more about meat than most trained butchers, and his sage-scented whole-hog sausage was so legendary that people would drive a hundred miles to get it. He could tell how well an animal had been treated and fed just from inspecting the carcass, and was known to reject a hog that had been passed by the USDA.

One reason for this skill at his job was that he was also an accomplished cook. Yes, being a butcher gave him an intimate connection to the meat he cooked, but being a cook helped him appreciate how to select, dry-age, and butcher a side of beef. A lot of what I know about meat and its cookery comes directly from him; I wish I'd listened more. Despite that, he was not a great meat eater. He was no Thomas Jefferson, who famously ate so little meat that he called it a condiment for his vegetables; his tastes were just too catholic to let any one thing dominate his plate. He appreciated a well-cooked steak as well as anyone else, but had an equal appreciation for a good tomato sandwich. The health problems that plagued his later life had less to do with an inordinate love of one thing than the fact that he loved everything.

My grandfather's omnivorous diet was actually typical for his day. The most widely held myth about Southern culture, fed no doubt by our very real obsession with barbecue, is that we've historically been a nation of carnivores who ate great quantities of pork, a little beef, a very little lamb and veal, and almost no vegetables at all. Actually, the opposite was true. Southerners of the past, even the few wealthy planters whose rare lives of privilege have been so romanticized, would be stunned by the massive daily portions of meat consumed by modern Americans. While Jefferson's wealthy contemporaries thought his eating habits strange, the balance of his diet was probably closer to the common man's than myth would have us believe.

Except for the occasional venison and other game, the red meat found on Southern tables today comes from farmed animals that were imported to this continent during the European conquest: cattle, sheep, and pigs. But because cattle and sheep eat grass and need a lot of grazing pasture, and most of our land was reserved for money crops like cotton and tobacco, large-scale ranching was uncommon. Pigs, on the other hand, will eat just about anything and are not very particular about where they eat it. Most Southern farms therefore raised a lot of swine, and thus began the myth that fresh pork was an everyday thing on Southern tables. It wasn't: Before refrigeration, hog slaughtering could only be done in cold weather, and most of the meat was salt-and-smoke-cured for prolonged storage; very little of it was eaten fresh. Today it's probably true that Southerners eat more than our share of fresh pork, but it's a modern habit.

Beef, for average families during the lean years of the late nineteenth century and Great Depression, came mostly from tough old animals that could no longer produce milk or pull a plow. Portions were small and were stretched with bread and rice. While the development of refrigeration, western cattle ranching, and the affluence that followed World War II changed the kind of beef that was available to us (and not always for the better—but that's another subject), our preference for the cooking methods that had previously been necessary didn't change. To this day pot roasts, stews, and slow-braised smothered steak are our best-loved beef dishes. With more luxurious cuts of better-quality beef becoming more widely available, the cooking methods found in early Southern cookbooks have of course made a comeback: rare grill-broiling and roasting, pan-broiling and quick sautéing. All the same, nothing satisfies the Southern palate quite like falling-apart-tender pot roast and slow-barbecued short ribs or brisket.

Nowadays veal can be quite expensive and isn't considered especially Southern, but until the mid-twentieth century it was not only cheap but commonplace. Lowcountry food historian John Taylor points to archaeological digs in Charleston's old rubbish heaps that reveal that the city's early residents ate more veal than any other red meat. Cookbooks of the period reinforced this, calling veal ordinary, everyday stuff. Until around the time of World War II, it was common dairy practice to take calves before they were weaned so the cow would keep producing; thus, veal was plentiful and inexpensive. Eventually, other ways of keeping the herd productive replaced this practice, and cheap veal became less common. Many lovely old recipes for it were forgotten. A renewed interest in French and Italian cooking during the last few decades has made veal fashionable and brought it back to our markets, though unfortunately with prices to match. With it has also come concern for the humane treatment of the calves destined for those markets. But as more farmers respond to the concerns, these handsome old recipes deserve to be revisited.

Lamb and mutton are also frequently generalized as not particularly Southern, and the rule of thumb in some of the Southern cooking schools where I teach is that lamb on the menu will kill class enrollment faster than roaches in the pantry. But in pockets of the South—Virginia, Kentucky, and Georgia particularly—these meats have always been loved. In her 1928 classic, *Southern Cooking*, Georgia's Henrietta Stanley Dull called lamb "ordinary, everyday food," and my Georgia-born mother still cooks it anytime she can get it.

The recipes that follow are the way Southerners cook these meats today. While they've been touched over the years by the influence of other cuisines, they haven't really strayed from the traditions first set down centuries ago by Virginia's Mary Randolph, Kentucky's Lettice Bryan, Carolina's Sarah Rutledge, Georgia's Annabella Hill, and, of course, dear Mrs. Dull. My grandfather would feel at home with any of them. I hope you will, too.

bourbon-grilled flank steak

The bourbon marinade is delicious not only for flank steak but for virtually any meat or poultry that is to be grilled. It's even good with strongly flavored, oily fish such as bluefish or sea trout.

½ cup bourbon

¼ cup red wine vinegar

1 large or 2 small cloves garlic, lightly crushed, peeled, and minced

¼ cup minced shallots or yellow onions (about 2 small shallots or ½ small onion)

1 ounce dried porcini mushrooms (not reconstituted), chopped fine

Whole nutmeg in a grater

Salt, ground cayenne, and whole black pepper in a mill

½ cup peanut oil

1 flank steak, about 1½ pounds

1. Whisk together the bourbon, vinegar, garlic, shallots, mushrooms, a generous grating of nutmeg, a large pinch of salt, a small one of cayenne, and a liberal grinding of pepper in a glass or stainless-steel bowl. Gradually whisk in the oil, cover, and set it aside for 30 minutes. (The marinade can be made several days ahead and in fact will improve as it ages. It can also be made in a food processor: Put the bourbon, vinegar, garlic, shallots, mushrooms, nutmeg, salt, cayenne, and pepper in the bowl of the processor fitted with the steel blade. Process until the onions and mushrooms are minced fine then, with the motor running, slowly pour the oil in through the small feed tube.)

2. Meanwhile, rinse the steak and pat it dry. With a sharp knife, make crisscross slashes about an inch apart on both sides of the steak. Put it into a shallow glass dish such as an oval or rectangular 3-quart baking dish. Pour the marinade over it and turn several times to coat it. Put it aside to marinate for at least 1 hour at room temperature, or for up to 8 hours or overnight, covered and refrigerated.

3. Prepare a grill with lump hardwood coals, or preheat the broiler for at least 15 minutes. When the coals are ready or the broiler is heated, position a rack about 4–6 inches from the heat. Drain the steak and place it directly on the grill rack, or place it on a rack fitted in a broiler pan or cookie sheet under the broiler. Broil until the steak is nicely browned on one side, about 4 minutes, then turn it and continue broiling until the steak is evenly browned and done to your liking—about 3–4 minutes more for medium-rare. Flank steak should never be broiled beyond medium or it will be tough. Remove it to a warm platter, loosely cover with foil, and let rest 10 minutes, then slice it across the grain at a 45-degree angle, as thin as possible. Serve at once.

Serves 4

pan-broiled tenderloin filet steaks with bourbon déglacé

Despite its posh reputation and corresponding cost, the tenderloin is the least interesting and flavorful cut of a cow. Its compensation is that the meat is always tender and there is very little waste from tip to tip. Fortunately, bourbon deepens the flavor of the most timid beef. Here it's used to deglaze the pan, releasing and distilling the cooking residue that remains in the pan. The resulting sauce infuses the steaks with their own concentrated juices, underscored by the rich caramel essence of whiskey.

4 beef tenderloin steaks (about 6 ounces each), cut at least 2 inches thick

Whole black pepper in a mill

Salt

2 tablespoons unsalted butter, divided

2 tablespoons minced shallot or yellow onion

¼ cup bourbon

½ cup Beef Broth (page 10)

1. Pat the steaks dry and sprinkle them generously with several grindings of black pepper. Press the pepper into the steaks on all sides.

2. Preheat a well-seasoned iron skillet over medium-high heat until it is almost smoking hot. Add the steaks to the pan and sear them well—about a minute per side. You will know when they are ready to turn: the steak will release itself from the pan. Reduce the heat to medium and continue cooking, turning once, until they're done to taste, about 2 more minutes per side for rare, 4 for medium-rare. Remove them to a warm platter and season well with salt.

3. Add 1 tablespoon of the butter and the shallots to the pan and sauté, tossing constantly, until they are golden-brown. Slowly pour in the bourbon, and, standing well clear of the pan, ignite it. Allow the flame to burn out, then add the broth and any juices that may have accumulated on the platter. Boil until the liquid is reduced and syrupy, stirring and scraping to loosen any cooking residue, about 2 minutes. Remove the pan from the heat, swirl in the remaining butter, pour the sauce over the steaks, and serve at once.

Serves 4

sunday pot roast with rosemary and onions

Nothing recalls the Sunday mornings of my childhood quite like the aroma of onions and beef baking slowly in a pot roast. It wasn't a time for lying around in our house: Because my father is a minister, it was the busiest day of his week. Mama had to help him prepare for the day, coax three boys out of shorts and into pressed shirts, polished shoes, and neckties, and somehow put together a traditional Southern Sunday dinner for us to sit down to as soon as we got home from church. More often than not, the main dish of that dinner was pot roast with onions. We were grown before we knew that the reason Mama made it so often was less because we loved it than because it was inexpensive, easy, and forgiving when the spirit moved Daddy to a longer than usual sermon.

3 large or 4 medium yellow onions, trimmed, peeled, and thinly sliced into rounds

3 large or 4 small cloves garlic, lightly crushed, peeled, and minced

2 tablespoons chopped fresh rosemary or 1 teaspoon dried rosemary

6 pounds (bone-in) beef chuck roast, trimmed of excess fat

Salt and whole black pepper in a mill

6 carrots, peeled and cut into 1-inch lengths

6 medium boiling potatoes, peeled and cut into quarters

1 tablespoon all-purpose flour kneaded into 2 tablespoons butter

1. Position a rack in the lower third of the oven and preheat to 325°F. Cover the bottom of a heavy Dutch oven with half the onions. Sprinkle with a third of the garlic and rosemary. Pat the roast dry with paper towels, season both sides with salt and pepper, and lay it on top of the onions.

2. Sprinkle another third of the garlic and rosemary over the roast and cover it with the remaining onions. Arrange the carrots and potatoes around it and season them with salt, pepper, and the rest of the garlic and rosemary. Cover and bake in the lower third of the oven until the beef is fork-tender, about 3 hours.

3. Transfer the beef a warm platter, loosely cover with foil, and let it rest at least 10 minutes before carving. Tip the pan and spoon off the excess fat from the roasting juices. Strain them into a saucepan, reserving the onions, and bring them to a simmer over medium heat. Whisk in the butter-flour mixture and simmer, stirring constantly, until thickened, about 4 minutes. Taste and adjust the seasonings and simmer a minute longer to blend the flavors. Turn off the heat and pour the gravy into a warm sauceboat.

4. Slice the roast thinly, across the grain, sprinkle the reserved onions over it, and serve with the gravy passed separately.

Serves 6–8

VEAL

georgia pot roast with tomato pan gravy

Annabella Hill was an indomitable matron from LaGrange, Georgia, who left us with one of the only printed records of antebellum Georgia's cooking, *Mrs. Hill's New Cook Book*, published in 1867. Mrs. Hill did not think much of veal, calling it "an insipid meat," but she knew exactly what to do with it. This pot roast is adapted from her work.

¼ **pound thick-sliced bacon, preferably applewood-smoked, divided**

1 **medium onion, peeled and chopped fine**

2 **tablespoons chopped parsley**

Whole white pepper in a mill

Ground cayenne

Salt

3 **pounds veal round**

1 **pound ripe tomatoes, blanched, peeled, and seeded as directed on page 35, roughly chopped, or 1 cup canned Italian tomatoes, drained, seeded, and roughly chopped**

1. Finely chop 2 slices of the bacon, setting aside the remainder. Mix the chopped bacon with the onion, parsley, a liberal grinding of white pepper, a small pinch of cayenne, and a large one of salt.

2. Wipe the veal well with paper towels or a clean cloth. Make several deep incisions into it with a sharp, thin knife such as a boning knife. Set aside 3 tablespoons of the bacon-onion mixture and pack the remainder into these incisions. Rub salt, white pepper, and cayenne to taste into all sides

of the roast and wrap it with the reserved slices of bacon, securing them with toothpicks or skewers. Put the roast in a heavy enameled iron Dutch oven or lidded roasting pan, cover, and set aside for at least an hour (or for up to 8 hours, refrigerated; but let it sit at room temperature for 30 minutes before cooking it).

3. Position a rack in the upper third of the oven and preheat to 450°F. Uncover the pot and roast until the meat is well browned, about 15 minutes. Pour the broth over the meat, cover, and reduce the heat to 325°F. Bake until the veal is fork-tender, about 2 hours.

4. Remove the roast to a warm platter, loosely cover with foil, and let rest 30 minutes before carving. Meanwhile, tip the pan, spoon off the excess fat from the pan juices, and set them aside. Put the reserved bacon-onion mixture in a large saucepan or skillet that will hold all the pan juices and tomatoes at once over medium-high heat. Sauté, tossing frequently, until the onion is translucent and the fat is rendered from the bacon. Add the tomatoes and stir until they're hot through, about 2 minutes. Add the reserved roasting juices, bring to a boil, and cook until the gravy is thick, about 20–30 minutes. Turn off the heat. Taste and adjust the seasonings. Thinly slice the veal across the grain, drizzle with some of the gravy, and serve at once, passing the remaining gravy separately.

Serves 4–6

grilled breaded veal chops

This handsome recipe is from Mary Randolph's *The Virginia House-Wife*, the first known cookbook to chronicle Southern food. What it illustrates so well is not only how wonderful historical cooking was, but how timeless it remains. These chops would be right at home on the hottest new restaurant menu and yet they satisfy all the requirements of a busy home cook: They are easy, elegant, showy, and, best of all, wonderfully good to eat. The seasonings are classic ones for veal—lemon zest, nutmeg, and white pepper—all reinforced and enhanced by a good hardwood fire. There is no more beautiful or satisfying way to cook veal, or, for that matter, to eat it.

The chops can of course be cooked using the oven broiler, or, if you really aren't worried about fat, are sumptuous when fried in clarified butter.

4 veal rib or loin chops, each about ¾ inch thick

Salt and whole white pepper in a mill

Whole nutmeg in a grater

Grated zest from 1 lemon

1 tablespoon chopped parsley

¼ cup all-purpose flour

1 egg, lightly beaten

1 cup dry bread crumbs

4 tablespoons (¼ cup or ½ stick) butter, melted

1 lemon, cut into 8 wedges, for garnish

1. If you're using rib chops, french the bone, scraping the meat and fat from the long end to leave only the meaty eye of the chop attached. Set the scraps aside for broth. Lightly beat the chops with a mallet or scaloppine pounder, until the meat is ½ inch thick. (If you're using loin chops, beat the tougher loin side well to tenderize it.) Sprinkle liberally on all sides with salt, white pepper, nutmeg, lemon zest, and parsley, pressing it into the meat.

2. Put the flour, egg, and crumbs in separate shallow bowls. Lightly roll each chop in flour, shaking off the excess, then dip it in egg until it is coated, letting the excess flow back into the bowl, and then roll it in the crumbs, patting the crumbs into all sides. Lay the chops on a wire rack for at least 30 minutes to allow the coating to set.

3. Prepare a grill with hardwood coals or preheat the broiler for at least 15 minutes. When the coals are glowing red but lightly ashed over, spread them and position a rack about 5 inches above them (in the broiler, about 5 inches below the heat source). Brush one side lightly with the butter and put them on the grill, buttered side toward the heat. Grill/broil until the crumbs are toasted golden-brown, about 3 minutes. Brush the uncooked side with butter, turn, and grill until they are evenly browned, about 3 minutes more for medium-rare. If you prefer the veal more done, move the chops to indirect heat and grill about 1–2 minutes more per side for medium. Don't overcook them or they will be tough. Serve hot, garnished with lemon wedges.

Serves 4

veal scallops with artichokes a la creole

Creole cooks know how to get the most out of veal, and these rich but delicate scallops are a luxurious example of this skill.

4 medium artichokes

1 lemon, halved

4 tablespoons (¼ cup or ½ stick) unsalted butter, divided

4 medium or 3 large scallions or other green onions, thinly sliced, white and green parts separated

Salt

1 cup heavy cream

1 pound veal round or sirloin scallops, cut about 2 inches across by ½ inch thick

Whole black pepper in a mill

1 tablespoon chopped fresh parsley

1. Put enough water into a large glass or ceramic bowl to cover the artichokes. Squeeze in the juice from one lemon half and drop in the spent rind. Trim the artichokes and remove the chokes as directed on page 185. Cut them into quarters, rubbing well with the other half of the lemon. Add them to the acidulated water as they're finished.

2. When they're all trimmed, drain well and put them in a large heavy-bottomed sauté pan or skillet with 2 tablespoons of the butter and white part of the scallions. Set the pan over medium-high heat and sauté, tossing frequently, until the scallion is wilted and the artichokes are hot and bright green, but not browned, about 2 minutes.

3. Add a healthy pinch of salt and the cream, bring to a boil, then reduce the heat to low, cover, and simmer, stirring occasionally, until the artichokes are tender, about 20–30 minutes. Turn off the heat, transfer the artichokes to a bowl, and wipe out the pan.

4. Meanwhile, spread a sheet of waxed paper or plastic wrap on a sturdy work surface. Lay the veal scallops on the paper or wrap and cover with a second sheet. Lightly pound them out with a mallet or scaloppine pounder to less than ¼-inch thickness.

5. Melt the remaining butter in the sauté pan over medium heat. When it's melted and bubbly, raise the heat to medium-high, add the veal, and sauté quickly, about half a minute per side. Season with salt and pepper and transfer them to a warm platter. Return the artichokes to the pan, stirring and scraping to loosen any cooking residue, and bring it to a boil. Turn off the heat, pour the sauce over the veal, and sprinkle the parsley and scallions over them. Serve at once.

Serves 4

veal scallops with oysters and country ham

Everywhere that there is a coastline in the South, there is an abundance of oysters. Coastal cooks use them prodigally during their traditional season (the months with an r in them), so they're mostly associated with winter cookery. Veal scallops with oysters is an old, old pairing with European roots, but in recent years the combination has not been as popular. So when a talented local chef proudly presented a similar dish as his creation, I didn't have the heart to tell him he hadn't invented anything. I was too glad to see another tradition coming back.

1 cup shucked oysters, with their reserved juices

1 pound veal round or sirloin scallops, cut about 2 inches across by ½ inch thick

Salt and whole white pepper in a mill

3 tablespoons unsalted butter, divided

¼ cup all-purpose flour, spread on a dinner plate

1 ounce wafer-thin-sliced country ham or prosciutto, cut into ½-inch squares

1 cup heavy cream

1 tablespoon chopped fresh chives or green onion tops

1. Drain the oysters in a wire sieve fitted over a glass or stainless bowl to catch their liquor. Spread a sheet of waxed paper or plastic wrap on a sturdy work surface. Lay the veal scallops on it, cover with a second sheet, and lightly pound with a mallet or scaloppine pounder to less than ¼-inch thickness. Lightly season with salt and white pepper.

2. Put 2 tablespoons of the butter in a large, heavy-bottomed skillet or sauté pan and turn on the heat to medium. When the butter is melted and bubbly, raise the heat to medium-high, lightly roll the veal in the flour, shake off the excess, and add it to the pan. Sauté, turning once, until golden-brown on both sides, about 1 minute per side. The veal should still be pink in the middle. Remove it to a warm platter and keep warm.

3. Add the remaining butter and the ham to the pan. Sauté, tossing constantly, until the ham loses its raw red color, about half a minute. Pat the oysters dry, add them to the pan, and sauté until they are plump and their gills begin to curl, about 1 minute. Remove them with a slotted spoon and pour the reserved oyster liquor into the pan. Bring it to a boil, stirring and scraping the pan, and boil until reduced by half. Add the cream, return it to a boil, and boil briskly until the cream is lightly thickened, about a minute.

4. Reduce the heat to medium-low, return the veal and the oysters to the pan, and turn several times in the sauce until they are lightly coated and just warmed through. Turn off the heat, transfer the veal to a warm platter, and pour the sauce and oysters over it. Sprinkle chives or green onion tops over all and serve at once.

Serves 4

lowcountry veal stew

The flavors in this elegant old Lowcountry stew are some of the loveliest of all for veal—the heady perfume of garlic, sage, and lemon peel simmering in a bath of wine. The Carolina Lowcountry is better known for its fish and shellfish cookery, but veal was once commonplace on Charleston tables, and this recipe is adapted from Sarah Rutledge's timeless bible of Charleston cookery, *The Carolina Housewife*. The choice of wine is up to you. Madeira or sherry lends a sweeter, mellower flavor; white wine is brighter and draws out the flavor of the lemon. They are equally delectable.

2 pounds 1-inch-thick veal chuck steak, bone-in

2 tablespoons unsalted butter

1 tablespoon extra-virgin olive oil

¼ cup all-purpose flour, spread on a plate

1 medium yellow onion, peeled and chopped

2 large or 3 small cloves garlic, lightly crushed, peeled, and minced

1 tablespoon chopped fresh sage
or 1 teaspoon crumbled dried sage

3–4 strips lemon zest, each 1 inch wide
(cut vertically from about half a lemon)

Salt and whole black pepper in a mill

1 cup dry white wine, Sercial Madeira, or dry sherry such as Amontillado

2 cups Carolina-Style Rice (page 77)

Fresh sage or parsley leaves, for garnish

1. Trim the excess fat from the veal and cut it from the bones. Set the bones aside and cut the meat into 1-inch cubes. Warm the butter and olive oil in a braising pan or deep, lidded skillet over medium heat. When the butter is bubbling, raise the heat to medium-high, quickly roll a third of the veal in the flour, shake off the excess, and add it to the pan. Brown well on all sides, turning often, about 2 minutes; remove it with a slotted spoon or tongs. Repeat this with the remaining veal in two batches, then add and brown the reserved bones.

2. Add the onion and sauté, tossing constantly, until it is golden, about 3 minutes. Add the garlic, sage, and lemon zest and toss until fragrant, about a minute more. Return the veal and its reserved juices to the pan; season well with salt and a liberal grinding of pepper. Add the wine, stirring well, and let it come to a boil.

3. Reduce the heat to low, tightly cover, and simmer, stirring occasionally, until the veal is fork-tender, about an hour. If at any point the stew appears to be getting too dry, add a few spoonfuls of water. Don't add more wine. If, on the other hand, there's too much liquid, turn up the heat and cook rapidly until the juices are thick, stirring frequently to prevent scorching. Taste and adjust the seasonings and turn off the heat.

4. Remove and discard the zest and bones. Mound the rice around the rim of a warm platter and pour the stew into the center. Garnish with sage or parsley, if you like, and serve at once.

Lowcountry Veal Shanks or "Osso Bucco": Use 4 meaty veal shank pieces cut about 2 inches thick. (Choose smaller shanks for this; the larger ones are from the joint and look meatier, but have more bone and connective tissue.) Cook the shanks whole, without removing the bones. They will take longer than the smaller, boned pieces of veal—about 2 hours. Serve them whole with a little of the sauce spooned over them.

Serves 4

roast lamb with bourbon and mint

Bourbon does wonderful things for any roast, but it's especially compatible with lamb. Its mellow, rich aroma mingles with the bright accent of mint, making a perfect complement for lamb. This is equally good served warm with Madeira Pan Gravy or Mint Butter, or cold with the Mint Butter or aioli.

Some cooks like to flame the bourbon before returning the roast to the oven, to prevent the alcohol from exploding in the oven's intense heat. I've never had this happen, but if you want to go on the side of caution, ignite the bourbon after you pour it over the roast, stand clear, and make sure there's nothing flammable (including you) near it. If you use hair spray, get someone else to do the flaming.

1 small whole bone-in leg of lamb (about 6–7 pounds)

Salt and whole black pepper in a mill

⅓ cup chopped fresh mint or ¼ cup crumbled dried mint

½ cup bourbon

Madeira Pan Gravy (page 163) and/or Mint Butter (follows)

1. Position a rack in the center of the oven and preheat to 500°F. Trim some of the excess fat from the lamb, but leave a thin layer of at least ⅛ inch of fat on all sides of the meat. Wipe it dry with paper towels or a clean cloth. Liberally rub it with salt and pepper, and press the mint over the entire surface.

2. Put the lamb directly on the bottom of a roasting pan and roast in the center of the oven for 15 minutes, or until the outside is seared and lightly browned. Remove it from the oven and slowly pour the bourbon over it. Return it to the oven, reduce the heat to 400°F, and roast, basting occasionally with the juices, until done to your taste, from 15 minutes per pound for medium-rare to 30 minutes per pound for medium-well.

3. Let the roast rest, covered with foil, for 20–30 minutes before carving it. Serve with Madeira Pan Gravy (page 163) or Mint Butter passed separately.

Serves 8–10

MINT BUTTER

Melt 6 ounces (¾ cup) unsalted butter over low heat. Put one loosely packed cup fresh mint leaves (preferably spearmint), 1 large crushed and peeled clove garlic, the juice of two lemons, and a pinch each of salt and sugar in a food processor fitted with a steel blade. Pulse until chopped, then, with the motor running, add the melted butter in a thin stream. Taste and adjust the sugar and salt (it should not be sweet), pulse to mix, and let stand until the butter begins to solidify, then turn on the machine and whip until the butter is fluffy.

lamb or mutton stew, hunter-style

As soon as a hint of autumn touches the air in the Deep South, you can almost hear the hunting rifles being cleaned and polished. Many Southern men (except for me) and not a few Southern women still love hunting, and venison is a favorite quarry. This hearty, rich stew is typical of the way Southern hunters like to prepare that lean, distinctive meat. Farm-raised venison is now sold in some specialty markets, but it isn't universally available, so for those who (like me) either don't hunt or couldn't shoot straight on a bet, this recipe substitutes lamb, another assertively flavored meat that stands up well to the complexity of flavors. If you want to try the stew with venison, up the drippings or oil to 3 tablespoons, and allow at least an extra half hour's cooking time.

2 pounds lamb (or venison), bone in, preferably from the shoulder

2 tablespoons bacon drippings or 1 tablespoon each unsalted butter and olive oil

¼ cup all-purpose flour, spread on a plate

1 medium onion, trimmed, split lengthwise, and chopped

2 large or 3 medium cloves garlic, lightly crushed, peeled, and minced

1 tablespoon chopped fresh sage or 1 teaspoon crumbled dried sage

1 whole fresh or dried pod hot pepper such as cayenne, serrano, or jalapeño

2 bay leaves

1 large sprig parsley

Whole nutmeg in a grater

Salt and whole black pepper in a mill

1 cup Madeira or full-bodied red wine

1 tablespoon red wine vinegar

2 cups Carolina-Style Rice (page 77), or Breakfast Grits (page 70), optional

1. Trim the excess fat from the meat and remove but reserve the bones. Cut it into 2-inch-square pieces. Melt the drippings in a braising pan, deep, lidded skillet, or an enameled iron Dutch oven over medium heat. When it is melted and hot, raise the heat to medium-high, roll the lamb a few pieces at a time in the flour, shake off the excess, and slip it into the pan. Do not overcrowd. Sauté, tossing often, until the meat is browned well on all sides. Remove it with a slotted spoon or tongs and repeat with the remaining lamb. Finally, add the bones and brown them.

2. Remove the bones, add the onion, and sauté, tossing, until it's pale gold, about 4 minutes. Add the garlic and sage and toss until fragrant, about half a minute. Return the lamb and bones to the pan with the whole pepper pod, bay leaves, and parsley. Season well with nutmeg, salt, and pepper, add the wine and vinegar, and bring to a boil. Reduce the heat to low, cover, and simmer, stirring occasionally, until the meat is fork tender, about 1–1½ hours (or up to 2½ hours for venison).

3. Tip the pan and spoon off the excess fat, remove and discard the bay leaves and hot pepper, then taste and adjust the seasonings. Simmer a minute longer and turn off the heat. You may either transfer the stew to a warm serving platter or serve it from the pan, passing Carolina-Style Rice or Breakfast Grits separately if you like.

Serves 4

lamb shanks with butterbeans

Shanks and beans are classic together, and can be found in most Western cuisines in one form or another. Here's the Southern take on the idea, made with our own sweet, tender butterbeans—which happen to be a particularly good complement for lamb.

4 meaty lamb shanks, about 3 pounds

2 tablespoons bacon drippings or 1 tablespoon each unsalted butter and olive oil

2 ounces (1 slice about 3 inches wide by ⅛ inch thick) country ham or prosciutto

1 medium onion, trimmed, split lengthwise, peeled, and chopped

1 large or 2 medium cloves garlic

1 pound fresh butterbeans, or frozen butterbeans (or small limas), about 3 cups, thawed

2 pounds Roma or other sauce tomatoes, blanched, peeled, seeded, and chopped (page 35), or 2½ cups whole canned tomatoes, seeded and chopped, with their juices

2 tablespoons chopped fresh sage or 2 teaspoons crumbled, dried sage

1 cup water

Salt and whole black pepper in a mill

1. Trim the shanks of excess fat and the tough outer membrane; pat dry with paper towels or a clean cloth. Melt the drippings in a braising pan, a deep, lidded skillet, or an enameled iron Dutch oven over medium heat. When the fat is melted and hot, raise the heat to medium-high, add the shanks, and brown them well on all sides, about 2 minutes per side. Remove them to a warm platter.

2. Add the ham and onion and sauté, tossing frequently, until the onion is golden, about 5 minutes. Add the garlic and sauté until fragrant, about half a minute more. Return the shanks to the pan along with the butterbeans, tomatoes, sage, and water. Season well with salt and liberal grinding of pepper. Bring to a boil, reduce the heat to low, cover, and simmer until the beans and shanks are very tender, about 1½ hours.

3. If the sauce is too thin, raise the heat, bring back to a brisk boil, and cook until lightly thickened. Tip the pan, spoon off any excess fat, taste and adjust the seasonings, and turn off the heat. Let it sit for a few minutes to settle, but serve hot.

Serves 4

grill-broiled lamb chops with eggplant, a la creole

All the traditional Southern cooks knew how to prepare lamb chops to perfection: Cut them thick, season simply, broil them over hardwood coals until they're crisp and brown on the outside, juicy and pink at the center, then simply sauce them with brown butter. Creole cooks took it another step, dressing up the presentation by bedding the chops on a crisp slice of fried eggplant. Why fool around with perfection? This is the traditional recipe, except that the eggplant is grilled instead of fried.

1 medium eggplant (about ¾ pound)

Salt

4 lamb loin chops cut at least ¾ inch thick (about 6 ounces each)

Whole black pepper in a mill

3 tablespoons chopped fresh mint, divided

¼ cup all-purpose flour

1 large egg, well beaten

1 cup fine cracker crumbs or matzo meal

6 tablespoons (¾ stick) unsalted butter

1 large or 2 small cloves garlic, lightly crushed and peeled, but left whole

1. Wash the eggplant under cold running water, peel, and slice it crosswise into eight ½-inch-thick slices. Lightly salt both sides, layer them in a colander set in the sink, and let stand for 30 minutes. Wipe dry with paper towels.

2. Meanwhile, wipe the chops with paper towels or a clean dry cloth and sprinkle both sides generously with pepper and 1 tablespoon of the mint. Put them on a clean, dry plate. Lightly roll the eggplant slices in the flour, shake off the excess, dip them in the egg, allowing the excess to flow back into the bowl, and roll them in the crumbs, patting the crumbs into the surface. Lay them on a wire cooling rack and let stand at least 15 minutes.

3. Gently simmer the butter and garlic in a small saucepan over medium-low heat until the cloves are colored pale gold, about 10 minutes. Turn off the heat and season well with salt.

4. About 30 minutes before you plan to cook the chops, prepare a grill with hardwood coals and light them or position a rack about 6 inches from the heat source and preheat the broiler. When the coals are ready, position the rack about 5 inches from them. Brush one side of the chops with butter and put them on the grill buttered-side down, or on a broiling pan fitted with a rack buttered-side up. Cook until the buttered side is browned, about 3–4 minutes. Brush with butter and turn (if you are broiling the chops, brush them after turning); cook until the second side is well browned and the chops are medium-rare to medium, about 4 minutes more. Set them on a warm plate.

5. Lightly brush the eggplant with the garlic butter and grill-broil until the crumbs are nicely browned, turning once, about 3 minutes per side. Put the eggplant (two slices per serving) on individual serving plates. Top one piece of eggplant with the chops, then arrange the second piece of eggplant to one side, overlapping slightly. Add the remaining mint and any juices that have accumulated from the chops to the remaining melted butter, stir, and spoon a little over each serving. Serve at once.

Variations: If you prefer, you may serve the chops sauced with Creole Sauce (page 172) or try Tarragon-Mustard Sauce: Substitute tarragon for the mint and whisk 2 tablespoons of Dijon mustard into the melted butter in step 5 with the herbs and juices.

Serves 4

PORK

roast pork with apples and mushrooms

When the weather turns crisp in the fall, seasonal apples, mushrooms, sage, and onions become the classic seasonings for pork. Here all of them are put to work at once in a traditional roast from the Carolina hill country. The recipe is adapted from the late chef Bill Neal's masterpiece *Southern Cooking*, but while it may look like a nouvelle concoction, it's literally as old as the hills from whence it comes. Don't be intimidated by the length of this recipe: It's more complicated in the telling than in the cooking.

1 fresh bone-in picnic ham (foreleg cut) of pork, about 8 pounds, bone in

2 tablespoons extra-virgin olive oil

Salt and whole black pepper in a mill

2 tablespoons crumbled dried sage leaves or ¼ cup chopped fresh sage, divided

6 green (underripe) tart apples (see notes)

1 lemon

¾ pound shiitake, crimini, portobello, Boletus edulis (porcini), or other fresh mushrooms (see notes)

3 medium yellow onions, trimmed, split lengthwise, peeled, and thinly sliced

3 large cloves garlic, lightly crushed, peeled, and minced

⅓ cup turbinado ("raw") sugar

1. Position a rack in the lower third of the oven and preheat to 500°F. Wipe the pork dry with paper towels or a clean, dry cloth. Rub all sides with olive oil and put it in a close-fitting roasting pan, skin-side up. Rub all sides well with salt, pepper, and half the sage. Roast in the lower third of the oven for 45 minutes without opening the oven door.

2. Check the roast to make sure the skin is crisping and not getting too brown. Baste well, reduce the heat to 375°F, and roast, basting occasionally, until the pork is cooked through and the juices run clear, about 20 minutes to the pound.

3. Meanwhile, peel, core, and thinly slice the apples. Put them in a glass bowl and toss them with the lemon juice. Clean the mushrooms with a dry cloth or paper towel, trim away any tough or dirt-encrusted stems, and thinly slice them.

4. Forty-five minutes before the roast is done, spoon 2 tablespoons of the drippings into a large, lidded sauté pan or skillet. Add the onions and put the pan over medium-high heat. Sauté, tossing often, until it's golden-brown. Add the garlic and sauté until fragrant, about half a minute more. Add the apples and toss until well mixed. Sprinkle in the sugar, a large pinch of salt, and the remaining sage. Toss well, cover, and reduce the heat to medium-low. Cook until the apples are tender, about 15–20 minutes, shaking the pan from time to time to prevent scorching. Turn off the heat and transfer them to a wide bowl.

5. When the pork is done, remove it to a platter. Degrease the pan juices and set aside, reserving 2 tablespoons of the fat. Deglaze the roasting pan with ½ cup water over medium heat and return the reserved roasting juices to the pan. Turn off the heat. Over medium-high heat, warm the reserved fat in the pan in which the onion and apples cooked. Add the mushrooms and sauté, tossing often, until golden, about 4 minutes.

6. Return the apples and onions to the pan and heat them through, shaking often. If there is any accumulated liquid, let it boil away. Turn off the heat, taste, and adjust the salt.

7. Cut away the crackling (skin) from the pork and break it up. Thinly slice the meat, spread it on a warm platter, and sprinkle it with the reserved pan juices. Surround it with the apple, onion, and mushrooms, garnish with the crackling, and serve at once.

Notes: The traditional mushrooms for this roast are honey mushrooms (Armillariella mellea), which are indigenous to the Southeastern United States; however, they are not available commercially. If you forage for mushrooms, make sure that you know what you are harvesting. Occasionally, Boletus edulis (porcini) mushrooms, which are also indigenous, turn up in the market. They are very expensive, but worth it—if that is, they are fresh. If you use cultivated mushrooms, they should have a sturdy, assertive flavor, so don't use delicate varieties such as white champignons, chanterelles, or oyster mushrooms. The apples should be tart and underripe or they will just fall apart when cooked. Granny Smith and Winesap are both good choices.

Serves 6–8

pork tenderloins with bourbon-mustard glaze

In parts of South Carolina and Georgia, mustard is the base for any barbecue sauce that will accompany pork. Other parts of both states (and most of the rest of the South) look on with abject horror. But those Carolinians and Georgians matter-of-factly ignore the shock because they're on to something and they know it: Mustard is a natural complement for pork. Not only does it enhance the flavor, it also helps tenderize and moisten the driest of cuts. Here the mustard is mixed with bourbon to form a simple but wonderfully savory-sweet glaze. It's lovely not only with tenderloins but with virtually any cut of pork, particularly boneless pork loin, and is also lovely on chicken or lamb.

1 pair pork tenderloins, about 2 pounds total weight

Salt and whole black pepper in a mill

¼ cup turbinado ("raw") sugar

¼ cup bourbon

¼ cup Dijon-style mustard

Fresh Apple Chutney (page 155), optional

1. Wash the tenderloins under cold water, then thoroughly pat them dry. Put them on an oblong platter, casserole, or bowl that will just hold them comfortably. Sprinkle the meat generously with salt and a few liberal grindings of pepper.

2. Dissolve the sugar in the bourbon and whisk in the mustard. Pour this over the pork, turning until all sides are well coated, and set aside for at least 30 minutes or up to 1 hour. Meanwhile, position a rack in the upper third of the oven and preheat to 450°F.

3. Lift the tenderloins from the glaze, allowing the excess to run off, and put them in a close-fitting roasting pan or shallow enameled iron casserole. Roast 15 minutes in the upper third of the oven, or until the glaze is beginning to brown. Reduce the heat to 400°F and roast, basting occasionally with the reserved glaze, until it reaches an internal temperature of 135°F, about 30 minutes longer. Stop basting 10 minutes before you think the pork is ready (when it reaches an internal temperature of about 110°F), since the glaze has been in contact with raw pork and will need to cook.

4. Remove the pork to a platter and let it rest for 15 minutes before carving it. Thinly slice it across the grain and arrange it on a warm platter. Return any accumulated juices to the roasting pan, stir the pan juices until they are smooth, and drizzle them over the pork. Serve hot or at room temperature with Fresh Apple Chutney, if you like.

Notes: The tenderloins can also be grilled. Prepare them up through step 2 and let them marinate for a full hour. Prepare a grill with hardwood coals, ignite them, and let them burn down. Spread the coals and position a rack about 6–8 inches above them. Grill the tenderloins, giving them a quarter turn every 10 minutes and brushing them with extra glaze, until they are just cooked through (an internal temperature of 135°F), about 30–45 minutes depending on the size of the tenderloins and how hot the coals are. Stop basting in the last 10 minutes (when they reach an internal temperature of 110°F).

To roast a boneless loin, you will of course need more time and gentler heat after the first

few minutes. Place the loin on a rack set in a roasting pan. After the initial searing, about 20 minutes, reduce the oven temperature to 375°F and pour just enough boiling water in the pan to completely cover the bottom by ¼ inch. Make sure the pork isn't standing in the water, but remains above it. Baste occasionally with the remaining marinade, and allow a roasting time of about 20 minutes to the pound. The water in the pan will absorb the drippings from the roast and make lovely pan gravy.

Serves 4–6

pork loin in milk

Trimmed boneless pork loin is the pig's equivalent of a chicken breast fillet: easy, convenient, and as boring as it is popular. The two lean cuts have the same problem: Without bones and outer fat to keep them moist, they can be dry and dull. Consequently, the way I prefer to cook boneless loin is slow and easy, in plenty of moist heat. Here it simmers in a tenderizing and fragrant bath of milk perfumed with sage, onions, and a few simple spices—a very old, traditional Southern way with pork that closely resembles a traditional roast from Emilia-Romagna, Italy's gastronomical center. It's just one of many parallels that these two cuisines share.

3 pounds boneless pork loin

1 tablespoon crumbled dried sage

Salt and whole black pepper in a mill

2 medium onions, peeled and thinly sliced

2 cups whole milk (do not use low-fat milk)

1 tablespoon all-purpose flour

Fresh sage leaves and curled strips of lemon peel, for garnish (optional)

1. Position a rack in the upper third of the oven and preheat to 450°F. Wipe the pork dry with paper towels or a clean, dry cloth. Rub all sides of it with the dried sage, and season well with salt and a liberal grinding of pepper.

2. Put a layer of onions over the bottom of an enameled iron Dutch oven. Lay the pork on top of them and roast, uncovered, in the upper third of the oven until seared and lightly browned, about 20 minutes. Scatter the remaining onions over the pork and pour the milk slowly over. Cover and return it to the oven. Reduce the heat to 325°F and bake until the pork is fork-tender, about 1½–2 hours longer.

3. Remove the pork and onions to a warm platter. Loosely cover and let it rest at least 15 minutes before carving. Meanwhile, tip the pot and spoon off most of the fat, reserving 1 tablespoon. Pour off but reserve the pan juices, then return the reserved fat to the pot and put it over medium heat. When it's hot, whisk in the flour and continue whisking until it smells toasty and is just beginning to color, about 3 minutes. Slowly whisk in the pan juices and bring them a boil, stirring constantly. Reduce the heat and simmer 3–4 minutes, or until it's lightly thickened. Taste and adjust the seasonings, then turn off the heat. Pour the sauce into a warm sauceboat or bowl.

4. Thinly slice the pork across the grain, surround it with the onions, and nap the meat with some of the gravy. Garnish with sage leaves and curls of lemon peel; serve warm, with the remaining gravy passed separately.

Serves 4–6

fresh apple chutney

This fresh chutney is lighter and less complex than slow-simmered ones, and makes a bright, colorful presentation at table. It is delicious not only with Pork Tenderloins with Bourbon-Mustard Glaze (above), but with any grilled or roasted meat, including Roast Lamb with Bourbon and Mint (page 144), Roast Chicken with Sage and Madeira Pan Gravy (page 163), or Braised Pork Chops with Sage and Madeira (page 157).

½ cup currants or raisins

¼ cup bourbon

2 medium, tart, underripe apples (Granny Smiths are fine for this)

1 tablespoon extra-virgin olive oil

1 small yellow onion, peeled and diced small

1 small green bell pepper, stemmed, seeded, and diced small

1 small hot red pepper, such as cayenne or serrano

1 large or 2 small cloves garlic, lightly crushed, peeled, and minced

2 quarter-size slices fresh ginger, minced

1 bay leaf

1 tablespoon whole yellow or white mustard seeds

Salt

2 tablespoons turbinado ("raw") sugar

¼ cup cider vinegar

1. Put the currants or raisins in a bowl and pour the bourbon over them. Set aside until the fruit is saturated, at least an hour. Meanwhile peel, core, and cut the apples into ½-inch dice. When you're ready to proceed, drain the currants but reserve the bourbon.

2. Warm the oil in a large sauté pan over medium-high heat. When it's hot, add the onion and both peppers and sauté, tossing often, until the onion is translucent but still firm, about 4 minutes. Add the garlic, ginger, bay leaf, and mustard seeds and sauté until fragrant, about half a minute, then add the apple and currants to the pan and toss until the fruit is hot. Season well with salt and sprinkle in the sugar. Sauté, tossing constantly, until the sugar is dissolved. Splash in the vinegar and reserved bourbon and toss until the apples are crisp-tender and the chutney is thick, about 2 minutes more. Turn off the heat. Taste and correct the seasonings, and serve hot or at room temperature.

Makes 3 cups

pan-broiled pork tenderloins with caramelized onions

Traditional Southern cooks prepare tenderloins by slicing them thickly, rolling them in seasoned flour, and quickly frying them in deep fat. Crackling-crisp on the outside, but sweet and juicy and tender inside, they are very satisfying to eat, especially when sandwiched in a hot biscuit. Here they are treated to the same seasonings, but instead of being fried they're pan-broiled and finished with a rich, mahogany blanket of caramelized onions. There's no crispy crust, but the flavor boost more than compensates for its loss.

1 pair pork tenderloins, about 2 pounds, total weight

Salt and whole black pepper in a mill

1 teaspoon dried crumbled sage

2 tablespoons extra-virgin olive oil

4 medium yellow onions, peeled and sliced as thinly as possible

1. Wash the tenderloins under cold running water and pat them dry. Season them generously with salt and liberal grindings of pepper. Rub them all over with the sage.

2. Put the olive oil in a large sauté pan or skillet and turn on the heat to medium-high. When the oil is hot, add the onions and sauté, tossing frequently, until they are wilted, dry, and beginning to color. Begin tossing constantly and continue sautéing until they are deep golden-brown but not scorched. Season the onions lightly with salt and a few grindings of pepper. Remove them from the pan with a slotted spoon or spatula. There will be a light film of fat and onion residue left on the bottom of the pan. Don't scrape this away.

3. Put in the tenderloins and brown them well on all sides. Reduce the heat to medium and sauté, turning them occasionally, until they are firm and their juices run clear, about 15–20 minutes more, depending on size and thickness. Return the onions to the pan and sauté until they are reheated, about 1 minute. Turn off the heat. Taste and correct the seasonings. Remove the pork to a cutting board and slice it on the diagonal about ¼ inch thick. Spread on a warm platter, scatter the onions over the top, and serve at once.

Serves 4–6

braised pork chops with sage and madeira

Thick pork loin chops were for a time a signature dish of nearly every upscale Southern restaurant in the region. All too often they were as disappointing as they were commonplace. This can be a lovely cut, but it presents a challenge to the cook. Attached to its T-shaped bone are two very different muscles, which react differently in cooking. The inner tender medallion will be good whether the chop is overcooked or undercooked, but without care the outer loin can end up dry and uninteresting if it's cooked past medium, especially on the grill—the favorite method employed by most restaurants. When cooked less than medium, its texture is frankly a bit scary. That's why I prefer to braise loin chops until both sides of the T bone are meltingly tender. Here a little wine further tenderizes the chops and helps to keep them juicy and flavorful.

4 center-cut bone-in pork loin chops (each 1 inch thick)

Salt and whole black pepper in a mill

¼ cup all-purpose flour, spread on a plate

2 tablespoons rendered bacon drippings or unsalted butter

¼ cup minced shallots (about 1 large or 2 medium) or yellow onions

1 tablespoon chopped fresh sage or 1 teaspoon crumbled dried sage

1 cup Sercial Madeira or medium-dry sherry such as Amontillado

1. Wipe the chops with paper towels or a clean, dry cloth and season all sides well with salt and pepper. Melt the drippings or butter in a large braising pan or skillet over medium heat. When it's hot, raise the heat to medium-high, quickly roll the chops in flour, shake off the excess, and add them to the pan. Brown well on both sides, about 3 minutes per side. Remove them to a platter.

2. Add the shallots and sage to the pan and sauté, tossing frequently, until the shallots are golden, about 4 minutes. Return the chops and with any accumulated juices to the pan and pour in the Madeira. Bring it to a boil, reduce the heat to low, cover, and simmer gently, turning the chops once or twice, until they're fork-tender, about an hour.

3. Remove the pork to a platter. Tip the pan and spoon off the excess fat. If the sauce is too thin, raise the heat to medium-high and cook, stirring and scraping to loosen any cooking residue from the pan, until lightly thickened. If, on the other hand, the sauce is too thick, thin it with a few spoonfuls of water and simmer for about 3 minutes more, again stirring and scraping to loosen the cooking residue so that the water can absorb all the flavors. Turn off the heat, pour the sauce over the chops, and serve at once.

Serves 4

CHAPTER SEVEN

CHICKEN AND OTHER POULTRY

When I was about two years old, my father accepted a call to the Baptist church at Grassy Pond, a rural farming community in Cherokee County, South Carolina. We moved into a rambling brick parsonage standing on a couple of shady acres that were surrounded by rolling fields, cow pastures, and woodlands. In that pastoral landscape, it was easy to embrace being country folk. My brothers and I happily ran wild and barefoot from March until October. My parents planted a garden that seemed to my child's eye as large as a football field, with everything from okra, corn, and tomatoes to field peas, eggplants, and sunflowers. And my father, for reasons best known only to him, decided to complete this cozy country-parsonage picture by raising chickens.

Henhouses went up behind the garage, an eerie, mad-scientist-like egg incubator appeared in our basement, and very soon the yard was filled with pullets, guinea fowl, and an extremely bossy red rooster. It didn't last long; the experiment came to an ignoble end with that rooster submerged in a tub of hot water, waiting to be plucked and stewed. After that brief brush with poultry farming, I never felt guilty about eating chickens. In case you don't know, they're unimpressive creatures: They have wings but can barely fly, and their brains are smaller than a shelled pecan, which means they're notoriously mean and stupid.

Yet the moment one has been plucked, cut up, rolled in flour, and dropped into hot fat, it becomes a source of fierce contention in any gathering that has more than one person with an ounce of Southern blood in his or her veins. We each have our own way of frying the bird, all of which are similar, most of which are perfection, and yet we each approach the subject with the conviction that (1) our ancestors single-handedly invented this iconic dish, and (2) those same ancestors have passed on to us (and us alone) the one true way of doing it right. When I once delivered an academic paper on the origins of this dish, it caused such a storm of controversy that I almost feared of being beheaded and fried myself.

Since Southern fried chicken is so much a cliché outside the South and a bone of contention within it, I used to resist the idea of it as an icon of Southern culture. There are so many other sides to Southern food, not to mention culture, and if it's impossible for Southern folk to find common ground on the dish's history—and, worse, its preparation—then why not just leave it alone? Well, when it comes down to it, nothing about the South is simple and neatly defined—so if we must have an icon, why not this bit of golden-fried perfection?

But let's leave frying the bird aside for a moment. Happily, there's a lot more to the Southern way with poultry than a disjointed chicken and a frying pan. Ducks, turkeys, and game birds of all sorts, including doves, quail, pheasant, and squab, might all turn up in that pan—not just fried, but also sautéed, fricasseed, braised, roasted, grill-broiled, and baked. In fact, many Southerners will be quick to point out that there are some glaring omissions here. There's no country captain—that spicy, tomato-based braise that is claimed for its own by every coastal town from Baltimore to Savannah—no stewed hen with dumplings, chicken bog, or chicken tetrazzini. There's no pan-fried quail or mahogany-skinned roast duckling. I can offer no defense but the explanation that most of those things have already been covered in my other books, and the techniques they involve are not fundamentally different from the ones that are included on the pages that follow.

And, honestly, I had to stop somewhere.

roast chicken with sage and madeira pan gravy

Roasting is one of the most elegant ways of cooking chicken there is—in all senses of the word. It is simple to do, requiring little of the cook's time, and yet no other cooking method produces more succulent or flavorful results. No matter how many exotic and interesting ways I learn to cook this bird (and after a whole book about frying chicken, I have learned plenty), it is roasting that still satisfies me most.

Today's chickens are oversize, especially the ones that are labeled as roasters, and tend toward dryness when they are the least bit overcooked. That is why I prefer a quicker, high-temperature roasting, use the smallest bird I can get, and never stuff it with anything other than a few flavor-enhancing, moisture-rich herbs and vegetables. Choose a very small chicken, preferably weighing no more than

3—certainly not more than 4—pounds. The flavors used here are the traditional ones for roasted poultry in the South—sage, onion, black pepper, and Madeira.

1 small young chicken weighing no more than 3½ pounds

Salt and whole black pepper in a pepper mill

1 tablespoon chopped fresh sage
or 1 teaspoon crumbled dried sage

1 medium yellow onion, trimmed, split lengthwise, peeled, and thinly sliced

Butter

Madeira Pan Gravy (recipe follows)

1. Position a rack in the center of the oven and preheat to 500°F. Remove the giblets and neck from the cavity of the chicken and freeze them for the next time you make broth. Rinse the chicken well inside and out under cold running water and pat it dry. Rub the inside with salt and several grindings of black pepper, and fill the cavity with the sage and sliced onion. Tie the legs together with kitchen twine and tuck the wing tips under the shoulders of the bird. Lightly butter the outside of the bird and liberally salt and pepper all sides of it.

2. Lightly butter an oval or rectangular roasting pan that will just hold the chicken with no more than an inch on all sides. (A tight fit will keep the pan juices from drying up.) Put the chicken in the pan breast-side up and put the pan on the center rack of the oven. Roast for 10 minutes, gently shaking the pan after 5 minutes to be sure the skin isn't sticking.

3. Remove the pan from the oven and turn the chicken breast-side down. You should still be able to handle it with your bare hands if you work quickly. If not, insert a carving fork into the cavity of the bird and flip it using the fork and a pair of tongs. Reduce the temperature to 450°F. Return the chicken to the oven and roast, shaking the pan gently once or twice more to be sure the skin isn't sticking, until the thighs are just cooked through, about 35–45 minutes. A meat thermometer inserted into the thickest part of the thigh should read 170°F. If the skin begins to get too brown before the bird is done, reduce the heat to 375–400°F. If the breast skin has, despite your efforts, stuck to the pan, don't worry. It will still be delicious. Gently pry it loose with a spatula. Using a carving fork and tongs as described above, turn the chicken breast-side up. Roast another 5 minutes or so until the skin is golden and crisp.

4. Remove the chicken to a warm platter and let it rest for 10 minutes before carving. Make the Madeira Pan Gravy while the chicken rests. Serve the chicken with the gravy passed separately.

Serves 4

MADEIRA PAN GRAVY

There's no better sauce for any roast than its own rich, concentrated pan juices, particularly when they are enhanced with Madeira. This delicious gravy is wonderful not only with roasted chicken, but with Roast Lamb with Bourbon and Mint (page 144) or Roast Pork with Apples and Mushrooms (page 150). Substitute Basic Broth (page 10) made from the meat you are roasting, or from beef.

Roasting juices left in the roasting pan

1 cup Madeira

1 cup Chicken Broth (page 10, see headnote above)

1 tablespoon chopped fresh sage, optional (use with chicken, turkey, or pork)

1 tablespoon unsalted butter

1. After the roast has been removed from the pan, pour off but reserve the pan juices. Let the juices settle and spoon off all the fat (or use a degreasing pitcher to do this). Put the roasting pan over direct, medium-high heat. Add the Madeira and bring it to a boil, stirring and scraping the pan to loosen any cooking residue. Let it boil for 1 minute.

2. Add the broth and bring the liquid to a vigorous boil. Boil it until it is reduced by half, about 3–5 minutes. Reduce the heat to medium, add the reserved roasting juices and optional sage, and bring the gravy to a simmer. Simmer until it is lightly thickened, about 2 minutes more. Turn off the heat and swirl or whisk in the butter until it is incorporated. Taste and adjust the seasonings.

Makes about 1½ cups

braised chicken with sweet potatoes

Sweet potatoes are a perfect accompaniment for poultry, though on modern Southern tables they're usually presented separately. Here they go right in the pot with the chicken, and all their best qualities as a savory vegetable are brought to the fore. This is a lovely, hearty stew that demonstrates the hand that so many unnamed, gifted African cooks have had in the transformation of Southern cooking. Though adapted from Mary Randolph's venerable classic *The Virginia House-Wife* (1824), its roots are almost certainly in the one-pot stews of Africa.

2 pounds small sweet potatoes

1 large leek

2 tablespoons butter

1 small frying chicken (2½–3 pounds), cut up as directed for frying (page 167)

2 ounces country ham or prosciutto, cut into thin strips (about ½ cup)

1 cup Chicken Broth (page 10) or ½ cup canned broth and ½ cup water (even if the label reads "use full strength")

1 bouquet garni, made with 1 bay leaf and 1 sprig each thyme, marjoram or oregano, parsley, and sage

Salt and whole black pepper in a mill

1 tablespoon chopped fresh parsley or sage or both, mixed

1. Wash, peel, and cut the potatoes into large chunks about 1 inch square. Wash the leek under cold running water, being careful to get all the sand from between the layers. Trim off the tough green leaves and set them aside for the stockpot. Thinly slice the leek.

2. Put the butter into a flameproof casserole or Dutch oven that will hold the potatoes and chicken in no more than two layers and turn on the heat to medium-high. When the butter is melted and hot, add the chicken and brown it well on all sides, turning occasionally, about 5 minutes. (Do this in batches if the chicken will not fit in one layer without being crowded.) Remove the chicken and tip the pan. Spoon off all but 2 tablespoons of the fat and add the leek. Sauté until it is softened and golden-colored, about 5 minutes. Add the ham and sauté until it loses its raw red color. Add the potatoes and toss until they are coated with the fat.

3. Return the chicken to the pot, add the broth and bouquet garni, and season well with salt and a generous grinding of pepper. Bring to a boil and reduce the heat to low. Cover and simmer until the potatoes and chicken are tender and cooked through, about half an hour. Shake the pot from time to time to be sure that the potatoes are not sticking, but don't stir or they'll start to break up.

4. Transfer the chicken and potatoes with a slotted spoon to a warm serving bowl. If the liquid is thin, raise the heat to medium-high and boil until reduced and thick. Remove the bouquet garni, pour the gravy over the chicken and potatoes, sprinkle with herbs, and serve at once.

Serves 4

buttermilk fried chicken

Nowhere is the eclectic nature of my cooking (and of Southern food in general) given away more fully than in the way I fry chicken these days. In it are combined both sides of my family's traditions, two years of research into a book on fried chicken from all over the world, and a lifelong love affair with Italy. The saltwater soak (from my paternal grandmother) makes for tender, juicy chicken; the buttermilk bath (from my maternal grandmother and mother) further enhances tenderness, gives the chicken a lovely flavor, and ensures a crackling-crisp crust that will stay that way even after the chicken is cold; and the garlic whispers of the Mediterranean.

Yet everything—including that garlic—is consistent with deep Southern traditions. Before you begin, here are some basic notes on successfully frying chicken:

+ The pan does not (here come the letters) have to be cast iron, but it must have a very heavy bottom—and for that, of course, cast iron is the best.

- The most important draining step occurs as you remove the chicken from the pan: Hold it over the pan until it no longer drips, then let it finish draining on a rack.

- If you must use absorbent paper to briefly blot the chicken, briefly is the operative word. Don't allow the chicken to remain on paper for more than a minute. Otherwise, the paper will do what it does best—absorb the moisture from inside the chicken, resulting in a soggy bottom crust and dry chicken.

- Though modern health regulations preach against it, the chicken should be allowed to lose the deep cold from the refrigerator or it will not cook evenly, inviting salmonella poisoning more readily than leaving it sitting out. Allow it to sit at room temperature for 15–30 minutes, and make sure that you cook it thoroughly.

1 frying chicken (2½–3 pounds or smaller), washed and disjointed for frying

Salt

2 cups whole-milk buttermilk or plain whole-milk yogurt diluted to buttermilk consistency with milk

5–6 large cloves garlic, crushed and peeled

Hot pepper sauce, such as Tabasco

3 cups all-purpose flour

1 tablespoon freshly ground black pepper

½ teaspoon ground cayenne pepper, optional

Lard or peanut oil, for frying

1. Put the chicken in a glass or stainless-steel bowl. Sprinkle a handful of salt over it and cover completely with cold water. Toss gently until the salt dissolves. Let the chicken soak, refrigerated, for at least 2 hours or as long as overnight.

2. Drain the chicken, discarding the brine, and pat dry. Pour the buttermilk over it (or if you are using yogurt, stir it until it's smooth and creamy and pour it over the chicken). Turn the chicken until well coated. Add the garlic and a generous sprinkling of the hot sauce. Toss until the sauce is mixed into the buttermilk. Let marinate for 30 minutes to an hour.

3. Combine the flour and a small handful of salt and both peppers in a large paper or ziplock plastic bag. Fold over the top to close it tightly and shake until well mixed. If you are serving the chicken hot, position a rack in the center of the oven and preheat to 150°F (or the warm setting). Fit a wire cooling rack into a rimmed baking sheet. Put enough lard or oil in a large, deep, cast-iron skillet or enameled iron Dutch oven to come halfway up the sides. Heat over medium-high heat until very hot but not quite smoking, about 375°F. Beginning with the thighs and drumsticks, lift the chicken out of the marinade a piece at a time, allowing the excess to flow back into the bowl, and drop the pieces into the bag of seasoned flour. Fold over the top and shake until the chicken is well coated. Lift them out, shaking off the excess, and slip them into the pan.

4. Fry until the outside is well sealed and beginning to brown, turning the chicken once. Reduce the heat to medium and continue frying, maintaining the fat temperature at 325°F, until the chicken is just cooked through and golden-brown, about 25 minutes for the thighs and drumsticks, 20 minutes for the breasts and

cutting up a chicken for frying

Although chickens already cut up for frying are available in most markets, buy a whole bird and do it yourself. Not only is it cheaper, most butchers cut the chicken into pieces that are too large for even frying. It's a simple operation. Joints in the muscle and fat leave natural guidelines that show you exactly where to cut. Once you get the hang of it, you'll be able to do it in 2 minutes or less. Unless a recipe specifically says not to, skinning the bird is up to you. Some cooks prefer it; others insist that the chicken can't be fried well if it's skinned. If you opt to skin it, you can do it while the bird is whole or wait and skin each piece—whichever is easier for you.

First, remove the packet containing the giblets and neck and save for the next time you make broth. Lay the chicken flat on its back on the work surface and bend back a leg. Under the skin, you will see a line where the thigh muscles join the hip. Cut through this line, bend back and cut through the hip joint, and remove the entire leg. Lay it flat, outer-side down. You'll see another line between the muscles of the thigh and drumstick at their joint. Cut through it with a cleaver or sharp knife. Set the thighs and drumstick aside. The wings have a similar ball joint at the shoulder. Cut through it and set the wings aside with the leg pieces.

The rib cage has joints up both sides where the back and breast rib bones meet. Cut through these joints and bend back the breast until the joints at the shoulder are exposed. Separate them with a cleaver or sharp knife. Turn the breast skin-side up. At the collarbone is the little Y-shaped bone that we call the wishbone. Reach under the collarbone and feel for the joints. Cut through them with a sharp knife, then find the joint at the neck end of the keel bone. Cut straight down at that point, cutting the wishbone piece away from the breast. Turn the breast over and, using a cleaver or heavy chef's knife, chop through the keel bone and long, pointed cartilage. Unless you are working with a very small bird, chop each breast in half crosswise with a cleaver or chef's knife. Traditional cooks split the back crosswise in half and fry it, too, but most modern cooks put the backs in the stockpot. Your bird is now ready to be fried.

wings, turning halfway. Remove the chicken pieces as they are done, drain well, and lay them on the prepared cooling rack. If you're serving it hot, keep the chicken in the warm oven.

Notes: You can deep-fry the chicken if you prefer; the chicken will be crispier and will take a little less time. Put enough fat in the deep fryer or deep, enameled iron Dutch oven to come a little less than halfway up the sides (never fill the fryer more than half full of fat) and maintain a steady temperature of around 350–365°F throughout the frying: about 15 minutes for breast meat, 10 minutes for wings, and about 20 minutes for the legs and thighs.

Feel free to doctor the seasonings, adding herbs (sage and thyme are traditional with chicken in the South—but chives, rosemary, oregano, and tarragon would all be compatible) and/or spices (ginger, nutmeg, cumin, and paprika all complement chicken nicely) as the spirit moves you. But don't overwhelm the chicken with too much: There is nothing worse than the overblown taste of too many herbs and spices.

Serves 4

CREAM (OR MILK) PAN GRAVY

The name for this pan gravy is misleading, since it doesn't actually have any cream in it. It's probably a holdover from the original gravy that accompanied Southern fried chicken—true cream lightly reduced in the pan in which the chicken was fried. Such an extravagance was not always possible, and flour-thickened milk gradually replaced the cream. Today this gravy has a bad reputation with the gourmet crowd because when it's badly done—and it sadly often is—it is gummy, lumpy, and unappetizing. Yet with care, particularly with the correct proportion of flour to milk, it can be a very good sauce.

2 tablespoons pan drippings from frying Buttermilk Fried Chicken (above), left in the skillet with the solid cooking residue

1 tablespoon all-purpose flour (you may use the leftover seasoned flour from Buttermilk Fried Chicken, page 165)

2 cups whole milk, preferably at room temperature

Salt and whole black pepper in a pepper mill

1. Turn on the heat under the skillet to medium and sprinkle the flour over the bottom of the pan. Stir it into the fat with a wooden spoon or whisk until smooth. Whisking or stirring constantly, slowly pour in the milk. Continue stirring, scraping loose the cooking residue that may be stuck to the skillet, until the gravy begins to boil and thicken. If you have not used seasoned flour, season with a large pinch or so of salt and several liberal grindings of black pepper.

2. Reduce the heat to low and simmer, stirring occasionally, until the gravy is as thick as you like it and the flour has lost its raw, pasty taste, about 4–8 minutes longer. If it should happen to thicken too much, thin it with a little water or milk and simmer another minute or so. Taste and adjust the seasonings. Pour the gravy into a warm sauceboat or serving bowl and serve at once.

Makes 2 cups

savannah cutlets

These breaded cutlets are enhanced by three classic flavors of a Savannah kitchen: Georgia pecans, bourbon, and Parmesan cheese. We love to cook with pecans, and we use bourbon as enthusiastically in our kitchens as we are reputed to drink it. Parmesan may look like a stretch to the uninitiated, but those who know appreciate that it has been imported into the old port city since the eighteenth century, and has long played a role in our cooking. What the trio does for chicken breasts must be tasted to be fully appreciated.

4 boneless, skinless chicken breast halves, about 6 ounces each

¼ cup bourbon

½ cup pecans

½ cup dry bread crumbs

½ cup plus 2 tablespoons freshly grated Parmigiano-Reggiano

¼ cup all-purpose flour, spread on a plate

1 large egg, lightly beaten, in a wide, shallow bowl

8 ounces (1 cup) clarified butter or 4 ounces (½ cup or 1 stick) unsalted butter mixed with 1 cup peanut or canola oil

1 lemon, cut into 8 wedges, for garnish

1. Put the chicken breasts between two sheets of plastic wrap or two flexible cutting boards and lightly pound them to a uniform thickness of about ¼ inch with a mallet or scaloppine pounder. Put them into a shallow stainless-steel or glass bowl that will hold them in one layer and pour the bourbon over them. Set aside to marinate for at least 30 minutes, or up to an hour.

2. In a food processor fitted with a steel blade or in a blender, grind the nuts to the texture of coarse meal. Don't overprocess: You'll release the oils and get pecan butter. Transfer to a shallow bowl such as a soup plate and mix in the bread crumbs and Parmigiano.

3. Drain the marinade from the chicken, shake off the excess, roll the pieces in the flour, shake off the excess, and dip into the egg. Let the excess egg flow back into the bowl and then roll the breasts in the crumb mixture one at a time, patting it well into all sides. Lay each breaded breast on a clean dry plate or wire rack. Set aside for at least 15 minutes to set the breading.

4. Melt the clarified butter in a large skillet over medium-high heat. When it's hot and its foaming has subsided, slip the cutlets into the pan. Fry each cutlet until the bottom is golden-brown, about 3 minutes, then turn and fry until it's cooked through and uniformly browned, about 3 minutes more. Serve hot with lemon wedges.

Note: You can make the cutlets several hours ahead up through step 3. Refrigerate until you are ready to cook, but let them sit at room temperature for 30 minutes before finishing them.

Serves 4

grilled chicken breasts with eggplant, creole-style

Lea Chase is the godmother of Creole cooking whose restaurant, Dooky Chase, was serving up traditional Creole food long before it was fashionable. She notes that Creole cooks love to stack things, though not in the overblown towers so many restaurants are serving up today. A grilled chop or, in this case, a chicken breast might be served atop a slice of fried eggplant or mirliton (see page 171), then finished off with a spoonful of sauce and maybe a sprinkling of herbs or green onion tops. This is not done merely to make the plate pretty: The elements literally build on one another, losing their individual identity in a perfectly balanced chord of flavors and textures. Take any of them away, and the chord becomes incomplete.

2 lemons

4 boneless, skinless chicken breast halves, about 6 ounces each

Salt and whole black pepper in a pepper mill

1 medium eggplant (about ¾ pound)

½ cup all-purpose flour, spread on a plate

1 large egg, well beaten, in a wide, shallow bowl

1 cup fine cracker crumbs or matzo meal, spread on a plate

3 tablespoons melted unsalted butter or extra-virgin olive oil

1 cup Creole Sauce (page 172)

2 tablespoons chopped fresh parsley

1. Grate the zest from 1 lemon and then juice both lemons through a strainer. Put the chicken breasts in a shallow stainless-steel or glass bowl and sprinkle them with the grated zest, a large pinch of salt, and several generous grindings of black pepper. Pour the lemon juice over them, turning several times to coat them, and set aside to marinate for at least 30 minutes or for as much as 8 hours or overnight, covered and refrigerated.

2. Wash the eggplant under cold running water. Peel and slice it lengthwise into four ½-inch-thick slices. Lightly salt both sides of the eggplant slices and put them in a colander set in the sink or over a plate. Let them stand for 30 minutes. If you are grilling the chicken, prepare a charcoal grill with coals and light it. When the coals are glowing red and are lightly ashed over, spread them and position a rack about 4 inches above them. Let the rack get very hot. Otherwise, position the broiling rack about 6 inches from the heat source and preheat the oven broiler at least 15 minutes before you plan to use it.

3. Meanwhile, wipe the eggplant with a paper towel and pat dry. Lightly roll each slice in the flour, shake off the excess, then dip it in the egg, coating all sides. Lift if from the egg, allowing the excess to flow back into the bowl, and then roll it in the crumbs. Shake off the excess and lay them on a wire rack.

4. Lift the chicken from its marinade and pat dry. Spread it on a platter in one layer and lightly brush it and the eggplant with the melted butter or olive oil. Put them both on the grill (or on

a broiling rack set in a roasting pan under the broiler), with the buttered side toward the heat. Grill-broil until the chicken and eggplant are browned on the side facing the heat, about 3–4 minutes. Brush them lightly with the melted butter or oil, turn them, and grill-broil the meat and vegetable until the chicken is cooked through and the eggplant slices are tender and browned on both sides, about 3–4 minutes longer, depending on how hot the fire or broiler is. The eggplant may be ready a little before the chicken. Place the eggplant on a warm platter, lay a chicken breast over each slice, and spoon Creole Sauce over them. Sprinkle with parsley and serve at once.

Serves 4

mirliton

Sometimes called chayote or vegetable pear because of its shape, this is actually a Native American squash. It flourishes in warmer climates, particularly Louisiana and the Southwest, where it is prized as a vegetable and widely used in Creole, Cajun, and Southwestern cooking. Mirlitons have a single large seed in the center and a skin that toughens as the vegetable matures. The seed and peel are usually removed before the squash is eaten. To substitute them for eggplant in Grilled Chicken Breasts with Eggplant, Creole-Style (page 170), steam or blanch them until they are nearly tender. Then peel, split lengthwise at the wrinkled bottom groove, and remove the seeds. Allow half a mirliton for each slice of eggplant.

creole sauce

Creole Sauce is an important element of many cuisines in the African Diaspora of the Americas and has many variations, from the simple salsa cruda (raw sauce) of the Caribbean to the suave, complex Sauce Creole of New Orleans's French Quarter. It enhances almost any fried vegetable, seafood, or poultry. Try it with Savannah Cutlets (page 169), Eggplant Fritters (page 205), Shrimp and Rice Croquettes (page 80), a plain omelet, or poached eggs (page 64).

2 pounds ripe tomatoes (preferable plum or Roma type), or 2 cups canned Italian tomatoes, seeded and chopped, with their juices

2 tablespoons extra-virgin olive oil

3 large or 4 medium shallots or 1 medium yellow onion, split, trimmed, peeled, and chopped

1 medium green bell pepper, stem, core, seeds, and membranes removed, chopped

1 small carrot, peeled and chopped

1 large clove garlic, lightly crushed, peeled, and minced

1 small red hot chile pepper such as cayenne, serrano, or jalapeño

1 bouquet garni, made from 1 leafy celery top, 2 bay leaves, 2 large sprigs thyme, and 1 large sprig parsley

2 ounces lean salt-cured pork or country ham, in 1 piece

½ cup dry white wine or medium-dry sherry (such as Amontillado)

Salt

1 large or 4 small scallions or other green onions, thinly sliced

1. If using canned tomatoes, skip to step 2. Blanche, peel, core, and seed the tomatoes as directed on page 35. Roughly chop the tomatoes and add them to the collected juices.

2. Put the olive oil, shallots, green pepper, and carrot into a heavy-bottomed saucepan and turn on the heat to medium-high. Sauté, tossing often, until the shallots are translucent but not colored, about 4 minutes. Add the garlic and sauté until fragrant, about a minute more. Add the tomatoes, hot pepper (left whole), bouquet garni, salt-cured pork, and wine. Bring the liquids to a boil, then reduce the heat to medium-low and simmer, stirring occasionally, until the tomatoes break down and the juices are thick, about an hour.

3. Taste and adjust the salt. Stir and let simmer for another minute or so and turn off the heat. Remove and discard the hot pepper, bouquet garni, and salt pork. The sauce can be made up through this point several days ahead. Cool and refrigerate in a tightly sealed container. Just before serving, reheat over medium-low heat. Stir in the scallions and serve at once.

Makes about 2½ cups

sautéed chicken livers with bacon, sage, and madeira

There's a sweetness to livers that comes to the fore when they are paired with onions and sweet wines. Here onion, Madeira, and garlic all conspire to bring out that sweetness, which is counterpointed by the savory flavors of sage and bacon. The combination is about as deeply Southern as it gets. These livers make a delicious and substantial winter main course for lunch or dinner, but can also be served as a first course over Dry Toast Points (page 40) instead of rice.

1½ pounds chicken livers

2 thick slices bacon or pancetta, diced

1 medium yellow onion, trimmed, split, peeled, and chopped

1 large or 2 small cloves garlic, lightly crushed, peeled, and minced

1 tablespoon thinly sliced fresh sage or 1 teaspoon crumbled dried sage

Salt and whole black pepper in a pepper mill

½ cup Madeira

2 cups hot Carolina-Style Rice (page 77) or Dry Toast Points (page 40)

1. Pick over the livers and cut away any fat or greenish spots. Cut them apart into individual lobes and cut the large lobes into halves so that they're a fairly uniform size. Rinse thoroughly under cold running water and drain well. Put them into a colander set in the sink.

2. Put the bacon or pancetta in a large skillet or sauté pan over medium heat and sauté, tossing often, until the fat is rendered and the bacon is golden. Raise the heat to medium-high and add the onion. Sauté, tossing often, until the onion is translucent and pale gold, about 5 minutes. Add the garlic and sage and sauté until fragrant, about a minute more.

3. Add the livers and sauté, tossing constantly, until they have lost their raw red color, about 1 minute. Season generously with salt and a liberal grinding of black pepper, and continue sautéing, turning often, until they are mostly cooked through but still pink at the center, about 4–5 minutes longer. Chicken livers tend to pop and splatter when sautéed. If this happens, loosely cover the pan, but leave the lid slightly askew so the steam can escape.

4. Pour in the wine, stir well, and bring to a boil. Reduce the heat to medium-low and simmer until the livers are just cooked through and the sauce is lightly thickened, about 2 minutes more. Taste and adjust the seasonings, then let simmer half a minute more and turn off the heat. Put the rice around the edges of a warm platter, pour the livers into the center, and serve at once.

Serves 4 as a main course, 6 as a first course

grilled duck breasts with warm peach-orange marmalade

Bourbon, sherry, and oranges are all traditional Southern flavorings for game birds, and all are particularly popular when the bird in question is a wild duck. Here all three are combined in a tenderizing marinade that cuts through the fat and does wonders even for farm-raised birds. The same marinade can, of course, be used for duck leg and thigh quarters that are to be grilled.

2 whole, boneless (but not skinned) duck breasts

1 large orange

⅓ cup medium-dry sherry (such as Amontillado)

⅓ cup bourbon

2 tablespoons freshly grated shallot or yellow onion

1 teaspoon Worcestershire sauce

1 rounded teaspoon salt

Whole black pepper in a pepper mill

Ground cayenne

1 cup Peach-Orange Marmalade (page 18)

1. Wipe the duck breasts dry with a clean cloth. Put them skin-side up in a wide, shallow glass or nonreactive ceramic dish (such as a gratin) that will hold them in one close-fitting layer. Grate the zest from the orange into a separate bowl. Cut the orange in half and juice it through a strainer into the bowl, then stir in the sherry, bourbon, shallot, Worcestershire, salt, a generous grinding of black pepper, and a pinch of cayenne. Pour this over the duck, turning it several times to coat; cover, refrigerate, and marinate for at least 1 hour, or preferably overnight.

2. If you are grilling, prepare a charcoal grill with coals and ignite them; if you're broiling, position a rack about 5 inches from the heat source, preheat the broiler for 15 minutes, and skip to step 3. When the coals are glowing red but lightly ashed over, spread them and position the rack 5–6 inches above the coals. Have on hand a clean spray bottle of cold water.

3. Warm the marmalade over low heat until it's melted and hot, and remove it from the heat. Lift the duck breasts from the marinade, letting the excess drain back into the dish. If you're grilling, put them on the grill skin-side down; if broiling, put them on a broiling pan skin up. Grill-broil until the skin is browned and crisping, 3–4 minutes. (If you are grilling them, the fat from the duck may drip onto the coals and can ignite. If it does, move the breasts away from the flame and lightly spray the coals with water until the flames extinguish.) Brush them with marmalade, turn, and brush the skin side with marmalade.

Grill-broil until they are done to suit your tastes: 2–3 minutes more for rare, 5–7 minutes for medium-well.

4. Just before taking them from the grill or broiler, turn the breasts so that the skin side faces the coals or heat source to crisp the skin, about 1 minute longer. Do not overcook. Remove the breasts to a warm serving platter, cut each in half at the center connective tissue, brush with more marmalade, and serve at once, passing the remaining marmalade separately.

Serves 4

roast turkey with sausage and pecan stuffing

When I began writing a regular feature for the *Savannah Morning News*, as Thanksgiving rolled around I began to think about what side dishes and desserts the column would feature, convinced that the last thing America needed was yet another recipe for roasting a turkey. I quickly learned otherwise: My recipe and tips have become an annual fixture that we dare not omit.

The trouble is that most of us only roast this large bird once a year and have forgotten that it was once the centerpiece for many other holiday celebrations all year long. We'd do well to learn that smaller turkeys are better than the monsters so many of us try to tackle at Thanksgiving; then perhaps we'd enjoy it more often. But even if you roast only one bird a year, there's no need for panic: It's really no more difficult than roasting a chicken; it just takes a little longer. The most important thing is to use a small bird. The smaller the bird, the easier it is to manage, and—more to the point—the more tender and better tasting it will be. If you're feeding a big crowd and have enough oven space, consider cooking two smaller turkeys, or roast a fresh turkey breast alongside the whole bird.

Stuffing versus dressing: In the South, until recently most cooks had drifted so far away from stuffing the bird that it was almost unheard of, but nowadays they're equally divided about whether or not to stuff the bird or cook the stuffing separately. I've done it both ways and each has its good points, but my mother and grandmothers never stuffed the bird, so cooking it separately is what I tend to prefer. You may do it either way; directions for both are included.

1 small young fresh turkey (about 12, and no more than 14 pounds)

Salt and whole black pepper in a pepper mill

1 pound bulk mild breakfast sausage, preferably seasoned with sage

1 large or 2 medium yellow onions, trimmed, split lengthwise, peeled, and chopped

2 large or 3 medium ribs celery, trimmed, strung, and chopped

2–3 tablespoons chopped fresh sage or 3–4 teaspoons crumbled dried sage (depending on whether the sausage is seasoned with sage), plus 8–10 whole fresh sage leaves for garnish, optional

6 cups stale crumbled Southern Skillet Corn Bread (page 256—made a day ahead)

4 cups stale crumbled Southern Breakfast Biscuits (page 260—made a day ahead), or soft white bread crumbs

About 2 cups Basic Broth (page 10), made with chicken or turkey (or both)

1 cup Toasted Pecans (page 232)

Butter

1. Choose a roasting pan just a little larger than the turkey, so that the roasting juices won't evaporate and burn in the corners, and fit it with a rack, if you have one. Remove the neck and giblets from the cavity of the turkey and use them to make Basic Broth. (This can be done a day ahead. Cover and refrigerate the turkey until you are ready to cook it.) Wipe the turkey thoroughly inside and out with a dry cloth. Rub the cavity

liberally with salt and pepper. Position a rack in the lower third of the oven and preheat to 500°F.

2. Crumble the sausage into a large skillet or sauté pan. Turn on the heat to medium and cook, stirring and crumbling the sausage, until it's nicely browned and no longer pink at the center, about 5–8 minutes. Remove the sausage with a slotted spoon and drain on absorbent paper. Tip the pan and spoon off all but 2 tablespoons of the fat. Add the onions and celery and raise the heat to medium-high. Sauté, tossing often, until the onions are translucent and the celery softened, about 5 minutes. Stir in the sage and sauté until fragrant, about half a minute. Turn off the heat.

3. Return the sausage to the pan. Add both breads, toss to mix, and season generously with salt and a liberal grinding of pepper. Moisten with broth until it's damp and clumping together. If you're using it as stuffing, don't make it soggy—the bird will add moisture as it roasts. You may not need all the broth. Stir in the pecans, taste, and adjust the seasonings. If you're stuffing the bird, turn on the heat to medium and cook, gently tossing and stirring almost constantly, until it's hot through, 2–4 minutes. Immediately spoon it loosely into the turkey and underneath the flap of skin at the neck end (the craw). If you're baking it separately, as dressing, make it quite wet with the broth, then add the pecans and adjust the seasoning. Instead of heating it, pour it into a buttered 3-quart casserole or deep gratin, level the top, and set it aside. To add flavor to the bird, stuff it instead with a quartered onion, a few leafy celery tops, and 1–2 sprigs of sage.

4. If you like, loosen the skin on the breast and arrange several sage leaves between the skin and meat—this isn't essential, but it does add flavor

and is a handsome garnish. Whether or not you've stuffed the bird, truss it with a trussing needle and twine or with small metal skewers. Rub the outside with butter. Put the turkey breast-side up on the rack if you're using one, or just rub the pan with butter and put the turkey directly on it.

5. Roast 20 minutes in the lower third of the oven, or until the skin is well seared. Rub with more butter and turn the bird breast-side down. (Use oven mitts and tongs to protect your hands if needed—often the bird will not yet be too hot to handle.) If the bird is on a rack, pour enough broth or water into the pan to cover the bottom by about ¼ inch. Reduce the heat to 400°F and roast, basting occasionally, until the bird is cooked through, about 1½–2 hours longer, or until a meat thermometer inserted into the thickest part of the thigh registers between 165 and 170°F. If you've stuffed it, the stuffing should register 165°F. If the skin is browning too quickly, reduce the temperature to 375°F. I turn the turkey breast-side up during the last 15 minutes to brown and crisp the skin, but it isn't essential.

6. Remove the bird to a warm platter and let it rest for at least 15 minutes before carving. If you're baking the dressing separately, reduce the temperature to 350°F and bake until it's browned and set, about half an hour. If you've stuffed the bird and are serving it within half an hour, you may leave the dressing in the bird and present it that way at the table, but it's safer to spoon all the stuffing into a warm serving bowl. Degrease the roasting juices and use them to make Madeira Pan Gravy (page 163). Cover and refrigerate any leftovers as soon after the meal as possible.

Serves 8–12

turkey cutlets with sage, lemon, and wine

This is a very old recipe from the Carolina Lowcountry; while it looks startlingly like an Italian dish and has undeniably European roots, it has been a part of Carolina cookery for the better part of two centuries. The original recipe used veal scallops (called "collops" in the old manuscripts), but it's an excellent way of preparing turkey. Etymology and history aside, the heady combination of sage, lemon, and white wine was just made for turkey.

1½ pounds turkey breast cutlets (page 179) or veal cutlets, cut ½ inch thick

1 tablespoon chopped fresh sage
or 1 teaspoon crumbled dried sage

Grated zest of 1 lemon

Whole nutmeg in a grater

Salt and whole black pepper in a pepper mill

2 tablespoons unsalted butter

1 tablespoon olive oil

1 whole clove garlic, crushed and peeled, but left whole

½ cup all-purpose flour, spread on a shallow bowl or dinner plate

2 tablespoons minced shallot or yellow onion

1 cup dry white wine

1. Put the cutlets between two sheets of plastic wrap or two flexible cutting boards on a sturdy, flat work surface and lightly pound them with a mallet or scaloppine pounder until they are a uniform thickness of about ⅛ inch. Sprinkle them evenly with the sage and zest, and season generously with nutmeg, salt, and a liberal grinding of pepper.

2. Put the butter, oil, and garlic in a large sauté pan or skillet over medium-high heat. Cook until the garlic is colored pale gold, then roll the cutlets in the flour, shake off the excess, and add them to the pan. Sauté, turning once, until lightly browned and just barely cooked through, about 1–2 minutes per side. Remove them to a warm platter.

3. Add the shallot to the pan and sauté until pale gold. Add the wine, stirring and scraping the pan to loosen any cooking residue, bring to a boil, and boil until it's reduced by half. Return the cutlets to the pan and turn them once or twice in the sauce until they are lightly coated and just warmed again. Transfer back to the platter, pour the sauce over them, and serve at once.

Serves 4

turkey cutlets

We think that turkey cutlets, taken from the boned turkey breast, are a new idea, but Georgia cookbook author Annabella Hill described exactly how to cut them from the bird back in 1867. It's easy to do: remove the skin and work the muscle loose from the rib bones with your fingers. With a thin, sharp knife, cut the muscle from the keel and wishbones. Separate the tender (the long, feather-shaped muscle) from the main breast muscle and set it aside for another use, then slice the larger muscle across the grain into ½-inch-thick cutlets. When it becomes too thin to slice, cut it in half horizontally.

turkey cutlets with pecan brown butter

Pecans, buttery-brown pan gravy, and fragrant lemon are three classic elements of roasted turkey in many Southern kitchens, particularly when the turkey is a wild one that has been provided by the family hunter. Here they lend their savory magic to turkey cutlets, adding depth and succulence to the tame flavors and textures of a domestically raised bird.

1½ pounds turkey breast cutlets (page 179) or veal cutlets, cut ½ inch thick

Salt and whole black pepper in a pepper mill

4 ounces (8 tablespoons or 1 stick) unsalted butter, divided

½ cup all-purpose flour, spread on a shallow bowl or dinner plate

½ cup sliced pecans

1 lemon, cut in half

2 tablespoons chopped fresh parsley

1. Put the cutlets between two sheets of plastic wrap on a sturdy, flat work surface and lightly pound them with a mallet or scaloppine pounder until they are a uniform thickness of about ⅛ inch. Season generously with salt and a liberal grinding of pepper.

2. Melt 4 tablespoons of the butter in a large sauté pan or skillet over medium-high heat. When it's hot, roll the cutlets in the flour, shake off the excess, and add them to the pan. Sauté, turning once, until lightly browned and just barely cooked through, about 1–2 minutes per side. Remove them to a warm platter.

3. Add 2 more tablespoons of butter and the pecans to the pan, and toss until the pecans are golden-brown, about 2 minutes. Add any juices that may have accumulated on the platter to the pan and squeeze the juice from one half of the lemon. Stir in the parsley and turn off the heat. Swirl in the remaining butter, taste and refresh the sauce with a squeeze more of lemon juice, and pour it evenly over the cutlets. Serve at once.

Serves 4

braised quail with mushrooms and country ham

Wild quail may be more flavorful than farm-raised birds, but they're not always tender, even when fattened up for the winter on summer's tasty seeds and berries. Consequently, traditional Southern cooks often braise them instead of roasting, giving them a slow simmer in a little aromatic liquid until they are meltingly tender. It is a treatment that even farm-raised quail take to well. This might as easily turn up under the name *alla cacciatore* in Italy, or *à la chasseur* in France—that is, hunter-style—because it's exactly how hunters deal with the catch almost anywhere that cured pork and mushrooms are also on hand.

If using frozen quail, first thaw them as follows. Dissolve a small handful of salt in enough cold water to completely cover. Add the quail and soak, covered and refrigerated, for at least 4 hours, or until they are fully thawed. Many hunters brine wild quail to tame their flavor and tenderize them. Follow the same procedure.

4 large (about 7 ounces each) or 8 small (4–5 ounces each) dressed quail

½ pound brown (crimini or baby portobello) mushrooms

Salt and whole black pepper in a mill

All-purpose flour in a shaker

2 tablespoons bacon drippings, unsalted butter, or olive oil

1 medium onion, trimmed, split, peeled, and thinly sliced

2 ounces lean country ham, cut into julienne (about ½ cup)

2 tablespoons chopped fresh parsley

½ cup Sercial Madeira

1. Wipe the quail with a dry cloth and look them over for pin feathers, removing any that you may find. Clean the mushrooms with a clean, dry cloth or paper towel and thickly slice them.

2. Season the birds inside and out with salt and pepper and lightly dust them on all sides with flour. Melt the bacon drippings in a large, deep, lidded, heavy-bottomed skillet or braising pan over medium-high heat. When the pan is hot but not smoking, put in the quail, breast-side down. Brown them well on all sides, and remove them to a warm plate.

3. Add the onion and sauté, tossing frequently, until golden-brown, about 5 minutes. Add the ham and toss until it loses its raw red color, about 2 minutes, then add the mushrooms and parsley. Sauté, tossing almost constantly, until the mushrooms are beginning to color, about 4 minutes. Return the quail to the pan, laying them on their sides, along with any juices that may have accumulated in the plate. Add the Madeira, bring to a boil, then reduce the heat to low and cover the pan. Simmer, turning the birds once or twice, until they're very tender, about an hour.

4. Remove them to a warm platter. If the gravy is thin, raise the heat briefly and cook it until it's lightly thickened. Taste and adjust the seasonings, and turn off the heat. Pour it over and around the quail, and serve at once.

Serves 4

grilled quail with oysters

Oysters and bacon are an old and popular combination for roasted birds in the South. This recipe has been around for the better part of two centuries, and once you've tasted it you will understand why. As the oysters heat, they throw off their briny juices, naturally basting the birds, while the bacon seals the outside and lends its smoky-sweet flavor in the bargain. They can be either grilled or roasted. Grilling comes closer to the flavor the old cooks achieved by roasting the birds on an open hearth, but the oven still does a respectable job if you prefer not to grill.

4 large (about 7 ounces each) or 8 small (4–5 ounces each) dressed quail

Salt and whole black pepper in a pepper mill

8–16 freshly shucked oysters

8–16 sprigs thyme

8 strips lean, thick-sliced bacon

1 recipe Breakfast Grits (page 70) or Carolina-Style Rice (page 77)

1. Wipe the quail dry with paper towels or a clean cloth. Season their cavities lightly with salt and generously with pepper, then stuff each bird with two or three oysters—as many as will fit. Tuck sprigs of thyme under the wings and thighs and tie the legs of the birds securely together with kitchen twine. Wrap a slice of bacon around each bird (you may need more than one for larger birds) and secure it with toothpicks or twine. Prepare a charcoal grill with coals and light them, or position a rack in the upper third of the oven and preheat to 500°F.

2. If you're oven-roasting, skip to step 3. When the coals are glowing red and ashed over, position the rack about 6 inches above the heat. Put the quail on the rack on their sides and grill until the bacon is browned and crisp, about 8 minutes. Turn them onto the opposite side and grill until the bacon is browned, about 8 minutes more. Turn breast-side down and grill until cooked through, about 8–12 minutes longer, turning them every few minutes to evenly distribute the heat. If the bacon begins to get too brown, move the rack farther from the heat. Remove them to a warm platter and serve hot with grits or rice.

3. If you're roasting, put them breast-side down in a lightly greased, close-fitting roasting pan and roast for 10 minutes, until the bacon begins to brown. Reduce the heat to 400°F and roast until the quail and oysters are cooked through, about 20 minutes longer, turning them breast-side up about 5 minutes before taking them from the oven. Remove the quail to a warm platter. Allow the pan juices to settle, then tip the pan, spoon off the excess fat, and pour the juices over the quail. Serve hot with grits or rice.

Serves 4

CHAPTER EIGHT

VEGETABLES

Fresh produce is to the South what pasta is to Italy. Anyone who doubts this need only drive down any highway south of the Mason-Dixon. From April through November roadside produce stands sprout like poke sallet after a hard rain, and throughout the region thriving local farmers' markets can be found in downtown parks and parking lots of even small towns, filled with fresh, local fruits and vegetables. From spring's first asparagus shoots through to autumn's mellow apples, the parade of fresh produce is steady and bountiful. Indeed, in the Deep South it never completely ends. Through the winter the roadside stands of Florida and Texas are bright with a rainbow of orange, pink, yellow, and green citrus fruit.

Historically, the litany of produce included many things that careless social historians would have us believe weren't eaten in the South until recent times: artichokes, broccoli, fava beans, mushrooms, parsnips, raspberries, salsify, shallots, and sorrel. Contrary to popular belief, these things used to be common on Southern tables. It was only in the mid-twentieth century that any of them became scarce, and actually, most of them never did.

As popular as roadside stands and farmers' markets have become, the place where our love of produce shines is in our backyards. Everywhere I've lived in the South, from urban Savannah to the rural Clover and Grassy Pond, my neighbors have been growing things to eat. It might be little more than a pot of basil or tomatoes, or a full-blown kitchen garden with neat rows of everything from corn to okra. The work may be grueling, the chances of harvest iffy, the yield either nonexistent or overwhelming, but when we pluck that first ripe tomato it always seems worth it.

You see, for all the attention that fried chicken and barbecue get, it's vegetables that really define the Southern table. Once, there would never have been less than three at any meal worthy of calling "dinner," and for really special occasions, especially at the height of summer, there might be as many as six. Even in our fast-food, grab-it-on-the-run age, a plate on which the meat portion dominates, with one lone vegetable keeping it company, is an oddity that few Southerners will tolerate. The vegetable chapters are always the longest in all my books, and my second book, *Beans, Greens, and Sweet Georgia Peaches*, was wholly given over to the subject, and yet I've barely scratched the surface.

It shouldn't surprise, then, that the way we cook vegetables has become the defining aspect of our cuisine, and not always in a positive way. Nothing else has been at once so praised and reviled. The lightning rod is our habit of seasoning with salt-cured pork. It used to amuse and distress me how so-called foodies would eagerly embrace the Italian way of braising vegetables with pancetta, yet turn up their noses at Southerners for doing the same just because our "salt pork" doesn't go by a catchy Italian name. It hasn't helped that many nouvelle Southern restaurants have gone to the opposite extreme, so undercooking vegetables that one needs a buzz saw to hack through a skinny little haricot vert. Happily, all that is changing as traditionalists broaden their repertory and the nouvelle crowd begins to recognize the wisdom of the ancients.

The parallels between Italian and Southern cookery are most apparent in the vegetable pot. Florentine and Roman cooks will immediately recognize our wilted greens and braised beans; Ligurians, our squash, eggplant, artichoke, mushroom, and green bean dishes. Bolognese cooks will be right at home with our use of salt pork, cream, and cheese, and Sicilians, our liberal use of tomatoes, garlic, and hot pepper. Yet I didn't choose these recipes to prove the point: I chose them because they're deeply characteristic of the Southern kitchen, and a matter of routine in mine.

understanding the artichoke

BASIC ARTICHOKE PREPARATION

Primary trimming: If the artichokes are to be cooked whole, trim off the discolored cut end of the stem, pull off the small tough petals (or "leaves") at the base and stem, rub the cut spots with the cut half of a lemon, and it's ready for the pot. There's no need to trim down or cut the tips of the petals; in fact, I find that cutting off the tips actually makes the artichoke more difficult to manage. Also, leave the stem attached: It's a little-appreciated fact that the stem is the most delicious part. Each diner can trim away the tough outer fibers, or you may cut them off with a paring knife before it's cooked: Once you've trimmed the cut end, it's easy to see where the tender core begins. Just pare off the tough outer fibers, rubbing the cuts well with the lemon half.

To boil artichokes: Use a 6- to 8-quart stainless-steel or enamel-lined stockpot for up to four artichokes. Fill it halfway with water and bring it to a boil over high heat. Add a small handful of salt and squeeze in the juice of half a lemon. Add the spent lemon rind and let the water come back to a boil. Add the artichokes, turning them with tongs until all sides have been submerged and turned bright green. Loosely cover, let the water return to a boil, and reduce the heat to medium. Simmer until the artichokes are tender, 30–45 minutes depending on the size, age, and variety of artichoke. Drain well and serve hot or at room temperature with Curried Mayonnaise (page 231), Lemon Butter (page 190), Honey-Lemon Bourbon Vinaigrette (page 236), or your favorite dipping sauce.

Additional trimming for braising: After the basic preparation and trimming outlined above, including peeling the stem, rub the artichoke well with a cut lemon, and begin pulling away the large outer petals. After the first two rows, place your thumb at the base of the petal; as you pull down, the petal will snap at the fleshy, edible part and pull away much of the tough fiber. Rub the surface periodically with half a lemon to prevent discoloration. Keep doing this until the center cone is pale yellow-green, about two-thirds of the way up. Cut off the dark green top with a sharp, heavy knife and rub the cut well with lemon. Take a very sharp paring knife (I like a tourné or bird's-beak peeling knife for this) and trim away any tough, dark green fibers that remain around the base, again rubbing the cuts with the lemon. Pull back the center petals, exposing the choke (a fine, purplish fuzz). Scoop it out with a melon baller or sharp-edged teaspoon, squeeze lemon juice into it, and rub it in with your fingers. The artichoke is now ready for the pan.

A PAIR OF
BRAISED ARTICHOKE RECIPES

Braising is a lovely way to cook artichokes, especially those that aren't as fresh as you'd like. Enrobed in its own reduced and lightly caramelized juices, the artichoke's flavor is concentrated and reinforced. Braising is also convenient for busy cooks; while trimming the artichokes down to size for the braising pan may be a little time consuming, they require very little attention once they get there.

braised artichokes and onions, creole-style

Artichoke and onion is a classic combination known not only to the Mediterranean basin but to the Gulf of Mexico's basin as well. The flavors here are pure Louisiana: onions and country ham caramelized in butter and brightened by that most Creole of herbs, thyme.

8–12 small white boiling onions, each no more than 1½ inches in diameter, or 4 medium white or yellow onions

Halved lemon used for trimming artichokes (page 185)

4 medium artichokes, trimmed for braising as directed on page 185

2 tablespoons unsalted butter

2 ounces country ham, cut into julienne

1 tablespoon chopped fresh thyme
or 1 teaspoon dried thyme

Salt and whole black pepper in a mill

½ cup Chicken Broth (page 10), or ¼ cup canned broth mixed with ¼ cup water (even if the can reads "use full strength"), or ½ cup water

1 tablespoon chopped parsley

1. If using boiling onions, fill a 3-quart stainless-steel or enameled pan with water, and bring it to a boil over high heat. Add the onions, cover, and count 1 minute. Drain, trim the root and stem ends, and slip off the peelings. If you're using large onions, you don't need to blanch them: Trim the root and stem, cut them lengthwise into quarters, and strip off the peeling. Half fill a large glass bowl with water, squeeze in the juice from half a lemon, and add the rind. Quarter the artichokes lengthwise, rub the cuts with lemon, and drop them into the lemon water.

2. Melt the butter in a large braising pan, sauté pan, or lidded skillet over medium heat. When it's bubbling, raise the heat to medium-high, add the onions and artichokes, and sauté, tossing, until they're beginning to color, about 4 minutes. Add the ham and thyme and sauté half a minute more. Season lightly with salt and pepper and add the broth. Cover, reduce the heat to medium-low, and braise until the vegetables are tender, about 30 minutes, shaking the pan occasionally and checking from time to time to make sure the pan doesn't get too dry. Replenish it with a few spoonfuls of water (not broth) as needed.

3. Remove the lid: If there is too much liquid, raise the heat and boil briskly until it's reduced and thick. Turn off the heat. Transfer everything to a serving bowl or platter and sprinkle with parsley. Serve hot or at room temperature.

Serves 4

braised artichokes and tomatoes

Braising in tomatoes is very traditional in Southern cooking. Okra and tomatoes is perhaps the best-known example, but it's only one of many such dishes. It's an especially nice way to cook artichokes. The recipe itself is easy, goes together quickly, and can be made as much as 2 days ahead. In fact, it actually improves with age and is even better on the second day. You may use canned tomatoes if the season for the two vegetables doesn't overlap where you live, but don't use canned or frozen artichoke hearts. Both are treated with ascorbic or citric acid to hold their color, which, unfortunately, does nothing for their flavor.

2 pounds ripe tomatoes, or 2 cups canned tomatoes, seeded and diced, with their juices

Halved lemon from trimming artichokes (page 185)

4 medium artichokes, trimmed for braising as directed on page 185

2 tablespoons unsalted butter

1 medium yellow onion, peeled and chopped

1 tablespoon chopped fresh thyme or 1 teaspoon crumbled dried thyme

Salt and whole black pepper in a mill

1. If using canned tomatoes, skip to step 2. Blanch, core, and peel the fresh tomatoes as directed on page 35. Halve them crosswise and scoop out the seeds into a sieve set over a stainless-steel or glass bowl to catch their juices. Cut into large dice and add them to their juices. Discard the seeds.

2. Half fill a large glass bowl with water, squeeze the juice from one of the lemon halves into it, and add the rind. Quarter the trimmed artichokes lengthwise, rub the cuts with lemon, and drop them into the lemon water.

3. Put the butter and onion in a large, lidded sauté pan or skillet over medium-high heat. Sauté, tossing often, until the onion is pale gold, about 4 minutes. Add the artichokes and sauté until they're bright green. Add the tomatoes and their juices and the thyme; season well with salt and a liberal grinding of pepper. Toss, bring the liquid to a boil, then cover and reduce the heat to medium-low. Braise, stirring occasionally, until the artichokes are tender, about 30 minutes.

4. If the sauce is thin when the artichokes are done, remove the lid, raise the heat to medium-high, and boil until thickened. Taste and adjust the seasonings, stir, and turn off the heat. Transfer to a serving bowl or platter and serve hot or at room temperature.

Serves 4

appreciating asparagus

There's one experience that I wish I could share with you firsthand. Imagine that it's early spring and we're in my mother's backyard. It has rained the night before and the new grass is wet, cold, and sweet smelling beneath our stubbornly bare feet. The enormous forsythia bush is an explosion of fragrant yellow sunshine, and somewhere at its center, a mockingbird's new brood is screaming for breakfast. She hops around us, trying to draw our attention away from them. Ignoring her, we kneel in the grass by the bush and carefully lift the lowest branches. There, in the yellow shadow, standing slim and pale and straight, are the first white asparagus of the season. Mama didn't plan on growing white asparagus; it just sort of happened. The beds spread like weeds, and forsythia, once established, will throw its fronds as far as you let it. Before she knew it, one whole end of the asparagus bed was under the bush.

Anyway, there it is—white asparagus. We gather all of it: Don't worry; the bed will keep producing. It snaps cleanly at the ground, and as its aroma meets our noses—the clean essence of spring—we eat half of our harvest on the spot. No salt; no lemon juice; no buttery hollandaise. Yet you will never taste anything else like it.

BUYING, STORING, AND PREPARING ASPARAGUS

Unless you have your own asparagus bed (with or without forsythia), or have access to a grower who cuts it fresh daily, the asparagus you buy will probably have been cut and refrigerated for several days. Here's how to get the most from it.

Look for tight, firm heads and stems that are firm and green without a trace of yellow. The cut end, though it will be scarred over, should not look dry or split, but white and full of moisture. Avoid any with wilted or partially open heads and wrinkled or yellowed stems. The thickness of the stem is no indication of freshness or youth, but of variety. I prefer those with fat stems; the pencil-thin ones can be tough halfway up the stem—which means you'll lose half the vegetable in the trimming since they're too thin to peel.

As soon as you get the asparagus home, trim off about an inch of the stems and stand it in a vase or bowl of cold water. Let it drink for at least half an hour to replenish the moisture it will have lost since it was cut. If you are not able to cook the asparagus the same day, you may keep it like this for up to 2 days in a cool spot away from direct sunlight, but use it as soon as possible.

When you're ready to cook the asparagus, don't do as many direct and just break off the tough part of the stem: You'll be wasting as much as a third of the asparagus. Peel it instead: It's not that much extra work and well worth it. Half fill a large bowl or basin with cold water. Lay an asparagus stalk on a cutting board or flat work surface with the top hanging over the edge. Holding the vegetable peeler perpendicular to the stem, peel away only the tough lower part of the skin, rotating the stalk as you go. Drop it into the basin of water and repeat until all of the asparagus is peeled. Leave it in the water until you are ready to cook it, but for no more than 2 hours.

basic asparagus

When asparagus is freshly cut and exploding with flavor, or when you prefer to serve it beside a more substantial main course that wouldn't be compatible with a complex sauce, this is how to cook it.

Salt

1½ pounds asparagus, trimmed and peeled as directed on page 188

2–3 tablespoons softened unsalted butter or Lemon Butter (recipe follows), optional

1. Put 1 inch of water in a large, deep sauté pan or lidded skillet, cover, and bring to a boil over high heat. Stir in a small handful of salt and add the asparagus by putting the stem end on the side closest to you then letting it fall away from you into the pan. Cover until the water returns to a boil, then uncover and cook briskly until the asparagus is firm to the bite but still bright green, 2–4 minutes, depending on the asparagus.

2. Immediately drain, using the lid to hold the asparagus in the pan, and turn it out onto a warm platter. Serve hot or at room temperature if you like, adding softened butter to the hot asparagus, and gently tossing until the butter has barely melted. You may also serve it with Lemon Butter passed separately.

Serves 4

lemon butter

This is an especially nice sauce for asparagus, but it's also lovely for dipping boiled artichokes (page 185), or seafood.

½ cup water

Salt

1 lemon, half the zest removed in one piece with a vegetable peeler

4 ounces (8 tablespoons or 1 stick) unsalted butter, cut into ½-inch chunks

1. Bring the water, a pinch of salt, and the lemon zest to a boil in a small heavy-bottomed saucepan over medium high heat. Reduce the heat to medium and simmer 5 minutes. Remove the zest and pour off all but 1 tablespoon of the water. Pat the zest dry and cut it into fine julienne.

2. Meanwhile, halve the lemon and juice it through a strainer.

3. Add 1 tablespoon of lemon juice to the pan with the water and let it warm over low heat. Gradually whisk in the butter, a few chunks at a time, adding more before the ones in the pan are completely melted and emulsified. When all the butter is added, it should have the consistency of thick heavy cream. Whisk in the zest and the remaining tablespoon of lemon juice. Pour it into a warm sauceboat and serve at once.

Makes about ½ cup

asparagus with lemon-pecan brown butter

Truly fresh spring asparagus, freshly cut and quickly cooked, is so delicious that it needs absolutely nothing, not even butter. Strong flavors like ham, leeks, garlic, and even lemon can be paired with it only with care and restraint. This rich, brown pecan and lemon butter sauce is the exception that proves the rule. Though complex and strongly flavored, it doesn't mask the flavor of really fresh asparagus, but reinforces it with a wonderful caramel undertone, and even gives back some of that bright, newly cut freshness to asparagus that is not as fresh as you would like.

Salt

1½ pounds asparagus, trimmed and peeled as directed on page 188

6 tablespoons (¾ stick) unsalted butter

½ cup pecans, cut lengthwise at the grooves into slivers

1 lemon, zest removed and cut into fine julienne, and halved

1. Put 1 inch of water in a large, deep sauté pan or lidded skillet, cover, and bring to a boil over high heat. Stir in a small handful of salt and add the asparagus by putting the stem end on the side closest to you then letting it fall away from you into the pan. Cover until the water returns to a boil, then uncover and cook briskly until the asparagus is firm to the bite but still bright green, 2–4 minutes, depending on the asparagus. Immediately drain, using the lid to hold the asparagus in the pan, and turn it out onto a warm platter.

2. Wipe out the pan, add the butter, and return it to medium-high heat. When the butter is melted and bubbly, add the pecans and sauté, tossing often, until the butter and pecans are a uniform golden-brown. Add the lemon zest and the juice from one of the halves. Cook for half a minute longer and remove the pan from the heat. Refresh the butter with another squeeze of lemon juice, taste and add salt as needed, then pour the sauce evenly over the asparagus. Serve at once.

Serves 4

butterbean and okra ragout

Here are two icons of the Southern summer table, paired in a very traditional vegetable stew that bears startling resemblance to the fava bean dishes of the Mediterranean basin. It's a very good example of how closely Southern cooking parallels that of Southern France, Italy, and Greece. Yet everything here is pure Deep South—and deeply delicious.

1 tablespoon unsalted butter

1 small yellow onion, split, peeled, and chopped

4 ounces (a ⅛-inch-thick slice) country ham or prosciutto, cut into julienne

1 small whole pod hot pepper such as cayenne or jalapeño

1 pound (about 3 cups) fresh shelled butterbeans, or frozen butterbeans or limas such as Fordhooks, thawed

½ pound very small, fresh okra, pods no longer than 2 inches

Salt

1. Warm the butter and onion in a lidded sauté pan or wide, shallow saucepan over medium heat. Sauté, tossing often, until the onion is translucent but not colored, about 4 minutes. Add the ham and toss until it loses its raw red color. Add the pepper pod (left whole) and beans, tossing until they're hot and bright green, then add enough water to barely cover them. Bring the liquid to a boil, loosely cover, and reduce the heat to medium-low. Simmer, stirring occasionally, until the beans are tender, about 20–40 minutes, depending on their freshness and maturity.

2. Meanwhile, rinse the okra under cold running water, gently rubbing to remove the outer fuzz, and trim the stem but leave the cap end intact.

3. Uncover the pan; if the liquid is still completely covering the beans, raise the heat briefly and boil until it only half covers them. Taste the beans and adjust for salt. Reduce the heat to medium, spread the okra over the top, cover tightly, and let the okra steam until it is crisp-tender, about 4–5 minutes. Stir the okra gently into the beans, cover once more, and simmer until the okra is done to your taste but still firm, no more than 3 minutes longer. Taste and adjust the seasoning, turn out into a serving bowl, and serve at once.

Serves 4

fava or windsor beans with bacon

Imported from Europe by the early English colonists, fava or—as they were called in those days—Windsor beans are the only beans in the Southern garden that aren't native to America. All the early Southern cookbooks had recipes for them, cooked plain in salted water but always served with slow-simmered salt pork. Sometime in the twentieth century, however, they disappeared from our tables, so when a renewed interest in Italian cooking brought them back to our attention, few Southerners realized that this "exotic" bean had once been part of their own heritage. Fava are seasonal in spring and, farther north, early summer. Always buy them whole, still in their pods, and count on about a cup of shelled beans from each pound of whole ones.

3 pounds fresh unshelled Windsor (fava) beans

3 tablespoons unsalted butter, divided

1 small shallot, trimmed, peeled, and minced

Salt and whole black pepper in a mill

2 extra-thick-cut slices of bacon, sliced crosswise into ¼-inch lardons

2 tablespoons dry bread crumbs, preferably homemade

1. Shell the beans and rinse under cold running water. Put a tablespoon of the butter and the shallot in a wide, lidded sauté pan or skillet over medium heat. Sauté, stirring often, until the shallot is translucent and beginning to color, about 4 minutes.

2. Add the fava beans, toss until hot, season well with salt and pepper, and add enough water to barely cover them. Bring to a boil, cover, and reduce the heat to low. Simmer gently until tender, between 6 and 15 minutes depending on the age and size of the beans.

3. Meanwhile, sauté the bacon in a small pan until browned but not crisp. Remove and drain it on absorbent paper. Spoon off all but a teaspoon of the fat and add the crumbs. Stir until lightly toasted and turn off the heat. Return the bacon to the pan and toss until it is coated with crumbs.

4. If, when the beans are tender, the liquid remaining in the pan is still thin, uncover, raise the heat, and quickly evaporate it to a thick sauce. Turn off the heat, add the remaining butter, and shake the pan to evenly coat the beans. Pour them into a warm serving bowl, scatter the bacon over them, and serve immediately.

Serves 4

young green beans with mushrooms and caramelized onions

A depressingly popular fixture at most covered-dish suppers in the South is a casserole made from three cans: one each of green beans, mushroom soup, and french-fried onion rings. Part of its popularity is owed, no doubt, to its effortless preparation, but part of it must be due to the fact that mushrooms, onions, and green beans are a splendid combination. This gives that combination a fresher approach, and yet is no more involved than that open-can-and-dump casserole.

1 pound young, tender green beans

Salt

2 tablespoons unsalted butter

2 medium yellow onions, split, peeled, and thinly sliced

1 large or 2 small cloves garlic, lightly crushed, peeled, and minced

½ pound brown crimini or portobello mushrooms, wiped clean with a dry cloth or paper towel and thickly sliced

Whole black pepper in a mill

1 tablespoon chopped parsley

¼ cup Buttered Crumbs (see below)

1. Rinse the beans under cold running water and snap off the stems, but leave the tails attached. Bring 4 quarts of water to a boil in large stockpot, add a small handful of salt, and let it come back to a boil. Add the green beans in handfuls, letting the water start simmering again before adding the next. Cover just long enough for the water to come back to a boil, then uncover and cook until the beans are crisp-tender but still a little underdone, about 2–4 minutes, depending on the beans. Drain and refresh them under cold running water to arrest the cooking.

2. Warm the butter and onions in a large sauté pan or lidded skillet over medium-high heat. Sauté, stirring often, until the onions are a rich golden-brown but not scorched, about 15–20 minutes. Add the garlic and toss until fragrant, about half a minute longer, then add the mushrooms and sauté, tossing, until they're wilted and beginning to color, about 4 minutes.

3. Add the beans and season with salt and a liberal grinding of pepper. Cover, reduce the heat to medium, and cook, shaking the pan frequently to prevent scorching, until the beans are just tender, about 5–8 minutes more. Remove the lid; if there's any liquid left in the pan, raise the heat and boil until it's evaporated. Stir in the parsley, taste and adjust the seasonings, and turn out onto a warm platter. Sprinkle the buttered crumbs over the top and serve at once.

Serves 4

BUTTERED CRUMBS

Buttered crumbs are a great little secret quick fix that dresses up just about any plain boiled or steamed vegetable.

1 tablespoon unsalted butter

¼ cup dry bread crumbs, preferably homemade

1. Melt the butter in a small skillet over medium low heat. Add the crumbs and toss until they have evenly absorbed the butter.

2. Continue stirring the crumbs over medium low heat until they are toasty. Turn off the heat and stir until cooled slightly, then sprinkle over the cooked vegetable and serve immediately.

Makes about ¼ cup

slow-cooked pole beans with parmesan

Pole beans, the large, flat, thick-skinned string beans, broken into bite-sized lengths and simmered slowly with a thick piece of salt pork, is one of the greatest and most misunderstood dishes in all Southern cooking. When properly done, there is nothing better. But for those who prefer to cook without pork, this meatless variation is equally rewarding. A well-scraped Parmesan cheese rind stands in for the meat, with caramelized onion supplying the subtle depth of flavor that is missing without salt-cured pork.

1½ pounds pole beans

1 medium yellow onion, trimmed, split lengthwise, peeled, and thinly sliced

1 tablespoon unsalted butter

1 well-scraped imported Parmigiano-Reggiano cheese rind at least 3 square inches (about 1 inch wide × 3 inches long)

1 medium whole hot pepper such as cayenne or jalapeño

Salt and whole black pepper in a mill

1. Break off the stem and tail ends of the beans and, if they have strings at the seams of the pods, pull them away. Snap them into 1-inch lengths and wash in several changes of water. Drain.

2. Bring a large teakettle full of water to a boil. Meanwhile, warm the onion and butter in a large, heavy-bottomed saucepan over medium-high heat. Sauté, tossing often, until the onion is a rich golden-brown with a few darker, chocolate-brown edges, but not scorched. (You'll know it's beginning to scorch if the rich onion aroma gives way to an acrid, burned-paper smell; if that happens, immediately remove it from the heat.)

3. Add the beans and toss until hot, then add enough boiling water to cover them by an inch (they'll float, so press them down with a spoon to test the depth). Add the cheese rind and whole pepper pod; season well with salt and black pepper. Bring to a boil, reduce the heat to a slow simmer, and loosely cover. Simmer gently until the beans are very tender but not mushy, as little as 45 minutes or as long as 1½ hours.

4. Taste and adjust the seasonings and simmer another minute. Remove and discard the pepper pod. The liquid should be considerably reduced and should no longer quite cover the beans. If it isn't reduced sufficiently, raise the heat and let it boil until sufficiently reduced, stirring from time to time to be sure that the beans don't scorch. Turn off the heat. The beans may be cooked to this point up to 2 days ahead. Transfer to a storage container, cool, cover, and refrigerate until you are ready to serve them. Reheat gently over medium-low heat and simmer 5 minutes.

5. Remove and discard the cheese rind, turn the beans out into a serving bowl, and serve at once.

Notes: Small, young vegetables are often laid on top of the slow-simmered beans to steam during the last few minutes of cooking. The most common are well-scrubbed and lightly skinned new potatoes, but baby summer squash and okra are also delicious additions. Allow a pound of new potatoes, a pound of very small yellow crookneck or pattypan squash, or half a pound of okra pods that are no more than 2 inches long, and cook only as long as it takes to steam them through, from about 5 minutes for the okra up to 20 minutes for the potatoes.

Serves 6–8

fresh black-eyed pea ragout

Fresh black-eyed peas have a delicate flavor and texture that is lighter and cleaner than that of dried peas. For one thing, some of the lighter overtones of flavor are lost; for another, the starchy quality that develops with drying is much less pronounced in fresh peas. That isn't to say that one is superior to the other; there are times when dried peas may even be preferred. This recipe, however, is not one of those times. If fresh black-eyed peas are not available where you live, they stand up well to freezing, and the frozen variety works well in this recipe.

1 tablespoon bacon drippings or olive oil

1 medium yellow onion, trimmed, split lengthwise, peeled, and chopped

1 medium green bell pepper, seeds and membranes removed, chopped

1 medium yellow bell pepper, seeds and membranes removed, chopped

2 large or 3 medium cloves garlic, lightly crushed, peeled, and minced

22 ounces fresh or thawed frozen black-eyed peas (see notes below)

4 medium fresh tomatoes, peeled with a vegetable peeler (page 35), seeded, and diced, or 1 cup drained, seeded, and diced canned tomatoes

2 cups Meat or Chicken Broth (page 10)

2 large sprigs thyme

2 bay leaves

1 whole pod hot pepper such as cayenne, serrano, or jalapeño

Salt and whole black pepper in a mill

4 small or 2 medium green onions such as scallions, trimmed and thinly sliced

1. Warm the fat, onion, and both bell peppers in a large, lidded skillet or wide, flameproof casserole over medium-high heat. Sauté, tossing frequently, until the onion is translucent but not colored, about 4 minutes. Add the garlic and toss until fragrant, about half a minute more. Add the peas and tomatoes and toss until they are hot.

2. Add the broth, thyme, bay leaves, and hot pepper pod (left whole); season well with salt and a liberal grinding of pepper. Bring to a boil, reduce the heat to medium-low, loosely cover, and simmer, stirring occasionally, until the peas are tender, about 20–30 minutes, depending on their size and freshness. Frozen peas will take less time; mature fresh ones will take longer.

3. Taste and adjust the seasonings, simmer a minute longer, then turn off the heat. Remove and discard the thyme, bay leaves, and hot pepper. The peas can be prepared up to this point up to 2 days ahead; reheat them gently over medium heat. Just before serving, stir in half the green onions, transfer the peas to a warm serving bowl, and sprinkle the remaining onions on top.

Notes: If you prefer a spicy-hot ragout, seed and chop the hot pepper and add it to the ragout with the other peppers at the beginning. Fresh black-eyed peas are available seasonally (late summer) and can be found at other times of the year in some specialty and natural food markets.

Serves 6

succotash

Probably the nicest image that the name of this underappreciated and truly American classic conjures is that of a lisping cartoon cat. And given what cafeteria steam tables have done to succotash, it's no wonder that it has come to have a dubious reputation. But when well made, there is no vegetable combination that is more satisfying to eat. This is how one does it well.

The optimum is to use only fresh vegetables in season, not only because they taste best, but also because adding a fresh corncob to the pot lends a subtle but distinctive flavor that can't be imitated. However, you can still make a very respectable succotash using good-quality frozen beans and corn.

¾ pound fresh ripe sauce-type tomatoes (such as Romas)

1 tablespoon bacon drippings or unsalted butter

1 medium yellow onion, trimmed, split lengthwise, and chopped

1 large clove garlic, lightly crushed, peeled, and minced

1 cup Chicken Broth (page 10), or ½ cup canned broth mixed with ½ cup water, or 1 cup water

2 ounces lean country ham

2 cups fresh or frozen butterbeans or small lima beans (such as Fordhooks)

2 cups sweet white corn kernels freshly cut from the cob (about 3 large or 4–5 small ears), reserving one of the cobs, or 1½ cups whole frozen white corn kernels such as Shoepeg

1 whole red hot pepper pod such as cayenne, serrano, or jalapeño

1 tablespoon chopped fresh sage or 1 teaspoon crumbled dried sage

Whole black pepper in a mill

Salt

1. Blanch, core, and peel the tomatoes as directed on page 35. Working over a wire sieve set in a bowl to catch the juices, cut them in half lengthwise and scoop the seeds. Roughly chop the tomatoes and add them to the collected juices. Discard the seeds.

2. Warm the drippings and onion in a large sauté pan or lidded skillet over medium-high heat. Sauté, tossing often, until golden, about 5–7 minutes. Add the garlic and toss until fragrant, half a minute longer. Add the tomatoes and their juices, broth, and ham; bring to a boil.

3. If you're using fresh butterbeans and corn, add the butterbeans, one of the corncobs broken into two or three pieces, the pepper pod (left whole), sage, and a liberal grinding of black pepper. Bring the liquid back to a boil, then cover, reduce the heat to a simmer, and simmer for 20 minutes, or until the butterbeans are almost tender but still a little underdone. Add the fresh corn, bring the liquids back to a simmer, cover, and cook until the vegetables are just tender, about 20 minutes more. If you are using frozen vegetables, add both corn and beans at once, bring to a boil, then reduce the heat to low, cover, and simmer until they are tender, about 20–30 minutes.

4. Taste and add salt if needed, then simmer for about 2 minutes more. Remove and discard the ham and corncobs; turn into a warm serving bowl, and serve hot. It can be made as much as a day ahead and reheated over medium-low heat. Cover and simmer for 4–5 minutes after it begins bubbling.

Serves 6

braised broccoli, georgia-style

A classic Georgia way of preparing bitter greens such as curly kale and collards is to wilt them with onions in bacon drippings and let them slowly braise until tender. That's exactly what happens here. Broccoli, a close relation of those greens, is sautéed with bacon and caramelized onions, then slowly braised. The broccoli loses its bright color, but—enrobed in onions and bacon—it also loses its sometimes sharp edge, and the natural sweetness is brought to the fore. Best of all, it's very easy to do and is forgiving if you need to prepare it ahead and reheat it.

1 pound fresh broccoli (about 2 large stalks)

4 ounces thick-cut bacon (about 2 slices), cut crosswise into ¼-inch-wide strips

1 medium yellow onion, split, peeled, and thinly sliced

Salt and whole black pepper in a mill

1. Wash the broccoli under cold running water and drain well. Using a sharp paring knife, cut off the cut end of the stem and peel away the tough outer skin. Slice the stem about ½ inch thick and separate the head into small florets. Set aside.

2. Sauté the bacon in a large sauté pan or lidded skillet over medium heat, tossing often, until it's browned but not crisp, about 4 minutes. Tip the pan and spoon off all but a tablespoon of the fat. Add the onion, raise the heat to medium-high, and sauté, tossing, until golden, about 4 minutes. Add the broccoli and toss until bright green and beginning to color, about 2 minutes.

3. Season lightly with salt (go easy if your bacon is especially salty; you can adjust it later) and a generous grinding of pepper. Add about ¼ cup water, cover, and reduce the heat to medium-low. Braise gently until the broccoli is tender but still firm, about 8 minutes. Taste and adjust the seasonings, let simmer half a minute more, then turn it out onto a warm platter or bowl and serve at once. Or, if you are making it ahead, transfer it to platter, let it cool, and cover until you are ready to reheat it. If you're making it more than 2 hours ahead, cover and refrigerate it. Add a splash of water and reheat it gently over medium-low heat.

Serves 4

creamed or fried corn

Both the names given to this dish are misleading—it is creamed even though there is no cream in it; fried even though it never sees so much as a sauté, and cooks with very little added fat. Yet both names are descriptive of what happens in the pan: The milky juices of the corn thicken with their own starches, forming a creamy sauce that coats the kernels. As for frying, the corn must be given the same attention as a stir-fry or sauté, and a wide, well-seasoned iron or nonstick frying pan with a heavy bottom is essential.

8 fresh ears corn, preferably white corn such as Silver Queen

2 tablespoons unsalted butter

½ medium yellow onion, trimmed, peeled, and finely chopped

Salt

Whole milk or light cream, if needed

1. Shuck the corn and scrub it with a vegetable brush under cold running water until all the silk is removed. Hold an ear over a large glass or stainless-steel bowl and cut halfway through the kernels in a downward stroke, removing only the top half of the kernels. Then turn the knife sharp-side out and, holding it at an angle to the cob, scrape firmly until all the inner parts of the kernels have been scraped away. This should produce a lot of juice, or "milk"; if it doesn't, the corn is beginning to get too mature and is probably not very fresh. But since you've come this far, work with it anyway. You will have to substitute cow's milk for the corn "milk."

2. Put the butter and onion into a well-seasoned iron skillet or heavy-bottomed nonstick pan. Turn on the heat to medium and sauté, tossing frequently, until the onion is translucent and pale gold, about 5 minutes. Add the corn and bring to a simmer, stirring frequently.

3. Stir in a large pinch of salt and reduce the heat to medium-low. Simmer, stirring and scraping the pan almost constantly, until the corn is tender, about 8–10 minutes. If there isn't enough liquid, or if the juices thicken before the corn is tender, add a little milk or light cream. Serve hot.

Serves 4

fresh corn cakes

Fresh corn is often folded into the batter for griddlecakes, giving them an interesting texture and moist, flavorful crumb. Here, however, the cakes are virtually all corn, with just enough meal and egg to bind the kernels together. They actually share more in common with potato latkes than griddlecakes. Yet if the corn is exceptionally fresh and sweet, you may omit the onion, herb, salt, and pepper and serve them as you would griddlecakes, dusted with superfine or caster (see page 404) sugar, passing syrup or jam separately.

4–5 ears sweet corn, preferably white corn (enough to make 2 cups kernels)

2 large or 3 small green onions, trimmed and minced

1 teaspoon chopped fresh or ½ teaspoon crumbled dried thyme

Salt and whole white pepper in a mill

Whole nutmeg in a grater

1 large egg, lightly beaten

¼ cup fine white cornmeal

2–3 tablespoons milk or half-and-half, if needed

Melted butter, for greasing the griddle

1. Shuck the corn and scrub it with a vegetable brush under cold running water until all the silk is removed. Hold an ear over a large glass or stainless-steel bowl and cut halfway through the kernels in a downward stroke, removing only the top half of the kernels. Then turn the knife sharp-side out and, holding it at an angle to the cob, scrape firmly until all the inner parts of the kernels have been scraped away. You should have at least 2 cups of corn kernels.

2. Add the green onions and thyme to the corn and season well with salt, a liberal grinding of white pepper, and generous grating of nutmeg. Stir in the egg and meal and mix until there are no lumps. Let the batter stand for a few minutes. If it seems too thick, add a few spoonfuls of milk.

3. Heat a griddle, well-seasoned iron skillet, or nonstick pan over medium heat and then brush it with butter. It's ready when a few drops of water dance and sizzle on the surface. Spoon the batter onto the hot griddle, allowing about 2 tablespoons per cake and spacing them an inch apart. Cook until the bottoms are golden-brown and steam holes begin to appear in the top, about 3 minutes. Turn and cook the other side until uniformly browned, about 3 minutes more. Serve hot.

Serves 4

eggplant fritters

Here is a traditional Southern dish that almost definitely comes from the hand of an African cook. Fritters are practically universal, of course, but it is in Africa that cooks have made little fried morsels of beans, rice, meat, or vegetables a high art. Historian Jessica Harris uses what she calls "the fritter factor" to trace the influence of the African Diaspora on the cuisines of the West, and it's a very reliable tool. Where savory fritters exist in the New World, there is almost certainly the mind of an African cook at work.

1 pound firm, purple eggplant
(about 2 medium)

Salt

2 large eggs, lightly beaten

About 2 tablespoons whole milk (or more)

1 large or 2 medium scallions or other green onions, trimmed and minced

Ground cayenne

½ cup all-purpose flour

Lard or peanut or canola oil, for frying

1. Cut the stems from the eggplant and peel them. Roughly chop and put them in a colander set in the sink. Lightly sprinkle with salt, toss until it's evenly distributed, and let drain 30 minutes.

2. Put the eggs and 2 tablespoons milk in a large mixing bowl and beat until evenly mixed and smooth. Add the onions, a large pinch or so of salt, and a small one of cayenne; stir in the seasonings and, a little at a time, beat in the flour with a whisk. Gently press the eggplant to extract the moisture, pat dry, and fold it into the batter. If the batter seems too thick, beat in another spoonful or so of milk. Set it aside in a warm, but not hot, spot.

3. Put enough lard or oil in a deep heavy-bottomed skillet or Dutch oven to come halfway up the sides. Warm it over medium-high heat until very hot but not quite smoking (around 375°F). Drop in the fritter batter by level tablespoonfuls and fry, turning once if they're not submerged, until golden-brown, about 3 minutes. Lift them out with a wire frying skimmer or tongs and drain thoroughly on a wire rack set over a rimmed baking sheet. Turn off the heat. The fritters can be made up to this point several hours ahead.

4. Just before serving, reheat the oil and refry the fritters a few at a time until crisp and golden, about 1 minute. Lift them from the fat, drain well, blot on absorbent paper, and serve at once.

Serves 4

managing eggplant

Even though eggplant has once again become popular in America, I find that many cooks don't know how to manage this strange vegetable in the kitchen. Before we get to the recipes, then, it is a good idea to take a moment to learn how to handle it. But first, a little of its history down South. Although eggplant can be found all around the Mediterranean basin and was well known in France, Spain, and England by the time all three countries colonized the West, it almost certainly found its way into Southern gardens and hearts by way of the African slave trade. Consider that it was popular in cotton- and rice-growing regions long before other parts of America (at least as early as the 1790s), and in Carolina it was nicknamed "Guinea squash" for the West African country from which many slaves had come. But the most telling evidence is the fact that many traditional Southern eggplant dishes parallel so many of those in West Africa.

In the early years several varieties of eggplants were grown in the South: We know this not only from records of vegetable markets, garden journals such as Thomas Jefferson's, and seed catalogs, but from cookbooks as well. But eventually, the milder, more widely preferred purple-skinned globe eggplant dominated the market. Today dozens of varieties have been introduced and reintroduced. Any of them will work fine in these recipes, but all of them, no matter what their color, size, or pedigree, should meet the following criteria: They should have taut, glossy skins, firm unbruised flesh, and a clear, green stem. The thing to avoid is what most of us want to avoid in our faces: wrinkles, brown spots, and mush.

There is a lot of back-and-forth about whether salting eggplant is necessary. Many scientists and Great Food Experts assert that there is no scientific evidence that it takes away the bitter, astringent aftertaste that many eggplants contain. I trust scientists in a lot of areas, but when I'm cooking, what I trust is my mouth. And my mouth tells me that if I don't salt eggplant before cooking it, particularly when there are a lot of seeds in the fruit, the end result will be a sharp bitterness underscoring a dish I have worked hard to make taste good. The method has been around for centuries and, I figure, not without reason. Therefore, I always lightly salt the cut eggplant and let it stand in a colander for half an hour before I cook it. Don't be concerned about excess salt; it stays on the outside, drawing moisture from the flesh to the surface, and is mostly wiped or rinsed away.

scalloped eggplant, creole-style

Eggplant marries happily with its nightshade cousins tomatoes and bell peppers, so it's no surprise that wherever all three can be found in the garden, one or more dishes combining them will be in the local cook's repertory. Here's the Southern version, in which that savory triad is underscored by another one essential to Creole cookery: salt-cured pork, thyme, and hot pepper.

1½ pounds eggplant

Salt

1 pound ripe tomatoes, or 1 cup canned Italian tomatoes, seeded, drained, and sliced thickly

3 tablespoons unsalted butter, divided

1 medium yellow onion, split, peeled, and diced small

1 medium green bell pepper, stemmed, seeded, and diced small

1 ounce country ham or thick-cut prosciutto (about ½ slice, ⅛ inch thick), cut into julienne

2 large or 3 small cloves garlic, lightly crushed, peeled, and minced

1 tablespoon chopped fresh thyme or ½ teaspoon crumbled dried thyme

1 tablespoon chopped fresh oregano or ½ teaspoon crumbled dried oregano

Ground cayenne and whole black pepper in a mill

½ cup dry bread crumbs

1. Wash the eggplant and cut off the stems. You may peel it if you like, but it isn't necessary. Cut it into 1-inch dice and put it in a colander set in the sink. Sprinkle liberally with salt, toss to coat well, and let drain 30 minutes.

2. If using canned tomatoes, skip to step 3. Blanch, core, and peel the fresh tomatoes as directed on page 35. Cut in half lengthwise and scoop out and discard the seeds (you don't need the juice, so don't bother with a sieve).

3. Position a rack in the center of the oven and preheat to 400°F. Put 2 tablespoons of the butter, the onion, and the bell pepper in a large sauté pan; turn on the heat to medium-high. Sauté, tossing often, until the onion is softened but not browned, about 4 minutes. Pat the eggplant dry with paper towels and add it to the pan along with the ham. Sauté, tossing frequently, until hot through and beginning to soften, about 4 minutes. Add the garlic, thyme, and oregano; sauté half a minute longer. Add the tomatoes and gently toss until they're hot. Season well with salt, a pinch of cayenne, and a liberal grinding of pepper. Turn off the heat.

4. Lightly butter a 2-quart casserole and pour in the eggplant. Pat it level with a spatula until evenly distributed, but don't flatten it. Wipe out the sauté pan and melt the remaining tablespoon of butter in it over low heat. Turn off the heat and mix in the crumbs. Sprinkle them over the top of the eggplant. Bake in the center of the oven until bubbly and golden-brown, about 20–30 minutes. Let it settle for 10 minutes if you're serving hot, or let it cool to room temperature.

Serves 4

spring greens with spring onions

This is more than merely a variation on the recipe for Wilted Winter Greens on page 210. Spring greens have a completely different taste and texture from the winter variety—even within their species. Not only are they more tender and delicate than winter greens, but their flavor is more forthright, brighter, and more intense, particularly when young spring onions are added into the equation. The traditional salt pork here lends understated but distinctive depth of flavor that tough winter greens can actually get along without. But if you prefer not to use pork, substitute 2 tablespoons of butter or olive oil.

2 pounds young mixed greens (about 3 bunches), such as dandelion (available in many organic and specialty produce sections), spinach, beet tops, chard, young mustard, watercress, or poke sallet (page 209)

2 ounces (about 3 thick slices) lean salt pork or unsmoked bacon such as pancetta

2 medium green onions, washed, trimmed, and thinly sliced, white and green parts separated

Salt

Pepper Vinegar (page 21), optional

1. Wash the greens in a basin of cold water, changing the water one or twice until they're free of any dirt or sand. When they're clean, one leaf at a time remove the tough stems along with any wilted or discolored leaves. Tear larger leaves into several pieces, but leave smaller ones whole.

2. Wipe the salt pork well with a dry paper towel and put it in a heavy-bottomed Dutch oven, preferably enameled iron, set over medium heat. Sauté, stirring frequently, until it's golden and the fat is rendered from it. Add the white parts of the onions and sauté until translucent, about 2–4 minutes longer.

3. Raise the heat to medium-high and begin adding the greens by handfuls, stirring with a wooden spoon until the greens wilt before adding more. Add the green onion tops, cover, and reduce the heat to medium-low. Simmer until the greens are just tender but still bright green, about 2–3 minutes. Taste and adjust the salt (if the pork is very salty, it may not need any), toss well, and turn off the heat. Transfer the greens to a warm serving bowl and serve at once, passing pepper vinegar separately, if liked.

Serves 4

about poke sallet

Poke sallet *(phytolacca americana)* is a native American plant. Though much loved by many Southerners and briefly cultivated in the nineteenth century, today it's found only in the wild. It's very hardy and flourishes practically anywhere, from pastures and roadside ditches to the grassy medians in the city. I've even had poke sprout in abandoned flower pots on my porch. It's a seasonal vegetable since only the young shoots and early leaves are believed to be edible. Poke develops a mild toxin as the plant matures that becomes more concentrated as the stem and leaf veins turn red and the flowers develop. The seeds, roots, and red stems are not edible. Don't forage for it on your own unless you know exactly what you are looking for, and never gather leaves that are tinged with red. A reasonable substitute is a mixture of chard and beet greens.

As added insurance, many old cooks would blanch poke sallet, supposedly to remove any toxins that it may contain, but mainly to tame its distinctive flavor. I don't find this necessary and never blanch it, but here is how to prepare it in the traditional way: After thoroughly washing the leaves in two changes of cold water, half fill a large stockpot with water. Bring the water to a boil over high heat and add the poke leaves, pressing them below the surface with a spoon. When they're wilted, but still bright green (about 2 minutes), drain and rinse under cold running water.

wilted winter greens

Slow-simmered winter greens (the kind with "pot liquor"—or as some folksy writers like to style it, "potlikker") is among the handful of traditional Southern vegetable dishes that's universally known (and misunderstood). It often overshadows some of the other traditional ways of preparing the sturdy, leafy greens of autumn and winter, such as this one. Here, instead of a long, slow simmer, they're wilted in a little fat and then undergo a brief braise until they're just tender. In this recipe olive oil replaces the more traditional rendered bacon fat, but the flavor is still homey and familiar. You need not feel limited to collards and kale: Spinach, beet tops, young mustard, dandelion, and watercress are all good candidates for wilting in this manner. Just make sure that the greens are as fresh as possible: There is nothing here to cover up the taste of indifferent produce.

3 pounds kale or very young collards, swiss chard, spinach, or other greens (see headnote above)

4 tablespoons extra-virgin olive oil, divided

1 medium yellow onion, trimmed, split lengthwise, peeled, and thinly sliced, optional

Salt and whole black pepper in a mill

1. Wash the greens in a basin of cold water, changing the water once or twice until they're free of any dirt or sand. When they're clean, one leaf at a time remove the stems along with any wilted or discolored leaves. Roll several leaves together and then slice them into thin chiffonade. (*Note:* Very tender young greens such as spinach or watercress can be cooked whole.) Continue until you have trimmed all the greens.

2. Heat half the oil in a heavy-bottomed Dutch oven, preferably enameled iron, over medium heat until it is almost at the point of smoking. Add the onion, if using, and sauté until it is golden, about 4 minutes. Start adding the trimmed greens by handfuls, with the water that's clinging to them. Stir vigorously with a wooden spoon until they're bright green and wilted.

3. Continue adding greens by large handfuls until all of them are wilted, then season well with salt and a liberal grinding of pepper. Add the remaining oil and stir well. Immediately reduce the heat to low. If there's no moisture in the pan, add about ¼ cup of water, cover, and braise for 3–5 minutes, or until the greens are just tender and the moisture is evaporated. Serve hot.

Serves 6–8

sautéed bourbon mushrooms

Really fresh mushrooms are, as Mary Randolph aptly noted in 1824, "too delicious to require aid from any thing." But, particularly when they are not freshly cut, a splash of bourbon does wonders for mild, domestic mushrooms from the market.

1 pound small brown (crimini) mushrooms, wiped clean (page 212)

3 tablespoons unsalted butter, divided

Salt and whole black pepper in a mill

¼ cup bourbon

1 tablespoon chopped parsley

1. Leave small mushrooms whole, but cut larger ones into halves or quarters, so that they're all about the same size.

2. Melt 2 tablespoons of the butter in a large skillet with sloping sides over medium heat. When the butter is melted and hot and the foaming subsides, raise the heat to medium-high and put in the mushrooms. Sauté, tossing constantly, until they're golden-brown, about 4 minutes.

3. Season with salt and a liberal grinding of pepper. Carefully add the bourbon, standing clear in case it accidentally ignites. Let it evaporate, shaking the pan constantly. Turn off the heat, add the remaining butter, and shake the pan until it is incorporated and has lightly thickened the cooking juices. Taste and adjust the seasonings, sprinkle with parsley, and serve at once.

Serves 4

buying and storing fresh mushrooms

Many different varieties of fresh mushrooms have become more widely available to Southern cooks, including such wild ones as Boletus edulis (cèpes or porcinis), chanterelles, and morels, all of which are native to our region, and all of which were known to traditional cooks who foraged for their own. But if these premium varieties aren't fresh, they're hardly worth the money or trouble, so if they don't pass muster, pass them over.

Here's what to look for when shopping for them: clear, dry caps without any damp spots; fat stems that do not look in the least withered. On small button mushrooms, the membrane below the cap should still be connected to the stem. On larger ones, such as portobellos, or on open varieties such as chanterelles, shiitakes, and oyster mushrooms, the gills should be dry and uniform in color. On any variety, the stems should be firm and dry. You notice a lot of "dry" here: dampness, especially dampness that is slippery, is a sign of decay.

Mushrooms are at their best used as soon as they're cut, but that's a luxury available only to those who forage for them or at least have a forager among the vendors of their local farmers' market. Most of us have to be content with market mushrooms, which will at best be a week from the field. Use them as soon as possible, preferably within 24 hours. For short-term storage (less than a day), keep them in an open basket in a cool, dark place. For more prolonged storage, put them in a covered, ventilated basket or fold them into a dry cotton or linen towel and put them in the produce bin of your refrigerator for up to 3 days.

Cleaning mushrooms for use: I don't care what all the so-called food scientists say about it: Yes, mushrooms are little sponges that are already full of moisture, but wetting their surface permanently changes the texture, especially if they're not very fresh. I never wash them, but clean them by wiping gently with a soft brush or dry cloth. If there's stubborn dirt clumped on the stem, trim it off.

mushroom-stuffed tomatoes

Mushrooms and tomatoes are one of the world's great combinations. Yet in some parts of the world, their seasons don't overlap. Consequently, either the mushrooms or the tomatoes will have been preserved in some manner. Because of our mild climate, however, tomatoes last well into the fall mushroom season in the South. This is a very old, traditional dish that illustrates how lovely and versatile the combination is. It can be served as a first course, side dish, or, accompanied by a simple green salad, main dish for a light, meatless lunch.

4 ripe medium tomatoes

salt

½ pound wild or brown (crimini or portobello) mushrooms, wiped clean (page 212)

3 tablespoons butter, divided

3 medium shallots or 1 medium yellow onion, peeled and chopped fine

1 large or 2 small cloves garlic, lightly crushed, peeled, and minced

1 ounce (about ½ slice) country ham, chopped

1 tablespoon chopped parsley

1 tablespoon chopped fresh thyme or 1 teaspoon dried thyme

1 cup soft bread crumbs

Salt, whole black pepper in a mill, and cayenne pepper

1. Wash the tomatoes under cold running water, pat dry, and slice off the stem end just below the stem scar. Scoop out and discard the seeds, and with a sharp spoon or melon baller scoop out the inner pulp, leaving the outer pulp below the skin to form a shell. Drain the pulp well and chop it roughly. Lightly salt the insides of the tomato shells, invert them in a colander set over the sink, and let drain 30 minutes.

2. Meanwhile, position a rack in the upper third of the oven and preheat to 375°F. Roughly chop the mushrooms. Warm 2 tablespoons of the butter and the shallots in a large skillet or sauté pan over medium-high heat. Sauté, tossing often, until the shallots are golden, about 5 minutes. Add the garlic and toss until fragrant, about half a minute longer. Add the ham and toss until it loses its raw red color, then add the mushrooms, parsley, and thyme and sauté until the mushrooms are wilted, about 3–4 minutes. Add the reserved tomato pulp, bring to a boil, and cook, stirring often, until the liquid is mostly evaporated. Turn off the heat.

3. Add the bread crumbs and season well with salt, pepper, and a pinch of cayenne. Toss to mix, then taste and correct the seasonings. Lightly butter a 9-inch square or round casserole. Pat the tomato shells dry inside and out and spoon the mushroom filling loosely into them. Set them in the casserole, dot with bits of the remaining butter, and bake in the upper third of the oven until the tomatoes are tender and the filling is hot through, about 20 minutes.

Serves 4

whole baby okra in olive oil

This dish is usually a revelation to the okra haters of my acquaintance, who turn up their noses at the whole idea of okra because all they've seen is okra boiled to a gooey mass of army-green slime. The bright green and firm, silky bite of this okra really turns their heads and palates. And as for the notion that all Southerners have always overcooked okra, this recipe dates back at least to Mary Randolph's *The Virginia House-Wife*, published in 1824. The only thing I have changed is the fat—from butter to olive oil.

1½ pounds fresh, very small okra pods (each no more than 2 inches long)

1 large or 2 small cloves garlic, crushed and peeled

2 tablespoons extra-virgin olive oil, divided

Salt and whole black pepper in a mill

1. Wash the okra under cold running water, gently rubbing them to remove the outer fuzz. Drain well and trim off the stem, leaving the cap intact. Set aside.

2. Put the okra, garlic, and 1 tablespoon of the olive oil in a lidded, heavy-bottomed skillet or sauté pan that will hold it all in one layer. Add a healthy pinch of salt, a generous grinding of pepper, and ¼ cup water; cover tightly and set it over medium-high heat.

3. Cook 3–4 minutes, giving the pan a good shake from time to time. Turn off the heat, taste and adjust the seasonings, and immediately pour the okra into a shallow bowl or platter. Drizzle with the remaining olive oil and serve hot, or let it cool and serve at room temperature.

Serves 4

okra with tomatoes and basil

This is the very essence of summer in the South: the sunshine of fresh, ripe tomatoes melded with the silky, mellow earthiness of okra and brightened by a touch of fresh basil. It is strictly a seasonal dish, since it can only be made with small, snapping-fresh okra, truly vine-ripe tomatoes, and just-snipped basil. The traditional fat is bacon drippings, which soften and round out the flavors, but olive oil is also very satisfying. If you use olive oil, splash a teaspoon or so more of fresh oil over the okra after it comes off the heat.

1 pound fresh, very small okra pods
(each no more than 2 inches long)

2 pounds ripe tomatoes

1 tablespoon bacon drippings
or extra-virgin olive oil

1 medium yellow onion, split, peeled,
and chopped

1 large or 2 small cloves garlic, lightly crushed,
peeled, and minced

Salt

1 small whole hot red or green pepper,
such as cayenne, serrano, or jalapeño

8 large or 12 small fresh basil leaves

1. Wash the okra under cold running water, gently rubbing them to remove the outer fuzz. Drain well and trim off the stems, leaving the caps intact. Blanch, peel, and seed the tomatoes as directed on page 35, then thickly slice them.

2. Warm the fat and onion in a large, heavy-bottomed sauté pan or skillet over medium-high heat. Sauté, tossing often, until the onion is translucent and pale gold, about 5 minutes. Add the garlic and toss until fragrant, about half a minute, then add the okra and toss until glossy and bright green. Season lightly with salt, toss, and add the tomatoes and hot pepper (left whole). Bring it to a boil, reduce the heat to medium-low, and simmer, stirring occasionally, until the okra is tender and the juices are thick, about 20–30 minutes. Taste and adjust the seasonings; turn off the heat. Remove and discard the hot pepper.

3. Tear the basil leaves into small pieces and scatter them over the okra and tomatoes, toss well, and serve hot or at room temperature.

Serves 4

green vidalia onions with lemon

Green onions in the South are most often used in salads or as a flavorful finishing garnish in Creole and Lowcountry cooking. They're a lovely vegetable on their own, especially welcome in late winter, when the selection of fresh green vegetables is somewhat limited. That's the season when Southern cooks look forward to the advent of green Vidalia Sweet onions. The trade began with the growers thinning their crops so that the onions could mature to full size. The slender, green culls were too good to discard, and the farmers started selling them in local markets. Once a strictly regional delicacy, green Vidalias are now nationally available. Of course, you needn't wait for Vidalias; this is a delectable treatment for any green onions, especially little spring scallions.

16 small green Vidalia onions or large scallions (or 24 small scallions)

1 cup Chicken Broth (page 10), or ½ cup canned broth mixed with ½ cup water (even if the label reads "use full strength")

4 tablespoons (½ stick) unsalted butter, divided

1 lemon, the zest cut into small julienne with a zester (or cut from the lemon with a vegetable peeler and cut into julienne with a knife), cut in half

Whole nutmeg in a grater

1. Wash the onions under cold running water, making sure to get any dirt that may be trapped between the leaves. Trim the root ends, trim any withered tips from the greens, and pull off any yellowed or withered leaves.

2. Put the broth and 2 tablespoons of the butter into a wide, shallow sauté pan or covered skillet that will hold the onions in no more than two layers. Cover and bring to a boil over medium-high heat. Carefully add the onions to the pan, sprinkling them with half the lemon zest and a generous grating of nutmeg. Cover and let it return to a boil, then reduce the heat to medium and cook until the onions are nearly tender but still bright green, between 4 and 8 minutes (less for scallions and small Vidalias, more for larger ones).

3. Remove the lid, raise the heat to medium-high, and cook briskly until the liquid is reduced and syrupy, about 3–4 minutes. Turn off the heat. Refresh with a squeeze of lemon juice and remove the onions with tongs or a slotted spatula to a warm serving platter or individual plates. Swirl the remaining butter into the cooking liquid, shaking the pan until it is dissolved. Pour the resulting sauce over the onions, sprinkle with the remaining zest, and serve at once.

Green Onions with Pecan-Lemon Butter: Add ½ cup sliced Toasted Pecans (page 232) to the sauce along with the butter in step 3.

Serves 4

baked vidalia sweet onions with ham

Stuffed onions are standard fare in many of the world's great cuisines, and small wonder: Just about anything a cook can imagine makes a delicious filling for them—lamb, poultry, rice, nuts, and even other vegetables such as greens or corn. Here is the Georgia version, making use of our local sweet onions and dry-cured country hams. Most Southern cooks love to mix salty and sweet flavors, and here the savory ham makes an ideal foil for the naturally sweet onions.

4 medium Vidalia or other sweet onions

1 cup soft bread crumbs

4 ounces country ham, trimmed of all fat and roughly chopped

1 tablespoon chopped fresh sage or 1 teaspoon crumbled dried sage

Whole black pepper in a mill

2 teaspoons unsalted butter

¼ cup fine, dry bread crumbs

½–1 cup Chicken Broth (page 10), canned broth diluted with water (even if the label reads "use full strength"), or water

1. Position a rack in the center of the oven and preheat to 400°F. Trim the roots so that the onions will sit flat, cut out their tops in a wide, inverted cone, and peel them. Put them top-side up in a close-fitting, lidded casserole. Cover and bake in the center of the oven until softened but still underdone, about 30 minutes. This step can be done in the microwave: Cook on high about 4 minutes, turn, and cook until softening but still underdone, about 3–4 minutes longer.

2. Let the onions cool enough to handle and, with a melon baller or sharp-edged spoon, scoop out their centers, leaving about ¼ inch of the outer layers and the root ends intact. Roughly chop the cores and put them in a bowl with the soft crumbs, ham, sage, and a liberal grinding of pepper. Mix well and taste and adjust the seasonings, adding salt if needed (most of the time the ham will be salty enough). Divide it among the onions, mounding it up a little on the top.

3. Melt the butter in a small skillet over medium-low heat. Stir in the dry crumbs until they have absorbed the butter evenly; turn off the heat. Sprinkle the crumbs over the stuffing. Pour just enough broth around the onions to come about a quarter of the way up their sides. Bake until the onions are completely tender and the crumb topping is golden-brown, about 30–45 minutes longer. Serve warm or at room temperature.

Serves 4

sautéed summer squash with green onions

The squashes associated with summer—yellow crookneck, pattypan, sunburst (a yellow variety of pattypan), and the ubiquitous zucchini—are sweet and delicate early in the season, more full-bodied as summer blossoms, then dense and often a little bitter tasting as the season draws to its close. If you can get young squash, freshly harvested, just steam them until they are barely tender (4–11 minutes, depending on the maturity and size of the squash), and serve them with salt, freshly ground black pepper, and butter. Here is how to get the best from them when they are not so fresh, sweet, and delicate.

2 pounds young yellow summer squash such as yellow crookneck, pattypan, or zucchini

2 tablespoons unsalted butter

4 large or 6 medium green onions, thinly sliced, white and green parts separated

Salt and whole black pepper in a mill

1. Scrub the squash well under cold running water and pat dry. Trim off the blossom and stem ends and slice thickly into rounds about ¼ inch thick.

2. Melt the butter in a large sauté pan or skillet over medium-high heat. When it is melted and hot, but not browning, add the squash, tossing until uniformly coated with the fat. Sauté, tossing often, until they're beginning to color, about 3–4 minutes.

3. Add the white parts of the onions and season well with salt and a liberal grinding of pepper. Sauté until the squash are golden-brown and tender, about 3–4 minutes more. Taste and adjust the seasonings, transfer the squash to a warm serving bowl, and scatter the green onion tops over them. Serve at once.

Serves 4

curried summer squash

Summer squash often last until the first really hard frost. In many parts of the South, that will not occur until early December. The later ones are not as delicate as early-summer produce, sometimes having a bitter edge that lends itself well to heftier seasonings than are usually associated with summer produce. Of course, curry and cream add a meaty depth to summer squash of any persuasion, and at any other time of year.

2 pounds summer squash such as yellow crookneck, pattypan, or yellow zucchini

1 tablespoon unsalted butter

1 medium yellow onion, split, peeled, and thinly sliced

1 teaspoon mild curry powder

Salt

¼ cup heavy cream

2 tablespoons snipped fresh chives or thinly sliced green scallion tops

1. Scrub the squash well under cold running water and pat dry. Trim off the blossom and stem ends and slice them crosswise into ¼-inch-thick rounds.

2. Warm the butter and onion in a large sauté pan or skillet over medium-high heat. Sauté, tossing, until the onion is pale gold, about 5 minutes. Sprinkle in the curry and stir until it is fragrant, just a few seconds. Add the squash and season well with salt. Toss until they're hot and lightly colored with the curry, about 1 minute. Cover the pan and reduce the heat to medium-low. Simmer slowly until the squash is just tender.

3. Remove the lid and raise the heat to medium-high. If there is a lot of liquid accumulated in the pan, let it evaporate until it's lightly thickened. Add the cream, bring it to a boil, and cook, tossing often, until the cream is lightly reduced, about 1 minute or less. Taste and adjust the seasonings, then transfer it to a warm serving bowl. Sprinkle with chives and serve at once.

Serves 4

summer squash casserole

Squash casserole is a standard of almost any Southern kitchen and a favorite for church covered-dish suppers or "dinner-on-the-grounds" picnics. Many traditional versions, while delicious, can be overwhelmingly rich and complicated. This one is lighter, fresher tasting, and easy to assemble, yet it does not skimp on the essential elements—squash, onions, and cheese.

2 pounds summer squash such as yellow crookneck, pattypan, or zucchini

2 medium yellow onions, split, peeled, and thinly sliced

2 tablespoons unsalted butter

Salt and whole black pepper in a mill

1 cup finely grated aged cheddar or gruyère

1. Scrub the squash well under cold running water to remove any grit that may be clinging to them. Put about 1 inch of water in a large lidded saucepan fitted with a vegetable steamer or into the bottom of a double-boiler-type steamer, and bring to a boil over high heat. Put the squash in the steamer basket, reduce the heat to medium, cover, and steam until the squash are just tender, about 10 minutes. Immediately remove them from the steam to prevent further cooking.

2. Meanwhile, warm the onions and butter in a skillet or sauté pan over medium-high heat. Sauté, tossing often, until the onions are beginning to color, about 5–7 minutes. Turn off the heat.

3. When the squash has cooled enough to handle, trim the stem and blossom ends and slice them into ¼-inch-thick rounds. Gently toss them with the onions; season well with salt and a generous grinding of pepper. Pour into a 9-inch square or round casserole. This can be prepared through this step up to a day ahead. Cover and refrigerate if you're making it more than couple of hours ahead.

4. Position a rack in the center of the oven and preheat to 450°F. Sprinkle the cheese evenly over the top of the casserole and bake in the center of the oven until it's bubbly and the cheese is melted and golden-brown, about 20 minutes. Let stand for at least 10 minutes before serving. Serve warm or at room temperature.

Serves 4

baked winter squash with sausage and goat cheese

Sweet winter squash are just made for sage, cayenne, and pork, so pairing them with sage-scented breakfast sausage is an old Southern tradition. The oldest recipes are exquisitely simple: The squash is halved, seeded, filled with bulk sausage, and baked until tender. Here those traditional flavors get fresh zip from the tangy flavor and creamy texture of goat cheese.

Butter

1 medium butternut or large acorn squash (about 2 pounds)

½ pound bulk breakfast sausage

1 medium onion, trimmed, split lengthwise, peeled, and chopped

1 tablespoon chopped fresh sage or 1 teaspoon crumbled dried sage

Salt and whole black pepper in a mill

Whole nutmeg in a grater

2 ounces soft goat cheese (chèvre)

1. Position a rack in the center of the oven and preheat to 375°F. Lightly butter a 9-inch square or round, lidded casserole. Peel and halve the squash lengthwise, scoop out and discard the seeds, and cut the flesh into 1-inch dice.

2. Roughly crumble the sausage in a sauté pan and set it over medium heat. Sauté, stirring occasionally, until the meat has lost its raw red color. Crumble it a little more with a fork as it browns, but leave most of it in ¾-inch lumps. Remove the sausage with a slotted spoon and drain it thoroughly on absorbent paper.

3. Spoon off all but a tablespoon of the fat and add the onion. Sauté, tossing frequently, until the onion is beginning to color, about 5 minutes. Turn off the heat. Return the sausage to the pan along with the squash and toss until both are well mixed with the onion. Transfer it to the prepared casserole.

4. Add the sage and season well with salt, a liberal grinding of pepper, and generous grating of nutmeg. Toss lightly until well mixed. Crumble the goat cheese over it, cover, and bake in the center of the oven until the squash is nearly tender, about 30 minutes. Remove the lid and bake until lightly browned, about 10 minutes longer. Serve hot.

Serves 4

whipped sweet potatoes with leeks

Sweet potatoes are native to the Americas, and there are dozens of varieties. The types of sweet potatoes preferred in the South are often confusingly called "yams" even though they're not remotely related to the true yams of Africa. They're the ones that have luscious deep orange flesh that is distinctly sweet; in fact, many of the ways they are prepared more closely resemble dessert than a vegetable side dish. Here they're paired with leek greens, which brings out their more savory side. The ideal sweet potatoes for this should have a deep orange to almost red-orange flesh, such as Louisiana "yams," jewels, or garnets.

2 pounds orange-fleshed sweet potatoes (see headnote above)

2 large or 4 medium leeks

½ cup heavy cream or half-and-half

1 tablespoon bourbon

Grated zest of 1 lemon

Salt and whole white pepper in a mill

Whole nutmeg in a grater

2 tablespoons unsalted butter

1. Scrub the sweet potatoes under cold running water. Put them in a large, heavy-bottomed pot and add enough cold water to cover them by 1 inch. Lift out the potatoes, cover the pot, and bring it to a boil over high heat. Carefully add the potatoes, let the water return to a boil, cover, and reduce the heat to medium. Simmer until the potatoes are tender and easily pierced with a fork or knife. Drain and set them aside, covered.

2. Meanwhile, split the leeks lengthwise and wash them under cold running water, root-end up, bending back the leaves to get all the dirt that is clinging to the inner layers. Pat dry, trim off the roots and any discolored leaves, and thinly slice them crosswise. Set aside.

3. Peel the sweet potatoes and put them through a potato ricer back into the pot in which they cooked, or cut them in chunks, put them into the pot, and mash until smooth with a potato masher. Add the cream and bourbon and return the pot to low heat. Beat until the potatoes are smooth and fluffy and thoroughly heated. Add the zest and season well with salt, a generous grinding of white pepper, and liberal grating of nutmeg. Turn off the heat, cover, and keep warm.

4. Warm the butter and leeks in a large skillet or sauté pan over medium heat. Sauté, tossing often, until the leeks are wilted and just tender, about 3–4 minutes. Turn off the heat.

5. Turn the sweet potatoes into a warm serving bowl and smooth the top. Spoon the leeks around the edges and serve at once.

Serves 4

sweet potato latkes with homemade applesauce and crème fraîche

These are neither traditionally Southern nor Jewish, and yet they are both. There are large Jewish communities all over the South, particularly in older cities like Charleston and Savannah. While many congregations adapted their culinary traditions to the cookery of their neighbors, blending and experimentation were inevitable. Here a quintessentially Southern ingredient goes into one of the icons of the Jewish table. But traditions aside, what matters is that these crispy potato pancakes are just plain delicious, either as a side dish or sprinkled with superfine or caster sugar (see page 404) and cinnamon and dolloped with applesauce and sour cream as a dessert.

The batter cannot be made ahead, as sweet potatoes start to throw off moisture after half an hour, making the batter soupy and difficult to cook.

1 pound sweet potatoes (the orange-fleshed "yam" variety)

2 large eggs, lightly beaten

¼ teaspoon cinnamon

¼ teaspoon freshly grated nutmeg

1 small pinch salt

3–4 tablespoons sugar, to taste

¼ cup all-purpose flour

Vegetable oil, for frying

Superfine or caster sugar (see page 404) and cinnamon, optional

Homemade Applesauce (follows) and Crème Fraîche (page 27) or sour cream

1. Grate the potatoes through the large holes of a box grater (or with the coarse grating blade of the food processor). Add the eggs, spices, salt, and sugar; stir until they are evenly mixed. Sprinkle the flour over and thoroughly mix it in.

2. Heat enough oil in a large, heavy skillet to come ¼ inch up the sides over medium-high heat until it is hot but not quite smoking (about 365°F). Add the batter in 2-tablespoons portions, flattening them with the back of the spoon or a spatula. Fry until golden-brown on the bottom, about 4 minutes, then turn and fry until uniformly browned and the edges are crisp. Blot on paper towels, sprinkle with superfine sugar and cinnamon if you are serving them as a dessert, and serve hot, passing applesauce and sour cream or crème fraîche separately.

Serves 6

homemade applesauce

Homemade applesauce isn't much trouble to make—and the rewards are large. The secrets to good sauce are to never peel the apples or add sugar before cooking them. The peel adds both flavor and pectin for body, and you cannot adjust the sweetening until you know how sweet the apples are after they cook. Tasting beforehand won't be reliable. Even if the apples are very tart, don't neglect to add lemon juice; it brightens the flavor. You may vary the sauce with other flavorings such as orange or lemon zest, a sprig of rosemary, or a couple of slices of fresh ginger, but keep these things subtle; the whole point is the concentrated flavor of apples.

2 pounds apples

⅓ cup water

Sugar

1 lemon, halved

Ground cinnamon, whole nutmeg in a grater, or cardamom, to taste, optional

1. Scrub the apples well, remove the stems, and cut each into six wedges. Don't peel or core them. Put them in a lidded, heavy-bottomed saucepan and add the water. Cover and bring to a boil over medium-high heat. Reduce the heat to low and simmer until the apples are soft, about 20 minutes.

2. Force the apples through a food mill or wire sieve while they're still hot. This will remove all peeling and seeds. Taste and add sugar and the juice from half the lemon. You may add spices to taste, if you like. Taste and adjust the lemon juice and sugar after adding them. Let the applesauce cool completely and store in a glass jar or bowl, covered and refrigerated.

Makes about 2–2½ cups

A PAIR OF
GREEN TOMATO RECIPES

Even if I didn't think Fannie Flagg was one of the best writers of our time, I would adore her for saving fried green tomatoes from oblivion. Once the brunt of rude jokes, thanks in part to Ms. Flagg's novel *Fried Green Tomatoes at the Whistle Stop Cafe*, they became almost chic during the comfort-food revivals of the 1980s. Today they're a standard in most upscale nouvelle Southern restaurants, served both on their own and in elaborately constructed dishes, topped with everything from poached eggs and crabmeat (wonderful) to beluga caviar (the silliest thing I ever saw). Fried green tomatoes are one of my favorite summer foods: crackling crisp on the outside, creamy but tart on the inside, they're hard to beat. But frying isn't the only way Southern cooks have of dealing with green tomatoes: There are pickles, relishes, and chowchows for the pantry, and braised and boiled ones for the dinner table.

braised green tomatoes with onions

The firm flesh and sharp, tart flavor of green tomatoes make them ideal for braising. They hold their shape and texture well, and while the tartness is blunted by heat, it doesn't altogether disappear and makes a lovely contrast with the golden, meltingly tender sweetness of the onions. A touch of ham underscores the union, pulling all the flavors together.

2 pounds green tomatoes

Salt

1 large yellow onion, peeled and thinly sliced

1 tablespoon extra-virgin olive oil

4 ounces (about a ⅛-inch thick slice) country ham or prosciutto, cut into julienne

1 tablespoon chopped fresh thyme, or 1 teaspoon crumbled dried thyme

1. Wash the tomatoes under cold, running water, cut out the stems, and cut them vertically into wedges—quarters, if they're small, eighths if large. Put them in a colander set in the sink. Sprinkle generously with salt, toss well, and let drain for 30 minutes.

2. Pat the tomatoes dry. Warm the onion and olive oil in a large sauté pan or lidded skillet over medium-high heat. Sauté, tossing often, until the onion is pale gold, about 4 minutes.

3. Add the ham and tomatoes and sauté, tossing often, until the tomatoes are lightly browned,

about 4 minutes. Sprinkle the thyme over them, cover, and reduce the heat to medium. Braise, shaking the pan occasionally to prevent scorching, until the tomatoes are tender but still in distinct wedges, about 10–15 minutes.

Taste and adjust the seasoning, toss once more, and turn off the heat. Serve hot or at room temperature.

Serves 4

grill-broiled green tomatoes

This is one of the most elegant ways of cooking tomatoes that I know. Grilling concentrates the sweetness of ripe tomatoes, and enhances the tartness of green ones. It is most flavorful when the broiling can be done over hardwood coals, of course, but they are delicious even when the heat comes from the oven broiler.

4 medium or 2 large green tomatoes

Salt

2 tablespoons bacon drippings or
extra-virgin olive oil

Whole black pepper in a mill

1. Prepare a grill with hardwood coals and light them; or position a rack about 6 inches below the heat source and preheat the oven broiler for at least 15 minutes. Wash the tomatoes under cold water, pat dry, and cut them crosswise in half. Lightly sprinkle the cut sides with salt, invert them in a colander set in the sink, and let drain for 30 minutes.

2. Wipe the tomatoes dry. Lightly brush the cut side with drippings or oil and sprinkle with a generous grinding of pepper. If you're using the oven broiler, skip to step 3. Put them on the grill cut-side down and grill until lightly browned, about 6–8 minutes. Brush with more drippings or oil, turn, and continue grilling until tender, about 8 minutes more.

3. If you're using the oven broiler, put the tomatoes cut-side up in a broiling pan. Broil until the cut side is nicely browned, about 8 minutes. Turn carefully, brush lightly with more drippings or oil, and continue broiling until the tomatoes are tender, about 8 minutes more.

Serves 4

CHAPTER NINE

OF LEAVES AND LEFTOVERS

While it is not true that everything named "salad" in the South is by definition smothered in mayonnaise or suspended in gelatin, mayonnaise-dressed and congealed salads are still popular fare on Southern tables. This is not without reason: A rich, creamy mayonnaise gives new life to leftover meat, and a delicate and carefully made aspic is an elegant yet comforting thing to have on hand when the weather turns sultry—as the weather down South is prone to do. And since few Southern cooks care to waste anything, salads are a frequent route through which many a cold, leftover meat, vegetable, or fruit passes on its way to its final resting place. Mayonnaise- and aspic-based salads are an ideal vehicles for such leftovers, and while they may seem a bit old-fashioned, they're well worth getting over any prejudices they engender.

Even so, there are dozens of traditional Southern salads that contain neither mayonnaise nor gelatinous binders: The Southern salad bowl is host to a far more varied fare than that. The salads included here reflect that variety. They're also very flexible, equally as at home as a main course for a casual lunch or supper as they are as a first or salad course for a more formal dinner. Not a few can even be served away from the table altogether, with sturdy chips, crackers, toast, or celery sticks alongside for guests to scoop as often as they like.

Before we begin with the recipes, however, the following are two ingredients that most Southern cooks consider essentials.

homemade mayonnaise

Though this staple isn't found in every salad bowl, there's not a single Southern refrigerator without a jar of it lying in wait—to be tossed with leftover chicken or fish, dolloped over cold vegetables or meat, or slathered over a juicy tomato sandwich. Down here, commercial mayonnaise far outdistances the sale of catsup and mustard, and brand loyalties have been known to divide marriages faster than adultery. Those loyalties notwithstanding, however, the dividing line between good and spectacular is homemade mayonnaise. Making your own by hand may be a lot of work, but once you start doing it you'll never look back.

None of the options in the ingredients are to be considered arbitrary: Each produces markedly different results. The one you choose will depend to a large degree on how you plan to use the mayonnaise. A sauce made only with yolks is creamier and more delicate than one made with whole eggs, but whole eggs stand up better to the food processor and make a fluffier, lighter sauce. The choice of acid will not affect texture, but the flavor and balance depend on it. For any fish and most vegetables, lemon juice is the best choice, while wine vinegar gives mayonnaise meant for cold meat or boiled vegetable salads heft. Cider vinegar produces the most characteristically Southern flavor and is compatible with poultry or pork. As for the oil, if you find olive oil is too assertive (and an extra-virgin olive oil often is), choose one with milder flavor, or mix extra-virgin with a mild oil. My own preference is a blend of peanut and olive oil.

2 large egg yolks or 1 whole large egg

1 teaspoon dry mustard or 1 tablespoon Dijon-type mustard

1 teaspoon salt

Ground cayenne

1 cup olive or peanut oil, or ¼ cup extra-virgin olive oil and ¾ cup peanut oil

Juice of 1 lemon, or 2 tablespoons wine or cider vinegar

HAND METHOD

1. Put the yolks or whole egg in a mixing bowl with the mustard, salt, and a pinch of cayenne. Whisk until smooth.

2. Put the oil in a container that has a good pouring spout. Pour a teaspoon of it into the yolk mixture and whisk until it's incorporated. Begin adding the remaining oil a few drops at a time, beating until each addition is thoroughly incorporated before adding more. Keep at it until you've added half the oil.

3. Add a teaspoon of the lemon juice or vinegar and whisk it in, then alternate between the vinegar and oil until both are completely incorporated into the sauce. Taste and adjust the seasonings. Transfer the mayonnaise to a covered storage container or jar, and keep it refrigerated.

FOOD PROCESSOR METHOD

1. Use the whole egg for this method: It's sturdier and withstands the speed and heat of the food processor's blade. Put the egg, mustard, salt, a tiny pinch of cayenne, and lemon juice or vinegar in the bowl of a food processor fitted with a steel blade. Process until smooth, about 1 minute.

2. With the processor motor running, add ¼ cup of the oil in a very thin stream, then slowly add the remaining oil until it's all used, which will take between 1 and 2 minutes. Let the machine run for a few seconds more, then stop, taste and adjust the seasonings, and pulse a couple of times to mix. Transfer the mayonnaise to a covered storage container or jar, and keep it refrigerated.

Makes 1½ cups

VARIATION: CURRIED MAYONNAISE

Curry-scented mayonnaise is popular in the South as a dipping sauce for cold, cooked vegetables such as asparagus or whole artichokes, as a topping for tomato aspic, and as a binding sauce for chicken salad. To make it, fold 1–2 teaspoons of mild or spicy curry powder, to taste, into Homemade Mayonnaise (above) or your favorite commercial mayonnaise. You may also add half a clove of garlic, chopped and then pureed to a paste with a tiny pinch of salt and the edge of a knife blade.

toasted pecans

Fresh pecans are a popular addition to salads in the South. If they are very fresh indeed, I never toast them, so that their rich yet delicate flavor can shine through. If, however, the pecans are not quite so fresh, or the salad needs a little more crunch to the texture, a light toasting gives them just the right lift. Don't confuse these with Roasted Pecans (page 38). You may toast only as many nuts as you need for the recipe, or as much as a whole pound. Store those you don't use right away in the refrigerator.

Position a rack in the center of the oven and preheat to 375°F. Spread as many pecans as you plan to toast in a single layer on a rimmed baking sheet or metal pie plate. Toast, stirring once or twice, until the pecans are just beginning to color, about 8–10 minutes.

ambrosia with fresh coconut and cherries

This lovely fruit salad is synonymous with Christmas in the South, and usually does double duty as salad and dessert. But there's no reason to wait until Christmas to enjoy it, since nowadays good pineapples, oranges, and coconuts are available at other times of the year, and in summer you can give tradition a fresh twist by scattering cherries among the layers. Many Southern cooks have traditionally done this with maraschino cherries—more for color than anything else—but fresh cherries accomplish the same thing without that harsh manufactured taste that maraschino cherries tend to have.

Through the years ambrosia has been updated and subjected to worse indignities than maraschino cherries—canned fruit, rum, gelatin, nondairy topping, and a few things you don't want me to mention. But some things don't need to be messed with, particularly not something named for the food of the gods. Here is the classic.

1 small, fresh coconut with plenty of juice sloshing inside it

1 fresh ripe pineapple (the skin should be mostly yellow, but the top still bright green and healthy looking)

6 large sweet oranges

1 cup halved, pitted dark cherries, in season (optional)

Sugar, optional (see step 6)

1. Fit a large, fine-meshed wire strainer over a glass or stainless bowl. Punch a skewer, ice pick, or Phillips-head screwdriver through the stem scars that make the little monkey face on one end of the nut, tapping with a hammer until the utensil goes through to the center. Turn the nut holes-down over the strainer and drain it. Before going any farther, smell the juice—it should have a clean coconut fragrance. If it is musty or fermented, the coconut is bad. Break the coconut

open as follows: Lay the nut sideways on an unbreakable surface (a patio, bare concrete floor, or the front walk) and hammer firmly around the middle, rotating the nut until it splits. Or you can just throw the nut against the surface and it will shatter, but use caution—the shell scatters like shrapnel. Turn each half domed-end up and tap until they shatter. Pry the white flesh from the shell and remove its brown hull with a paring knife or vegetable peeler. Shred the nutmeat with the fine holes of a grater, rotary cheese grater, or fine-shredding blade of a food processor.

2. Holding the pineapple over the bowl of coconut juice to catch the juices, cut off the stem and sprout ends and peel it on the diagonal—this will get most if not all of the hard, brown dimples in the outer edges of the fruit. If it doesn't, scoop them out with the potato-eye scoop of a vegetable peeler or a V-shaped garnish-cutting tool.

3. Cut out the core and slice the pineapple into ¼-inch-thick pieces. The easiest way to do this is to cut the pineapple flesh from the core in vertical wedge-shaped sections. You can also use a special tool—a kind of corkscrew on steroids that's designed for the purpose. If your grocer has a commercial coring machine, they will peel and core the pineapple for you, which will save you the work and allow you to cut the pineapple into rings.

4. Cut off the stem and blossom ends of the oranges, cutting all the way through to the flesh, then, holding the fruit over the bowl of juices, peel them with a paring knife, just barely cutting through the outer membranes of each section. Cut the oranges crosswise into ¼-inch-thick slices and remove the seeds.

5. Cover the bottom of a glass serving bowl with a layer of oranges, sprinkle it well with a handful of the coconut, and cover it with a layer of pineapple. Scatter a few cherries among the pineapple (if you are using them) and sprinkle them well with coconut. Repeat with more oranges, coconut, and pineapple until all the fruit is used up. Reserve enough coconut for a thick finishing layer on the top.

6. Stir the reserved coconut, pineapple, and orange juice and taste it. Sweeten it with a few tablespoons of sugar, if needed, then pour it evenly over the ambrosia. Sprinkle the remaining coconut over the top and let the salad stand for an hour or so before serving. Store ambrosia in the refrigerator if you are not serving it soon thereafter.

Serves 6–8

tossed green salad with apple and pecans and clemson blue cheese buttermilk dressing

This salad is delicious made with other blue cheeses and the most commonplace of green onions, scallions; but it steps into another dimension when the cheese is Clemson Blue (see page 46), and the onions are green Vidalia Sweet onions, which have a bright, herbal flavor that the mature onions do not. Green Vidalia onions are seasonal in midwinter and early spring. Originally, both ingredients were only regionally available. But happily, nowadays they are enjoying a wider, national distribution. If you can't get them, scallions or other green onions make an acceptable substitute, and any blue other than stilton may be substituted for the Clemson Blue.

If the pecans you are using are very fresh (and you will know because they will be meaty and have a clean, mild flavor), use them raw. But if they are not as fresh as you would like, toast them as directed on page 232 or substitute walnuts in their stead.

1 firm, tart apple, such as McIntosh, Empire, Black Arkansas, or Granny Smith

4 medium green onions or scallions (see headnote above)

1 large head Boston or other leaf lettuce, or 5 cups mixed salad greens

1 tablespoon each chopped fresh thyme and sage, or ½ teaspoon each crumbled dried thyme and sage

1 cup Blue Cheese Buttermilk Dressing (recipe follows)

½ cup fresh pecans

Salt and whole black pepper in a mill

1. Wash and peel the apple, core it, and cut it into ½-inch dice. Wash and trim the green onions and thinly slice them.

2. Put the apple, onions, salad greens, and herbs in a large salad or mixing bowl. Pour the dressing over them and toss until they are lightly coated. Add the pecans, tossing until the pecans are mixed in and lightly coated with the dressing. Taste for salt and pepper, adjust the seasoning, and give the salad one last toss. Serve at once.

Serves 4

CLEMSON BLUE CHEESE BUTTERMILK DRESSING

This dressing is lighter and fresher tasting than most blue cheese dressings, due mainly to the fact that the acid used is buttermilk, which lends both a tart and a creamy element without adding a lot of fat. It not only is a wonderful dressing for the Tossed Green Salad with Apple and Pecans, but makes a fine dip for raw vegetables, and gives an interesting fillip to chicken salad.

4 ounces crumbled Clemson Blue cheese, or gorgonzola, Roquefort, or Danish blue cheese

¼ cup extra-virgin olive oil

1 medium clove garlic, mashed, peeled, and minced

¼ cup Dijon-style mustard

1½ cups whole-milk buttermilk

Salt and whole black pepper in a mill

1. Put half of the cheese in a mixing bowl. Mash the cheese with a fork, and gradually mix in the oil until smooth and creamy. Add the garlic and mustard and whisk until smooth.

2. Gradually beat in the buttermilk. Season with salt and a liberal grinding of pepper and mix until they're incorporated. Cover and let stand for at least 1 hour before using, then taste and adjust the seasonings. It can be made up to 3 days ahead; keep it covered and refrigerated.

Makes about 2½ cups

asparagus pecan salad
with honey-lemon bourbon vinaigrette

Asparagus is perennially a favorite ingredient in spring salads, and lightly cooked asparagus doused with a simple oil-and-vinegar dressing is a French and Italian classic that endures. Southern cooks love to pair the sprightly herbal flavors of this vegetable with a mix of sweet and tangy flavors. Here the tang comes from lemon, a natural complement for asparagus, the sweet from local honey, and the spice from a characteristically Southern dollop of mustard. The whole is underscored by the subtle, buttery bass note of toasted pecans. Use a light hand with all of them—asparagus is subtle, and needs subtle treatment if it's going to really shine.

FOR THE VINAIGRETTE:

¼ cup freshly-squeezed lemon juice

1 tablespoon Dijon mustard

1 tablespoon honey

1 teaspoon bourbon

½ teaspoon salt

Whole black pepper in a mill

½ cup extra-virgin olive oil

1 tablespoon finely chopped chives
or green onion tops

1 tablespoon chopped fresh thyme
or 1 teaspoon dried thyme

FOR THE SALAD:

1½ pounds asparagus, trimmed and peeled as directed on page 188 and cooked as for Basic Asparagus (page 190)

2 medium green Vidalia onions or scallions, trimmed and thinly sliced

½ cup sliced Toasted Pecans (page 232)

1. In a glass or stainless-steel bowl, whisk together the lemon juice, mustard, honey, bourbon, and salt. Add several liberal grindings of pepper and whisk it in. Gradually whisk in the oil, a spoonful at a time, until it is incorporated and emulsified. Whisk in the chives or onions and thyme and set aside for at least 20 minutes. Taste and adjust the seasonings, whisking until the seasoning is incorporated.

2. When you are ready to serve the salad, spread the asparagus on a platter or divide it among individual salad plates. Scatter the green onions and pecans over the asparagus and drizzle half the dressing over it. Serve at once, passing the remaining dressing separately.

Note: The vinaigrette can be made a day or so ahead. Cover and refrigerate until needed, but let it stand at room temperature for 30 minutes before serving. If it should separate, whisk until the oil is smooth again.

Chicken, Asparagus, and Pecan Salad: Chicken-pecan salad is a Southern classic that can be found on countless luncheon menus throughout the region. Give the classic a twist by using the previous recipe as a base. Cut the asparagus into 1-inch lengths and add 3 cups diced, cooked chicken and ½ cup each sliced green onions and diced celery. Toss all the ingredients with ½ cup dressing and mound it on four plates lined with lettuce leaves. Garnish with sliced green onion tops and pass the remaining dressing separately.

Serves 4

sweet potato salad with apples and raisins

Sweet potatoes are one of those vegetables that have always straddled the line between savory vegetable and sweet dessert. This salad straddles the line along with them, combining the classic flavors of a Southern autumn in a savory-sweet mix that is the perfect complement for the hefty stews and roasts of fall and winter.

2 pounds orange-fleshed sweet potatoes (sometimes labeled "yams")

¼ cup sherry vinegar or red wine vinegar

4 medium green onions (such as scallions), trimmed and thinly sliced

½ cup raisins

1 orange

1 tart apple such as Winesap or Granny Smith

Salt, sugar, and whole black pepper in a mill

1 tablespoon chopped fresh mint

1. Scrub the sweet potatoes under cold running water and put them in a large pot that will hold them in one layer. Add enough water to cover them by an inch and then lift out the potatoes. Cover and bring the water to a boil over high heat. Carefully slip the sweet potatoes into it, cover, and let it to return to a boil. Reduce the heat to medium and simmer until the potatoes are barely tender (a knife should go through without resistance). Drain well and let the potatoes cool enough to handle. They should still be very warm. Peel them and cut them into ½-inch cubes.

2. While the sweet potatoes are still warm, put them into a glass bowl. Sprinkle them with half the vinegar, toss gently, and then sprinkle on the rest. Add the onions and raisins and toss gently until they are well mixed. Cut the zest from the orange in thin strips with a bar zester or remove it with a vegetable peeler in wide strips; cut the strips into fine julienne. Add it to the salad. Cut the orange in half and have it close at hand. Peel, core, and cut the apple into dice a little smaller than the potatoes. Put the apple in a small bowl and squeeze some of the orange juice over it. Toss until it is coated, then add the apple to the salad. Squeeze a little more orange juice over the potatoes and toss carefully. Toss, taste, and season as needed with salt, sugar, black pepper, and orange juice. Let stand until cooled. It can be served at room temperature, or cover and refrigerate it if you are making it ahead or want it cold. Just before serving, add the chopped mint and gently toss until it is mixed in.

Serves 4

tomato and vidalia onion salad

This is one of the simplest and yet most satisfying summer salads in the world. It is very easy to make, exquisitely beautiful to look at, and delicious to eat, so long as the tomatoes are ripe and sweet and are seasoned with a light and careful hand.

4 medium or 3 large ripe tomatoes

Salt and whole black pepper in a mill

1 medium Vidalia or other sweet onion, trimmed, split lengthwise, peeled, and sliced as thinly as possible

Extra-virgin olive oil

Sherry vinegar (available at specialty grocers and kitchen shops)

½ cup loosely packed fresh basil leaves

1. Wash the tomatoes under cold running water. Cut out the stem, then core and peel them with a vegetable peeler. Slice them crosswise ¼ inch thick. Remove and discard the seeds, and spread the slices on a serving platter or four individual salad plates. Season lightly with salt and pepper.

2. Trim off the root and sprout ends of the onion, cut it in half lengthwise, peel each half, and slice it paper-thin. Scatter the onion evenly over the tomatoes. Season them lightly with more salt and pepper. The salad can be made half an hour ahead through this step.

3. Just before serving, sprinkle the tomatoes and onions to taste with olive oil and sherry vinegar. Cut the basil into fine chiffonade, scatter it over the entire salad, and serve at once.

Serves 4

florida chicken salad

Reminiscent of the lime-cooked seviches found throughout the Caribbean and Gulf rim, this chicken salad whispers of trade winds and sunshine, even on the dullest, iciest winter day. It's at its very best made with key limes, but such glories are only available for short periods of time, so it's a comfort to know that regular Persian limes work almost as well. The secret to any chicken salad is a light, judicious hand with the mayonnaise. Start with less than you think you will need and add it by teaspoonfuls until you have just enough to coat the chicken.

2 large, whole boneless chicken breasts

4–5 limes (see step 2), 1 thinly sliced for garnish

2 cups chicken broth

Salt

¾ cup finely chopped Vidalia or other sweet onion

⅓ cup Homemade Mayonnaise (page 230) or commercial mayonnaise

Whole black pepper in a mill or ground cayenne pepper

4–8 lettuce leaves

2 tablespoons thinly sliced chives or green onion tops

½ cup fresh raw pecans, or Toasted Pecans (page 232), sliced lengthwise in slivers

1. Trim the fat and cartilage from the chicken and rinse under cold running water. Pat dry.

2. Grate the zest from one of the limes and remove half the zest from a second one in large strips with a vegetable peeler. Cut the limes in half and juice them. Measure the juice and juice enough additional limes to make ½ cup plus 1 tablespoon juice.

3. Put ½ cup of the lime juice, the large strips of zest, and broth in a pan that will just hold the chicken comfortably in one layer. Bring it to a simmer over medium heat. Add a generous pinch of salt and slip in the chicken breasts. Bring to a simmer, reduce the heat to low, cover, and gently poach until the chicken is just cooked through, about 5–7 minutes. Turn off the heat (if you have an electric range, remove the pan from the burner) and let the chicken cool in the poaching liquid. Remove the chicken, strain the broth, and refrigerate it for another use.

4. Cut the chicken into bite-size pieces and mix it with the onion in a glass or stainless-steel bowl. Stir together the mayonnaise, reserved lime juice, and zest until smooth. Gradually fold about two-thirds of the dressing into the chicken, then add more by spoonfuls until the chicken is lightly coated. Taste and correct the salt; season to taste with black pepper or cayenne and mix well. Cover and refrigerate until ready to serve. The salad can be made a day or two ahead.

5. To serve, spoon the chicken onto the lettuce leaves and sprinkle with chives or green onion tops and pecans. Garnish with thinly sliced limes and serve at once.

Serves 4

savannah crab salad

Blue crabs are abundant in the marshes that surround Savannah, and fresh crab salad—a luxury elsewhere—is a standard here on restaurant, home, and picnic menus throughout the summer months, though nowadays the crab often comes from somewhere else. Good crab salad depends on two things: excellence in the crabmeat in the bowl and restraint in the cook. This is a delicate and sweet shellfish, so the seasonings that go into it must be carefully balanced. Strong flavors such as garlic, pickles, and hot pepper can all too easily overwhelm and bury that flavor.

The bonus is that the best meat for salad is the claw meat, which is also the least expensive. Although it requires more work (claw meat always has more bits of shell and cartilage that must be picked out), it's sweeter and more flavorful than premium lump backfin meat.

1 pound crabmeat, preferably claw meat

½ cup minced green onions (about 4, including both white and green parts)

2 tablespoons minced white celery (about 1 stalk from the heart of the head)

2–3 tablespoons drained nonpareil capers, optional

1 lemon, halved

2–3 tablespoons Homemade Mayonnaise (page 230) or commercial mayonnaise

Cayenne pepper and salt

6–8 small basil leaves

4–8 Bibb or Boston lettuce leaves, or 2 ripe avocados, peeled, split, and pitted

1. Pick through the crab for bits of shell and cartilage. Put it in a glass serving bowl, add the onions and celery, and capers (to taste) if using, and gently toss until they're evenly mixed.

2. Cut the lemon in half and squeeze the juice from one of the halves over the crab. Add 2 tablespoons of the mayonnaise and a pinch of cayenne. Toss gently until the mayonnaise is very lightly coating the crab. It should still be loose and crumbly, but if it's too dry, add just enough to make a very light coating—no more than a tablespoon. Taste for lemon juice, cayenne, and salt, adding more of each if needed. Cover and refrigerate until you are ready to serve. The salad can be made to this point as much as 6 hours ahead.

3. Just before serving, tear the basil into very small pieces and add them to the salad. Toss gently and taste one last time, adjusting the cayenne and salt if needed. Serve as soon as possible after the basil is added, over lettuce leaves or scooped into avocado halves. If you want to use avocados more decoratively, slice them and serve the salad on lettuce, with the sliced avocado decoratively arranged over or around each serving.

Serves 4 as a main course, 8 as a first course

duck and jerusalem artichoke (or celery) salad

This salad comes from Henrietta Stanley Dull, who was for decades the home economics editor of the *Atlanta Journal Sunday Magazine* and Atlanta's premiere authority on cooking. Her cookbook, simply titled *Southern Cooking*, first published in 1928 and revised in 1941, is still in print and is widely regarded as one of the most comprehensive records of Southern gastronomy. What is so striking about the book is not so much its rich store of historical recipes, but rather how fresh and contemporary the recipes remain today.

That's because Mrs. Dull was never afraid of going forward, and looked back to the past only as a means of keeping her equilibrium. This salad exemplifies that sensibility; the flavors here are very traditional and yet contemporary. While I've added my own touches, what you will taste is what Mrs. Dull intended that you should.

⅓ cup plain or tarragon red wine vinegar

1 teaspoon salt

Whole black pepper in a mill

1 tablespoon chopped fresh tarragon
or 1 teaspoon dried tarragon

⅔ cup extra-virgin olive oil

2 cups thin-sliced cooked duck, such as Grilled Duck Breasts with Warm Peach-Orange Marmalade (page 174), or 2 whole fresh duck breasts, boned but not skinned

2 tablespoons freshly squeezed orange juice (only if using fresh duck)

1 pound Jerusalem artichokes, or 8 ribs celery

4 green onions or scallions, trimmed and thinly sliced on the diagonal

1 small head leaf lettuce such as Boston or Bibb

2 tablespoons chopped parsley

1 large ripe orange, split lengthwise (but not peeled) and thinly sliced

1. Stir together the wine vinegar, salt, several liberal grindings of pepper, and tarragon in a stainless or glass bowl. Gradually whisk in the olive oil a few drops at a time until it is emulsified. If you are using leftover cooked duck, skip to step 4.

2. Wipe the fresh duck breasts with paper towels and put them in a shallow glass or stainless-steel bowl. Combine the orange juice and 2 tablespoons of the dressing and pour it over the duck. Cover and marinate, refrigerated, for at least an hour, or as long as overnight.

3. Drain the duck, discarding the marinade. Warm a large, nonstick skillet over medium heat. Do not add fat of any kind. When it is hot, raise the heat to medium-high, add the duck skin-side down, and sear well, about 2 minutes. Turn and sear the other side, about 2 minutes more. Lower the heat to medium-low and cook, turning occasionally, until done to suit you, about 1–2 minutes for rare, up to 10 minutes for medium-well. Be careful not to overcook. Remove the duck from the pan, allow it to cool completely, and thinly slice it crosswise.

4. Scrub the artichokes under cold running water, peel them, and cut them into bite-size dice. If you're using celery instead, wash and string it, then cut it into bite-size dice. Put the artichokes or celery in a glass or stainless-steel bowl with the green onions. Spoon half the dressing over them, tossing until lightly coated. Pour the remaining dressing over the duck and let it marinate for at least 30 minutes.

5. Separate the lettuce leaves and divide them among individual plates. Arrange the duck and marinated vegetables separately over the greens, sprinkle the parsley over all, and garnish with the sliced orange. Serve at once.

Serves 4

marinated shrimp and cucumber salad

Shrimp marinated in a spicy vinaigrette (locally called "pickled" shrimp) are standard fare on Carolina and Georgia Lowcountry tables throughout the summer. Many cooks keep a jar of them in the back of the refrigerator for emergencies or when it is just too hot to even think about dinner. We serve them for lunch, as an elegant supper on sultry summer evenings, and as a wonderful hors d'oeuvre either with drinks before dinner or at the table as a first course.

1½ pounds (headless weight) shrimp

Salt

½ cup freshly squeezed lemon juice

1 cup thinly sliced Vidalia or other sweet onions (about ¼ large onion)

2 tablespoons minced celery
(about 1 small stalk)

2 large or 3 small cloves garlic, crushed and peeled but left whole

1 small pod red hot chile peppers such as cayenne or serrano, stemmed, split, seeds and membranes removed, and minced

2 bay leaves, chopped if fresh, crumbled if dried

1 tablespoon chopped fresh thyme or oregano

1 tablespoon yellow or white whole mustard seeds

2 tablespoons extra-virgin olive oil

Whole white pepper in a mill

1 large or 2 small cucumbers

Bibb or Boston lettuce leaves, optional

1. Rinse the shrimp under cold running water and drain thoroughly. Fill a 4-quart pot about two-thirds full of water and bring it to a boil over high heat. Add a small handful of salt. Slip the shrimp into the water, cover, and count 2 minutes. They should be curled and pink; if so, they're done. Immediately drain and rinse them well under cold running water.

2. Mix together the lemon juice, onions, celery, garlic, chile pepper, bay leaves, thyme or oregano, and mustard seeds, and oil in a large glass or stainless-steel bowl. Peel the shrimp and add them to the bowl. Season them with salt and white pepper and toss gently until they are well coated with all the seasonings. Cover and refrigerate for at least 1 hour or up to 2 days.

3. Just before serving the salad, peel and thinly slice the cucumber. Toss it in a spoonful or so of shrimp marinade, and use it to garnish the salad. Serve cold, directly from the bowl, offering toothpicks or salad plates and cocktail forks, or line individual salad plates with lettuce, spoon the shrimp over them, and garnish with the cucumber.

Serves 4 as a main course, 6 as a first course, 8–10 as an hors d'oeuvre

classic shrimp salad

Shrimp salad is without doubt one of the great dishes of summer in the Deep South. It can, of course, be had at any time of year, and some regional restaurants offer it as a permanent fixture on their menus, but wise cooks know that it can only be at its best in summer, when the shrimp are in season and at their sweetest.

Making this classic is not complicated, but like most things that are simple, doing it well requires care with the details. The shrimp must be freshly caught, never frozen, and care must be taken to be sure they're properly cooked: "Boiled" in this case is not literal. They must cook quickly, but gently, and never actually boil.

The other main element is the dressing. When you've gone to the trouble of getting the best shrimp, and have cooked them with care, why spoil things with indifferent mayonnaise? Regardless of the brand slogans we're always hearing, the best is not going to come from a jar on the grocer's shelf. You're going to have to make it yourself. Once you have those details in hand, and use good judgment with the mixing and last-touch seasonings, the shrimp salad that comes to your table will be something to remember.

2 pounds (headless weight) shrimp

Salt

**¼ cup minced Vidalia Sweet onion
or ½ cup thinly sliced small green onions**

½ cup small-diced heart of celery

½–¾ cup Homemade Mayonnaise (page 230)

Ground cayenne pepper

1. Rinse the shrimp under cold running water and drain thoroughly. Fill a 4-quart pot about two-thirds full of water and bring it to a boil over high heat. Add a small handful of salt. Slip the shrimp into the water, cover, and count 2 minutes. They should be curled and pink; if so, they're done. Immediately drain and rinse them well under cold running water. Peel and, if they're large, cut them into two or three pieces, but leave small to medium shrimp whole.

2. Toss together the shrimp, onion, and celery in a large serving bowl until well mixed. Fold in enough mayonnaise to lightly coat the shrimp (you may not need all of it). Taste and season with salt and a dash or so of cayenne, toss well, then cover and refrigerate 30 minutes. Taste and adjust the seasonings, and return to the refrigerator until ready to serve.

To serve as a first course/appetizer (larger shrimp preferred for this): Divide the salad among eight scallop shells or washed and dried whole Bibb or Boston lettuce leaves. Lightly sprinkle with paprika and sprinkle with 1 tablespoon each minced parsley and thinly sliced chives. Serve with crackers, cheese straws, or buttered toast points.

To serve as a main dish: Serve exactly as the appetizer portions, but dividing evenly among only four to six plates (depending on what is to be served with it).

To use as a sandwich spread: Use only small shrimp or roughly chopped medium to large shrimp. Mix in 1 tablespoon chopped parsley or basil. Spread onto trimmed white or whole wheat bread, top with a second piece of trimmed bread, and cut on the diagonal into two triangles for luncheon portions, four for tea or reception portions.

Adding up: When the shrimp are perfect, they don't need to be complicated by too many things in the salad, but you might add a large, ripe tomato, peeled, seeded, and small-diced, or a cup of halved (or, if large, quartered) grape or cherry tomatoes. A tablespoon of finely chopped basil or chives is also a fine addition. Some love to add a couple of diced hard-cooked eggs, or a few boiled potatoes, cut into large dice.

Serves 4–6 as a main dish, 8 as an appetizer

CHAPTER TEN
THE SOUTHERN BREAD BASKET

Mama's Bread: They are simple words, homey and even a little saccharine; yet for Southerners nothing is more powerfully evocative than the idea of bread baked by our mother's hands. Whether it was cloud-light breakfast biscuits that virtually floated out of the bread basket, fragrant, buttery dinner rolls, velvet-smooth white bread sliced thick for toast or wafer-thin for dainty tea sandwiches, or a lusty brown loaf, rich with nutty whole meal and molasses, it lingers in our memories, firing the imagination. The notion is so powerful that the mere words beguile even those who have no actual memory of morning biscuits or still-hot homemade yeast bread.

Southern novelist and essayist Lee Smith captured this when she spoke in her soft, gentle drawl of her own mother's bread one crisp fall morning at a Southern Foodways Alliance symposium in Oxford, Mississippi. One the South's most lucid wordsmiths, Lee was at her fullest power as she poignantly talked of the aroma of that baking bread filling the autumn air, meeting her all the way at the school bus with the very essence of her mother's warmth and love. As she explained how, in baking that bread today, she brings a bit of her mother back to her, even the toughest curmudgeons were sniffling back tears. When she held up a handful of recipes, the old courtroom erupted like a feeding frenzy in a fish tank. Mind you, these were people who had never met Lee's mother nor caught as much as a whiff of her bread.

Part of that reaction was no doubt owed to a gifted novelist's way with words, but there's more to it than that. Because the South remained mostly rural until well into the twentieth century, good bakeries were historically rare, and the responsibility for the daily bread fell to the homemaker. "Lady"—that title once so highly prized by Southern women as a mark of grace, good manners, and breeding—literally means "the bread giver," and down here that subtext rings peculiarly true. Well into my living memory, when a mushy pre-sliced supermarket loaf had become a staple in every Southern pantry (some still insist that you can't make a decent tomato or pimiento cheese sandwich without it), women who weren't satisfied to put such insubstantial stuff in front of company, let alone their children, continued to make their own bread.

Unhappily, Lee's and my generation are the last to grow up with a baking mother or, for that matter, father. Today stay-at-home parents are rare, and as good bakeries pop up even in small towns across the region, home baking is becoming at best an occasional hobby. A colleague once remarked that this didn't worry him, because restaurants were keeping scratch-made biscuits alive. Ah, but no, they aren't. It's true that nowadays a basket of house-baked yeast bread and biscuits is standard fare on many public dining tables, and almost every fast-food diner offers biscuits by the sackful. But even if these could touch the goodness of home-baked bread—and they rarely do—I doubt seriously that our children's children will be slipping into misty-eyed eloquence over a restaurant yeast roll, let alone a drive-through biscuit.

A less attractive reason that home bread making, especially of biscuits, has lost ground, however, has less to do with time than sheer intimidation. For some reason people who have no fear of jumping headfirst out of an airplane are scared to death of biscuit dough. If you're one of them, take comfort in two things: The skills required are not difficult, and there's no such thing as a natural-born bread maker. I pride myself on being very good at it now, but my first biscuits were so dense they could have been used as targets for skeet shooting. The difference between that first batch and the ones pictured on page 261 is nothing more than a little patience and practice.

The recipes that follow are basics that anyone aspiring to be called a good Southern baker should master. They're by no means comprehensive, because every baker brings his or her own tastes, traditions, and prejudices to the bread bowl. All they require of you is a little time; what they give back may not be fully measured for a generation. But it won't be measured at all unless you take them into your kitchen, roll up your sleeves, and brave getting a little flour in your hair. So get in there and make some memories of your own.

The Keys to Good Southern Baking: Soft-Wheat Flour and Stone-Ground Cornmeal

Many ingredients essential to Southern baking, such as fresh buttermilk, lard, drippings, and first-quality butter, are necessary for all good Southern cooking, and a brief discussion of them can be found in the pantry section on pages 26–32. Ingredients that are unique to yeast bread are discussed where they're needed, with the yeast breads later in the chapter. However, there are two key ingredients without which a Southern baker would have a rough time: soft-wheat flour and stone-ground cornmeal, and we do well to begin with a little about them.

Soft-wheat flour: Whenever this subject comes up in one of my classes, people get confused because they see the word "wheat" next to flour and automatically think "whole grain flour." In this instance, we are not talking about unbolted, whole-grain flour but flour milled from a particular kind, soft winter wheat. The protein and gluten content of this grain is very low compared to those of hard red summer wheat, which is the kind from which bread flour is milled. Soft wheat is the type used for pastry flour and the fine double-zero flour used in Emilia Romagna's famed fluffy egg pasta. Once, soft winter wheat was the kind used all over the world, because red wheat was too hard for most millstones. It's still preferred in the South because its low gluten content is better for pastries, cakes, and bread leavened with baking powder.

All leavening in baking is achieved by trapped gas or air expanded by heat. In yeast dough, the gas is produced gradually by a living organism and requires an elasticity in the dough that gluten provides. Baking powder, on the other hand, produces the gas with an instant chemical reaction between an acid and an alkali; a strong, elastic dough would get in its way. Elasticity is also the enemy of tender pastry. Consequently, low-gluten soft-wheat flour is preferred for quick breads and pastries. Actually, it also makes excellent yeast bread: The bread may not rise quite as spectacularly, but it will have much more flavor.

American all-purpose flour is a blend, with flours from both types of wheat mixed together to get the best of both. With care, you can make very good biscuits, pastry, and cakes, with all-purpose flour, but for the best results, soft-wheat flour will help ensure perfect results every time. There are many regional brands within the South, but White Lily and Martha White brands are both nationally available, at the very least by mail order if you cannot find them locally (see page 417 for sources). Another good alternative is any national brand of pastry flour, since it is also made from soft-wheat.

Stone-ground cornmeal: Stone-milling (as opposed to modern steel roller-milling) corn is preferred because the stone crushes the kernels whereas steel rollers squeeze it. There's a distinct difference in texture. Water-stone-ground means that the millstone has been powered by water, as in those picturesque mills with a big water wheel. Those who swear by water power say it makes a difference because it's slower, but frankly I don't think that a kernel of corn can discern what powers the stone that is grinding it to bits.

There's a lot of debate about which is "truly" Southern: white or yellow meal. These debates are often heated and always entertaining, but in the end, silly. Both kinds of meal have historically been common in the South: while white was often considered the nicer of the two in most places, the preference for one over the other varied across the region. The real issue with cornmeal is freshness; it's far more important than color. It has more natural oils than bolted flour, making it far more perishable. While I personally prefer white meal, there have been times when I've actually chosen yellow because it was fresher than the white. Let your own tastes and local availability guide you and don't let some "authority" take you to task for it. If you can't get quality meal of any color, mail order sources can be found on page 417.

Plain versus self-rising: Flour and meal pre-mixed with baking powder and salt are very popular in the South. They're convenient and many good bakers swear by them, so what could be wrong in using them? Unfortunately, a lot: they're always over-leavened to prolong their usefulness, since baking powder goes stale quickly and loses its potency, and too much baking powder gives baked goods a harsh aftertaste. That's why I don't use or recommend them.

Baking powder: Too many people assume that baking powder is baking powder, but they're not all the same. The earliest form was single-acting, which means it worked through only a single, liquid-activated chemical reaction between an acid and an alkali—usually cream of tartar and baking soda. All modern baking powder is double-acting, which means it reacts in two stages: the first is liquid activated; the second is heat activated, causing a second rise in the oven. Unfortunately, it often leaves a harsh aftertaste, especially if it's overused. The recipes in this book were tested with both types, though I prefer the single-acting powder. If you use double-acting, however, look for an aluminum free brand such as Rumford for the best results and flavor.

Single-acting powder is no longer manufactured commercially. Fortunately, it's easy enough to make at home and a recipe follows. It's not as strong as modern double-acting powder, so if you're substituting it in a modern recipe, use roughly a third more single-acting powder than the double-acting powder called for. Regardless of which kind you use, always give the container a shake before you open it and measure out the powder: That which is on the very top of the can goes stale more quickly from having had more exposure to air, so shaking it up ensures that you'll get an even dose of potent powder.

single-acting baking powder

This does not keep well, so don't make it in any larger quantity than you will use in a month of making it.

3 tablespoons cream of tartar, available in many markets and drug stores

2 tablespoons bicarbonate of soda (baking soda)

3 tablespoons rice flour, cornstarch, or all-purpose flour

1. Combine all the ingredients in an airtight container and shake until thoroughly mixed.

2. Store tightly covered and away from moisture.

Makes ½ cup

southern skillet corn bread

For nearly two centuries, this skillet bread was the Southern staff of life and a staple on home tables and meat-and-three diners throughout the region. Often called egg bread because the batter was enriched with eggs (an ingredient rarely found in other Southern cornmeal breads), what set it apart and made it "Southern" was the fact it never contained flour or sugar. This is no longer true: Though there are still plenty of Southerners who staunchly maintain that corn bread should never contain either ingredient, there are a lot of our region's bakers, both at home and in restaurants, who produce corn bread so puffy and sweet that it more resembles cake than bread. But while I can no longer argue that "real" Southern corn bread "never" contains sugar or wheat flour, I don't have to like it. My first bite of those soft, sweet corn breads brings sharp disappointment; the second, weariness; the third (if I get that far) downright annoyance. What follows is the traditional bread: Its only unorthodox ingredient is olive oil, which makes surprisingly good corn bread for those who are avoiding animal fat.

2 cups fine stone-ground cornmeal

1 teaspoon salt

1 tablespoon Single-Acting Baking Powder (page 255) or 2 teaspoons double-acting baking powder

2 large eggs

1½ cups buttermilk or plain whole-milk yogurt thinned to buttermilk consistency with milk

4 tablespoons melted bacon drippings, unsalted butter, or extra-virgin olive oil, divided

1. Position a rack in center of the oven and preheat to 400°F. Heat a well-seasoned iron 10-inch skillet, 12-cup muffin pan, or two cornstick pans in the oven for at least 10 minutes. Meanwhile, sift or whisk together the meal, salt, and baking powder in a mixing bowl. In a separate bowl, whisk together the eggs, buttermilk, and 2 tablespoons of the fat.

2. Make a well in the center of the meal and pour in the liquids. With a wooden spoon quickly stir them together, using as few strokes as possible. It can be a little lumpy.

3. Remove the heated pans from the oven and put the remaining fat in the skillet or brush it generously into the wells of the muffin or cornstick pans with a heatproof pastry brush. Quickly add the batter, pouring it into the skillet or spooning it nearly level with the tops of the wells: it should sizzle as it hits the pan, or the pan isn't hot enough. Bake in the center of the oven until golden-brown and a toothpick inserted into the center comes out clean, about 30 minutes for the skillet cake, 20–25 minutes for muffins or cornsticks. Immediately invert the skillet over a plate and remove the bread, or invert the muffin/cornstick pans over a cloth-lined bread basket or clean towel. Serve hot with plenty of butter passed separately.

Crackling Skillet Bread: Cracklings are the solids left from rendering pork fat into lard. Using them to flavor bread goes all the way back to some of the great regional breads of Europe, and they've been used in corn bread at least since the early days of the Republic. To make crackling bread, substitute 1 cup cracklings, broken or chopped into small ½-inch pieces, for the 2 tablespoons fat in the batter of the preceding recipe, and cut the amount of fat for the skillet to 1 tablespoon. Mix the cracklings into the meal after whisking it together with the baking powder, soda, and salt.

Bacon and Onion Bread: Omit the drippings and add 4 extra-thick slices of bacon, diced; 1 onion, trimmed, split lengthwise, peeled, and diced; and 1 tablespoon chopped fresh sage or 1 teaspoon crumbled dried sage. Sauté the bacon in a skillet over medium heat until browned and crisp. Spoon off and reserve the fat, leaving 2 tablespoons in the pan. Add the onion and sauté, tossing often, until pale gold, about 5 minutes. Mix the bread as directed above up through step 2, adding the sage to the dry ingredients. Stir the bacon and onion and fat remaining in the pan into the batter. Finish as directed in step 3, using 2 tablespoons of the reserved bacon drippings as the fat in the skillet in which the bread will bake.

Makes one 10-inch round skillet cake or about 16 cornsticks or muffins, serving 4–6

hoecakes

These homely cornmeal griddle cakes are one of the oldest corn breads in the South, but they did a sad disappearing act for a time when America rediscovered crusty loaves of European-style breads and bakeries offering them began to be commonplace in the South. Fortunately, hoecakes have made a comeback and are nowadays offered even in many of our elegant white-cloth restaurants. You don't have to wait to visit one of those places to enjoy them, since they're very easy to make at home.

Traditionally, hoecakes were served as a bread accompaniment for the midday meal or supper, but they make excellent breakfast fare served with melted butter and syrup, molasses, jam, or honey. They're especially good served with greens of any sort, bean soup, gumbo, or any hearty meat or vegetable stew.

2 cups stone-ground cornmeal

1 teaspoon salt

1 tablespoon Single-Acting Baking Powder (page 255) or 2 teaspoons double-acting baking powder

2 large eggs, lightly beaten

2 cups whole-milk buttermilk or plain whole-milk yogurt thinned to buttermilk consistency with milk

4 tablespoons melted bacon drippings, unsalted butter, or extra-virgin olive oil, divided

1. Sift or whisk together the meal, salt, and baking powder in a mixing bowl and make a well in the middle. In a separate bowl, beat together the eggs, milk or yogurt, and 2 tablespoons of the fat, then pour it into the dry ingredients. Quickly stir it together into a fairly smooth batter, but don't worry if it is a little lumpy. Set aside for 10 minutes.

2. Warm a griddle or wide, shallow skillet over medium heat. When it is hot (water droplets flecked onto it should sizzle and dance), lightly brush with fat. Stir the batter again and pour it onto the griddle from the end of a large spoon in 2-tablespoonful-size rounds, leaving about an inch between. Cook until air bubbles begin to break the top surface at the center and the edges are beginning to set and brown. Turn and continue cooking until golden-brown on both sides. Remove the cakes to a warm platter and keep them warm while you cook the remaining batter.

Serves 4–6

southern breakfast biscuits

From at least the beginning of the nineteenth century until the middle of the twentieth, biscuits were standard breakfast fare in most Southern households. They were rarely seen at any other meal—and were never served at dinner. Today, while they're still a popular breakfast bread, they're also turning up in the bread basket of the most formal of dinners. Fast-food restaurants all over the South do a booming business in "from scratch" breakfast biscuits; white-cloth restaurants offer them all day long. But as they become more commonplace outside the home, the place that they're actually becoming rare is within it. This is too bad, because once you get the knack, they're very easy to make, and people always think you've gone to a lot more trouble than you have.

2 cups Southern soft-wheat flour or soft-wheat pastry flour

1 tablespoon Single-Acting Baking Powder (page 255) or 2 teaspoons baking powder

1 teaspoon salt

4 tablespoons (¼ cup) chilled lard (don't argue with me), cut into small bits

¾–1 cup whole-milk buttermilk or plain whole-milk yogurt thinned with milk to buttermilk consistency

1–2 tablespoons melted butter or milk, optional (see step 4)

1. Position a rack in the center of the oven and preheat to 500°F. Sift or whisk the flour, baking powder, and salt in a mixing bowl. Add the lard, and cut it in with a pastry blender or two knives until it's the texture of grits or polenta meal with lumps the size of small peas. Do not overblend; small lumps of shortening are what make biscuits flaky.

2. Make a well in the center and pour in most of the buttermilk. (You may not need quite all of it; a lot depends on the moisture content of the flour, the humidity of the day, and how good you have been. Biscuits are very judgmental.) Mix with as few strokes as possible until the dough clumps together and pulls away from the sides of the bowl, adding milk by the spoonful until the dough is no longer crumbly.

3. Turn it out onto a lightly floured work surface and pat out 1 inch thick. Fold it in half and pat it flat again. Repeat this twice more, then lightly flour the surface and roll it out ½–¾ inch thick. Using a 2-inch biscuit cutter dipped in flour before each cut, cut straight down without twisting into 12 biscuits. When cutting at the edges, be sure that there is a cut side all the way around the biscuits or they won't rise evenly. Lay them on an ungreased baking sheet; for very light, fluffy biscuits with soft edges, let them touch; for crisper biscuits (the kind I prefer), space them at least ½ inch apart.

4. There will be leftover scraps. To rework them, lightly gather them into a lump, gently fold it over itself, and pat flat. Pat and fold as before about three times, just until the scraps hold together, then pat it out ½–¾-inch thick and cut. To help the tops brown, you may brush them with milk or melted butter. Bake until they're risen and golden-brown on top, about 8–10 minutes. Serve piping hot.

Makes 12 biscuits

mama's olive oil biscuits

My mother, the Low-Fat Queen of the Universe, is always looking for ways to cut fat (especially animal fat) from her cooking. When good olive oil became readily available in the South, she started making biscuits with it and has never looked back. Most really traditional cooks raise a brow and shake their heads at the mention of Mama's biscuits—until, that is, they see how light, fluffy, and delicious they are.

2 cups Southern soft-wheat flour (see page 253) or soft-wheat pastry flour

1 tablespoon Single-Acting Baking Powder (page 255) or 2 teaspoons double-acting baking powder

1 teaspoon salt

2 tablespoons extra-virgin olive oil

¾–1 cup whole-milk buttermilk or plain yogurt diluted with whole milk to buttermilk consistency, divided

1–2 tablespoons melted butter or milk, optional (see step 4)

1. Position a rack in the center of the oven and preheat to 500°F. Sift or whisk together the flour, baking powder, and salt in a mixing bowl. Stir together the olive oil and ⅔ cup of the buttermilk.

2. Make a well in the center of the flour and pour in the buttermilk. Mix with as few strokes as possible until the dough clumps together and pulls away from the sides of the bowl, adding the remaining milk by spoonfuls until all the dough is no longer crumbly. You may not need quite all of the liquid; as with traditional biscuits, a lot depends on the moisture content of the flour and the humidity of the day.

3. Turn the dough out onto a lightly floured work surface and pat out 1 inch thick. Fold it in half and pat it flat again. Repeat five or six times, then lightly flour the surface and pat it out ½–¾ inch thick. Using a 2-inch biscuit cutter dipped in flour before each cut, cut straight down without twisting into 12 biscuits. When cutting at the edges, be sure that there is a cut side all the way around the biscuits or they won't rise evenly. Lay them on an ungreased baking sheet; for very light, fluffy biscuits with soft edges, let them on touch; for crisper biscuits (the kind I prefer), space them at least ½ inch apart.

4. There will be leftover scraps. To rework them, lightly gather them into a lump, gently fold it over itself, and pat flat. Pat and fold as before about three times, just until the scraps hold together, then pat it out ½–¾ inch thick and cut. To help the tops brown, you may brush them with milk or melted butter. Bake until they're risen and golden-brown on top, about 8–10 minutes. Serve piping hot.

Makes 12 biscuits

bacon and cracked pepper biscuits

A popular fixture of diner breakfast menus in the South is a fluffy breakfast biscuit stuffed with thick slices of bacon. That's not what we have here: These are crisp short biscuits made with bacon drippings for shortening. They were the pride of Miss Laurie LeGrand, the most unusual and eccentric neighbor I've ever known. Every election year, she ran for president on her own ticket, the National Maturity Party, which had, so far as we know, only one member: Laurie. Of all her eccentricities, the one I remember best was her deep and abiding affection for very dry martinis and almost anything that contained bacon fat.

Laurie unexpectedly died before sharing her recipe; this as close as I've been able to get. Rich with bacon fat and containing less leavening than most biscuits, these are crisp, flaky, and dangerously addictive. They're my tribute to her and to my other favorite fallen belles: Jill Conner Browne and her troupe of Sweet Potato Queens in Jackson, Mississippi.

2 cups Southern soft-wheat flour (see page 253), pastry flour, or all-purpose flour

1 teaspoon Single-Acting Baking Powder (page 255) or double-acting baking powder

1 teaspoon salt

6 tablespoons chilled bacon drippings (see notes)

½–⅔ cup whole milk

Whole black pepper coarsely ground

1. Position a rack in the upper third of the oven and preheat to 500°F. Put the flour, baking powder, and salt into a mixing bowl. Whisk together well, then cut in the fat with a pastry blender, fork, or knives until the dough takes on the overall texture of coarse grits or polenta, with occasional lumps the size of small peas.

2. Make a well in the center and pour in ½ cup of the milk. Mix with as few strokes as possible until the dough clumps together and pulls away from the sides of the bowl, adding more milk as needed by spoonfuls until the dough is no longer crumbly.

3. Turn onto a lightly floured work surface and pat out ½ inch thick. Liberally grind pepper over the dough and fold it in half. Pat it flat again and sprinkle with more pepper. Repeat twice more, omitting the pepper unless you want them really peppery.

4. Lightly flour the surface once more and roll or pat the dough out about ¼ inch thick. Using a 1½-inch-diameter biscuit cutter dipped in flour before each cut, cut the dough straight down, without twisting, into 12 biscuits. The scraps can be reworked with care (see Southern Breakfast Biscuits, page 260). Gather them together, lightly fold the dough over itself, and pat it flat about three times, until the scraps just hold together. Then pat the dough flat and cut as above. Put the biscuits on an ungreased baking sheet spaced ½ inch apart and bake until golden-brown, about 8–10 minutes. Serve piping hot.

Notes: An average piece of thick-sliced bacon (not the extra-lean kind, which is in general not worth your notice) will yield at least a tablespoon of rendered fat. Store drippings for the short term (3–4 weeks), well sealed, in the refrigerator, or for up to 3 months in the freezer. Frankly, they never last that long around here.

Makes about 12–16

flannel cakes

Also known as velvet cakes, these enriched, yeast-leavened griddlecakes were another commonplace on the American table that has all but disappeared. They fall somewhere between crumpets and a modern pancakes. Eaten hot off the griddle, with their delicate, velvety centers and crisp edges they are terrific for breakfast, supper, or—if you have that kind of leisure—an afternoon tea. They don't hold up well if they're allowed to cool or sit for too long in a warm oven, but they do reheat beautifully on a griddle, so you will want to save leftovers (or make an extra batch) and store them, well wrapped, in the refrigerator or freezer, for a quick breakfast or suppertime treat.

¼ teaspoon active dry yeast
or ½-ounce cake compressed fresh yeast

¼ cup lukewarm water

2 cups whole milk

2 tablespoons unsalted butter, plus more for greasing the griddle

2 large eggs, lightly beaten

10 ounces (about 2 cups) unbleached all-purpose flour

½ teaspoon salt

1. Dissolve the yeast in the water and let proof for 10 minutes. Meanwhile, scald the milk and 2 tablespoons butter in a heavy-bottomed saucepan over medium heat until the butter is just melted. Remove the pan from the heat and let it cool to less than 110°F.

2. Beat the eggs into the milk and stir in the water and yeast. Whisk the flour and salt together in a large mixing bowl, and gradually beat in the liquids. It will be the consistency of a standard pancake batter. Cover with plastic wrap and set in a warm place until doubled, about 3 hours.

3. Heat a griddle or wide, heavy-bottomed skillet over medium heat. Generously brush the griddle with butter and drop the batter onto it from the pointed end of a large spoon in 2-tablespoonful portions, forming cakes about 3 inches in diameter. Bake until lightly browned, about 4 minutes, then turn and bake until evenly browned and set at the center.

Yeast-Raised Waffles: This batter can also be used to make very good waffles. Heat the waffle iron to medium (about 350°F) and grease with butter or oil. Pour in the batter, leaving enough room on the edges for it to expand. Close the iron and bake until the steam no longer rises from the edges of the iron and the waffle smells toasty and is uniformly golden-brown, about 5–8 minutes.

Makes about 2 dozen 3-inch cakes, serving 4–6

cinnamon pecan drop biscuits

Cinnamon rolls are among the loveliest of breakfast breads, especially in autumn, when the crisp air picks up the rich, spicy aroma of cinnamon and toasted pecans and carries it more cleanly than at any other time of year. But yeast dough requires advance planning—something I have never been very good at. These biscuits have all the best elements of yeast rolls, but can be thrown together in minutes with almost no advance notice and without the tedious rolling and cutting into spiraled rolls.

1 small tart apple, such as Winesap, Arkansas Black, Empire, or Granny Smith

Juice from ½ lemon

½ cup raisins

½ cup chopped pecans

2 cups all-purpose flour

1 tablespoon Single-Acting Baking Powder (page 255) or 2 teaspoons double-acting baking powder

½ teaspoon salt

1 teaspoon cinnamon

½ cup light brown sugar

3 tablespoons cold unsalted butter, cut into small bits

1 cup buttermilk or plain whole-milk yogurt thinned to buttermilk consistency with milk, divided

Brown Sugar Glaze

1. Position a rack in the center of the oven and preheat to 450°F. Lightly butter a large baking sheet. Peel, core, and cut the apple into small (about ¼-inch) dice. Put it in a glass bowl with the lemon juice and toss well. Add the raisins and pecans and toss to mix.

2. Sift or whisk together the flour, baking powder, salt, cinnamon, and sugar. Cut in the butter with a pastry blender or two knives until it's the texture of grits or polenta meal with lumps the size of small peas. Do not overblend; small lumps of shortening are what make biscuits flaky. Add the apple, raisins, and pecans and toss until they're coated. Make a well in the center and pour in ¾ cup of the buttermilk. Quickly and lightly stir the mixture into a dough, adding milk by spoonfuls until it's no longer dry and crumbly.

3. Drop by 2-tablespoonful lumps onto the prepared baking sheet, spacing ½ inch apart. Bake in the center of the oven until golden, about 12 minutes. While still warm, drizzle with Brown Sugar Glaze and serve warm. They can be made a couple of hours ahead and reheated in a 250°F oven, but don't add the glaze until you're ready to serve them.

Makes 12 biscuits

BROWN SUGAR GLAZE

½ cup (tightly packed) light brown sugar

½ cup granulated sugar

½ cup whole milk

1 teaspoon Homemade Bourbon Vanilla (page 17) or vanilla extract

1. Stir the two sugars and the milk together in a small, heavy-bottomed saucepan until smooth. Bring it to a boil over medium heat, and cook until it barely reaches the soft-ball stage (230°F on a candy thermometer). Stir in the vanilla and remove the pan from the heat.

2. Cool for 3 minutes and immediately pour over the baked goods that are to be glazed.

Makes about 1 cup

sour cream cheddar drop biscuits

Drop biscuits are just about the easiest ones for novices to master. They require very little handling, so there's also very little chance of overworking the dough, and they are the most forgiving of an imperfect balance of moisture. These are doubly easy since, unlike most drop biscuits, there's no shortening to cut in: It's all contained in the liquid.

2 cups Southern soft-wheat flour (see page 253), pastry flour, or all-purpose flour

1 tablespoon Single-Acting Baking Powder (page 255) or 2 teaspoons double-acting baking powder

1 teaspoon salt

1 cup (about 4 ounces) shredded sharp cheddar

1 cup sour cream

2–4 tablespoons buttermilk (as needed— see step 2)

1. Position a rack in the center of the oven and preheat to 450°F. Lightly grease a 9 x 13-inch baking sheet. Sift the flour, baking powder, and salt into a mixing bowl. Add the cheese and toss until it is evenly distributed and lightly coated.

2. Make a well in the center and add the sour cream and 2 tablespoons of the buttermilk. Quickly and gently work the wet ingredients into the flour mixture, using as few strokes as possible. The dough will be firm but not crumbly. Work in a spoonful or so more buttermilk as needed until the dough is holding together. Drop in heaping 2-tablespoons-size mounds onto the prepared baking sheet, spacing them about an inch apart, and bake until risen and golden, about 8–10 minutes.

Makes 12

old-fashioned popovers

These are so easy to make it's almost embarrassing—so easy, in fact, that one can't help wonder why they are rarely seen nowadays. Don't take them seriously: Being too careful and overmixing will result in bread that's too even to "pop" into the airy, hollow puffs that give the bread its name and make it so delightful to eat. Traditionally served for breakfast or tea, popovers make delicious dinner rolls, and are a fine thing to have with lunchtime soup or salad.

Unsalted butter

1 scant cup all-purpose flour, measured by spooning flour into cup after sifting or whisking it (page 273)

1 teaspoon salt

2 large eggs

1 cup whole milk

1. Position a rack in the center of the oven and preheat to 450°F. Generously butter an eight-well standard muffin tin and put it in the oven to heat.

2. Whisk together the flour and salt. In a separate bowl, beat the eggs until light but not too fluffy. Stir in half the milk until smooth. Gradually mix in the flour, then the remaining milk. Don't use a whisk or beat the batter at this point—overbeating will give the bread a texture that is actually too even and regular. Pour the batter into the hot muffin tin, filling the wells only two-thirds full. Bake in the center of the oven for about 15 minutes without opening the oven.

3. Again, without opening the oven, reduce the heat to 350°F and bake until the popovers are crisp and golden-brown, about 20–25 minutes longer. If you take up the popovers before they are done, they will collapse, so make sure the sides are firm and crisp. They'll still taste good, but won't have the wonderful airy quality that is the hallmark of a well-made popover. Serve hot.

Makes 8

yeast bread

Yeast Bread Basics

Unlike baking powder breads, which depend on a chemical reaction for leavening, yeast bread is a living thing. All yeast, even the active dry variety, is a live organism. As it grows, feeding on the moist bread dough, it produces gas that is trapped by the elastic strands of gluten. The yeast of course dies in the oven, but it needs to stay alive until its last wild burst of growth, so the dough must be given proper care. If you are an experienced yeast bread baker, you probably don't need any of the following notes, but they'll be useful for novices and occasional bakers.

The Ingredients

Yeast: There are three types of yeast used in modern baking—active dry yeast, compressed fresh yeast, and homemade sourdough starter. All have unique properties of their own, but first, a few words about using modern yeast in general. After active dry yeast was introduced in the last century, it became almost axiomatic that most American yeast bread recipes contained too much of it. Why is open to speculation, but most likely it was in part a misreading of old recipes that used weaker, less stable homemade yeast cakes, and in part a failure to understand just how powerful and active dry yeast actually is.

Homemade "patent" yeast used in early America was made with a fermented paste of water, hops, flour, cornmeal, and brewer's yeast. It was spread on a pan, dried slowly in a shady spot, and cut into small, even cakes. To use it, one of these cakes was dissolved in the water or scalded and cooled milk needed for the dough, which is why recipes often called for "a tumbler of yeast." While it was fairly stable and reliable, it wasn't nearly as powerful as active dry yeast. The equivalent of a cake of patent yeast is a mere ¼–½ teaspoon of active dry yeast. Fortunately, modern bakers have a better understanding of dry yeast, and are using much smaller doses. Just keep in mind that while the first rising is slow, it occurs on its own time, requiring nothing of the baker but a warm, draft-free spot and protection from drying out. It can mostly be left unattended to work its magic while you go about your business. During that first rise, the yeast multiplies on its own, so the final rise after the shaping will go quickly.

Here are a few pertinent notes on the yeast varieties used in this book.

Active dry yeast: This is the kind of yeast most of us have to be content with, the kind most commonly found in every supermarket. It works fine as long as it isn't overused. A scant quarter teaspoon of active dry yeast (roughly equal in strength to a modern ½-ounce cake of fresh compressed yeast) is ample to leaven dough made up with up to 20 ounces (4 cups) of flour. Look for preservative-free yeast (most of them are nowadays), make sure the expiration date is at least 6 months ahead of the purchase date, and only buy as much as you will use in a short period. You can freeze it, but that doesn't save it indefinitely. Make sure that the yeast has been stored properly in the store, preferably on a lower shelf (where it's usually kept cooler), away from direct sunlight. The best place to keep it at home is in the refrigerator, especially after it's opened.

Rapid-rise or instant dry yeast: This type of active dry yeast has been engineered to grow like mad during the first rise so that it takes much less time without the sour bite of over-yeasting. Many good home bakers—my mother included—have used it successfully, but I rarely care how long the first rise takes, and I adhere to the belief that a slow fermentation makes better bread in the long run, so I've never really used the stuff.

Compressed fresh yeast: The kind used by professional bakers, fresh yeast is superior to active dry yeast, but it's no longer easy to come by. A few specialty markets still sell it and it's available through some baker's catalogs, but it's highly perishable and therefore few supermarkets carry it. Once professional bakers could be persuaded to sell you a little, but nowadays even that's rare. If you do find a source for fresh yeast, buy only what you can use within a couple of weeks and keep it refrigerated. Look for an even creamy tan color and a clean yeasty smell. Avoid any that is dry, crumbly, gray, and sour smelling.

Sourdough: This homemade yeast is a soupy batter made with potato and sometimes flour. Because it's fermented, it lends a mild tanginess to the finished loaf, hence the name. It's discussed in some detail in the section on breads that are made with it.

Flour: Contrary to popular belief, bread flour is not always the "best" flour for yeast baking. While it is true that its high gluten content makes for well-risen bread, volume is not the only mark of a well-made loaf. Each type of flour has its own advantages: Soft-wheat flour gives bread a fine texture and superior flavor; hard wheat's high moisture absorption increases the bread's shelf life; for some breads, a blend of the two (all-purpose flour) strikes the best balance of volume, texture, and flavor. Each recipe will tell you which type to use. But what matters most is quality and freshness. Flour is an organic substance that eventually decays and goes rancid. Make sure that it is sweet and "wheaty" smelling: If it smells sharp and a little sour, throw it out.

Water: The most elemental ingredient in all cooking, water is often taken too much for granted. Yet its quality can affect all cooking and drastically affects yeast baking. If you use treated water (and nowadays, most of us do), it's a good idea to filter it or use bottled spring- or distilled water for yeast baking; while some lingering chemicals in treated water may not harm you, they can harm yeast. Many American recipes specify heated water—or, worse, warm tap water, which usually contains traces of the anti-corrosive chemicals that domestic water heaters contain. Yeast seems healthiest when dissolved in water that is at room temperature (between 70 and 75°F) and in any case less than 110°F. If you are making bread in the winter and the water is cold, or you want to give the yeast a boost, warm it briefly and let it cool to less than 110°F.

Milk: Often used in enriched breads, milk produces a lighter, softer crumb that keeps fresh longer. It also adds subtle flavor. All the old recipes called for the milk to be scalded because it contained enzymes and organisms that inhibit yeast growth. Pasteurization has taken care of that, but the yeast will still perform better if the milk is warmed first. Always let it cool to less than 110°F before adding the yeast.

Salt: While salt adds flavor to bread, and a certain amount of it helps control the fermentation, too much of it can damage or even kill the yeast, so take care not to overuse it. Use pure sea or kosher salt. The latter is flaked and won't measure the same as table or fine salt, so if you use it, crumble it between your fingers before measuring. I generally use kosher salt for cooking and refined sea salt for baking.

Sugar and other sweeteners: The only thing any sweetener properly lends dough is sweetness. It's neither necessary nor desirable as food for the yeast. In part because of the lower natural sugar content of modern milled flour, many began adding small doses of sugar to boost the initial rise, but the yeast doesn't need it, and I find the artificial stimulation does the bread no good in the long run. Unless the bread is meant to be sweet, sugar is unnecessary.

The Process

Measuring: Most of the recipes in this and the cake and pastry chapter use weight measures, because it's by far and away the more dependable method of measuring flour. Even that isn't absolutely foolproof: moisture content (which affects weight), and absorbency (which affects the ratio of liquid to flour), can vary a little, even within the same bag of flour. A lot depends on how well-sealed the storage container is and on the ambient humidity of the day. But weighing is far less likely to lead you astray. In the end, however, the best and only truly reliable measure is the feel of the dough. That is one reason I always recommend a brief hand kneading for any dough that is made in a machine. The machine can't tell you when the dough is too slack or too stiff, but an experienced pair of hands will detect instantly. Take the time to learn not only how the dough should look, but how it should feel under your fingers.

Sifting and whisking dry ingredients: Sifting does two things: It evenly mixes dry ingredients and aerates the flour. In yeast baking, aerating the flour (as sifting before volume measuring is intended to do) is rarely necessary; the object here is simply to mix, and that's more easily done with fine wire whisk in the bowl.

The sponge: In classic French, English, and early American bread making, the yeast was often activated in a thin batter or sponge. Within that moist, warm environment, the yeast thrives and multiplies naturally, making for a stronger, more active yeast growth all around. The sponge also makes it possible to leaven dough with far less processed yeast. You can make acceptable bread by omitting the sponge process, and not all the recipes in this chapter call for it, but almost any bread is the better for having been started with one. In the bread recipes that call for a sponge, it's buried in the rest of the flour, both to prevent its surface from crusting and to facilitate the final mixing. I often mix the sponge in the food processor and put the flour on top, but the more traditional method is to bury it within the bowl, with a third of the flour on the bottom, the sponge in the middle, and most of the remaining flour on top. Hold back a little to use in the kneading.

Mixing and kneading: Food processors and mixers are fine gadgets, saving a lot of labor and making the modern cook's job easier. Few of us make breads and cakes often enough to have the strength and stamina in our hands to cream butter, beat cake batter, or stir flour into a dough that is too slack to knead by hand. However, they do have their drawbacks, especially in bread making. They cannot tell you when the dough is too slack or too stiff (unless of course the dough is so stiff that it stops the motor), and it is possible, though not likely, to overwork dough in a machine. They're great for mixing a soupy sponge, batter, or sticky dough such as Sally Lunn or challah. But even with those, the machine doesn't make the process carefree: You still need to pay attention  and sometimes get your hands a little sticky by feeling the dough or batter to be sure of its consistency. Food processors especially can make overworking the dough more likely, overheating and damaging the glutens. Even when I've used one to mix the dough, I still turn it out and finish the kneading by hand. The mixer's dough hook will do a better job of kneading than the food processor's dough blade, but you should still give it a few turns by hand, just to make sure of its consistency. Whether you do all or only part of the kneading by hand, this is not a time to have a temper fit or take out your aggressions because the dough will suffer for it. I put on music that will get me in a good mood if I'm not already in one, and help me set a good rhythm in the kneading. Next, find a rhythm and motion that's comfortable for you. There's really no single right one—the object is to evenly distribute the moisture and activate the glutens. I put the dough on a lightly floured surface, take the heels of both hands and push it away from me to stretch and flatten it, and then I double back the end that is farthest from me, like folding a sheet of paper or a towel, press it down with the heel of my hand, and give it a quarter turn. I repeat this until the dough settles into a smooth ball and its surface springs back when pressed with a finger.

Preparing the oven: While a baking stone offers real advantages to all baking, it's all but essential to good yeast baking. It will make all the difference between merely good and great bread. Even pan-molded loaves and rolls bake more evenly on the stone's even, radiant heat. To outfit your oven with it, position a rack to the lowest position in the cold oven and put the baking stone on it. Set the oven to the temperature required in the recipe and preheat at least half an hour. Never put the stone into an oven that is already hot (this could cause it to break), and always allow time for it to heat completely. If you need to take it out of the oven, let it cool completely before doing so. To even out an especially erratic oven chamber, you can just leave your stone in the oven all the time. The only time I take mine out is when I'm doing high-temperature roasting.

To create the supplemental steam needed for yeast bread baking that the old domed chambers trapped naturally, spray the bread itself and the oven floor with a little water in a clean spray bottle, or put a small rimmed metal pan on the floor of the oven and toss about ¼ cup water into it after you've put the bread on the stone. Be careful not to throw large amounts of cold water directly on the stone or heating element.

When is it done? The most common way of judging doneness is when a tap on the bottom of the loaf gives off a hollow sound. It will work if you bake enough, but it can lead you astray, especially with enriched, dense breads. The most foolproof way is to use a reliable instant-read thermometer to gauge the internal temperature.

classical southern wheat bread

This is the bread that the European colonists brought with them when they settled along the eastern seaboard. It had been the daily bread of the European upper classes at least since the fourteenth century, and until the mid- to late nineteenth century it was our daily bread as well. As the old brick ovens gave way to cast-iron ranges and then mechanized bakeries, however, this bread also gave way to pan-molded loaves of increasing puffiness and decreasing character. Today, as artisan bakers bring back many wonderful breads, this deserves its place among them.

This dough formula was the standard one in all the old cookbooks, used for all the early hand-molded loaves, from Mary Randolph's topknotted hard rolls to the baguettes of French Creole New Orleans. Following it are directions for molding and baking a few of the common shapes. Though I prefer to bake directly on the stone, it can also be baked in loaf pans if you want a more regular, compact loaf to slice for sandwiches.

Wheat, in this case, just means "wheat flour": Since corn bread was so commonplace, Southerners historically distinguished yeast-leavened bread from it by variously calling it white, light, or wheat bread. That last is especially confusing for modern Americans, since today "wheat" automatically means whole grain. But while I've included a little whole wheat flour in the dough, it's only to approximate the character that it would have had when made up with the kind of stone-milled white flour that early American cooks would have had: it's still "white" bread.

¼ teaspoon active dry yeast, or ½-ounce cake compressed fresh yeast

1½ cups water, at room temperature

20 ounces (about 4 cups) unbleached all-purpose flour or bread flour, including 1 ounce (about ¼ cup) whole wheat pastry flour

1 rounded teaspoon salt

1. In a large glass or ceramic mixing bowl, dissolve the yeast in the water and let proof for 10 minutes. Stir in 1½ cups of the flour, beating until smooth, and cover it with all but 1 cup of the remaining flour. Sprinkle the salt over the top and cover the bowl with a damp, double-folded linen towel or plastic wrap. Let it sit in a warm draft-free spot until the starter has doubled and made deep fissures in the dry flour, about 4 hours.

2. Work in the top flour, then turn the dough out onto a lightly floured work surface and knead it until it's elastic and smooth, gradually adding the remaining cup of flour as needed, about 8–10 minutes. It should spring back when you press it with a finger. These first two steps can be done in a food processor fitted with a plastic blade. Refer to the notes at the end of the recipe.

3. Gather the dough into a ball, lightly flour it, and put it back into the bowl. Cover with a damp double-folded towel or plastic wrap. Let it rise until doubled, about 4–6 hours. In a fairly cool spot, it can be left to rise overnight.

4. When the dough has doubled, turn it out onto a lightly floured surface and knead it lightly for a minute or two, until it is smooth again, but don't work it too much at this stage. It is now ready for shaping and baking as directed in any of the recipes that follow.

Notes: The mixing and initial kneading can be done in the food processor. Fit the processor bowl with the dough blade and put in the yeast and water. Pulse to mix and let it proof for 10 minutes. Add 1½ cups flour and process until smooth, about half a minute. Scrape down the sides, add all the remaining flour, sprinkle the salt on top, and replace the cover. Let it stand until the starter is doubled. Process until the dough forms into a ball. Let it knead for a minute in the machine, then turn the dough out onto a floured surface and finish the kneading by hand: That's the only way to know for certain that it's the proper consistency, and I think it produces a better texture.

The following are three of the most common ways that this dough was shaped and baked. For all of them, you'll need water in a clean spray bottle that hasn't been used for cleaning or laundry sprays, a baking stone, and a baker's peel (pizza paddle).

For 1 round loaf, 2 baguettes, or about 12 large rolls

the round cast loaf

This is the simplest loaf to accomplish with the basic dough. It makes a lovely, crusty round that is very satisfying to eat as is, but also makes wonderful toast and croutons.

1 recipe Classical Southern Wheat Bread dough (page 276)

1. After the second kneading in step 4 of the dough recipe, shape the dough into a ball, pinching where it was gathered to seal it, and lightly dust all sides with flour. Put it pinched-side down on a baker's peel lightly dusted with coarse meal, rice flour, or semolina, cover with a damp towel, and let rise until doubled. (I do this on top of the range while my oven heats; it takes about an hour. It will take longer if your oven isn't under the cooktop.)

2. Meanwhile, prepare the oven with a baking stone and pan as directed on page 275. Preheat it at 450°F while the bread does its final rise, but no less than half an hour.

3. Slash the dough in a tic-tac-toe pattern with a single-edged razor, batard knife, or sharp chef's knife. Slide the peel onto the baking stone and with a quick, sure jerk pull it out, leaving the dough on the stone. Lightly spray the bread and oven floor with water, being careful not to spray the heating element or stone.

4. Bake 15 minutes. Reduce the heat to 400° and bake 15 minutes more, then check to make sure that the bread is not browning unevenly. If it is, put on a pair of oven mitts and turn the loaf carefully. If it's browning too quickly, reduce the temperature to 350°F. Bake until it is nicely browned and reaches an internal temperature of 200–210°F or gives off a hollow thump when you tap the bottom, about 15 minutes more. Cool the loaf on a wire rack.

For 1 round loaf

old virginia hard rolls

This is the way bread came to the table in the upper-class households of old England, where the rolls were called manchets, and later, in Colonial Virginia, where Mrs. Randolph recorded the method in *The Virginia House-Wife*. The top of the dough was slashed in a circle, so that the finished loaf had a topknot. You can simply slash them in an X if that's easier for you: The history police aren't going to come after you. Originally, the rolls baked directly on the brick oven floor, which is still the best way, but it takes a little finesse to accomplish, and you may bake on a parchment-lined baking sheet if you prefer.

1 recipe Classical Southern Bread dough (page 276)

1. After the dough has been kneaded the second time in step 4 of the master recipe, above, pull off small handfuls and make them into balls about 2 inches round. Place them on a baker's peel lightly dusted with cornmeal, rice flour, or semolina flour, or onto a lightly greased baking sheet. Cover it with a damp linen towel and let it rise until it is doubled once again.

2. Prepare the oven with a baking stone and pan as directed on page 275. Preheat it at 450°F for at least half an hour while the rolls go through the final rise.

3. Be ready to work quickly, so as not to let the oven lose too much heat. Quickly slash the center of each roll in a deep circle (this will form a topknot) or simply slash with an X. Slide the rack with the stone carefully out as far as it will go without tipping. With a quick jerk of the peel, deposit the rolls on the stone, or quickly put them on it one at a time, allowing space around each for the final bursting rise. Slide the rack back into the oven and spray the rolls and oven floor with water, being careful not to spray the heating element. (Using the peel for rolls takes practice, but it's the best way if you can master it. If you prefer, you may bake them on a parchment-lined baking sheet, placing the pan directly on the stone.) Bake until the rolls are well browned and give off a hollow thump when tapped or reach an internal temperature of 200–210°F, about 20 minutes. If they're browning too quickly, turn the heat down to 400°F.

For about 1 dozen large rolls

creole baguettes

In the Creole communities of New Orleans, it isn't just the cooking that mirrors old France; the daily bread reflects French practice as well. Under the surface it was the same basic dough as was baked into the round loaves of England and early Virginia.

1 recipe Classical Southern Wheat Bread dough (page 276)

1 large egg white beaten with 1 tablespoon water, optional

1. After the last kneading in step 4 of the master recipe, divide the dough in half. Lightly flour a work surface and pat each half into a long rectangle about 12 inches long and ½ inch thick. Roll the two long sides inward to the middle, then gently pinch them together at the seam. Lightly roll each loaf into a sausage shape a little thicker than 1 inch. Lay them on a baker's peel lightly dusted with cornmeal, rice flour, or semolina, cover with a damp linen towel, and let rise until doubled. Meanwhile, prepare the oven with a baking stone as directed on page 275 and preheat at 450°F for at least half an hour.

2. Check to be sure the baguettes aren't sticking to the peel. If you want a glossy finish, brush lightly with the egg-white-and-water mixture. With a single-edged razor, batard knife, or sharp chef's knife held almost parallel to the surface, make three or four quick, sure diagonal slashes in each. Deposit them onto the baking stone with a quick jerk of the peel and spray the bread and oven floor with water, being careful not to spray the heating element or stone. Bake 15 minutes, lower the heat to 400°F, and bake until they're nicely browned and reach an internal temperature of 200–210°F or sound hollow when thumped on the bottom, about 15–20 minutes more.

Notes: Baguettes can be baked on a parchment-lined baking sheet or in trough-shaped pans specially made for baguettes, but I prefer the character that baking directly on the stone achieves.

Makes 2 baguettes

carolina rice bread

This is one of the world's finest regional breads. Low-country cooking authority John Martin Taylor says it was once the daily bread of Charleston, and has crusaded for years to restore it to its place. Almost every Charlestonian who tastes it can't imagine how a city that lives on traditions could have let one this delicious slip through its fingers.

The practice of supplementing expensive wheat flour with other, less costly grains or mealy potatoes, nuts, or peas is ancient. Historian Karen Hess, who wrote a thorough, loving history of this bread in *The Carolina Rice Kitchen*, believed that adding rice originated in colonial Carolina. Here the rice does much more than just add bulk; its inherent moisture makes a remarkably tender loaf that keeps moist and sweet for at least a week—no small feat in the Lowcountry's hot, humid climate. The recipe is from Sarah Rutledge's *The Carolina Housewife*, 1847. The only change I've made is to cut the original quantities by half, which I find easier to handle and is about as much bread as my small household can eat in a week.

1 quart water

½ pound long-grain rice, washed and drained (see notes below)

2 teaspoons salt

½ teaspoon active dry yeast, or ½-ounce cake compressed yeast

2 pounds (about 7 cups) unbleached all-purpose flour, including ¼ cup whole wheat pastry flour

1. Put the water in a large, stainless-steel pot that will later hold all the ingredients; bring it to a boil over medium-high heat. Stir in the rice and salt. Let it come back to a boil and reduce the heat to a slow simmer. Cook, uncovered, until the rice is soft and most (if not all) of the liquid is absorbed. Remove the rice from the heat and let it cool to less than 110°F. (The center should be warm but not hot when you stick your finger into it.)

2. Gently stir the yeast into the rice and let it stand for about 10 minutes. Add about half the flour and work it in. You'll think something is terribly wrong, that you'll never get it all worked in, but keep at it: The rice will be sticky and soft again in no time. Keep adding flour by the handfuls until the dough is too stiff to stir, then sprinkle a work surface with flour and turn the dough out onto it. Gradually knead in the rest of the flour. Again, at first you will feel as if something is terribly wrong, that you'll never get that much flour worked in, but keep at it.

3. When all the flour is worked in, knead 8–10 minutes. It will be slightly sticky, but don't add more flour than is necessary to keep it from sticking to the work surface. Gather into a ball, dust with flour, and put into a large ceramic bowl. Cover with a damp, double-folded linen towel or plastic wrap and set aside until doubled.

4. Punch down and turn onto a lightly floured work surface. Give it a light kneading, 1–2 minutes. Shape it into either a single ball for a cast loaf or two ovals for pan loaves, and dust it with flour. Put the single ball on a baker's peel lightly

dusted with rice flour or semolina; put the ovals in two lightly greased 9-inch loaf pans. Cover with a damp towel and let it rise until doubled (I do this on top of the range while the oven preheats). Prepare the oven with a baking stone as directed on page 275 and preheat for at least 30 minutes to 450°F.

5. Slash the tops with a single-edged razor blade, batard knife, or sharp chef's knife, a tic-tac-toe pattern for the round, or down the center for pan loaves. Slide the round onto the stone with a sharp jerk of the peel or put the pans directly onto it. Spray the dough and oven floor with water, being careful not to spray the heating element or stone, and bake 15 minutes. Reduce the temperature to 400°F, bake 15 minutes more, and check: If it seems to be browning too quickly, reduce the heat to 350°F. If you're baking in pans, for a crustier finish John suggests removing the bread from the pans and returning it to the oven "naked" for the last half hour. Bake to an internal temperature of 180–190°F, or until golden-brown and hollow sounding when thumped on the bottom, about 30 minutes more. Let cool on a wire rack before cutting.

Notes: Carolina Gold is expensive and only available regionally; I prefer an aromatic Southeast Asian long-grain rice for this bread such as basmati and jasmine rice, both of which have a fairly consistent absorption rate and add a lovely hint of nuttiness. Regular long-grain rice will work, though it has less character and its absorption can vary: it may need a little more water. Keep a teakettle of simmering water on hand until you know the absorptive properties of your rice. Rice bread keeps remarkably well, up to 8 days in cool weather, but loosely wrap it; sealed plastic or foil will trap the abundant moisture that remains in the crumb and makes the bread mold faster.

Makes one large round or two 9-inch pan loaves

"irish" potato bread

Rub half a dozen Irish potatoes, peeled, through a coarse sieve; mix them thoroughly with twice the quantity of flour; add one egg, a tablespoonful of butter, a teaspoonful of salt, a tumbler of tepid water or fresh sweet milk, in which has been dissolved a tablespoonful of leaven; make a smooth dough, and, after being well risen, mould into loaves or long rolls; bake in a rather quick oven. This bread keeps well.

— Annabella P. Hill,
Mrs. Hill's New Cook Book, 1867

The bread that Mrs. Hill was so lucidly describing did not, of course, have anything to do with Ireland. Throughout the Deep South, sweet potatoes have been a staple for more than three centuries, so much so that, well into my living memory, they were simply called "potatoes" and regular potatoes were called "Irish" to distinguish them. Mrs. Hill took for granted that anyone would know that, just as she took for granted that you'd have sense enough to cook the potatoes before trying to press them through a sieve. Potato bread remains popular in the South to this day. It makes a light but satisfying loaf, and as Mrs. Hill observed, it does keep well.

14 ounces baking potatoes (about 1 large or 2 medium)

1 cup whole milk

½ teaspoon active dry yeast or ½-ounce cake compressed fresh yeast

20 ounces (about 4 cups) all-purpose flour or bread flour, including ¼ cup whole wheat pastry flour

1 teaspoon salt

2 tablespoons unsalted butter, softened, plus more for brushing the loaves

1 large egg, lightly beaten

1. Scrub the potatoes under cold running water. Put them in a close-fitting heavy-bottomed pot with water to cover, and bring to a boil over medium-high heat; reduce the heat to medium and simmer until they're easily pierced with a paring knife. Drain and let cool enough to handle.

2. Scald the milk in a small saucepan over medium heat, remove it from the heat, and cool it to less than 110°F. Stir in the yeast and proof for 10 minutes. Set aside a cup of flour for kneading, then whisk together the remaining flour and salt in a large mixing bowl. Peel the potatoes while they're still quite warm and put them through a ricer. You should have about 2 cups. Work the butter into them. Beat the egg into the milk and yeast, and then gradually beat it into the potato.

3. Make a well in the center of the flour and pour in the milk and potatoes. Work it into a smooth, soft dough. Turn it onto a lightly floured work surface and knead until elastic and smooth, about 8 minutes, using the remaining flour as needed. Clean the bowl and put the dough back in it, cover with a damp, double-folded linen towel or plastic wrap, and let it rise until doubled, about 4 hours.

4. Lightly butter two 9-inch loaf pans or a large baking sheet. Punch down the dough and knead it for a minute. This dough is soft and a little sticky: You may need to sprinkle it with a little flour. Divide it in half, shape it into ovals, and put it into the two loaf pans. To make rolls, the dough is a little easier to handle if you chill it before punching it down and shaping it. You may roll it out ½ inch thick, cut it with a 1½-inch biscuit cutter, and make a crease down the center of each, fold them over, and place them on the baking sheet, leaving about an inch between them, or shape it into cloverleaf rolls in buttered muffin tins, or cluster rolls (see French Rolls, below). Loosely cover with a damp towel and let rise until doubled again, about 1–1½ hours.

5. Position a rack in the upper third of the oven and preheat to 450°F. If you are baking the bread in loaves, slash each down the center with a single-edged razor blade, batard knife, or sharp chef's knife. Regardless of shape, brush the tops lightly with butter.

6. For loaves, bake 10 minutes, reduce the heat to 375°F, and bake until golden-brown, or to an internal temperature of 180°F, about 20–25 minutes. Turn out onto a wire cooling rack and let cool before cutting. For rolls, bake at 450°F until golden-brown, about 16–18 minutes. Serve warm.

Makes two 9-inch loaves or about 24 rolls

french rolls and creole brioche

A recurring theme in old Southern cookbooks, from Mary Randolph right into the twentieth century, were "French" rolls, buttery dinner rolls enriched with eggs, milk, and butter. Though they bear more than a passing resemblance to brioche (and were even called that in Creole New Orleans), they actually had nothing in common with the daily bread of France, but give away the lingering English influence on the language of American baking. In the early years of the American colonies, enriched breads like these were called "French" bread in England, a practice that continued in Colonial America. Today they're often just called butter rolls.

There are a number of ways to shape this dough. In the old days French rolls were baked in a buttered round pan in concentric circles. Creole Brioche was done the same way (rather than in fluted cups with the jaunty topknot of the brioches of France), except that the center roll was twice the size of the others. It can also be baked as individual rolls in a muffin pan, and Southern Jewish bakers braided it into challah, the quintessential loaf for Sabbath dinners and bar/bat mitzvahs. Several of these variations are included here.

Egg-enriched dough is usually soft and sticky, making it a challenge to handle in the final shaping unless it has been thoroughly chilled first.

1 teaspoon active dry yeast
or 1-ounce cake compressed fresh yeast

1 cup water

1 cup whole milk

½ cup sugar

40 ounces (about 8 cups) bread flour or unbleached all-purpose flour, including ¼ cup whole wheat pastry flour

2 teaspoons salt

4 large eggs, lightly beaten

8 ounces (1 cup or 2 sticks) unsalted butter, softened

2 ounces (¼ cup or ½ stick) unsalted butter, melted, or 1 large egg beaten with 1 tablespoon water, for finishing the bread

1. Dissolve the yeast in the water and let it proof for 10 minutes. Meanwhile, scald the milk in a heavy-bottomed saucepan over medium heat. Remove it from the heat and stir in the sugar until it is dissolved. Let it cool to 110°F, then stir in the dissolved yeast.

2. Whisk together the flour and salt in a large mixing bowl and make a well in the center. Lightly beat the eggs into the milk and yeast and pour this into the center of the flour. By hand or with a mixer fitted with a paddle, gradually stir the flour into it until it becomes almost too stiff to stir, then work in most of the rest of the flour. The dough will be very soft—almost too soft to handle.

3. Work the cup of softened butter into the dough by hand or with the mixer fitted with a dough hook, kneading until it's elastic and smooth, about 8 minutes. Put it into a large bowl rubbed with 2 tablespoons of the melted butter, turning it until it is coated on the outside, then cover with plastic wrap and leave it to rise until it is doubled, about 4–6 hours. Refrigerate until thoroughly chilled.

To make French Rolls: Rub three 9-inch round cake pans with butter and lightly flour your hands and a work surface. While the dough is quite cold, divide it into three equal parts and roll each into a long cylinder about 1½ inches round. Pinch off lumps of equal size and roll each into a ball. Put the balls of dough into the buttered pans in concentric circles, slightly touching one another, and loosely cover with damp linen towels. Let rise until doubled—about an hour. Another classic shape is created by baking the rolls in muffin tins. Lightly butter three 12-well standard muffin tins. Pinch off small handfuls of dough and roll into ½-inch-diameter by 6-inch-long cylinders. Coil them into the cups of the muffin tin, forming a spiral with the center sticking up slightly. Cover with damp linen towels and let rise. Position a rack in the center of the oven and preheat to 350°F. Lightly brush the rolls with the remaining melted butter and bake in the center of the oven until they are golden-brown and reach an internal temperature of 180°F, about 18–20 minutes.

To make Creole Brioche: While the dough is quite cold, punch it down and turn it out onto a floured work surface. Butter three 9-inch cake pans, punch down the cold dough, divide it into three parts, and roll each into a 1½-inch cylinder. Divide the cylinders into balls about the size of an egg, but make three of them twice the size of the others. Put a large ball in the center of each pan and arrange the others around it, barely touching, in concentric rings. Cover with a damp towel and let it double, about an hour. Position a rack in the center of the oven and preheat to 400°F. Instead of butter, brush them with the egg solution and bake until they reach an internal temperature of 180°F and are a glossy golden-brown, about 30 minutes.

To make Creole "Bullfrogs": This colorfully named variation on shaping brioche dough comes from the 1901 classic *Picayune's Creole Cook Book.* Instead of baking them in a round pan, the rolls are baked two abreast in a long chain. Line a large baking sheet with parchment paper and put the rolls onto it in lightly touching rows two rolls wide and as long or short as you like. Brush them with the egg solution and bake as for Creole Brioche.

To make braided challah: Line a large baking sheet with parchment. Divide the chilled dough in half, and then divide each half into six even pieces. Roll each out in a long sausage-like cylinder about 1 inch in diameter. Braid three of them together (the outside pieces alternate, always crossing them to the middle) and put it on the prepared baking sheet. Braid the remaining three together and lay them on top of the first braid. Repeat with the second piece of dough. Cover loosely with a damp cloth and let it double, about an hour. Position a rack in the center of the oven and preheat to 350°F. Brush the loaves generously with the egg solution and bake in the center of the oven until they reach an internal temperature of 180°F and are golden-brown and hollow sounding when tapped, about 30 minutes.

Makes about 3 dozen rolls or 2 large challah loaves

monticello muffins

These are not the puffy, cupcake-like "muffins" of our day, but the classic griddle bread that we know as English muffins; they were commonplace in our country at least through the early days of the Republic, and have an interesting and little-known place in the history of American baking. They were a specialty of Monticello's master cook, Peter Hemings, and Jefferson so loved them that, when his French chef at the President's House couldn't make them, he wrote to his daughter Martha: ". . . Pray enable yourself to direct us here how to make muffins in Peter's method. My cook here cannot succeed at them, and they are a great luxury to me."

Despite that early popularity, by the third quarter of the nineteenth century griddle-baked muffins were on their way out, having been displaced by the sweet, cupcake-like thing that we know as muffins today. And by the century's end, they were so little known that when a bakery reintroduced them, they had to be marketed as "English" to save confusion.

After Jefferson's day, most griddle-baked muffins contained egg, and many of them were made up with milk; in fact, about the only difference between later recipes for muffins, crumpets, and Flannel Cakes (page 265) was the proportion of egg and liquid to flour. But eggs make a rather heavy muffin for my taste; this follows the example of the older cooks like Monticello's Peter Hemings.

¼ teaspoon active dry yeast,
or ½-ounce cake compressed fresh yeast

2 cups tepid water

20 ounces (1¼ pounds, about 4 cups) unbleached all-purpose flour, including ¼ cup whole wheat pastry flour

1 rounded teaspoon salt

Rice or corn flour, or fine white cornmeal, for dusting

1. Dissolve the yeast in the water and let proof 10 minutes. Whisk or stir together the flour and salt in a mixing bowl. Make a well in the center, add the yeast and water, and gradually stir it into the flour. Beat until the dough is cohesive and smooth—almost too stiff to stir but too slack to knead by hand. Cover with a damp, double-folded towel or plastic wrap and let rise until almost doubled, about 3 hours or—if covered with wrap and left in a cool spot—overnight.

2. Lightly dust a baking sheet, wooden board, or laminate counter with rice or corn flour or cornmeal. Beat the dough down with a wooden spoon. Dust your hands and the top of the dough with flour and scoop up small, even handfuls, shaping them into round flat cakes about 2½ inches across. Put them on the prepared surface, spacing at least an inch apart, and let rest 15–30 minutes. If they rose overnight, they'll only need a few minutes to begin recovering volume.

3. Warm a griddle or wide, shallow skillet over medium-low heat. With a wide, thin-bladed spatula, place as many muffins as will comfortably fit on the griddle with at least an inch on all sides. Bake slowly until the bottom is delicately browned, about 8–10 minutes; then turn, lightly pressing each muffin flat with the back of the spatula, and bake until uniformly browned and set but still moist at the center, about 8 minutes longer.

Makes about 16 muffins

the art of eating muffins

The fine art of buttering and eating muffins hot off the griddle was a skill well understood within the Jefferson household. According to family lore, no less than Dolley Madison was instructed in this art by toddler Benjamin Franklin Randolph: "Why you must tear him open, and put butter inside and stick holes in his back. And then pat him and squeeze him and the juice will run out!" I cannot improve on that except to add that the tearing goes easier when the edges are loosened by piercing them with the tines of a fork. In today's cholesterol- and saturated-fat-conscious society, it is not for the faint of heart, but it sure is rewarding. You need not, as little Ben directed, put holes in the muffin, but if butter doesn't run out the edges when you bite into it, you didn't use enough. Muffins don't keep well, but happily they do freeze well and toast beautifully. They should not, as is often done in this country, be split open, but as directed above be pierced with the fork to loosen the edges, and toasted whole. They are then and only then split open and buttered as little Ben so lucidly instructed.

mama's bread

After that memorable reaction to novelist Lee Smith's talk on her mother's bread, described at the opening of this chapter, I began to pay attention to the way people reacted to the mere mention of the words Mama's bread. Among those of us who grew up in the 1960s or earlier, Lee's story was echoed often: the warm aroma of home-baked bread meeting them almost at the door of the school bus, perfuming cool autumn air, like the changing leaves and waning sunlight, filled with golden promise and ageless comforts. These memories were so powerful that I decided right then that they should be preserved, and started collecting both stories and recipes. Though many of those breads overlapped, I could easily have filled an entire book with unique recipes. Here are a few that have been particularly close to my own heart.

lee smith's mama's bread

It turns out that Lee's mother's bread was nothing more than a variation on the enriched "French" rolls found on page 286, but for Lee, and for the people who shared her memories that afternoon, the fact that it was not unique did not—and never will—matter. This delicate yet robustly flavored loaf is very satisfying eating with or without the nostalgia, fresh from the oven, toasted the next day, or as the base for French toast once it is past its prime. It also makes very nice rolls, yielding about three dozen, depending on the shape.

½ teaspoon active dry yeast
or ½ ounce cake compressed fresh yeast

¼ cup lukewarm water

2½ cups whole milk

3 tablespoons sugar

1 teaspoon salt

¼ cup (4 tablespoons) lard, butter, shortening, or oil

2 large eggs, well beaten

40 ounces (about 8 cups) unbleached all-purpose flour

About 2 tablespoons unsalted butter, softened

1. Dissolve the yeast in the water and proof 10 minutes. Put the milk, sugar, salt, and shortening in a heavy-bottomed saucepan over medium heat. Bring it almost to a simmer and pour it into a large mixing bowl. Let it cool until lukewarm (less than 110°F), then stir in the eggs and yeast. Gradually stir in the flour until the dough is too stiff to stir (about 6 cups), then turn the dough out onto a floured work surface and work in the remaining flour. Knead lightly 2–3 minutes—just until the dough is uniform—then clean the mixing bowl and return the dough to it, cover with a damp double-folded towel or plastic wrap, and leave it in a warm, draft-free spot to rise until it has doubled in volume, about 4–6 hours.

2. Turn the dough out onto a lightly floured work surface, punch it down, and knead until it is elastic and smooth, about 8 minutes. Lightly grease two 9-inch loaf pans. Divide the dough in half and shape it into loaves. Place the dough in the pans and cover them with a double-folded damp cloth. Let rise until doubled and clearing the tops of the pans, about 2–4 hours.

3. Position a rack in the center of the oven and preheat to 350°F. Bake to an internal temperature of 180°F, or until the loaves are well browned and hollow sounding when thumped, about 35–40 minutes. Turn them out of the pans onto a wire cooling rack, turn right-side up, generously butter the tops while still hot, and let them cool before cutting.

Makes two 9-inch loaves

mama's buttermilk bread

Buttermilk makes a tender, sweet-tasting bread that keeps well, freezes well, and—even after it has begun to go a little stale—still makes terrific toast. This is my mother's all-purpose yeast dough, used for the biscuit-like rolls at Thanksgiving, Christmas, and any other special meal, for small loaves to give away to a shut-in, ailing, or grieving neighbor, or just to have for toast. It's those small, neat loaves that say home and love best for me.

2 pounds (about 7 cups) unbleached all-purpose flour or bread flour, including ¼ cup whole wheat pastry flour

2 tablespoons sugar

1 teaspoon baking soda

1 teaspoon salt

2 cups buttermilk

½ cup water

4 tablespoons (¼ cup) butter or oil, plus more for greasing the pans

½ teaspoon active dry yeast
or 1-ounce cake compressed fresh yeast

1. Reserve 1 cup of flour to use during the kneading. Whisk or sift together the remaining flour, sugar, soda, and salt. Heat the milk, water, and butter or oil until just warm (110°F) and stir until the butter is melted. Let it cool slightly and dissolve the yeast in it. Proof for 10 minutes.

2. Make a well in the center of the dry ingredients and pour in the liquid. Work it together into a soft, cohesive dough. Lightly sprinkle a work surface with some of the reserved flour and turn the dough out onto it. Knead about 8 minutes, adding the reserved flour as needed, until the dough is elastic and smooth.

3. Clean the mixing bowl and return the dough to it, cover with double-folded damp towel or plastic wrap, and let rise in a draft-free spot until doubled, about 4 hours, or lightly oil the bowl before putting the dough in, cover with plastic wrap, let it rise in the refrigerator overnight or for at least 8 hours, keeping it refrigerated until you are ready for the final shaping and rising.

4. Lightly grease four small (7½ x 2¼-inch) loaf pans with butter or olive oil. Punch the dough down and lightly knead for about 1 minute. Divide it into quarters, shape each one into an oblong loaf, and put them into the greased pans. Cover with a double-folded damp towel and let rise in a warm spot until the loaves are doubled and clearing the tops of the pans, about 1–1½ hours.

5. Meanwhile, position a rack in the center of the oven and preheat to 375°F. Uncover the loaves and bake 20 minutes in the center of the oven, then increase the oven temperature to 400°F. and bake until the loaves are well browned, reach an internal temperature of 190°F, and sound hollow when tapped, about 15 minutes longer. Turn out of the pans and cool on wire racks.

Buttermilk Rolls or Yeast Biscuits: Mama cuts them into simple yeast biscuits, but you can shape them in any way you like. For biscuits, roll the dough out ¼ inch thick, cut with a 2- to 2½-inch biscuit cutter, and put on a greased baking sheet, spacing a little apart for separate rolls or slightly touching one another for clusters. Cover with a damp towel and let rise until doubled, then bake at 450°F until browned, about 12–15 minutes. For pocketbook rolls, press the biscuits firmly down the center with a knife, fold over, and place on a lightly greased baking sheet, not touching; cover, let rise, and then bake as above.

For cloverleaf rolls, flour your hands, pinch off 1-inch lumps of dough, and roll them into tight smooth balls. Lightly butter a standard twelve-well muffin tin and put three balls into each well. Cover, let rise, and bake as above.

Whole Wheat Buttermilk Bread: Substitute from 1 to 3 cups of whole wheat flour for the regular flour. Mama varies the amount depending on whether she is making it for herself or for a neighbor whose tastes will determine how mild or intensely wheaty the bread needs to be. Most whole wheat flour tends to be a little on the thirsty side: You may need a little more liquid for the dough, so have about ¼–½ cup of room-temperature water close at hand as you mix the dough, adding a little at a time as the dough needs it.

....

Makes four small (7-inch) loaves, three 9-inch loaves, or about 3 dozen rolls

mama edith's bread

An interesting aspect of bread making is the way a loaf will often take on some of the character and personality of its baker. Edith Wakefield was all country gingham and lace, sentimental and tenderhearted to a fault, and yet tough and wise in ways that defy the usual preconception of sentimentality. She came into my life by way of her exquisitely beautiful daughter, Kathy, one of my lifelong closest friends. Edith in turn became a dear friend, one of the "Mamas" in every Southern man's life who is as important as she is impossible to explain, and we remained close until she died. Edith's bread is a distillation of her essence: warm and earthy as whole wheat and molasses, simple and old-fashioned and yet wise and forward looking, always meeting and embracing the world as she found it. Neither Kathy nor I remember lecithin or canola oil in her earlier bread—both found their way into the mix later on—but that, too, was typical of her adaptable nature. As age challenged her, making her more conscious of health issues, she met the challenge head-on.

FOR THE SPONGE:

¼ teaspoon active dry yeast or 1-ounce cake compressed fresh yeast

1½ cups lukewarm water

1 tablespoon granulated lecithin (available at any natural food grocery), optional

1 tablespoon salt

2 tablespoons unsulfured molasses

10 ounces (about 2 cups) unbleached all-purpose flour

FOR THE DOUGH:

½ cup water

3 tablespoons canola oil

½ cup unsulfured molasses

20 ounces (about 4 cups) whole wheat flour, preferably organic

About 2 tablespoons melted butter

1. To make the sponge, dissolve the yeast in the water and let it proof 10 minutes. Stir in the lecithin, salt, and molasses, then gradually whisk in the all-purpose flour until it forms a smooth, thick batter. Cover with plastic wrap and let rise in warm place until doubled.

2. To make the dough, bring the remaining water to a boil and remove it from the heat. Stir in the oil and remaining molasses, let it cool to lukewarm, and then mix it into the sponge. Gradually stir in the whole wheat flour until it's too stiff to stir and then sprinkle some of the flour

onto a work surface, turn the dough out onto it, and work in the remaining flour by hand until the dough is no longer sticky but still fairly soft. Knead it until it is elastic and smooth, about 8 minutes.

3. Clean and dry the mixing bowl and rub it liberally with oil. Put in the dough and turn it several times to lightly grease all sides. Cover with plastic wrap or a damp, double-folded linen towel and let it rise until doubled, about 4–6 hours.

4. Lightly oil two 9-inch loaf pans. Punch the dough down, cut it in half, and lightly knead each half until smooth again—about 2 minutes. Shape into loaves and invert the prepared pans over them. Let rest for 15 minutes, then turn the pans faceup and put the loaves into the pans, cover with a damp cloth, and let rise until the tops of the loaves clear the tops of the pans.

5. Position a rack in the center of the oven and preheat to 350°F. Uncover and bake in the center of the oven until the tops are uniformly brown and they reach an internal temperature of 180–190°F, about 40–45 minutes. Turn out of the pans and put right-side up on a cooling rack. Brush the tops with melted butter while still quite warm. Let cool before cutting.

About lecithin: This is a natural emulsifier found in foods such as egg yolks. It holds fat in suspension in things like mayonnaise and oil-and-vinegar dressing and is also used as a dietary supplement. In bread making it's used as a dough enhancer and to improve the bread's shelf life. If you can't find it, a large egg yolk may be substituted—or it can just be omitted altogether.

Makes two 9-inch loaves

hot-water corn bread

This is the ancient bread that more properly goes by the name hoecake. Scalding the meal with hot water softens it and gives the bread a more delicate consistency. Nita Dixon, a traditional Lowcountry cook who for years ran a café in downtown Savannah, used to serve this bread with her deeply Southern fare. Nita learned to make it from her sister, Joan Simmons, a lovely artist and free spirit who has lived all over the map. One warm spring morning, Joan finally shared her secret with me.

About 1¾ cups water

¼ cup thinly sliced green onion
(about 2 small scallions)

1 cup stone-ground white cornmeal

1 teaspoon salt

Bacon drippings or vegetable oil,
or a mixture of both, for frying

1. Bring the water to a boil in a heavy-bottomed saucepan over medium heat. Stir together the onion, meal, and salt in a heatproof bowl.

2. Gradually stir the hot water into the meal, beginning with 11/2 cups and adding more by spoonfuls until the batter is quite thick, almost stiff.

3. Film the bottom of a wide, well-seasoned iron skillet with oil or drippings about 1/8 inch deep. Warm it over medium-high heat until the fat is almost smoking hot, then drop in the batter in 2- to 3-tablespoons-size lumps. Spread it with the back of a spoon or spatula and cook until golden-brown on the bottom, about 4 minutes; turn and cook until golden-brown and firm. The cake should be slightly moist in the center but not mushy.

Makes about 12, serving 4–6

savannah cream biscuits

Despite their richness, cream biscuits are surprisingly light and delicate. Best of all, they're simple to make and are one of the easiest breads for novices to master. They're perfect for ham, jam, or just about any sweet or savory filling, and when cut small they make an ideal biscuit for cocktail buffets. Delicate, easy, and delicious with cocktails: That's probably why they have a long history in Savannah.

1¾ cups Southern soft-wheat flour (see page 253), pastry flour, or all-purpose flour

1 tablespoon Single-Acting Baking Powder (page 255) or 2 teaspoons double-acting baking powder

1 teaspoon salt

1 cup heavy cream

1. Position a rack in the center of the oven and preheat to 500°F. Sift or whisk together the flour, baking powder, and salt in a mixing bowl.

2. In a separate bowl, whip the cream until it is quite thick and beginning to peak but not stiff. Fold the cream into the flour mixture until it is thoroughly combined.

3. Turn the dough out onto a lightly floured work surface and pat out 1 inch thick. Fold in half and pat flat; repeat twice more. Lightly flour the dough and surface and roll or pat it out ½ inch thick. With a plain or decorative biscuit cutter (1½–2 inches round) dipped in flour before each cut, cut without twisting into 12–16 biscuits, depending on the size of the cutter. The scraps may be lightly reworked and cut into biscuits (see Southern Breakfast Biscuits, page 260). Put them on an ungreased baking sheet spaced ½ inch apart and bake until golden-brown, about 8–10 minutes. Serve piping hot.

Makes 12–16

sourdough starter

People who make sourdough bread are usually glad to give away some of their starter, especially if they don't make bread every week, since feeding it without taking some away makes huge volumes of the stuff. That's why a variation of sourdough is often called Friendship Loaf—because the starter thrives on being spread around. If you don't know someone who makes sourdough, however, and are wary of depending solely on such wild yeasts as inhabit the air of your kitchen, you can create a starter using packaged yeast. It will take a few weeks for it to hit its prime, so be patient with it. Eventually, the natural wild yeast in the air will impregnate even a starter begun with commercial yeast, giving it a character unique to your kitchen.

Some of the recipes in this section are designed with starter that does not contain flour, and the ingredients list will call for Sourdough Starter II if that is the case, but either starter can be used. To substitute one for the other, refer to the notes on page 299.

½ cup sugar

2 cups warm (110°F) water

¼ teaspoon active dry yeast
or ½-ounce cake compressed fresh yeast

1 medium potato, boiled soft, peeled, and mashed, or 6 tablespoons instant potato flakes

10 ounces (about 2 cups) unbleached all-purpose or bread flour, optional

1. Dissolve the sugar in the water. Sprinkle in the yeast and let stand until the yeast is dissolved and creamy. Stir in the potato. Sprinkle in the flour, if using, and stir until it is smooth. Some bakers prefer a thin, flourless starter, and some prefer the thicker batter-like starter. The latter is thought to be more durable and forgiving of uneven feeding.

2. Loosely cover (using loose foil with holes punched into it with a carving fork, a damp linen towel, or plastic wrap stretched tight and punctured with a carving fork—it must be able to breathe) and let it stand at room temperature for 24 hours. Cover and refrigerate until you're ready to use it.

Feeding the starter: Sourdough starter is a living thing. To keep it healthy and vigorous, feed it once a week, especially while it's still young. After a few months, it'll get more forgiving, and will tolerate longer intervals between feedings, but try to maintain a regular schedule, and feed it no less than every 2 weeks if you don't make bread regularly. Stir together 1 cup of warm (less than 110°F) water, ½ cup sugar, and 3 tablespoons instant potato flakes, then whisk in 5 ounces (about 1 cup) unbleached all-purpose flour (if your starter contains flour). Let the starter stand at room temperature for at least half an hour, then stir the feeding mixture into it, loosely cover (a glass lid set askew, punctured foil, or tea towel will all work), and let it ferment 8–10 hours. Take up 1 cup of the starter to make bread, or give it away if you aren't making bread right away. Cover and refrigerate until you are ready to use it again.

Substituting sourdough starters in bread recipes:
Whether or not you feed your starter with flour (which makes a starter the consistency of thin pancake batter), it can be used in any sourdough bread recipe. To substitute one starter for the other, here are some basic rules of thumb. If your starter is flour-based and the recipe calls for the thinner starter without flour, just hold back ½ cup of the flour called for. If your starter doesn't contain flour and the recipe calls for a starter with flour, allow an extra ½ cup of flour. Almost any bread recipe can become sourdough by substituting starter for the regular yeast and some of the liquid: Allow a cup of starter for 4–8 cups of flour. Omit the yeast and proofing liquid and hold back ½ cup of the liquid called for in the recipe (for starter with flour), or a cup of the liquid if the starter doesn't contain flour.

Makes about 5 cups

basic sourdough bread

The uses for this basic dough are limited only by your imagination. It makes wonderful dinner rolls, a fine, compact sandwich loaf, or a satisfyingly crusty round cottage loaf; with a few additions it can be put to use in sweet breads for breakfast or brunch. Adding oil to the dough helps to increase its keeping qualities: Well wrapped in both waxed paper and foil, the loaves last up to a week, and are still good for toasting for a few days after that.

1 cup Sourdough Starter (with flour, page 298)

1½ cups warm (110°F) water

¼ cup oil (olive, canola, or another vegetable oil)

28 ounces (about 6 cups) unbleached bread flour or all-purpose flour, including ¼ cup whole-wheat pastry flour

1 tablespoon salt

1. Combine the starter, water, and oil in a large work bowl that will allow the volume of the dough to double without overflowing. Gradually stir in the flour and beat until the dough is too stiff to stir, then turn it out onto a lightly floured work surface and work in the salt and remaining flour until the dough is smooth and no longer sticky but still fairly soft. Knead 8–10 minutes or until elastic and smooth. Put the dough back in the mixing bowl, loosely cover with a damp, double-folded towel or plastic wrap, and let rise until doubled, 8–10 hours or overnight.

2. Punch down and let it rest 10 minutes, then turn it onto a lightly floured work surface and lightly knead until smooth again, about 2 minutes. Cut it in half and shape each half into an oval or round loaf. Lightly oil a large baking sheet and place the loaves on it, leaving at least 3 inches between them and 2 inches on the other sides, or put them into 2 lightly greased 9-inch bread pans. Cover with a double-folded damp towel and let them rise until doubled (about 3–5 hours; let pan loaves rise until they clear the tops of the pans).

3. Position the rack in the center of oven and preheat to 350°F. Make three diagonal slashes across the top of each free-form oval loaf, or lengthwise down the center of the pan loaves, with a single-edged razor blade or sharp knife. Place the pan(s) on the center rack of the oven and bake about 35–40 minutes, or until the bread sounds hollow when thumped. Remove the loaves from the pans and cool them on a wire rack.

Sourdough Cloverleaf Rolls: Make the dough as directed in step 1. After the initial rise, turn it onto a floured work surface, punch down, and knead for a minute. Butter two standard twelve-well muffin pans. Lightly flour your hands, pinch off walnut-size (1-inch) lumps of dough, and roll them into uniform balls. Put three in each well of the pan. Cover with a double-folded damp cloth and let rise until doubled and clearing the top of the pans. Position the rack in the center of oven and preheat to 350°F. Lightly brush the rolls with melted butter and bake in the center of the oven about 30 minutes.

Sourdough Cast Cottage Loaves: This bread can also be baked directly on a baking stone (see page 275). Make the dough as directed in step 1; if the dough seems slack, add enough flour to make it hold its shape without a pan. After a couple of times, you will know how it should feel under your hands. After it has gone through the initial rise, punch it down and divide it in half, lightly knead each half, and shape it into a ball. Lightly flour each ball and place it on a baker's peel dusted with a little semolina flour. Cover with a damp towel. Let it rise until it is doubled, then slash and bake it as directed on page 300.

Makes 2 loaves

mary lizzie's whole wheat sourdough

After Mary Lizzie Kitchengs came to Savannah from Bainbridge, Georgia, to live with her daughter, Maryan, and granddaughter, Mary Margaret, the trio quickly became known to all of us as "The Three Marys," which had a biblical sound that suited Mary Lizzie's dry sense of humor. What a privilege it was to know this lovely lady, share her love and wisdom, and, when her life had come full circle, be at her bedside with the other two Marys as she died. As long as she could stand at the table to knead it, this was the daily bread of their household—and of mine, too. It's a fairly sweet bread: If Mary Lizzie had a fault, it was a raging sweet tooth. Feel free to adjust the sugar to suit your taste.

1½ cups Sourdough Starter II (without flour, page 298)

½ cup sugar

½ cup oil (olive, canola, or peanut)

1¼ teaspoons salt

1½ cups lukewarm water

20 ounces (about 4 cups) unbleached bread flour

10 ounces (about 2 cups) whole wheat flour

About 3 tablespoons unsalted butter, melted

1. Mix together the starter with the sugar, oil, salt, and water. Whisk the flours together in a large mixing bowl, make a well in the center, and pour in the liquids. Gradually work it into a smooth, stiff dough. Turn it out onto a lightly floured work surface and lightly knead until elastic and smooth, about 6 minutes. Clean the bowl, return the dough to it, and cover with a double-folded damp towel or plastic wrap. Let it rise until doubled, about 6–8 hours or overnight.

2. Lightly grease three 9-inch loaf pans. Punch the dough down and divide it into three equal portions. Knead each until it is elastic and smooth, about 5 minutes, and put them into the prepared pans. Cover with double-folded damp towels and let them rise until doubled, about 6 hours.

3. Position a rack in the center of the oven and preheat to 350°F. Uncover and bake in the center of the oven until golden-brown and hollow-sounding when tapped, or to an internal temperature of 180–190°F, about 35 minutes. Turn the loaves out of the pans, put them right-side up on a cooling rack, and brush their tops generously with the melted butter. Let them cool before slicing.

Makes three 9-inch loaves

lyn's rosemary sourdough bread

Sourdough starter can almost become a member of the family. My own starter was given to me by my late friend Lyn McDonald, who, when her family moved to Savannah a few years ago, had carefully nursed it all the way from Alabama in its own cooler. Lyn's starter had been given to her by her next-door neighbor, and was therefore an important link back to that friendship. When Lyn was diagnosed with cancer, she was almost as worried about who would look after her starter as her sons and husband. True to her generous nature, my starter was accompanied by a loaf of this, her favorite bread, delicately flavored with honey and fragrant with rosemary.

1 cup Sourdough Starter with flour (see page 298)

1½ cups warm (110°F) water

¼ cup olive oil

¼ cup honey

28 ounces (about 6 cups) unbleached bread flour or all-purpose flour

1 tablespoon salt

1 rounded tablespoon chopped fresh rosemary

1. Combine the starter, water, oil, and honey. Whisk together the flour and salt in a large mixing bowl. Make a well in the center and add the liquids, then work it into a smooth dough. Loosely cover with a damp cloth and let it rise overnight (8–10 hours).

2. Punch down and let rest for 10 minutes. Turn it out onto a lightly floured work surface, knead 5 minutes, and sprinkle the rosemary over it. Continue kneading until the herb is incorporated and the dough is elastic and smooth, about 2 minutes longer. Cut into two equal portions and shape into oval loaves. Lightly oil a large baking sheet and place the two loaves on it, leaving at least 2 inches clear on all sides. Cover with a damp cloth and let rise until doubled in bulk, 3–5 hours.

3. Position the rack in the center of the oven and preheat to 350°F. Make three diagonal slashes across the top of each loaf with a single-edged razor blade, batard knife, or sharp chef's knife. Bake 35–40 minutes in the center of the oven, until the loaves are golden-brown and hollow sounding when thumped, or they reach an internal temperature of 190°F. Remove the loaves to a wire rack to cool.

Makes 2 oval loaves

cinnamon raisin and pecan sourdough bread

This quintessential breakfast bread is good hot from the oven, but when it really shines is later, toasted and slathered with butter or cream cheese. Sourdough gives it a subtle bite that counterpoints the sweet spiral of brown sugar and raisins, but if the slow rise is longer than you would wish, the loaf can be made with almost any enriched bread dough such as Mama's Buttermilk Bread (page 292) or Lee Smith's Mama's Bread (page 291).

1½ cups whole milk

6 tablespoons (¾ stick) unsalted butter, divided

1 cup Sourdough Starter (with flour, page 298)

½ cup honey

28 ounces (about 6 cups) unbleached bread flour or all-purpose flour, including ¼ cup whole wheat pastry flour

2 teaspoons salt

½ cup raisins

1 cup light brown sugar

2 teaspoons cinnamon

½ cup roughly chopped Toasted Pecans (page 232)

1. Scald the milk with 4 tablespoons of the butter until the butter is melted; let it cool to less than 110°F. Stir in the starter and honey. Whisk together the flour and salt in a large mixing bowl. Make a well in the center, add the liquids, and work it into a cohesive dough. If it seems dry, sprinkle in a little water. Turn out onto a lightly floured work surface and knead until it is elastic and smooth, about 8 minutes. Clean the bowl and return the dough to it. Loosely cover with a damp, double-folded linen cloth and let it rise until doubled, about 8 hours or overnight.

2. Put the raisins in a heatproof bowl. Bring 1 cup water to a boil, pour it over them, let plump for 10 minutes, and drain. Lightly butter two 9-inch loaf pans. Punch it down and turn it out onto a lightly floured work surface. Lightly knead 2–3 minutes, or until elastic and smooth again. Divide it in half and flatten each half into a rectangle almost as thin as pizza crust. Sprinkle evenly with the sugar, cinnamon, raisins, and pecans. Roll each into a cylinder from the short side, carefully pinching it together at the seam and ends. Put the dough into the prepared pans, cover with a damp cloth, and let rise until the dough clears the top of the pans, about 2–4 hours.

3. Position the rack in the center of oven and preheat to 350°F. Make a longitudinal slash down the center of each loaf with a single-edged razor blade, batard knife, or sharp chef's knife and brush with the remaining 2 tablespoons melted butter. Bake in the center of the oven 35–40 minutes, until the loaves sound hollow when thumped or reach an internal temperature of 180–190°F. Turn the loaves out of the pans onto wire racks to cool.

Makes 2 loaves

apple-pecan sticky buns

You can certainly make sticky buns with any yeast dough, but the slow-rising characteristics of sourdough make it ideal for preparing them ahead; well covered, they go through a slow 24-hour rise in the refrigerator before baking. This calls for half the amount of the Basic Sourdough Bread (page 300); I always make a full recipe, using half for a regular loaf of bread and the remaining half for these buns. If you are cooking for a crowd, of course, you can also double the recipe and use a full recipe of bread dough.

¾ cup (firmly packed) light brown sugar

½ cup honey

2 ounces (¼ cup or ½ stick) unsalted butter

½ cup broken pecans

1 lemon

1 small or ½ large tart apple such as Winesap, Arkansas Black, or Granny Smith

Sugar

2 pounds (½ recipe) Basic Sourdough Bread dough (page 300)

1 teaspoon cinnamon

¼ cup finely chopped crystallized ginger

1. Butter a 9 × 9 × 2-inch baking pan or the wells of two 6-well jumbo muffin pans. Combine the brown sugar, honey, and butter in a small saucepan over medium heat. Simmer 2 minutes and pour the mixture into the pan or divide it equally among the wells of the muffin pans. Sprinkle the nuts evenly over the syrup. Grate the zest from the lemon and then cut it in half. Peel, core, and cut the apple into quite small (¼-inch) dice. Put it into a bowl and squeeze the juice from half the lemon over it. Add a sprinkle of sugar to taste and lightly toss until evenly coated.

2. Roll the dough on a lightly floured work surface into a 15 × 8-inch rectangle. Sprinkle with cinnamon and lemon zest, then scatter the ginger and apple over it. Roll it up from one of the long sides and with a sharp knife cut into nine (or twelve, if you're using muffin pans) equal slices. Place them spiral-up in the prepared pan. Cover with plastic wrap and let rise until doubled, about 3–5 hours, depending on the warmth of the room, or cover well and refrigerate for 24 hours.

3. Position a rack in the center of the oven and preheat to 375°F. Bake about 25 minutes if using muffin tins or up to 35 minutes if cooking them in a square pan, until golden-brown. Remove the buns from the oven, carefully loosen any edges of the buns that may be sticking to the sides, and invert the pan over a flat platter or baking sheet. Carefully lift the pan away from the buns. Spoon any pecan syrup that runs to the sides back on top of the buns. Let stand until just warm and the syrup is set. Serve warm or at room temperature.

Makes 9–12 buns

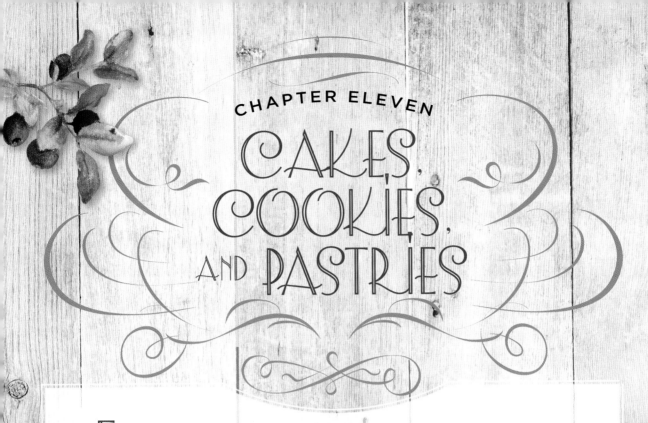

CHAPTER ELEVEN

CAKES, COOKIES, AND PASTRIES

For Southern cooks, cakes are part and parcel of our identity. A cake is often the first thing that we learn to make, even before biscuits. And it's the quality of our cake baking that gives us our culinary identity. A cake is an event in itself: Dessert at the end of the meal is just dessert, but a cake turns it into a celebration. Nothing gets more attention at a Southern covered-dish supper. Not only do they disappear in a hurry, nothing else will be more talked of than whether the baker will part with her recipe—and if so, whether the recipe she shares will be missing her real secret. Until recently, "What's your secret?" was the most frequently asked question, but today, as whole generations grow up without bakers at home, the questions have become more elemental, and all too often conclude with "Can you make it from a mix?"

There's a lot of speculation about why mixes have become so commonplace, and the most usual argument involves time, some variation on "People have busy lives; most women work; nobody has time to bake from scratch anymore." But a mix doesn't really take appreciably less time than a scratch-made batter: What it does take less of is skill. The dry ingredients are pre-measured and assembled in one box; their mixing is completely artless. The reason most people use a mix is less speed than fear: They think they don't know enough to make a cake from scratch, and a mix gives them the confidence to go where they would otherwise fear to tread.

If you are one of the fearful, take heart: Though cake making does take a certain amount of skill, that skill is honed with practice, and is not as complicated as it seems. Remember: It has for thousands of years been accomplished by thousands of ordinary people. Julia Child once said of her popularity as a cooking teacher that it had less to do with her own knowledge and skill than her very ordinariness: "They look at me and think, 'if she can do it, surely I can do it.'"

Do you know what? She's right.

Cake-Making Basics

- Have all the ingredients, especially the eggs and butter, at room temperature. If you've ever tried to cream cold, hard butter, you know partly why this is important, but egg whites also whip better when they're not refrigerator-cold, and both hold volume better at room temperature. To speed up the warming process, eggs (in the shell) can be submerged in hot tap water for a minute, and butter can be cut into small bits. Never try to warm eggs or soften butter in a microwave: Not only does it not work, it is inviting disaster.

- Use the freshest eggs you can get. Freshly laid eggs are heavier than week-old eggs, because eggs lose moisture as they age and as a result their ability to hold air when beaten is compromised.

- Get a reliable scale and weigh the flour: There are too many variables in volume measures, including ambient humidity, moisture content within the flour, and compacting in the storage bin. Experienced bakers can tell when a cake batter is too thin or too thick at a glance, but most of us don't bake often enough to have that kind of eye.

- If you are making an old-style pound cake, consider weighing the eggs, too, and get as close to a pound as you can, since too much moisture can upset the balance of this kind of cake and cause sad streaks (when part of the cake collapses, resulting in a heavy, damp streak in the cake).

- If you must rely on a dry measuring cup, measure the flour for a cake by spooning it into the cup, then sweeping off the excess with a knife or pastry scraper. This will measure a little lighter than scooping directly out of the canister or bag.

- The initial creaming is the single most important step in ensuring volume and lightness in a cake, especially pound cake. Although beaten egg whites are sometimes used to leaven cakes, most of the trapped air in a batter that is essential for giving the finished cake texture and height is that which is caught in the fat, not the eggs.

- If you are a worrier, this will be hard for you, but develop a habit of leaving the oven door alone. Too much peeking will cause too much fluctuation in the oven temperature, causing the cake to collapse.

- Bake often. The best way to perfect cake baking is to do it over and over until you know exactly how the batter should look, feel, and smell. The prize bakers of my childhood were not champions because they were always tinkering with some new recipe, but because they had a favorite that they were known for, and they cooked it over and over again. After a while, you'll also know by smell when a cake is done. Some traditional cooks, like the late Edna Lewis, develop an ear for baking, too. Ms. Lewis put an ear to the cake and listened: When it stopped "singing" to her, she knew it was done.

The Technique

Karen Barker, an award-winning pastry chef who with her chef-husband, Ben, owned the legendary Magnolia Grill in Durham, North Carolina, observes in her dessert book *Sweet Stuff* that cake making is more of an exacting science than breads and pastries, relying less on technique than on precision in measuring. However, she points out three techniques that are essential to success: creaming, whipping, and folding. When a cake has failed, nine times out of ten it's because the baker has fallen short with one of these three techniques. Without going into a dissertation, here is what home bakers need to know about them.

Creaming: The single most important step in ensuring the correct volume and texture in a cake is this frequently used technique. It is the process of beating the fat—usually with the sugar—until it is thoroughly aerated. Sometimes the creaming is done in two steps: The fat is beaten until it is soft and fluffy, then the sugar is gradually beaten into it. It accomplishes two things: Obviously, it traps air in the batter, but it also helps to form a smooth emulsion, keeping the fat evenly suspended in the batter. Before chemical leavening came on the scene, this step was very important indeed, but it's no less important for a baking-powder-leavened cake. The fat, especially when it's butter, must be at room temperature (around 70°F), softened but still holding it shape and not in the least oily looking. If it's too warm, it won't suspend the sugar and air, and will oil rather than fluff. Creaming can be done with a mixer fitted with rotary beaters or a paddle, a rotary eggbeater, or a wooden spoon. Obviously, hand creaming will take longer than a mixer, but the most useful gauge for judging when the fat has been well creamed isn't time but appearance: Properly creamed fat will change color, getting lighter (even shortening and lard will look whiter), and will look very fluffy and hold its shape well.

Whipping: This technique involves beating eggs, cream, or sometimes the entire batter to incorporate air, thereby introducing further volume. Whipping can be done with a fork, a wire whisk, a rotary eggbeater, or a mixer fitted with whisk or beater attachments. The specific techniques for whipping eggs and cream are discussed elsewhere in this book but as a reminder, they don't react in at all the same way, and their condition for optimum whipping is an exercise in extremes. While cream must be quite cold to whip properly, egg whites must be at room temperature or even a little warm. Underwhipping cream or egg whites is possible, but in some ways more damage can be done by overwhipping them: Overbeaten cream can break and turn into butter, and overbeaten egg whites become stiff and brittle. Neither will fold evenly into a batter nor hold its volume well.

Folding: The second most common failure in baking is the misunderstanding of this simple technique in which whipped egg whites, cream, dry ingredients, and sometimes floured solids like fruit and nuts are incorporated into a batter. It's called "folding" because that is exactly what happens: The heavier batter is literally folded around the lighter ingredient, just as you would fold a letter around a picture. This differs from stirring or mixing in that it requires a light, gentle, and yet quick hand. Here's how to do it: The ingredient to be folded into the batter (usually the lighter or drier of the two parts) is laid on top. Dip down into the center with a large mixing spoon or, better, a flexible spatula, going all the way to the bottom of the bowl and scooping up batter as you go. Bring it up

the side closest or farthest from you (whichever is the most comfortable), twisting so that it's parallel with the batter as you bring it out. Bring the spatula up and gently flip it over, letting the batter fall over the ingredient that is to be folded in. Slightly rotate the bowl and repeat this until the ingredient is evenly incorporated.

When the folded ingredient is full of trapped air, as in whipped cream or egg whites, it helps to mix a little into the batter first so that it's lighter and looser, making it easier to fold around the aerated ingredient. Scoop about a quarter of the whipped ingredient onto the batter and mix it in. You'll find that the remainder is much easier to incorporate evenly after that.

Evening things out: Once the cake batter is in the pan, it will need to be leveled and, though it may seem a contradiction after all that creaming and whipping, large pockets of air will need to be removed. There are several techniques for doing this. Spooning the batter (especially a hefty one like a pound cake) rather than pouring it into the pan is a big help. You may then level it off by smoothing the top with a spatula or, as *Baking in America* author Greg Patent suggests, by grasping the pan firmly with both hands and half rotating it first in one direction and then in the other. Some bakers tap the pan firmly on the counter, which both levels the batter and knocks loose any large air pockets. This is my method, but I do caution not to get too slaphappy and knock it too hard or you'll lose the even distribution of minuscule air bubbles that give the cake its texture and volume. Another way to remove those big air pockets in cakes baked in tube, loaf, or bundt pans is to run a table or palette knife through the batter in an S pattern.

Preparing the pan: Cake pans must be coated with fat and flour to keep the cake from sticking. For further insurance, many bakers line the bottom with a piece of buttered waxed paper or cooking parchment. To grease and flour a pan, save those butter wrappers: There's usually just enough butter film left on them to coat a couple of 9-inch round pans. Lightly rub the pan with butter or shortening until it's completely coated, then put in a tablespoon of flour. Gently turn and tap the pan until the entire surface is coated; turn out the excess. Bundt pans release best if you use dry bread or cake crumbs instead of flour. Substitute about ¼ cup dry crumbs for the flour for a full-size bundt pan, about a tablespoon for a mini bundt pan.

Pound Cakes

Pound cake is a very old European confection, already ancient when the Americas were first colonized. But over the last four centuries, Southerners have made this cake peculiarly our own. While baking powder layer cakes, with their multiple cloud-like layers bound together by rich, creamy frosting, have become icons of Southern baking, pound cakes still set the standard. Maybe that is because they can be tricky, temperamental, downright ornery creatures. The preceding notes are important for any cake, but they're especially important for pound cakes. If you're a novice, please make yourself familiar with them before attempting a pound cake.

Pound cakes follow one of two basic formulas: the traditional formula based on weight and the newer one based on volume measurements. The traditional formula is where the cake got its name: a pound of everything, including, ideally, the eggs. The modern volume cakes are sweeter and a little lighter, using sugar and flour in equal volumes, with half the volume of butter. Instead of weighing the eggs, they proportion the eggs to flour in volume, which generally works out to two eggs for every cup of flour. Despite the accuracy of weighing, the volume formula is sometimes less temperamental because it's lighter and sometimes includes a touch of baking powder to help ensure against a sad streak.

The old formula, dense, rich, and substantial, survives among traditional cooks, and remains the classic and best base for just about any fruitcake. Yet the fact that it is treated almost as an anachronism in community cookbooks—appearing under such names as "Grandma's," "Old-Fashioned," or "Old-Time"—is telling. It deserves a place of respect in any home baker's repertory other than as a charming anachronism.

Pound cakes were originally leavened only with the air that was beaten into the batter, mainly into the fat: That's why the old recipes directed to beat the heck out of the butter and sugar. Some also included separately beaten egg whites, like a genoise, which made for a cake that was lighter but more prone to sad streaks. The whites can contract a little as they cool, causing the cake to fall a little, the same way a soufflé sinks as it cools. At any rate, with or without beaten egg whites the old cake didn't need baking powder, but many of the modern ones, with their low ratio of fat and a high ratio of liquid, do.

Some Southerners actually love a good sad streak and will go to some wild extremes to have one, including adding more eggs to the batter, banging the oven door, jumping up and down in the kitchen, and poking the cake with a finger to make it fall. My mother had a string of fallen pound cakes one year and couldn't understand it until our the church choir director, a frequent guest in our house, moved away; the sad streaks mysteriously stopped. It was only years later that Mama's problem was explained. That choir director finally broke down and confessed that he loved a chewy sad-streak better than anything, and had been sneaking into the kitchen to stick his finger in the middle of the baking cake so it would fall.

classic pound cake

This is the old, original formula—made up with a pound of everything. Some of the old recipes were so specific about equal weights that they went so far as to recommend weighing a dozen eggs and used this weight to proportion the butter, sugar, and flour. It isn't as sweet as most modern cakes, but its richness and body are deeply satisfying.

1 pound (4 sticks or 2 cups) unsalted butter, softened

1 pound (2 cups) sugar

Salt

8 large eggs (see headnote above)

1 pound (about 3½ cups) Southern soft-wheat flour or unbleached all-purpose flour

½ cup cream

1 tablespoon Homemade Bourbon Vanilla (page 17) or rose or orange flower water, or 1 teaspoon vanilla extract and
2 teaspoons bourbon

1. Position a rack in the center of the oven and preheat to 325°F. Butter and flour a tube pan or two 9-inch loaf pans (see page 314). With a wooden spoon or mixer fitted with a paddle or rotary beaters, cream the butter, beating until light and fluffy, then beat in the sugar and a small pinch of salt. Cream until very light and fluffy.

2. Beat in the eggs one at a time, alternating in small amounts with the flour, until both are incorporated. Don't overbeat it at this point. Finally, stir in the cream and liquid flavoring, and pour the batter into the prepared pan(s). Slip a table knife blade into the batter and run it through in a back-and-forth S motion to take out any large air bubbles. Give the pan a couple of firm taps on the counter—just enough to bring large air pockets to the surface.

3. Bake 1½–2 hours, depending on the shape of your pan, until a straw inserted into the center comes out clean. Don't open the oven door for the first hour and 15 minutes. Make sure the cake is completely done before taking it from the oven, but don't overcook it or it will be dry and heavy. Cool the cake for 15 minutes in the pan, then turn it out onto a cake plate and let it cool completely before cutting it.

Makes one 10-inch tube or two 9-inch loaf cakes, serving 12–16

bourbon pound cake

This is the traditional cake, in which all the ingredients except the flavoring liquid are weighed. Bourbon lends a subtle, rich flavor to the crumb and a lovely aroma to the air as it bakes. It makes an ideal base for other desserts (see pages 16–17). This is also my standard base for all my fruitcakes (see page 326), in which I generally substitute sherry for half the bourbon to round out the flavor and complement the dried fruit. To vary the flavoring, substitute ½ cup sherry or milk for the bourbon, and substitute another flavoring extract for the vanilla.

1 pound (4 sticks or 2 cups) unsalted butter, at room temperature

1 pound (2 cups) sugar

1 pound (about 3½ cups) Southern soft-wheat flour or pastry flour

½ teaspoon salt

1 teaspoon baking powder

8 large fresh eggs, weighing just over a pound in shell, at room temperature, whites and yolks separated

½ cup bourbon

2 teaspoons Homemade Bourbon Vanilla (page 17) or 1 teaspoon pure vanilla extract

1. Position a rack in the center of the oven. Butter and flour a tube cake pan or two 9-inch loaf pans (see page 314).

2. Whisk together the flour, salt, and baking powder. With a wooden spoon or mixer, cream the butter and then beat in the sugar until the butter is light and fluffy. Alternating, gradually beat in the egg yolks and flour, adding one yolk and a small amount of flour at a time, and beating well after each addition. Stir in the bourbon and vanilla and mix well.

3. In a separate metal bowl, beat the egg whites a wire whisk or clean mixer until they form soft peaks. Fold a little of them into the batter, and then gradually fold the remaining whites into the batter. Pour the batter evenly into the tube or loaf pans, run a knife through the batter in an S pattern to release any large air bubbles, then firmly tap each pan on the counter several times to force the bubbles to the surface.

4. Place the cake in the center of the oven. If there is more than one pan, make sure they do not touch. Turn oven on to 325°F and bake for about 1½–2 hours, without opening the oven door for the first hour. The tube cake may take the entire 2 hours; loaf cakes may take little more than an hour. The cake is done when a straw or bamboo skewer stuck into the center comes out clean. With practice, you will be able to tell when the cake is done by the smell and by the way the cake sounds when you put your ear close to the top of it. Meanwhile, the straw test is not a bad one. Turn off the oven and let the cake cool in the oven for 30 minutes, then open the oven door and let it cool completely before you remove it from the pan and slice it. This will help ensure that there is no sad streak where slightly underdone cake collapses in the center. This can happen even if the cake is essentially done if it cools too rapidly or if you take it out of the pan and cut it while it's still warm.

Makes one round tube cake or two 9-inch loaf cakes

indian pound cake

The name of this very old-fashioned cake has nothing directly to do with Native Americans but rather with the fact that it is made with cornmeal, which was often called Indian meal until late in the nineteenth century. The formula is still an old European pound cake. Recipes for it were common until late in the nineteenth century, but virtually disappeared over the course of the last century, except in such rare historically slanted collections as Bill Neal's classic *Biscuits, Spoonbread, and Sweet Potato Pie* and Greg Patent's handsome *Baking in America*. Perhaps one reason it fell from favor is that it doesn't keep well, but its toothsome crumb and delicate flavor make it very satisfying eating—a terrific foil for fresh fruit and cream—and leftovers are terrific slathered with butter and toasted. It deserves to be returned to an honored place in the modern American repertory.

Either white or yellow cornmeal will work in this cake—the choice is yours. Yellow meal gives the cake a rich golden color and its flavor is a little sweeter and more pronounced than white meal, but they provide exactly the same structure. It is delicious with either one.

2 cups extra-fine cornmeal or corn flour (see headnote above)

1 cup Southern soft-wheat flour or cake flour

1 teaspoon cinnamon

1 teaspoon freshly grated nutmeg

Salt

½ pound (1 cup or 2 sticks) unsalted butter

2 cups sugar

7 large eggs

¼ cup bourbon

1 tablespoon Homemade Bourbon Vanilla (page 17), or 1 teaspoon vanilla extract and 2 teaspoons bourbon

Superfine or confectioners' sugar, for dusting

1. Position a rack in the center of the oven and preheat to 325°F. Butter and flour a 10-inch tube or two 9-inch loaf pans (see page 314). Whisk or sift together the meal, flour, spices, and a small pinch of salt. With a wooden spoon or mixer fitted with a paddle or rotary beaters, cream the butter until light and fluffy, then gradually beat in the sugar and cream until very light and fluffy.

2. Beat in the eggs one at a time, then stir (don't beat) in the flour in three or four additions. Stir in the bourbon and vanilla and pour it into the prepared pan. Slip a table knife into the batter and run it through in a back-and-forth S motion to take out any large air pockets. Give the pan a couple of firm taps on the counter—just enough to bring those air bubbles to the surface.

3. Bake for about 1¼ hours, until a straw inserted into the center comes out clean. Don't open the oven door for the first hour. Remove the pan to a wire rack and let it cool for 10–15 minutes, then loosen from the pan and invert it onto a cake plate. Cool completely and dust generously with confectioners' sugar. Use a serrated knife to cut the cake.

Makes one 10-inch tube or two 9-inch loaf cakes, serving 12–16

bonnie's sour cream pound cake

Sour cream pound cake has become a standard in the Southern baker's repertory and is often one of the first cakes a young woman will venture to make on her own. Once you taste it, you will know why: It is moist, rich, and heavenly. This version comes from my pound cake mentor, Bonnie Carter, an accomplished home baker who has helped me bake through all the pound cakes in this book. Bonnie's advice on pound cakes is not to fuss with them too much and to relax: "Pound cakes," she says, "know when you're afraid."

3 cups unbleached all-purpose flour

Dash salt

Dash baking soda

½ pound (1 cup or 2 sticks) unsalted butter

3 cups sugar

6 large eggs

1 cup sour cream

1 teaspoon almond extract, Homemade Bourbon Vanilla (page 17), or vanilla extract

1. Position a rack in the center of the oven and preheat to 325°F. Butter and flour a tube pan (see page 314). Whisk or sift together the flour, salt, and baking soda. With a mixer at medium speed, cream the butter and sugar until very light and fluffy—about 2 minutes.

2. Mix in the eggs one at a time and then the sour cream. Mix in the flour in several additions until smooth. Stir in the flavoring. Pour the batter into the prepared pan, run a knife through it to get out any large air pockets, and give it a few solid taps on the counter to bring big air bubbles to the surface.

3. Bake in the center of the oven about 1¼ hours, or until a straw, toothpick, or cake tester inserted in the center comes out clean. Remove the cake to a wire cooling rack and cool it in the pan for 10–15 minutes, then invert it onto a plate and let it cool completely before cutting. Bonnie always inverts her cake onto a plain plate, then lays a cake plate onto the bottom and inverts it again so that the crusty top is faceup.

Makes one 10-inch tube cake, serving 12–16

aunt margaret's fresh apple pound cake

This cake follows the modern volume pound cake formula but with an unorthodox twist: The batter contains oil instead of solid shortening, which makes an exceptionally moist cake. Otherwise, it's a straightforward, old-fashioned fruitcake—that is, a pound cake batter studded with fruit and nuts. Along with a steaming mug of coffee or tea, it's the perfect thing to savor by a warming fire on a cool autumn afternoon or evening.

FOR THE CAKE:

2 cups sugar

1½ cups vegetable oil

4 large eggs

3 cups unbleached all-purpose flour

1 teaspoon baking soda

1 teaspoon salt

2 teaspoons Homemade Bourbon Vanilla (page 17) or 1 teaspoon vanilla extract

3 cups peeled, cored, and diced tart pie apples (such as Winesap, Arkansas Black, or Granny Smith)

1 cup grated coconut

1 cup chopped pecans

FOR THE TOPPING (OPTIONAL):

¼ pound (½ cup or 1 stick) unsalted butter

1½ cups (firmly packed) brown sugar

½ cup chopped pecans

1 tablespoon milk

1. Position a rack in the center of the oven and preheat to 325°F. Butter and flour a tube pan (see page 314). Combine the sugar and oil in a mixing bowl and beat until well mixed. Beat in the eggs one at a time.

2. Set aside ¼ cup of the flour and sift or whisk together the remainder with the soda and salt. Beat it a little at a time into the sugar, oil, and egg and beat in the vanilla. Put the apples in a mixing bowl and lightly sprinkle them with the reserved flour. Toss to coat, add the coconut and pecans, and toss to mix. Fold this into the batter and pour it into the prepared pan. Run a knife through it in an S pattern and lightly tap the pan on the counter several times to get out any large air bubbles.

3. Bake in the center of the oven for 1 hour and 20 minutes, or until a straw or cake tester inserted into the center comes out clean. Do not open the oven door during the first hour of baking. Cool the cake in the pan for about 15 minutes and then remove it from the pan to a serving plate. Cool the cake completely before topping it.

4. To make the topping, melt the butter in a heavy-bottomed saucepan over medium heat. Add the sugar, nuts, and milk, stirring until the sugar is melted. Raise the heat to medium-high and bring to a boil. Cook, stirring frequently, until it reaches the soft-ball stage (234–240°F on a candy thermometer). Let it cool until it is just warm and pour it over the cake. The cake is also good without the topping, and you may omit it if you prefer it to be less rich.

Makes one 10-inch tube cake, serving 12–16

maryan's chocolate pound cake

Chocolate pound cake has been a standard in the Southern baker's repertory for the better part of a century. It's nothing more than the cook's favorite pound cake with ½–¾ cup cocoa powder substituted for an equal volume of the flour. My own favorite is friend Maryan Harrell's version. Her secret is Mexican vanilla extract. Not only is it more concentrated than American extract, but it's made from the bean of a different strain of orchid than the one we're accustomed to. For years, Mexican vanilla was not exported into our country, but today it's more widely available. The second best choice is Homemade Bourbon Vanilla (see page 17). The formula here is the modern one: equal volumes flour and sugar, then half the volume in shortening. Maryan substitutes vegetable shortening for some of the butter for a lighter crumb, and uses evaporated milk for moistness. Cream won't substitute for it.

½ **pound (2 sticks or 1 cup) unsalted butter, softened**

¼ **pound (½ cup) all-vegetable shortening (see headnote above)**

3 **cups sugar**

6 **large eggs**

2½ **cups Southern soft-wheat flour or soft-wheat pastry flour**

½ **teaspoon baking powder**

1 **teaspoon salt**

½ **cup cocoa**

1 **cup evaporated milk**

1 **teaspoon Mexican vanilla extract, Homemade Bourbon Vanilla (page 17), or pure vanilla extract**

1. Butter and flour a 10-inch tube pan or two 9-inch loaf pans (see page 314), then shake out the excess flour. Using a mixer or wooden spoon, cream the butter and shortening in a large mixing bowl. Add the sugar and cream until light and fluffy. Beat in the eggs one at a time, beating well after each addition until the batter is lemony and very fluffy.

2. Sift together the flour, baking powder, salt, and cocoa. Alternating between the two, gradually mix the flour and evaporated milk into the batter, beating well between each addition. When all the flour and milk are incorporated, beat in the vanilla extract. Spoon the batter into the tube pan or divide it equally between the loaf pans.

3. Run a knife through the batter in an S pattern to release any large air bubbles, then firmly tap each pan on the counter several times to force the bubbles to the surface. This will help ensure an even texture. Position a rack in the center of the oven and put the pan on the rack. Set the oven temperature at 300°F and turn it on. Bake the cake for 1½–2 hours, until a straw inserted in the center comes out clean. (Loaf cakes will be done a little sooner than a tube cake.) Turn off the oven and leave the door slightly ajar. Allow the cake to cool in the oven.

Makes one ring cake or two 9-inch loaf cakes

candy's blueberry pound cake

This lovely cake has become a modern American classic. Its rich, dense, velvety, and yet delicate crumb, studded with contrasting deep purple-blue, tart-sweet berries, is a perfect study in balanced contrast. This version comes from friend Candy Hall in Virginia, a fine cook and baker whose two amazing and beautiful daughters are among the great joys of my life. This cake was once strictly a summer sweet, made during the blueberry season that can be as early as June in the Deep South and as late as September to the north, but Candy and *Baking in America* author Greg Patent both say that individually quick-frozen berries work fine here. Don't thaw them first, but dust them with flour and fold them into the batter while they're still frozen solid.

1 pint blueberries, washed and well drained

14 ounces (about 3 scant cups) unbleached all-purpose flour

1 teaspoon baking powder

½ teaspoon salt

½ pound (1 cup or 2 sticks) unsalted butter, softened

2 cups sugar

4 eggs

1½ teaspoons pure vanilla extract or 1 tablespoon Homemade Bourbon Vanilla (page 17)

Freshly squeezed lemon juice, to taste

1. Position a rack in the lower third of the oven and preheat to 325°F. Butter and flour a 10-inch tube pan or two 9-inch loaf pans (see page 314). Dust the berries with ¼ cup of the flour. In a separate bowl, sift or whisk together the remaining flour, baking powder, and salt.

2. With a mixer fitted with a paddle or rotary beaters, cream the butter until fluffy. Gradually add the sugar, creaming at medium speed until fluffy and very light. Beat in the eggs one at a time, beating well after each addition, then beat in the vanilla and lemon juice.

3. Fold the flour into the batter a little at a time until well blended; gently stir in the berries. Pour it into the prepared pan(s), run a table or palette knife through, and tap firmly on the counter a couple of times to take out any large air bubbles.

4. Bake in the lower third of the oven for about 1 hour and 10 minutes or until a cake tester or straw inserted into the center comes out clean. Do not open the oven during the first hour. Cool the cake in the pan on a wire rack for 10 minutes, then remove it from the pan.

Makes one 10-inch tube or two 9-inch loaf cakes, serving 12–16

great fruit cake

Fruitcake used to be the essential cake for any celebration—and with good reason. When well made, there is nothing to equal it. The recipe is called "Great" because it often appeared in the old books as "great cake." While their intention was "enormous" and not, as it is nowadays, "terrific," our looser modern use of the word is, in this case, appropriate. If you think otherwise, you've probably never had a real, homemade fruitcake, with a rich pound cake base and succulent, flavorful preserved fruit. If fruitcake brings to your mind those drab commercial blocks of lurid candied fruit that are all too common around the holidays, it is past time that you got acquainted with this cake. Ever since I started making them while researching *Classical Southern Cooking*, I've never let a Christmas pass without them. My family met the first effort skeptically, but today they beg for it.

1 pound raisins

1 pound golden raisins

1 pound currants

1 pound dried dark cherries

1 pound Crystallized Citrus Peel (page 24), made from oranges

½ cup bourbon, plus more for aging the cakes (optional)

1 pound (4 sticks or 2 cups) unsalted butter, at room temperature

1 pound (2 cups) sugar

1 pound (about 3½ cups) Southern soft-wheat or pastry flour, plus about ¼ cup for dusting the fruit

1 teaspoon each cinnamon and freshly grated nutmeg

8 large fresh eggs, at room temperature

½ cup dry sherry

1 tablespoon Homemade Bourbon Vanilla (page 17) or 1 teaspoon vanilla extract

1 pound pecans

1. Put the raisins, currants, cherries, and candied orange peel in a heatproof, nonreactive metal or glass bowl. Bring a teakettle of water to a boil and pour it over the fruit. Let it stand for 10 minutes, then drain thoroughly. Add the bourbon and toss well. Let cool, cover, and let it macerate for at least an hour; overnight is better. The whiskey should be almost completely absorbed.

2. Position a rack in the center of the oven and preheat to 325°F. Butter and flour two 10-inch tube cake pans or four 9-inch loaf pans (see page 314), shake out the excess flour into the next pan, and repeat until all the pans are floured.

3. With a wooden spoon or mixer fitted with a paddle or rotary beaters, cream the butter and sugar until light and fluffy. Sift or whisk together the flour and spices, then, alternating, gradually mix the flour and eggs into the butter and sugar. Mix well after each addition. Stir in the sherry and vanilla.

4. Lightly sprinkle the fruit with ¼ cup flour and toss until coated. Fold the fruit and pecans into the batter until all is uniformly distributed; spoon the batter evenly into the prepared pans. Run a knife through in an S pattern and firmly tap the pans on the counter several times to force any air bubbles to the surface.

5. Bake in the center of the oven, not touching one another, for about 1½ hours without opening the oven door, then check the cakes and continue baking until they are done and a straw or bamboo skewer stuck into the center comes out clean. A tube cake will be done in about 2 hours;

loaf cakes may take a little less time. Turn off the oven, crack the oven door, and let the cakes cool in the oven. Let cool completely before removing from the pan.

6. If you like, you may soak cheesecloth or clean, undyed cotton cloths in bourbon, wring them out thoroughly, and wrap these around the cakes, then wrap the cakes tightly with plastic wrap or put them in an airtight tin for at least 2 weeks before using them.

Makes two tube cakes or four 9-inch loaf cakes

pound cake sandwiches

Toasted pound cake is a popular, if somewhat home-spun, Southern breakfast sweet, but when the cake is filled with a variation on every child's favorite sandwich, it takes on a whole new dimension. Think of this as a PBJ with an attitude.

If you really want to gild the lily, serve it with a small scoop of ice cream on the side or pass a pitcher of Bourbon Custard (see page 329). For variety, you may also substitute chopped almonds or peanuts.

8 thin (about ⅓-inch thick) slices Bourbon Pound Cake (page 318)

¼ cup blackberry or raspberry preserves, or ¼ cup orange marmalade

⅓ cup finely chopped pecans

2 tablespoons unsalted butter, melted

1. Position a rack about 4 inches from the broiler heat source and preheat the broiler for at least 10 minutes.

2. Thinly spread one side of all the slices of cake with the preserves or marmalade. Sprinkle half of them evenly with the chopped pecans, then top these with the remaining slices, preserve-coated-side down.

3. Lightly brush both sides of the sandwiches with butter and broil them, turning once, until both sides are golden-brown. Serve hot.

Serves 4 as a dessert, 6–8 at tea

bourbon custard

Whether you call it by its elegant French name, "crème anglaise," or by its more prosaic and artlessly inaccurate Southern name "boiled custard," this delicate sweet sauce is practically ubiquitous throughout the entire Western world. For Southern cooks, it's the sauce to have on hand, especially in summer. It's incomparable over sliced fresh or poached fruit, homey bread pudding, fruit pies, and cobblers, and it cuts the intensity of rich chocolate or tart, acidic desserts.

2 cups half and half

⅔ cup sugar

6 large egg yolks, lightly beaten

2 tablespoons bourbon, or 1 tablespoon Homemade Bourbon Vanilla (page 17) and 1 tablespoon bourbon

1. Prepare the bottom of a double boiler with 1 inch of water, cover, and bring to a boil. Reduce the heat to medium. Stir together the half-and-half and sugar in the top half of the double boiler. Bring it almost to a boil, stirring constantly, over direct medium heat.

2. Place the pan over the simmering water. Slowly beat half a cup of the hot half-and-half into the egg yolks. Add this to the remaining half-and-half and cook, stirring constantly, until it coats the back of the spoon. It will be only lightly thickened, so take care not to overcook it. It will continue to thicken as it cools.

3. Remove the custard from the heat and stir until it is slightly cooled. Stir in the flavoring and keep stirring for another minute. Let it cool completely before serving or refrigerating. Serve chilled or at room temperature.

Makes 2 cups

plain, or 1-2-3-4 cake

The name for this traditional all-purpose yellow layer cake is an easy-to-remember shorthand for the proportions of its main ingredients: 1 cup of shortening, 2 of sugar, 3 of flour, and 4 eggs. It's the cake our grandmothers used as their basic yellow layer cake, the name and character of the finished cake depending entirely on what was slathered over it: Rich fudge frosting made it chocolate cake, snowy layers of coconut-crusted Seven-Minute Frosting or sour cream frosting made it coconut cake, and so on. This recipe was so commonplace that it often appeared as nothing more than a title and list of ingredients with no directions whatsoever, as if any baker worth her mixing bowl would know what to do.

To make the cake lighter and more delicate, separate the eggs. Add the yolks to the batter where indicated in step 1. Beat the whites in a separate bowl until they form firm but not dry peaks. Fold a little of the batter into them, and then fold the whites into the batter. The rise will be a little higher, but the cake will also settle a little as it cools, like a soufflé.

½ pound (1 cup or 2 sticks) unsalted butter

2 cups granulated sugar

4 large eggs

14 ounces (about 3 cups) all-purpose flour

2 teaspoons baking powder

1 teaspoon salt

1 cup whole milk

1½ teaspoons Homemade Bourbon Vanilla (page 17) or vanilla extract

1. Position a rack in the center of the oven and preheat to 350°F. Butter and flour three 9-inch round or two 9-inch square cake pans (see page 314). In a large mixing bowl, cream the butter and sugar until fluffy, light, and lemon-colored. Beat in the eggs one at a time.

2. Sift or whisk together the flour, baking powder, and salt. Alternately beat the flour and milk into the batter in four additions, beating well between each addition. Stir in extract.

3. Divide the batter equally among the prepared pans, then tap them sharply on the counter several times to make any large air bubbles rise to the top. If the oven won't hold all the pans on one rack without touching, stagger them on two racks in the middle of the oven. Bake for 25–30 minutes, or until a toothpick inserted in the center comes out clean.

4. Remove them to a wire rack and let cool completely before taking them out of the pans and icing them.

For three 9-inch-diameter or two 9-inch square layers

mama's coconut cake

This is my maternal grandmother's recipe for a cake that, since at least the last quarter of the nineteenth century, has been traditional at Christmas in Carolina and Georgia. Its rich moistness and deep coconut flavor are owed to the fact that MaMa saved the fresh coconut juice to baste over each layer before she frosted it. Except for the brief heating to melt sugar into that juice, no part of the coconut was cooked, so it stayed lively and fresh. Both my grandmothers made this cake—a fact that my father's side of the family did not fail to point out when I first published MaMa's recipe. Well, with all due respect to Granny, who was hands-down the best chicken fryer I ever knew, MaMa had the real touch when it came to baking.

1 recipe 1-2-3-4 Cake (page 330), baked in 3 layers

1 medium fresh coconut, with plenty of juice (it should slosh when shaken)

2–3 tablespoons sugar

1 recipe Seven-Minute Frosting (page 337), not made ahead, but where indicated in step 2

1. Prepare the coconut: Pierce all the holes at one end with an ice pick or other pointed object such as a screwdriver, tapping it with a hammer. I do this sitting down with the coconut held firmly between my knees. Drain the juice through a strainer into a bowl, shaking the nut gently to get it all. Lay the nut on its side on a concrete floor or brick-paved patio or door stoop and tap it firmly with a hammer at the middle. Roll it, tapping steadily until it splits in half. Turn each half dome-side up and tap at the top until it cracks and breaks apart. Slip a wide sturdy blade such as that of an oyster knife between the shell and the meat and pry it loose. Peel off the brown skin with a vegetable peeler, rinse the white meat, pat dry, and grate it using a rotary cheese box grater, or the fine shredding blade of the food processor.

2. Measure the reserved coconut juice. If there's less than a cup, add enough water to make a full cup of liquid. Put it in a saucepan with 2–3 tablespoons of sugar, to taste, and warm it over a medium-low heat, stirring occasionally until the sugar dissolves. Turn off the heat. Make the frosting according to the recipe on page 337.

3. Invert the first layer of cake over the plate and carefully remove the pan. Spoon about ¼ cup of the coconut juice over it, gently spread it with a thin layer of frosting, and sprinkle a quarter of the coconut evenly over it. Invert the second layer over it and remove it from the pan. Spoon another ¼ cup plus a tablespoon of juice over it, frost and sprinkle it with coconut as before, and then invert the final layer and spoon another ¼ cup of the juice over the top.

4. Frost both the top and sides of the cake, turning it as you work to ensure an even cover. Pat the rest of the coconut evenly over the top and sides and spoon the remaining juice slowly over it, letting each spoonful soak in before adding more. Cover with a cake dome or an improvised dome of aluminum foil that does not touch the cake and let it rest for 24 hours before cutting it. Once it is cut, keep it well covered and, after the second day, refrigerated.

Makes one 9-inch, 3-layer cake

white layer cake

Sometimes this delicate cake, pale because it contained only the whites of the eggs, could be found in old cookbooks and manuscript recipe collections under evocative, picturesque names like "lady" or "silver" cake. Its pale color of course is not truly white unless the baker has used lard or shortening instead of butter, but let's not split hairs. It's the ideal base for many of the elegant layer cakes filled with fruit, including the legendary Lady Baltimore Cake of the Carolina Lowcountry or Emma Rylander Lane's Prize Cake that now carries her name, and for those curd- and custard-"jelly"-filled confections of the late nineteenth century that carried patriotic names like Robert E. Lee Cake.

7 large egg whites (yolks set aside for another use such as lemon curd, page 340)

½ pound (1 cup or 2 sticks) butter

2 cups sugar

12 ounces (about 2⅔ cups) all-purpose flour

1 tablespoon Single-Acting Baking Powder (page 255) or 2½ teaspoons double-acting baking powder

½ teaspoon salt

1 cup milk

1 lemon, or 1 tablespoon Homemade Bourbon Vanilla (page 17), or 1 teaspoon commercial vanilla extract

1. Position a rack in the center of the oven and preheat to 375°F. Butter and flour two or three 9-inch round cake pans (see page 314). Put the egg whites in a metal or glass bowl. With a mixer set on medium speed, cream the butter and sugar until light, fluffy, and lemon-colored.

2. Sift or whisk together the flour, baking powder, and salt. Gradually add this alternating with the milk to the butter and sugar, beating well after each addition. Stir in the flavoring. (If you are using lemon, grate the rind into the batter and then the juice of the fruit into it through a strainer.)

3. With a whisk or the mixer refitted with cleaned beaters or a whisk attachment, whip the egg whites to soft peaks. Carefully, but thoroughly, fold them into the batter. Divide it equally among the pans and bake in the center of the oven (make sure that the pans don't touch) for 25–30 minutes, or until a toothpick inserted into the center comes out clean.

Makes 2 thick or 3 thin 9-inch layers

old-fashioned lemon jelly cake

Jelly cakes made in layers rather than rolled spirals are rarely seen anymore, and may nowadays be thought a bit old-fashioned, but once they were the prize of Southern housewives from Virginia to Mississippi. Variations on the theme can still be found in historical collections going by such regionally patriotic names as Robert E. Lee Cake. But they live in more than history, even among those who grew up in the last half of the twentieth century. Seven-Minute Frosting really makes this cake shine, though it will mean that there will be a lot of leftover yolks, even after you've made the lemon curd, so if you prefer frost it with Mock Lemon Buttercream.

1 recipe White Layer Cake (page 334), baked in 3 layers

About 1½ cups lemon curd (page 340)

1 recipe Seven-Minute Frosting (page 337), flavored with lemon, or Mock Lemon Buttercream (page 340) not made ahead but at the point indicated in step 3

½ cup Candied Citrus Threads, made with lemon (page 343)

1. Allow the cake layers to cool and take them carefully out of the pans. If the cakes have "domed" a little in the center, you can carefully slice off the excess to level the layers with a serrated bread knife. Place one layer top-side up on a cake plate. Cover the top thickly with lemon curd, leaving about ½ inch uncovered at the edges (the filling spreads when the next layer is added). Invert the second layer over it and carefully set it in place.

2. Thickly cover the top of the second layer with curd, again leaving about ½ inch around the edges uncovered. Invert the third layer over it and set it in place.

3. Make the Seven-Minute Frosting and immediately spread it evenly over the top and sides of the cake, swirling it decoratively with the spatula. Let the cake stand for at least an hour to allow the frosting to set. Sprinkle it with Candied Citrus Threads just before serving.

Orange or Key Lime Jelly Cake: Substitute orange curd (page 341) and Candied Citrus Threads made with orange zest, or key lime curd (page 341), either using lemon zest or green Persian lime zest for the Candied Threads—or omitting them. Either frosting can also be flavored with orange.

Makes one 9-inch, 3-layer cake

brown velvet cake with dark fudge frosting

One of the most popular and legendary cakes in modern American baking is red velvet cake—a light cocoa-flavored cake whose naturally ruddy color is enhanced by a whopping dose of red food coloring. There are a couple of popular legends about the origins of the name that have no basis in fact and are not worth going into. (The Southern creed is to never let the truth stand in the way of a good story.) But legends aside, this cake's legendary, velvet crumb has nothing to do with its color, but with the leavening combination of buttermilk and baking soda. Most version of the cake—whether red or brown—are usually iced with a plain white sugar frosting, which is as pretty to look at as it is boring to eat. A cake with velvet in its name deserves a finish that is equally luscious and indulgent, and rich, silky old-fashioned fudge frosting fits the bill handsomely.

2 cups Southern soft wheat flour or pastry flour

2 teaspoons baking soda

½ teaspoon salt

3 ounces (3 squares) unsweetened chocolate

8 ounces (1 cup or 2 sticks) unsalted butter, softened

1½ cups (firmly packed) light brown sugar

2 large eggs

1 cup whole-milk buttermilk, or plain whole-milk yogurt thinned to buttermilk consistency with milk or water

1 tablespoon Homemade Bourbon Vanilla (page 17) or 1 teaspoon vanilla extract

1 recipe Old-Fashioned Dark Fudge Frosting (page 338), not made ahead, but where indicated in step 3

1. Position a rack in the center of the oven and preheat to 350°F. Butter and flour two 9-inch layer cake pans (see page 314). Whisk or sift together the flour, baking soda, and salt. Melt the chocolate in a double boiler over simmering water, then remove it from the heat but keep it warm.

2. Cream the butter until fluffy, then add the sugar and cream until fluffy and light. Beat in the eggs one at a time, and then stir in the melted chocolate. Mix in the flour and milk a little at a time, alternating, beginning and finishing with the flour, and stir in the vanilla. Divide the batter between the prepared pans, tap them lightly on the counter to force any large air bubbles to the surface, and bake in the center of the oven for about 20 minutes, or until a straw or cake tester inserted into the center comes out clean.

3. Set on wire racks and let the cake cool in the pans before removing and frosting them. While they cool, make the frosting. Invert one layer over a cake plate and carefully remove the pan. Cover it thickly with about a third of the frosting. Invert the second layer over it, remove the pan, and then frost the top and sides with the remaining frosting. Let the frosting set before cutting, at least an hour.

Makes one 9-inch, 2-layer cake

seven-minute frosting

This frosting is of course called Seven-Minute because that's how long it cooks. It's also artlessly called "boiled" icing in some old cookbooks, a name that's misleading, since, as is true of "boiled" custard or ham, it would be ruined if it actually boiled. It's a good all-purpose frosting, and its variations unlimited. My maternal grandmother taught me to make this, and just as creaming butter and sugar brings her back, whipping up a batch of Seven-Minute Frosting is filled with good memories. Modern recipes often contain a little cream of tartar or tablespoon of corn syrup to help stabilize the frosting, but since MaMa never used either, neither do I. Make this only when you are ready to frost the cake, as its surface hardens and crusts over as it cools.

4 large egg whites

1 pound (2 cups) sugar

9 tablespoons water

Flavorings (see variations, following)

1. In the bottom pan of a large double boiler, bring 1 inch of water to a simmer over medium heat, then reduce the heat to a simmer. Off the heat, combine the egg whites, sugar, and water in the top pot and beat until the sugar dissolves.

2. Put the pan over the simmering water, making sure that the water doesn't touch it, and beat for 7 minutes with a whisk or handheld mixer at medium speed, or until it stands in soft peaks.

3. Immediately take it from the heat and beat in the flavoring, then beat until it's thick enough to spread. Use at once.

Vanilla Seven-Minute Frosting: Add 1 tablespoon Homemade Bourbon Vanilla (page 17) or 1 teaspoon commercial vanilla extract.

Lemon Seven-Minute Frosting: Grate the zest of 1 lemon and substitute a tablespoon of its juice for an equal amount of the water. Add the zest where directed in step 3. You may color it with saffron or yellow food coloring, but I leave it snowy-white and garnish it with Candied Citrus Threads (page 343) made with lemon zest.

Orange Seven-Minute Frosting: Follow the procedure for lemon icing, using the grated zest of half an orange and substituting its juice for the water. (If you can get Seville oranges, their tart juice and bright rinds make an even better icing than regular oranges.) Beat the zest into the icing as directed in step 3. As with the lemon frosting, above, you may color it orange with food coloring, but I prefer a garnish of Candied Citrus Threads (page 343).

Peppermint Seven-Minute Frosting: So it's hokey and retro—get over it: It also happens to be really good. Fold in a cup of finely crushed peppermint stick candy, or just sprinkle the candy over the frosting after it has been put onto the cake.

Makes enough for three 9-inch layers

old-fashioned dark fudge frosting

The first chocolate cakes were not really chocolate, but yellow cakes covered with simple chocolate icing, a confection that survives to this day in towering cakes whose six to eight (or more) layers are bound with fudge frosting. The earliest had a much simpler topping—grated chocolate sprinkled over whipped cream or a meringue similar to Seven-Minute Frosting—much as we would finish a cake today with confectioners' sugar. The next logical step was to fold the chocolate into the cream or meringue. All of these were fragile and not nearly as good as rich, dense fudge frosting, so they disappeared almost as soon as it came on the scene. This is the perfect frosting for Brown Velvet Cake (page 336), old-time 1-2-3-4 Cake (page 330), or your favorite plain or chocolate cupcakes.

3 cups sugar

1 cup cocoa

1 teaspoon salt

1½ cups heavy cream

4 ounces (8 tablespoons or 1 stick) unsalted butter

4 ounces bittersweet chocolate, roughly chopped, or bittersweet chips (about 1 cup)

1 tablespoon Homemade Bourbon Vanilla (page 17) or 2 teaspoons vanilla extract

1. Whisk together the sugar, cocoa, and salt in a heavy-bottomed saucepan. Slowly whisk in the cream and bring it to a boil over medium heat, stirring occasionally. Add the butter and chocolate, stirring until melted and smooth. Let it come back to boil and cook, stirring occasionally, until it reaches the soft-ball stage (234°F on a candy thermometer), about 2–3 minutes.

2. Remove from the heat and stir in the vanilla. Let it cool, undisturbed, until just warm (no more than 110°F), then beat the frosting with a mixer or wooden spoon until it's thick enough to spread. Immediately frost the cake.

Makes about 6 cups

real buttercream frosting

This sumptuous frosting lifts any cake from the mundane to the spectacular. It's a genuine French-style buttercream in which softened and whipped butter is beaten into egg yolks that have been thickened and tempered with hot sugar syrup. The syrup should simmer long enough to reach the thread stage (235°F on a candy thermometer), and the custard must cool to room temperature or even slightly cooler or it will not set up properly. Any cake iced with this buttercream should be kept cold until served.

¾ cup sugar

¼ teaspoon cream of tartar

¼ teaspoon salt

⅓ cup water

5 large egg yolks

½ pound (1 cup or 2 sticks) unsalted butter, softened to room temperature

Flavorings (see variations, below)

1. Combine the sugar, cream of tartar, and salt in a small saucepan and whisk to mix. Stir in the water and place the pan over medium-high heat. Bring it to a boil, stirring occasionally, and reduce the heat to medium. Simmer 5 minutes, or until it reaches 235°F on a candy thermometer. Meanwhile, beat the yolks with an electric mixer fitted with rotary beaters at medium speed until light, thick, and almost doubled in volume, about 3 minutes.

2. Pour the boiling syrup into a heatproof measuring cup and immediately beat it into the egg yolks in a thin, steady stream. Continue beating at medium speed until it reaches room temperature and is no longer at all warm. You may want to refrigerate it for a few minutes.

3. Cream the butter in a separate bowl until light and fluffy, then beat it gradually into the custard a tablespoon at a time. It should begin to thicken suddenly as you add the last ¼ cup butter. Beat in the flavorings. If at this point buttercream is not thick and holding peaks, chill it for about 30 minutes, or until it is very cool and quite thick, then beat it until it's thick enough to spread. Spread the frosting at once.

Vanilla Buttercream: Beat in 1 tablespoon Homemade Bourbon Vanilla (page 17) or 1 teaspoon vanilla extract and 1 tablespoon bourbon.

Lemon or Orange Buttercream: Beat in the grated zest of a lemon or orange and 2–3 tablespoons of lemon or orange juice or orange liqueur.

Makes about 4 cups, enough to frost a 2-layer cake

mock orange or lemon buttercream

Cruder and not nearly as delicate as true buttercream, the big drawback of this frosting is the cornstarch that is contained in American confectioners' sugar, which often lends a raw, pasty aftertaste. It is a good quick fix for a strongly flavored cake, however, and flavorings like lemon or orange go a long way toward covering up its deficiencies. As with true buttercream, any cake frosted with this must be kept refrigerated.

¼ pound (½ cup or 1 stick) unsalted butter, softened to room temperature

⅛ teaspoon salt

2¼ cups confectioners' sugar

Grated zest of 1 lemon or orange

¼ cup lemon or orange juice or orange liqueur

3–4 tablespoons heavy cream

1. Cream the butter until light and fluffy with a mixer at medium speed. Add the salt and sift in the sugar. Beat the sugar into the butter at medium speed until it is thick and fluffy.

2. Beat in the zest and juice and then gradually beat in enough heavy cream, a tablespoon at a time, to make the frosting light and spreadable. Spread it at once.

Makes about 3½ cups, enough for one 2-layer cake or a dozen cupcakes

lemon curd

The nicest and most traditional filling for lemon pies, tarts, and old-fashioned jelly cakes, lemon curd is singularly wonderful all on its own slathered over hot biscuits or toast. This makes enough for one 9-inch lemon meringue pie, a dozen pre-baked tartlet shells, or the filling for a 9-inch round Old-Fashioned Lemon Jelly Cake (page 355). It will keep, covered and refrigerated, for up to a month—or so I'm told: It has never lasted that long in my house.

To make Lime or Key Lime Curd, simply substitute lime juice and zest for the lemon.

¼ pound (½ cup or 1 stick) unsalted butter

½ cup freshly squeezed lemon juice (about 4–5 lemons)

4 teaspoons grated lemon rind—or more, to taste

1 cup sugar

Salt

2 whole large eggs and 4 large egg yolks

1. Prepare the bottom pot of a double boiler with 1 inch of water and bring it to a boil over medium heat. Reduce the heat to a slow simmer. Put the top pot over direct, medium heat and put in the butter. Barely melt it, and then stir in the lemon juice, grated rind, sugar, and a small pinch of salt, stirring until the sugar and salt are dissolved. Put the pot over the simmering water, making sure it doesn't touch the water.

2. Beat together the whole eggs and yolks until smooth. Slowly stir them into the butter and cook, stirring constantly, until the curd is quite thick and the spoon leaves a distinct path in it, about 8 minutes. It will continue to thicken as it cools, but it won't reach the stiff consistency of a bottled curd until it's cold, so don't overcook it. Remove it from the heat.

3. Keep stirring the curd until it has cooled somewhat and then pour it into another container and let it cool completely. Cover and refrigerate until thoroughly chilled before using.

Notes: This is a simple recipe—but working with butter and egg custards can be a tricky business unless you pay attention every second. Take care not to allow the butter to get too hot before the eggs are added or they could curdle. If at any point it looks as if it's getting too hot, take it off the heat and beat in a little cold butter.

Key Lime Curd: Substitute the juice and zest of key limes for the lemon. If you can't get real key limes, a plausible substitute can be made using equal amounts of juice from lemons and Persian limes.

Orange Curd: Substitute orange juice for all but a tablespoon of the lemon juice (for tartness), and use orange instead of lemon zest.

Makes about 2½ cups

custard cream for layer cakes and pastries

This custard is basically a classic crème patisserie (pastry cream). It's the only proper custard to bind that quintessential Southern trifle, banana pudding (see page 405), and is a fine base for a fresh fruit tart.

5 large egg yolks

½ cup all-purpose flour

1 cup sugar

3 cups whole milk

1 tablespoon Homemade Bourbon Vanilla (page 17) or 1 teaspoon vanilla extract

1. Beat the yolks in a heatproof bowl until light and smooth. Prepare the bottom half of a double boiler with an inch of water and bring it to a simmer over medium heat. In the top pot, whisk together the flour and sugar. Slowly whisk in the milk and place the pot directly over medium heat. Bring it almost to a boil, stirring constantly.

2. Whisk ½ cup of the hot milk mixture into the yolks to temper them and then slowly whisk the yolks into the remaining milk. Place it over the simmering water and cook, stirring constantly, until it is thickened, about 5–8 minutes. Remove it from the heat, stir in the vanilla, and stir for a minute more to cool it slightly. Set aside to cool completely.

Makes about 3½ cups

candied citrus threads

This delicate candied peel is different from the one on page 24 that's used for fruitcakes and sweet buns. Thin, crisp, and delicate, these threads make a beautiful garnish for pies and cakes, especially those topped with a snowy Seven-Minute Frosting, meringue, or whipped cream. They are also delicious served as a last sweet bite after dinner—on their own or as condiment for coffee. I learned to make it from soul food diva Joyce White, who likes to add a touch of vanilla.

3 large oranges or 4 large lemons

1¼ cups sugar, divided

1 teaspoon Homemade Bourbon Vanilla (page 17) or ½ teaspoon commercial vanilla extract (optional)

1. Wash the fruit and pat it dry. Remove the zest with a vegetable peeler in ½-inch-wide strips, avoiding any white pith. If there is any pith on the back of the zest, gently scrape it away with a sharp paring knife. Cut the zest into thin straw or matchstick strips, put them in a medium saucepan with enough cold water to cover them by an inch, and bring to boil. Boil for 5 minutes, drain into a wire sieve, and rinse well with cold water.

2. Return the zest to the pan, cover with cold water, and bring to boil. Reduce the heat to a slow simmer and cook until the peel is tender, about 20–25 minutes. Drain it and return to the pan. Add 1 cup of the sugar, 1 cup cold water and the optional vanilla (if you want a pure citrus flavor, you may want to omit it). Bring it to a simmer over low heat and simmer until the zest is translucent and the syrup somewhat reduced and thickened, 20–30 minutes. Drain through a wire sieve, reserving the syrup—it's one of the best things about the whole recipe.

3. Spread the peel on waxed or parchment paper and place it in a warm spot to dry for 1 hour. Toss the peel in the remaining ¼ cup sugar to coat, spread it on clean paper, and leave it to dry for several hours. When it's dry, store it in an airtight container. Keeps about 1 week or up to a month, refrigerated.

Makes about 1 cup

COOKIES AND BARS

The only possible explanation for why the serpent used fruit to tempt Eve is that cookies had not yet been invented. It is for certain that had she presented Adam with a cookie instead of some suspicious-looking fruit, he'd have bitten right in and asked questions later. Ever since these little morsels came along, they've been used by temptresses the world over—by brides to please a new husband and win over a reticent mother-in-law or nosy neighbor, by mothers and grandmothers to tame unruly children, by little girls (of all ages) to lure little boys into a modicum of civilized behavior (or trouble, depending on how old they are). Well, no matter what the motive, nothing succeeds quite like a plate of homemade cookies.

Often called "little cakes" in old cookbooks (*cookie*, adapted from a Dutch word, didn't become common until late in the nineteenth century), these sweet bites have been a part of American baking from the beginning, but not in the commonplace, taken-for-granted role they occupy today. Once reserved for special occasions, today commercially made cookies fill entire aisles of most supermarkets, and have become our easy answer to virtually every daily whim. Ready-baked confections satisfy quick fixes, but they can't replace the irresistible aroma of cookies baking in your own oven, which is probably why as much as half the dairy case is taken up with cylinders of prepared cookie dough, ready to slice off and bake—or, as is often the case nowadays, to pinch right off the cylinder and eat raw.

The puzzling thing about the proliferation of this ready-to-bake dough is that homemade cookies are not much more work opening a tube of dough and slicing it, and they're a lot more rewarding. Cookies require no special skills and are accessible to the most inexperienced baker. All they require is first-rate ingredients, carefully measured, a little care in the mixing, and a very little of the cook's attention once they go into the oven. About the hardest thing about cookie baking is remembering not to wander off and forget them until that unmistakable and depressing odor of overbrowned flour and sugar brings you running back—too late—to the kitchen.

Beyond simply paying attention while the things bake, here are a few cookie basics:

- Have everything, especially the butter and eggs, at room temperature unless noted otherwise.

- All-purpose flour is fine for most cookies: Only a few benefit from the low glutens of soft wheat flour, and I've so noted where it applies.

- A kitchen timer is useful in helping you not to forget a baking batch, but only after you have gotten used to your oven and know how hot or cool it tends to run. Set the timer for a minute or two before the time given in the recipe.

- After a while your nose will be the best indicator of doneness: You'll know by smell when the cookies are still underdone, just right, or beginning to overcook. Pay attention to those smells: Once you get accustomed to them, they will never fail you.

- Most cookie dough (except bar cookies and wafers) can be made ahead and refrigerated or frozen. You can make a batch to have on hand, or bake part of a batch and store the leftover dough to use later and have fresh-baked cookies all along. Often, chilling the dough makes it easier to handle, and I've indicated as much in the pertinent recipes.

bourbon pecan squares

This rich kissing cousin to lemon squares combines two famed Southern baking traditions in one sumptuous mouthful: Southern-style shortbread laced with a little cornmeal topped with a brown sugar, bourbon, and pecan custard reminiscent of pecan tassies (page 379). Best of all, they are even easier than tassies to make—and dangerously irresistible.

2 cups whole pecan halves

10 ounces (about 2 cups) Southern soft wheat or all-purpose flour, plus 1 tablespoon

2 tablespoons extra-fine white cornmeal

1 cup sugar

Salt

10 ounces (1¼ cups or 2½ sticks) unsalted butter, softened, divided

3 large eggs

½ cup (tightly packed) light brown sugar

2 tablespoons bourbon

1. Position a rack in the center of the oven and preheat to 375°F. Spread the pecans on a baking sheet and toast in the center of the oven until beginning to color, about 8 minutes. Let the pecans cool and roughly chop them. Reduce the oven temperature to 350°F.

2. Sift together 2 cups of the flour, the cornmeal, ½ cup of granulated sugar, and a small pinch of salt. Add 8 ounces (1 cup, or 2 sticks) of the butter and work it into the flour until smooth. You may do the first part of this step in a food processor fitted with a steel blade: Put in the flour, meal, sugar, and salt and pulse several times to sift. Add the butter and process until the mixture resembles coarse meal. Turn it out into a mixing bowl and finish blending by hand. Wrap and chill for 30 minutes.

3. Press the dough into a 9 × 13-inch pan in a uniform layer over the bottom and about ½ inch up the sides. Lightly prick it with a fork and bake in the center of the oven for 20 minutes, or until it's beginning to color, then remove it from the oven and let it cool slightly.

4. Melt the remaining butter, let it cool slightly, and beat it together with the eggs, the remaining granulated sugar, the brown sugar, and a small pinch of salt. Stir in the bourbon and pecans. Sift in the remaining tablespoon of flour and stir until smooth. Spread evenly over the crust and bake until golden and set, about 25 minutes. Cool in the pan on a wire rack before cutting into 24 squares.

Makes about 2 dozen

aunt margaret's congo squares

Southern families are endlessly convoluted, and sorting them out is not helped by the fact that most of us grew up with "aunts," "uncles," "Big Mamas," "Ma-Mas," "Paw-Paws," and "Grannies" that weren't blood relatives—at least, not in any way that was ever acknowledged. Margaret Queen Snelgrove was not my mother's sister, but her best friend; still, I never knew her as anything but "Aunt." If you are Southern, you already understand, and if you aren't—well, explaining why is far too complicated. Aunt Margaret was a terrific old-fashioned Southern cook and baker, and any visit to her house always included plenty of good things to eat. For us children, that usually meant a big stash of these luscious, chocolate-studded blond brownies—or so I used to think. It was only when I asked Margaret's daughters for this recipe that my mother confessed that the reason they were always on hand was because they were her favorite. There are several folk explanations for this cookie's name, some more complicated than explaining Aunt Margaret, but the most plausible is that they're named for New Orleans's Congo Square.

¾ cup (6 ounces or 1½ sticks) unsalted butter, melted

2¼ cups (firmly packed) light brown sugar

3 large eggs, well beaten

2¾ cups all-purpose flour

2½ teaspoons baking powder

½ teaspoon salt

6 ounces (1 cup) semisweet chocolate chips

1 cup Toasted Pecans (page 232), broken up or roughly chopped

1. Position a rack in the center of the oven and preheat to 325°F. Lightly butter and flour (see page 314) two 7½ × 11-inch pans (that's what Aunt Margaret used) or one 9 × 13-inch pan. In a large mixing bowl, stir together the butter and sugar until smooth. Stir in the eggs one at a time, mixing well until they are completely incorporated.

2. Sift the flour, baking powder, and salt onto a large sheet of waxed paper or into a separate bowl. Gradually stir it into the batter, a little at a time. By the end, it'll be fairly stiff, like cookie dough. Fold in the chocolate and pecans. Scrape the batter into the prepared pan, level it with a spatula, and bake in the center of the oven for 25–30 minutes, or until lightly browned and set in the center. The smaller pans will cook more quickly and produce slightly thinner cookies than the sheet cake pan. Cool in the pan on a wire rack before cutting into 24 uniform squares.

Makes about 2 dozen

jerome's cookies

Variations on these graham cracker layer cookies are frequent in community cookbooks all over the Southeast, and often come with a claim that the recipe originated with the author. In consequence, the true origin has become a tangle that is virtually impossible to unravel. The version my family has used for three generations came from my cousin Dot Merritt in Hartwell, Georgia. She got the recipe from a co-worker named Jerome, who often made them for the office, hence our name for them.

Until my grandmother died, these cookies were a given at Christmas in our family, and at the heart of a heated battle she had with my mother. Jerome toasted the coconut topping by running the cookies under the broiler. My grandmother faithfully followed old Jerome; Mama never did. So when people asked Mama for her recipe, she never mentioned that step and MaMa would have a fit. That the recipient wanted the recipe as my mother made it fell on deaf ears. She'd cross her arms and hotly insist, "You're s'posed to toast it!" Well, God rest her: I'm on my mother's side. I never do it, either, but you can make MaMa happy in heaven if you want.

1 (16-ounce) box whole graham crackers

8 ounces shredded coconut, divided

1 cup pecans, chopped

¾ cup (6 ounces or 1½ sticks) butter

1 cup sugar

1 large egg

½ cup milk

FOR THE BUTTERCREAM FROSTING:

1 cup confectioners' sugar

½ stick butter, softened

3–4 tablespoons milk

1 teaspoon Homemade Bourbon Vanilla (page 17) or ½ teaspoon vanilla extract, optional

1. Line the bottom of a 9 × 13-inch pan with whole graham crackers, cutting if necessary to fit the pan. Set aside enough crackers to cover the top and crush enough of the remainder to make 1 cup. Mix the crushed crackers, 7 ounces of the coconut, and all the nuts together in a mixing bowl.

2. Melt the butter in a small saucepan over medium heat and stir in the sugar. Lightly beat the egg into a separate bowl and then beat in the milk. Stir this into the butter and sugar and bring it to the boiling point, stirring constantly.

3. Add the custard to the crumb, coconut, and nuts, and mix well. Pour it into prepared pan and spread it evenly over the crackers with a spatula. Top with the reserved whole crackers, pressing them lightly into it, completely covering the filling. Again, trim the crackers if necessary.

4. To make the frosting, beat the sugar into the softened butter and add milk by tablespoonfuls until it's spreadable. Stir in the vanilla extract if using. Immediately spread over the crackers and sprinkle with the remaining coconut. Cover and refrigerate until firm, about 4 hours. Cut into 1 × 2¼-inch bars. Keep refrigerated.

Makes about 4½ dozen

old-fashioned tea cakes

Everything about these cookies seems old-fashioned: The very name whispers of Victorian parlor sets, floral china teapots, and grandmother—as if anyone's grandmother nowadays is sitting around in the parlor serving forth tea and cakes. That may be why this simple cookie is so frequently neglected by serious bakers. It may not be flashy, but it's well worth adding to any baker's repertory, for there's no basic dough more simple or versatile. Dozens of different cookies can be made from this simple base, merely by varying its flavorings or toppings—or, as is done in the Coconut Tea Cakes recipe that follows, by mixing in nuts.

1 pound (2 cups, or 4 sticks) unsalted butter, softened

1 pound (2 cups) sugar

3 large eggs, lightly beaten

Grated zest of 2 lemons or 1 orange, optional

1 tablespoon rose or orange flower water or Homemade Bourbon Vanilla (page 17), or 1 teaspoon vanilla extract

28 ounces (about 5½ cups) unbleached all-purpose flour

2 teaspoons Single Acting Baking Powder (page 255) or 1½ teaspoons double-acting powder

½ teaspoon salt

1. Cream the butter and sugar in a large mixing bowl until fluffy. Beat in the eggs one at a time. Stir in the zest, if using, and the flavoring extract (if you're using the citrus zest, use rose or orange water with lemon zest, orange water with the orange, or any of them if not using zest).

2. Whisk the flour, baking powder, and salt in a separate bowl, or sift them onto a large sheet of waxed paper. Gradually work it into the butter, sugar, and egg, mixing until the dough is smooth, stiff, and no longer sticky. Cover and chill at least half an hour.

3. Position a rack in the center of the oven and preheat to 375°F. Lightly butter a baking sheet. Dust a work surface with flour and roll out the dough fairly thin (no more than ³⁄₁₆ inch—thinner, if you can manage it). Cut with a round or fancy-shaped cutter, and transfer the cookies to the baking sheet with a thin spatula. Bake, in batches if necessary, until they are lightly browned, about 15 minutes.

Sugar Cookies: Dust the tops with granulated sugar, colored sanding sugar, or turbinado sugar just before baking. They can also be frosted with your favorite icing.

Orange Chocolate Tea Cake Sandwiches: These are lovely with Sweet Potato Ice Cream (page 412). Flavor the tea cakes with the finely grated zest of 1 orange and 1 tablespoon orange flower water or orange liqueur such as Grand Marnier; roll the dough to the thickness of a piecrust (about ⅛ inch). Cut into 1½-inch rounds or symmetrical shapes such as stars or hearts. While the cookies cool after baking, melt 4 ounces dark bittersweet chocolate in a heavy-bottomed saucepan over low heat, stirring often. While it's still warm and soft, spread a dab on the bottom of a cookie, leaving the edges clear. Press a second cookie into the chocolate bottom-side in, pressing until the chocolate comes to the edges but isn't running out. Repeat with the remaining cookies, let cool completely (or chill in the refrigerator until the chocolate is hard), and store in an airtight container at room temperature.

Makes about 8 dozen

coconut tea cakes

Coconut tea cakes are another longtime standard for Southern bakers; they first began to turn up in Southern cookbooks in the second quarter of the nineteenth century, and remain popular to this day. Most of the old recipes called for freshly grated coconut, and that is what I faithfully used for years, but nowadays I've come to actually prefer the dried grated coconut that is sold in bulk in health food and special bulk sections of some supermarkets. Though it loses some of the subtlety of freshly grated coconut, its flavor is more concentrated, and the low moisture content makes a much more consistent dough.

1 pound (2 cups, or 4 sticks) unsalted butter, softened

1 pound (2 cups) sugar

3 large eggs

4 cups unsweetened fine-grated coconut, preferably dried (see headnote above)

2 teaspoons baking powder

½ teaspoon salt

About 10 ounces (around 2 cups) all-purpose flour (see step 2)

6 ounces roughly chopped bittersweet chocolate (1 cup)

1. Cream the butter and sugar in a large mixing bowl until fluffy. Beat in the eggs one at a time. Mix in the coconut, baking powder, and salt.

2. Gradually work in enough flour to make a smooth, moderately stiff dough that's no longer sticky—you probably won't need to use all of it. Cover and chill for at least half an hour.

3. Position a rack in the center of the oven and preheat to 375°F. Lightly grease a baking sheet. Dust a work surface with flour and roll out the dough ¼ inch thick. Cut with a round or fancy-shaped cutter and transfer to the baking sheet with a thin spatula. Bake in batches until lightly browned, about 14–16 minutes. Cool on the pan on a wire rack.

4. While the cookies cool, melt the chocolate in a heavy-bottomed saucepan over medium-low heat, stirring occasionally until smooth. Put it in a squeeze bottle or keep it warm over the hot water. Line the counter with waxed paper and put the cookies on a wire cooling rack over it. Squeeze thin crisscrossed lines of chocolate over the cookies or scoop up small amounts on a spatula and flip it over them in irregular ribbons.

Notes: Unsweetened, dried coconut is available in bulk at natural food grocers, most Asian markets, and even a few supermarkets. Grated fresh or frozen, unsweetened coconut can be substituted, but the moisture content in both will require more flour.

Makes about 8 dozen

southern shortbread

From France to Scotland, England to America, everyone loves these buttery-rich and yet delicate cookies—and everyone seems to have a favorite variation. Perhaps shortbread's popularity is due in part to the fact that it is an easy, artless confection, made up of little more than softened butter, flour, and sugar rubbed together with no particular care or technique—as easy to make as they are to gobble down by the handful. In the South many cooks give the crumb a toothsome crunch by adding a handful of stone-ground cornmeal. For a more delicate cookie, you can substitute an equal volume of corn flour or cornstarch for the meal.

10 ounces (2 cups) Southern soft-wheat flour or soft-wheat pastry flour

2 tablespoons very fine white cornmeal

½ cup confectioners' sugar

Salt

½ pound (1 cup or 2 sticks) unsalted butter, softened

1. Position a rack in the center of the oven and preheat to 325°F. Sift or whisk together the flour, meal, sugar, and a small pinch of salt. With your fingers or a pastry blender, work the butter into the flour until it forms a smooth dough. This step may also be done in a food processor fitted with a steel blade: Put the flour, meal, sugar, and salt in the bowl of the processor fitted with a steel blade and pulse to sift. Then add the butter and process until the mixture forms a ball.

2. You may pat the dough out to a little less ¼ inch thick on an ungreased baking sheet and prick it at regular intervals with a fork, or pinch off a small (1-inch-diameter) piece, roll it into a ball between your hands, then lay it on a baking sheet and press it flat with a cookie stamp or the palm of your hand. The dough can also be chilled for half an hour, turned onto a floured work surface, lightly floured, rolled out, and cut with a cookie cutter. Space individual cookies an inch apart.

3. Bake in the center of the oven for 14–20 minutes, until the edges are lightly browned. If you've baked the shortbread in one large piece, cut into pieces about 1 inch wide by 2–2½ inches long while still very warm and soft. Let it cool before you remove it from the pan.

Makes twenty 3-inch round or thirty small cookies

pecan shortbread

Commonly known as Pecan Sandies, this is a classic variation on the shortbread theme. Nuts are the distinguishing ingredient, but it's the kind of sugar used that makes the real difference. Turbinado or "raw" sugar isn't fully refined and still contains some of the molasses, so its flavor is more distinctive than that of white sugar. It's not the same as brown sugar, and they can't always be substituted for one another. This is one such recipe. Brown sugar won't work here.

⅔ cup demerara or turbinado sugar,
or ½ cup granulated sugar

10 ounces (2 cups) unbleached all-purpose flour

Salt

1 cup finely chopped pecans

½ pound (1 cup or 2 sticks) unsalted butter, softened

1. Position a rack in the center of the oven and preheat to 325°F. Pulverize the sugar until very fine, either in a mortar and pestle, or in a blender or food processor fitted with a steel blade.

2. Sift or whisk together the sugar, flour, and a small pinch of salt in a mixing bowl. Mix in the pecans and then work the butter into the dry ingredients until a smooth dough is formed. You can do this in a food processor, pulsing until the mixture resembles coarse meal, being careful not to overprocess. Turn the dough out into a mixing bowl and finish working the butter in by hand.

3. Pinch off a 1-inch piece of dough and roll it into a ball between your hands. Put it on an ungreased baking sheet and lightly press into a ¼-inch-thick round, with either a cookie stamp or the palm of your hand. Repeat with the remaining dough, spacing the cookies about an inch apart. You may also roll and cut this dough. Gather it into a ball, patting until it's compact, wrap it in plastic wrap, and refrigerate 30 minutes, or till firm enough to handle. Turn it onto a lightly floured work surface, flour it, and roll it out a little less than ¼ inch thick. Cut it with the cookie cutter, and transfer to an ungreased baking sheet about 1 inch apart.

4. Bake in the center of the oven until lightly browned at the edges, about 20–22 minutes. Cool them on the baking sheet before removing them, and store in an airtight container.

Makes twenty 3-inch round or thirty small cookies

chocolate chip pecan wedding shortbread

Growing up, my favorite store-bought cookies in the world were those fancy little Danish wedding cookies (also sometimes called Mexican wedding cookies)—dainty shortbread nuggets studded with nuts and bits of dates or chocolate and rolled in confectioners' sugar. They're kissing cousin to kourabiedes, the highly addictive sugar-dusted butter cookies from Greece, and to the South's own pecan shortbread. These airy little morsels, studded with pecans and bits of bittersweet chocolate, are my own version of that childhood favorite. You do not, needless to say, have to wait for someone to get married to enjoy them.

12 ounces (about 2¼ cups) Southern soft-wheat flour or pastry flour

¼ cup cornstarch

½ teaspoon salt

1 teaspoon cinnamon

½ teaspoon freshly grated nutmeg

½ cup sugar

½ pound (1 cup or 2 sticks) unsalted butter, softened

½ cup finely chopped Toasted Pecans (page 232)

½ cup bittersweet chocolate mini morsels

About 1½ cups confectioners' sugar, for coating the cookies

1. Whisk together the flour, cornstarch, salt, cinnamon, nutmeg, and sugar. Add the butter and work it into the flour with your fingers or a pastry blender until it resembles coarse meal. Continue working the dough until it is smooth. Sprinkle in the pecans and chocolate chips and work them in until they are evenly distributed. Gather the dough into a ball, flatten it into a 1-inch-thick disk, wrap well with plastic wrap, and refrigerate for at least 30 minutes.

2. Position a rack in the center of the oven and preheat to 325°F. Working in batches, break off about a quarter of the dough, keeping the rest refrigerated. Pinch off a small, ¾-inch round lump and roll it between your hands into a ball; put these on the baking sheet about 1 inch apart.

3. Bake 18–20 minutes, or until the edges and bottoms are lightly browned. Let cool until they are no longer soft and crumbly, and while still slightly warm, roll them in confectioners' sugar until well coated. Cool completely and store in airtight tins.

Makes about 5–5½ dozen

crunchy peanut butter chocolate chip cookies

That perennial American favorite, old-fashioned peanut butter cookies, with the characteristic ridges or tic-tac-toe pattern pressed into their tops with the tines of a fork, are really nothing more than shortbread enriched with peanut butter. These take a trip over the top with the added crunch of chopped peanuts and chocolate chips. They were made for eating with an ice-cold glass of milk—and I am not talking about the skimmed kind, either.

1 cup unbleached all-purpose flour

½ teaspoon salt

1 teaspoon baking powder

4 ounces (½ cup or 1 stick) unsalted butter, softened

1 cup (firmly packed) light brown sugar

1 large egg

1 cup all-natural peanut butter, preferably fresh-ground (see notes below)

½ cup roasted, unsalted peanuts, roughly chopped

¾ cup milk chocolate chips

1. Position a rack in the center of the oven and preheat to 375°F. Whisk together the flour, salt, and baking powder. In a separate bowl, cream the butter and sugar until fluffy. Beat in the egg and then the peanut butter.

2. Add the flour in three parts, mixing well after each addition. Work in the peanuts and chocolate chips until evenly distributed. Pinch off a 1-inch lump of dough and roll it into a ball between your palms. Put them on an ungreased baking sheet about 1¼ inches apart. Press the balls flat with the backside of a regular dinner fork, then press the tines crosswise to make a tic-tac-toe pattern. Bake until golden-brown, about 10–12 minutes. They will still be quite crumbly when they first come out of the oven; cool them on the pans on a wire rack before transferring them to an airtight storage container.

Notes: All-natural peanut butter is preferred for these cookies because it contains nothing but peanuts—there's no added sugar, salt, or oil other than peanut. Freshly ground peanut butter, available from specialty grocers (especially natural food markets), will not only taste fresher, but also gives the cookies a richer, more intensely peanutty flavor.

Makes about 3½–4 dozen

lemon-ginger scented benne wafers

A lingering reminder of the slave trade with West Africa, benne (or sesame) seeds have become practically indigenous in the Carolina and Georgia Low-country, and almost every cook has her own version of these delicate cookies. Some are more like brittle candy than a cookie; some are so airy and delicate that they practically evaporate on your tongue. These tend toward the latter variety—delicately scented and yet intensely flavorful. You can usually find sesame seeds in the spice aisle of supermarkets, but they are fresher and much more economical at Asian and natural food markets, where they are often sold in bulk. The kind of seeds you want for this cookie are white or hulled sesame.

¾ cup white (hulled) sesame seeds

¾ cup unbleached all-purpose flour

¼ teaspoon salt

¼ teaspoon baking powder

6 ounces (¾ cup or 1½ sticks) unsalted butter, softened

1½ cups (packed) light brown sugar

1 large egg, lightly beaten

Grated zest of 1 lemon

1 tablespoon grated fresh ginger

1 tablespoon freshly squeezed lemon juice

1. Position a rack in the center of the oven and preheat to 350°F. Spread the sesame on a 9-inch metal pie plate or cake pan and toast in the center of the oven, stirring often, until they're a rich golden-brown. Let cool. Reduce the oven temperature to 300°F. Line two large baking sheets with parchment or silicone baking pads (parchment can be reused once).

2. Whisk together the flour, salt, and baking powder in a bowl, or sift them onto a large sheet of waxed paper. In a separate mixing bowl, cream the butter and sugar until fluffy. Beat in the egg and then mix in the flour a little at a time, then the sesame, lemon zest, ginger, and lemon juice. Drop by scant ½ teaspoonfuls onto the parchment or silicone pads, leaving at least an inch between them (the cookies will spread more on the pads).

3. Bake in batches until nicely browned, about 10–12 minutes. Cool completely on the pans set over wire racks. Carefully peel the cookies off the parchment or pads and store in airtight tins.

Makes about 14 dozen

chocolate irish lace

These cookies are a specialty in Savannah, host to one of the largest St. Patrick's Day celebrations in the country. Each shady square along the parade route in the historic downtown is overrun with picnickers, whose hampers are filled with treats that sport Irish names and sometimes even contain Irish ingredients. These delicate and delicious lace cookies are about as Irish as Queen Elizabeth, but they're crunchy with Irish oats and mellowed with a judicious dose of good Irish whiskey.

¼ pound (½ cup or 1 stick) unsalted butter, softened

½ cup sugar

½ cup (packed) light brown sugar

1 large egg

1 teaspoon Homemade Bourbon Vanilla (page 17) or vanilla extract

2 teaspoons Irish whiskey (your choice, but I am a Jameson man, myself)

¼ teaspoon salt

2 tablespoons all-purpose flour

1 cup quick-cooking oats

4 ounces bittersweet chocolate

1. Position a rack in the center of the oven and preheat to 350°F. Line four large baking sheets with parchment or silicone baking pads.

2. Cream the butter and both sugars until fluffy. Beat in the egg, vanilla, whiskey, and salt. Add the flour and oats and mix well. Drop by level ½ teaspoonfuls onto the prepared pans, leaving at least 1½ inches between (these spread a lot, especially on silicone pads).

3. Bake in batches to a rich golden-brown, about 7 minutes. Cool on the pans set over wire cooling racks. Meanwhile, melt the chocolate in a heavy-bottomed saucepan over medium-low heat, stirring occasionally. Remove it from the heat.

4. When the cookies are cooled, spread a dab of melted chocolate on the bottom of one, leaving space on the edges for the chocolate to spread. Gently press another cookie into the chocolate, bottom-side in, until it spreads to the edges. Cool until the chocolate is hardened (you may do this in the refrigerator), and store the cookies at room temperature in an airtight tin.

Makes about 4½–5 dozen

PIES AND PASTRIES

Like most American baked goods, pastry was not invented on our continent; those that we enjoy today have their roots in Europe and the Middle East. But the history that interests us here is what happened to those pastries once they landed on our shores. The phrase "as American as apple pie" was not coined without reason, and over the last four centuries we've made this pie indubitably our own: It is our symbol of ultimate comfort, our measure of national pride, and at least in popular song has even became a symbolic reminder of our complacency. The consternation among lovers of real French cooking over the thick, pie-like quiches that have dominated American brunch menus since the 1970s has always amused me: Well, no, they're not authentic French quiche— they're American, and what, after all, is the matter with that?

Pie was and is my favorite baked sweet: As a boy, I'd choose it over cookies, cakes, or brownies any day, and pastry making is still my favorite kind of sweet baking. The proudest I've ever been was when an African American friend told me I made piecrust "like a black woman." Now, I learned to make it from a collection of white women— my mother, grandmother, and Julia Child—but the compliment was not lost on me, because African American women have a reputation for flaky, delicate piecrust like no one else's, and I accepted it with pleasure.

The compliment can as easily be yours, because making a decent crust (especially if you own a food processor) is, if you'll pardon the cliché, easy as pie. Actually, most clichés become such because they are mostly true, and this one is no exception. Making good pastry is not hard, and not nearly as complex and prone to failure as cakes, breads, or even cookies. The most complicated kind to make is puff pastry, and that's because it's time consuming and a little tedious—not because it is at all difficult. All that a good hand at pastry requires is a little knowledge, a modicum of care, and practice.

Easy as Pie: Pastry-Making Basics

With rare exception, keeping cool is the key to good pastry: not just your kitchen, but your temperament and everything else—especially the fat. If the fat warms enough to begin melting, it won't suspend in the dough in the small, cohesive bits that flatten as the pastry is rolled out, creating the characteristic flakiness of a well-made piecrust. Instead of crisp, delicately flaky, and dry pastry, the results will be greasy, uneven, and heavy.

That's why the chilled fat and liquid are kept ice-cold, but it's also why everything else must stay cool, too: Overhandling the dough with warm hands can be just as damaging. Old recipes, written when air-conditioning in the average kitchen consisted of opening a window or knocking the chinking out from between the logs in the wall, directed the baker to make up pastry in the cool of the morning, in a cold ceramic bowl, and on a cold work surface like marble. Some old cookbooks from the Deep South went so far as to suggest that the housewife give up pastry making in summer. With air-conditioning practically universal, modern cooks rarely have to deal with extreme temperatures, but the caution in those old recipes remains a word to the wise. With them in mind, here are some key techniques and tips for making pastry like a pro:

- Have the fat and liquid ice-cold. Chill the fat both before and after cutting it into the smaller bits required of the recipe, and always use thoroughly chilled liquids.

- Use a cool or cold utensil to cut the fat into the flour. There are experienced pastry cooks who can work butter into a pastry with their fingers, but they are the exception that proves the rule: For most of us, our hands and fingers are too warm, and handling the fat too much with them will make the pastry greasy and tough.

- Mix the dough in a cool ceramic or glass bowl and work it up on a cool surface to minimize warming.

- Chill the dough after mixing it, to give it a chance to relax and evenly absorb moisture, but always let it warm slightly to make it pliable enough to roll it out.

- Chill yourself out, too: Get in a good mood, be patient, and handle the pastry lightly. Like most things in this life, pastry does not respond well to rough or careless handling.

Rolling and Placing Pastry in the Pan

The only challenge in rolling pastry is to use a light, quick hand. Rolling it too vigorously or stretching it when you are both rolling and placing it in the pan will lead to certain failure. Stretched dough will try to return to its original shape when heated, which means your pie shell will be shrunken, uneven, and, in some cases, unusable.

- Let the dough sit at room temperature for 5–10 minutes before trying to roll it.

- Lightly flour a cool or neutral work surface (polished stone, wood, or plastic laminate all work fine, but the grout joints in tile make that surface unsuitable). Keep it lightly dusted with flour while you are working to prevent the pastry from sticking.

- Lightly flour the top of the pastry. If the rolling pin begins sticking to the pastry, give it another light dusting, but use no more flour than is absolutely necessary.

- Begin rolling from the center outward with light pressure. The intention is to gradually flatten the dough, not stretch it. Give it a quarter turn and roll again. Continue rolling, regularly giving the pastry quarter turns until it's the thickness needed for the recipe.

- There is no single "correct" thickness for a pastry shell: Each recipe will indicate the thickness required, but for standard pies, a good rule of thumb is slightly less than ⅛ inch thick; for tarts and a few pre-baked shells, it should be ⅛ inch or slightly thicker.

- To transfer the pastry to a pie plate or tart pan, fold it in quarters. Place the point dead center in the pan and unfold gently, letting the pastry fall into the edges. Gently press (never stretch) it into the edges of the pie plate or into the edge and flutes of the tart pan.

- To trim the excess dough from a pie shell, gently hold it in place by laying your hand on the dough at the flat rim. Cut away the excess with a sharp knife held against the side rim of the plate. To trim a tart crust, roll it with a rolling pin until the sharp edges of the pan cut the crust away, taking care in the process not to stretch the dough. Don't hold a pie plate in the air and cut away the excess as you've seen models doing in those old nostalgic baking ads: That's a sure way to stretch the dough at the edge.

- When you trim the edges, save any scraps; you may need them for patches or for decorating the edges or top crust.

basic pastry for pies and tarts

Butter gives pastries a wonderful flavor and richness, but it needs the help of a little lard to keep the pastry flaky and light. Vegetable shortening doesn't work nearly as well, but it can be substituted if you cannot use lard, or you can make an all-butter pastry by substituting an ounce more of butter for the lard.

It's beyond me why so many cooks are afraid of making pastry. As long as you use good ingredients and don't overwork the dough, pastry is not at all difficult to make, and it makes all the difference in the world between a good pie and a great one. As Southern food maven Nathalie Dupree always tells her students, the ingredients here are not expensive, so if your first try isn't perfect, who cares? Just practice until you get it right.

10 ounces (about 2 cups) Southern soft-wheat flour or soft-wheat pastry flour

½ teaspoon salt

4 ounces (8 tablespoons or 1 stick) chilled unsalted butter, cut into small pieces

1 ounce (2 tablespoons) chilled lard, cut into small pieces

½ cup ice water

1. Sift or whisk together the flour and salt in a large work bowl. Add the butter and lard, handling them as little as possible. Work them into the flour with a pastry blender or two knives until it is the texture of raw grits or polenta.

2. Add ⅓ cup of the ice water and lightly stir it into the flour. Add more water by tablespoonfuls until the dough gathers into a clump, but is still loose and not sticky. Lightly dust the dough and your hands with flour and gather it into a ball. Wrap it with plastic wrap and refrigerate half an hour.

3. Lightly flour a cool, smooth work surface (marble, wood, or plastic laminate) and roll out the pastry for use as directed in the individual recipe.

Food Processor Pie Dough: Once you make pastry in a food processor, you'll never do it any other way. The only tricky part is to keep from overheating the fat. To help prevent this, chill the steel blade in the freezer for 5 minutes before using it. Fit the chilled blade into the processor and put in the flour and salt. Pulse a few times to sift, then add the butter and lard. Pulse until the flour reaches the coarse polenta stage. Add ⅓ cup ice water and pulse again until it is mixed. Then add water in tablespoonfuls, pulsing to mix each addition in, until the dough just gathers into a rough ball.

Makes one 9-inch double-crusted pie or two open-faced 9-inch pie shells

puff pastry

Light, delicate, and airy, this pastry used to be the standard for the best company piecrust. It is not difficult to make, if you keep everything as cold as possible and weigh all the ingredients carefully. The old instructions were to make up the pastry in a cool place, preferably early in the morning—still sound advice, even in our days of artificially cooled houses. The recipe makes about 2 pounds of dough. If it's more than you need for the recipe you are making, it will keep, well wrapped, in the refrigerator for up to a week. It can also be frozen for up to 3 months. If neither option is feasible, you can cut the recipe in half.

1 pound (2 cups or 4 sticks) unsalted butter, divided

20 ounces (about 4 cups) Southern soft wheat flour or pastry flour, divided

1 teaspoon salt

About ¾ cup ice water

1. If the butter is in one big block, cut it into quarters. Cut three of the quarters in half (into 2-ounce, or 4-tablespoon chunks) and put them back into the refrigerator. Cut the remaining quarter into bits. Chill it briefly in the freezer until it is firm again.

2. Set aside ⅔ cup of the flour and whisk the remainder with the salt in a large, cool mixing bowl. Add the ¼ pound of butter cut into bits and cut it into the flour, using a pastry blender or two knives. The texture should be like damp raw grits or polenta meal.

3. Make a well in the center and add ½ cup of the ice water. Stir it in lightly with a fork and keep adding water by tablespoons until the pastry is smooth and no longer crumbly, but not wet or sticky. Dust your hands and the pastry with some of the reserved flour and gather it into a ball. Wrap it well in plastic wrap and refrigerate it to let it rest for half an hour. The pastry can be made to this point in a food processor. Follow the method for Basic Pastry, page 364.

4. Meanwhile, take the remaining 2-ounce chunks of butter from the refrigerator and thinly slice them on sheets of waxed paper. Let them soften but don't let them get oily. Roll the dough out into a rectangle about ½ inch thick. Spread one portion of the sliced butter evenly over two-thirds of the pastry with a palette knife or pastry scraper, dust lightly with a little reserved flour, and fold the blank, unbuttered third over the center, then fold the other side over it, like a letter. Dust with a little flour and roll it out ½ inch thick. Spread another 2-ounce portion of butter over two-thirds of it, flour, triple-fold it as before, and roll it out ½ inch thick. Repeat until the butter and flour are used. If at any point in this process the dough seems to be getting too soft, cover and refrigerate it for half an hour.

5. Roll the pastry ½ inch thick, fold it, and roll it out one last time. Fold the pastry, wrap it up, and refrigerate for at least an hour before using it. Ideally, this pastry should stay cold right up to the moment it goes into the oven.

For 2 pounds of dough, enough for 4 open-faced (or 2 with top crust) 9-inch pies

pre-baking a pastry blind (without filling)

"Blind" baking a pastry means that it's partially or fully baked before the filling is added. Even pastries that will be filled and baked often benefit from pre-baking to help ensure a light, delicate crust that doesn't get soggy.

About 1½–2 cups raw dried beans or ceramic or metal pie weights

1 sheet aluminum foil or parchment large enough to cover the pastry plus 2-inch-wide strips of foil for covering the edges (if fully baking the pastry)

1. Position a rack in the center of the oven (you may use a baking stone, if you like) and preheat to 375°F. Roll out the prepared pastry to the thickness called for in the recipe and line a pie plate or tart pan with it (see the notes above).

2. Trim or crimp the edges according to the recipe. Generously prick the bottom with a fork. Butter the foil, if using, and put it over the pastry buttered-side down, or put a sheet of parchment over the pastry. Gently press it into the corners, being careful not to mash the edges of the pastry or tear it. Pour in the weights and gently shake it to level them. Bake on the center rack or stone for about 20 minutes. The exposed edges should be barely beginning to color.

3. Remove the pastry from the oven, carefully lift out the foil and weights, and return it to the oven. For a partially baked pastry, bake until it is beginning to color and the bottom looks dry, about 10 minutes longer. If the pastry bubbles up (as it will sometimes do), gently prick the bubbles with a fork. Cool it on a rack before filling it. For a fully baked shell, cover the edges with strips of foil to prevent overbrowning and bake until uniformly golden-brown, about 5–10 minutes more. For pre-baked individual tartlets, do them in exactly the same way. Put them on a large baking sheet, not touching, and bake exactly as you would a full-size pie shell. They may take slightly less time, though in some ovens they may actually take a little longer.

For each 9- or 10-inch piecrust or 9- or 12-inch tart

a pre-baked puff pastry top crust

Sometimes all a pie filling needs is a showy top crust. When that is what is called for, there's nothing more impressive than a towering puff pastry.

Puff Pastry (above) or commercial puff pastry, as needed for the individual recipe

1 egg white beaten with 1 tablespoon water

1. Position a rack in the center of the oven (if you have a baking stone, put it on the rack—it makes a real difference with puff pastry), and preheat to 400°F. Roll out the pastry to slightly under ¼ inch thick and cut it into the shape and size required by the recipe.

2. Line a baking sheet with cooking parchment or lightly butter it and lay the pastry on it. If you like, cut the leftover scraps into decorative shapes, brush their bottoms with water, and arrange them on the top of the pastry. Brush the pastry with the egg white wash and prick it through in several places with a fork. Bake until the pastry is puffed and golden, about 20 minutes for pies that will undergo further baking, 30 minutes for fillings that are fully cooked. Cool it on a rack before placing it on top of the pie unless the pie is to be served hot, in which case transfer the hot pastry to the pie and serve at once.

For large or single-serving individual pies in any amount

pre-baked puff pastry shells, or vol-au-vents

For fully cooked or cold fillings, these showy cases are easy to make, once you've mastered the puff pastry itself, and they make a big splash. Their big advantage is that, unlike baking regular pastry blind, they don't have to be weighted in the initial baking: The whole point of them is to have a shell that is spectacularly puffed and delicate.

I recipe Puff Pastry (page 365)

1 large egg white, beaten with 1 tablespoon water

1. Position a rack in the upper third of the oven and preheat to 400°F. Roll out the pastry ¼ inch thick. Cut it into sixteen 3-inch circles with a fluted or plain round cutter. Using a 2½-inch cutter of the same shape, cut out the centers of eight of the circles, setting aside the centers for another use.

2. Brush the bottoms of the rings with water and place them over the remaining rounds, aligning any pattern in the cut edges. Brush the edges of the rings with the egg white wash. Lightly butter a baking sheet or line it with parchment, lay the pastry shells on it, and bake them until they are puffed, a rich golden-brown, and dry at the center, about 25 minutes.

Makes 8

raised pastry for cobblers and potpies

The leavening in this pastry produces a light, soft dough that's traditionally used for cobblers and potpies. It also makes nice flat dumplings (called "slipperies" in many parts of the South) when rolled thin, cut into strips, and dropped into simmering, well-seasoned broth. Lard is the preferred fat, as it contributes both lightness and tenderness, but butter will also work fine, and vegetable shortening will do if you prefer not to use lard. Though this pastry is easier to manage when made up by hand, with care it can be made in a food processor. The leavening makes for a light, airy, and delicate crust, but it also makes the pastry extremely brittle and difficult to work with. Keep it well dusted with flour when rolling it out and handle it carefully.

10 ounces (about 2 cups) all-purpose, soft-wheat flour

½ teaspoon salt

1 teaspoon baking powder

½ teaspoon baking soda

6 ounces (¾ cup) chilled lard (or butter), cut into bits

⅓–½ cup cold buttermilk or plain whole-milk yogurt thinned to buttermilk consistency with milk or water

1. Whisk together the flour, salt, baking powder, and soda in a metal or ceramic bowl. Add the fat, handling it as little as possible, and work it into the flour with a pastry blender or two knives until it's the texture of damp raw grits or polenta, with lumps no bigger than small peas. If using a food processor, put the dry ingredients in the bowl fitted with the steel blade and pulse several times to mix. Add the fat and pulse until it resembles coarse meal with larger lumps no bigger than small peas, and then turn it out into a mixing bowl.

2. Add ⅓ cup of the buttermilk, and lightly stir until the dough clumps together and is soft and smooth, but not sticky, adding more by the spoonful as needed. The pastry will be soft—more like biscuit dough than pie pastry. Lightly dust it with flour and gather it into a ball. This pastry should be rolled and used right away.

Makes enough pastry for one 9-inch deep-dish pie

the chess pie family

Chess pie is a lingering legacy of a form of pastry that the English settlers brought into America during the early days of the seventeenth-century colonization. Its enigmatic name, also a part of that heritage, has been the subject of legends and tall tales that are as numerous and popular as they are false. Some of them—like the notion that it is derived from a modest baker's protest, "Aw shucks, it's jes' pie"—are jes' plain silly. The confusion that has led to the popular legends and tales of the tall-tale tellers can be laid at the door of the uneven and often uncodified spellings of Elizabethan and Jacobean English. As unromantic as the truth may be, chess is nothing more than an archaic spelling of cheese, which was once used to mean "curd," even when it was not made from curdled milk or cream. Those early curds were the precursors of modern chess pie, cheesecake, and all the butter-and-egg custards that survive on the modern Southern dessert board. Like any good Southern family, this one has many branches and confused interconnections, from the standard and now classic variations that carry the name to lemon meringue pie, cheesecake, and the transparent custards like pecan pie.

lemon buttermilk chess pie

Buttermilk pie is an old standby in Southern baking that had until recent years been neglected as old-fashioned and somewhat anachronistic, but it's happily making a comeback, both with home bakers and professional pastry chefs. Delicious all on its own, its handsome balance of sour and sweet also makes it an ideal foil for just about any fresh seasonal fruit or fruit sauce.

1 partially baked 9-inch pie shell (page 366) made with ½ recipe Basic Pastry (page 364)

1 large lemon

2 ounces (4 tablespoons or ½ stick) unsalted butter, softened

1½ cups sugar

4 large eggs

1 tablespoon all-purpose flour

2 tablespoons fine white stone-ground cornmeal

Small pinch salt

¾ cup buttermilk

Fresh Raspberry Bourbon Sauce (recipe follows), or lightly sweetened fresh seasonal fruit such as blueberries, blackberries, strawberries, or sliced peaches, nectarines, or plums

1. After the pie shell is partially baked, adjust the oven to 350°F and put the pastry aside on a wire rack to cool completely.

2. Grate the zest from the lemon, then halve and juice it through a strainer. Cream the butter in a large mixing bowl and gradually add the sugar, beating until light and fluffy. Beat in the eggs one at a time and then the flour, meal, and salt. Stir in the buttermilk, lemon juice, and zest.

3. Pour the custard into the prepared crust and bake 10 minutes in the center of the oven, then reduce the heat to 325°F and bake until the pie is set but still slightly jiggly in the center (a straw or toothpick inserted into the center will come out clean), about 45–55 minutes. Cool it on a wire rack and serve at room temperature or slightly chilled, plain, or with Fresh Raspberry Bourbon Sauce or seasonal fruit.

Makes one 9-inch pie, serving 6–8

fresh raspberry bourbon sauce

This recipe can be also be used to make a different sauce with blackberries, blueberries, pitted and halved cherries, or sliced peaches or mangoes. These will not break down as the raspberries will, so stop as soon as the flame dies out, and omit the straining step.

½ **pound fresh raspberries**

2 **tablespoons unsalted butter**

3–4 **tablespoons sugar, to taste**

¼ **cup warm bourbon**

1. Gently rinse the berries under cold running water and drain well. Melt the butter in a large sauté pan over medium-high heat. When it's hot but not browning, add the berries and sprinkle in the sugar. Cook, shaking the pan constantly, until they begin to dissolve, about a minute.

2. Add the bourbon, and, leaning well away from the pan, ignite it. Shake or stir the berries with a long-handled utensil until the flame dies out. Continue until the berries break down completely.

3. Strain the sauce to remove the seeds through a fine-meshed sieve set over a warm serving bowl, pressing well on the berries to extract as much of the juice and solids as possible. Discard the solids, stir the sauce well, and serve warm or at room temperature.

Serves 4

brown sugar, or butterscotch chess pie

Real butterscotch is made of sugar caramelized in butter; brown sugar blended with butter is a latter-day substitute that doesn't taste at all the same, but it's a rich, wonderful flavor on its own that has a long tradition in Southern baking. Delicious in its pristine, ungarnished glory, it's also wonderful served with fresh fruit, either in a sauce like Fresh Raspberry Bourbon Sauce (page 371) or simply sweetened and served on the side. Try it with fresh slices of banana and Bourbon Whipped Cream (page 402). For a mellow lemon chess variation, substitute the grated zest and half the juice of one lemon for the bourbon.

1 partially baked 9-inch pie shell (page 366) made with ½ recipe Basic Pastry (page 364)

¼ pound (½ cup or 1 stick) unsalted butter, softened

1½ cups (firmly packed) light brown sugar

4 large eggs

1 tablespoon all-purpose flour

2 tablespoons fine white stone-ground cornmeal

Small pinch salt

1 tablespoon bourbon

1. After the pie shell is partially baked, adjust the oven temperature to 350°F and set the pastry aside on a wire rack to cool completely.

2. Cream the butter and sugar in a large mixing bowl until light and fluffy. Beat in the eggs one at a time. Beat in the flour, meal, salt, and bourbon.

3. Pour into the prepared crust and bake in the center of the oven 10 minutes, then reduce the heat to 325°F. Bake until the pie is set but slightly jiggly at the center (a straw or toothpick inserted in the center will come out clean), about 35–40 minutes longer. Cool the pie on a wire rack and serve it warm, at room temperature, or chilled.

Makes one 9-inch pie, serving 6–8

chocolate fudge chess pie

This rich, chocolaty custard has nowadays been displaced by silky modern chiffon, cream, and black-bottom pies, and more commonly turns up with a layer of pecans on top, baked in the same way as Bourbon Pecan Pie (page 377), but it is the grand-daddy of them all and has distinct charms of its own. To make this into Chocolate Fudge Pecan Pie, add 1¼ cups slivered Toasted Pecans (page 232) just before pouring the filling into the pastry in step 3.

1 partially baked 9-inch pie shell (page 366) made with ½ recipe Basic Pastry (page 364)

3 ounces bittersweet chocolate

¼ pound (½ cup or 1 stick) unsalted butter, softened

1 cup sugar

½ cup (firmly packed) light brown sugar

2 tablespoons all-purpose flour

Small pinch salt

4 large eggs, lightly beaten

1 tablespoon Homemade Bourbon Vanilla (page 17) or 1 teaspoon vanilla extract

Bourbon Whipped Cream (page 402)

1. After the pie shell is partially baked, adjust the oven temperature to 350°F and set the pastry aside on a wire rack to cool completely.

2. Melt the chocolate and butter in a heavy-bottomed saucepan, stirring often, over medium-low heat. Whisk together the sugars, flour, and salt in a large mixing bowl. Stir in the eggs and mix until smooth, then stir in the chocolate and butter and then the vanilla.

3. Pour the filling into the prepared pastry and bake in the center of the oven 10 minutes. Reduce the heat to 325°F and bake until set (a straw or toothpick inserted in the center will come out clean), about 35–40 minutes longer. Cool on a wire rack and serve at room temperature or cold, with a dollop of Bourbon Whipped Cream on each serving.

Makes one 9-inch pie, serving 6–8

coconut chess pie

Rich, chewy, and dense with coconut, there is nothing timid about this pie. It's a real coconut lovers' confection, and as best I've been able to trace, it's the forerunner of the more delicate coconut custard and cream pies that have come along in the last century. Early versions were sometimes made only with the whites of the egg, but those are a bit tricky and had pretty much vanished by the middle of the nineteenth century. Though unorthodox by traditional standards, this pie really shines when it is served on a thin pool of Dark Chocolate Bourbon Sauce or is simply drizzled with melted bittersweet chocolate.

1 partially baked 9-inch pie shell (page 366) made with ½ recipe Basic Pastry (page 364)

¼ pound (½ cup or 1 stick) unsalted butter

1 cup sugar

4 large eggs

¼ cup whole-milk buttermilk or plain whole-milk yogurt

1 teaspoon Homemade Bourbon Vanilla (page 17) or vanilla extract

1 tablespoon light rum

Small pinch salt

1 cup freshly grated fresh coconut or unsweetened frozen coconut

Dark Chocolate Bourbon Sauce (below) or 2 ounces bittersweet chocolate, melted

1. After the pie shell is partially baked, adjust the oven temperature to 350°F and set the pastry aside to cool completely.

2. Cream the butter and sugar in a large mixing bowl until light and fluffy. Beat in the eggs one at a time, and then the buttermilk, vanilla, rum, and salt. Fold in the coconut and pour it into the prepared pastry.

3. Bake in the center of the oven 10 minutes, then reduce the heat to 325°F and bake until just set and a straw inserted into the center comes out clean, about 35–40 minutes longer. When it begins to puff, it's overdone, so check it after it has been baking for 40 minutes (including that initial 10 minutes). Cool on a wire cooling rack and chill thoroughly before serving. Film the serving plates lightly with a pool of Dark Chocolate Bourbon Sauce or drizzle with bittersweet chocolate and top with the pie.

Makes one 9-inch pie, serving 6–8

dark chocolate bourbon sauce

This good, basic bittersweet chocolate sauce is the perfect finishing accent for the Coconut Chess Pie that precedes it here, but it also lifts a slice of pound cake or almost any custard pie from ordinary to special. And it's wonderful drizzled over ice cream or orange sherbet. Tailor it to a particular dessert by changing the flavoring, using any of the suggestions given at the end of the recipe.

1¼ cups water

⅓ cup sugar

8 ounces bittersweet chocolate, roughly chopped, or 8 ounces semisweet chocolate morsels

1 teaspoon Homemade Bourbon Vanilla (page 17), or 1 teaspoon bourbon and ¼ teaspoon commercial vanilla extract

1. Stir the water and sugar together in a 2-quart saucepan until the sugar is almost dissolved. Put the pan over medium-low heat and add the chocolate. Heat, stirring, until the chocolate is melted and smooth and almost simmering, about 5 minutes. Still stirring, simmer 2–3 minutes, until the sauce takes on the smooth consistency of thin cream or custard. Don't overcook or it will taste scorched and sharp. Remove it from the heat.

2. Stir in the flavoring, and keep stirring until it is cooled slightly. Strain it through a fine-meshed strainer into a serving or storage bowl or jar and let it cool to room temperature before serving. It can be made ahead: Cover and refrigerate, but let it warm almost to room temperature before serving. It will thicken considerably as it cools, so if you plan to float the sauce on the plate or pass it separately for pouring, you may need to thin it with a little water before using.

Variations: Try adding a pinch of cinnamon after adding the vanilla, or substitute raspberry or orange liqueur for the vanilla and add a little grated orange zest.

Makes about 2 cups

damson custard pie

While my father was pastor of Grassy Pond Baptist Church in Gaffney, South Carolina, we enjoyed the privilege of a previous gardening pastor's passion. There was practically a grove of pecan trees, a sour cherry tree that was great for climbing (what other jungle gym has a built-in snack for the grabbing?), and, best of all, a damson plum tree, which every year produced plenty of this lovely blue-black fruit for tart jam and for baking fresh in pies and cobblers. This pie, richly flavored with damson jam, became one of my mother's specialties and my very favorite dessert, even though most of the time I have to make it with store-bought preserves. If you cannot find damson plum preserves, wild blueberry preserves make a fine substitute.

1 partially baked 9-inch pie shell (page 366) made with ½ recipe Basic Pastry (page 364)

4 large eggs

1 cup sugar

¼ pound (½ cup, or 1 stick) butter, melted

Small pinch salt

1 teaspoon Homemade Bourbon Vanilla (page 17) or ½ teaspoon commercial extract

1 cup damson plum preserves, at room temperature

Bourbon Whipped Cream (page 402), optional, for serving

1. After the pie shell is partially baked, adjust the oven temperature to 350°F and set the pastry aside on a wire rack to cool completely.

2. Lightly beat the eggs in a large mixing bowl. Beat in the sugar and then the butter until light and smooth. Stir in the salt and vanilla. Stir a little of the custard into the preserves to soften them and then mix them into the remaining custard. Pour the filling into the prepared crust. Bake in the center of the oven until puffed, lightly browned, and set (a toothpick inserted into the center should come out clean), about 35–40 minutes. Cool the pie on a rack; it will deflate as it cools. Serve at room temperature or cold, plain or with Bourbon Whipped Cream.

Makes one 9-inch pie

bourbon pecan pie

The pecan pies that are common throughout the South are direct descendants of chess pie; they're just a buttery custard with nuts folded into them. Recipes for these custards go back at least into the early nineteenth century. The earliest recipes for pecan pie were made with sugar, butter, and eggs, but most modern pies contain large doses of corn syrup, which can be good, but for my taste are rather heavy and toothachingly sweet. This one harks back to those older pies, adding a suave splash of bourbon for mellowness.

1¼ cups pecan halves

½ recipe Basic Pastry (page 364)

3 large eggs, lightly beaten

1½ cups (tightly packed) light brown sugar

Small pinch salt

2 ounces (4 tablespoons or ½ stick) unsalted butter, melted and cooled

1 tablespoon Homemade Bourbon Vanilla (page 17) or 1 teaspoon vanilla extract

2 tablespoons bourbon, plus 2 additional teaspoons if using vanilla extract

1. Position a rack in the center of the oven and preheat to 375°F. Spread the pecans on a rimmed baking sheet and toast in the center of the oven 10 minutes, stirring occasionally to be sure that they cook evenly. Set them aside to cool.

2. Meanwhile, line a 9-inch pie plate with pastry, prick the bottom well with a fork, and decorate the edges by fluting with your fingers or the tines of the fork or cut bits of pastry. Weight and partially bake it as directed on page 364. Let it cool before filling it.

3. Stir together the eggs, sugar, and salt until smooth. Mix in the butter, vanilla, and bourbon, stirring until just smooth. Fold in the pecans and then pour the filling into the prepared pastry.

4. Bake in the center of the oven for 10 minutes. Reduce the heat to 325°F and bake until the filling is set in the center (a sharp knife blade, toothpick, or straw inserted into the center should come out clean). Cool on a wire rack and serve it cold or at room temperature.

Makes one 9-inch pie, serving 6–8

lemon pecan pie

Two standards of the Southern pastry cook's repertory are chess and pecan pie. Though they taste and look very different, they're actually closely related, both being derived from the old butter-and-egg custard "cheese" cakes of England (chess is, in fact, an old spelling of cheese). There are a lot of rude jokes about cousins intermarrying in the South, but here is one time when such a marriage is not only a good idea, but downright magical. The rich flavor of toasted pecans and butter is transformed when counterpointed by the bright, tart bite of lemon.

1½ cups roughly chopped pecans

½ recipe Basic Pastry (page 364)

4 large eggs

¾ cup granulated sugar

½ cup (firmly packed) light brown sugar

¼ teaspoon salt

Grated zest of 1 lemon

¼ cup freshly squeezed lemon juice
(about 2 lemons)

1 tablespoon all-purpose flour

2 ounces (¼ cup or ½ stick) unsalted butter,
melted and cooled

1. Position a rack in the center of the oven and preheat to 375°F. Spread the pecans on a baking sheet and toast in the center of the oven until they are fragrant and beginning to color, about 10 minutes, stirring occasionally to ensure that they toast evenly. Set them aside to cool. Meanwhile, line a 9-inch pie plate with the pastry, prick the bottom well with a fork, and flute the edges with your fingers or the tines of the fork. Line it with parchment, weight it with pie weights, and bake 10 minutes. Remove the parchment and weights and bake 10 minutes longer. Set it aside on a wire rack to cool.

2. Beat the eggs in a large glass or ceramic mixing bowl until lightly mixed. Add both sugars and the salt; beat until the sugar and eggs are creamy. Beat in the lemon zest, juice, and flour. Stir in the butter, then the pecans, and pour the filling into the prepared pastry.

3. Bake in the center of the oven 10 minutes. Reduce the heat to 325°F and bake until the filling is set in the center (a sharp knife blade or toothpick inserted into the center should come out clean). Don't overcook or the filling could curdle. Cool on a wire rack and serve it cold or at room temperature.

Makes one 9-inch pie, serving 8

golden bourbon pecan tassies

These delicate, golden-brown morsels are a standard for receptions all over the South. Though dainty and bite-size, there's nothing timid about their flavor. Almost everyone has a special person and memory connected with pecan tassies—their wedding day, graduation, or just their mama or grandmother's kitchen table on a cool autumn day after school. For me, they inevitably call to mind Southern cooking maven Nathalie Dupree, who wrote so warmly of them in her classic book *Southern Memories,* and with whom I have been privileged to enjoy an enduring friendship. It is she who taught me to make them, and this recipe owes much to her.

1 recipe Cream Cheese Pastry for Tassies and Tartlets (below), chilled

1 large egg

¾ cup (firmly-packed) light brown sugar

1 tablespoon bourbon

Small pinch salt

2 tablespoons unsalted butter, melted and cooled

½ cup roughly chopped Toasted Pecans (page 232)

1. Divide the pastry into twenty-four equal balls (about an inch in diameter). If the pastry begins to soften too much, lay them on a baking sheet lined with waxed paper and chill for a few minutes. Put a ball of pastry into each well of an ungreased mini muffin tin (with wells about 1¾ inches in diameter). With flour-dusted fingers or a tart tamper dipped in flour, press the pastry into the bottom and sides of each well until it is level with the top. Refrigerate while you make the filling.

2. Position a rack in the center of the oven and preheat to 350°F. Lightly beat the egg in a mixing bowl and then beat in the brown sugar, bourbon, salt, and butter, beating until smooth.

3. Divide the pecans among the shells and spoon about 1½ teaspoons of the filling into each. Bake until golden-brown and set, about 25 minutes.

Chocolate Pecan Tassies: Roughly chop ¼ cup bittersweet chocolate chips until they are about one-quarter their original size, or chop a 1½-ounce block of bittersweet chocolate to small bits. Toss the chocolate with the pecans, divide it among the tart shells, then fill and bake as directed in step 3.

Lemon Pecan Tassies: For a miniature variation of Lemon Pecan Pie (page 378), add the grated zest of a lemon and substitute 2 tablespoons of its juice for the bourbon.

Makes 24

cream cheese pastry for tassies and tartlets

This rich, delicate pastry is the classic one for pecan tassies, but it's also good for any tartlet with a rich, very sweet filling. Try it filled with lemon curd (page 340).

3 ounces (1 small package) cream cheese, softened

4 ounces (½ cup or 1 stick) unsalted butter, softened

¼ teaspoon salt

1 tablespoon sugar

1 cup all-purpose flour

1. With a mixer, cream the cheese and butter until light, fluffy, and smooth. Whisk together the salt, sugar, and flour, then work this into the creamed cheese and butter until the pastry is smooth. This can be done in a food processor: Process the butter and cheese until fluffy and light, then add the salt, sugar, and flour and pulse until the dough is smooth.

2. Scoop the dough onto a sheet of plastic wrap, fold the wrap over it, and press it into a flat 1-inch-thick disk. Chill until the dough is firm, at least 2 hours. The dough can be made several hours or a day before you plan to use it.

Makes 24 shells

gingered apple shortbread tart

The great thing about shortbread crusts is that they are rich tasting and impressive while requiring absolutely no skill from the baker to put together. The combination of apples, ginger, and lemon is pretty near perfect on its own, but when you add crisp, buttery shortbread to the mix, it becomes downright magical.

10 ounces (about 2 cups) Southern soft-wheat or all-purpose flour

2 tablespoons extra-fine white cornmeal

½ cup sugar

Salt

½ pound (1 cup or 2 sticks) unsalted butter, cut into small bits

2 lemons

6 large or 8 small to medium tart apples such as Arkansas Black, Braeburn, Rome, Winesap, or Granny Smith

¼ cup chopped crystallized ginger

2–4 tablespoons turbinado ("raw") sugar

¼ cup bourbon

Whole nutmeg in a grater

Buttered Pecan Caramel Ice Cream (page 413), or your favorite vanilla or dulce de leche ice cream (optional)

1. Position a rack in the center of the oven and preheat to 375°F. Sift or whisk together the flour, meal, sugar, and salt. Add the butter and work it into the flour until smooth. (You may do this in a food processor fitted with a steel blade.

Pulse together the flour, meal, sugar, and salt several times to sift. Add the butter and process until it resembles raw grits or polenta. Turn it out into a mixing bowl and finish blending the dough by hand.)

2. Put the dough in a 12-inch removable-bottom tart pan and press it into a uniform layer over the entire surface and up the sides. Lightly prick it with a fork and bake it in the center of the oven 10 minutes. Let it cool on a wire rack while you prepare the apples.

3. Cut the zest from both lemons in fine strips with a bar zester or remove it with a vegetable peeler and cut it into fine julienne with a sharp knife. Halve the lemons and squeeze their juice through a strainer into a large glass or stainless-steel bowl. Peel and core the apples and slice them ¼ inch thick. As they're ready, add them to the lemon juice, tossing to coat them.

4. Arrange the apple slices in a single layer of overlapping circles on top of the shortbread crust, scattering the ginger among them as you go. Sprinkle them with the raw sugar, lemon zest, and bourbon; generously grate nutmeg over the top.

5. Bake until the apples are tender and golden, about 40 minutes. Serve warm or at room temperature with, if liked, a scoop of vanilla, caramel, or dulce de leche ice cream.

Serves 6

fried apple pies with rosemary and ginger

Fried fruit pies are a perennial favorite almost everywhere the South, but what is called "fried pie" varies from place to place. The only common denominator is that they're traditionally made with dried fruit. My grandmother's pies, encased in a modified biscuit dough, were not really fried at all, but griddle-baked in a skillet with just enough butter to keep them from sticking. Elsewhere, the crust is a true pastry and is really deep-fried. The pies offered here can be done either way. The traditional filling has been given a contemporary lift with a touch of rosemary and fresh ginger, but it's still the same satisfying homespun pastry that homesick Southerners crave.

8 ounces dried apples

⅓ cup sugar

2 large sprigs fresh rosemary (at least 3 inches long; do not use dried)

2 quarter-size slices fresh ginger

1 lemon

2 ounces (½ stick or 4 tablespoons) unsalted butter, cut into teaspoon-size bits

1 Recipe Basic Pastry (page 364)

Butter, peanut, or vegetable oil, for frying

Confectioners' sugar in a shaker, optional

1. Put the apples in a heavy stainless or enameled saucepan with the sugar, rosemary, ginger, and enough water to completely cover; bring to a boil over medium-high heat. Reduce the heat to medium-low and simmer, stirring occasionally, until the apples are tender and the liquid has mostly evaporated, about 45 minutes. Remove and discard the rosemary and ginger. Grate in the lemon zest. Cut the lemon in half, squeeze in the juice from one half, taste, and add more as needed. Roughly crush with a potato masher and mix in the butter until dissolved.

2. Divide the pastry into twelve equal balls. Roll each out on a lightly floured surface into a circle about 5 inches across and ⅛ inch thick. Put a rounded tablespoon of apples in the center of each, brush the edges with a little water, and fold the pastry over the filling to form a half circle, gently pressing the edges together with the tines of a fork. If the edges are a little ragged, even them up by trimming them with a knife or zig-zag pastry wheel.

3. The pies may be either sautéed or fried in deep fat. To sauté, heat a heavy-bottomed skillet over medium heat, brush it with butter, and sauté the pies until they were golden-brown, about 4–5 minutes per side. The pastry will be soft but flaky.

4. To fry, put about 1 inch of oil in a heavy-bottomed Dutch oven at least an inch deep but no more than halfway up the sides and heat it to 375°F (almost smoking hot) over medium-high heat. While it heats, fit a wire cooling rack over a rimmed baking sheet. When the fat is ready, put in enough pies to fill the pan without crowding.

Fry until the bottoms are nicely browned, about 3 minutes; turn and fry until uniformly browned, about 3 minutes more. Drain well on the wire rack. If you like, dust them lightly with confectioners' sugar. Serve hot or at room temperature.

Fried Peach Pies with Orange: Substitute dried peaches for the apples, omit the rosemary and ginger, and season the peaches with a generous grating of nutmeg and tablespoon of bourbon. Use orange zest and juice instead of lemon.

Makes 12

mama's sweet potato custard pies

Sweet potato custard pie has been a defining standard for Southern baking at least since Mary Randolph published a recipe for it in *The Virginia House-Wife* of 1824 through to Bill Neal's modern classic *Biscuits, Spoonbread, and Sweet Potato Pie*. For me, it has a special place in my heart: My grandmother's sweet potato custards were a holiday standard in my family for at least four generations. Like sturdy bookends, this pie and her coconut cake defined our Christmas dessert board, and while she often made pumpkin pie at Thanksgiving, she would not have let the day pass without at least one of these pies, even when the turkey shared the table with candied yams. No matter the time of year that I taste it, every bite whispers of autumn leaves, frosted windowpanes, and mistletoe all at once.

For more than a decade and through four cookbooks, I've tried to reproduce that special something that was MaMa's touch, both while she was at my side to coach me and in the years since she left us with only memories to guide. I don't know if I've completely succeeded, but if I had to try to describe her to you in a single taste, it would be this one, so I think it's pretty close.

3 pounds (5–6 medium) sweet potatoes

1 recipe Basic Pastry (page 364)

1 cup sugar

1 ounce (2 tablespoons) unsalted butter

4 large eggs, lightly beaten

Salt

1 teaspoon cinnamon, optional

½ teaspoon freshly grated nutmeg, optional

1 tablespoon Homemade Bourbon Vanilla (page 17) or 1 teaspoon vanilla extract

About ¼ cup heavy cream or evaporated milk

Bourbon Whipped Cream (page 402)

1. Scrub the potatoes well under cold running water. Put them in a large, heavy-bottomed pot and add enough cold water to cover by 1 inch. Bring to a boil over medium-high heat, reduce the heat to a steady simmer, loosely cover, and cook until the potatoes are tender (a fork or sharp knife should easily pass through). Drain and let cool enough to handle.

2. Meanwhile, position a rack in the center of the oven and preheat to 375°F. Line two 9-inch pie plates with pastry and partially bake them (see page 366).

3. While they're still hot, peel the sweet potatoes and puree them through a ricer or sieve into a large mixing bowl, or cut them in chunks, put them in the bowl, and mash them well with a fork or potato masher. Mix in the sugar and butter, stirring until the potatoes absorb them, then stir in the eggs, a small pinch of salt, spices, and vanilla. Beat in enough cream or evaporated milk to make the filling smooth and barely pourable—it should still be quite thick and not at all soupy.

4. Pour the custard into the prepared pastry, smooth the top, and bake in the center of the oven until the filling is set at the center and the pastry is nicely browned, about 40 minutes. You may need to rotate the pies midway if your oven is uneven. Cool on wire racks and serve either at room temperature or chilled, with a healthy dollop of lightly sweetened whipped cream.

Makes two 9-inch pies

bourbon cherry pie

Bourbon is a natural paring for cherries, far superior to brandy or cognac in cherries jubilee. In a pie, it mellows out tart sour cherries and gives kick to delicately sweet ones. Of course, cherries are the main event here, and bourbon cannot completely cover the taste of indifferent fruit, so use only the ripest and best that you can get. If they are very sweet and completely lacking tartness, the bourbon may need the help of a squeeze of lemon juice to give the pie the right balance.

1 recipe Basic Pastry (page 364)

1 cup plus 1 tablespoon sugar

4 cups pitted and halved dark cherries
(about 2 pounds whole cherries)

Salt

2 tablespoons bourbon

3 tablespoons unsalted butter, cut into bits

3 tablespoons all-purpose flour

1. Position a rack in the center of the oven and preheat to 450°F. Divide the pastry in half and roll out one half ⅛ inch thick. Line a 9-inch pie plate with it and prick the bottom well with a fork, but don't trim off the excess dough. Sprinkle the bottom with 1 tablespoon of the sugar. Roll out the remaining pastry and cut it with a knife or fluted pastry wheel into ½-inch-wide strips.

2. Toss together the cherries, remaining sugar, a tiny pinch of salt, bourbon, and butter in a mixing bowl. Sprinkle in the flour and toss to mix. Pour the fruit into the prepared pastry and level it with a spatula.

3. Weave the lattice top as follows: Lay strips of pastry ½ inch apart on top of the pie. Fold back every other strip and lay a strip crosswise along one edge over the strips that remain. Unfold the folded strips and fold back the ones that had not been folded before to the point where the crosswise strip covers them. Lay another strip of pastry ½ inch from the other, unfold the folded strips, and repeat until the surface is covered. Trim off the excess at the edges of strips, brush their undersides with water, and lightly press them into the bottom pastry to make them stick. Brush the edges of the pastry with a little water and fold the excess bottom pastry over the edges of the lattice. Press into place and flute the edges with your fingers.

4. Put the pie in a large, rimmed cookie sheet and bake in the center of the oven 15 minutes. Reduce the heat to 350°F and bake until the top is golden-brown and the filling is bubbly to the center and thickened, about 30 minutes more.

Makes one 9-inch pie, serving 6

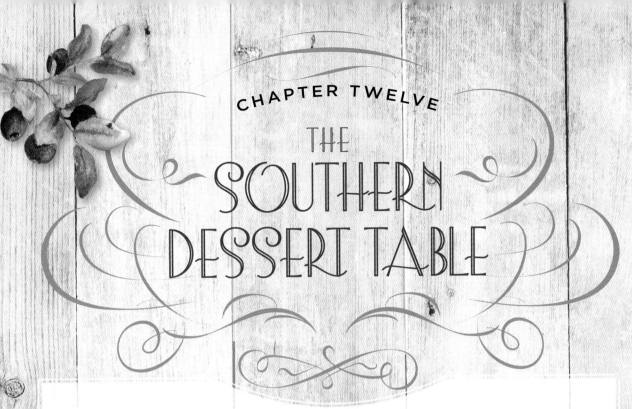

CHAPTER TWELVE

THE SOUTHERN DESSERT TABLE

One of the great fantasy figures of our time is the Southern grandmother, bustling about her kitchen in her flour-dusted apron, smelling of vanilla and cinnamon, conjuring up an endless progression of cakes, cookies, pastries, and dainty creams. Unhappily, if such a woman ever really existed outside our imaginations, she's long gone, and we no longer take homemade desserts for granted. Before the South became widely urbanized in the mid-twentieth century, however, when two-income households were rare and dinner was a midday institution, serving a meal without dessert was as unnatural to a Southern cook as flying. She might make the world's flakiest biscuits, fry up the most golden, juicy chicken, cook vegetables to a turn, and brew iced tea as clear and sweet as ambrosia, but her reputation rested on the end of the meal and she knew it. That's probably how that fantasy grandmother came to be, and certainly why as much as half of any community cookbook from down South is devoted to sweets.

Even when the meal is nothing but a sandwich, most Southerners still want to finish it with a bite of something sweet, even if it's nothing more than a moon pie. This habit has drawn a lot of fire in recent times and maybe we've overdone it in the past, but most of the rich confections that have lately been vilified were never everyday fare on home tables, even for the wealthy. And as for the sweets that were offered every day, we got away with them because portions were smaller and lives were more active. Many argue that our increasingly sedentary lives have made this sweet habit unhealthy, but the truth is it's our lack of restraint that needs to be reined in, not the dessert table.

For better or worse, the art of dessert making in the South has nowadays become a hobby rather than a daily occupation, and many traditional Southern sweets have given way to fashionable newcomers. Such things as tiramisu, Sacher torte, and something amorphously called "death by chocolate" have become almost standard repertory even among traditional cooks, while a real banana pudding, made with rich homemade custard and topped with a genuine, delicately browned meringue, has become as rare as a bikini in the Antarctic.

This chapter revisits those older desserts, and is organized into three basic types: those made with fruit; composed desserts, such as that banana pudding, made up of multiple elements; and the delight of anyone born and bred in a hot climate, frozen ices and creams. Baked sweets such as cakes, pies, and cobblers can be found in chapter 11.

gingered peaches

As cooks in the Carolina and Georgia peach country have always known, ginger and peaches were made for each other. The pungent spice of ginger intensifies the delicate, sunny fragrance of the fruit, adding depth without overwhelming the natural flavors.

6 ripe medium peaches

1 lemon

1 cup water

⅔ cup turbinado ("raw") sugar or white sugar (do not use regular brown sugar)

¼ cup chopped crystallized ginger

2 tablespoons bourbon

1 pint vanilla ice cream, or 1 cup chilled heavy cream or Bourbon Custard (page 329)

1. Bring a teakettle of water to a rolling boil. Rub the peaches well under cold, running water and put them into a heatproof bowl. Completely cover with boiling water and let stand for 1 minute. Drain and refresh them under cold running water. Slip off the peelings, halve them and remove the pits, then cut them into thick wedges. Cut the zest from the lemon in strips with a bar zester or remove it with a vegetable peeler and cut it in fine julienne. Halve and juice the lemon.

2. Stir the water and sugar together in a large stainless-steel or enameled pan and bring it to a boil over medium-high heat, stirring occasionally. Add the ginger and lemon zest, reduce the heat to medium, and simmer for 5 minutes. Stir in the lemon juice and bourbon and turn off the heat.

3. Put the peaches into the syrup and let it sit until it's completely cooled. Serve at room temperature over ice cream or in bowls with a cold pitcher of cream or custard passed separately.

Serves 6

apple-pecan crumble

Crumbles may be old-fashioned, too, but there's nothing like a warm apple crumble for comfort when the weather suddenly turns crisp in the fall. Best of all, they're a snap to put together, and turn a plain family dinner into a company meal.

6 Golden Delicious, Gala, or Honey-Crisp apples

Grated zest and juice of 1 lemon

1½ cups (lightly packed) light brown sugar, divided

Salt

1½ teaspoons cinnamon, divided

Whole nutmeg in a grater

1 rounded tablespoon cornstarch

10 tablespoons unsalted butter, cut into ¼-inch chunks, divided

7 ounces (about 1½ cups) unbleached all-purpose flour

½ cup slivered pecans

Ginger Ice Cream (page 411), Bourbon Custard (page 329), or 1 cup heavy cream, optional

1. Position a rack in the center of the oven and preheat to 375°F. Peel, core, and thinly slice the apples. Put them in a large glass bowl and toss with the lemon juice and zest. Add ¾ cup of the brown sugar, a pinch of salt, 1 teaspoon of the cinnamon, a generous grating of nutmeg, and the cornstarch; toss gently to mix. Add 2 tablespoons of the butter chunks and toss again.

2. Butter a 2-quart gratin or shallow casserole, put in the apples, and level the top. In a separate bowl, whisk together the flour, a pinch of salt, and the remaining brown sugar and cinnamon. Add the remaining butter and work it into the flour until it resembles coarse wet sand with large crumbles. Add the pecans and toss to mix. Sprinkle evenly over the apples and bake until bubbly and golden-brown, about 45 minutes. Serve warm with Ginger Ice Cream or chilled Bourbon Custard, or pass cream separately.

Serves 6

baked apples with ginger and pecans

Baked apples are very old-fashioned, homey, warming, and comfortable as a favorite old sweater. Their sweet, spicy aroma whispers of crisp air and the rustle of bright leaves at our feet, even if the nip in the air comes only from the air conditioner. You may be thought a bit old-fashioned yourself when you serve them, but never mind: No one ever has any trouble eating them. Here, they get a little dressed up with ginger and pecans, making them special enough for company. You can dress them up even more by serving them with a pitcher of chilled Bourbon Custard (page 329) or heavy cream passed separately.

4 tart apples

¼ cup chopped crystallized ginger

¼ cup chopped pecans

5 tablespoons turbinado ("raw") sugar
or light brown sugar

Zest from 1 lemon

¼ cup bourbon

4 teaspoons unsalted butter

1. Position a rack in the center of the oven and preheat to 350°F. Wash the apples under cold running water and pat dry. Cut out the stem end and, using a melon baller or apple corer, scoop out and discard the core of each apple without penetrating the bottom. Mix the ginger, pecans, sugar, and lemon zest in a bowl and stuff this into the cavities of each apple, lightly mounding a little of it on the top.

2. Butter an 8-inch round or square baking dish and put in the apples. Spoon the bourbon into their centers and top with teaspoon of butter. Pour enough water into the dish to come about ¼ inch up its sides. Bake in the center of the oven until the apples are tender but not collapsing and the pecans are golden-brown, about 30–40 minutes. Serve warm or at room temperature.

Serves 4

baked peaches with pecans

In midsummer, when sweet, yellow peaches are at their ripest and most fragrant, they do not need much to make them really delicious. Southern cooks usually do little more slice them, add a suggestion of sugar, and douse them with cream, spoon them over ice cream, or pile them into an old-fashioned short-cake. When they are not, perhaps, quite as sweet and ripe as we would like, here is how we infuse them with some of that mellow, sun-ripened flavor.

2 large, slightly underripe peaches

2–4 tablespoons turbinado ("raw") sugar, depending on the sweetness of the peaches

¼ cup chopped pecans

¼ cup bourbon

4 teaspoons unsalted butter

1 pint vanilla ice cream, 1 cup chilled heavy cream, or Bourbon Custard (page 329), optional

1. Bring a teakettle full of water to a rolling boil. Rub the peaches under cold, running water and put them into a heatproof bowl. Completely cover them with the boiling water and let them stand 1 minute. Drain and refresh the peaches under cold running water. Slip off the peelings, cut them in half lengthwise, and remove the pits.

2. Position a rack in the center of the oven and preheat to 350°F. Lightly butter an 8-inch square or round baking dish and put in the peaches, cut-side up. Sprinkle the pit cavities with a little sugar, then mound the chopped pecans into them. Sprinkle the peaches evenly with bourbon and the remaining sugar. Put a teaspoon of butter over the pecans on each peach and bake in the center of the oven until they're tender, about 45 minutes.

3. Let them rest at room temperature for at least 10 minutes or let them cool to room temperature before serving. If you like, you may put a scoop of vanilla ice cream on the side or pass a pitcher of cold heavy cream or custard separately.

Serves 4

southern macerated summer fruit

The advent of congealed salads made from flavored gelatin and canned fruit cocktail caused mixed fruit salad to sink, in many people's estimation, into something that is not quite nice. Yet when the fruit is carefully chosen and judiciously seasoned, there is no dessert in the world that is more satisfying to eat than a fragrant bowl of mixed fruit. This is the South's own version, sweetened with mountain honey and splashed with rum. It's a kissing cousin to Italy's Macedonia di Frutta. And just as Italian cooks sometimes add rum to the bowl along with their more traditional maraschino liqueur, I don't know a single Southerner who would quibble if you chose to add ¼ cup of cherry liqueur to our traditional rum.

2–3 medium oranges (see step 1)

2 lemons

2 firm, crisp apples such as Winesap, Pink Lady, Fuji, or Granny Smith

2 firm but ripe Bosc or Bartlett pears

2 ripe peaches or mangoes (or both)

1 cup halved and pitted dark cherries

1 cup halved and pitted white grapes

1 cup diced cantaloupe or honeydew melon

¼ cup golden rum

¼–⅓ cup honey, preferably sourwood honey (page 397)

2 ripe but firm bananas

1. Grate the zest from half an orange into a large glass bowl that will comfortably hold all the fruit. Juice enough oranges through a strainer to make 1 cup juice and add it to the bowl. Grate the zest from one of the lemons into the bowl, and then juice both lemons into it through a strainer.

2. Peel, core, and dice the apples and pears, adding them to the orange juice and tossing well to coat the fruit as you go. Peel, pit, and dice the peaches or mangoes, add them to the juice, and toss well. Add the cherries, grapes, and diced melon and stir well.

3. Add the rum and ¼ cup of the honey, stir well, then taste and adjust the honey. Let the fruit macerate for 30 minutes, then taste and adjust the sweetness, adding either honey or a little sugar if it needs to be sweeter. (If you are using a strongly flavored honey such as sourwood, more could be somewhat overpowering. In that case use sugar.) If you're not planning to serve the fruit right away, cover and refrigerate it. You may prepare it up to 2 days ahead through this step.

4. Half an hour before serving, peel and slice the bananas ¼ inch thick. Add them to the fruit and toss well, carefully stirring up from the bottom with a wide, shallow spoon. Don't overmix, as too much tossing could cause the fruit, especially the bananas, to bruise and break down. Let it sit at room temperature until you are ready to serve it. Serve cool or at room temperature.

Additions and subtractions: As the season progresses, you may change the mix, adding strawberries, blueberries, or plums as they come into season, or substituting other fruits for the cherries and/or peaches when they're not available. Some cooks add ½ cup pecans or walnuts just before serving.

Sourwood Honey: Found only in the Appalachian Mountain regions of the South, this honey comes from the pollen of sourwood tree blossoms. While its distinctive flavor has no equal, any good-quality honey can be substituted for it. Acacia and lavender honey are two especially good substitutes.

Serves 6–8

pears in white wine

Many luscious, juicy varieties of pears are now grown in the South, and good Bosc and Bartlett pears are available in most markets. They make a wonderful dessert just as they are, with maybe a few pecans and a creamy blue cheese on the side. The old varieties of pears that were most often found in Southern orchards were too hard for that kind of eating, so pears are more often found on traditional Southern tables in the form of chutney, relish, or sweet preserves—or poached in wine, as is done here. The very earliest cookbooks presented such dishes as a sweet relish to serve with meat, but they make a wonderful dessert as well.

2 large ripe but very firm Bosc or Bartlett pears

2 tablespoons butter

2-3 tablespoons turbinado ("raw") sugar, depending on the sweetness of the pears

1 cup dry white wine

1 large lemon, half the zest removed in 1 or 2 pieces and reserved

Whole nutmeg in a grater

1 cup Bourbon Custard (page 329), chilled, or chilled heavy cream

1. Peel the pears and halve them lengthwise. Cut out the cores with a coffee spoon or small melon baller. Melt the butter in a sauté pan or lidded skillet over medium heat. When it is melted and hot, raise the heat to medium-high, add the pears, and sauté, turning once or twice, until they are just beginning to color. Sprinkle them with the sugar and sauté until they're lightly browned.

2. Add the wine, lemon zest, and a generous grating of nutmeg. Bring to a boil, reduce the heat to low, and loosely cover. Simmer, turning the pears once about halfway through, until they're tender but still firm, about 20–30 minutes.

3. If, when the pears are tender, the cooking liquids are very thin, raise the heat to medium-high and boil until they are syrupy. Turn off the heat. Cut the lemon in half and squeeze the juice from one of the halves over the pears. Shake the pan gently to distribute the juice, then taste and adjust the lemon juice. Serve warm or at room temperature, passing custard or heavy cream separately.

Serves 4

old-fashioned southern shortcake

Shortcake is a summer favorite almost anywhere you go in America. In the South, where many still stubbornly resist the manufactured angel-food-cake cups that appear next to the strawberries each spring in the supermarket, the usual cake onto which the fruit is spooned is really just a light, sweet biscuit, but sometimes it's a crisp, buttery shortbread cookie. Both have their charms. But the real charm of this simple, homey dessert is that it can be made completely new by changing the filling. Almost any berries or summer fruit will work, so while I've included several options here, feel free to experiment with the fresh berries and fruits that you might have on hand.

THE SHORTCAKE:

SOUTHERN BISCUIT SHORTCAKE

This is the traditional shortcake that most Southerners remember from their childhood. It needn't be relegated to the dessert table: It also makes a delectable carrier for savory fillings, and since they're closely related to scones, they're delicious served the same way, slathered with clotted cream or butter and Peach-Orange Marmalade (page 18) for breakfast or tea.

2 cups all-purpose Southern soft-wheat flour or soft-wheat pastry flour

2 teaspoons baking powder

¼ cup sugar

½ teaspoon salt

3 tablespoons chilled unsalted butter, cut into bits

1 tablespoon chilled lard (or omit and increase unsalted butter to 4 tablespoons)

¾–1 cup whole-milk buttermilk or plain whole-milk yogurt thinned to buttermilk consistency with regular milk

1. Position a rack in the upper third of the oven and preheat to 450°F. Sift or whisk the flour, baking powder, sugar, and salt together in a mixing bowl. Add the butter and lard, cutting them in with a pastry blender or two knives until the mixture is the size of small peas. Make a well in the center and pour in ¾ cup of the buttermilk. Using a very light hand and as few strokes as possible, combine the ingredients into a soft dough. If it's too crumbly and dry, add more milk by the spoonful until the dough is soft but not wet and sticky. Gather it into a ball and lightly flour it.

2. Lightly flour a work surface and turn the dough out onto it. Pat it out ½ inch thick. Fold it in half, pat it flat again, and repeat three or four more times, using as light a hand as possible. If the dough gets sticky, lightly flour it, but use as little flour as possible. Pat out one last time ½ inch thick. Dip a 2½-inch round biscuit cutter in flour and, pushing it straight down without twisting, cut the dough into rounds. Any leftover scraps can be lightly reworked and cut or baked as they are for cook's treat. Lay the cakes on an ungreased baking sheet.

3. Bake in the upper third of the oven 8–12 minutes, until lightly browned. Cool on a rack and, if they are made ahead, store them in an airtight tin or plastic container.

Makes 8–10 shortcakes

THE FILLINGS:

BOURBON-MACERATED STRAWBERRIES AND OTHER FRUITS

Bourbon and lemon are a classic Southern combination that sends so many desserts into another dimension. Their marriage with strawberries is downright magical, but also gives a lift to blackberries, blueberries, and peaches. The bourbon almost disappears, surrendering its sharp alcoholic edge while lending a rich, mellow undertone. It makes even indifferent berries that were picked a little too green and ripened in storage taste richly of spring and sunshine.

STRAWBERRIES (MASTER RECIPE)

1 pound (about 2 pints) ripe strawberries

1 lemon

About ½ cup turbinado ("raw") sugar

¼ cup bourbon

Fresh mint leaves, for garnish

1. Rinse the berries under cold running water, drain, and then stem and core them. Thickly slice large berries and halve the smaller ones. Cut the zest from the lemon in long julienne with a bar zester, or remove the zest with a vegetable peeler and cut into fine julienne. Halve the lemon.

2. Put the berries in a glass or ceramic bowl and add ⅓ cup of the sugar, the bourbon, and the lemon zest; squeeze in the juice from one of the lemon halves. Toss until the sugar evenly coats the berries. Let macerate 30 minutes.

3. Taste the berries and adjust the sugar and lemon juice (they may not need more; a lot will depend on the ripeness of the berries and the strength of the lemon juice). Let sit until the sugar is completely dissolved, about 20–30 minutes more. Use them as a shortcake filling, spoon them over your favorite vanilla ice cream, or serve them just as they are or topped with a dollop of whipped cream.

Blackberries or blueberries: Substitute 2 pints black- or blueberries for the strawberries. Wash the berries in cold water and pick them over to remove any stems and mushy or shriveled berries.

Peaches, plums, or apricots: Substitute 4 cups peeled, pitted, and sliced fruit for the berries. If you like, substitute orange zest for the lemon zest and add a squeeze of orange juice with the lemon juice.

Serves 4

CRANBERRY PRESERVES

Based on old recipes from several antebellum Southern cookbooks, this old-fashioned conserve is perfection in its traditional role as a relish for turkey or game meat, but needn't be confined to the sauce bowl. It's sumptuous on toast, and makes a delicious holiday variation for shortcake, simply substituted for the fruit filling. It can also be spooned into pre-baked tart shells, over sliced pound cake, or even a scoop of Buttered Pecan Caramel Ice Cream (page 413).

24 ounces (6 cups) fresh cranberries

1 pound (2 cups) demerara, turbinado, or brown sugar

Zest from 1 orange, cut into fine julienne

3 tablespoons bourbon

1. Pick through the berries and discard any soft or damaged fruit. Wash in cold water and drain. Put 2 cups in a 3- to 4-quart stainless-steel or enameled saucepan. Lightly crush them with a wooden spoon and pour in just enough water to barely cover them. Bring gently to a boil over medium heat, skimming away the foam that rises. Reduce the heat to low and simmer, uncovered, until the berries have collapsed and the juice is thick, about 45 minutes. Turn off the heat.

2. Pour the cooked fruit into a jelly bag or clean piece of muslin set in a sieve over a bowl. Force the juice through the bag (or muslin) into the bowl and discard the pulp. Put the juice back in the pan, stir in the remaining berries and the sugar, and bring it back to a boil over medium heat. Skim away the foam as it rises. Reduce the heat to the barest simmer and cook until the berries are very tender and transparent, about 45 minutes. Turn off the heat and stir in the zest and bourbon. With a clean, stainless-steel utensil, spoon or ladle the berries into a clean glass bowl or, for prolonged storage, sterile glass jars. It will keep, covered and refrigerated, for up to 6 weeks. This can also be canned for prolonged storage.

For 6–8 servings as a shortcake or tartlet filling, 12–16 as a condiment

THE TOPPINGS:

OLD-FASHIONED CLOTTED CREAM

½ cup sugar

1 pint (2 cups) heavy cream (minimum 36% milk fat)

1 lemon

Whole nutmeg in a grater

1. Stir the sugar and cream together until the sugar dissolves. Grate in the zest from the lemon, then halve the lemon and squeeze in the juice from one of the halves through a strainer. Stir until the cream thickens to the consistency of a thick cream sauce.

2. Season with a generous grating of nutmeg and stir well. Cover and let sit for at least 30 minutes at room temperature, then refrigerate for at least 4 hours or overnight. The cream should be the consistency of sour cream, and the longer it sits, the thicker it will be. If, however, it is not thickened enough when you're ready to serve it, lightly whisk it, being sure the cream is well chilled, and be careful not to overbeat it or you'll turn it into butter.

Makes about 2½ cups

BOURBON WHIPPED CREAM

1 pint (2 cups) cold heavy cream

¼–½ cup sugar

1 tablespoon bourbon, rum, or Homemade Bourbon Vanilla (page 17), optional

1. Beat the cream in a chilled glass or stainless bowl with a wire whisk or electric mixer until it begins to thicken.

2. Sprinkle in the sugar (exact amounts will depend on how sweet you want the cream to be) and continue beating until the cream holds soft peaks. Fold in the optional flavoring and continue beating until the cream holds stiff peaks. It can be made up to an hour ahead. Keep chilled.

Makes 2½–3 cups

PUTTING THE SHORTCAKE TOGETHER

8 Southern Biscuit Shortcakes (page 399), or 16 Southern Shortbread cookies (page 353), or 16 Pecan Shortbread cookies (page 354)

1 recipe Bourbon-Macerated Strawberries and Other Fruits (page 400), or Cranberry Preserves (page 401)

1 recipe Clotted Cream (page 401) or Bourbon Whipped Cream (above)

8 fresh berries, curls of orange zest (for cranberries), and/or mint sprigs, for garnish

1. If you're using biscuit shortcakes, split them. Put the bottom half or one shortbread cookie on each of eight individual serving plates.

2. Spoon the fruit filling over the shortcake, reserving a few spoonfuls for garnish if you like. Add a small dollop of the cream. Cover with the top half of the shortcake or another cookie and finish with a generous spoonful of the cream. Garnish as desired and serve at once.

Serves 8

mrs. randolph's quire of paper pancakes

For those who think that dear Julia Child introduced America to crepes, the delicate, paper-thin pancakes of France, please note that this recipe, from Mary Randolph's landmark cookbook *The Virginia House-Wife*, dates back to the early days of the American Republic, and was even known in Colonial America. Until the twentieth century, pancake was the name used for crepes; what we call pancakes today were then called griddlecakes. Eventually, old-fashioned griddlecake disappeared from American usage. At any rate, regardless of what you call them, you might say that Mrs. Randolph's quire is an all-soprano chorus—made as it is of a stack of delicate, lacy-edged crepes flavored with wine and nutmeg. Some old recipes call for each crepe to be spread with a little bit of jam: They won't need a sauce if you opt to do that.

Have everything at room temperature. Let the eggs sit out until they are no longer chilled, or put them (in shell) in a bowl of hot tap water for 2–3 minutes before using them.

1 cup milk

3 large eggs, room temperature

2 ounces (4 tablespoons or ½ stick) unsalted butter, melted

2 ounces (a generous ½ cup) unbleached all-purpose flour

Whole nutmeg in a grater

½ cup sugar

¼ teaspoon salt

¼ cup dry white wine or sherry

Superfine sugar (see notes below), for dusting

Fresh Raspberry Bourbon Sauce (or one of its variations, page 371), sautéed seasonal fruit, wine sauce, or Bourbon-Macerated Strawberries and Other Fruit (page 400)

1. Scald the milk in a heavy bottomed saucepan over medium heat and let it cool to around 110°F. Lightly beat the eggs in a mixing bowl, then gradually beat in the milk and butter until smooth. In a separate bowl, sift or whisk together the flour, a generous grating of nutmeg, sugar, and salt. Gradually stir the egg and milk into the dry ingredients, being careful not to let the flour lump. Stir in the wine. The batter will be quite thin. Let it rest, covered, for at least 1 hour.

2. Warm a plate and lightly dust it with superfine sugar. Heat a seasoned crepe pan or 9-inch nonstick pan over medium-high heat. Brush lightly with butter. Pour in just enough batter to thinly coat the bottom, swirling until it's uniformly coating the bottom of the pan, and cook until the edges are browned, the bottom is golden, and the top is set and completely opaque, about 35–45 seconds. These crepes don't require turning. Loosen the edges, invert the pan over the warm plate, and let the crepe fall onto it. Lightly sprinkle with superfine sugar.

3. Repeat with the remaining batter (you won't need to grease the pan after the first pancake), stacking them one on top of the other, with a dusting of sugar between each. Serve warm, cutting into wedges like a cake, with fruit sauce, syrup, sautéed seasonal fruit, or wine sauce. They're eaten as soon as they're made, but if you need to make them ahead, instead of stacking

them on top of one another, invert them onto squares of waxed paper as you take them up. Cool, stack, and store in a plastic zipper-locking bag. They can be rewarmed for a few seconds one at a time, top-side down, in a crepe pan or non-stick skillet over medium-high heat.

Notes: Superfine sugar is the consistency of American 4x confectioners' sugar, but the cornstarch that our confectioners' sugar contains makes it a poor substitute as it lends a pasty consistency and has a raw aftertaste. Superfine sugar is available from professional bakers' suppliers and mail-order catalogs such as the *King Arthur Flour Company's Baker's Catalogue*. Failing that, pulverize granulated sugar to a powder in the food processor.

Variation: Instead of stacking the crepes, you can spoon some macerated fruit into each crepe, fold or roll the crepe around it, and top with some of the syrup and a dollop of Bourbon Whipped Cream (page 402).

Makes about 2 dozen, serving 4

shortbread banana pudding

Banana pudding is a simple, homey, and sadly under-appreciated dessert. When it is well made, there is nothing more satisfying to eat: creamy, cool, and comforting, its rich, intense banana filling is counterpointed by a cloud of lightly browned meringue. Only someone who hates bananas can ever resist it. Unfortunately, nowadays it's seldom made well. Far too often, everything but the bananas—from the custard to the artificial nondairy topping—has come out of a box, and inevitably tastes as if the box is still in it. These substitutes take a little less work than a traditional pudding, but in the end are never worth the effort they do take.

Before you begin, a few notes on the elements are in order here. While boiled custard doesn't need starch to it to make it thicken, custards that will undergo further cooking or that will bind uncooked fruit do need added reinforcement or they'll be watery. The meringue topping often intimidates novices, and can be tricky in humid weather, but it's not really difficult. A little cream of tartar helps stabilize it and keep it from collapsing or shrinking. But even with that reinforcement, humidity and both over- and undercooking can cause a baked meringue to collapse or weep, so choose a dry day and pay close attention while it's in the oven.

5 eggs

½ cup all-purpose flour

1⅓ cups sugar, divided

3 cups whole milk

1 teaspoon Homemade Bourbon Vanilla (page 17) or vanilla extract

1 recipe Southern Shortbread (page 353), or 1 package all-butter shortbread cookies—or, for a more traditional take, vanilla wafers flavored with real vanilla

4–5 ripe bananas

1 teaspoon cream of tartar

1. Separate the eggs, putting the whites in a copper, stainless-steel, or glass bowl and the yolks in a heatproof glass or ceramic bowl. Prepare the bottom half of a double boiler with 1 inch of water and bring it to a simmer over medium heat. Mix the flour and 1 cup of the sugar together in the top pan and slowly whisk in the milk. Bring this to a simmer over direct medium heat, stirring constantly. Lightly whisk the egg yolks to mix and then whisk ½ cup of the milk mixture into them. Slowly whisk this into the remaining milk and transfer the pan to the simmering water. Cook, stirring constantly, until the custard is quite thick, about 5 minutes. Remove the pan from the heat, stir in the vanilla, and stir for a minute more, then set it aside to cool completely.

2. Line the bottom of a 9-inch square or round deep casserole dish with shortbread cookies, breaking them to fill in the gaps until the bottom of the dish is covered. Peel and slice the bananas ¼ inch thick. Cover the cookies with a single layer of bananas. Spoon half the custard over them, then add another layer of shortbread, reserving a cookie or two. Finish with the remaining bananas and custard. Crush the reserved cookies to fine crumbs and sprinkle them over the top.

3. Position a rack in the center of the oven and preheat to 375°F. With a whisk or electric mixer, beat the cream of tartar into the egg whites and continue beating until they form very soft peaks. Gradually beat in the remaining ⅓ cup sugar and beat until the peaks are firm and glossy. Spread the meringue evenly over the pudding and bake in the center of the oven until the meringue is golden-brown, about 10–12 minutes. Remove it promptly and let it cool completely. Refrigerate if it's not to be served within the hour, or—if you prefer it cold—chill it for 2 hours before serving. It can be made as much as 12 hours ahead, and some believe it's actually better the second day.

Serves 6–8

lillie's little lemon puddings

Lillie King was a Southern Lady in all the best senses of the term, and was widely known in her hometown of Talladega, Alabama, for her baking. Though Miss Lillie is no longer with us, her legend lives on and her sons and nieces and nephews still get glassy-eyed when they talk of these warm little puddings that often awaited them at the end of a cold winter's school day. The charm of these puddings is that the batter separates into distinct layers when it is baked: a creamy, luscious, lemony custard settles to the bottom while a feather-light, sponge cake layer rises to the top. They are wonderfully comforting served warm, fresh from the oven, with their tops still puffed like a soufflé, but are equally good at room temperature or even chilled. The top layer of course sinks as the pudding cools, but that doesn't interfere with their lovely texture and flavor.

2 large eggs

1 large lemon

2 tablespoons all-purpose flour

1 cup sugar

Salt

1 cup whole milk

1 teaspoon Homemade Bourbon Vanilla (page 17) or ½ teaspoon vanilla extract

1. Position a rack in the center of the oven and preheat to 350°F. Bring a teakettle full of water to a boil. Separate the eggs, putting the whites in a large copper, stainless-steel, or glass bowl and the yolks in a glass or ceramic mixing bowl. Grate the zest from the lemon into the yolks, then halve and squeeze in its juice through a strainer. Whisk until smooth.

2. In a separate bowl, mix together the flour, sugar, and a small pinch of salt. Gradually beat this into the yolks, then stir in the milk and vanilla.

3. Beat the egg whites with a whisk or electric mixer until they form stiff peaks. Gradually stir them into the batter. Set five individual custard cups in a roasting pan or 9 x 12-inch baking pan with sides at least 2 inches deep. Divide the pudding batter among the cups, and pull out the center rack of the oven and put the pan on it. Carefully pour boiling water into the pan around the cups until it comes halfway up their sides. Bake until the puddings are set and lightly browned on top, about 30–35 minutes. Carefully lift the custard cups from the pan and let the water cool before removing the pan from the oven. Serve the puddings warm, at room temperature, or cold.

Serves 5

chocolate charlotte

The original charlottes were a simple, homey molded dessert, composed of stewed fruit encased in toasted stale bread or cake. Charlotte Russe, which came along in the nineteenth century, took the idea to a more elegant level. The stewed fruit was displaced by a rich Bavarian cream and the casing became ladyfingers or sponge cake. In the South the casing often disappeared altogether, and the cream was set in an unlined mold or individual stemmed glasses. A classic Southern Charlotte Russe was snowy white and flavored with sherry, but other flavorings did turn up, including strawberries, lemons, oranges, and, of course, chocolate.

This is the kissing cousin of chocolate mousse, that quintessential dessert from the gourmet 1970s. The primary difference is that the cream is set with gelatin, but the essentials are the same. I've streamlined the traditional recipe and taken advantage of modern kitchen equipment, but the sumptuous elegance of the old charlotte remains.

1 egg

6 ounces semisweet chocolate, roughly chopped

⅛ teaspoon salt

4 tablespoons sugar, divided

1 tablespoon unflavored gelatin

2 pints (4 cups) heavy cream, divided

2 tablespoons bourbon

1. Combine the egg, chocolate, salt, and 2 tablespoons of the sugar in a blender. Process at moderately high speed for 20 seconds, or until the chocolate is nearly smooth.

2. Soften the gelatin in 2 tablespoons cold water. Bring ¾ cup of the cream to the boiling point and pour it over the gelatin, stirring until the gelatin completely dissolves. Put it back into the pan and bring it back to a simmer, then, with the blender motor running, slowly add it to the chocolate custard. Add the bourbon and pulse to mix. Let it cool to room temperature, pulsing the machine occasionally to keep it from setting on top.

3. Put the remaining cream in a metal or glass bowl. Beat until light and fluffy. Sprinkle the remaining 2 tablespoons of sugar over it and continue beating until the cream holds firm peaks.

4. A few spoonfuls at a time, fold the chocolate custard into the whipped cream. Refrigerate until it is beginning to set, about an hour, then spoon it into stemmed glasses and chill until set, at least 2 hours. Serve with a Pecan Shortbread cookie (page 354) inserted upright on one side of the bowl, garnished, if you like, with mint and/or flowers. Alternatively, you may line the bottom and sides of a charlotte mold or trifle bowl with ladyfingers or sliced Maryan's Chocolate Pound Cake (page 322), fill it with the cream, and cover the top with more ladyfingers or cake. Chill until set, about 4 hours, and unmold onto a cake plate. Serve cut into wedges as you would a cake.

Serves 6–8

roman punch

We are accustomed to thinking of punch as something to drink; this punch, however, is an old-fashioned ice or sherbet. It harkens back to the Renaissance-era wine sherbets of Italy, which is probably the source of its name. During the nineteenth century Roman Punch was a popular palate cleanser between the fish and meat courses at elegant formal dinners. Though few people eat such meals today, this sherbet fits nicely at the end of a modern meal as a refreshing finish to almost any meal featuring fish, pork, roasted poultry, or game.

Because of its alcohol content, Roman Punch does not freeze solid like most sherbets, but remains slightly slushy. Just think of it as a snow cone with attitude.

1¼ cups sugar, divided

Grated zest of 2 lemons

1 cup freshly squeezed lemon juice

¼ cup rum

2 cups chilled champagne

3 large egg whites

1. Stir 1 cup of the sugar, 2 cups water, and the zest together in a saucepan until the sugar dissolves. Bring it to a boil over medium-high heat and boil for 2 minutes. Turn off the heat, allow it to cool, and stir in the lemon juice and rum. Refrigerate until thoroughly chilled, about 2–4 hours.

2. Stir in the champagne and freeze in an ice-cream freezer, following the manufacturer's directions, or put it in shallow containers and put it in the refrigerator's freezer compartment, stirring occasionally to keep the ice broken up. When the ice is frozen, whisk the egg whites until frothy, sprinkle in the remaining ¼ cup sugar, and whip until they form soft peaks.

3. (If you have not used an ice-cream freezer, put the ice in the food processor and pulse until it is fluffy.) Fold the egg whites gradually into the ice. Pack it in a freezable container and freeze again until the ice is set.

Makes about 2 quarts

ginger ice cream

Although ginger can have a powerfully peppery edge, this unusual ice cream is surprisingly subtle and smooth—as fragrant and delicate as the blossoms of the lily whose root is the source for the spice. It makes a refreshing finish for a meal whose main course was fish or shellfish, or anything spicy, especially curry or barbecue.

2 cups whole milk

1 whole vanilla bean, cut in half and split lengthwise

1 cup sugar

6 large egg yolks

2 cups heavy cream (minimum 36% milk fat)

Salt

1 generous tablespoon freshly grated gingerroot

⅔ cup chopped crystallized ginger or preserved ginger in syrup, drained

1. Bring 1 inch water to a simmer in the bottom of a double boiler over medium heat. In the top pan, over direct medium heat, bring the milk and vanilla bean to a simmer. Add the sugar and stir until it is completely dissolved. Whisk the egg yolks in a heatproof bowl and gradually whisk in a cup of the hot liquid. Put the top pan over the simmering water and gradually stir in the yolk mixture. Cook, stirring constantly, until it thickly coats the back of the spoon. Remove it from the heat.

2. Stir in the cream, a small pinch of salt, and both kinds of ginger. Stir until completely cooled, remove the vanilla bean (it can be rinsed, dried, and reused), and chill at least 2 hours. You can make the base a day ahead and chill it overnight.

3. Freeze the cream in an ice-cream freezer, following the manufacturer's instructions, until it is the consistency of commercial soft ice cream (set, but still not quite hard). Pack it into a deep container and put it in the freezer to ripen and harden. The flavor of this ice cream really develops when it has ripened for at least 6–8 hours.

Makes 1½ quarts, serving about 6

sweet potato ice cream

The flavors of this ice cream are traditional ones for sweet potatoes—lemon, nutmeg, and bourbon—but when they're mixed into a creamy base and frozen, that traditional combination takes on an added dimension. No one flavor is pronounced, not even the sweet potatoes, yet all of them are suggested at once, underscored with a distinctly floral aftertaste.

Orange Chocolate Tea Cake Sandwiches aren't an absolutely essential accompaniment, but they do send this right over the top. Of course, they'd send just about anything over the top.

1 pound (about 2 medium) mature, orange-fleshed sweet potatoes such as Louisiana "yams," jewels, or garnets

1 cup sugar

Salt

3 cups half-and-half

1 cup heavy cream

1 tablespoon bourbon

Grated zest of 1 lemon

Whole nutmeg in a grater

½ cup chopped Toasted Pecans (page 232)

Orange Chocolate Tea Cake Sandwiches (page 350), optional

1. Scrub the sweet potatoes under cold running water, remove any root tendrils, and pat dry. Put them in a large, heavy-bottomed saucepan and add enough water to cover them by 1 inch. Remove them, bring the water to a boil over medium-high heat, and return the potatoes to the pan. When the water is boiling again, reduce the heat to a simmer and cook until the potatoes are tender and easily pierced with a knife, about 45 minutes. Let them cool enough to handle, then peel and, while they're still warm, force them through a potato ricer. You should have at least 1 cup of puree. Stir in the sugar and a small pinch of salt and let it cool completely.

2. Gradually whisk in the half-and-half and then the cream; continue whisking until it's the consistency of a thick custard. Add the bourbon, lemon zest, and a generous grating of nutmeg. Mix well, cover, and refrigerate until well chilled, at least 2 hours or overnight.

3. Freeze in an ice-cream freezer according to the manufacturer's directions until it's the consistency of soft-serve ice cream. Pack it into a freezable container, cover, and let it solidify and ripen in the freezer for at least 2 hours. If you like, you may serve it sprinkled with the chopped pecans or pralines, with or without an Orange Chocolate Tea Cake Sandwich cookie on the side.

Makes about 2 quarts

buttered pecan caramel ice cream

Buttered pecan ice cream used to be a standard fixture of any church ice-cream social almost anywhere in the South. Those socials have practically vanished, however—and in my opinion that's a serious theological mistake, because they were better at soul saving than a dozen tent revivals. Face it: If buttered pecan ice cream won't send you straight to heaven, nothing will.

2 cups whole milk

2 cups heavy cream

1 whole vanilla bean

1 cup sugar

½ cup (tightly packed) light brown sugar

Salt

6 large egg yolks

1 cup Toasted Pecans (page 232)

1. Bring 1 inch of water to a simmer in the bottom half of a large double boiler over medium heat. Bring the milk, cream, and vanilla bean to a simmer in the top pan over direct medium heat. Let this simmer 3–4 minutes. Add both sugars and a tiny pinch of salt, stirring until dissolved, then put the pan over the simmering water.

2. Whisk the egg yolks in a heatproof bowl. Whisk a cup of the hot liquid into them, then whisk them into the remaining liquid. Cook, stirring constantly, until it lightly coats the back of the spoon. Take it off the heat and continue stirring it until it's slightly cooled, about 5 minutes. Remove the vanilla bean (it can be rinsed, dried, and reused) and let the mix cool to room temperature, stirring occasionally. Cover and refrigerate until thoroughly chilled, at least 2 hours or overnight.

3. Freeze in an ice-cream freezer, following the manufacturer's instructions, until it's thick but not quite to the stage of soft-serve ice cream. Add the pecans and freeze to soft-serve consistency. Pack the ice cream into a freezable container, cover, and put it in the freezer to ripen and harden, at least 2 hours.

Makes 1½ quarts, serving about 6

 # ACKNOWLEDGMENTS

My first book was dedicated to the four women who shaped the way I think about food: Marcella Hazan, Karen Hess, my mother, and my maternal grandmother, known to me as MaMa. Though Karen and MaMa are no longer with me, these four, joined since by Nathalie Dupree, remain the greatest influences on my cooking, writing, and teaching. I've talked of Marcella and Nathalie elsewhere in this book, but hope you'll indulge me in a brief word on the other three.

MaMa died in the early summer of 1997 while I was finishing my second book. As I sat with her in the hospital checking copy edits and knowing she would never see it finished, I talked to her about it as if she could hear—and I hope she did. The rhythms of her kitchen will always be a part of mine, and I still hear her voice every time I make a cake, whip up a sweet potato pie, or mix a batch of pimiento cheese. Ten years later, almost to day, Karen Hess died at the ripe age of eighty-eight; it was like losing my grandmother all over again. Though we didn't talk every day, I still miss her every day, and don't know what I would've accomplished without her scholar's mind, strict fidelity to fact, and vast knowledge. But what I miss most is her friendship, her irreverent sense of humor, and her passion for living. Her voice is still in my ear when I taste a recipe for balance—or anytime that I'm tempted to get sloppy with scholarship.

My mother, thankfully, can still be found puttering in her garden every day from early spring until after the first frost, hoeing, weeding, gathering, and at times talking to the pest-devouring lizards and toads that have almost become her pets. We often associate our mothers with a fragrance of some kind, and for me that fragrance will always be the smell of freshly turned earth. Mama's garden is still where she gives me her best advice, shares her own dreams, and, most important, reminds me to be honest. I wish I could be in it more than I am. I realize as I write this that I never mention her partner in life of more than sixty years: my father. Yet his voice, his strong ethics, and his wry sense of humor are an indelible part of my own voice as a writer and teacher.

I've heard some writers complain that this is a lonely business, but I have never felt less alone than when I am working. Whenever I sit down at my desk, the presence of the dozens upon dozens of friends and colleagues is palpable. To name everyone both alive and dead who has over the last three decades had a hand in shaping me as a writer, cook, and teacher, and who has therefore had a hand in the contents of this book, would more than double its size.

But I must mention the forty-nine other Southern food champions who included me in the founding of the Southern Foodways Alliance. And I feel especially lucky to have known the friendship, guidance, and inspiration of fellow Southern food writers Jean Anderson, Sheri Castle, Paula Deen, John Egerton, Martha Foose, Camille Glenn, Vertemae Grosvenor, Rebecca Lang, Edna Lewis, Ronni Lundy, Martha Giddens Nesbit, Louis Osteen, Janis Owens, Scott Peacock, Joe Randall, Julia Reed, Sallie Anne Robinson, Marie Rudisill, Frank Stitt, John Martin Taylor, Elizabeth Terry, Toni Tipton-Martin, Jim Villas and his indomitable mother, Martha Pearl, and Virginia Willis. And if it were not for Boss Sweet Potato Queen Jill Conner Browne and her royal troupe of Queens, I would've given up a long time ago.

Finally, there are four other women whom I've never met, who had in fact been dead for nearly a century before I was born, but who have nonetheless had a great deal to do with the book you hold in your hands. I like to call them the Four Gospel Writers of antebellum Southern food: Mary Randolph, author of *The Virginia House-Wife* (1824); Lettice Bryan, *The Kentucky Housewife* (1839); Sarah Rutledge, *The Carolina Housewife* (1847); and Annabella Hill, *Mrs. Hill's New Cook Book* (1867). Almost from the day that I decided to turn my hand to food writing until now, these four women have, through their books, been a lively presence in my kitchen.

Oh, and one more: Thank you, Amy Lyons, for believing in this work, and for joining a long line of great editors who have kept me focused. More or less.

RESOURCES

One of the lovely things about good Southern cooking is that it doesn't require much in the way of specialty ingredients. Most of the ingredients called for on these pages are available at just about any local market in America. For the few products that tend to be strictly regional, I've suggested substitutes where appropriate, and many of them are readily available by mail order. Here are a few key sources.

Southern Soft Wheat Flour

Daisy Organic Flour
PO Box 299
Lancaster PA 17608
(800) 624-3279
www.daisyflour.com

King Arthur Flour
PO Box 876
Norwich, VT 05055
(800) 827-6836
www.kingarthurflour.com

Martha White Foods
PO Box 751030
Memphis, TN 38175
(800) 663-6317
www.marthawhite.com

White Lily Foods
4740 Burbank Road
Memphis, TN 38118
(800) 595-1380
www.whitelily.com

Grits and Cornmeal

Freeman's Mill
518 Country Club Road
Statesboro, GA 30458
(912) 852-9381
www.freemansmill.com

Hoppin' John's
(Online only)
www.hoppinjohns.com
Logan Turnpike Mill
3485 Gainesville Hwy.
Blairsville, GA 30512

(800) 844-7487
www.loganturnpikemill.com

Old Mill of Guilford
1340 NC Hwy 68 North
Oak Ridge, NC 27310
(336) 643-4783
www.oldmillofguilford.com

Carolina Gold Rice

Anson Mills
1922 C Gervais Street
Columbia, SC 29201
(803) 467-4122
www.ansonmills.com
Anson Mills also offers organic whole corn grits, cornmeal, soft wheat flour, other specialty grain products, and Sea Island red peas, the pea originally used for authentic Hoppin' John.

Southern Dry-Cured (Country) Hams and Other Cured Pork Products

Benton's Country Hams
2603 Hwy. 411
North Madisonville, TN 37354
(423) 442-5003
www.bentonscountryhams2.com

S. Wallace Edwards & Sons, Inc.
PO Box 25
Surrey, VA 23883
(800) 222-4267
www.virginiatraditions.com

W.G. White & Company
2119 Hwy. 601 N.

Mocksville, NC 27028
(866) 600-4267
www.wgwhite.com

Pecans

Ellis Brothers Pecans, Inc.
1315 Tippettville Rd.
Vienna, GA 31092
(800) 635-0616
www.werenuts.com

Pearson Farms
5575 Zenith Mill Rd.
Fort Valley, GA 31030
(888) 423-4374
www.pearsonfarm.com
Pearson Farms also grows and sells quality Georgia peaches in season.

Sunnyland Farms, Inc.
Jane Wilson
PO Box 8200
Albany, GA 31706
www.sunnylandfarms.com

Sourwood Honey

Blue Ridge Honey Company
Bob & Suzette Binnie
PO Box 15
Lakemont, GA 30552
www.blueridgehoneycompany.com

Savannah Bee Company
Ted Dennard, Beekeeper
211 Johnny Mercer Blvd.
Savannah, GA 31410
(800) 955-5080
www.savannahbee.com

INDEX

PREACHING, BUILDING, AND BURYING

CAROLINE BRUZELIUS

Preaching, Building, and Burying

FRIARS AND THE MEDIEVAL CITY

Yale University Press ~ New Haven and London

Designed by Charlotte Grievson
Printed in China

Library of Congress Cataloging-in-Publication Data

Bruzelius, Caroline Astrid.

Preaching, building, and burying : friars in the Medieval city / Caroline Bruzelius.

pages cm

Includes bibliographical references and index.

ISBN 978-0-300-20384-4 (hardback)

1. Architecture and society-Europe-History-To 1500. 2. Architecture, Medieval-Europe. 3. Space (Architecture)-
Europe-History-To 1500. 4. Friars-Europe-History-To 1500. 5. Cities and towns, Medieval. I. Title.

NA2543.S6B755 2014

726'.70940902-dc23

2014008876

A catalogue record for this book is available from The British Library

Frontispiece: Treviso, Santa Caterina, detail of the fresco of Saint Catherine and the unfinished church (detail of fig. 11).
Page vi: Lodi, San Francesco, the tomb of Antonio Fissiraga, upper section (detail of fig. 73).
Page viii: Naples, San Lorenzo, view of the chevet (detail of fig. 10).

For Peter Fergusson

CONTENTS

PREFACE AND ACKNOWLEDGMENTS

This book began as a walk in Pisa, a walk that started with San Francesco, moved to the Dominican church of Santa Caterina, and ended up at the Camposanto. At the Franciscan church, the tombs beneath my feet seemed to resonate with the construction of the walls, and as I moved from the two convents to the cathedral cemetery, I wondered whether in the Middle Ages these three sites might have been connected through the importance of strategic burial and effective intercessory prayer. Could the great cemetery added to the episcopal complex in the late thirteenth century have been a response to the popularity of burial in the friars' churches? Did these buildings – and their tombs – therefore exist in a dynamic relationship with each other, one that may once have been emphasized in the themes of their fresco decoration? Did the type of competition between religious institutions that seemed to exist in Pisa occur in other cities? This set of questions had to do with how medieval cities accommodated new religious orders and the invasion of middle-class burials.

The issue of changing social practices in burial, however, brought up questions about other matters that might also have affected the design and construction of mendicant convents. Rituals of death and burial concern not only spiritual, but also social and economic systems: last rites, funerals, and burials were all important sources of clerical income, and these in turn enhanced the ability of the friars to build. Other mendicant innovations, such as outdoor preaching (often from portable pulpits) and visiting the laity in homes, created a new kind of relationship between clergy and the public, with the result that patrons sometimes took a personal and immediate role in construction, if only out of self-interest (the location of the tomb and intercessory prayer reduced purgatorial suffering). In time I also came to wonder whether, by the late thirteenth century, the role of certain convents as seats of the Inquisition may have helped to pay for construction. Taken together, this line of inquiry began to present another kind of narrative about the architecture of the friars, one that engaged with these remarkable and distinct buildings as a reflection of the friars' unique relationship to the public in urban and private spaces, and the odd mixture of hope (salvation) and tension (disputes over land, money, bodies, and authority) that seemed to hover around their settlements.

So I began to read. Accounts of body snatching, such as the theft in 1288 of a Florentine merchant's corpse and the subsequent sacking of the Franciscan church of Salerno (by the canons of the cathedral, no less), seemed to confirm my ideas. The documents concerning

Pisa provided a range of examples of bitter contestation over burials. Battles over bodies, both legal and physical, that concerned the income derived from funerals and tombs, in addition to clerical disputes over the donations left in wills and legacies, often set the friars in bitter conflict with the parochial and episcopal clergy – not to mention each other! As I worked further on this topic, the intimacy of friars with families in domestic space, sometimes culminating in the formal language of wills, but much more vividly emerging in the stories of Boccaccio and Chaucer, added to my sense that the capillary presence of friars in medieval cities and in the daily lives of their inhabitants was intimately linked to life and space within the friary: the friar in "The Summoner's Tale" not only squeezes the fine bosom of the young wife, orders up a good dinner, and hectors the ailing and cranky husband (Thomas), he also specifically asks for gold with which to complete his cloister. Other poems, especially those emerging from Wycliffites in England, describe the sumptuous and colorful ornaments of the friars' churches, funded by patrons less cynical than Thomas. This evidence from literature is particularly important because most churches were stripped of their decoration in the Reformation, the Enlightenment, the Revolution, or by the zeal of restorers: we now often receive these churches as hulking empty spaces, whereas they were once filled with tombs, altars, paintings, shields, flags, and other paraphernalia.

Conversations with historians such as Ronald Witt, Roberto Rusconi, Randolph Starn, André Vauchez, Michael Robson, Frederick Paxton, Guy Geltner, and Mauro Ronzani have helped shape my thinking, and I am grateful for their patience with what may have seemed a naïve line of questioning. Teaching a course on the mendicant orders in collaboration with Fiona Somerset brought to my attention evocative literary descriptions of mendicant churches in the late Middle Ages. Robert Hunt and my son, Anders Wallace, suggested readings in cultural anthropology that (perhaps!) enhanced the sophistication of my thinking.

I have tried my ideas out on many colleagues in art and architectural history, and have benefited immensely from their thoughts and observations, especially as I began to develop notions about the social topography of church space in relation to burial, commemoration, portable pulpits, and lay access to the choir. Conversations or correspondence with many colleagues including Francesco Aceto, Michele Bacci, Damien Berné, Louise Bourdua, Sarah Brooks, Jean Pierre Caillet, Joanna Cannon, Gemma Teresa Colesanti, Thomas Coomans, Donal Cooper, Glynn Coppack, Paul Crossley, Michael Davis, Peter Fergusson, Sean Field, Julian Gardner, Gianmario Guidarelli, Seth Adam Hindin, Fabienne Joubert, Peter Kurmann, Brigitte Kurmann-Schwartz, Michalis Olympios, Doralynn Pines, Philippe Plagnieux, Serena Romano, Alessandra Rullo, Frithjof Schwartz, Elizabeth Smith, Charlotte Stanford, Kurt Sundstrom, Giovanna Valenzano, Eliane Vergnolle, Irene Winter, and many others helped to refine and improve my thoughts. My Franciscan friend, Fra Agnello Stoia, has always been a source of inspiration. I thank Byron Stuhlman for reading an early version of this manuscript, and Kelley Tatro and Justin Sanduli for helping with the bibliography.

Teaching my advanced students Meagan Green, Rachael Deagman, Matthew Woodworth, Jim Knowles, Erica Sherman, and Alexandra Dodson has brought further depth to my reflections into the history and architecture of certain convents or the dynamics of mendicant construction in specific towns. I owe special thanks to Alexandra Dodson who read through the entire manuscript. With the support of the Radcliffe Institute, Leonard Bliss helped with the bibliography and Julian Rooney with illustrations. Cosimo Monteleone provided a series of schematic reconstructions. I thank Andrea De Marchi, Alick McLean, Thomas Coomans, Alexandra Dodson, Serena Romano, Wolfgang Schenkluhn, Richard Sundt and Stefano Zaggia for several pictures. Bonnie MacLachlan generously gave me days of her time for proofreading.

I have spent a lot of time in the past ten years in libraries. At Duke University I would especially like to thank the interlibrary loan staff. Lee Sorensen, the librarian for Visual Studies, has helped me enormously. I also thank John Taormina, Director of the Visual Media Center and Jack Edinger, Imaging Specialist, for help on many aspects of this book and many of its images. In addition, I am grateful for the use of the Widener and Fine Arts Libraries at Harvard University.

My research has also been supported by the generosity of numerous scholarly institutions and their staffs: the National Humanities Center, the Center for Advanced Studies in the Visual Arts at the National Gallery in Washington, the Radcliffe Institute and the American Philosophical Society for supporting research travel in Poland.

The anonymous reader for Yale University Press was more than kind in the comments provided. Once again it is an immense pleasure to have put this book together with Gillian Malpass, and with the infinite grace and patience of Charlotte Grievson, who shepherded the volume through layout and to completion.

In the ten years or so that I have worked on this book, I have repeatedly thought this line of inquiry might founder. But, for me at least, the topic has seemed more interesting with each twist and turn, so much so that it is hard to declare it finished and consign it to print. It is my hope that the reader will find it so as well.

INTRODUCTION

FRIARS IN THE CITY

Go to almost any Italian city, to Siena, Naples, or Venice. Looming over the urban landscape will be a mendicant church: San Domenico in Siena, Santa Chiara in Naples, or Santi Giovanni e Paolo in Venice (figs. 1, 2 and 3). These massive structures are only the most visible part of large convents and adjacent preaching piazzas that created new axes of power and influence within medieval cities. Mendicant institutions redirected attention and focus toward the urban periphery: at Santa Croce in Florence (see fig. 6) toward a low-lying industrial zone inhabited by a recently arrived immigrant population of the working poor; in Venice to reclaimed land in need of development on the north side of the city; and in Naples toward a new center of royal authority, the Castel Nuovo. Above all, convents became centers of spiritual and intellectual renewal that reached from hovel to palace, the most visible signs of a movement that had profound implications for the character of late medieval spirituality and for art, architecture, urban environments, and literature.

Yet ironically these gigantic buildings and large-scale institutions were inspired by the ideal of the poverty of Christ and the apostles, a model independently interpreted by two pivotal figures of medieval spirituality, Saints Dominic and Francis. The new types of religious communities came to be known as the mendicant, or begging orders because they renounced the usual sources of income that supported the other sectors of the clergy – tithes, rents, income from property, and customary fees offered for the sacraments – in order to live from charity. This was a radical return to the pre-Constantinian origins of the Church, and the notion of poverty inherent in the mendicant movement was to cause conflict not only within the orders themselves but also with the clergy in parishes and the ecclesiastical hierarchy. To distinguish themselves from parish priests and monks, members of the new orders came to be known as *fratres*, or friars, and wore distinctive habits. In addition, friars sought to distinguish their architecture from that of other churches and religious communities.

How was the ideal of poverty as conceived by Saints Francis and Dominic transformed into monumental buildings? How could evangelical poverty be reconciled with these large churches that were once richly decorated with stained glass, altars, and paintings? These questions are the story of this book. It is a narrative about *process* rather than about *project*: it is about how the structures we see and discuss today emerged from decades or centuries

2   Naples, Santa Chiara from above.

of construction and expansion that reflected changes in the spiritual ideals and social norms that shaped urban and sacred spaces. *Process* underlines every aspect of this narrative, which seeks to understand and explain mendicant architecture in relation to the friars' complex roles in the rapidly evolving spiritual, social, and economic structures of their time. The buildings as we experience them now must be imagined as structures that were a singularly organic response to change. Indeed, precisely because the mendicant movement was based on the friars' active engagement with the public, it became uniquely susceptible to the desires and aspirations of the laity; as the thirteenth century progressed, the public had an increasingly strong voice in decisions about these churches and their decoration. The results of this process survive in fragments of tombs and paintings in the churches and convents that we see today, but often what remains of this decoration hangs on the walls of our museums as isolated works of art, deracinated, decontextualized, and desacralized. The contrast between an eighteenth-century and a modern plan of San Francesco in Bologna is highly instructive in this regard (figs. 4 and 5).

3 Venice, Santi Giovanni e Paolo from the south.

The mendicant movement represented a new element in the traditional order of the church, hitherto mostly divided between two categories of clergy: "seculars" in parishes and cathedrals, and "regulars," monks living according to a rule within a monastery. The former were in cities, towns, and villages, while the latter were primarily rural. Monasticism was based on the idea of isolation from communities of the living, an isolation that added value to monastic prayer. This isolation was enhanced by the character of monastic architectural planning, which enclosed buildings in order to create introverted environments centered on lives of study and devotion in church and cloister. Monastic spatial forms articulated, enhanced, and protected strict rhythms of daily life centered on the liturgical hours and regulated patterns of action within the community. The place of the secular clergy, on the other hand, was to engage with lay people in towns and villages. Priests therefore usually lived in houses beside or near the church or chapel in which they officiated; their daily needs were provided for by servants or housekeepers. Bishops lived in palaces that were frequently adjacent to their cathedrals, and their residence formed part

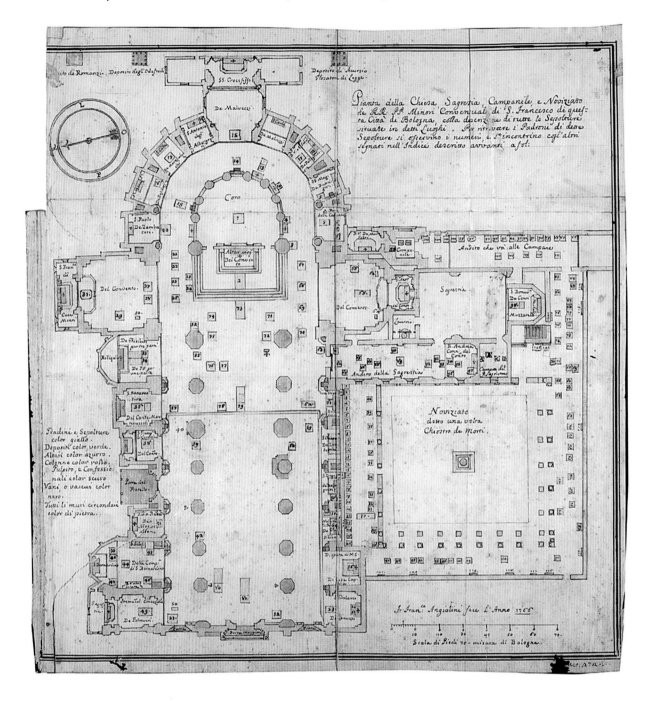

of a much larger complex that at times included a distinct zone for canons, creating a monumental episcopal precinct.

As members of the clergy, friars, however, were *in between* social, religious, and spatial systems. They engaged with the public, but lived in a community according to a rule. They proposed a new role for the clergy and reshaped the concept of the place of religion in the lives of the public and in the city. In the early years, much of their action was in

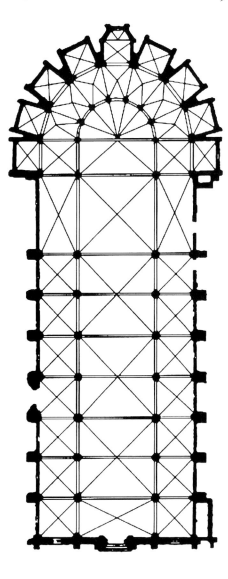

OPPOSITE PAGE 4 Bologna, San Francesco, eighteenth-century plan, with the permission of the Ministero dei beni e delle attività culturali e del turismo, Archivio di Stato di Bologna, Fondo Demaniale, Conventuali di San Francesco, ms. 212–4344, authorization no. 1084.

RIGHT 5 Bologna, San Francesco, after its restoration in the nineteenth century. Wolfgang Schenkluhn, *Architektur der Bettelorden.* Darmstadt: WBG 2001, p. 70.

the open spaces of towns and cities in order to convert heretics. They also visited lay people in their homes, an activity that spurred great hostility on the part of their clerical critics. By engaging with the public in their secular spaces, both public and private, friars offered city people a new and more intimate connection to the sacred and a new form of access to salvation. They not infrequently presented a more educated and thoughtful approach to reconciling the complexities of modern life with spiritual salvation, entering into a different kind of relationship with lay people in homes and with families. The activities of friars were supported by pious confraternities inspired by the mendicant examples of charity and penitence, and these associations often dedicated themselves to promoting the interests of specific convents by attracting new followers, encouraging donations in wills, and raising funds for the convent. By espousing poverty, friars set a model of good works and renunciation that gave them the claim to a closer, purer, relationship to God. Evangelical poverty meant that mendicant prayer was considered a highly effective aid for the soul in purgatory, and in this exchange friars came to supplant a function usually associated with monks. Prayer became an increasingly important medium of exchange in the economy of salvation, and with the coming of the friars early in the thirteenth century prayer seems increasingly to have taken place outside the consecrated spaces of the church: in the *campo*, in the piazza, in the private house. In his sermons on the mendicants, Federico Visconti emphasized the extent to which mendicant prayer represented continuous beneficent action for the residents of Pisa, whether at home or at sea.[1] Mendicant prayer, preached Visconti, could save from illness and death and from barbarians: it presented a constantly engaged action of protection for each moment of a citizen's life.[2]

Decades earlier, in the 1234 bull of canonization for Saint Dominic, Gregory IX had highlighted the contrast between the mendicants and earlier religious groups, such as the Benedictines and Cistercians, by stating that God had inspired Dominic to take on the role of preaching in order to strike fear into the hearts of heretics and restore the church and its institutions. In promoting the canonizations of Anthony of Padua (1231), Dominic (1234), and Elizabeth of Hungary (1235), the pope promoted mendicant communities as a new public-facing and evangelical model of Christian engagement against the combined evils of heresy and indifference among the laity.[3]

In taking on this externalization of religion and outreach to lay communities, however, friars destabilized the traditional roles of the secular and regular clergy. They encroached on the prerogatives of parishes as they expanded into cities, preaching and converting in open spaces. Their active externalization of religious life meant that religion was no longer confined to the traditional consecrated spaces of church and baptistery, or to hierarchical rituals and processions.[4] Within twenty years of their inception, the orders were able to administer the sacraments and to bury patrons in their churches and cemeteries. Floods of donations and bequests to the new orders from patrons grateful for this additional benefit deflected resources away from parish and cathedral. Thus, ironically, by espousing poverty and reaching out to the public, friars came to be rich. And as men and women flocked either to join the orders or to worship and be buried in their churches, friaries were enlarged to accommodate these growing communities. A movement inspired by the idea of apostolic poverty, and driven by the rejection of property and possessions, came to generate great convents that dominated entire quarters of towns and cities.

As early as the 1220s, mendicant friars (and particularly the Dominicans, or Friars Preachers) began to adopt the forms of monastic architecture: chapter houses, dormitories, refectories, cloisters, and reserved choirs. Most importantly, by c. 1250 both orders brought this architecture – *into* cities, wedging the spatial volumes of conventual architecture into densely populated towns. At the same time, at least in Italy, friars systematically began to add their own dedicated piazzas for preaching to the complex of church and convent, as at Santa Croce in Florence thus coming to occupy enormous terrain in the urban fabric (fig. 6).

Mendicants thereby created new types of urban institutions, ones that sometimes placed considerable stress on the communities that hosted them even as their presence guaranteed redemption and salvation. And there were consequences: friars competed with residents and traditional urban institutions for physical space (lots and houses), they contested with the secular clergy for the devotion of the public and for financial resources, and their

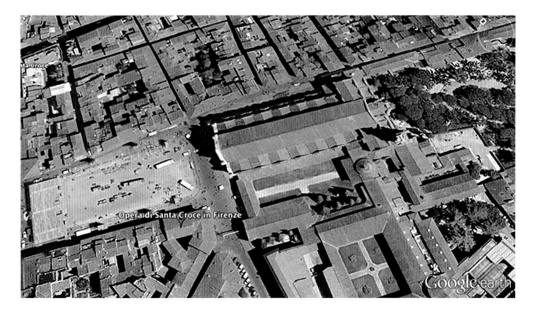

6   Florence, Santa Croce, from Google Earth. Image copyright 2014 DigitalGlobe.

convents challenged the hegemony of bishops as the center of spiritual life in the medieval city. In addition, friars recalibrated the equation between religious institutions and the public within cities: they engaged with lay men and women in public spaces by preaching in piazza, market, and street, and visited parishioners in the private spaces of homes. Because of the perceived power of mendicant prayer as interceding on behalf of the soul in purgatory, friars came to play a vital role in funerals and burials – so much so that in time their churches and cloisters became vast cemeteries within cities already densely packed with the living (fig. 7).

This study will focus on the first two orders of friars that emerged in the early decades of the thirteenth century, the Franciscans and Dominicans.[5] These orders are called for their founders, Francis and Dominic, but these denominations are not entirely correct: Francis insisted that his followers be called Friars Minor, and Dominicans are technically known as the Order of Preachers, a name that reflects their original purpose as a clerical order founded to deflect lay people from heresy. In his biography of Dominic, Jordan of Saxony suggested that Bishop Diego of Osma was as much the inspiration for the Order of Preachers as Dominic and emphasized the corporate origins of the order, a feature brilliantly reflected in its earliest constitutions.[6] As early as 1222 Jacques de Vitry described Dominican preachers as "the new canons of Bologna."[7]

Francis's earliest followers, on the other hand, were laymen who took the Gospel as their guide, with little or no initial idea of formal structure or association. This was a movement, not an order. In the 1220s and 1230s, however, the Friars Minor became primarily clerical as the order developed an institutional structure, adopting some of the models of the Preachers in matters of internal organization and architectural planning.

New social institutions generate new types of social space. Friars entered into a late medieval world undergoing a constellation of changes, especially in cities: population

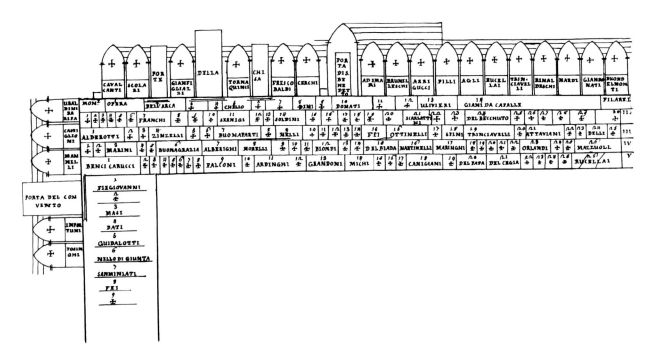

7   Florence, Santa Maria Novella, locations of the tombs outside the west front, from the *Libro delle Cappelle e Sepulture*, Archivio di Santa Maria Novella, with kind permission of Padre Emilio Panella, OP.

growth, the development of manufacturing, a flourishing market economy, new systems for banking and the circulation of wealth, and, above all, the development of communal governments (a phenomenon particularly striking in central and northern Italian cities). At this time of change, and in part because of it, the early thirteenth-century papacy (especially under Innocent III) sought to establish its absolute primacy (*plenitudo potestatis*) in all secular and spiritual matters. In the face of flourishing heresies, the papacy felt the need to impose universal orthodoxy of religious belief. At the same time, an increasing public consciousness of the doctrine of purgatory stimulated a new type of contractual relationship between priests and laity, one in which prayer could be offered in return for contributions, and strategic burial could enhance the possibilities of salvation. These concepts introduced, in effect, ideas from the marketplace (the "debits" of sins versus the "credits" of good works), engaging the public and clergy in a web of actions intended to negotiate the fate of the soul after death. And while marketplace concepts came to inflect religious transactions, the wealth from commerce came to finance friars' convents and the decoration of their churches.

Friars were at the heart of many of the radical changes of the thirteenth century: they capitalized on the reactivation of open space by communes (markets and piazzas) to use them as theaters for preaching. They "penetrated homes" by engaging with parishioners in the private and secluded territory of the house, away from both the sacred territory of the church and the public zone of the piazza. Their critics claimed that this also involved an inappropriate "penetration" of the conscience and "inner thoughts" of parishioners, particularly those of women, perceived to be more susceptible to influence of all kinds (there are many reflections of this in the literary sources). Friars thus represented and spearheaded a new and capillary action of the church in reclaiming a primacy that had been threatened by social change, increasing wealth, various heretical movements, and the growing power and authority of communal governments. In this, the mendicant orders were successful beyond anyone's dreams.

What does all this have to do with cities and buildings? It is tempting to answer "everything," because built space inevitably reflects social practice. The Lateran Council of 1215 had stipulated annual confession and penance, as well as the importance of preaching. The mendicant practice of visiting the homes of parishioners, for example, meant that friars were at the bedsides of the sick and dying, moments when confession and penance were at their most important. Words of comfort and prayers that were intended to help negotiate the passage from life to death, and provide some measure of comfort and assurance about the fate of the soul, could easily slip into transactions that were economic as well as spiritual. For example, additional prayers for the soul by "busy, chaste, and charitable friars"[8] could be stimulated by donations and bequests left in wills, and the prospects for salvation could be enhanced by the strategic location of a tomb. The friars' practice of visiting homes could thus have direct consequences for the construction of churches and convents. At the same time, preaching against heresy in the public areas of cities also meant that, at least in the early years, space designated for laymen within the churches of the friars was not essential, especially as preachers were on occasion assisted by other ordained friars who could receive penitents and offer absolution. Preaching was indeed intended to achieve precisely this: contrition, confession, and redemption, and these would happen outdoors. The externalization of religious practice that brought spiritual issues into public (and private) spaces meant that for friars completion of a church with space for the lay public was not an urgent priority: spiritual life and the word of God could be, and were, literally "in the world," as well as in church and cloister.

Friars thereby reversed a long tradition of the internalization of religious life that had begun in the early Christian period. They moved religion into public spaces (streets, markets, piazzas) and homes, and yet within the public sphere they addressed their message to the private conscience of the individual. They engaged with the city in a way that was new and different from their clerical predecessors in the secular and regular clergy. Therefore, a central argument of this book will be that friars were instrumental in developing a new approach to both internal and exterior space. Their impact was not only in how space was conceived and designed, but also in how it was created – a deliberately episodic and long-term process.

A Rapid Overview of the Literature in the Field

Generations of exceptional scholars have written about the art and buildings of the friars, starting with the groundbreaking work of Henry Thode published in 1885.[9] This was followed by important studies by Kurt Biebrach (1908), Richard Krautheimer (1925), Louis Gillet (1939), Wolfgang Krönig (1938), and Renate Wagner-Rieger (1957–8). More recent publications on architecture by Angiola Maria Romanini, Antonio Cadei, Wolfgang Schenk-kluhn, Achim Todenhöfer, Corrado Bozzoni, Richard Sundt, Panayota Volti, Renato Bonelli, Gabriella Villetti, Giovanna Valenzano, and Thomas Coomans are fundamental.[10] In 2009 Frithjof Schwartz published a study of the architecture and tombs of Santa Maria Novella in Florence, a book that coincided with the writing of this study. The recent publications of Jens Röhrkasten, some of which also overlapped with the completion of this volume, are important for their analysis of the Europe-wide phenomenon of Franciscan urbanization. For the visual arts, Joanna Cannon, Serena Romano, Dieter Blume, Julian Gardner, Andrea De Marchi, Louise Bourdua, Michele Bacci, Chiara Frugoni, Donal Cooper, Janet Robson, Anita Moskowitz, and many others have changed and enriched the ways we can understand the friars' innovative and powerful use of imagery.

Most of the literature specifically on mendicant architecture, however, is taxonomic: it fails to address buildings in context, as *process*, and as a reflection of social and religious practice. Church plans are sometimes separated out from the rest of the convent and treated like botanical specimens on a page (fig. 8). These taxonomies ignore the umbilical relation of the church to the other community buildings, such as the sacristy, chapter house, and cloister. The typological analysis also does not take into consideration the simple fact that the locations, shapes, and scale of mendicant convents and their piazzas were changed and renegotiated over time – and sometimes for as long as two or three centuries. These spaces were conditioned not only by the varying availability of funding and needs of the communities, but also (as noted above) by the social and economic phenomena that tied friars to laymen and to city governments through deep and abiding systems of spiritual and economic exchange.[11]

There are essentially three broad types of study in the field of architectural history. The first focuses on an individual site, either a church alone or a convent as a whole (as can be seen in the recent studies of San Francesco in Pistoia by Lucia Gai (1993), Joan Barclay Lloyd's remarkable work on Santa Sabina in Rome (2004), or the important new volume on Santa Croce in Florence edited by Andrea De Marchi and Giacomo Piraz (2011). On rare occasions these concern the acquisition of property, as in Marie-Humbert Vicaire's study of 1974. A second category is the general survey that covers regions and/or extended chronological periods, such as Herbert Dellwing's volumes on the Veneto, Thomas Coomans's book on the mendicants in the Low Countries of 2001, and Wolfgang Schenk-kluhn's ambitious volume of 2000. Panayota Volti's book on mendicant architecture in northern France and southern Flanders of 2003 and Achim Todenhöfer's 2010 volume on mendicant architecture in Saxony are two recent examples of excellent broad surveys.

A third type of study was introduced in 1946 by Giles Meersseman with a groundbreaking article on the legislation and architectural practice of the Friars Preachers, an approach that since has been applied to specific orders, to particular buildings, and to the entire phenomenon of mendicant building practice. This early work was expanded by his article of 1966 in the *Archivum fratrum praedicatorum*, and further important work on this topic was published by Richard Sundt in 1987 and 1989. An additional and deeply interesting current of research concerns the administration and labor force of mendicant building sites and their decoration, exemplified in the work of Joanna Cannon and Panayota Volti (both 2004).

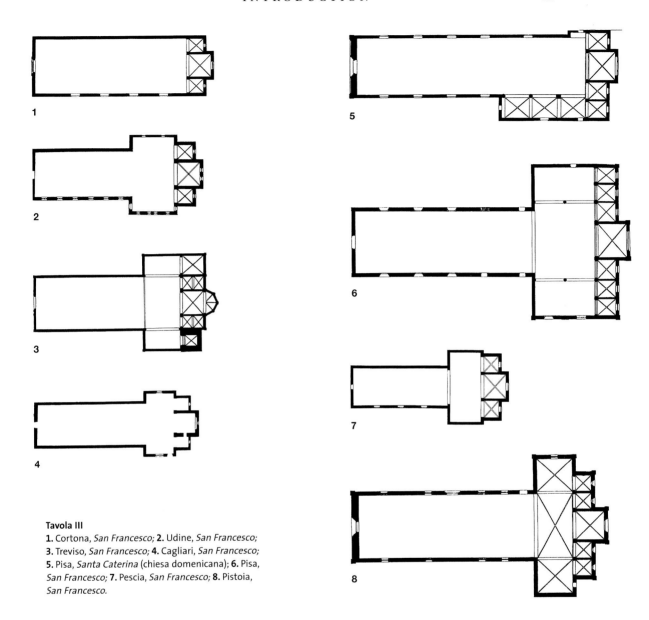

Tavola III
1. Cortona, *San Francesco;* **2.** Udine, *San Francesco;*
3. Treviso, *San Francesco;* **4.** Cagliari, *San Francesco;*
5. Pisa, *Santa Caterina* (chiesa domenicana); **6.** Pisa,
San Francesco; **7.** Pescia, *San Francesco;* **8.** Pistoia,
San Francesco.

8   Mendicant plans. Wolfgang Schenkluhn, *Architektur der Bettelorden.* Darmstadt: WBG. 2000, p. 64.

A recent group of studies has engaged with choir screens, an issue of fundamental importance for our understanding of mendicant space and its decoration. Among these are various articles by Marcia Hall (1974 and 1978), Joan Barclay Lloyd (2004), Monica Merotto Ghedini (2000 and 2002), Giovanna Valenzano (2003), Andrea De Marchi (2003, 2008, and 2011), and Donal Cooper (1999, 2001, and 2009). Although the evidence is often fragmentary (most of the internal divisions were demolished in the sixteenth century), an understanding of their location, structure, and decoration is fundamental to reconstructing not only the character of mendicant church space, but also the sequence of construction.

Legislation on buildings was generated by the need to reflect the notion of visible poverty in the architecture of the new orders. As the mendicant movement expanded with rapidly growing numbers of friars and lay followers, enlarging buildings became an increasingly urgent necessity, and longer churches required some measure of greater height. At the same time, however, creating large enough interior spaces for these communities put the notion of architectural poverty at risk, a process that regulations were only intermittently able to control. There was pressure from local confraternities, guilds, and private patrons for lavish decorations on the interiors; such interventions were sometimes supported or encouraged by members of the religious communities, either to solicit donations from laymen or as a demonstration of the success and prestige of their convent or order.[12] Volti's wide-ranging study of 2003 is a subtle contextualization and expansion of the theme of architectural legislation that brings to bear evidence such as Bernard Gui's *De fundatione et prioribus conventuum provinciarum tolosanae et provinciae ordinis praedicatorum*, Bonaventure's encyclical letters and the *Determinationes quaestionum*, as well as visual imagery (such as the scene of the Apparition at Arles from the Upper Church at Assisi), in order to examine how regulations played out in practice.

The phenomenon of architectural legislation was not new to the friars, and its failure to halt architectural excess in even the most rigorous religious orders (the Cistercians, for example) is striking. For the friars, however, a further complication lay in the fact that their buildings were the result of an ongoing, organic and long-term process: legislation and construction have to be imagined in synchrony, in an ongoing dialectic of architectural gesture and legislative response. As Trachtenberg notes in *Building in Time*, architecture exists in time distinct from "man-made" time of days, weeks, months, and years.[13] In this "other," ongoing flow of building time, we might imagine that architectural legislation was to buildings what traffic rules are today to driving: locally accepted infractions become a behavioral norm, and driving, like making buildings, is form in practice rather than form universally frozen in place by rules.

Whereas the study of an individual site is ideally the result of archaeological excavation or (less frequently) a multidisciplinary analysis of structures and what survives of their furnishings (including tombs and paintings), the broad overview continues the tradition of long-established models for the analysis of monastic architecture (especially that of the Cistercian order). This type of study emerged early in the twentieth century and concentrated on the identification of systematic approaches to architectural planning and design, especially church plans arranged by type (see fig. 8), as noted. This is useful for understanding the diffusion and meaning of certain architectural concepts and their possible symbolic associations, as well as the evolution of distinct local architectural variants. But how frequently and in what way were the concepts embedded in a ground plan comprehensible to the contemporary user of the space in the Middle Ages, or even today? Surely plans were adopted and developed by the clergy more in relation to the effective liturgical requirements of a building than for their symbolic content, especially in a world in which the two-dimensional representation of architectural space (the drawing or plan) was exceedingly rare. The tendency to create taxonomies of types in medieval architecture may distort the central point of architectural space, which is that above all it must be useful in addition to reflecting (if possible) an effective statement of ideals or meaning.

Overviews on occasion depend upon the work of the local scholars and archaeologists (who are sometimes the authors of the surveys themselves) who through deep acquaintance with a region and its history elucidate the histories of individual sites. Coomans (2001) and Schenkluhn (2000) focus on the architecture of extant churches and their chronological and stylistic relationships over a wide chronological span and in relation to regional preferences. This is also true of the recent volume by Achim Todenhöfer (2010), although here the author does much to reconstruct the lost patrimony of destroyed sites, including many damaged or lost in the Second World War. In taking on the synthetic approach these authors can engage with the international character of the mendicant orders while simultaneously identifying strong local characteristics (regional social and economic factors, materials, feudal or communal systems), which they discuss within an international context. One of the disadvantages of the broad survey is that the granularity of the complex process of construction at any one site, often the key to understanding what we now see, tends to be absent.

The studies of Todenhöfer and Volti have the great merit of considering entire convents (not only the churches) within the city. Volti's interest in the social and urban role of the friars and their active reconfiguration of the civic environment in its multiple political, spiritual, economic, and topographical senses (what she calls "macrotopographie") represents an important new approach; her interests range from the liturgical and decorative disposition of the friar's choir to the locations of the laundry and the chicken coops.[14]

The archaeologically oriented, in-depth study that engages with archival sources is essential for understanding mendicant building practice, especially in the decades from c. 1220 to 1270, a period during which the small early buildings were consistently replaced by larger structures. Archaeology is therefore a fundamental tool in this field, especially for the first generation, but it presents difficulties precisely because friars settled in urban areas that are usually still densely inhabited. For example, publication of the post-flood excavations at Santa Croce in Florence revealed the relationship between the small church of the mid-thirteenth century and the vast edifice begun in 1294 that we see today (fig. 9).[15] The protracted construction of the new church has been illuminated by new research on the fragments of the painted cycle, and a reconstruction of the location and decoration of the choir screen.[16] My earlier work on the Franciscan church of San Lorenzo in Naples also demonstrated how, starting probably in the 1250s or 1260s, the Friars Minor renegotiated the spaces of an early Christian basilica in a series of episodic additions that resulted in the architectural volumes visible now (fig. 10); the original sixth-century church underwent multiple expansions and additions over a roughly eighty-year period, and was demolished beginning c. 1324 (see fig. 41).[17]

There are numerous analyses that propose systems of ideal proportion in the setting out of mendicant churches.[18] Although proportional relationships (repeated modular units for the nave, the ratio of width to height, for example) are detectable in buildings as we receive them in the present, that kind of argument was not, I shall argue, a driving force in the shaping of mendicant space, which was instead motivated by institutional and economic forces: expansion took place when sufficient funds became available through loans or the contributions of patrons. In Chapter Three, I show how in some cases the terrain to be

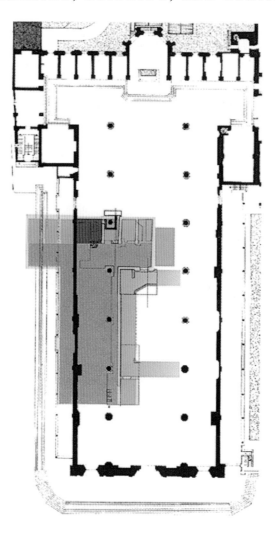

9   Florence, Santa Croce,
archaeological plan, after Rocchi
Coopmans de Yoldi, 2004, p. 254.

eventually occupied by a church may have been set out in advance with low or foundation
walls that were raised to full height at a later date, as at San Francesco in Pisa.

My approach to this topic depends above all on social and economic history. In these
fields the work of Antonio Rigon, Cécile Caby, André Vauchez, Luigi Pellegrini, Mauro
Ronzani, Jacques Chiffoleau, Lorenzo Paolini, Jacques Le Goff, Robert Rusconi, and
Sylvain Piron has exerted a profound influence on my interpretation of how buildings
played a central role in the process of institutionalization, as well as in the creation of a
distinct identity for the mendicant orders (as separate from other religious architecture).
Notarial and communal records from many sites attest to the financial and administrative
ties between friars and local communities, ranging from symbiotic collaborations (friars
advising communes on everything from coinage to hydraulics and diplomacy) to the fundamental role of friars as political operatives.

It is ironic that for religious communities that – at least in principle – renounced wealth
and possessions, much of this book concerns money or property. In spite of the difficulties
of documentation, reflections on this topic have recently become possible through the

10   Naples, San Lorenzo,
view of the chevet.

remarkable publications of economic and social historians in Italy and France.[19] Antonio
Rigon and others have published systematic analyses of local archives and notarial records
and, in particular, editions of the inquiries into the offices of the Inquisition at Sant'Antonio
in Padua and Santa Croce in Florence. These records unveil the turgid financial dealings
of the inquisitors in those two cities, and as a result we can now see at work a modus
operandi that diverged profoundly from the theory of poverty as articulated in mendicant
legislation. After c. 1255 documents attest to extortion, usury, usurpation of inheritances,
and false (or politically or financially motivated) persecutions. Sadly, the voices that have
mostly been lost – if indeed these were ever heard above a whisper – are those of the rigorous friars who were anguished by what was occurring within their own communities. One
of the few surviving testaments to a *cri de coeur* from a harassed opposition is that of Angelo
Clareno (c. 1255–1337), whose reliability as a source, however, has been questioned.[20]

   This book frames mendicant architecture as the product of spiritual, social, and economic negotiations between convents and urban populations, lay and clerical. I set out a
concept of mendicant building as ongoing process – as a negotiation of spatial prac-

tice – rather than as concrete and defined projects. As far as possible, I consider church and cloister as parts of a conceptual whole, a unity of structures intended to support and reflect a way of life, not as a series of disaggregated structural or spatial elements. The missionary activities of friars, their externalized action achieved through preaching out-doors and visiting homes, profoundly inflected the ways in which their communities (churches and convents) were conceived and built: architectural interventions existed at an uneasy and restless intersection of (changing) self-representation, progressive institution-alization, and (the dream of) an historical and ideological commitment to poverty, an ideal always conditioned, however, by the realities of funding and local circumstances. Buildings were an expensive enterprise, and space within cities was hard to find. All these elements in combination shaped the appearance of convents and the process of their construction. Indeed, many projects remained in a state of semi-perpetual incompletion, sometimes for centuries, a situation that reflected not only the vast, unaffordable ambitions of certain factions within the religious communities, but also, perhaps, what we might call a strange "ostentation of poverty" via the medium of incompletion. Santa Croce in Florence, even after its consecration in the mid-fifteenth century, is a case in point. For this reason, I have produced a number of schematic diagrams that show process and change. I ask the reader to "peel back" the finished structures we see today to imagine unfinished walls, ragged joints, and the bricks or planks that would have closed off usable space from the incomplete lower walls (fig. 11). Dante and his contemporaries would have seen the looming hulk of the new Santa Croce closed off and partially supported by scaffolding while parts of the small older church remained dwarfed below. Indeed, Florence, like many other Italian cities, would have been "tutto un cantiere" in the fourteenth century.

*   *   *

This book focuses primarily on the architecture of the Franciscans and Dominicans in Italy. Because the evidence that a medievalist has at his or her disposal is often so frag-mentary, however, and because the mendicant phenomenon was deeply international, I include materials from other countries, particularly France and England and occasional examples from elsewhere. I use archaeological evidence where it exists, and literature or wills from sources where they can enhance or support this narrative. The reader will, I hope, accept and forgive a certain profligacy in this matter.

The first chapter presents an overview of the evolution in mendicant approaches to architecture and building from c. 1220 up to roughly 1300. The following two chapters consider a series of specific sites, the construction process, and topographical positioning. These chapters will propose alternative views about mendicant buildings, ones that touch on issues of inside/outside and the notion of building campaigns, including some thoughts on the nature and function of sacred space. Chapter Four engages with urban contexts, while Chapter Five considers how the social action of the friars, their relations with the lay public, and their economic resources affected buildings. In this last chapter, I ask how the friars' social action of preaching, burial, and will-making, along with the reciprocal influence exerted by laymen, shaped architectural practice and the appearance of buildings. In this chapter especially, where it can be useful, I use literary texts to enrich or expand our understanding of the role of the friars within homes, cities, and communities. Although

11   Treviso, Santa Caterina, detail of the fresco of Saint Catherine and the unfinished church, with kind permission of Andrea De Marchi.

many of these texts are satirical (Chaucer, Boccaccio, for example), they describe the social practices and impact of friars in homes as they forged the relationships with supporters that became indispensable for their success (and the construction of their buildings). Wills are often the lasting expression of these relationships. Other types of sources, such as images, treatises, and sermons, inform the "apostolic" role of friars in the spaces of cities.

There is no attempt in this book to provide a systematic survey of mendicant architecture. The purpose of each chapter is rather to suggest a series of approaches to understanding the places and the spaces that friars created. The focus is on key sites where enough physical or documentary evidence survives to suggest representative types of buildings and construction strategies.

I

THE INVENTION OF A NEW TYPE OF CLERGY: STRUCTURES, INSTITUTIONS, IDEOLOGIES, AND SPACE

In the *De conformitate vitae B. Francisci ad vitam Domini Iesu*, Fra Bartolomeo of Pisa described Fra Giovenale degli Agli, one of the principal friars to whom the reconstruction of Santa Croce in Florence is attributed, as punished for eternity by being beaten upon his head with two hammers: "sunt duo mallei, qui eius caput percutiunt."[1] But could this comment on the vast scale of the building, and its distance from the Franciscan ideal of humility and poverty, also reflect the "eternal" enterprise of mendicant construction, as well as the "eternal" quest for funds?[2]

It may be possible to imagine that systematic incompletion could be useful for attracting financial support. An unfinished building was in itself a visible testament to poverty. Although for the medieval viewer incompletion was characteristic of many large-scale structures, this would have been particularly striking in the monumental churches of the friars. Even the most richly endowed "mega-churches," such as Santa Chiara in Naples (see fig. 2), took about forty years to complete, and the nave of Santa Croce was finished about 150 years after the east end was initiated. Other buildings underwent constant modification and enlargement: the two primary mendicant churches of Venice (the Frari and Santi Giovanni e Paolo; see fig. 3) are excellent examples. With the great leap in scale of mendicant architecture in the late thirteenth and fourteenth centuries, unfinished hulks loomed over neighborhoods as a normal fact of life. The 1294 choir at Santa Croce, raised on an elevated foundation, continued to dwarf the small older church of c. 1252 for well over a century; during that time the old nave may have been used by the lay community while the friars worshipped in the new choir and crossing, and their wealthiest patrons and donors decorated and were buried in the transept and eastern chapels (fig. 12). The dramatic juxtaposition of the two churches – the older one increasingly truncated, the newer unfinished – would, of course, have been the medieval experience of the convent.

In this chapter we shall consider how the extended and incremental processes of institutionalization and conventualization, as well as the simple fact of success, inflected the location, construction process, and design of friaries from the origins of the movement early in the thirteenth century to c. 1320. Specific examples and building strategies will be considered in Chapters Two and Three. Although the Franciscan and Dominican orders differed profoundly in many respects, they approached the planning and design of build-

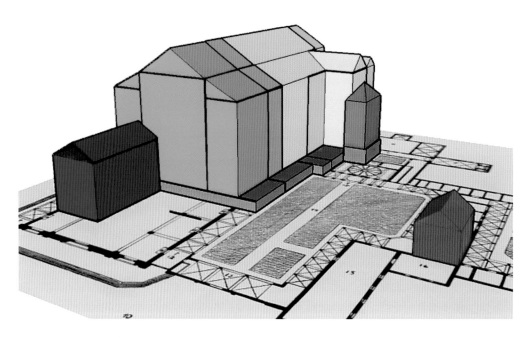

12   Florence, Santa Croce, hypothetical reconstruction of the state of construction c. 1341 by Alexandra Dodson and Laura Fravel. (The church of c. 1252 is in blue; the Cerchi chapel is in red).

ings and convent spaces in similar ways, especially after c. 1240, with the Dominicans usually taking the lead. In addition, although Francis's and Dominic's views on, and experiences with, architecture are a vital point of departure, little remains of the buildings from the first decades, as most sites were subsequently enlarged and reconstructed. My narrative primarily concerns surviving buildings, the earliest of which for the most part date to after c. 1240. Because of the constraints of the evidence, much of what is deduced here is interpretive and conjectural.

The emergent groups that came to be identified as the Franciscan and Dominican orders were in the process of formation until c. 1240.[3] The transformation was most dramatic for the Franciscans, or Friars Minor, who evolved from a small band of itinerant lay preachers begging for food and shelter to an order housed in conventual complexes similar to those of the monastic orders. Their original rule, the *Regula primitiva*, for which Francis and his early associates secured papal approval in 1209–10, was little more than a selection of passages from the Gospels. In the following decade, however, the order grew so rapidly that by 1217 Franciscan communities were organized into provinces, each with its appointed minister. In 1221 leadership passed to Elias of Cortona, who became Minister General of the order. The production of a new rule in 1221 and its revision, the *Regula bullata*, which received papal approval in 1223, marked the transition to a more formally structured order, one that would eventually acquire extensive conventual complexes (held in trust for the friars by third parties in order to maintain the appearance of poverty). The types of spaces offered to the Franciscans as lay preachers in the first years – huts, porches, old or abandoned hospitals or chapels, and other structures – rapidly became inadequate for growing communities: by the 1220s and beyond, Friars Minor required more stable and permanent arrangements in order to carry forward a mission that was ever more ambitious and increasingly clericalized.

The Dominican Order, or Friars Preachers, as a reform movement within the clergy, offers a more conventional and coherent model of creation and development. Unlike Francis, Dominic was a priest who became a canon of the diocese of Osma in Spain in 1199 under a bishop, Martin de Bazan, who established a strict discipline for the canons with the rule of Saint Augustine. Dominic remained in this community, of which he became the head, until 1203, when he joined Diego, the new bishop of Osma, on a preaching mission against the Albigensians in Languedoc. In 1206 Dominic founded a convent for women converted from heresy in Prouille. Count Simon IV of Montfort put the castle of Casseneuil at his disposal in 1214, and here the plans to found an order of priests living in community dedicated to the conversion of the Albigensians began to take more concrete form. A year later Dominic secured recognition for his order from the bishop of Toulouse, and in 1216 he obtained authorization from the papacy, in time adopting a version of the rule of Augustine supplemented by a set of customs for canons regular. Two general chapters in 1220 and 1221 at Bologna further determined the new order's institutional structure. Unlike the Friars Minor, Dominicans were clerical from the start, and devoted to study and preaching. Like their mendicant counterparts, however, they were committed to corporate poverty and had no possessions other than the convents and churches, which they held communally. Dominic's activities as a founder of convents attests to his recognition that buildings and property were essential.

By the 1230s both orders had evolved, with the Friars Minor becoming more clerical and committed to life in community in fixed residences. Over time, vertiginous growth, lavish patronage, and the need for ever larger conventual buildings came to undercut the commitment to poverty, and in particular radically transformed the Franciscan movement. Nevertheless, in both orders the broad concept of apostolic poverty and the public mission in the cities, as well as the need to establish a distinct mendicant identity in architecture, prompted similar approaches to the design and construction of buildings, especially as the Friars Minor became increasingly institutionalized. Pressures to develop a more conscious articulation of corporate identity and institutional presence became particularly strong toward the middle of the thirteenth century, a phenomenon that ironically expressed itself in the adoption of the architecture of monasticism – cloisters, refectories, and dormitories. Yet even as friars adopted these architectural norms – and it is especially important to note that they usually did so within urban environments – they nonetheless needed to express a clearly defined difference from other types of religious institutions such as parishes, cathedrals, and urban monasteries. Institutional identity required the visible declaration of spiritual values through clothing and architecture. Ideally, these visible signs would also entail the notion of poverty, particularly visible in the cord and undyed wool habits of the Friars Minor.

Thus starting in the 1230s or even before, both orders sought to develop an architectural language that inserted them into legitimizing genealogies of architectural form for religious institutions, ones adapted to reflect the friars' unique institutional dedication to poverty. As the more organized and structured order, the Preachers took the lead in refining and

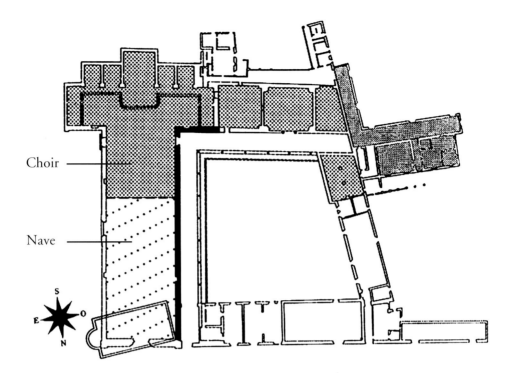

Choir

Nave

13   Pistoia, San Francesco, with the older church of Santa Maria al Prato indicated in the lower left-hand zone, plan after Gai, 1993, p. 56.

defining institutional representation through their buildings; their architectural and spatial concepts were subsequently the inspiration of many Franciscan sites.

It is, of course, an obvious fact that structured religious communities require shelter for themselves and their liturgy, but in the early years the two orders addressed this need in different ways. As ordained members of the clergy (and technically canons), the Preachers required altars (as well as chapels and oratories) from the outset. Until they received the privilege of portable altars in 1220, they sought out consecrated spaces where altars already existed. This authorization was therefore vital for the expansion of the order, which could thus move forward to found new communities.[4] On the other hand Franciscans, as a lay movement, did not require either altars or churches: in the early years their participation in the Mass depended upon the presence of ordained clergy in existing churches or chapels. Nevertheless, in 1222 Honorius III granted them the right of portable altars and oratories; around the same time he also exempted both orders from episcopal control.[5]

Formalization and internal organization were gradual processes among the followers of Francis, however. Whereas early documents that refer to the Preachers describe them as a legally constituted order, these types of sources are far less precise about the Friars Minor,[6] who were difficult to distinguish from other autochthonous groups of pious laity devoted to preaching and caring for the sick and poor. Indeed, many larger towns had numerous groups of men and women who spontaneously affiliated themselves with the Franciscan

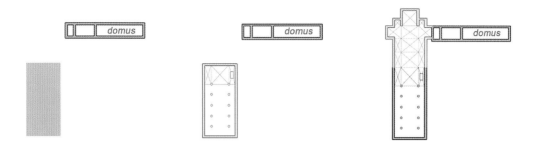

14   Bologna, San Domenico, hypothetical reconstruction of initial construction phases based on Alce, 1972a (Caroline Bruzelius with Julia Rooney and Cosimo Monteleone).

ideal. But through various papal authorizations, and certainly by c. 1230, the Friars Minor had become publicly identifiable as a religious group separate and distinct from other pauperistic movements, as we shall see below. In addition, the wild appeal of the Franciscan movement in the early decades of the thirteenth century meant that it was no longer practical for the many adherents to the movement to beg for shelter. The types of spaces offered to them in the first years had rapidly become inadequate for larger communities: Friars Minor now required more stable and permanent housing in order to carry forward an increasingly clerical mission. As they formalized their organizational structure and crystallized their objectives, they also began to attract a new level of patronage.

The design and construction of mendicant convents, however, needs to be understood in relation to the multiple purposes of friaries. Spiritual engagement with the lay public and a commitment to the extirpation of heresy were primary activities, much of which took place outside the convent. On the other hand, the daily life of the community included reserved and regular liturgical offices and patterns of communal life based on that of the traditional religious orders: meetings in chapter, collective meals, and collective prayer. Since the liturgical choir was integral to life within the convent, the setting out and construction of the choir took priority over the spaces designated for lay worship, specifically the nave of the church (fig. 13).

In the quadrilateral plan of a normally arranged convent (insofar as urban topography and available terrain permitted), the wing adjacent to the choir was often the first part of the complex to be erected, often on its south side. This wing contained the core structures (sacristy, chapter house, and dormitory above) for a functioning community. Although evidence is often fragmentary because of destruction, reconstruction, and restoration, this approach has been documented at numerous houses, as at the Franciscan convent of Pistoia (see fig. 13). Alce and others have suggested that this type of sequence took place in the early 1220s at San Domenico in Bologna, possibly the earliest example of such planning and building procedure (fig. 14).[7] Friars engaged in a pragmatic process of expanding buildings as a series of progressive and incremental steps that focused initially on the needs of the conventual community.

The choir and its adjacent residential structures were thus the point of departure for setting out a convent, an integral part of the essential operation for the community. In contrast, and as the example of San Francesco in Pistoia demonstrates, the nave often was one of the last parts of a convent to be completed (though it is true that sometimes the lower walls may have been partially erected to enclose the site: see Chapter Three). The increasing importance after c. 1230 of the separation of mendicant churches into two separate volumes, the choir (or internal church) for the religious community and the nave (or external church) for laity, often articulated this sequence of construction, with the screen serving as a temporary wall between the choir and the area projected for the future nave.[8] Choir screens thus did double service, initially as a provisional closure, and subsequently as the separator between the internal and external churches. In some instances, where an older church survived, it continued to be used for lay services (probably at Santa Croce in Florence [see fig. 12] and the old parish of Santa Maria al Prato in Pistoia [see fig. 13]), with the result that there was considerably less urgency to complete the nave. In other examples, the area of the nave was enclosed with a low wall to create a precinct, perhaps the case at Santa Maria Novella in Florence (discussed in the following chapters). In examples where an enclosed open-air precinct existed, we may be able to imagine that both burials and preaching took place within these spaces: there are possible analogies with the "open-air" churches of Central America.[9]

At the same time that they were concerned with establishing adequate residences and oratories, friars were also conscious of the symbolic importance of architecture, the very existence of which could be (and was) understood as contrary to evangelical poverty. The earliest Dominican architectural legislation (1220) concerned the expense of construction and the worry that sumptuous buildings would scandalize "seculars or religious." Francis in turn repeatedly warned his followers against buildings as a visible contradiction of poverty. The issue was particularly sensitive because both orders had taken on the mission of preaching against heresies characterized by rigorous opposition to clerical wealth and possessions. Many of those considered to be heretics viewed churches as examples of misplaced clerical ostentation;[10] among these groups the Petrobrusians were particularly explicit, stating that prayers were as effective in a stable as in a church, and that a bale of hay could serve as an altar. Others objected to the monetization of the relationship between laity and the church in the form of tithes and customary oblations, both of which began to be more strictly enforced in the thirteenth century.[11] The construction of churches and convents could easily be interpreted as a deflection of precious resources toward clerical display. Although the initial rigorous opposition of the mendicant orders to tithes and clerical fees thus separated them sharply from the other clergy and enhanced their cause in the conversion of heretics, the construction of convents had the potential to undermine one of the chief distinctions of their movement.

Thus, even though their communities naturally needed shelter, property, buildings, and architecture, these were fraught with complexity for friars. The construction of churches and convents presented a delicate dilemma that was exacerbated by the exponential growth of the communities. In Paris, for example, within seven years after their arrival, there were already well over a hundred Preachers at the Dominican community of Saint-Jacques.[12] The establishments of the friars in the university centers of Paris, Bologna, Oxford, and Naples had the particularly steep challenge of obtaining large enough spaces for communities that included teachers, classrooms, books, and students. Although there is some evidence that teaching sometimes occurred outside – see Ambrogio Lorenzetti's fresco of the *Effects of Good Government* in Siena – or in homes (Eloise and Abelard), there is also some evidence that the friars played an important role in creating the institutional spaces of teaching.

An Approximate Chronology of Mendicant Construction[13]

PHASE I: FROM THE FOUNDATION ERA THROUGH THE 1230S

The early years were characterized by outdoor preaching in piazzas and markets, or as guests in parish churches. Friars were frequently welcomed by the secular clergy and offered the use of local churches by bishops, local patrons, and communal governments.[14] Often they occupied chapels and hospitals that had been abandoned. The Preachers required consecrated altars in oratories for their daily liturgy, and their communities were primarily centers for training and preparing novices to preach. As the residence of the community was a point of departure for external action, they did not initially require churches to accommodate laity.[15] Indeed, in sites such as Santa Sabina where they were provided with a church already equipped with parish clergy, it can be assumed that the parish continued parallel to the presence of the Preachers.[16]

As we have seen, in the early phase the differences between the two orders were profound: the clerical character of the Preachers stood in sharp contrast to the informal association of the followers of Francis, who by contrast were a mixed collection of devotees inspired by a common ideal but with no coherent institutional structure. Friars Minor were itinerant, a movement that Rigon has described as "wandering and adventurous."[17] They usually inhabited humble structures outside the margins of towns, often without a recognizable altar or chapel: the case of Naples is exemplary, for here the Friars Minor first settled in the remains of a Roman villa well outside the walls of the city at Santa Maria ad Palatium, where the Castel Nuovo was later constructed in 1279. Only in 1234 was a new separate and urban community of Franciscans founded within the city at the old basilica of San Lorenzo. Whereas Preachers were recognized as a religious order with an urban preaching mission and the need for institutional architecture from the outset, communal documents refer to Friars Minor, if at all, as generally indistinguishable from the miscellany of other poverty-minded groups who camped in temporary quarters.[18]

Because of their clerical character and their choice of the Augustinian rule, by c. 1220 the Preachers adopted the model of monastic architecture. Even before his arrival in Italy, Dominic had acquired experience in setting up new communities: in the first decade of the thirteenth century he had established residential structures for women converted from heresy (Prouille and Fanjeaux). He subsequently created appropriate spaces for his own order, first in pre-existing buildings as at Saint-Romain in Toulouse in 1216, and at Santa Sabina in Rome in c. 1221. Under Dominic's direction, these complexes were reconfigured with certain elements of monastic planning, and the new buildings were arranged around a cloister. For example, at Santa Sabina, Barclay Lloyd has demonstrated that the initial nucleus of structures added to the complex starting in 1221 was framed around a claustral space.[19] By 1228 a document refers to a church and cloister of San Nicolò in Bologna "ad edificationem fabrice ecclesie et claustri Beati Nicolai."[20] Texts concerning the new settlement at Toulouse in 1229 also refer to a *claustrum*, indicating that a rectilinear cloister with cells, a library, and refectory were important components of the new foundation.[21] Thus, in the early 1220s Dominicans had begun to incorporate the essential elements of monastic planning into their residences, and this process seems to have been systematic even within the early foundations.

At the same time, the Preachers were also developing their first legislation on buildings: "Let our brothers have moderate and humble houses so that they should neither burden themselves with expenses, nor that others – secular or religious – should be scandalized by our sumptuous buildings."[22] Dominic had moved the Toulouse community from their early residence in the palace of Pierre de Sella precisely because he was concerned with the issues of visible ostentation and luxury: aside from the problems of expense and potential debt, life in a palace was not easy to reconcile with the apostolic mission of the order.[23] The synchrony of settlements and legislation indicates that Dominic and his followers engaged in remodeling existing buildings or creating new ones as part of an institutional process controlled by legislation and careful planning.

By the early 1220s the Dominican approach to buildings seems to have been largely defined by the transformation of San Nicolò delle Vigne into the new church that was to become San Domenico. The first general chapter of 1220, held in Bologna, emphasized the uniformity of the order.[24] As members of the clergy with a strong element of clerical reform, Preachers understood the need for institutional architecture from the outset. Their models (architectural as well as administrative) were in part derived from the Cistercian order, an appropriate choice because of a common concern with renewal and reform.

Although the principles of Dominican architectural planning – as well as their institutional structure – subsequently influenced the choices made by Franciscans, theirs was a far more complex evolution, one which from its inception lacked a unanimity of vision. If we are to believe Angelo Clareno, within two decades of its foundation the Franciscan movement was already fraught with conflict over poverty, property, and buildings,[25] and certain episodes from Francis's life suggest this was true. This was, after all, a lay movement at its inception, and both the saint's ideals and his example inhibited a systematic approach to organizational and institutional thinking. For the Friars Minor, it was a struggle to move beyond the conflicted leadership offered by the founder to confront issues of structure and administration, as well as an institutional presence as reflected through buildings.

In 1216 Jacques de Vitry described the early communities of the followers of Saint Francis thus: "during the day they come into the cities and towns, exerting themselves to bring others to the Lord; at night they return to their hermitages or solitary places to devote themselves to contemplation."[26] The early followers of Francis seem not to have been

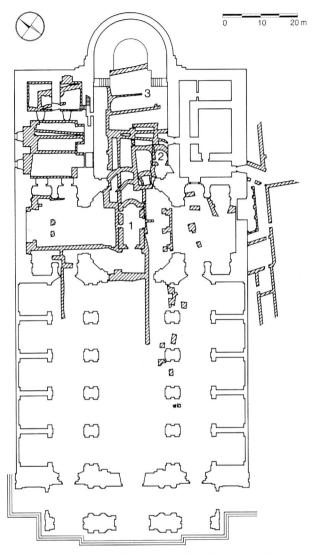

1. Porziuncola. 2. Cappella del Transito. 3. Casa del Comune.

15   Assisi, Santa Maria degli Angeli (Porziuncola), excavation plan after Cadei, 1991, vol. 2, p. 630.

visibly distinct from any number of other pauperistic movements; at Treviso, for example, the commune supported the foundation of a Franciscan community in 1231 as an association of paupers whose presence was an act of charity that would benefit the city, whereas an analogous document in favor of the Preachers in the preceding year referred to their institutional role as defenders of the faith.[27] We can imagine the structures at the Porziuncola, a rustic accumulation of simple buildings, as was typical of the earliest Franciscan settlement, as a sort of camp on the outskirts of a city (fig. 15). Florence is a good example of a city in which the Friars Minor moved from outside the walls (their first known settlement was a hospital at San Gallo, founded in 1218) to the industrial area of dyers that was to become the site of Santa Croce c. 1221.[28]

Whereas initially Friars Minor had been described as the poor among the poor, this situation changed rapidly in the 1220s and 1230s.[29] Between c. 1230 and 1240 they began to be called upon as witnesses, guarantors, and advisors.[30] Written evidence of permanent urban settlements begins to appear after 1230, and by mid-century, Matthew Paris described the Friars Minor as "living in towns and cities" ("habitant in urbibus et civitatibus").[31] Although little evidence of the early settlements remains above ground, the Cerchi chapel at Santa Croce in Florence may represent the type of simple oratory used by Franciscans in the 1220s, even if in this instance there is evidence of substantial patronage that enabled the construction of a permanent stone structure (see fig. 12).[32]

For both orders, but especially for the Franciscans, the election of Gregory IX was of profound importance: this pope's activation of the articles of the Fourth Lateran Council of 1215 involved the new orders in the administration of penance and confession. As members of the clergy, the Preachers were the first to be enlisted, followed c. 1230 by the Friars Minor.[33] Around 1228 Friars Minor were entrusted with antiheretical activities in Bassano and Milan. Under Saint Anthony of Padua's leadership they played an important role in preaching in the Veneto, and became active in the Alleluia movement of 1233.[34] Indeed, 1228 was a year of major developments for the Franciscans, as they founded houses in Prato, Pisa, and Lucca, and work was under way at the complex of Santa Croce in Florence. Most importantly, the first stone was laid for the basilica in honor of Saint Francis at Assisi. Individual patrons also began to play a role in the foundation and construction of new settlements: as early as 1227 a will executed in Trani left funds for the construction of a house for the Friars Minor.[35]

Early mendicant architecture includes the two exceptional monuments in which the founders of the orders were buried, the basilica of San Francesco in Assisi and the reconstruction of San Nicolò delle Vigne (later San Domenico) in Bologna, and these require special comment. The reconstruction and enlargement of the old parish church of San Nicolò was initiated by Dominic before his death to serve the rapidly expanding community of Preachers in Bologna; it was therefore conceived as a convent and a center for training and learning for Preachers. Assisi, on the other hand, was begun in 1228 by the papacy as a shrine for the recently canonized Saint Francis.[36] Although both churches now serve as shrines to their founders, this function was not the original purpose of San Nicolò, and, indeed, the Preachers initially reacted with anxiety and resistance to popular veneration and pilgrimage to the tomb of Dominic. They "did not respond with gratitude" to the flood of votive offerings from the laity cured at his tomb. Jordan of Saxony, writing c. 1232–3, suggests that many of the brethren, "under the guise of poverty," were reluctant to publicize miracles at the tomb for fear that they would be accused of trying to make money from the relics.[37] Tugwell suggests that Jordan and some contemporaries were concerned that the focus on the thaumaturgic presence of Dominic might result in an attribution of sole credit to him as founder of the order, and therefore misrepresent the evolutionary process that involved first and foremost Diego of Osma.[38] In addition to Dominic, there were other early and profoundly charismatic leaders within the order, chief among them Reginald of Orléans, a vitally important figure for the Preachers' presence in Bologna.[39] In spite of these concerns, by 1233 or 1234 Jordan of Saxony seems to have reconciled the community to the idea that miracles at Dominic's tomb and the promotion of his canonization would serve the long-range goals of the order.[40] The translation of Dominic's remains to the new external church at San Nicolò in 1234 may well reflect a reformulation of the foundation narrative of the order to accentuate the primacy of Dominic as founder.[41] If this gesture was partially driven by what we might now call "public relations," it was successful, for six weeks after Dominic's body was moved, Gregory IX initiated canonization proceedings. He was declared a saint on July 3, 1234.

Dominic's somatic and thaumaturgic presence in Bologna became central to the order, to the convent, and to Bologna. Bitter rivalries between the two orders for resources and patrons had already begun to emerge in the late 1220s, and the canonization of a second Franciscan saint, Anthony of Padua, in 1232 probably served as an additional stimulus for the Preachers to identify, exalt, and promote Dominic as their primary founder. Nevertheless, San Nicolò, in addition to its role as a shrine, remained primarily a major center of Dominican identity and teaching. Most importantly for our purposes, its architecture seems to have established the model for many other convents of the order.

The push to develop a founder's cult in Bologna may have reflected events in Assisi. The foundation of the basilica and convent of San Francesco after the death of Francis in 1226 represented a dramatic alternative to the normal pattern of a Franciscan settlement. While he was alive, Francis had been the object of intense and urgent devotion; his followers, the papacy, and the city of Assisi were poised to promote his canonization even before his death. Under direct papal patronage, the convent at Assisi became a papal chapel and pilgrimage site with the promotion of the cult as a primary function. In the century after its inception in 1228, the basilica was transformed into a magnificent church filled with lavish decoration that conditioned and prepared the pilgrim for the particular messages of Franciscan spirituality.[42] Although the fresco cycles at Assisi were crucial for the development of Franciscan painting, precisely because the role of the church as a unique and special shrine its architectural influence was limited: Santa Chiara in Assisi, San Francesco in Perugia, and a few other examples.[43] San Francesco in Assisi was indeed an *ecclesia specialis*, not a generalized model for the rest of the order, although there were a few imitations in plan and vaulting, as for example in Perugia.[44]

The mendicant establishments of Bologna and Assisi therefore played very different roles. San Francesco in Assisi was a "one off" monument with a relatively small architectural impact. San Domenico in Bologna (known as San Nicolò until the 1240s), on the other hand, was founded by Dominic himself and seems to have become an architectural prototype for the order: its flat-ended chevet and rectangular transept chapels, modeled on the plans of Cistercian churches, were repeated in numerous new foundations, such as Santa Maria Novella in Florence, and came to influence the architecture of the Franciscans as in the c. 1250 church of Santa Croce (see fig. 9). The Preachers' broad fidelity to this model reflects their institutional character, Dominic's personal role in the early stages of its reconstruction, and the rapidly emerging importance of the convent as a pilgrimage place. After his canonization in 1234, the increasingly powerful tradition of Dominic as the founder of the order and the community in Bologna placed him in a position roughly parallel with that of Francis. The monumental tomb for Dominic, the *arca* produced by Nicola Pisano and his workshop in the 1260s, concretized this tradition.

To conclude: in the first decades (with the exception of San Francesco in Assisi) friars settled into pre-existing chapels, churches, or hospitals,[45] which they progressively modified to serve their needs. For the Preachers in particular, these were often existing parish churches, as at Santa Sabina in Rome; here the local clergy continued to officiate in a church separated into two parts.[46] This was also the case in the first years of the Preachers at San Nicolò in Bologna (where the local priest soon joined the order, however). Similar arrangements sometimes also emerged for Franciscan communities, as at San Francesco in Pisa, where a community of friars shared the church with a priest under the jurisdiction of a community of canons regular.[47] Where there was no previous church or chapel Gregory IX, starting in 1228, authorized the founding of provisional oratories adjacent to the residential quarters. At an early date Dominic established convents for his followers on a monastic model, first introduced at Saint-Romain in Toulouse (1216), followed soon thereafter with Santa Sabina in Rome and San Nicolò in Bologna (beginning c. 1221). Later, the second and permanent settlement of Toulouse (the Jacobins, c. 1229) was also conceived with a cloister.[48] Choir screens became an early and important phenomenon, especially in those churches where there was a pre-existing parish.

PHASE 2: CONVENTUALIZATION IN THE LATE 1230S AND 1240S[49]

By the second and third decades of their existence, mendicant friars had settled into stable communities across much of Europe. Their presence in cities was palpable, attracting a devoted following from the public and the brightest students and teachers to their centers of theological study. The ever-growing devotion of middle-class patrons and donors led to the foundation of pious associations and lay confraternities attached to mendicant communities. In the case of Franciscans, lay supporters often took on roles as their financial administrators and legal advisors (procurators). At the same time friars began to have an impact on communal governments,[50] and in some cities they were entrusted with the activities of the Inquisition. In Italy in particular, friars increasingly became implicated in factionalism, such as the Guelph–Ghibelline conflict, which complicated their expansion into southern Italy and inhibited their activities in certain towns in the years prior to 1250.[51]

Within the orders vertiginous growth imposed a growing need for structure and institutionalization: friars now needed spaces that could accommodate and reflect the stable presence of large communities that were now both topographically and socially embedded within the urban fabric. As it signified permanence and authority, architecture was at the crux of this process. Dominicans as clerics were in the forefront of this tendency, for they were more prepared than the early followers of Saint Francis to think institutionally and to accept the necessity of fixed houses in permanent materials. Yet by the early 1230s the Friars Minor also began to adopt the principles of monastic planning in order to authenticate – perhaps even to legitimize or "ennoble" – an enterprise that had started off as a movement of itinerant lay preachers, an initiative that was, as we have noted, sometimes hard to distinguish from autochthonous and poverty-minded groups. Indeed, as will be seen below, part of the challenge for the institution of the Friars Minor was to solve the problem of the multiple autonomous male communities that called themselves Franciscan in cities such as Verona and Rome.

Early Dominican legislation indicates that in addition to the choir, the convent as a whole was considered consecrated ground: "claustrum ipsum divino cultui dedicatum."[52]

THE INVENTION OF A NEW TYPE OF CLERGY

Although both topographical and economic constraints frequently determined the precise configuration of buildings, studies of the architecture of the Preachers in Toulouse and Bologna reveal that in the first years of a foundation these friars systematically engaged in purchasing property with the intention of acquiring enough land for residential complexes based on a monastic model (see the discussion of Toulouse in Chapter Two, as well as fig. 34). In the case of Bologna, this also included space in front and on the north side of the church for preaching and burial, activities that specifically reflected the friars' public mission. As noted above, the oratories and adjacent structures for the community (the *claustri*) were conceived as integral units, often as a transverse wing to the south side of the choir;[53] this was the nucleus and point of departure for what would later be developed into a cloister and other ancillary buildings on the north, west, and south (see figs. 14 and 24).

The growing popularity and increasing stability of the orders in the 1230s and 1240s also imposed the need to build with a view to accommodating the public. Growing numbers of lay followers meant that the friars needed to separate the liturgical space of the religious community from that of laity. This was achieved by the erection of walls (choir screens, or *tramezzi*) across the width of the nave, creating the "internal" church for the religious community to the east of the "external" church for the lay community. The creation of two successive religious spaces separated by a choir screen was an early phenomenon for the Preachers: the screen at Santa Sabina in Rome was in existence by 1238 although perhaps much earlier, and that of Sant'Eustorgio is documented in 1239 by Galvano Fiamma.[54] Dominican statutes of 1243 articulated the need for a "locum . . . ad capiendos homines in praedicationibus."[55]

The creation of two contiguous liturgical spaces for separate communities subsequently influenced the design and conception of churches, with each space distinguished by different types of supports (for example, piers versus columns) and coverings (wooden truss ceilings versus vaults). This arrangement can still be seen at San Giovanni a Canale, Piacenza (fig. 16), probably modeled on the disposition of San Domenico in Bologna (c. 1220–21 to 1251), the first church in which such a typological articulation of space seems to have occurred (see fig. 25). Dominican legislation permitted vaulting in the choir,[56] suggesting that vaults were understood as a marker of the greater sacrality of this space. Their acoustic properties were probably also important.

Conventualization had broad implications. It meant that friars needed to acquire increasingly large tracts of land, an expensive and diplomatically challenging undertaking in crowded cities. This frequently created conflict with neighborhoods and parishes, as property acquired by friars was not taxable and was held in mortmain (could not be sold). In order to have adequate terrain on which to plan and to build large convents, friars sometimes moved to the periphery of a town from a more central location (the Preachers in Toulouse in 1229 and at Oxford in 1236). On other occasions, however, they did the reverse, as with the Franciscans in Piacenza, who moved to the center in 1278. The acquisition of a central location was sometimes the result of a political process that may have involved the expropriation of property by a bishop or commune from political rivals or from those convicted of heresy.

Construction within cities or their immediate surroundings required financial support. Sites that bridged city walls were often chosen because there was the potential for utilizing

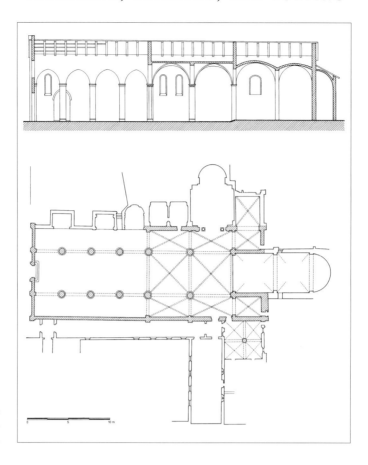

16   Piacenza, San Giovanni a
      Canale, after Segagni
      Malacart, 1984, pp. 566–7.

the "dead" space adjacent to the walls (the Jacobins in Toulouse, the Franciscans in Paris), and this land seems to have been more easily available. Founding a convent in a city generally required the destruction of houses (Bologna, Piacenza) or the reconfiguration of existing buildings (Paris, where the Preachers occupied the site of a hospital and adapted it to their purposes). The constraints of urban or semi-urban sites at times led to eccentric ground plans, as in the parallel naves of the Dominican church (fig. 17) or irregularly shaped cloisters at the Franciscan church (fig. 18) in Paris.

Yet the acquisition of urban properties often entailed conflict with neighbors, parishes, other pre-existing religious orders, or sometimes all three. By the 1230s and 1240s friars were also in stiff competition with each other for space, resources, and patrons. As their convents increased in scale, they began to have problems with debt, an issue anticipated by Dominic in 1220 and later much lamented by Bonaventure and Humbert of Romans. Indebtedness (frequently caused by the building programs) exposed both orders to accusations of hypocrisy on the issue of poverty, and made them more likely to compete for donors and become more responsive to patrons' requests for tombs and chapels in return for donations.

The Friars Minor officially redefined themselves as a clerical order in 1239. This was the result of a long process of transformation, one perhaps best described by Raoul Manselli in 1974. Clericalization enabled these friars to affirm their legitimacy in the face of growing

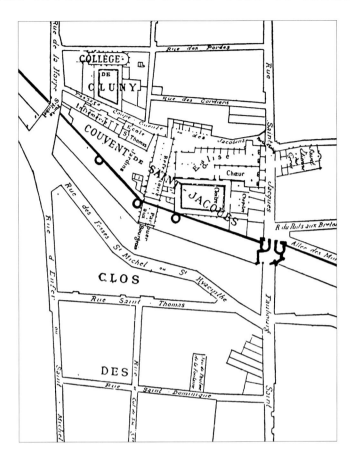

17 Paris, the site of Saint-Jacques (Dominican), after Volti, 2003, plate XXIII.

hostility from the secular clergy and increasing competition for resources from the Preachers.[57] It was a process supported by the papacy, as it authenticated the Franciscan movement and distinguished it from the other poverty-minded religious groups. As a result of this transformation, the Friars Minor became more inclined to adopt monastic plans for their convents, in this imitating the example set by the Dominicans. The mid-thirteenth-century church of Santa Croce in Florence, known from the excavations of the 1960s, is an early example of the use of a cloister by the Franciscans (see fig. 9).[58]

The church of San Francesco in Cortona, usually dated from c. 1245 to 1253, is a surviving example of a Franciscan church from this period: a simple unarticulated rectangular hall 44 by 15 meters in dimension, covered by a wooden truss ceiling, and culminating in three rib-vaulted chapels to the east, the central one of which is larger and projects more deeply. With the exception of the rib vaults of the eastern chapels, the structure is entirely utilitarian (fig. 19; see fig. 8, plan 1). This is similar to the plan of the church of Santa Croce (c. 1252), and was typical, in larger or smaller versions, of much of the architecture of the order.

Clericalization had other broad implications for Franciscan religious space and led to important changes, especially in the major churches of the *studia*. The presence (and dominance) of priests in the order imposed the need for subsidiary altars and secondary chapels for the daily private masses of the clerical members of the community. Other

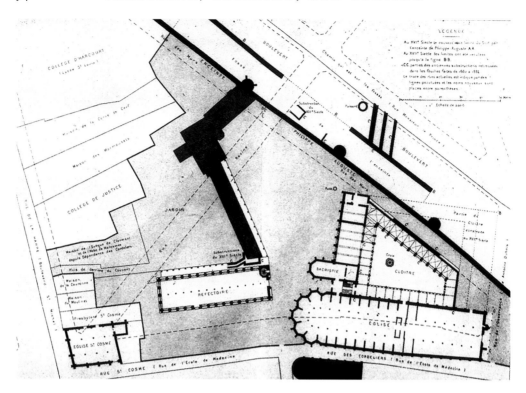

18   Paris, the convent of the Cordeliers (Franciscans), from D.L. Tisserand, *Topographie historique du Vieux Paris*, IV Paris, 1887.

structures, such as chapter houses, became increasingly important elements of Franciscan convents, along with dormitories and refectories.

Haymo of Faversham, elected Minister General in 1240, was a fundamental figure in the process of institutionalization in the Franciscan order. He was behind the creation of a coherent liturgy for the Friars Minor, and insisted upon consistency within the order in the words and the actions of the Mass.[59] His liturgical manual, the first of its kind, subsequently had enormous influence, and was eventually adopted for the church as a whole under the Dominican pope Pius V. According to the Franciscan chronicler Salimbene, Haymo's successor, John of Parma, continued the systematization of the liturgy, requiring all friars to bring their devotional practices into conformity.[60] The Preachers initiated similar but far more protracted liturgical reforms in the mid-1240s, a process completed in 1256 with Humbert of Romans' decree that all Dominican liturgy was to be based on the master text at Saint-Jacques in Paris.

By the 1230s (and even earlier for certain sites, especially those that had previously been active cemeteries) there is considerable evidence that lay patrons were requesting tombs and burials in and around friars' churches and cloisters. Requests for burials and memorials sometimes included altars and commemorative sculpture or paintings. As early as 1240 the Preachers began to legislate against interior decoration and sculpted monuments;[61] we can assume that such legislation existed because of increasing external pressures for tombs in churches and convents. In 1243 the provincial chapter of Narbonne required the removal of crosses, shields, and banners from Dominican churches,[62] and in Paris in 1245 the

19   Cortona, San Francesco, view toward the altar.

Preachers issued a regulation against tombs sculpted with ostentatious decoration.[63] Elsewhere this stricture was repeated with apparently minimal success.

   In this period of institutionalization in the 1230s and 1240s, the Franciscans attempted
to concentrate and exert order over the many independent, spontaneous, and multiple
foundations that claimed affiliation with the order. Because Franciscanism had emerged as
a movement rather than a structured religious institution, organizational mechanisms and
hierarchies needed to be imposed retrospectively. Many cities (for example, Verona, Rome,
and Venice) had multiple Franciscan communities, reflecting the often independent and
unstructured character of the early foundations prior to a centralized process for the authorization or approval for new houses. The situation of multiple competing Franciscan convents
within the same city not only created competition for donors and patrons, but also presented
the question of which community legitimately represented the order. In Rome in 1249 the
Franciscan communities at Santa Maria del Popolo and San Biagio in Trastevere were
consolidated at Santa Maria in Aracoeli on the Capitoline, a prestigious and centralized
position. A decade later, in 1260, the Franciscan communities of Verona, spread between

San Gabriele, Santa Croce, and Santa Maria delle Vergine (where they attended a community of Clarissas), were united at the previously Benedictine convent of San Fermo. The reduction in the number of foundations in large cities coincided with the tendency to acquire more prestigious and visible locations in urban centers if sufficient space was available; for Franciscans, this often meant the acquisition of an older and sparsely populated Benedictine convent. It is not difficult to imagine that this was a contentious and fraught process,[64] but it had the great advantage of providing the Friars Minor with a "ready-made" conventual complex, frequently one already equipped with the requisite structures of church and conventual buildings (San Fermo in Verona, the Aracoeli in Rome).

In spite of the effort to concentrate and centralize Franciscan communities at one site, multiple Franciscan convents nevertheless continued to exist: in Rome, for example, the community at San Francesco a Ripa persisted in Trastevere as a community parallel with the more prestigious foundation of Aracoeli. In Naples, San Lorenzo Maggiore flourished in spite of the continued existence of the older foundation of Santa Maria Nova on the margins of the city (not to mention the later foundation of Santa Chiara). It is tempting to suppose that the different and multiple Franciscan establishments reflected the divergent tendencies within the order for greater or lesser rigor in the interpretation of the Franciscan model, but evidence for this is not clear, and surely the situation must have fluctuated from decade to decade.

PHASE 3: THE CONFLICTS OF THE LATE 1240S AND 1250S

Toward the middle of the thirteenth century the success of the friars presented an increasingly serious threat to the secular and regular clergy, who by the 1240s had become acutely aware of the diminishing allegiance of the laity to their parishes. It was evident to the secular clergy that the arrival of the mendicants had vast implications for parochial structures and the system of financial support that oblations had once guaranteed. There were conflicts over the authority to preach and the right to administer the sacraments (including the funerals and burial of laity): friars' visible, permanent, and conspicuous presence in urban life had become a threat to the hegemony of the secular clergy, above all to their exclusive rights to preaching and the sacraments. The ensuing controversy, spearheaded by William of Saint-Amour and the cathedral school of Paris in the 1250s, threatened the new orders with extinction.[65]

It is perhaps a measure of the seriousness of the threat that Franciscans and Dominicans put aside their differences to craft a common response to the challenge from the secular clergy. In spite of decades of competition for space, patrons, and other resources, the leaders of both orders recognized the need to make common cause against their critics.[66] In a joint letter of 1255, the Ministers General John of Parma and Humbert of Romans agreed to avoid bickering.[67] Many of the issues addressed in their letter – the scramble for urban space in strategic locations, the cultivation of donors, the gratuitous criticism of each other, and the attempts to deflect bequests to the benefit of each order – were important for the financing of churches and convents. Franciscans may also have tempered the increasingly bitter internal debate over issues of property and building.[68]

Hostility from the secular clergy had practical implications: it meant that parishes were no longer lent to friars for preaching, a situation that created additional pressure on the new orders to create their own (indoor and outdoor) spaces for preaching. Urban monasteries were also in conflict with the mendicants, and, as noted above, this was a particularly acute phenomenon among the Benedictines, who had lost numerous houses to Franciscan encroachment (Rome, Verona). The same was true of parishes and churches administered by other types of regular clergy, such as canons.

In Italy there were additional tensions in these decades, driven by the political conflict between the papacy and the empire. Because friars were enlisted by the papacy as anti-imperial agents, Frederick II had expelled them from the Kingdom of Sicily in the 1230s. Until Charles of Anjou's victory over the Ghibellines in 1266, towns that supported the Holy Roman Emperor, such as Ferentino (Lazio), opposed the friars and literally dismantled their buildings. This was also the case in Sicily, where pro-imperial laity and clergy in Catania and Palermo resisted mendicant settlements with violence.[69]

In the hostile climate of the 1250s that challenged the very existence of the mendicant movement, it is easy to imagine some mendicant building projects may have been postponed or suspended. Yet there is evidence that others, such as the 1252 church and convent of Santa Croce in Florence,[70] were completed during this period (see fig. 9).

The challenges of the 1240s and 1250s may have inspired some of the particularly creative approaches to construction that characterize mendicant architecture, and these dates roughly coincide with the first evidence for the addition of lateral chapels to the flanks of naves, as well as other types of extensions and additions to older churches. Chapels provided space for secondary altars (San Lorenzo in Naples, Sant'Eustorgio and San Francesco in Milan), a phenomenon for which the earliest visible remains seem to date to soon after c. 1250. Adding chapels to extant buildings was a way to enlarge without rebuilding, a way to expand a church without the ostentation or expense of an entirely new construction project. In these difficult years, necessity had perhaps become the mother of architectural invention.

In the Franciscan order, however, tension over architectural excess and conflict over the burial of laity remained not far from the surface, and these phenomena were intimately connected to the expansion of churches in whatever form. After his election as Minister General in 1257, Bonaventure was explicit about the dangers that architectural expansion represented for the Friars Minor. His first encyclical letter lamented that "the residences of the brothers are being changed frequently and at great expense, often impetuously and with considerable disturbance to the surrounding territory. This denotes capriciousness and compromises our poverty."[71] He also stated that "the construction of buildings on a lavish and extravagant scale is upsetting to many brothers, becoming a burden to friendly benefactors, and leaving us prey to hostile critics." In this same letter Bonaventure noted violations of the regulations on burials: "See to it . . . that the new constitution on burials is observed more strictly."[72] In a second letter a few years later, the Minister General associated extravagant construction with the decay of morals within the order.[73]

Under Bonaventure's direction the 1260 Constitutions of Narbonne addressed issues of construction and debt: "we firmly prohibit any contract or loan to be entered upon for the purpose of constructing buildings or for relocating or enlarging a friary. . . . However, if there are sufficient funds held or offered by spiritual friends without entering any contract or debt, and where it is necessary, construction may take place with the permission of the provincial minister."[74] There was also a provision about the character of church architecture: "Our churches shall in no way be vaulted, except for the apse; and in the future their belfries may nowhere be constructed in the shape of a tower."[75] This was reinforced by the additional decrees issued by the chapter of Narbonne in the same year: "Henceforth, there is to be no vaulting in our churches, except over the altar, without the permission of the general minister."[76] Other articles of the Constitutions prohibited stained glass windows except for the principal window of the choir.[77]

In addition, article 22 of the Constitutions specifically addressed issues related to burial: "The burial of the brothers is to be strictly reserved, so that no one whom they could refuse without notable scandal is to be admitted there." A previous article (21) stipulated that brothers "may not dwell in any place having a parish cemetery or baptistery attached, if it would thereby fall to them to bury the dead or baptize children."[78] As Monti observed, the obligatory fees for both rituals would have inserted the friars into the system of offerings that characterized parish activity, thus depriving local priests of an important source of income.[79] Bonaventure's second encyclical letter of 1266 expanded on the problem of burials: "A contentious and greedy intrusion into the domain of burials and legacies . . . has made us exceedingly hated by many clergy,"[80] and he repeated his injunctions on this matter in the first encyclical of 1257: "Brothers are all too eagerly invading the area of burials and legacies, causing no small annoyance to the clergy, especially parish priests."[81] It is interesting that the injunctions about burials almost always precede those on architecture.

Thus by the 1250s it was officially recognized that Friars Minor were allowing lay burial and expanding convents and churches. They accepted large donations to do so, yet were nonetheless incurring debts. The construction of "lavish and extravagant" churches was cited by Bonaventure as a cause of envy from other religious orders: construction had become a lightning rod for hostility, a generator of debt, and a convenient symbol of hypocrisy for enemies (as numerous fourteenth-century literary sources, especially from England, attest). Yet aside from San Francesco in Assisi (subsequently significantly modified), few buildings from this important and transitional early period survive intact. In spite of this absence, texts and regulations appear to confirm that the late 1250s represented a turning point in mendicant architecture, and indeed the themes enunciated by Bonaventure – as well as the vituperative rhetoric of the archcritic of the new orders, William of Saint-Amour – confirm this impression. The problems articulated by Bonaventure were to resonate for centuries. In later chapters we shall see echoes of this in the comments of fourteenth-century critics of mendicant churches and their decoration.

PHASE 4: AFTER 1256 – MONUMENTALIZATION

Although in October 1256 Alexander IV reaffirmed the friars' right to preach in public and administer the sacraments without episcopal permission,[82] disputes with the secular clergy were to persist as a form of *basso continuo* through the remainder of the thirteenth century. The concerns over burials and relations with the parish clergy expressed by Bonaventure remained central. As a result of the continued challenges and protests from the secular clergy addressed to the papacy, it became clear that friars themselves needed sustained access to the curia and papacy in order to cultivate support. This gave special importance to the convents in Rome, especially the Franciscan house of Santa Maria in Aracoeli and the two Dominican communities, Santa Sabina and (later) Santa Maria sopra Minerva.

An additional factor important for the process of institutional affirmation emerged in the 1250s. At papal request, and as early as the 1220s, mendicants began to be involved in the Inquisition. In 1252 Innocent IV created permanent regional tribunals planted in certain major mendicant convents in Italy. After 1254 Franciscans were entrusted with a majority of these. Responsibility for the tribunals of the Inquisition provided friars with a critically important function within the ecclesiastical structure of the church, so much so that Paolini has proposed that the survival of the new orders at the Council of Lyons in 1274 may in part have been the result on their indispensability to the papacy as the special guardians of orthodoxy.[83] Within convents, the offices of the Inquisition were increasingly independent of the priors and provincial ministers; though physically planted within the religious communities in which they lived, inquisitors were essentially autonomous. For Franciscans, this must have exacerbated the growing tensions between rigorist and conventual factions, and may indeed have become an instrument in suppressing the former in the prisons in which some of the most poverty-minded friars were condemned.

The houses that hosted the Inquisition were obliged to guarantee adequate quarters for the inquisitor and his staff.[84] Specific zones of convents were designated for this purpose (offices, tribunals, locked archives, prisons), and as we shall see in a later chapter, these quarters came to occupy a significant proportion of the convents thus engaged.

On other fronts, the process of institutionalization continued across a wide spectrum of activities, presided over by the Ministers General of the two orders, Bonaventure and Humbert of Romans. They emphasized stability and conformity of practice and identity,[85] including the continued systematization of liturgical practice, for Franciscans confirming and concluding the process begun in c. 1240 by Haymo of Faversham. Humbert of Romans reflected on the need for uniformity: "Established religious orders . . . show uniformity not only in their observances, but also in their habits and in their buildings and such like. It makes me groan to think how far from achieving this we are, for they have churches and conventual buildings of the same shape, organized in the same way, while our churches and buildings are of all types and arrangements."[86]

For the Friars Minor, the election of Bonaventure in 1257 to replace John of Parma signaled the victory of the Franciscan faction committed to intellectual and pastoral activities. The Franciscan legislation on buildings adopted in the Constitutions of Narbonne of 1260 may have been driven in part by the need to reaffirm the legitimacy of the order and to create a clear and visible institutional identity.[87] This Franciscan legislation echoes earlier Dominican documents on building (though it is also possible that it reflected earlier Franciscan ordinances that no longer survive). In addition to regulating the height and complexity of buildings, the regulations of Narbonne prohibited "anything enticing or superfluous" in painting, sculpture, pavements, or in any other medium that might distract from the order's dedication to poverty.[88]

Growing division and factionalism over the issue of poverty among the Friars Minor in the third quarter of the thirteenth century was perhaps a response to this process of institutionalization. It may also have been exacerbated by a new era of confidence after Alexander IV's bull of 1256 in favor of the mendicants. Bonaventure's election to the position of Minister General closely followed a (temporary) triumph over the secular clergy, and his election confirmed important aspects of how the process of institutionalization was reflected in architecture.[89] New instructions by Bonaventure legitimized the use of stone buildings as more permanent and fireproof; this, of course, meant recognition of a permanent institutional presence by Franciscans in cities, a concept in direct conflict with the early notion of itinerancy. Bonaventure's compromises on buildings stimulated a new level of intensity in the debate over the issue of property.[90] Later, at the 1274 Council of Lyons, the rumor that the order would be forced to accept ownership of property stimulated radical opposition from a core group of the rigorists, some of whom were subsequently imprisoned.[91] This episode initiated a cycle of intense repression of dissidence within the order, one in which the prisons provided by the Inquisition may have proved useful for internal reasons. Although it cannot be my purpose here to engage in the tragic story of strife among the Franciscans, the acceleration in the scale of convents became in itself a cause for conflict and dissent: indeed, visibility and increasing ostentation in buildings was perhaps the most tangible sign of the transformation of the order by mid-century.

Concerns similar to those of Bonaventure emerge in Dominican legislation under Humbert of Romans. In 1263 the Minister General addressed issues of conformity and consistency in a new edition of the Constitutions that was explicitly concerned with architecture and its decoration.[92] Sundt has noted that the Constitutions promulgated in 1263 expanded in more detail and with greater rigor the architectural legislation of five years earlier: "mediocres domos et humiles habeant fratres nostri," and he associates these dispositions with Humbert's "passion for order and legal clarity."[93] In 1258 the provisions had required annual visitors to denounce all infractions in the meetings of the general chapter.[94] But the Constitutions of 1263 expanded the regulations further to include decoration: "nothing notably enticing or superfluous in sculpture, paintings, pavements or other such similar things should be made that defile our poverty."[95] Humbert was clearly concerned by the pressures exerted by lay patrons on the integrity, austerity, and simplicity of conventual spaces.[96] It is worth noting in addition that the earlier legislation of 1249 on choir enclosures indicates that naves for the lay public were already broadly in use, and that choir screens served to preserve the sanctity of the choir.[97]

Humbert's attention to the suitability of locations for preaching reflects an emerging awareness of the need for dignified and appropriate spaces for this central activity. Aquinas recognized that not only did architecture require large expenditures, but also that magnificence was connected with holiness and teaching.[98] Images of Dominican preachers from the fifteenth and sixteenth centuries show them in monumental spaces, in the piazzas in front of churches, or in front of the well-ordered arcades of city squares.[99] The preacher usually speaks from a portable wooden pulpit, as is visible in the frontispiece for Girolamo da Padova's *Confessione* (fig. 20; for an extended discussion of pulpits, see Chapter Four). A few (post-medieval) examples of external pulpits in stone survive, often attached to the

20 A Dominican preaching from a wooden pulpit while another friar offers confession, from Girolamo da Padova, *Confessione*, Venice, 1515, frontispiece.

facades of churches or other parts of churches, as at Sant'Eustorgio in Milan (fig. 21) and San Domenico in Naples (see fig. 71).

For both orders, the continued conflict with the seculars after 1256 generated an environment in which friars understood the need to affirm their permanence and institutional

21   Milan, Sant'Eustorgio, the facade and external pulpit.

authority in substantial buildings. There may also have been a concern to emphasize their unique role as international orders with a capillary presence both within the church hierarchy and on the local level: institutional affirmation of the orders needed to face both "up" and "down." In this regard, few gestures would have been more effective than the large churches and adjacent piazzas that confirmed the prestige and permanence of the new orders.[100] Although, as we have seen, Bonaventure complained about large-scale and constantly changing construction projects, evidence from the years of his administration as Minister General after 1256 indicates that these statements coincided with a distinct tendency toward an increased scale, permanence, and complexity in architecture that he himself justified.

Yet if systematic monumentalization affirmed the presence, permanence, and institutional authority of the new orders, it also presented a unique and somewhat contradictory challenge: how to convey authority and permanence and yet maintain a visible evocation of poverty? It is this particular combination of challenges (scale and identity) that generated the characteristics of large-scale mendicant architecture as we perceive it today. Starting in c. 1260 there was a distinct interest in using traditional Gothic elements (pointed windows and arches, for example) in combination with large, open, "barn-like" interiors, as in the Franciscan church of Pisa (see fig. 46). Choirs were almost always rib vaulted, and naves covered with wooden truss ceilings. Where internal supports existed, they tended to be circular or octagonal. Sculptural decoration was restrained or nonexistent, towers largely absent, and facades were plain. In towns of importance, these buildings often dominated the urban landscape: this can be seen in fifteenth-century city views such as that of the Tavola Strozzi at the Capodimonte Museum in Naples, where mendicant churches prominently define the urban horizon.

Mendicant architecture in the second half of the thirteenth century was thus characterized by a wave of new buildings conceived of as "grand monuments," such as Santa Corona and San Lorenzo in Vicenza, San Francesco in Pisa, and San Domenico in Siena (see fig. 1). These can be read as deliberate signifiers of the permanence and authority of the mendicant mission in the cities, the importance of their educational institutions, their central role in tending to the spiritual life of the lay public through preaching and confession and, on occasion, with the inquisition. Antonio Cadei described pivotal monuments such as San Lorenzo in Vicenza as representing the "stabilization" of mendicant architecture in northern Italy,[101] and, indeed, the uniformity of the mendicant churches of the Veneto confirms this suggestion.[102] I suggest in addition that the struggles of the 1250s served as a "refining fire" to generate consciousness within the orders of the need for an authoritative presence in the city. In any event, the conflicts with the seculars seem to have launched a desire to be more, not less, visible in important centers, a process that entailed strategic choices of location as well as in the scale of buildings. And as will be seen in the following chapters, in spite of the wide variety of mendicant building practices and the use of local builders and materials, certain salient characteristics emerged in their architecture in this period.

From roughly 1260 to 1270, therefore, the die was cast for the future of the new orders, one that concretized in architectural form the changes of the previous decades. As will be discussed in Chapter Five, the openness of friars, the Franciscans in particular, to the middle class and the marketplace involved a radical extension of the exchange of prayer for donations. The economic survival of the orders was viscerally linked to the emerging and rapidly changing financial structures of the day.[103] This was especially true of the Franciscans, as attested by wills and testaments.[104] In response to the challenges posed by this period of change and the obvious difficulties that it presented for issues such as poverty, dominion, and property, Bonaventure in 1269 proposed a formal solution in the *Apologia*.[105] For the first time in the debates over apostolic poverty and the sequence of documents on the papal ownership of Franciscan possessions, the Minister General used Roman civil law to support the Franciscan position on physical possessions: he argued that the Friars Minor were in the juridical position of children in relation to their parental home and, as "minors," could have the "use" and "enjoyment" of parental property with no claim to "dominion" or "ownership."[106] The parent/owner was the papal see. With a rationale planted not only in biblical precedent but also in Roman jurisprudence, the administration of the order after 1269 could proceed with impunity in architectural matters, replacing the hodgepodge agglomerations of "add-on, take-off" convent structures with large new buildings. In the process, they also largely erased the first decades of Franciscan architecture.

The last third of the thirteenth century thus presents for both orders a generation of churches designed as monumental from the outset, as, for example, at Santa Maria Novella in Florence, Santa Maria sopra Minerva in Rome, Santa Corona in Vicenza, San Francesco in Piacenza, and the Franciscan and Dominican churches of Siena.[107] The reconstruction of the Dominican church of Rieti beginning in 1263 also belongs to this period. Bernard Gui's chronicle mentions over and over again churches, dormitories, refectories, chapter houses, and sacristies that are "bonum et pulchrum" or "valde pulchrum"; the friars at Brives admired new walls "non mediocriter elevati."[108] Montagnes notes that the prior of Brives, in office 1273–4, was described as "promotor aedificiorum conventus industrius et sollicitus toto tempore quod vixit."

Is it possible to call this new generation of buildings after c. 1260 "triumphalist"? André Vauchez described this phase of mendicant history as afflicted with "une veritable 'maladie' de la pierre,"[109] a malady that was supported by a network of financial arrangements with lay donors and confraternities who largely funded the explosion of mendicant communities and their buildings.

New construction erased the small churches and chapels used by the friars in the early years, the sites of which were absorbed into or replaced by the larger new structures (Santa Maria Novella in Florence, San Francesco in Pistoia, San Lorenzo in Naples, for example). The collective memory of the modest origins of the orders was thus also replaced through a process not unlike the systematic effort to erase the early narrative lives of Saint Francis after the composition of Bonaventure's official version. Yet in many cases the older churches continued to be used while the new structure, usually the friars' choir, was under way. On occasion an original church or chapel remained in use for the lay community as the "external church," sometimes for many decades, while the friars celebrated services in the new "internal church" (the choir to the east). This was the case for the Franciscans in Pisa and Florence (see fig. 12). In other instances, traces of the earlier church survived adjacent to a new choir, as is the case of the chapter house at San Nicolò in Treviso.

As noted earlier, the years after 1260 are striking for the number of Benedictine communities displaced by Franciscans. This occurred in Rome (Santa Maria in Aracoeli), Verona (San Fermo), and Ferentino (the church formerly known as Santi Fabiano and Sebastiano). It was also true of women's communities (San Sebastiano at Alatri, San Pietro in Vineis at Anagni). Scarcely populated Benedictine convents, especially those in or near city centers, seemed particularly suitable as "ready-made" complexes that could be modified as needed for the needs of the friars (or enclosed Clarissas). Thus, the Benedictine church of the Aracoeli was rebuilt by the end of the century and the old nave became the transept of the new building. At San Fermo in Verona the inner supports were eliminated to create a larger unified interior volume (see the next chapter on construction strategies).

Issues of institutional authority and political exigency also stimulated the promotion of the founders in new types of decorative programs produced at San Domenico in Bologna and San Francesco in Assisi. The tomb of Dominic of 1264 (the Arca di San Domenico), and the first cycle of frescoes in the Lower Church of Assisi, dated between the early 1250s and 1260s, are both from the years immediately after the first formal protests from the secular clergy. As part of their new institutional identities, friars exalted their founders in word and picture; by so doing they "crisped up" and codified their public image. Visual arts came to play a fundamental role in conveying the ideology of the orders: Francis and Dominic were presented as modern parallels of traditional "founding" saints. The unique phenomenon of Francis's reception of the stigmata led the Franciscans to promote him as *alter Christus*.[110] In the 1260s both orders thus commemorated the founders in startlingly new forms of monumental art. The frescoes of Assisi, Bonaventure's authoritative biography of Francis, and the powerful suggestion of early Christian "apostolicity" in the tomb of Dominic created by Nicola Pisano in 1264 were powerful and effective gestures in public hagiography.[111] In 1263, the remains of the second Franciscan saint, Anthony (can. 1232), were also translated to a new marble tomb raised on columns.[112] In the rapidly evolving appropriation of the visual arts as ideological instruments, the two orders surely had a sharp eye on each other's activities.

Convents rebuilt after c. 1260 represented and symbolized the institutional authority of the new orders. Local and stylistic variations notwithstanding, friars set out distinct identities through their architecture, and as a result their churches are rarely confused with those of other religious institutions. Certain features such as wooden truss ceilings in naves, flat wall surfaces, the absence of architectural sculpture, and consistently unfinished facades were used as architectural signifiers of poverty and austerity. Although the new large-scale churches came to accommodate multiple communities (friars, lay public, and increasingly the dead), these were also statements of permanence, power, and authority. The legislation of the orders on architecture and its decoration thus had a double purpose: it articulated identity, certainly, but it also can be read as an attempt to control the ostentatious funerary displays of patrons anxious to be associated with the piety and increasing prestige of the new orders.

The world was aware. As Alexander Murray has noted, Archbishop Federico Visconti of Pisa, who knew the friars well, spoke of them often, and not infrequently preached in their churches in the 1260s, made little if any mention of institutional poverty but rather focused on the need of the Franciscans to have an "honorable" church.[113] From the perspective of a Benedictine monk, however, a description of the new orders could be more negative, as in the mid-thirteenth-century observations of Richer of Senones, in reference to the friars:

> For they went around visiting the rich, the robbers, and the public moneylenders, and if they found things that had been acquired by them through some ambition for worldly things or by means of theft or even interest on a loan, they made sure that they gave [these things] to their monasteries, which they had begun to build in very large form. And in this way through middle men they turned those things to the advantage of their own buildings or their sustenance, although they were not ignorant of the fact that the plunder and interest should not have been turned over except to those from whom they had been extorted.[114]

It is true, of course, that Benedictines were often the jealous rivals and the unsuccessful competitors of friars; as noted, Benedictine communities were frequently displaced by new mendicant (especially Franciscan) communities. But the buildings speak also, and in their scale confirm the acerbic comments of Richer of Senones.

PHASE 5: C. 1300 AND BEYOND

The largest churches of the mendicant orders – such as Santa Croce in Florence, Santa Chiara in Naples, San Nicolò in Treviso, Sant'Anastasia in Verona, and the mendicant basilicas of Venice – date largely to the decades after 1290. Wealth, papal patronage, and increasing prestige led to a final phase of gigantism in convent architecture. While the churches of the Veneto form a distinct group with strong common characteristics, others, such as Santa Croce in Florence and Santa Chiara in Naples, are highly original designs. In smaller towns or at more constrained sites, the late thirteenth and the early fourteenth centuries were marked by a more common type of mendicant church, either simple rectangular halls, or more ambitious structures that "grew like Topsy," with a series of consecutive additions to an older core (San Lorenzo in Naples, Sant'Eustorgio in Milan). In some cases, older churches were voided out to make larger interior volumes: at San Fermo in Verona and San Lorenzo in Naples the colonnade between nave and aisles was eliminated, conserving the outer envelope. Many churches were extended to both east and west (San Lorenzo again). Almost universally chapels were added to exterior walls except those flanking cloisters and conventual buildings; this additive and progressive approach to expansion will be discussed in Chapter Three.

What accounted for this change in scale? Clearly there were many more friars, and their increasing parochial activities entailed the need for additional space for altars and tombs. The role of friaries as centers for theological training and teaching brought many young scholars to their communities as novices or students. In certain cities, the role of the mendicant orders as centers for the Inquisition meant that space was needed for offices, archives, and prisons; sometimes the Inquisition could be "helpful" in obtaining the financing or property for architectural expansion, as we shall see in the final chapter. Preaching to the public increasingly occurred in interior, rather than exterior, spaces, so both the "internal" and "external" churches of the friars thus needed to expand in size. And progressive institutionalization and conventualization required new types of architecture.

Yet the quantitative leap in the size of churches starting in the 1290s reflects, I believe, other factors as well. One was the systematic acceptance of *inter vivos* bequests for individual friars as well as the role played by friars as executors in wills and testaments.[115] The 1260 Constitutions of Narbonne had forbidden these activities, but by 1279 the Constitutions of Assisi permitted friars to act as "counselors" for the ill and dying, and the provincial Constitutions of Tuscany in 1292 explicitly permitted both practices; *inter vivos* bequests were allowed if the provincial minister approved the donation.[116] Ubertino de Casale recalled that Bonaventure had strictly forbidden friars to act as executors; he also noted Bonaventure's attempt to stop the practice of burying laity.[117] Yet it is precisely in these years that these practices had become so common that even some of the rigorist Franciscans (often known as Spirituals) also served as executors, as Piron has noted.[118]

This type of legacy meant increasing personal bonds between individual friars and donors. It meant that gifts – even those that were designated for the foundation of an altar or a chapel – had a powerful personal advocate within the mendicant community. Ultimately, the practice of *inter vivos* bequests created a political structure of internal pressures that are, perhaps, not unlike that of lobbyists within the American Congress. In this way, a patron acquired a personal advocate who would "see to" the areas of interest driven by his or her desires for grandiose commemorative structures – which could be the church itself.

Burials risked incurring the charges of cupidity and simony. Peter John Olivi, who resided briefly at Santa Croce (1287–9), wrote in strong terms about the burial of laity in convents as an avenue toward corruption, observing that burying and burial fees were opposed to poverty.[119] Olivi noted that the laity would fail to appreciate the grandeur of evangelical poverty if with their own eyes they could observe that the rich were more willingly buried (and more rapidly saved?) than the poor. Although he did not live to see them, nothing would have been a more flagrant demonstration of his concerns than the Bardi and Peruzzi chapels.

Franciscans legalized procurators in the general chapter of Milan in 1285, confirming the provisions of Martin IV's *Exultantes in domino* of 1283, a bull that permitted houses to appoint "special persons" with full authority to receive money in the name of the church and use it for the needs of the order. These articles allowed procurators to take full legal action against those who obstructed legacies, and to prosecute debtors.[120] At Santa Croce, the role of procurator was institutionalized in the 1290s and included the appointment of a full-time notary, Opizo de Pontremoli, whose documents fill three volumes that cover the period 1296–1311.[121] (Opizo and his successor also served as part-time notaries for the office of the Inquisition at the convent.)

It cannot be a coincidence that these permutations of the rule occur at the moment when many new buildings were under way. Plans for the new church at Santa Croce were initiated in 1292, for example. Two of the unique features of this church were a crypt and long external galleries on the flanks of the nave (fig. 22 and see figs. 9 and 80): both seem to have been designed as burial places from the outset. If that is the case, this church, perhaps more than any other before it, was intended to include a vast indoor/outdoor cemetery designed to accommodate a broad range of the public. We might even wonder if on some level this magnificent church might have been intended as a *response*, something of a slap in the face, to the crochety rigorism of Peter John Olivi, Ubertino da Casale, and other poverty-minded friars. Burr and Piron have both remarked on the extent to which Olivi was attacked within his own order specifically on the point of burials, and this function, I suggest, was very much at the core of the concept of Santa Croce.[122] The 1283 censure against Olivi indicates that burial within and around church and convent was by this time not only common practice, but indeed also an indispensable element in the economy of mendicant communities.

Within the Order of Preachers, Ministers General after Humbert of Romans (John of Vercelli [1264–83], Munio of Zamora [1285–91], and Stephen of Besançon [1292–4]) turned a blind eye to infractions of the legislation on buildings. Finally, Niccolò Boccasini (1296–9) eliminated all architectural legislation from the Constitutions in 1300,[123] and it

22   Florence, Santa Croce, the exterior gallery on the south side. With kind permission of Alexandra Dodson.

is no surprise that he presided over construction of the great Dominican church of San Nicolò in Treviso (fig. 23). Proscriptions on decoration remained, however, and, as noted above, perhaps continued to serve a useful means of managing requests from lay patrons for intrusive memorials.

It is interesting that at least among the Friars Minor, the late thirteenth and the four-teenth century began to be characterized by increasing withdrawal into a type of monastic isolation: did the conventualization of communities have a predictive component that led to a tendency to restrict contact with the external world? The Constitutions of 1331 forbade friars from going into town more than once a week, and young brothers could go only once a month. Friars were prohibited from keeping secular clothes in their cells.[124] Travel from one house to another required a letter of permission.[125] At the Assisi chapter in 1338 a rule of silence was imposed on cloister and dormitory. Around 1340 Franciscan officials were ordered not to leave the area of their jurisdiction (obviously, the old model of itin-

23   Treviso, San Nicolò, view toward the altar. © DeA Picture Library/Art Resource, NY.

erancy was in direct contradiction with the new restrictions that kept friars within convents). In some places popular agitation against the friars as inquisitors may have made it dangerous for them to go into the city, as in Siena (see Chapter Five). Most crucially, the mission to the poor became severely compromised: Benedict XII (1334–42) needed to enjoin the ministers, custodians, and guardians of the order to hear the confessions of the poor as well as those of the rich.

Scale had immediate consequences for the capacity of convents to complete projects. Many sites existed for decades with scaffolding and lifting devices, with a new church looming over a small, older structure still in place and in use. General chapters attempted to promote completion: in 1290 the Preachers issued a directive urging their communities to finish work on their cemeteries and churches. On the other hand, the inception and construction of large-scale buildings may also be seen as a response to Bonaventure's complaint about impetuous and frequent change that suggested capriciousness and compromised poverty.[126] Rather than proceed as a series of additions and extensions, new "coherent" large-scale building projects such as Santa Chiara in Naples and Santa Croce in Florence might be seen as efforts to achieve organic unity and to obviate the problem of episodic and inconsistent additions.

What now distinguished a mendicant convent from that of the traditional monastic orders, we might ask? The new orders were, of course, urban, and education and training were central to the identity of friaries. Preaching and conversion would always remain a major part of their mission, especially when friars later engaged with Asia and the New World. But the aura of prestige, security, and legitimacy expressed in architectural form became a significant factor in the long and vituperative invective against the friars that emerged over the next few centuries, especially north of the Alps. Within the Franciscan movement this period of architecture (what in French we might describe as *envergure*) led to heightened intensity in the controversy over *usus pauper* (the restricted use of goods) and culminated in the burning of four friars on the stake in Marseilles in 1318.[127] For decades, "poverty-minded" friars had been pitted against those who accepted property and buildings.

The construction of mendicant buildings was contingent upon the episodic accumulation of donations, bequests from donors or in the codicils of wills, yet we need to be skeptical of the use of documents for dating mendicant buildings: if a will existed, was it successfully executed against the contrary claims of heirs, and when might the funds have become available?[128] Francis's emphasis on itinerancy and his fierce resistance to the idea of fixed residences meant that Friars Minor, if anything, underplayed the "establishment" or "foundation" of a convent; in the early years it is often not certain when a community may have been established. In addition, for an architectural practice that was inherently incremental and additive, to which phase of construction should a "known" date, such as a donation in a will or a foundation document, apply? If work was funded, projected, and planned, can we be confident that it was actually executed?[129] It will be the argument of this book that mendicant churches and convents were *always* under construction, always in a *process of becoming*. Friaries should thus perhaps be understood as "continuously negotiable" spaces that could change and grow in relation to emerging circumstances that could include growth of the community, the acquisition of new property or new donors, the changing complexion of the urban fabric, and shifting papal or internal institutional leg-islation. Yet beyond financial and practical concerns, in organizations that emphasized corporate poverty, it may be that we can identify what might best be called an "institutional culture of incompletion": the unfinished building in itself as an ideological strategy and demonstration of community values.

2

THE PROCESS OF INSTITUTIONALIZATION:

DOMINIC, FRANCIS, AND THE EARLY BUILDINGS

Over the course of the thirteenth century the new orders evolved from clusters of like-minded itinerant preachers living in provisional quarters and devoted to evangelical poverty into residential communities with large urban convents. They often transformed old neighborhoods or created new ones. The process was driven by many factors, among which was the exponential growth of communities, the friars' shifting roles in their mission to the lay public, and the need for both the representation of institutional identity and space for teaching and administration. Episodic papal interventions alternately expanded or constricted the friars' ministry and juridical status, as did the friars' wide variety of relations with local hierarchies, both religious and secular. This chapter will examine how evolving structures and institutionalization specifically affected approaches to the construction of convents.[1] It will set out how the clearly distinct "architectural cultures" of the Preachers and Friars Minor in the early decades of their existence were gradually subsumed into a common approach to building as the thirteenth century progressed, so much so that their buildings came to look very much the same (as at the Dominican church of Santi Giovanni e Paolo and the Franciscan Santa Maria Gloriosa dei Frari in Venice). By the end of the thirteenth century, and probably well before, a distinctly mendicant architectural identity was largely shared by Dominicans and Franciscans; this aesthetic in turn shaped the character of buildings in the other mendicant orders. How did this process occur?

Buildings and Spaces for the Friars Preachers

As wandering preachers and laymen Francis and his followers initially sought only provisional shelter. But from the outset the Preachers as an order of canons required oratories for liturgical services. As a canon, it was natural for Dominic to formulate his concept for a preaching order in institutional terms, and over the course of his ten years in Languedoc, as he developed the initial organizational structure of the new order, he must also have considered what kinds of buildings would be appropriate for the new community.

Even before the formal constitution of the Preachers, Dominic had been concerned with housing his ministry of conversion from heresy. Some elements of his concept, such as

OPPOSITE PAGE Toulouse, view of the nave from the west (detail of fig. 34).

itinerant preaching, poverty, and the renunciation of wealth, were strongly reminiscent of heretical practice, and it would seem that part of Diego of Osma and Dominic's radical intuition was to embed these similarities within their movement as fundamental principles. Because the Fourth Lateran Council of 1215 prohibited the foundation of new orders, however, Dominic and his followers adopted a modified version of the rule of Saint Augustine, which they adjusted for their use with certain strictures on food and clothing. The Augustinian rule did not require physical permanence at one place (*stabilitas loci*, an essential feature of Benedictine monasticism), and its special emphasis on spiritual perfection suited the new initiative. Dominic received powerful support from Fulk, Bishop of Toulouse, who offered the old church of Saint-Romain for the community. In 1216 Fulk was instrumental in helping Dominic obtain authorization to found his order as the Ordo Fratrum Praedicatorum.

Although their urban and apostolic mission differed radically from the central purposes of traditional monasticism, the Preachers nonetheless adopted many features of monastic planning, in particular from the Cistercian and Premonstratensian orders, in whose convents Diego of Osma and Dominic had stayed on various occasions during their travels.[2] They visited Cîteaux while on a mission to Scandinavia for King Alfonso of Castile, and around 1220 Dominic seems to have modeled certain features of San Nicolò in Bologna on the Cistercian model. There appear to be three ways in which Cistercian design inflected Dominican planning. First and foremost, the architecture of the new convents needed to convey the concept of reform.[3] Cistercians conveyed this idea primarily through flat-ended chevets and austerity in their buildings, both of which were utilized, for example, at Santa Maria Novella in Florence. More broadly, the adoption of the convent plan around a cloister, as well as the division of the church interior into two successive spaces (one for lay members, the other for the ordained clergy), may also have derived from Cistercian models.

Dominic's first experiences in planning religious communities started with the creation of convents for women at Prouille and Fanjeaux, founded around 1206–7, neither of which survives in medieval form. These were establishments for women converted from heresy who had left heretical families or needed to enter a religious community after their homes had been expropriated or destroyed.

There are references to the construction of Dominican houses with cloisters for his male followers already in the 1220s (Bologna starting in 1221, Toulouse in 1229). The early texts that pertain to individual foundations refer to monastic spaces, such as chapter houses, dormitories, and refectories. At Saint-Romain in Toulouse the Preachers built a cloister and cells for studying and sleeping soon after 1216 and by c. 1220 they had adopted a monastic plan for San Nicolò (later San Domenico) in Bologna. At San Nicolò the friars' choir of c. 1228–38 was attached to an earlier wing of conventual structures on the south that included a chapter house and dormitory, referred to as the *domus* (fig. 24 and see fig. 14). As an initial component of a future convent, the "L-shaped" configuration of choir and eastern range was a common feature of early Dominican planning, and indicates that liturgical and living space were conceived at the same time. Dominicans were thus "conventualizing" almost from the start.

This architectural typology was not only functional, however. The plan of San Nicolò in Bologna appears to have established an important model for the order, one often

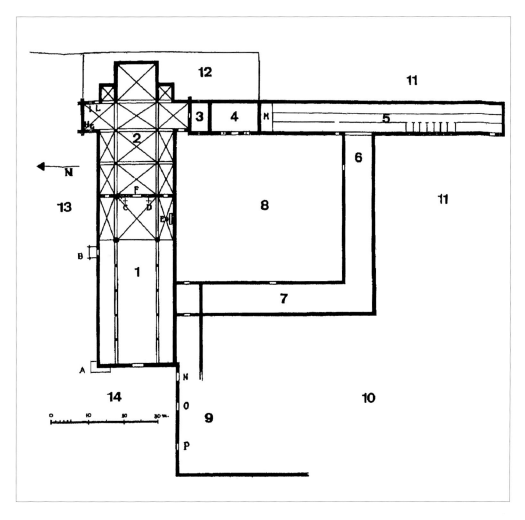

24 Bologna, San Domenico, reconstructed plan after Alce 1972a, fig. 15.

KEY: 1. Lay church; 2. Friar's choir; 3. Sacristy; 4. Chapter House; 5. Dormitory; 6. Area for the novices and students; 7. Refectory; 8. Cloister; 9. Classroom area; 10. Area of the Infirmary; 11. Orchard and garden; 12. The friars' cemetery; 13. The lay cemetery; 14:. The piazza; A. The external pulpit; B. The lateral portal; C. The altar of the Virgin; D. The altar of Saint Peter Martyr; E. The tomb and altar of Saint Dominic; F. The doorway between the lay church and the friars' choir; G. The altar of Saint Catherine; H. The tomb of King Enzo; I. The altar of Saint Lawrence; L. The portal from the friars' choir to their cemetry; M. The *parlatorio;* N. The entrance to the convent; O. The entrance to the friars' school, or *studium*; P. The entrance to the general school.

repeated in major houses such as Santa Maria Novella in Florence. As we shall see in greater detail below, these architectural choices confirm the efforts of the Dominican Ministers General, and especially those of Humbert of Romans, to establish consistency and clear institutional identity through architectural forms. The choices made by the Preachers were thus ideological as well as functional, conveying a distinctive character of reform and institutional poverty through an integrated model that was both practical and austere.

One of the primary purposes of a Dominican house was the preparation of preachers: convents were schools for the theatre of the public square. The development of the Dominican establishments at Toulouse and Bologna suggests a process of planning that was driven by the need to create a spiritual and utilitarian nucleus of action, a place for training and teaching from which the friars would emerge to engage with the world. Although the evidence is fragmentary, it may be useful to think of early Dominican struc- tures as oratories attached to a communal residence and utilitarian spaces for teaching. At both Toulouse and Bologna a chapter house seems to have been an integral part of the first nucleus of structures; could it also initially have served as a teaching space? Such a function might partly inform the painted cycles of famous Dominican preachers, scholars, and teachers in chapter houses, as at San Nicolò in Treviso. On the other hand, in the early communities providing church space for the laity seems initially not to have been an important consideration except in instances of its pre-existence as an earlier parish, as at Santa Sabina in Rome.[4]

Between 1215 and 1220 Dominic and his followers adopted a more explicitly articulated model of austerity, one closer in some respects not only to that of the early Franciscans but also, for that matter, the Cathars, who generally rejected the idea of church property. As early as 1216, when the Preachers were offered the church of Saint-Romain in Toulouse, they expressed the concern that this would bring with it "worldly responsibility and worries."[5] Their concern led to the first regulations of 1220: "let our brothers have moderate and humble houses so that they should neither burden themselves with expenses nor that others – seculars or religious – should be scandalized by our sumptuous buildings."[6] On his return from an absence to see the new dormitory of San Nicolò delle Vigne shortly before his death in 1221, Dominic is reported to have asked his brethren in tears whether they "wished to relinquish poverty to such an extent as to build large palaces?"[7] Within a few years of his death, however, the need to expand the convents in Toulouse, Bologna, and Paris for growing communities meant that the need for buildings was rapidly outpacing the early strictures on architecture, stimulating more specific language in the constitutions composed between 1228 and 1235. Clothing and buildings, were to be "parvas, humiles, viles":[8] "Let our brothers have moderate and humble houses in such manner that the walls of houses without a loft should not exceed 12 *pedes* in height and with a loft, 20; the church [should not exceed] 30. Neither should it be vaulted in stone, except perhaps over the choir and the sacristy. If anyone contravenes [these regulations] in any way, he will be subject to punishment corresponding to the more griev- ous fault."[9]

As noted in the previous chapter, it is clear that mendicant attitudes toward architecture evolved rapidly after c. 1220. The immense popularity of the new orders meant that ad hoc arrangements were no longer satisfactory. Communities were faced with floods of postulants and an ever-growing role within the spiritual life of cities. Lay patrons began to make donations in return for spiritual benefactions, and requested burial in or adjacent to the church and cloister. Donors expressed their support by contributing to the construc- tion of buildings. In addition, the competitive spirit that so vigorously animated medieval economic and urban life came to drive patrons' ambitions for the communities they patronized, which were induced to build larger and more prominent structures. The friars clearly benefited from the pious and well-meaning interventions of donors, but this process also transformed the character of the orders.

Increasing involvement with lay communities created a need for space to serve the growing lay congregations. Beginning in c. 1230 with San Nicolò delle Vigne in Bologna, the Preachers divided church interiors with choir screens that created the two aligned spaces of the choir and nave for laity. San Nicolò was probably the first example of a mendicant church that adopted the Cistercian church plan of two successive liturgical spaces.[10] The nave was finished by c. 1233 when Dominic's remains were translated there from the friars' choir, which in turn was probably in use by c. 1238.[11] In the interval the friars may have created a reserved choir in the nave or north aisle of the new structure, a solution in some respects similar to that of the first church of the Jacobins at Toulouse. Although by around 1220 the Preachers had acquired the historical basilicas of Santa Sabina in Rome and Sant'Eustorgio in Milan, both sites were shared with a pre-existing parish; Bologna was therefore the first church entirely rebuilt by the Preachers,[12] and the separation between the two parts of the community was an essential characteristic of the structure. The conjunction of a nave for laity with an extended choir resulted in an exceptionally long church (about 81 meters) and, as we shall see below, this length is conceptually extended by the "preaching piazza" created in front of the church.

The screens between the internal and external churches soon became substantial masonry structures: at Santa Sabina it was 12 *palmi* tall (2.68 meters).[13] Other early examples were the dividing wall that separated the two parallel naves of Toulouse (after 1229) and the screen added in 1239 to Sant'Eustorgio in Milan.

Preachers took the concept of separate liturgical spaces to a new level, however, and used structural form to demarcate and create hierarchies of spatial zones. Although the situation at San Nicolò delle Vigne in Bologna is poorly understood because of later reconstruction, the two liturgical spaces seem to have been differentiated by distinct types of covering: reconstructions suggest that the choir was vaulted and the nave wooden-roofed (fig. 25). The shapes of the piers differentiated each part of the church, as can still be seen at the church of San Giovanni a Canale in Piacenza, generally dated to the 1230s (see fig. 16). This was also visible in churches north of the Alps, as in the Dominican church of Louvain (fig. 26). A doorway in the north flank of the church of San Nicolò gave access to the lay nave and was covered by a porch. This arrangement is echoed at San Giovanni a Canale in Piacenza, the best surviving example of the early standardized Dominican type in Italy.

The concept of interior and exterior churches as two aligned liturgical spaces is analogous to a pair of railway freight wagons. But these volumes were not entirely separate, as choir screens did not rise up the full height of the building, and the screens in many ways appear to have served as a hinge between the greater and lesser sacrality of spaces. For the most part, screens were destroyed in the Counter-Reformation, as in San Nicolò in Treviso; much later restoration often "completed" church interiors by creating uniform roofing systems along the length of the nave. This may have been the case at the Dominican church of Santa Corona in Vicenza where rib vaults now cover the entire length of the church but appear not to have been original in the nave (fig. 27).

The systematic destruction of choir screens in the sixteenth century has conditioned our vision and interpretation of Dominican sacred space and obliterated the enclosed and

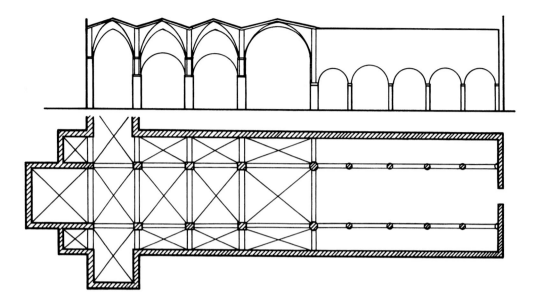

25   Bologna, San Domenico, reconstructed plan and longitudinal section. Wolfgang Schenkluhn, *Architektur der Bettelorden*. Darmstadt: WBG. 2001, p. 34.

semi-reserved quality of choirs.[14] Where they are still visible, however, differentiated supports and nave coverings even today continue to emphasize the two spaces. Over the life of a church, painting and sculpture would also have contributed to this architectural and decorative differentiation: access to the choir became the privilege of wealthy patrons whose presence, in life and in death, imposed upon its private and exclusive character,[15] and whose monuments were more ornate; the choir chapels at Santa Maria Novella in Florence are an excellent example. Choirs became a privileged zone for the tombs and chapels of the wealthiest or noblest donors. The remarkable reconstruction of the tombs in the Franciscan church of London (Greyfriars) illustrates some aspects of this social topography of death that by the late fourteenth and fifteenth centuries came to dominate the interior volumes of many mendicant churches (fig. 28).[16]

   Although monastic architecture may have inspired the prototypes of institutional identity and prestige for Dominican communities, the space required for the differentiated areas of a monastery (cloisters, refectories, dormitories) was difficult to obtain within cities. The adoption of the monastic plan in the 1220s at Bologna and Toulouse therefore greatly complicated the planning, construction, and financing of buildings. Locating a mendicant house on the periphery of a city, even when it meant straddling the fortifications (Toulouse, Paris), perhaps facilitated matters, as land in these zones was cheaper, more available, and presented fewer conflicts with neighbors and the local clergy (see figs. 17 and 18).[17] Nevertheless, by the middle third of the thirteenth century, many friaries were established in city centers, sometimes at an older church (San Domenico in Naples), sometimes in place of houses and shops (San Francesco, Piacenza), and almost always presenting immense challenges for the acquisition of adequate space (and, as we shall see below, also introducing conflicts with neighbors and parishes).

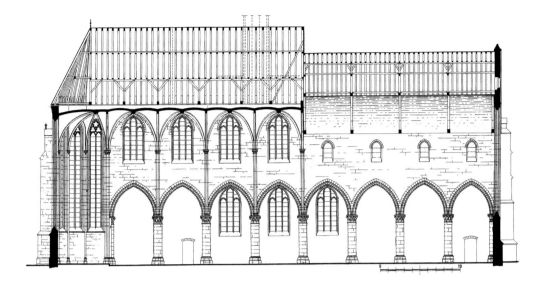

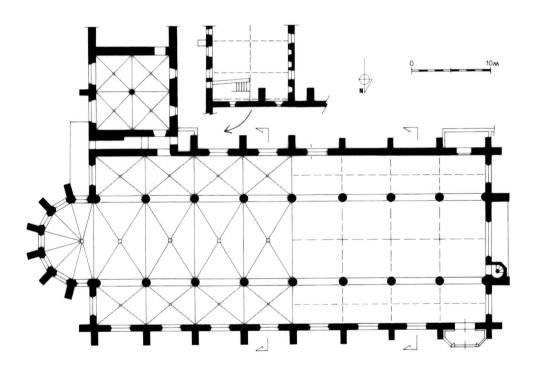

26   Louvain, the Dominican church, after Coomans, 2006b, p. 185.

The externalized mission with its focus on outdoor conversion, and the need to demonstrate poverty in buildings (as well as in clothing and lifestyle), imposed certain strategic
choices on Dominic and his companions. The use of older or abandoned churches had
initially been a good solution. Jordan of Saxony recounts that in 1216 Dominic sought to
create an example of clergy living in poverty and humility within the city by moving the
nascent Dominican community from the noble residence of Pierre de Sella to Saint-

27   Vicenza, Santa Corona, interior view from the west. Scala/Art Resource, NY.

Romain, acquired from the canons of the cathedral of Toulouse. Yet here the Preachers soon added cells and a cloister.[18] In keeping with the mission of scholarship and study, the friars' cells were large enough for a bed and a table, a deviation from rigorous monastic practice where individual cells were either rejected entirely (the early Cistercians) or only large enough for a bed.[19]

The process of conventualization in the Dominican order has been described for Santa Sabina in Rome by Joan Barclay Lloyd. The friars initially used an older nucleus of parochial buildings to the west of the church and later extended them to the south and the east (fig. 29).[20] The structures adopted from the older parochial community can still be

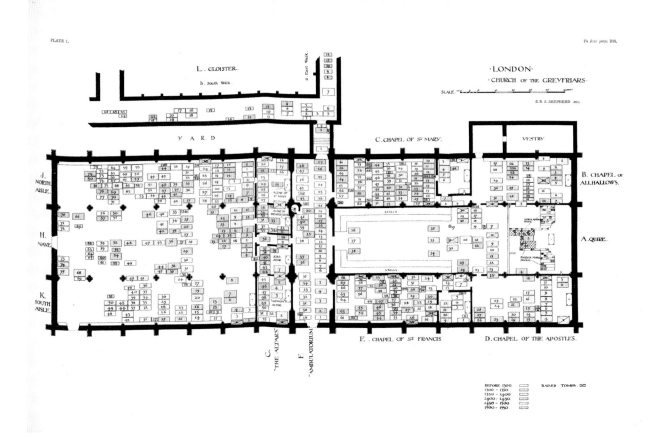

28 London, Greyfriars, reconstructed plan with burial locations after Shepherd, 1902, plate 1.

seen today in an aerial view that shows the early wing extending to the west in front of the (later) tower (fig. 30).

The absence of legislation on architecture in the first years suggests that it was understood that an oratory and living space were essential from the outset. For Preachers, the difficulties lay not with the existence of buildings but rather with their scale when enlarged for growing communities. As the order of Preachers expanded in size and began to acquire new land for settlements rather than remodeling older sites,[21] concerns over scale and austerity became more acute. The issue was aggravated by the desire of lay followers to attend religious services within the Preachers' church, and the increasing numbers of lay people imposed the need for altars as well as for burials. These changing concerns imposed a reconsideration of the function of original convent structures, as can be seen in the successive changes to the Dominican church in Toulouse as reconstructed by Leff and Sundt (fig. 31).

These changing circumstances meant that the ad hoc approach to housing and oratories needed regulation. Under Humbert of Romans (Minister General 1254–63) legislation on architecture formed part of more general dispositions on uniformity of observance in habits and buildings, as we have seen, but the need for uniformity was also reflected in Humbert's

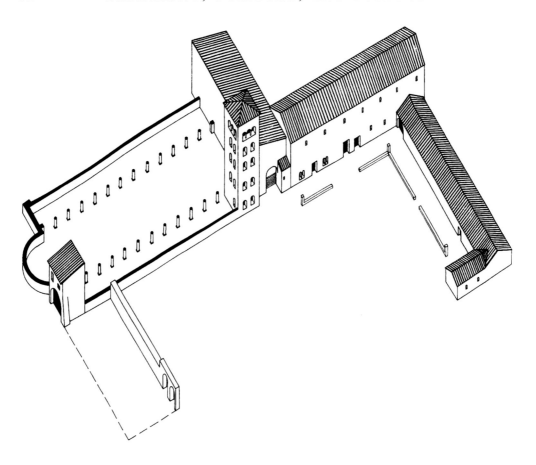

29   Rome, Santa Sabina, after drawing by Jeremy Blake, in Barclay Lloyd, 2004, p. 285.

touching remark that the character of the order's buildings at mid-century differed from that of other approved religious orders, which had churches and monastic buildings all conforming to the same pattern and arranged in the same way. As the Minister General noted, "we have almost as many different patterns and arrangements of our churches and buildings as we have houses."[22] Humbert's lament reflects a concern with institutional identity and the need for standardized and identifiable architectural models, a phenomenon that is broadly typical of his administration. It was also a response to the urgent need to affirm the presence of the order in response to the crisis with the secular clergy that erupted in the mid-1250s.

Humbert's comparison with the monastic orders and his concern for uniformity reflected the challenges presented by the rapid evolution of the order. The monastic model had been developed for rural settings; it was far more complex to insert this spatial concept into tightly packed urban environments and peculiarly shaped sites that were often pressed against city walls (Toulouse, Paris) or were constrainted by pre-existing properties. Yet by 1243, tense relations with parish clergy, who first had welcomed the friars into their churches, increasingly imposed the need for protected preaching spaces and lay churches "ad capiendos homines in praedicationibus."[23]

30   Rome, Santa Sabina, from Google Earth. Image copyright DigitalGlobe.

Humbert's lament about "different patterns and arrangements" reflected the fact that the friars adjusted older structures to their needs, or built on oddly shaped and placed lots (San Domenico in Naples, the Jacobins in Paris). The reuse of old buildings and limited urban space constrained the design and construction of Dominican convents. This impeded the creation of an institutional architecture that was identifiably "Dominican," a problem exacerbated by the fact that many new houses and their piazzas remained as partially constructed or "fragmentary" complexes for many years.[24]

Dominican buildings thus negotiated between the exigencies of urban sites, the need for conformity and identifiability, and rapidly changing social circumstances. The growth of communities had meant larger "internal" churches for the friars as well as the creation of "external" churches for laity, as has been seen. The simple fact of making buildings long enough for these separate groups became in itself a challenge to the strictures on their height: long and low buildings without some proportional elevation would create tunnel-like spaces. Certain elemental rules of proportion as well as aesthetic and acoustic considerations meant that Dominican churches needed to become tall as well as long. Churches built after around 1250 soon surpassed their own restrictions on maximum height (c. 11.40 meters). The great historian of Dominican architecture, Gilles Meersseman, cap-

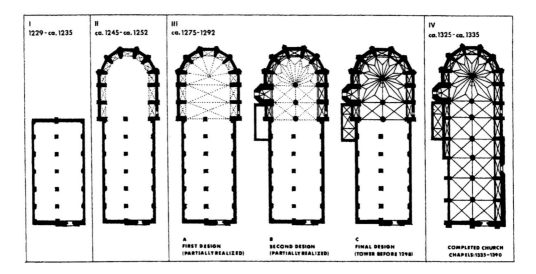

31　Toulouse, construction sequence at the church of the Jacobins, Fred Leff, commissioned by and based on research by Richard Sundt, 1989, p. 188, plate 4.

tured the tensions well by describing the process of evolution in Dominican architecture as a "painful birth followed by a rebellious adolescence." He cited the dream of Gérard de Frachet of around 1260, in which a building-loving friar from Bologna was condemned for eternity to measuring a cloister on all fours while being beaten by demons, and the "edifying" example of the sub-prior of Orthez, whose passion for construction relegated him to eternal purgatory.[25]

The general chapter of 1258 in Toulouse attempted to halt the construction of excessively large or ornate buildings: "Let them not make buildings except lowly ones and in moderate fashion and according to the form of the foundation document [of the order]" ("Non faciant edificia nisi humilia et mediocre et secundum formam constitutionis"). The chapter of 1261 (Barcelona) punished friars who constructed a high dormitory and forced the Preachers of Cologne to lower the vaults of their choir. In this last example, however, the prior who initiated the reconstruction of the choir was none other than Albertus Magnus, recently promoted (1260) as bishop of Ratisbonne, and who therefore could not be reprimanded. Indeed, in 1271 he requested papal dispensation to donate jewels and money to complete the convent. When Albertus Magnus eventually returned to Cologne in 1279, the community had already outgrown the choir of c. 1260, and views of the church made prior to its destruction suggest that the new polygonal choir was taller than the nave (fig. 32).

Dominican legislation on architecture was stimulated in particular by the exceptional expansion of the primary houses of the order: Toulouse, Paris, and Bologna. In Bologna, the rapid growth of the community[26] and the development of a cult at the tomb of Saint Dominic (d. 1221) precipitated the reconstruction of the church and important changes in its function. The tomb of the founder, located between two eastern altars in the choir ("inter due altaria"), had begun to attract throngs of pilgrims, interfering with the liturgy and threatening the privacy and seclusion of the friars in the choir. Indulgences were

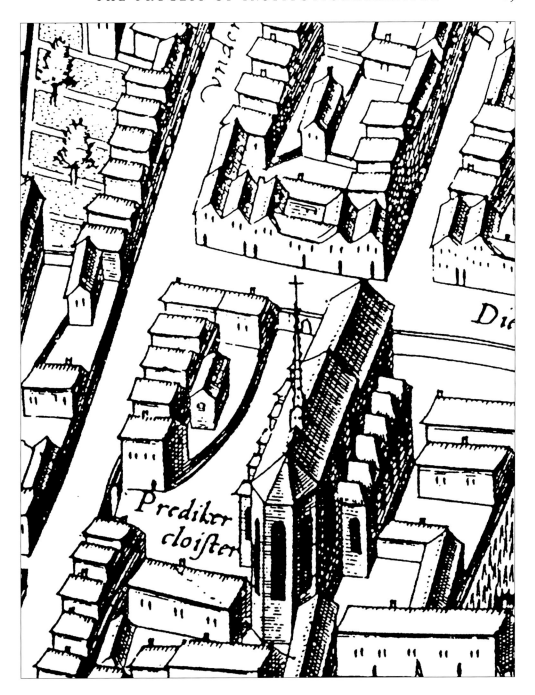

32   Cologne, view of the Dominican church, after Wolfgang Schenkluhn, *Architektur der Bettelorden.* Darmstadt: WBG. 2000, p. 116.

declared in September 1228 for the reconstruction of the old church (where Dominic's tomb remained temporarily) and the completion of the cloister.[27] The first translation of the remains took place during the night of May 23–24, 1233, on the occasion of the general chapter of the order, and numerous miracles took place in the succeeding months.[28] After little more than a year (July 3, 1234) Dominic was canonized. Three decades later, the new tomb carved by Nicola Pisano was commissioned.[29] It is worth considering that Francis's canonization in 1228, and the vast new basilica erected over his tomb in Assisi, may have stimulated the Preachers to create a more adequate setting for Dominic's tomb, and in this matter the role of Gregory IX was of fundamental importance for both projects.[30] A review of significant early Dominican foundations highlights some of these issues and shows the process of institutionalization at these sites.

TOULOUSE: THE FIRST SETTLEMENTS AND THE JACOBIN CHURCH (1229)

The history of the Dominican convent in Toulouse has been exceptionally well studied by M.-H. Vicaire (1974) who focused on the successive acquisitions of property, together with Richard Sundt's analysis of the construction sequence of the building (see fig. 31). The beauty and prominence of the church attest to the historical importance of this foundation for the Preachers. Yet the early years in Toulouse were anything but tranquil: the Preachers were twice forced to abandon the city, first in 1217 as a result of the tumult around the Albigensian Crusade, and again between 1235 and 1236 when they were exiled because of their inquisitorial activities. After acquiring the first house at Saint-Romain, founded by Dominic in 1215, the community moved twice before settling definitively on land purchased for them in 1229 by the usurer Pons de Capdenier as restitution for *male ablata*.[31]

The foundation in 1229, as elucidated by Vicaire and Sundt, exemplifies many characteristics that were to become standard features of Dominican houses:

1   The convent was located on the fringes of the city on land adjacent to the fortifications, and initial support came from middle-class patrons involved in commerce and banking (see fig. 33).

2   It was conceived and built in a series of "phased campaigns" that anticipated expansion into adjacent areas as land and funds became available. Under the direction of its first *operarius* (building manager), the friars built strategically and provisionally, anticipating the eventual need for the expansion and transformation of temporary early structures. From the outset of the 1229 campaign, however, the architectural model was that of monastic space with a cloister, chapter house, refectory, and dormitory.

3   Building campaigns alternated with periods of land acquisition;[32] it is worth noting in this connection that by 1278 the institution was seriously burdened with debt.[33]

In spite of the presence of a cloister, the first design of the complex represented, nevertheless, some modifications to traditional monastic planning. The church consisted of two parallel naves, that of the friars' adjacent to the cloister, and that of the lay community adjacent to the street, in closer proximity to the city (fig. 33 and see fig. 31).[34] The church for the laity was flanked by an external portico on the west and south sides of the church.[35] This complex was in use by 1232.[36] Vicaire suggests that strong community support for the

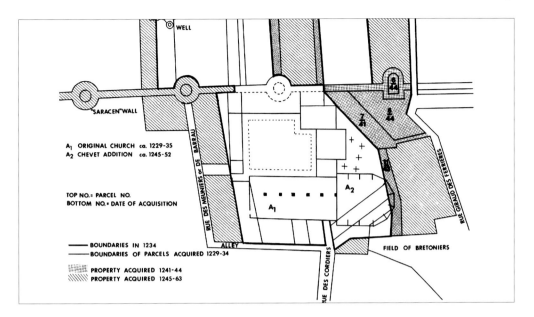

33   Toulouse, land acquisition for the Jacobins, Fred Leff and Richard Sundt, 1989, p. 198, fig. 16. After Vicaire, 1974.

Dominican friars in Toulouse within two years (1234) stimulated a series of land acquisitions in order to expand the lay church, a project supported by donations from wealthy and noble patrons.[37] The extension to the east with a large new polygonal chevet with shallow radiating chapels was built between c. 1245 and c. 1252 over the earlier cemetery.[38] The absorption of the cemetery, in addition to the fact that Innocent IV allowed the Order of Preachers to bury patrons who requested internment with the order, may suggest that the extension was intended to provide space not only for secondary chapels and a larger lay congregation, but also, and even at this early date, for tombs and private family chapels.[39] This structure was radically remodeled after about 1275 with a fan vault supported by central columns; the coats of arms that decorate the upper walls and windows attest to the patronage of rich and noble families. A final period of reconstruction in the first third of the fourteenth century unified and vaulted the entire structure (fig. 34). A series of lateral chapels were subsequently built on the south side of the nave to replace the earlier porch, a project completed in the 1390s.[40] During these successive interventions, and in spite of continued growth in the size of the religious community, the friars' choir continued in its original and historical location, a feature that confirms the public function of the extensions.

The chronology of the Jacobin church of Toulouse is exceptionally important because it reflects a certain modus operandi for the order: a restrained and pragmatic approach to construction was combined with a programmed sequence of additions and extensions driven by requests from lay patrons. There was also a willingness to experiment with innovative solutions in response to the constraints imposed by finances and the configuration of the property at their disposal. Sundt is correct in rejecting symbolic and "iconographic" meanings of the parallel naves at Toulouse in favor of arguments pertaining to poverty and an institutional preference for pragmatism.[41]

34   Toulouse, the Jacobin church, view of the nave from the west. With kind permission of Richard Sundt.

PARIS: SAINT-JACQUES, AFTER 1217

The Preachers arrived in Paris in 1217, first renting space near the Hôtel-Dieu, and a year later moving to their definitive location near the Porte D'Orléans, a site which had also previously been a hospital (see fig. 17).[42] Demolition of the convent in 1849 prohibits a detailed discussion of the site or its architecture, but it may be reasonable to suppose that

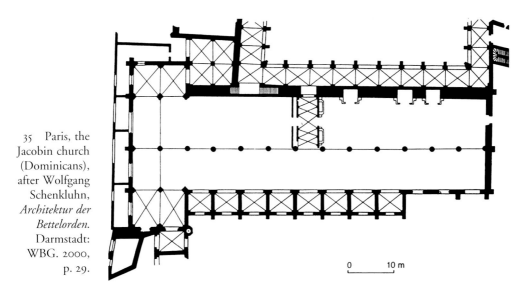

35 Paris, the Jacobin church (Dominicans), after Wolfgang Schenkluhn, *Architektur der Bettelorden.* Darmstadt: WBG. 2000, p. 29.

0   10 m

the large rectangular hall used by the hospice of Saint Jacques was simply adapted to become the Dominican church (fig. 35). A trapezoidal cloister to the south aligned with the parallel naves suggests that at least one of the naves existed already and conditioned the alignment of the other conventual structures inserted at this awkwardly shaped site.[43] Some scholars have dated the church to after 1221; a seventeenth-century historian placed its construction between 1241 and 1263. As Sundt notes, at about 20 meters wide its dimensions were similar to those of Toulouse; it was also asymmetrical, with the south nave wider than that on the north.[44] If we are concerned here with the survival of a pre-existing hospital structure, the complex in Paris, however, might well have provided the model for the disposition in Toulouse.

BOLOGNA: SAN NICOLÒ DELLE VIGNE (SAN DOMENICO), AFTER 1219

Preachers arrived in Bologna in 1218, and first settled in a hospital near Santa Maria della Mascarella. A year later (March 1219), under the charismatic leadership of Réginald of Orléans, they acquired the property of San Nicolò delle Vigne, close to the city walls on the southern border of the city. This site included the small church that belonged to the Carbonesi family.[45] Réginald of Orléans, with the assistance of the parish priest Rudolph of Faenza (who later joined the order), began further purchases of land from the Carbonesi, rapidly extending the new holdings to cover roughly 4,000 square meters. The *praefectus operum* may well have been Rudolph himself.[46] The parish priest seems to have been a central figure in the rapid purchase of properties, which extended the friars' holdings from the church to the city walls.[47] Indulgences began to be issued in 1220, suggesting that planning for a new community residence must have started forthwith, and was from the outset conceived of as a series of integrated structures (chapter house, school, refectory, infirmary, dormitory).

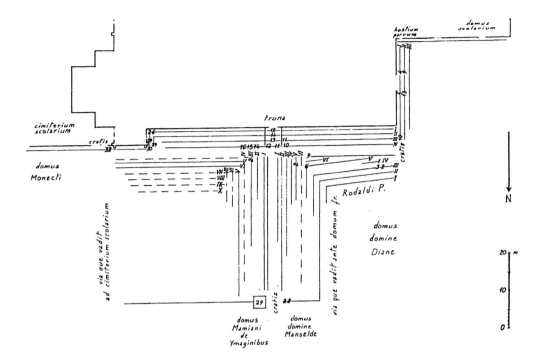

36   Bologna, San Domenico, reconstruction of the tomb locations, after Breveglieri, 1995, plate 1.

In contrast with the more troubled situation in Toulouse, the Dominican settlement in Bologna flourished from its earliest days. The presence of magnetic preachers such as Réginald attracted students and townspeople; the continued presence and conversion of Rudolph must have been of great assistance in practical and logistical considerations.[48] The convent was soon integrated into the city's hierarchy of religious institutions. Even before Dominic's canonization, his body was the object of popular veneration and in the 1220s the convent's exterior cemetery a prized location for burial (fig. 36).

The site was reconfigured in a series of phases designed to guarantee liturgical continuity, although not all went smoothly.[49] Prior to the translation of Dominic's remains in 1233, his tomb was exposed to the elements. Jordan of Saxony, as we have seen, also noted that the friars at the convent were initially skeptical of the demonstrations of popular devotion at Dominic's tomb.

Eighteenth-century restorations of the church by Dotti now entirely conceal the interior of San Domenico. Alce identified numerous fragments of the exterior walls and suggests that the Dominican reconstruction of the church early in the thirteenth century was an essentially homogeneous process.[50] Subsequent additions and modifications impede the clear identification of building phases, but occasional references in the documents indicate that completion of the friars' choir followed the reconstruction of the old church, presumably for the lay public and the tomb of Dominic (see figs. 14 and 24). The (heavily restored) facade reflects the dimensions of the early church, while fragments of the upper nave walls visible from the cloister and the north flank indicate the level of the roof at least by the fourteenth or fifteenth century. Alce suggests that the choir was vaulted from the outset,

THE PROCESS OF INSTITUTIONALIZATION

but the nave was meant to be covered with a wooden truss ceiling. As noted above, and like San Giovanni a Canale in Piacenza, both spaces may have featured differentiated supports (see figs. 16 and 25).

The reconstruction of San Nicolò has been described in two exemplary studies by Venturino Alce, both published in 1972. After construction of the *domus* for the community, which probably contained the first teaching and training spaces, attention turned to reconstructing the church; Alce believes that this work began only after the indulgence of 1228 (see fig. 14).[51] Although much remains uncertain at San Domenico, the brickwork of the upper walls suggests that the structure of San Nicolò was entirely replaced in the thirteenth century as part of a fairly continuous process.[52] The reconstruction must have been complicated, however, by the combined needs of providing a liturgical choir for the religious community, access to the tomb of Dominic, and space for the rapidly growing lay community.

A plausible chronology suggests that the old structure of San Nicolò was replaced by the new nave (the external church) for the lay public (see fig. 14). Yet because the south transept is closely aligned with the east wing of the conventual buildings (see fig. 24), the entire plan for the new church was probably projected from the outset. In 1230 there are references to the church as *noviter facta*, and in 1233 there is mention of the *domus* of the friars. A portico (*truna*) mentioned in the 1220s was added along the north flank of the church (see fig. 24); it was perhaps associated with burials on the north side, a practice that began in the same years and was officially authorized in 1227.[53] The cemetery came to link the conventual complex to the city to the north, while the cloister and community buildings extended to the east and south. The eastern portion of the cemetery was reserved for the use of the friars and prelates (see fig. 36). By 1291, however, tombs of distinguished citizens began to invade the cloister, though apparently without the systematic allotment of space that was established on the north flank of the church.[54] Distinct burial zones were reserved for students, prelates, and nobles.[55] By the end of the thirteenth century, the external cemetery contained several hundred tombs in parallel rows;[56] their arrangement, recorded in the sepultuary of 1291, mirrored in large measure the social strata of the city.[57] Prior to 1291, the tombs inside the church were restricted to five notable burials: Enzo (d. 1272), the son of Frederick II, the Polish archbishop Martin, and the Dominican bishop Teodorico of Faenza; two more tombs, one now anonymous, were located in front of the altars of the Blessed Virgin and Saint Peter Martyr at the choir screen.

In 1233 the remains of Saint Dominic were translated to the south aisle of the exterior church (in the presence of 300 members of the order).[58] Work probably continued on the new choir, which, because it was vaulted, took longer to complete. An indulgence for the completion of the church issued in 1235 by the patriarch of Aquileia referred for the first time to San Domenico.[59]

The cost of land acquisition and construction weighed heavily on the community. In 1238 the patriarch of Aquileia again facilitated matters by declaring that debts to his own bishopric could be absolved by donations to the friars of Bologna, and that all such contributions would be designated for the construction of their *domus*. As this document does not mention the church, it may have been complete.

The early phases of San Domenico may be summarized as follows:

1219–24 Construction of the first nucleus of the conventual buildings on the site of San Nicolò.

1228–38 Reconstruction of the church, beginning with a nave for the laity to replace that of San Nicolò, completed in 1233.[60]

1238 Completion of the choir, or "internal" church.

1233–43 Reorganization of the spaces around the church and conventual complex, the principal buildings of the convent (cloister, refectory, dormitory), and the creation of the orchard. This may have entailed the destruction of the first building (the *domus*) erected by the friars, no longer adequate for the needs of the greatly enlarged community.

1251 Consecration of the church by Innocent IV.

If the translation of the relics (1233) to the south aisle marked the completion of the "outer" or lay church, the Preachers may provisionally have used the nave or north aisle while the liturgical choir was erected to the east. The completion of the choir in 1238, however, almost certainly included a *tramezzo*, or choir screen, to separate the shrine of Dominic and the lay church from the choir; this would have been in keeping with the similar arrangement in the two succeeding years at Santa Sabina in Rome and Sant'Eustorgio in Milan.

Properties in front of the west facade were acquired in 1231.[61] In 1240 more land was purchased in that area.[62] A pulpit was built into the facade, as attested in the *Libellus funerum* of 1291 (demolished when the Ghislardi chapel was built in 1524). The families who sold the land took on the responsibility of demolishing the buildings located on these properties. Adjacent to the pulpit was a metal grate that perhaps served for the public exhibition of heretics. By the middle of the century, the space in front of the church was identified as the Piazza San Domenico. The pulpit integrated into the facade of the church probably dates to the construction of the exterior (lay) church – completed by the time of the translation of Dominic's relics in 1233 – and seems to have been integral to the conception and function of the complex with its piazza. This pulpit is mentioned in 1267 on the occasion of the second translation of the remains of Dominic to the new sarcophagus/reliquary designed by Giovanni Pisano and his workshop. On that occasion, the bishop of Vicenza carried the head of the saint to a "corner pulpit of the church . . . in a piazza with a praiseworthy crowd of the faithful present" ("in angulari pulpito ecclesie . . . in platea exteriori presente laudabili fidelium multitudine").[63]

In the second half of the thirteenth century, work continued on the conventual complex and altars were added to the church (Saints Peter Martyr, the Blessed Virgin, and Dominic). Dominic's altar was located in front of his tomb.[64] Although tombs proliferated on the exterior north flank and western piazza, the interior remained restricted to the burials of the most prestigious and influential donors.

Difficult though it is to reconstruct, the church of San Domenico in Bologna became increasingly important as a major center for the order because of the political disruptions in Toulouse. It seems likely that by the time the friars began the reconstruction on the church around 1228, the order had fully appropriated the architecture of reform monasticism, including most likely a flat-ended termination for the choir and a cloister flanked by chapter house, dormitory, and refectory. San Domenico in Bologna is therefore probably the first mendicant example of a double church constructed largely *ex novo*, with a vaulted "interior" church to the east and a wooden-roofed "exterior" church to the west. The solution may have received special impetus at this site because of the challenges presented by public devotion to the shrine of Dominic, and seems to have become a disposition that was to influence generations of subsequent Dominican church architecture.

By c. 1228–30 the importance of the Preachers' ongoing project in Bologna as a model for other new foundations is confirmed at various sites. San Giovanni a Canale in Piacenza, begun in the 1230s, may reflect its disposition (see fig. 16). A late example is the Dominican church of Louvain (see fig. 26). The Bolognese model may also have informed some aspects of the subsequent structures at Toulouse, such as the choice of octagonal or cylindrical supports in brick. The early incorporation of a cemetery on the north and west sides of San Domenico in the early 1220s may also have set a strong and prestigious precedent for the integration of burials with convents.

Several salient points emerge from the example of San Nicolò delle Vigne in Bologna: reconstruction was approached in an episodic manner that revolved around practical necessities, such as providing separation and enclosure for the enlarged friars' choir. The efficient progress of the work (financial difficulties notwithstanding) and the general coherence of the plan suggest that the friars began the reconstruction with a fairly well-developed concept of the entire project, even though the enterprise needed to absorb and enhance the evolving cult of the founder while also expressing institutional poverty. It should be noted that although the form of the original termination of the east end is uncertain,[65] a flat terminal wall behind the altar would have been in frank imitation of Cistercian models, and this feature became a consistent element of Italian Dominican houses up to at least c. 1280 (as at Santa Maria Novella in Florence).[66] If suppositions about the sequence of construction are correct, San Domenico may also have been one of the first mendicant churches provided with a choir screen.

ROME: SANTA SABINA (C. 1218–1220)

The church of Santa Sabina on the Aventine Hill was acquired by the Preachers c. 1218–20. Hinnebusch observes that Dominic may have pressured Honorius III for this site because the early Christian basilica well suited the concept of an "apostolic" renewal.[67] In the event, the original structure of the basilica never underwent significant reconstruction, though chapels were added to its flanks and various additions made to the interior (for the most part expunged in nineteenth- and twentieth-century restorations). From the outset this church had an important strategic role for the order,[68] and its association with the papacy remained strong through the thirteenth century: Gregory IX dedicated the new high altar in 1238, and Urban IV donated an altar in 1263. Although the Aventine Hill is removed from the bustle of the city, and therefore is in keeping with some of the peripheral sites chosen by the Friars Preachers in the early decades, by the middle of the thirteenth century the changing political environment for the new orders required a different approach. Although the convent remained one of the most important houses of the order (especially as a *studium*, library, and archive), the location of Santa Sabina was too distant from the city center for a mission of public outreach. It is probably for this reason that in the 1260s the Preachers acquired the site at Santa Maria sopra Minerva, adjacent to the Pantheon in the heart of the city.[69]

Honorius III's transfer of Santa Sabina to the Preachers preserved the integrity of the pre-existing parish: the secular clergy kept control of part of the church, the baptistery, and some flanking buildings to the east. The arrangement thus foresaw the continuity of the parish and its clergy, preserving the parochial relationship to the local community as well as the traditional fees presumably paid to the parish priests.[70] Constrained by a precipitous cliff off its north flank, the friars added cloisters and conventual buildings to the west of the church starting c. 1219, creating the first sides (west and north) of what was to become the cloister (see figs. 29 and 30).[71] The choir screen was added in 1239, especially important at this site precisely because of the continued existence of the parish.

MILAN: SANT'EUSTORGIO, 1220

Dominic stayed in Milan, a city notorious in the Middle Ages for its heresies, in various periods between 1217 and 1220. In 1219 he sent two friars there to establish a community. After a brief interval at San Nazaro they acquired the ancient basilica of Sant'Eustorgio, a site officiated by a small group of canons (who remained *in situ* until at least 1227). The site is distinguished by several important historical associations: it was the shrine of Bishop Eustorgio (344–50) and a historical cemetery: the friars acquired the rights to continue burials here in 1227. The complex also contained the legendary fountain where Saint Barnabas had baptized the first Christians of the city. In addition, the relics of the Three Kings were at Sant'Eustorgio until Frederick Barbarossa removed them to Cologne in 1164. The fourteenth-century historian of the Preachers in Milan, Galvano Fiamma, described the church and its ancillary buildings when the Preachers arrived as in ruinous condition and the area as swampy.[72] In spite of these challenges, Sant'Eustorgio represented a site of great strategic importance just south of the city gates on the north–south *cardo* toward Pavia.

The Dominican presence at Sant'Eustorgio has the exceptional good fortune of a fourteenth-century description of the convent and early years of the community, a text published by G. Odetto as *La cronaca maggiore dell'ordine domenicano di Galvano Fiamma*, in the *Archivum Fratrum Praedicatorum* of 1949. Analysis of the text for understanding the chronology of architectural interventions, however, is complicated by additions to the buildings after Fiamma's descriptions as well as a heavy-handed restoration in the nineteenth century; a detailed chronology of the church is in any event beyond the scope of this study.[73] In spite of these complexities, Sant'Eustorgio is an important example of an early medieval church that was the object of almost continuous intervention and reconfiguration by the friars: only the nucleus of the four eastern bays remains from the building as it was adopted in 1220 when they arrived. The exterior walls and side chapels, apse, south transept arm, and the three western bays are all the result of later interventions (figs. 37 and 38).

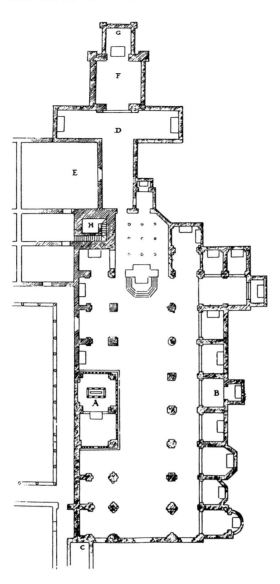

37 Milan, Sant'Eustorgio, plan from the Raccolta Bianconi, vol. 5, fol. 10b. Archivio Storico Civico Biblioteca Trivulziana. © Comune di Milano.

The early modifications at the site were the construction of a dormitory and cloister, work that, according to Fiamma, was entirely supported by the donations of the faithful. Among the early works was the creation of what would appear to have been a raised choir from which all parts of the church were visible.[74] At the same time, a wooden pulpit was installed outside the church, later replaced by the permanent structure now visible (see fig. 21).

Other early changes were relatively modest: the transept to the south of the main altar appears to have been one of the first additions to the fabric of the church and entailed the insertion of a portal, subsequently suppressed by the addition of a chapel.[75] A further series of interventions occurred after the canonization of Peter Martyr in 1253, which transformed Sant'Eustorgio once again into a major pilgrimage site, second only to the tomb of Dominic in Bologna. The tomb of Peter Martyr became an active stimulus for patronage

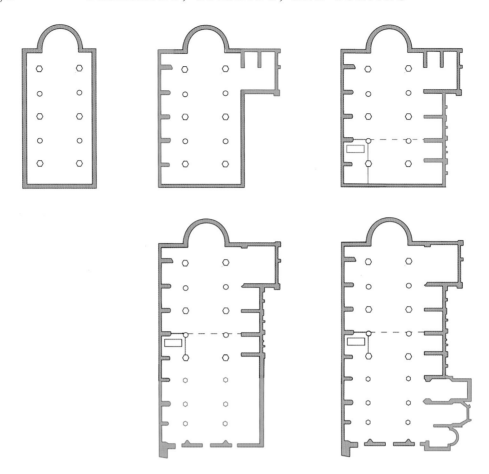

38   Milan, Sant'Eustorgio, schematic and hypothetical reconstruction of sequence of major additions (Caroline Bruzelius with Julia Rooney and Cosimo Monteleone).

and donations as well as for pressures on the community to accommodate burials in proximity to the tomb. As a result, and probably starting in the thirteenth century, the south flank of the church was reconstructed to create a series of lateral chapels for private donors, especially members of the Visconti family.[76] In the process, the vaults of the south aisle were reconfigured with slender and pointed rib vaults. On the north flank of the church, the construction of the cloister can be associated with the addition of shallow chapels along the length of the adjacent north wall. The extension of the church to the west with three additional bays and the construction of a new facade probably took place in the second half of the thirteenth century, a project that had the dual purpose of enhancing access to the tomb of the martyr (located in the western bays of the nave) and creating more space for burials and private chapels. Indeed, over the course of the thirteenth century, additions to the core of Sant'Eustorgio were so extensive and complex that no part of the structure seems to have remained untouched.

Angiola Maria Romanini put it well: "The Romanesque fabric of the extramural basilica has been enclosed, that is to say, embedded like a kernel in a series of extensions, transformations and additions that were not exclusively of the thirteenth century but rather continued to be added piecemeal from the first half of that century through to the late fifteenth."[77]

Contradiction and Conformity: Franciscans and Buildings

Francis never intended to found an order, much less an international movement of extraordinary importance. His was an intensely personal search for a spiritual ideal directly inspired by the New Testament. The vocation was individual, not institutional. Although the force of this personal vision was to explode and become one of the most powerful spiritual movements of its time, the founder himself was on an essentially solitary journey, which was an individual quest for salvation and redemption. Yet this journey had such compelling power that it still attracts followers and disciples. In stark contrast with Dominic, Francis was not an institution builder, and, indeed, his withdrawal from leadership of the movement in the 1220s may have reflected his inability to reconcile his initial concept of itinerant preaching on an apostolic model with what was emerging as a powerful social movement.

In contrast to the Friars Preacher, Francis was largely opposed to buildings and fixed settlements: his community and his followers were to live as "pilgrims and strangers," receiving food and shelter from charity. In the rule of 1223, the saint stated: "The brothers shall not acquire anything as their own, neither a house nor a place nor anything at all. Instead, as pilgrims and strangers in this world who serve the Lord in poverty and humility, let them go begging for alms with full trust."[78] Within three years, however, Francis issued instructions for settlements in cities:

> When the brothers go to any city where they have no house and they find someone who wants to give them enough land for them to build a house and have a garden and whatever is necessary for them, they ought first to consider how much land will suffice, always bearing in mind the holy poverty which we have promised and the good example which we are bound to show to others in all things. . . . Afterwards . . . they ought to go to the bishop of that city . . . and say to him . . . we have come first to you . . . for we would like to build there with God's blessing and with yours. . . . Let them go then and have made a boundary ditch . . . and let them plan there a good hedge instead of a wall as a sign of holy poverty and humility. Afterwards let them have poor hovels prepared, made of loam and wood, and some other small cells where the brothers can sometimes pray . . . and let them also have small churches built. The brothers ought not to have large churches made for preaching to the people, or for any other reason, since it is more humble and gives a better example when the brothers go to other churches to preach.[79]

Francis's recognition of the practical need for shelter is reflected in his final testament of 1226, in which he warned his brethren against receiving "churches or poor dwellings for themselves, or anything that was built for them, unless they were in harmony with the poverty that we have promised in the rule."[80] The document suggests that by this time Francis was reconciled to the need for providing for basic shelter (churches and poor dwellings) while at the same time affirming poverty in buildings. This was a significant shift from his earlier statements on permanent settlements. It is a salutary reminder of the rapidly shifting character of the Franciscan ideal – and of Francis's own evolution – from the early years of the movement, a process in which the saint himself needed to confront the new realities of the order as it was transformed over the previous decade.

During the lifetime of Francis it is thus impossible to speak of "Franciscan architecture," or indeed to identify with any real security the existence of such a phenomenon before the late 1230s at the earliest.[81] Yet as we have seen, Francis's instructions to his followers on matters of buildings evolved during his lifetime, and within a few years of his death the order's rapid expansion and clericalization imposed new pressures in relation to forms of life and liturgical practice that resulted in dramatically changed attitudes toward permanent settlements.[82]

Not all friars were reconciled to change, however: the transformation of Francis's ideal brought with it the seeds of controversy within many aspects of the movement, not the least of which was the character and scale of buildings. Francis himself had offered a contradictory example, shifting from episodes of wandering, preaching, and doing good works to periods of retreat for hermetic contemplation in rustic sheds. Even within the context of his itinerant practice, he created a meeting place and occasional center for his brethren at the chapel of the Porziuncola and repaired the vaults of the crumbling church of San Damiano.[83] On the other hand, when confronted with buildings erected for the Friars Minor by the commune at the Porziuncola and in Bologna, the saint tried to dismantle them with his own hands until stopped by local authorities.

Starting in the 1230s, Franciscan architecture began to follow loosely the example of the Preachers.[84] Franciscans increasingly adopted or accepted the use of older churches (San Lorenzo in Naples, San Fermo in Verona) that they reconfigured in similar ways to the transformations that the Preachers instituted at Sant'Eustorgio in Milan. When necessary, they erected new churches and convents, which in the early decades of the thirteenth century were typically simple rectangular halls (Cortona, Pola); at a slightly later date, the Friars Minor began to introduce plans with transepts (San Francesco in Pisa, San Francesco in Siena) or add them to pre-existing structures (San Francesco, Treviso). These typically had several flat-ended chapels on the eastern wall. The central apse and side chapels were often vaulted, but on occasion, as at the Cordeliers in Paris, there were no vaults whatsoever. After about 1250 a small number of Franciscan churches in Italy that were associated with *studia* (San Francesco at Bologna, San Francesco in Piacenza, Sant'Antonio in Padua, San Lorenzo in Naples) were expanded with ambulatories and radiating chapels; in all these examples the rib vaults of the interior were supported by external flying buttresses. It is striking, however, that both rib vaults and flyers were absent from one of the most prestigious churches of the order and the greatest international center of Franciscan learning: the church of the Madeleine (the Cordeliers) in Paris.

As within the Dominican order, there was often a range of possible plans and designs, as well as a close association with local architectural practice. At the same time, however, even in the first half of the thirteenth century there must have been a distinct "family resemblance": imagine how the two major mendicant churches of Paris, large, austere, and utilitarian, must have stood out as sharply distinct from other religious institutions. The homogeneity of solutions within the orders can be attributed in part to friars who were master builders and traveled from place to place.

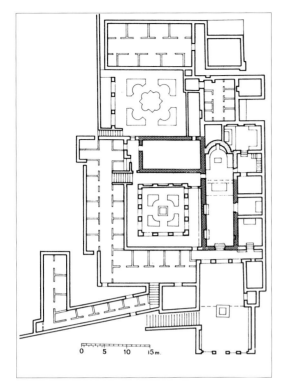

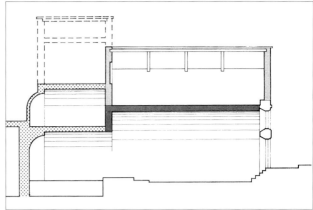

39 Assisi, San Damiano, plan after
I. Baldelli and A. M. Romanini, *Francesco,
il francescanesimo e la cultura della nuova
Europa*, Rome, 1986, fig. 21.

40 Assisi, San Damiano, section after
I. Baldelli and A. M. Romanini, *Francesco,
il francescanesimo e la cultura della nuova
Europa*, Rome, 1986, fig. 22.

These principles are confirmed in what we can glean of the early architecture of the Friars Minor. Excavations at the Porziuncola indicate a disaggregated cluster of dwellings (see fig. 15). The small chapel, now known as the Cappella del Perdono, and the nearby room in which Francis died are among the few surviving early structures from the thirteenth century utilized (not necessarily constructed) by the Franciscans. There are no indications of a coherent or systematic organization of what appear to be haphazardly placed mud and wattle huts, some on stone foundations. The nearby house built by the commune of Assisi was entirely of stone and located behind the chapel in a roughly trapezoidal shape aligned with the apse of the present church. There is nothing here from the earliest phase that suggests the least interest in the organization of space analogous to that of a monastic complex, and the concept of a self-contained and partially enclosed cluster of buildings seems indeed remote.

The situation at San Damiano is different, however, as Francis in his repairs anticipated its use by a community of women. As a pre-existing structure, the complex probably consisted of not only the church but also some sort of residence for the parish priest. In the early years after the arrival of Clare and her companions, an oratory and dormitory for the women were superimposed above the church (figs. 39 and 40). The structures to the east of the apse behind the main altar and nuns' choir were probably erected sometime after the women moved to the site after 1212 (these areas are now normally not accessible and appear to have been substantially reconstructed). The cloister and conventual buildings on the north side were perhaps created toward the middle of the thirteenth century. The facade clearly indicates the additions to the church that enlarged it to accommodate the community of women. Later, additional structures were added or reconfigured on the right flank of the church, part of which may have been commeomorative chapels. Although issues related to San Damiano and its community pertain primarily to the realm of architecture intended for enclosed communities of women,[85] the church remained a parish while the nuns worshiped in an enclosed choir attached to the east end. This established a pattern for enclosed Franciscan women: the lay public was welcomed into the nave while the religious community participated in a separate space near the altar. (Indeed, the regulations established for the enclosure at San Domenico created a model not only for the later legislation on *clausura*, but also for the design of liturgical space for women religious.)[86]

For male communities, the monastic prototype of buildings arranged around a cloister was introduced by the mid-thirteenth century: at Santa Croce in Florence around 1250, the friars adopted a plan with cloister and conventual buildings on the south side, known from the excavations undertaken after the flood of 1966 (see fig. 9). The flat-ended chevet was flanked by three chapels on either side.[87] The nave had no aisles. The disposition of San Francesco in Cortona (c. 1246–54), though not a completely enclosed cloister, shows a similar arrangement to the north of the church.

Santa Croce presents the first evidence that survives of a cloister flanking a Franciscan church, although other examples may have existed that no longer survive. By the mid-thirteenth century, the flat-ended chevet was typical of Franciscan buildings, as at both Santa Croce in Florence and San Francesco in Cortona (see fig. 19). The church could be expanded with transepts, as at Treviso, but in other examples these were an integral part of the layout from the start (Pisa, Pistoia, Udine). Transepts, when they existed, often functioned as a corridor to the conventual structures as well as space for additional altars.

NAPLES: SAN LORENZO, FOUNDED 1234

San Lorenzo, a sixth-century basilica in the center of Naples transferred by the bishop of Aversa to the Friars Minor in 1234, is an example of the process of the transformation of an earlier building and "organic growth" analogous to that of Sant'Eustorgio in Milan.[88] The postwar discovery of the foundations of the early basilica permits a new interpretation of the successive Franciscan interventions at the site, changes that were similar to those at San Francesco Grande in Milan. As at San Fermo in Verona (see fig. 58), the old church was eventually "voided out," leaving only its exterior envelope to enclose a large single nave unarticulated by internal supports.

At San Lorenzo chapels were added to the exterior aisle walls in small groups at around the same time that a partial cloister may have been constructed on the south side of the church (fig. 41b).[89] This work probably took place sometime around the middle of the thirteenth century and perhaps c. 1260. The chapels would have been essential for secondary altars for the ordained friars, who increased in number as the *studium* became established. However, with the growth of the community the number of secondary altars was probably not sufficient, and as a result, probably beginning in the late 1270s, the church

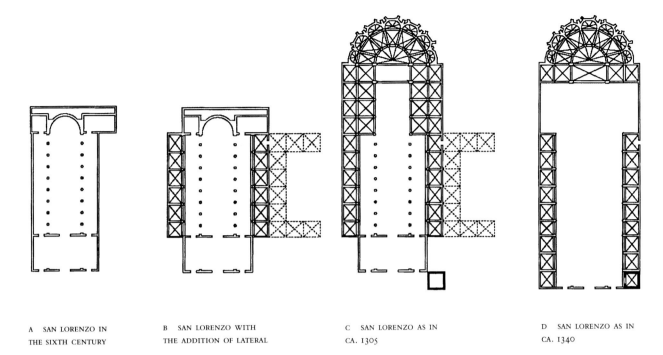

A SAN LORENZO IN
THE SIXTH CENTURY

B SAN LORENZO WITH
THE ADDITION OF LATERAL

C SAN LORENZO AS IN
CA. 1305

D SAN LORENZO AS IN
CA. 1340

41 Naples, San Lorenzo, hypothetical reconstruction of sequence of major additions.

was extended to the east with a magnificent Gothic choir that closed off one of the narrow north–south streets (*vicoli*) of the ancient grid plan (figs. 42 and 43). There are no documents on the closing of the street, and we can only imagine that this took place through the intercession of the convent's procurator or possibly the political intervention of the local administrative unit, the Seggio di Montagna, which met at the abbey.[90]

The choir doubled the length of the old basilica and consisted of an ambulatory with radiating chapels. Construction was probably delayed by the outbreak of the War of the Vespers in 1282, although in 1284 a fine of 400 *once* exacted from the Rufolo and Della Mara families of Ravello provided significant new funding. The eastern extension and Gothic chevet (see fig. 10) were complete by c. 1300, when members of the royal family were buried in its southern side aisles and Montano d'Arezzo decorated the area with frescoes.

The church, thus extended with double aisles that joined the old basilica to the new chevet, would have looked strikingly similar to the Franciscan church in Paris (see fig. 18) and not dissimilar from San Francesco in Bologna (see figs. 4 and 5). Neither San Lorenzo nor the Madeleine had a transept that interrupted the continuity of the internal supports from the nave through the apse, and thus in both cases we might imagine a continuous horizontal roof, something like the reconstructions provided here (see figs. 42 and 43). The presence of radiating chapels in these Franciscan convents would thus have sharply differentiated them from the churches of the Preachers, none of which reflected plans with a constellation of radiating chapels: as Schenkluhn noted in his important study of 1985, this feature remained unique to the Friars Minor.

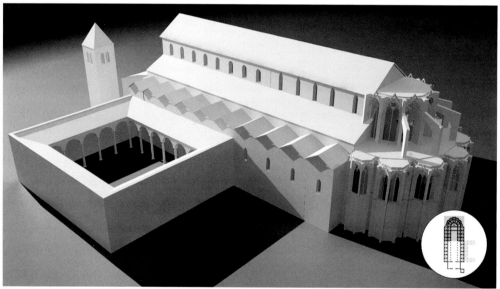

TOP 42 Naples, San Lorenzo, reconstruction of the Gothic choir as a continuation of the early Christian basilica (Caroline Bruzelius with Umberto Plaja).

BOTTOM 43 Naples, San Lorenzo, reconstruction of the Gothic choir from the exterior as a continuation of the early Christian basilica (Caroline Bruzelius with Umberto Plaja).

OPPOSITE PAGE 44 Naples, San Lorenzo, reconstruction of the inserted transept and reconstructed nave after c. 1324 (Caroline Bruzelius with Umberto Plaja).

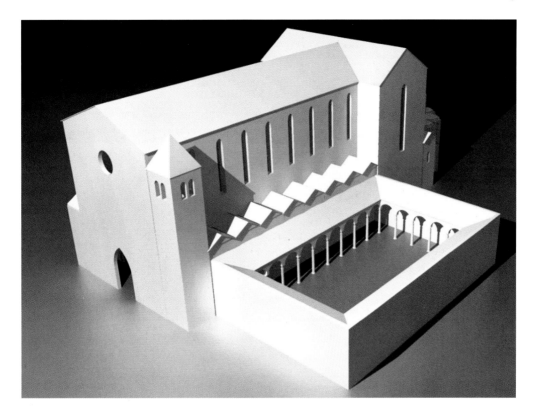

Starting c. 1324, however, San Lorenzo underwent a radical transformation with the destruction of the sixth-century nave, the extension of the church to the west, and the removal of the intermediate piers connecting the chevet to the nave in order to insert a transept (fig. 44; and see fig. 41d). The "voiding out" of the interior at San Lorenzo was not new within the order: the Friars Minor at San Fermo, Verona, performed a similar operation by removing the piers between the nave and side aisles and extended the nave into the atrium to create a much longer church. Most sources date this work to the late thirteenth century.[91]

MILAN: SAN FRANCESCO GRANDE (C. 1249)

Until its destruction between 1809 and 1813 to make way for army barracks, San Francesco Grande in Milan must have been one of the most prominent Franciscan houses of Italy (fig. 45). A building chronology of modifications to the early Christian basilica at the site was proposed by Romanini in her 1964 study of Lombard architecture, and I summarize her chronology here.[92] In 1249, twenty-eight years after their arrival in Milan (1221), the Friars Minor were provided with the use the ancient fourth-century basilica of Santi Nabore e Felice by the archbishop, an arrangement confirmed by Alexander IV in 1256. Their earlier residence and oratory, however, seem to have been adjacent, perhaps directly in front of, the old basilica, as a document of 1235 refers to a house to the south of both

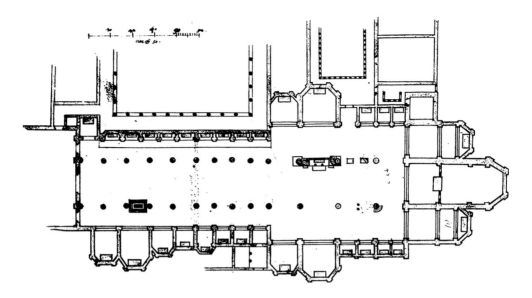

45 Milan, San Francesco Grande. Raccolta Bianconi, vol. 5, fol. 13b. Archivio Storico Civico Biblioteca Trivulziana. © Comune di Milano.

churches ("a meridie ecclesia Sancti Francisci sive Sancti Naboris.")[93] After 1256 the friars extended the old basilica to the east with a new choir, one that might have had a flat-ended chevet and lateral chapels similar to the c. 1252 church at Santa Croce in Florence. As Romanini observes, the altar of the old church remained in its original location until it was transferred to the vast and much later polygonal apse of 1570. In the intervening years, numerous chapels were added to the old nave, many of which are recorded in wills and testaments of the thirteenth and fourteenth centuries.

The complete destruction of the complex prohibits a more detailed analysis of the site. For our purposes, however, several points are important: the friars settled in proximity to a prestigious ancient basilica which they acquired several decades later. Their additions and reconstructions expanded upon the ancient core, perhaps preserving parts of the old church, probably until the complete demolition of the convent. As has been seen, the insertion of a Franciscan church within an older institution occurred frequently in mid-thirteenth-century Franciscan foundations in cities of importance, as attested by Santa Maria in Aracoeli (Rome), San Lorenzo Maggiore (Naples), and San Fermo (Verona). In all these cases, elements of the older buildings were preserved and incorporated into later additions. As with the Dominican settlements at Santa Sabina and Sant'Eustorgio, this had the advantage of associating the mendicant house with a prestigious older foundation, one sometimes in the heart of a city, or at other times adjacent to or including a venerable cemetery.

*   *   *

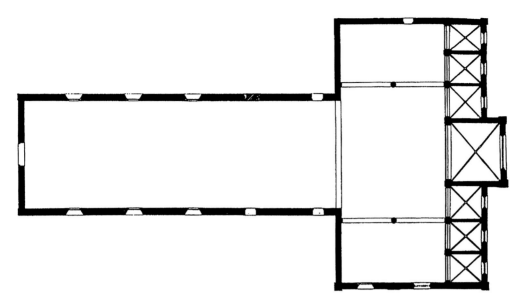

46   Pisa, San Francesco, plan from Wolfgang Schenkluhn, *Architektur der Bettelorden*. Darmstadt: WBG. 2000, p. 64, plate III, no. 6.

PISA: SAN FRANCESCO (C. 1228)

The convent of San Francesco in Pisa reflects the complex process of settlement and institutionalization that occurred even in wealthy cities with substantial episcopal and public support.[94] At Pisa the Friars Minor had difficulties establishing a permanent presence in the city, and long periods were spent securing space and building the convent.

According to tradition, Francis was in Pisa in 1211. Two friars are mentioned in a document of 1219 as possibly living in a hospice associated with the oratory at the Casa del Ponte. In 1228 arrangements were made for a group of Friars Minor to acquire the church of Santa Trinità in Sopracastello; actual possession, however, was obstructed by the parish priest and local residents. By 1233 the dispute appears to have been partially resolved by the construction of a church or chapel nearby, and by this time relations with local residents and the commune seem to have improved. Yet, local support notwithstanding, possession of Santa Trinità continued to be obstructed by the archbishop. In 1238 an *operaio* was assigned to the convent by the communal government, but only in 1247, with direct papal intervention, was an agreement reached that guaranteed the friars the use and possession of Santa Trinità, and this on the condition that Edmond, the parish priest, continue to live and officiate there until his death. It appears that the latter expressed his views on this cohabitation by ringing the parish bells at inappropriate intervals.

The first small church of the friars, mentioned as in existence in 1233, was expanded in 1241. In 1259, the friars acquired the right to enlarge their church over a street, and Alexander IV granted them an indulgence of 100 days for the works. This is probably the project for which Archbishop Visconti laid the cornerstone in 1261 and encouraged parishioners to make contributions toward construction (fig. 46). Donations were made for the works on the church in 1273, and in 1305 Napoleone Orsini allowed the Friars Minor to receive 500 golden florins of *incerta* for its continued construction. A variety of wills left donations for the addition of chapels, such as that of 150 lire in 1302 "pro faciendo fieri et construi unam cappellam," and the commune offered funds for construction of the roof in 1318. A large segment of the nave and the facade were only finished three centuries later.[95]

PISTOIA: SAN FRANCESCO (C. 1249–1250)

Like San Francesco in Pisa, the Franciscan settlement at Pistoia, which was the focus of a 1993 study by an Italian team of scholars[96] and a conference in 2000,[97] is a salutary reminder of the protracted process of construction of many mendicant houses (fig. 47 and see fig. 13). Because of its spacious location outside the walls, San Francesco became the largest of the mendicant churches of Pistoia, but its contruction was protracted and sporadic.

The friars of Pistoia initially settled at Santa Croce (the location of which is unknown), and in 1249–50 were authorized to move to a larger site, Santa Maria al Prato, a highly visible and prestigious site outside the city walls. Here they utilized the older church (which may have continued to function as a parish) and lived in the nearby hospital of Santa Maria Maddalena. The new location appears to have offered much more space for a growing community; it also faced onto the large open *prato del comune*. In spite of indulgences conceded in 1250 "ecclesiam cum aliis edificis suis usibus caeperint construere";[98] there is no evidence of work on the present complex of buildings before 1289, and even then it proceeded slowly: the old parish church continued to be used until well into the fourteenth century.

It would appear that the friars for many decades lived in the old hospital at the site – arranged with spaces for the dormitory, refectory, and chapter house – prior to the completion of the choir of the new church and the new eastern wing of the conventual complex. The trapezoidal plan of the convent may reflect the alignment of the earlier buildings. References to an *operaio dei frati minori*, mentioned in 1252, and the "Opera di Santa Maria al Prato e di San Francesco" in 1274 suggest that some work on the new complex was taking place, but it is not clear whether this concerned the church or the conventual buildings.[99] The coherence of the post-1289 layout, and the succession of dates associated with the chancel, sacristy, dormitory, and chapter house, suggests that, although the process of building went forward over many decades, the eastern range of large new convent was planned and broadly executed as a unified complex.

* * *

In this chapter I have sought to examine how the move toward institutionalization affected the type and organization of several mendicant buildings in the first decades of the orders. The example of the Friars Preachers in adopting the normative forms of monastic planning subsequently inspired the solutions of the Friars Minor. By the 1230s both orders had developed a taste for the acquisition of older, often early Christian, basilicas (Santa Sabina in Rome, San Lorenzo in Naples, the basilicas of Milan), most with ancient cemeteries.

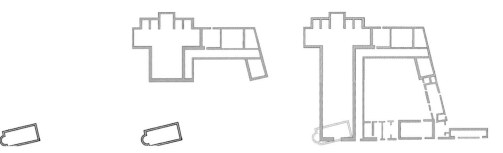

47   Pistoia, San Francesco and Santa Maria al Prato, hypothetical reconstruction of major building phases based on Gai, 1993, p. 56 (Julia Rooney and Cosimo Monteleone).

Some of the older churches were in urban centers, and their adaptation to the needs of the friars imposed particular challenges.

Under the guidance of Saint Dominic, the Preachers introduced the concept of conventualization in c. 1220. Sometime in the 1240s (for example, at Santa Croce, Florence) this model was adopted by the Friars Minor. Conventualization required the acquisition of space for a cloister and other regularly situated buildings, imposing strains on local communities and sometimes considerable expense for the friars.

Choir screens separating churches into two spatial compartments, an inner and outer church, were introduced in the early 1230s. This reflected the increased need of the friars to provide liturgical space for lay congregations. During the 1220s the public began to request burial in or around mendicant churches, a phenomenon conspicuous in Bologna and at Toulouse. While it is true that in some houses, such as San Domenico in Bologna, the church interior was reserved for only the most distinguished burials, by mid-century such requests presented growing challenges for both orders, which they attempted to manage through legislation against intrusive tomb monuments and the other forms of commemoration.

The following chapters will engage with three broad questions. What kinds of strategies did the friars develop in relation to the expansion and construction of convents within the constraints of both the building sites and restricted finances? How did friaries relate to urban populations and how did this affect the character and building process of convents? How did social practice and funding condition the relations of the mendicants to their own buildings and to the cities in which they were located?

MENDICANT CONSTRUCTION STRATEGIES

Mendicant churches and convents were constantly undergoing modification and expansion. Churches were enlarged to the east, to the west, or both, and encrusted with aisles or chapels on their north and south flanks (fig. 48; see figs. 41 and 45). They were often razed to make way for new, larger structures (Santa Croce in Florence or San Francesco in Pistoia; see figs. 9 and 13). Chapels were added, removed, and added again as patrons founded new altars and old families died out; sometimes corridors were erected to provide secure access to family chapels so that the choir would not be disturbed (San Francesco a Folloni, fig. 49). In other instances, there were successive additions to an original, smaller core, as at the Franciscan churches of Salzwedel and Oxford (figs. 50 and 51). Sometimes an older building was wrapped with a new exterior, as in the late example of San Francesco in Rimini (fig. 52). Friars used a combination of all these possibilities, simultaneously or in succession: their architecture had an amoeba-like mobility that responded to requests by donors for altars and chapels as well as to broader changes in social, economic, and spiritual circumstances. The architecture of the new orders was by definition work in progress molded to their changing institutional character (for example, the clericalization of the Friars Minor) and the conventualization of their settlements.

The challenge of finding space in urban centers stimulated ingenious and inventive approaches to construction. Pressure to acquire property and buildings rivaled other community needs such as food and clothing: these competing demands were particularly challenging for large convents with a hundred friars or more. In view of these multiple and sometimes conflicting concerns, friars evolved pragmatic strategies of adaptation, modifying older buildings to their requirements, or adding to them in a series of progressive steps as property and funds became available. This chapter identifies a series of building strategies that conceived of construction as an ongoing enterprise – reusing spaces, walls, and materials whenever possible.

Whether new or old, mendicant building projects were thus protracted and episodic. Extensions were tacked on to original cores over decades, even centuries. Large new churches, such as Santa Maria Gloriosa dei Frari in Venice, extended only slowly to occupy a site that expanded as land was acquired through purchases or gifts. The nave of the Frari was constructed as donors gave one column at a time, and this process gradually erased all

48   Milan, Sant'Eustorgio, view from above, from Google Earth. Image copyright 2014 DigitalGlobe.

traces of the earlier and smaller structures on the location. Throughout this process mendicant building sites were "eternal," as seen in the description of the constant hammering
that persecuted the friar at Santa Croce (Chapter One). Yet within the conceptual frame
of long-term ongoing construction, certain consistent approaches to enlarging or rebuilding emerge. In some cases projects were designed to respond to the straightforward need
for a larger choir or nave; in others, they reflected the specific requests from patrons or
confraternities for space to accommodate burials and dedicated chapels. These motivating
factors were often interconnected, however, and the latter often helped to finance (and
even promote) the former. In other words, works on different parts of a convent could be

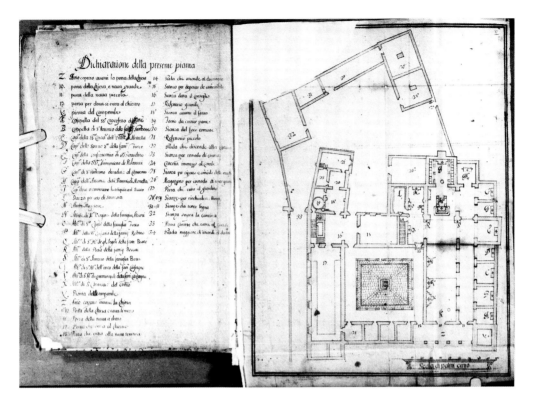

49   San Francesco a Folloni, the plan of 1720, after Strazzullo, 2000, p. 26.

linked through fungible income sources. It is also reasonable to imagine that important additions to a mendicant church (the choir, the nave) could often be built speculatively, projected on hoped-for subsidies from wealthy patrons who desired a family chapel or altar within the nave or chancel; a specific instance of this practice would be the donations made prior to the reconstruction of Santa Croce in Florence.

The building strategies discussed here, however, did not originate with the mendicant orders; they were not infrequent in medieval building practice more generally.[1] But because friars were uniquely dependent upon episodic funding sources for construction, they were particularly consistent in their utilization of these approaches for building, which can be considered a defining characteristic of mendicant architecture (even though completion and/or restoration eventually obliterated or concealed traces of this episodic process). This chapter concludes with some general hypotheses about planning and building one of the most important and monumental churches of the orders in the last years of the thirteenth century.

Redefining the Perimeter

Over the course of the thirteenth century, and especially in the decades after c. 1260, lateral chapels were frequently added to the side flanks of churches.[2] In existing buildings, the flat wall surfaces between the bay divisions were cut away, and where present, the buttresses

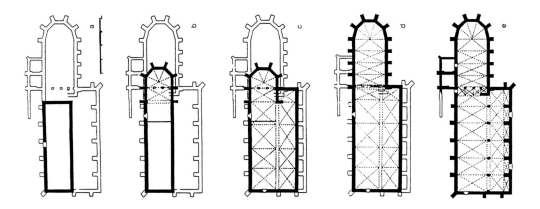

50   Salzwedel, the Franciscan church, reconstruction of building phases, after Leineweber, 1992, p. 74.

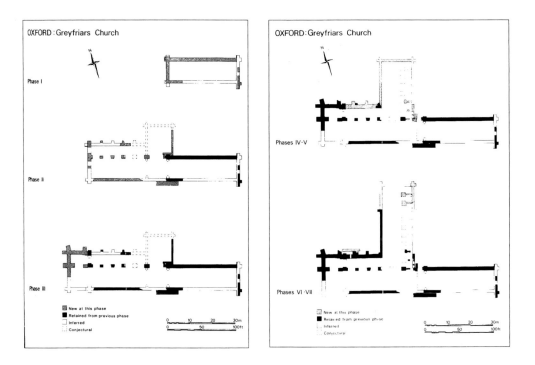

51   Oxford, Greyfriars, archaeological plan after Hassall, Hapin, and Mellor, 1989, p. 183.

behind the wall responds acquired a new role in dividing the projecting chapels. These buttresses were frequently extended outwards to create the chapel's deeper volume. Vault structures on the interior could thus be maintained intact even though the intermediate walls were dismantled. In this process, of course, original windows were obliterated along with the external wall, and new windows were placed on the new external wall. In effect, a new box was erected against the exterior of the church.

52   Rimini, San Francesco (Tempio Malatestiano), from Google Earth. Image copyright 2014 Digital Globe.

The practice was to become common in both large and small churches of the late Middle Ages, mendicant or not; for example, chapels were added to the naves of many French cathedrals, as at Paris, Amiens, Noyon, and Laon. The spread of this phenomenon in late thirteenth- and fourteenth-century church architecture might provoke the question of whether the mendicants with their efficacious cultivation of lay patrons stimulated the broader practice. It seems likely that friars, who had their fingers on the pulse of social change, were indeed in the avant-garde in this matter, especially as significant parts of their buildings were erected in direct response to exchanges with patrons and donors.

The concept of walls as malleable or negotiable surfaces may have inspired new thinking about the entire perimeter of a church, a phenomenon stimulated by lay and clerical pressure for family chapels and secondary altars. Indeed, a wall could be negotiated over and over, as lay families died out and new patrons offered funding for an updated, or larger chapel. In the 1740 plan of San Francesco a Folloni, for example (see fig. 49), the corridor along the south flank of the nave providing access to a major confraternity chapel added to the south transept in 1482, probably replaced an original row of lateral chapels. To this corridor a second row of chapels was later added in the sixteenth century.

53   Milan, Sant'Eustorgio, the east flanks of the nave, south side.

Sant'Eustorgio in Milan is an important example of successive interventions that started at an early date, as noted previously. Here the Dominicans retained the Romanesque nave but in a series of progressive actions peeled away the exterior walls on both flanks of the church. After the reconstruction of the apse and the insertion of a transept on the south side, the friars added a series of matching chapels in the eastern bays (see figs. 37, 38, and 48); when the nave was later extended to the west, the new span of wall on the south side of the church received three additional lateral chapels (fig. 53). In the process, the flanking aisle was modified with the addition of rib vaults. The core of the Romanesque church was preserved within a completely reconfigured exterior envelope. Although this chronology has not been facilitated by the vague descriptions of Fiamma in the fourteenth century, it seems evident that the extension of the church to the west, together with the western chapels, was subsequent to those on the east, and the south aisle received its rib vaults at the time that the westernmost chapels were inserted.[3] No doubt the growing importance of the cult of Peter of Verona, located between the choir and the western bays of the nave, was part of the reason for the western extension. The north flank of the nave was also reconstructed with a series of shallow chapels that were added during the construction of the cloister. These chapels were part of the continued reconfiguration of the church around the tomb with the construction of an elaborate iron screen erected in 1253.[4] At Sant'Eustorgio in Milan, as at San Domenico in Bologna, the prominent burial of an important saint of the order added what we might call "sacred value" to the lay, or exterior, church and would later enhance the authority of the convent in matters such as the Inquisition.

Alberti's redesign of the Franciscan church of Rimini in 1450 (the Tempio Malatestiano) reflects an analogous approach, one that was, however, systematically applied from the

54 Padua, the Eremitani (Augustinian friars), exterior. With kind permission of Stefano Zaggia.

outside in (see fig. 52). Here the older structure was encased with a new classical carapace that consisted of round-arched niches open to the exterior, each of which contained a cenotaph. Alberti folded the concept of the private family chapel "inside out" to create a monumentalizing architectural motif that faced outwards rather than inwards to emphasize the ducal tombs. The Gothic building was thus hidden from view and its exterior updated on radical Renaissance principles – in this example the exterior was entirely co-opted and turned into a memorial to its magnificent patron, Sigismondo Malatesta. For all its modernity, however, Alberti may have been inspired by the rebuilt west end of the church of the Eremitani in Padua, where the nave was elongated by a structure characterized by deep external burial niches (fig. 54).

Treating walls as malleable surfaces is typical of mendicant architecture everywhere in Europe. The extension of churches is particularly true in cases of choirs north of the Alps. The destroyed church of San Francesco Grande in Milan, primarily known from a sixteenth-century plan from the Raccolta Bianconi (see fig. 45), offers an Italian example of this type of procedure. On the basis of this plan and Romanini's analysis[5] it can be supposed that the original core of the early Christian church of San Nabore may first have

55   Florence, Santa Maria Novella, the Chiostro de' Morti.

existed at the eastern corner of the cloister, perhaps extended by the Franciscans with a flat-ended (Cistercian) type of chevet. They may also have absorbed an atrium to the west to create the full length of the nave. To this structure were added a cloister to the north and the easternmost nave chapels on the south. The church was radically expanded again in the sixteenth century when it was doubled in length and ambitious polygonal chapels added to its flanks.

Another common mendicant building strategy was the construction of a low precinct wall around the area projected for the nave. Evidence for such a building process may be visible at San Francesco in Pisa, where a foundation of large ashlar blocks marks out the entire periphery of the church (see fig. 46). In the first phase of construction in the 1260s only the eastern chapels and transept seem initially to have been brought to their full height. At Santa Maria Novella in Florence, the low precinct walls that include tomb niches still visible on the exterior were eventually extended upwards to create the nave (fig. 55).[6] The internal piers erected inside the main vessel could have been inserted within the perimeter box at a later point, only then permitting the friars to complete and vault the nave.[7]

There are many examples of choirs with their vaults brought to completion while the naves continued as simple roofed halls undifferentiated by aisles. The latter were often added at a later date (both the Franciscan and Dominican churches in Chelmno, Poland, seem to be examples of this practice). In these instances the outer walls were erected as a box around the projected nave. Outer walls could have been encrusted with the systematic insertion of tomb niches, or *avelli*, from the outset, and the interiors, enclosed as a precinct, were also available for burials. San Domenico in Prato may be an example of the former approach (the tombs once placed against the facade have been removed). Incorporating the tombs of donors into the walls was, in effect, a visual attestation of their commitment to the institution: their memorials, prominently displayed to the public, literally supported the walls of the church (fig. 56). An interesting reflection of this practice can be seen in the ruined interior of the Dominican church at Roscommon, Ireland (fig. 57).

Construction of the nave in successive phases, the first of which simply set out the walls and the second of which added piers to create a nave and aisles, may have been a practice especially prevalent north of the Alps, where colder and wetter climates made outdoor preaching less practical. An interesting and late reflection of this approach to building church space would be the sixteenth-century open-air churches of Mexico, where a roof or covering became entirely superfluous.[8] Here what had been a process of sequential additions or modifications as practiced in Europe was interrupted *in medias res* by leaving the enclosed space of the nave open to the sky.

Lay and clerical pressure for secondary altars and private family chapels thus inspired new attitudes toward the perimeter walls, which took on importance as visible sites of family commemoration. External surfaces (the walls at aisle level) were now perceived as permeable: they could be penetrated and reconfigured, and as we have seen this sometimes occurred repeatedly as families died out and new potential patrons offered funds for an updated or reconstructed chapel.

At the same time that the external walls and lateral spaces were activated by lay patrons, spatial zoning of church interiors also became more complex, and the choir screen itself was transformed into a site for private altars and burials, becoming a tender and charged barrier between the secular and the more reserved zones of a church. The interior pulpits on the choir screen operated as a dynamic force in the spiritual intersection between the inner church (the choir) and the outer church (the nave for the lay community), as has recently been demonstrated by Donal Cooper.[9] These dynamics were affirmed in the decorative programs that embellished these spaces. The monumental crucifixes suspended on axis with the altar over choir screens are examples of painted decoration as a transactional medium: the levitating image of the bleeding Christ on the cross served as a powerful visual connector for the laity to the Eucharistic sacrifice at the (invisible, or partially visible) main altar of the choir.

Addition by Subtraction

In Italy mendicant communities created large interior volumes from early Christian basilicas by removing the interior supports. As noted, San Lorenzo in Naples (see figs. 10 and 41) and San Fermo in Verona (fig. 58) are examples of this approach. In both the interior space was at some point also extended to the west either by the absorption of an atrium (San Fermo) or by annexing a narthex, a privately held garden, and (possibly) part of the old market (San Lorenzo in Naples).[10] In each case, these annexations permitted the crea-

56   Prato, San Domenico, exterior flank of the church with avelli, north side. With kind permission of Alick McLean.

57   Roscommon, Ireland. With kind permission of Thomas Coomans.

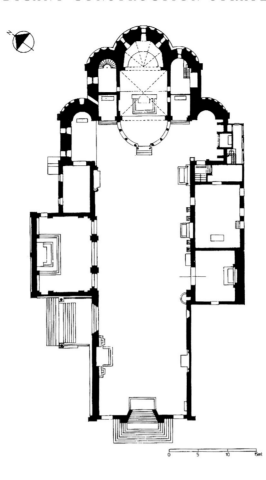

58 San Fermo, Verona, plan of the interior, after Suitner Nicolini, 1991, p. 583.

tion of a large single-nave church within, or adjacent to, a densely inhabited urban fabric where the acquisition of new terrain was probably difficult or impossible. At both churches the addition of a lateral portal provided public access to the "external" church (the laity's nave) from the street on the north flank.

Expansion of a church into an atrium or narthex presented few difficulties because the space was already part of the church complex. A private house or garden or a public piazza was different, however, and would have required special arrangements. In Naples this involved royal intervention to expropriate the garden and some houses owned by Andreas Cannutus de Napoli in order to complete the extension; the royal protonotary, Bartolomeo di Capua, paid for much of the reconstruction, including the new western portal and upper extension to the western tower, decorated with his coat of arms.[11] This project was integral to the reconfiguration of the interior space into a single united volume; sixteenth-century sources describe the di Capua coat of arms as everywhere in the church.[12] The reconstruction of the nave and transept of San Lorenzo, which involved considerable change to the urban fabric around the convent, thus entailed negotiations with and support from the highest authorities in the kingdom, a process in some respects analogous to the creation of "preaching piazzas" by communes as in Florence (discussed in the following chapters).

Voiding interior spatial divisions was a remarkably efficient way to create single unified volumes from more traditionally configured church interiors with naves and aisles. The process permitted friars to maintain the walls of the exterior envelope while renegotiating interior volumes, just as elsewhere they had reconfigured external surfaces. The resulting large and open spaces were ideal for the accretion of activities and monuments within mendicant church interiors, activities that included not only preaching but also tomb monuments, altars, votive paintings, and other forms of pious and family memorials. These practices also attest to the high value of real estate and reflect the complex relations of mendicant houses with their neighbors in tightly packed cities. We might note that the example of San Lorenzo, which invaded a piazza and appropriated a garden (not to mention the earlier closing of the narrow *vicolo* to the east when the choir was expanded), reflects the importance of powerful royal or noble patrons, just as elsewhere it might involve the support of a communal government.

Ninety-Degree Rotation

There are several examples of churches in which the primary axis was rotated by ninety degrees, transforming what had been a nave into a transept at right angles to a new structure. Santa Maria Novella in Florence and Santa Maria in Aracoeli in Rome are conspicuous examples of this practice. This approach to enlarging a church reflected a strategic decision to provide a nave appropriate for public functions while maintaining a choir in roughly its original location. At Santa Maria Novella the original small church had the main altar to the west while the portals faced the city to the east. The construction of the new nave at a ninety-degree angle shifted the alignment so that the altar is to the north and the façade faces south (fig. 59). The reorientation of the church permitted the Dominicans not only to greatly expand the dimensions of the church, but also to face what was to become the vast open expanse of the new piazza in front, a piazza designated by the commune in 1287 for public preaching in perpetuity. The earlier piazza, created some forty years previously east of the former church, probably continued to provide access to the basilica until the later construction of private chapels in that area. Santa Maria Novella thus represents a fully developed example of the spatial formula created at an early date by the Dominicans: the sequence of the inner church (the choir), the outer church (the nave), and the exterior space for public preaching, were all aligned as a series of sequential volumes. It is tempting to suppose that from the outset the reconstruction of Santa Maria Novella beginning in 1279 was to some extent envisioned as similar to those aligned spaces that were developed at San Domenico in Bologna. What had perhaps begun at Bologna as an ad hoc arrangement to promote the cult of Dominic and engage in external preaching developed into the systematic spaces visible at Santa Maria Novella.

At Santa Maria in Aracoeli, the old church became the transept of the new building, a project financed at least in part by bequests for private burial chapels.[13] A will executed in 1296, while the new church would have been under construction, suggests some aspects of how requests for burials could aid in the more general process of construction. The merchant Eduardo di Pietro Sassone, who lived in the San Marco quarter, offered the com-

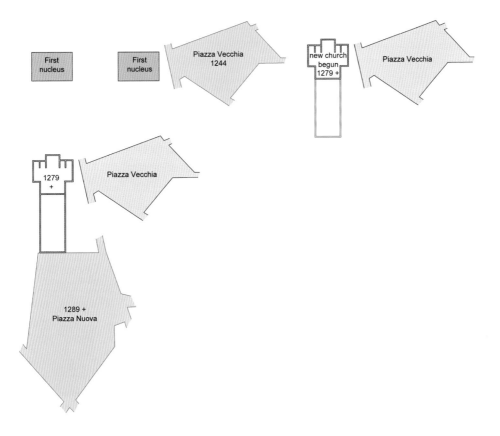

59   Florence, Sta. Maria Novella and its two Piazzas. Schematic and hypothetical reconstruction of major phases (Cosimo Monteleone).

munity of friars at Aracoeli 15 florins for the fabric, in addition to 100 florins for the construction and endowment of a chapel, on the condition that the friars identify a location in their church for its construction.[14] If the friars did not build the chapel, they would receive neither the 100 nor the 15 florins (on this type of arrangement more generally, see Chapter Five).

The rotation of a church axis was by no means exclusive to the friars. Beginning in 1294 Naples rebuilt its cathedral at right angles to the old basilica of Santa Restituta, absorbing the atrium and orienting the main altar toward the east.[15] The old church of Santa Restituta was transformed into a large chapel on the north side after c. 1310. The most famous example of such practice is the cathedral of Siena, where a vast new nave undertaken early in the fourteenth century was (conspicuously) abandoned by the middle of the century.

Raising the Roof

The exteriors of mendicant buildings often contain traces of successive interventions in the upper walls that reveal the progressive transformation of earlier and smaller churches into

more monumental structures. A striking example is San Francesco in Siena, enlarged beginning in 1326 by raising the walls to a greater height and extending the church to the west. Traces of this process and the modified windows can still be seen on the south flank of the nave facing the cloister (fig. 60). In this approach the peripheral walls are preserved and simply extended upwards to create a taller building. An analogous process, also in Siena, is visible on the facade of Santa Maria dei Servi (fig. 61). San Francesco at San Miniato also reveals the dimensions of the previous building in its facade. The ghostly traces of rooflines and gables often permit an schematic reconstruction of the original church.

In these types of extensions, the wall adjoining the cloister was often preserved, as change on this side would have disrupted the living quarters and internal rhythms of the community. Cloisters once erected often tend to fix the angle between the projecting transept and the nave. Obviously, extensions to the other sides of a church were also often constrained by buildings, streets, topographical features (steep changes in elevation, as in Siena), and piazzas. The enlargement of a church was therefore frequently controlled by pre-existing elements that were either internal to the community (cloister, sacristy, chapter house, and dormitory, often located on the south) or external, such as privately held properties, squares, markets, and city streets. The intercession of powerful patrons and the community's procurator (legal representative) in the acquisition of new properties for expansion would have been a common feature of conventual life.

Yet again, these types of structural expansions were not unique to the new orders. Indeed, many examples of similar approaches to reconstruction come readily to mind:

OPPOSITE PAGE 60 Siena, San Francesco, right flank of the church.

LEFT 61 Siena, Santa Maria dei Servi, facade. With kind permission of Alexandra Dodson.

William of Sens did much the same at Canterbury after the fire of 1174 when he preserved the lower walls of the choir and the entire substructure of Anselm's crypt and with great ingenuity absorbed the tribune windows of Anselm's choir into the aisles. The reuse of older walls and foundations expedited the reconstruction of Saint-Denis beginning in 1231, as it did also at Chartres after the fire of 1194. Building on top of lower walls and foundations not only accelerated the reconstruction process, but also saved time, materials, and money. It also meant that the footprint occupied by a structure could be preserved, minimizing disruption to other adjacent spaces.

Hall churches in central and northern Europe permitted another kind of inventive expansion upwards, one with perhaps fewer practical advantages but certainly strong aesthetic ones. There are a number of structures in Poland and Germany where aisle vaults were removed and the external walls extended upward in order to create a hall church out of what had initially been a basilica (a tall nave flanked by lower aisles). This can be seen, for example, in the cathedral of Tolún and in Saint Mary's at Gdansk, although in the latter case the project also entailed redefining the perimeter by adding wider exterior walls with shallow lateral chapels. At Saint Mary's, the expansion of the church created space for the private chapels of wealthy burghers, an important source of funding for the project, but the upwards extension of the cathedral of Tolún seems to have been driven by the desire for increased verticality. It may not be a coincidence that both churches are built in brick in important cities of the Hanseatic League: collective identity and civic pride may have been at stake in remodeling, and great wealth may have facilitated its execution.

Building materials were a precious commodity and a major expense in all large-scale projects; they were particularly important for religious communities that depended upon the largesse of patrons. The commune of Siena encouraged the friars to expand their churches by contributing materials to the Carmelites, Franciscans, Augustinians, and Servites, starting in 1262. Different quanitites of bricks were allotted annually to the various mendicant communities: 10,000 for the Carmelites, 50,000 for the Augustinian hermits, 25,000 for the Franciscans, and 50,000 for the Servites.[16]

Within the new orders patterns of funding imposed a need for the reuse of materials and structures. There may also, however, have been an ideological component that emphasized the preservation of and continuity with older or original churches. Mendicant building practice was therefore inventive and resourceful, especially in the decades up to about 1290. The mendicant approach to architecture might best be described by words that are rarely applied to buildings: elastic, organic, and flexible. A phenomenon that may have started as the practical and ideological revitalization of the church by using old buildings was put under pressure by the episodic interventions of lay patrons through bequests in wills and last testaments. This social phenomenon, motivated by the desire for salvation and remembrance, inspired new attitudes toward the perimeter walls, which were increasingly perceived as permeable surfaces that could be penetrated and reconfigured. On occasion the renegotiation of the perimeter occurred over and over, as families died out and new potential patrons offered funds for an updated or recycled chapel – as we have seen at San Francesco a Folloni and Sant'Eustorgio in Milan.

Documents confirm the long-term state of incompletion of mendicant churches and convents. At Pistoia the will of Lanfranco del fu Giusto, preparing himself for a trip to the Holy Land, left a bequest in his will "pro opere ecclesie Sancte Crucis que fit pro fratribus minoribus."[17] Yet later in the same will the donor also left six lire for the candles before the main altar of the church:[18] it would appear that construction continued while services were taking place. The document confirms a situation analogous to what has been observed above: the friars' choir, with its altar, was complete and in use, but work continued on other parts of the building, for the completion of which the first donation was directed. This is the situation we see expressed in different ways in reconstruction images (see figs. 12 and 13).

Endemic incompletion had its uses. It evoked poverty and a lack of cash. It could be part of a rhetorical argument in a plea for funds, as we shall see in the following chapters. But there is this consideration: once churches *were* completed – as at the Frari and Santi Giovanni e Paolo in Venice in the fifteenth century (after multiple changes and additions that were in some measure in dialogue or competition with each other) – the long, slow, episodic process of construction was forgotten. As modern viewers we perceive (and study) the looming end products of completed structures; scholars have tended to think of building campaigns as an organized series of interventions rather than as part of an achingly slow, ongoing, interrupted work. Our modern perception of mendicant architecture sees it as consisting of "projects"; rather it should be seen as belonging to a long grey zone of "process."[19]

Thinking about mendicant building as "process" reconfigures in some important ways how we may understand medieval construction, and especially that of the new urban orders. Construction phases may be far more complex, contested, protracted, and discontinuous than previously considered. An intellectual frame that looks at medieval building practice as a result of the early modern ideal of design and proportion may often misrepresent the medieval, and especially mendicant worksite.[20] With mendicant buildings we are often confronted not with building campaigns as such, but rather with building as an ongoing, elastic enterprise. Building campaigns as a notion presuppose an overall plan and essential ideal homogeneity of structure, in sharp contrast with a building culture that was dominated by interruption and disjunction. Would it be possible to suggest that our understanding of medieval building process was led astray by the architects of the early modern period, and especially Alberti?

It also appears that breathing space was often essential to construction: there is evidence of phased approaches that were integrated into the planning process, as at San Francesco in Pistoia or, indeed, Santa Croce in Florence. There may have been a culture of incompletion,[21] or, at least, a willingness to construct and think about buildings as an ad hoc enterprise in dialogue with the urban context as well as with the exigencies of funding. For friars, a visibly incomplete church was perhaps useful as a rhetorical and ideological demonstration of apostolic poverty.

The choir screen often delimited completed areas (usually the choir for the residential community) from the open, unfinished volume projected for the nave. The latter could serve multiple functions while awaiting completion (even as a cemetery), or could continue as the location of a smaller, earlier church which might remain partially intact for some time, as at Santa Croce in Florence (see fig. 12) or San Francesco in Pistoia (see fig. 13).

A view of mendicant building practice as one in which completion was not an immediate and urgent goal stimulates reflections on the traditional art-historical enterprise of dating buildings through documents such as wills. These were often contested. In addition, because the orders themselves often delayed the execution of works funded through a bequest, donors came to insist that donations would be made only if construction took place within a certain number of years, usually five or ten. Dating mendicant buildings on the basis of legacies, especially wills, is therefore unreliable, and the austerity of these buildings, in particular the frequent absence of decorative detailing (such as moldings or capitals that can be roughly indexed through their style), exponentially increases the difficulties. If we think of the mendicant convent as in a continuous process of *becoming*, as part of an organic and additive approach to architecture, we find ourselves participating in a mental frame that understands construction as part of a flow, continuous or episodic, conditioned by any number of internal or external factors.[22] What is important to see is this: scaffolding everywhere, buildings in motion, architecture as malleable.

4

INTO THE CITY

"Un lieu d'échanges dynamique": Chiffoleau's description of a medieval parish could be applied to entire thirteenth-century cities as well.[1] Royal and imperial authorities, civic governments, religious institutions and associations – not to mention neighborhoods and political factions – were in rapid change, and the shifting equilibrium was different in each place. The ubiquitous action of friars came to form a systemic part of Innocent III's effort to reclaim the hegemony of the church in the face of growing heretical movements and the development of autonomous communal governments. And yet in supporting thriving mendicant establishments, the papacy undermined some aspects of traditional ecclesiastical authority as represented through the system of parishes, bishops, and cathedrals.

In Italy, communes seeking to establish their institutional identity after the Peace of Constance of 1183 created new types of urban spaces that combined monumental administrative buildings (*palazzi del comune*) with open spaces (piazzas) for meetings and commerce.[2] Communes often supported the new mendicant orders because they brought honor and glory to a city and could offer an alternative to parish priests who frequently were not adequately trained for the complexities of modern life. At the same time that cities (usually) encouraged the new orders, however, they also reinforced the traditional cults of local saints to validate regional and institutional identity.[3] Between the old and new civic and religious institutions there emerged a constantly changing equilibrium of collaboration, exchange, and rivalry that manifested itself differently in each place. A city absorbed (and sometimes did not) the new religious orders in its own way and for its own (often fluctuating) spiritual or political ends.[4] The established secular clergy, especially cathedral and parochial priests, were profoundly involved in all these processes, sometimes as enthusiastic collaborators and sometimes as spectators; by the mid-thirteenth century, however, many of the secular clergy had become entrenched enemies of the friars. In Italy, especially after the pro-papal triumph of Charles of Anjou in 1266 and the ensuing polarization between Guelph and Ghibelline factions, the pro-imperial communes in some cities were associated, or even considered synonymous, with heresy and anti-papal (Ghibelline) sympathies, and friars as the agents of orthodoxy (and also later as inquisitors) came to play an active role in their suppression. Yet in spite of the wide range of variation and possibilities, certain common

OPPOSITE PAGE 62   *Saint Bernardino of Siena preaching in front of the church of San Francesco* (detail). Opera della Metropolitana, Siena, Aut. N. 554/2013.

elements emerge. The mendicant movement was profoundly local and profoundly international at the same time.

This chapter considers issues related to the friars and the spaces of urban life, moving from questions of their physical activity and presence within the city (their occupation of open and public civic space) to their "invasion" of domestic and private spaces (the home). I will use examples from literature to help tell this story because much of what I describe has to do with ephemeral social action: action, however, that was to have an impact on buildings, as I shall demonstrate.[5] This chapter therefore describes activities that went in two opposite directions: from the convent into the city's public and private spaces and, conversely, from the city into the convent. And this two-way traffic applied not only to the living but also to the dead.

Friars represented a concerted activation of private and public space in the service of religious orthodoxy (figs. 62 and 63). Some of their practices such as religious poverty and visiting homes seem close to those of heretical groups. Other activities such as the Inquisition were largely new. The important point is that the friars aimed at a capillary presence in the city: engaging the laity not only in the open – in public squares – but also in the enclosed and private environment of domestic space. To aid in this purpose mendicant convents were places of preparation and renewal, for teaching and training in order to engage with the world outside. It should be noted, however, that a broad variety of encounters with lay people also took place in the friars' churches and cloisters.

The practice of visiting the homes of laymen and women might appear to have little to do with architecture. But this practice, which included the presence of friars at the bedsides of the ill and dying, created intimate bonds between friars and the lay public. Visiting the homes of the ill and dying was important in the formulation of the lists of pious legacies in wills, encouraging donations to fund the construction of convents. It was also important for questing for generic support, but the practice scandalized some contemporary secular clergy and was emphasized as improper by William of Saint-Amour. It was also the inspiration for numerous ribald tales by Boccaccio, Chaucer, and others. Indeed, it is from literature that we have the best evidence for this practice in action.

In northern Italy cities underwent rapid change as a consequence of the shift in power after the Peace of Constance. Charles of Anjou's defeat of the Ghibellines in the battle of Benevento in 1266, a victory reaffirmed in the battle of Tagliacozzo of 1268 and the execution of Conradin, effectively sealed the fate of the empire, leaving some pro-imperial cities adrift or within volatile and sometimes fragile coalitions and the Guelphs with renewed strength. Irrespective of political alliances, however, after 1183 communal palaces began to be erected at the highly visible intersections of major arteries (Bologna) and right in the center of a city (Piacenza). Space for these new civic interventions entailed the expropriation of lots and the demolition of houses or shops. In these major urban interventions of the late twelfth and early thirteenth centuries, the historical seat of religious authority, the cathedral, sometimes remained on the margins, as at Siena. At times the cathedral was on a very distant edge, as in Piacenza or Venice.[6] Although Miller has pointed out that the construction of new walls in the twelfth century often repositioned cathedrals at the center of enclosed urban space (for example, Florence),[7] by c. 1230 this process was often undermined by the installation of communal palaces adjacent to market areas. On occasion the

63   Florence, Santa Maria Novella, the west facade. Photograph courtesy Scott Gilchrist/Archivision Inc.

centralization of the cathedral was further diminished by the magnetic and centrifugal forces of friaries on the edges of urban agglomerations (Florence again). By the middle of the thirteenth century new friaries attracted vast numbers of lay devotees and inspired the foundation of affiliated confraternities. Large, and sometimes multiple, piazzas were specifically constructed for preaching and burial: one of the earliest examples is the eastern piazza at Santa Maria Novella (see figs. 59 and 70) of 1244, where associations of lay supporters inspired by the preaching of Peter of Verona (later Peter Martyr) gathered to hear his sermons.[8]

Friaries were often supported by communal governments. At Siena, the dispersion of friaries on the ridges around the city surrounded the center with a constellation of sacred sites in which the preaching and prayer of mendicant friars created a sanitizing barrier between country and city, open road and urban street. Here, as noted in the previous chapter, the commune provided bricks for the construction of many of these institutions. In numerous cities, friaries located in peripheral areas provided charity and parochial services to new and squalid suburbs, as at Santa Croce in Florence.

It is important to this narrative to recall that since the eleventh century, medieval cities – especially those in areas contiguous to the Mediterranean basin or associated with the wool trade and Hanseatic League in the north – were growing at a vertiginous pace. By around 1300 populations were at levels not to be seen again for 600 years: estimates suggest that inhabitants of Florence numbered about 120,000, those of Siena about 52,000, Pisa 40,000, and Arezzo 20,000.[9] New walls were built to accommodate the swelling cities, and the vast dimensions of these enclosures anticipated a continued growth of population.

The range and variety of city dwellers had expanded exponentially as the result of increased immigration, trade, and travel. Differences between rich and poor became more visible.[10] In north Italian cities, much of the growth came from immigrants from the countryside, attracted by the prospect of employment and wealth in the new and flourishing trades. Whatever their hopes, however, immigrant workers often found themselves living in considerable squalor in the least desirable parts of town – on the swampy east side of Florence, for example. On the other hand, the middle-class population of foreign traders and merchants, especially in port cities, were often obliged to live within separate and often enclosed zones on the model of the Islamic *funduk*; the best known example of these to survive is perhaps the Fondaco dei Tedeschi in Venice. The foundation of urban churches and convents often needs to be understood in relation to these social and economic strata, and the new populations for whom new religious centers were created were frequently on the margins of urban centers in industrial zones or adjacent to markets.

Property became more valuable with population growth; the foundation of new convents therefore entailed either a donation of property or the transfer of an abandoned or little-used church or religious community.[11] On occasion lots and houses were expropriated to make space for convents. Sometimes this was a political negotiation, as appears to have been the case in Piacenza, where a new centrally located Franciscan convent was built on properties acquired from the Ghibelline Ubertino Landi. It was therefore no small matter to make way for the convents of the friars in crowded cities. In addition, at least in Italy, land was also needed for the piazzas and open squares in which friars preached. The long process of surveying and expropriating houses after 1289 for the creation of the Piazza Nuova at Santa Maria Novella is a case in point.[12]

The revival of trade, the growth of manufacturing, and the press for supplies and materials produced in workshops, such as leather and cloth, changed the nature of work toward an industrial model, a phenomenon that can still be seen in the buildings of the Arsenale in Venice. With trade and industry, ideas spread easily from place to place. In workshops large and small these new trends and concepts were discussed and debated, and in the densely packed and often squalid neighborhoods of expanding cities, where the poor struggled for both physical and spiritual solace, messages that emphasized the virtue of poverty from preachers inspired by the New Testament had special and intense appeal.[13]

The mendicant orders thus emerged, and responded to, a period of intense change in medieval cities, which over the course of the twelfth and early thirteenth centuries had become volatile and multi-vocal communities.[14] Meanwhile, bishops in their palatial residences and in magnificent cathedrals represented a form of ecclesiastical and aristocratic authority that in some respects had been left behind by the rapid change and growth of the world around them (at the same time that they benefited exponentially from the increase in income brought in by tolls and taxes on travel and trade). In parishes, priests were often illiterate and incapable of addressing the new types of questions posed by the rapidly changed economic and social fabric.[15] And the regular clergy – mainly monks in rural monasteries whose lives were (in principle) devoted to prayer and penitence – were for the most part removed and distant from urban environments; their prayers in any event were primarily for the souls of their benefactors, mostly their aristocratic patrons. Who within the church then, was going to speak to and for the people in the shops, streets, mills, and factories? And who within the church was competent to address the meaning of issues such as poverty, profit, property, and commerce?

New types of preachers and clergy emerged in response to these questions. Heretical groups that emphasized poverty, such as the Umiliati, Waldesians, and Cathars, had an immediate and profound appeal in part because they were tightly knitted to the communities of workers and the poor.[16] It was clear to Innocent III that the traditional clergy, whether parochial or monastic, was not prepared to meet the new challenges of cities, especially in matters of orthodoxy and religious conformity. Although the Fourth Lateran Council of 1215 had recognized the problem, it was not adequately addressed within the existing structures of the church or the statutes of the Council. Thanks to Innocent III's creative intuition, one of the heretical groups, the Umiliati, which was closely connected to cloth production, was partially integrated within the church: its more literate members received papal permission to preach on non-doctrinal matters in the streets and sometimes, with the consent of the local prelate, even in parochial churches.

In Diego of Osma, in Dominic, and, with his more eccentric voice, in Francis, the western church found an inspired response, one that expanded and evolved with the astonishing success of their movements. The theological training of the Dominicans, in particular, was central to the promotion of religious orthodoxy. It will be the argument of this chapter (and the book overall) that the mendicant revolution – the "invention" of an orthodox evangelism that echoed the New Testament – was to have a lasting impact on the urban fabric of cities, on buildings, and on social and spatial practice.

In many ways the methods of heretics seem to have influenced the strategies and methods of the friars, who adopted some of their social activities: debating, outdoor preaching, and visiting homes. Jordan of Saxony, second Minister General of the Preachers, describes how Diego of Osma and Dominic in their first encounters with the heretics of the Languedoc repeatedly debated them in public, and for days on end. In one episode, it was not the beauty and clarity of Dominic's rhetoric that won the contest for the Preachers but rather the miracle of his book that would not burn when the competing texts were put to the test of fire. Indeed, as Jordan of Saxony notes, the heretics suggested to Diego and Dominic that they had much to learn from heretical practices. Although Diego and

Dominic were, of course, not converted to heresy, they responded by adopting some of their methods. As Diego recommended, "use a nail to drive out a nail."[17]

The most important element that friars had in common with heretics was the dedication to poverty, however. In contrast to other clergy, who were supported by tithes, emoluments from the sacraments, and income from properties and donations, friars in the thirteenth century depended on the resources of cities. In the early decades their renunciation of traditional clerical income and their reliance upon voluntary donations and charity freed them from a network of responsibility, obligations, and property management. Their income from begging depended upon an economy based on cash and urban property, in cities this was the economy of commerce.[18]

The friars' quest in cities was also for souls. In this matter they expressed their goals with great clarity. Humbert of Romans, writing sometime between 1254 and 1263, stated that preaching was quantitatively more effective in towns because there were more people.[19] Cities were also more in need of preachers because they were more sinful, for "there are many sins there [ibi sunt plura peccata]," says Humbert. He added that cities set the pattern for the countryside:

Likewise, lesser places that are around cities adapt to the cities, rather than the other way around, and for that reason the benefit of preaching that is done in the city is channeled off into those places, rather than the other way around, and for that reason one must endeavor to produce fruit through preaching in the cities more than in other, lesser places. (Item minora loca, quae sunt circa civitates, magis conformantur civitatibus quam e converso, et ideo fructus praedicationis, qui fit in civitate magis derivatur ad ista loca quam e converso, et ideo magis conandum est facere fructum per praedicationem in civitatibus quam in aliis locis minoribus.)

The *Determinis quaestionum* attributed to Bonaventure states:

However, in towns or villages where food is plentiful, many people can band together and be sustained better, and among many people greater benefit is expected, and those by whom more of this world's necessities are supplied to us in alms ask us, all the more, to repay them with spiritual necessities. (In oppidis autem seu villis, ubi abundant victualia, plures possunt confluere et melius sustenari, et inter plures maior fructus speratur; et a quibus ministrantur nobis plura temporalia in eleemosynis, plus etiam requirunt, ut eis spiritualia rependamus.)[20]

Bonaventure went on to state that cities provide not only physical protection but also economic security because abundant goods are in circulation.[21]

The explicit focus on urban settings and preaching expressed by Bonaventure and Humbert characterizes their generalships in the 1250s and 1260s and reflects the mature phase of the mendicant movement; for the Friars Minor in particular, it articulated in formal language their institutional move to cities. This reaffirmation of the importance of the city may also have been expressed with new clarity because of the emerging competition from other new mendicant groups (Augustinians, Carmelites, and Friars of the Sack), and the broader initiative toward conventualization and institutionalization in the face of the challenges presented by the secular clergy, as discussed in Chapter Two.

The Order of Preachers focused their urban mission on the largest cities, especially those with universities.[22] Among the Friars Minor matters (as usual) were more complex: Francis himself spent long periods in rural hermitages, and his life was marked by periodic withdrawals into remote areas for spiritual renewal; the hermetic impulse was to remain a strong component within certain factions of the order.[23] Franciscans founded houses not only in large cities but also in smaller towns; in the first years and in larger agglomerations they settled in hermitages on the fringe, as at Santa Maria al Palazzo in Naples. Itinerancy was also a fundamental Franciscan concept: friars were to be "as pilgrims and strangers," which in the first years was part of their broader refusal of lodging that was not in accordance with their vows of holy poverty.[24] Itinerant Friars Minor were to preach, work, visit churches, submit themselves to the clergy, and, above all, venerate the consecrated host.[25] Le Goff and others have noted the particular Franciscan predilection for locations on roads or by gateways, at the edges of towns;[26] Franciscans were to be *in viam*, "on the road" in every sense. In cities such as Florence and Bologna, mendicant houses marked the arteries into the city. In Bologna the Friars Minor acquired land just west of the city walls at the confluence of three large arteries (fig. 64). The acquisition of this particularly strategic site was a joint effort by the community of friars, their supporters in the communal government, and the papacy. Locations by roads and gates gave access to those entering the city, for example farmers and merchants with goods for the market, but in the broader sense friars also became mediators, or points of juncture, between countryside and city.[27] This is especially striking in the locations of the mendicant houses of Bologna.

By the 1230s, however, both orders also began to acquire old churches in the center of town: in Naples in the 1234 acquisition of San Lorenzo Maggiore (Franciscan) and Sant'Angelo a Morfisa (Dominican) (fig. 65). At San Lorenzo the centrally located site adjacent to the old market square was probably a strategic gesture of an archbishop concerned with heresy.[28] In other instances, as at Cortona, the commune worked closely with Brother Elias to negotiate an exchange with the Benedictines of Sant'Egidio for a strategically located property in the city center, one close to both the Palazzo del Popolo and the Palazzo della Ragione.[29] These types of exchanges, and sometimes expropriations, were rarely smooth transactions, however: the church reassigned to the Friars Minor in Pisa was contested for several decades, so the friars settled nearby and built a small chapel.[30] They began to acquire further property around the site in successive years: 1233, 1238, 1239, and 1241. The early chapel of c. 1233 was enlarged in 1241 and again in 1259; in 1255 the friars were able to close off an adjacent street in order to enlarge the church, and in 1260 Archbishop Visconti preached in order to raise funds for its construction (as noted in the preceding chapter, the structure initiated at that date may be the transept and presbytery of the present church).[31]

Acquisition of land inside the walls often prompted hostility from local clergy and governments. At Ferentino, the Franciscans moved to a location inside the walls in 1255–6. But the town was strongly allied with the Ghibellines (whereas friars were supported by the papal or Guelph faction), and when the Franciscans began to reconstruct the old convent in 1263, their work was denounced by the bishop and clergy. Papal intervention on behalf of the friars in 1264 stimulated more violence by the local clergy and townspeople,

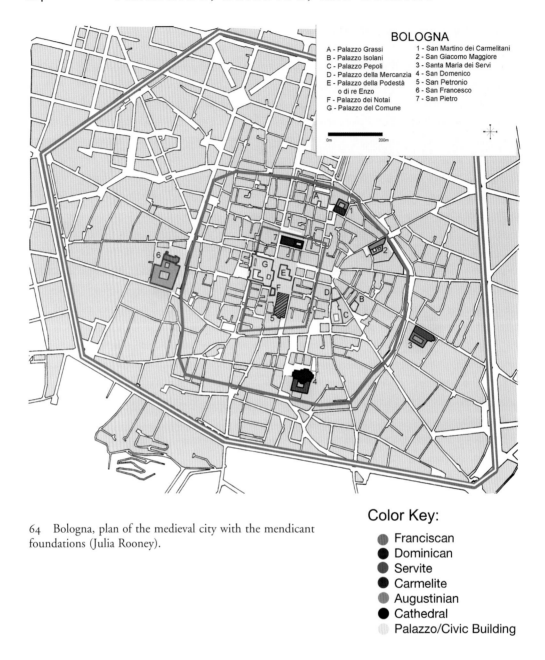

BOLOGNA

A - Palazzo Grassi
B - Palazzo Isolani
C - Palazzo Pepoli
D - Palazzo della Mercanzia
E - Palazzo della Podestà
    o di re Enzo
F - Palazzo dei Notai
G - Palazzo del Comune

1 - San Martino dei Carmelitani
2 - San Giacomo Maggiore
3 - Santa Maria dei Servi
4 - San Domenico
5 - San Petronio
6 - San Francesco
7 - San Pietro

0m   200m

64   Bologna, plan of the medieval city with the mendicant foundations (Julia Rooney).

Color Key:

● Franciscan
● Dominican
● Servite
● Carmelite
● Augustinian
● Cathedral
● Palazzo/Civic Building

who attacked and severely damaged the convent and its vineyard.[32] Further papal support and the Guelph victory of 1266 created an environment in which the friars thought they could renew work on the buildings, only to be attacked a second time by the bishop and clergy, who destroyed the roof and the new work accomplished since 1264. The attackers carried away the bell. Only the appointment of a new *podestà* loyal to the papal cause in 1267, a year after the Guelph victory at Benevento, restored order. Nevertheless, the relentless bishop excommunicated the workers at the site. A peaceful co-existence of the city with the Friars Minor came only with the intervention of Nicholas III in 1278, after more than twenty years of strife.

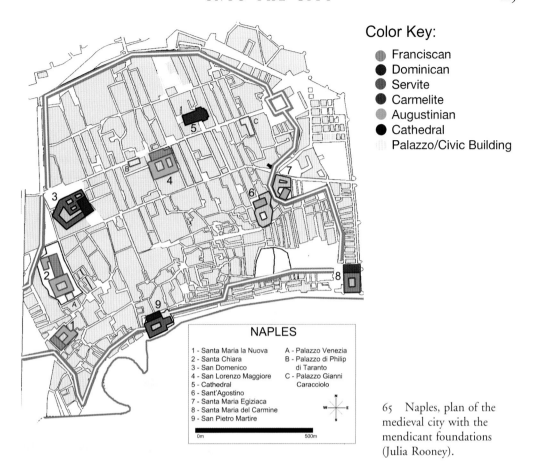

Color Key:
- Franciscan
- Dominican
- Servite
- Carmelite
- Augustinian
- Cathedral
- Palazzo/Civic Building

NAPLES

1 - Santa Maria la Nuova
2 - Santa Chiara
3 - San Domenico
4 - San Lorenzo Maggiore
5 - Cathedral
6 - Sant'Agostino
7 - Santa Maria Egiziaca
8 - Santa Maria del Carmine
9 - San Pietro Martire

A - Palazzo Venezia
B - Palazzo di Philip di Taranto
C - Palazzo Gianni Caracciolo

65 Naples, plan of the medieval city with the mendicant foundations (Julia Rooney).

Similar strains occurred elsewhere in Europe as well. At Limoges the Benedictine monastery of Saint-Martin objected to the construction of the nearby Franciscan convent. After thirty years of litigation, the mendicants moved to a new site and entirely rebuilt their complex.[33] Nevertheless, controversy continued over funerals and burials between the Benedictines and the friars.

This second Franciscan friary of Limoges is also an example of long-range strategic planning in the acquisition of land contiguous to an original conventual core. After the church was complete (1257) the friars purchased a series of adjacent properties: in 1264 a garden and open land from Jacques Gérard, in 1279 a garden and a house purchased from his heirs, and a year later the rights to the rents of the same house.[34] More nearby property was acquired in 1331, and a year later they absorbed the small road that separated the convent from this property.[35] Lands and houses were thus aggregated to the central nucleus of the convent of 1243–57 in a long-term process of purchase and exchange that also interrupted the street system. Although no documents survive that attest to what was probably a deeply politicized process of property acquisition, something similar must have occurred at San Lorenzo Maggiore in Naples. Embedded in the center of the densely inhabited city, the convent expanded in the last quarter of the thirteenth century across the small north–south street (*vicolo*) located in the area of the transept between the sixth-century basilica and the new choir constructed to the east (see fig. 41).

Urban Topography

Population density and the cost of land meant that available lots for friars were often located adjacent to, or outside, city walls (Toulouse, Paris) and sometimes between older and newer rings of fortifications (Florence). Coomans and others have demonstrated that this was also the case beyond Italy.[36] Toward the middle of the thirteenth century there was a tendency to relocate, or consolidate, multiple foundations of the same order at one site in the city center: this was a particular issue for the Friars Minor, whose communities had often originated with autochthonous groups of pious laymen and women. At Verona, for example, various Franciscan houses were merged at San Fermo in 1261; in 1249 several Roman communities joined to occupy (and displace) the formerly Benedictine convent of the Aracoeli.[37] These efforts at centralization were at times supported and promoted by communal governments (Piacenza, 1278), or by the episcopacy (San Fermo in Verona after 1249), each of which might have had an interest in reducing the numbers of independent religious communities. In other instances, communities of friars might be appropriated by a wealthy donor: Countess Marguerite of Constantinople moved the Dominicans of Ypres into the count's palace in 1268, in spite of strenuous protests from the local canons of Saint-Martin.[38] North of the Alps, Preachers in particular obtained devoted support from the nobility and as a result flourished in major cities such as London and Paris. Franciscans were particularly adept at attracting the attention of noble and royal women, as attested by foundations in London, Naples, and Barcelona.

The locations provided to friars were sometimes on sites that nobody else wanted, on the far-flung fringes of a town, or in low-lying land prone to flooding. The land given by Giovanni Badoer to the Franciscans at what is now Santa Maria Gloriosa dei Frari was swampy and low.[39] Their fellow Friars Minor in Rome complained of the "pestilent air" on their low-lying convent prior to the move to the Aracoeli.[40] In Florence, even the high foundation of Santa Croce as reconstructed after 1294 could not save the church from the disastrous floods of 1966 (fig. 66).

Providing land for the foundation of a mendicant house could be useful for expanding a city in a certain direction, stabilizing local communities (possibly the case with Santa Croce in Florence), or neutralizing (sanitizing) politically problematic areas. The last may have been the case in Prato, where in 1228 the Friars Minor were provided with land next to Frederick II's castle and former Ghibelline stronghold, "prope castrum Prati."[41] Although our knowledge of heretical communities is fragmentary, in some instances bishops such as Archbishop Pietro di Sorrento of Naples deliberately founded or installed mendicant communities in areas suspect for heresy: he fostered the arrival of the Preachers in 1231 and a new community of Franciscans in 1234. In Naples an additional factor in the archbishop's efforts may have been the creation of centers for theological study to counter Frederick II's University of Naples.

Locations adjacent to, or bridging, walls were part of the aggressive urban expansion in the thirteenth century, and these included the rapidly growing suburban or semi-suburban zones crowded with immigrant populations. Peripheral and newly populated locations may also have solved the problem of overlapping authority with local priests, as in these areas there was rarely an existing network of parishes. In 1246 the Preachers were

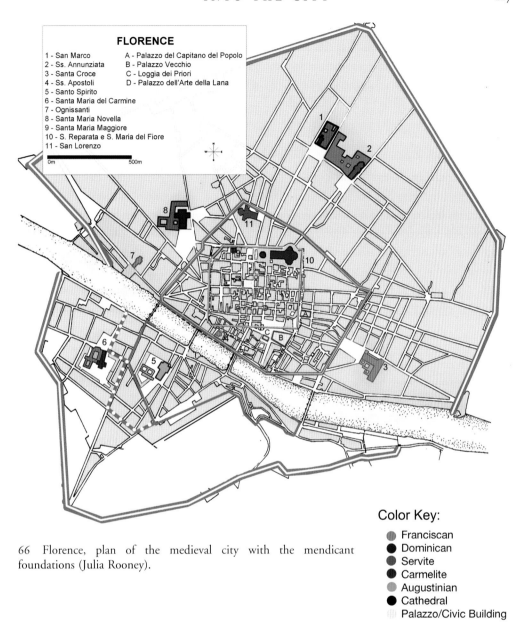

FLORENCE

1 - San Marco
2 - Ss. Annunziata
3 - Santa Croce
4 - Ss. Apostoli
5 - Santo Spirito
6 - Santa Maria del Carmine
7 - Ognissanti
8 - Santa Maria Novella
9 - Santa Maria Maggiore
10 - S. Reparata e S. Maria del Fiore
11 - San Lorenzo

A - Palazzo del Capitano del Popolo
B - Palazzo Vecchio
C - Loggia dei Priori
D - Palazzo dell'Arte della Lana

0m   500m

Color Key:
- Franciscan
- Dominican
- Servite
- Carmelite
- Augustinian
- Cathedral
- Palazzo/Civic Building

66 Florence, plan of the medieval city with the mendicant foundations (Julia Rooney).

given terrain to the north of the Rialto of Venice, on the upper edge of the city, an area they subsequently expanded through landfill to create two large cloisters. The donation was inspired by Doge Jacopo Tiepolo's dream of a flock of white doves over the lagoon, but we might well imagine that in addition to the spiritual vision, the doge understood the practical importance of developing this side of the city, especially as the expansion of the Arsenale was attracting workers and traders to an area used for the delivery of supplies (such as timber) from the mainland. The population in this location would have consisted of manual laborers engaged in making, repairing, and provisioning ships, as well as traders and sailors returning after exposure to foreign (and potentially unorthodox) ideas. Thus, Tiepolo's positioning of the Preachers here might have provided a measure of social management. Similar examples existed north of the Alps, as Thomas Coomans has noted: at Kampen friars were located at the intersection of the two main roads that connected the docks to the city at a gate that came to be called Broederpoort.[42] These areas were often those of most rapid development because of the increase in manufacturing and trade.

Communes

We noted many instances of the communes supporting friars.[43] Aside from bringing honor and distinction, they helped to take the temperature of, and control, dissent within local populations (initially through confession, and later additionally via the Inquisition). Friars often served as civic administrators, agents, ambassadors, or construction supervisors.[44] At times friaries functioned as counterweights to the episcopacy, thus changing the dynamics of power within cities; this seems to have been especially striking in the large dioceses of France and England, where the antifraternal movement was particularly strong late in the thirteenth century and into the fourteenth. For communal governments the mendicant dedication to apostolic poverty suggested that friars were perceived as suitable to serve as disinterested financial advisors: in Perugia in 1266, for example, a Franciscan was the consultant on coinage and the city market.[45] Franciscans were used as accountants and scribes, and communal documents were often kept in the sacristies of convents. Mendicants functioned as hydraulic engineers, notaries, jurists, and military experts for communal governments. They served in communal administrations and acted as ambassadors in missions to other cities for civic business, sometimes in sets of pairs (two Franciscans and two Dominicans). In addition, mendicant schools of theology were on occasion integrated with the city university: in Perugia, for example, there was an agreement for collaboration in 1285 between the city university and the *studium* of the friars.[46]

Mendicant poverty was central to the friars' roles in civic governments and made them attractive acquisitions for a city. Treviso supported the construction of the church and convent of the Preachers in 1230, and a year later that of the Friars Minor. The communal records attest how the poverty of the Friars Minor could serve a city:

> In the honor of omnipotent God and the glorious Virgin Mary and Saint Francis and all the saints. As nothing will be lacking for those who fear the Lord and because charity to the poor is among the highest of all virtues. . . . We, for the salvation and prosperity of the city of Treviso . . . establish with this constitution that the podestà and commune of Treviso will . . . pay one thousand lire . . . to the order of Friars Minor who are truly paupers.[47]

Franciscan poverty thus represented an investment in well-being and continued prosperity; their poverty guaranteed prosperity and salvation for the commune and its citizens.

Mendicants (and especially mendicant saints) were important for civic prestige. In Padua the commune took on the role of promoting the cult of Saint Anthony, after 1256 designating the vast sum of 4,000 lire annually for construction of the church of the Santo (fig. 67).[48] The design of the building evolved from a simple single-nave church to a monumental structure that in its later form imitated St. Mark's in Venice. Architecture

67 Padua,
Sant'Antonio,
reconstruction of
the church after
Lorenzoni, 1981,
plate 281.

articulated the apostolic nature of Saint Anthony and his relics, an association that would
have been apparent to any sophisticated viewer in the Veneto. The Paduan commune also
supported the Dominicans at regular intervals, and encouraged the foundations of the
other mendicant orders.[49]

As we have seen, Bologna in 1236 offered space to the Friars Minor and, at the instigation of Gregory IX, subsidized construction of a church begun the same year.[50] In addition,
the city supported work on the Augustinian convent of San Giacomo starting in 1252,
continuing subsidies to the church again after 1267; the church with its rows of tombs still
flanks a major artery.[51] In effect, Bologna ringed itself with mendicant houses, especially
on the south, east, and west sides (see fig. 64), a phenomenon still visible in Siena, which
also subsidized the construction of the mendicant communities. In Florence, the communal government contributed to the construction of Santa Croce and Santa Maria
Novella with annual subsidies.[52] In addition, as will be examined in the next chapter, both
the Friars Minor of Santa Croce and those of Sant'Antonio in Padua benefited from
properties and goods expropriated from heretics.

Mendicant churches and convents often served as meeting places, and townspeople fre-
quented certain parts of mendicant space. This is especially striking in Umbria, where the
buildings for communal administration (*palazzi del comune*) were erected later than those
in Lombardy, and required provisional arrangements for periods of time that sometimes
stretched to many decades.[53] The commune of Perugia met in the church of the Preachers
and used their sacristy to store its books and archives. The Franciscans of Città del Castello

hosted the meetings of the commune at least through 1373, and this even after the construction of the Palazzo Comunale beginning in 1335. They also stored tax and customs records, notarial documents, and other communal archives at the friary.[54] Albertano da Brescia mentions in a sermon that around 1250 the city's lawyers were "in their customary meeting in the House of the Friars Minor."[55] In Naples two of the local *seggi* (local administrative units ruled by the urban patriciate) met in the convents of San Domenico and San Lorenzo: through this familiarity with élite local administrators the friars enhanced their ties to the urban patriciate, who in turn patronized their construction projects.[56] Members of the *seggi* may have served as financial administrators or procurators for the communities in question and obtained burial in the church or cloister. We can imagine a symbiotic relationship between civic (or commercial) organizations and friaries, with the latter offering convenient, centrally located, and dignified settings for meetings that in turn acquired the aura of authority and prestige by virtue of being held in the convent.

Communes took an interest not only in providing space for mendicant convents, but also in sponsoring the urban voids that were necessary for outdoor preaching (Santa Maria Novella, Santa Croce in Florence, San Fermo in Verona, and the various mendicant churches of Siena: see fig. 62). Communes constructed roads to give access to convents (Pistoia and Florence).[57] In Siena roads were put in to facilitate access to San Domenico, San Francesco, and Sant'Agostino.[58] Communes thus engaged in a planning process that could be understood in several possible ways: as decentralizing the city, giving new significance to the mendicant houses on the periphery that often ringed the urban center, or as affirming and stabilizing the city margins with the stable presence of new religious communities. In any of these cases, we might imagine that the mendicant chorus of prayer was perceived as a beneficial form of protection for the entire community: "for the salvation and prosperity of the city," as the town fathers of Treviso put it.

The close ties of mendicant religious institutions to neighborhoods became increasingly important as itinerancy diminished and friaries were bound even more by family ties to local communities. This, however, meant that convents increasingly participated in the factionalism of urban environments.[59] After the battles between the Filippeschi and the Monaldeschi in Orvieto in 1313, the dead of each faction were respectively taken to one or the other of the mendicant churches. Cities were divided in areas of influence closely tied to family loyalties and to neighborhoods. Piron has confirmed how important local ties were for the daily life, as well as the ambitions, of the community of Santa Croce in Florence.[60] Ostentatious building thus acquired a political resonance within the local frame.

In view of the frequent instances of mutual support between communes and the friars, it is perhaps not surprising that their respective buildings sometimes echo each other in style, sharing a general austerity and sometimes using the same materials; as Romanini observed in 1964, this is a characteristic of mendicant architecture in Lombardy.[61] The "Gotico," or communal palace of Piacenza, begun within a few years of the Franciscan church across the piazza, is a case in point, although the use of marble facing on the palazzo's lower story displays high prestige materials absent from the Franciscan church. The central location offered to the Friars Minor in Piacenza precipitated violent conflict with the nearby clergy over competition for parishioners, however.[62] A papal inquest was instigated against the new foundation. In a memorable episode of strife, the friars' crucifix was thrown into a latrine. The parish and cathedral clergy authorized the practice of launching stones at the new mendicant establishment. It may be that the wall built around the site mentioned in the inquest existed in order to defend the friars against attacks from the secular clergy as well as to enclose the worksite and create the boundaries of the future convent. In spite of the disruptions, the friars at Piacenza expeditiously erected a church and cloister modeled on San Francesco in Bologna with an ambulatory and curiously compacted radiating chapels, as well as flyers on the exterior. The vaults of the nave were completed in the second half of the fourteenth century. The ostentatiously Gothic style of the church was perhaps a deliberate effort to affirm the connection with the communal government across the piazza, but it may also have served to proclaim the importance and permanence of the Franciscans at this contested site, and their significance in comparison with the small fractious parishes that surrounded them.

Communal benevolence was not guaranteed, however. In Strasbourg the friars acquired so much land that the commune (created in 1262) resisted their encroachment within the walled city.[63] Here as in other cities the land was held in mortmain (as a perpetual endowment of a religious institution that could not be alienated) and could not be taxed. In 1283 the commune of Strasbourg presented a list of demands to the mendicant communities to limit their acquisition of property, burial rights, and legacies. Although the Franciscans agreed to the terms, the Dominicans refused to sign the agreement. The commune forbade the Preachers to offer the sacraments or receive alms and sent an armed guard to close the church. A cadre of local women devoted to the Preachers attacked the city's constables with rolling pins and clogs. After the melée, the Dominican community left town to seek support and the city was placed under interdict. Within a few years, however, they returned in triumph and reclaimed their property. The long history of tension and conflict continued, and the Preachers were exiled again between 1331 and 1333. In this instance, the commune worked in concert with the local secular clergy against the aggressive land acquisition of the Dominicans.[64]

City Centers

Friaries were not always on the margins. As noted above, in some cities mendicants obtained centrally located property, either through astute purchases and legacies (as in the case of the Preachers in Strasbourg)[65] or through the agency of patrons, bishops, or communes. The insertion of a mendicant convent inside a city, however, often led to heightened conflict over land or parochial rights, and sometimes, as in Strasbourg, one order or another, reinforced by determined local supporters, might be flagrant in its contempt for local concerns. In other instances, because of the constraints of urban space, the mendicants abandoned sites in the city center for larger parcels outside the walls, as was the case with both the Franciscans and Dominicans in Oxford. Yet in spite of the difficulties and stress of acquiring land for expansion, a centrally located position was often too precious a prize to give up, and as communities expanded in size, conflicts over rights and property were increasingly acute. As has been seen, this problem was exacerbated by the conventualization of friaries toward the middle of the thirteenth century.

As noted in Chapter Two, a basilica of San Lorenzo in Naples (presumably with its parochial functions) and ancillary buildings were used by the initial group of Franciscans who settled there in 1234 (see fig. 41). But the growth and increasing clericalization of the community required the addition of lateral chapels to the nave around 1260–70. Within a few decades, the old church and the conventual spaces were probably too small for the growing communities of friars and lay supporters, especially in view of the function of the convent as a *studium*. The expansion of the convent over the narrow city street to the east permitted the construction of the large Gothic choir and a vast new refectory. The site plan suggests a policy of almost continuous expansion around the original core of the old church in centuries of piecemeal acquisition (through purchase, exchange, and, on occasion, expropriation) that permitted a series of episodic additions: the creation of a cloister adjacent to the row of nave chapels, the new chevet with ambulatory and radiating chapels, and later the expanded transept terminations of the fourteenth century.

San Lorenzo was the second Franciscan foundation in Naples; an earlier settlement existed simultaneously southwest of the city at the site of Castel Nuovo. It is possible that the new foundation in the city center reflected Archbishop Pietro di Sorrento's interest in imposing authority or orthodoxy on the urban population: the convent flanked one of the main *decumani* that traversed the city from east to west and faced the old market, an ideal location for a mission of preaching and conversion. It is tempting to speculate whether the facade of the old church, where there is also archaeological evidence of tombs, may have been used as a backdrop for preaching, but there is no surviving evidence of this. The Preachers in Naples had been provided with a central location in 1234 when the same archbishop arranged for them to acquire the strategic site of the old hospital of Sant'Angelo a Morfisa, in this instance located above the lower *decumanus*, adjacent to the western city walls (see fig. 65). The mendicant foundations were probably part of the archbishop's strategic (anti-imperial) plan and intended to counter the secularism of the law faculty at the university. After 1266 both houses were patronized by the Angevin kings: Charles II and Robert the Wise were particularly devoted supporters. The convent of San Domenico became the center for the Inquisition in the kingdom and continued to be closely allied with royal interests (see Chapter Five).

Preaching spaces have been mentioned above in relation to streets and roads, but they deserve a repeated note of emphasis here. As well as the widening or increased emphasis upon certain roads and gates, preaching stimulated the creation of new open spaces, as is most visible still for Santa Croce and Santa Maria Novella in Florence. The extent to which mendicant preaching was held to be of vital importance for urban communities is attested by the cavities of the piazzas (see fig. 62).

The Proliferation of Mendicant Houses and Zoning Regulations

Friars were in competition with each other for space, financial resources, and patronage. The faithful often left bequests in wills to multiple institutions (and therefore did not necessarily privilege one community over another, except in their choice of burial location), and sometimes oscillated in their preferences between the orders. A well-known example is Guglielmo di Castelbarco of Verona, who gave support to both the Friars Minor at San Fermo and the Preachers at Sant'Anastasia.[66]

It therefore made sense to establish houses as far away from each other as possible, in different zones of a city, as in Florence (see fig. 66). Through this process mendicant houses became intimately tied to specific neighborhoods and local associations.[67] Competition for resources was sometimes exacerbated by the existence of multiple Franciscan foundations in the same town as has been seen for Rome (they settled first at San Biagio, later at San Francesco a Ripa in 1229; at San Cosimato, a convent for Poor Clares, in 1234; and at Santa Maria del Popolo in 1227). By c. 1315 in Naples there were at least three Franciscan houses: Santa Maria al Palazzo founded c. 1217 (re-established as Santa Maria Nova after 1279), San Lorenzo founded in 1234, and Corpus Domini (later Santa Chiara) founded in 1309. There were also other women's institutions affiliated with the order, such as Santa Maria Donnaregina. In Verona the Friars Minor by 1225 had establishments at Santa Croce (later known as San Francesco) and at San Gabriele by c. 1229. In addition, Franciscan friars were attached to communities of the Poor Clares at Sant'Agata (1224) and at Campomarzo (1226).[68]

Multiple foundations were a natural consequence of the unstructured and spontaneous character of the Friars Minor in their early years. We have already seen that toward the middle of the thirteenth century there were attempts at consolidation in Rome and Verona, and often a Benedictine convent was used to house multiple communities of Friars Minor. In Rome, both San Biagio and Santa Maria in Capitolio (the Aracoeli) had been Benedictine. Not surprisingly, previous monastic occupants did not cede their properties willingly.[69] But in other cities, as in Naples, various Franciscan houses continued to exist independently.

The proliferation of friaries of the same order presented a complicated situation for Franciscans, and the problem was exacerbated toward the middle of the thirteenth century with the arrival of the Carmelite, Servite, and Augustinian orders. Increased competition for space and donors prompted papal legislation concerning distances between mendicant institutions. In November 1265 Clement IV, in *Clara merita sanctitatis*, specified that there should be a distance of 300 *canne* (approximately 600 meters) as the crow flies ("mesurandarum per aream") between each mendicant foundation.[70] Similar legislation had already appeared on a local level earlier the same year at Assisi and Bologna. In 1268 the required distance was reduced to 140 *canne* (approximately 280 meters). But legislation did not obviate controversy: Trevisan noted that the friars of San Fermo in Verona, by this point securely installed at the former Benedictine abbey, carried on fierce litigation over the construction of the new Servite convent of Santa Maria della Scala across the river.[71] Such tensions were present in many towns. At Pistoia the Franciscans vigorously objected to the foundation of a Carmelite community in 1291, and were able to suspend construction of the new church (the ruins of which were still visible in the seventeenth century). There Carmelites were ultimately obliged to begin a new establishment at a site 140 *canne* from San Francesco.[72]

*   *   *

Open Civic Space: Piazzas and Markets

Friars co-opted public space for preaching, and from an early date piazzas and external pulpits (permanent or portable) formed part of their architectural planning and strategic positioning in cities. External pulpits were incorporated into the facades of churches, as at San Domenico in Bologna (no longer extant) and Sant'Eustorgio (in reconstructed form) (see fig. 21). Elsewhere, portable wooden pulpits were the norm, as is attested by numerous images (fig. 68; and see figs. 20 and 62). In 1233 the citizens of Parma created a piazza for Dominican preaching,[73] a phenomenon repeated in many cities, most famously at Santa Maria Novella in Florence, noted above. At the Franciscan church of Pola (Istria) the external pulpit hovers over a narrow street in steep descent (fig. 69).

In Italy the active voiding out of urban space in order to create piazzas emerged from the new developments of civic and communal life in the previous half-century. Communes had created open public spaces along with communal palaces and markets as symbols and expressions of communal authority and identity. As Miller has noted, these palaces and piazzas were probably inspired by those of twelfth-century bishops,[74] and sprang up quickly after the Peace of Constance of 1183. By 1194 a communal palace and piazza were under construction in Modena, and in Brescia four years later. In Bologna the first of three communal palaces on the major city piazza, the Palazzo del Podestà, was begun in 1200.[75]

The new communal piazzas were for the public performance of civic life; they represented not only a physical claim to urban space but also a reactivation of the ancient practice of using the outdoor public realm for political, mercantile, and religious activities. In the thirteenth century friars renegotiated this concept by adding a fourth, spiritual dimension to these urban voids: they activated the urban piazzas to engage open space as a field for preaching and confession. Whereas early Christianity had internalized the practice of religion by moving it into interior spaces strictly reserved and enclosed for converts,[76] friars (consciously or not) returned to ancient practice by restoring religious life to external space.

Outdoor preaching introduced a new element to the equation between laity and religion. Along with public preaching, friars also offered confession and absolution in the open spaces of the city. Toward the middle of the thirteenth century, piazzas began to be created *ex novo* for the friars. One of the earliest examples is that created in 1244 on the east side of Santa Maria Novella (the Piazza Vecchia) to accommodate the dense crowds attracted by the preaching of Peter of Verona (Peter Martyr).[77] After 1288 the commune authorized a new piazza to the south, provided in perpetuity for the use of the Preachers:[78] "the piazza, which extends from the surface of the wall on the west side of said church in a straight line up to the gate of Saint Paul and on the other side from the property of the aforesaid friars, which is next to the road through which one passes to the Trebbio Gate in a straight line up to said gate of Trebbio" ("platea que protrahatur a pariete muri dicte ecclesie parte occidentali secundum rectam lineam usque ad portam Sancti Pauli, et ex alia parte a terreno predictorum fratrum, quod est iuxta viam per quam itur ad portam de Trebbio, secundum rectam lineam usque ad dictam portam de Trebbio").[79] At Cortona, in the 1240s, the friars were tightly linked to the creation of the central piazza and commune, and given permission to preach there and in the area preceding the *pieve* of Santa Maria.[80]

Coment cantal'parta de roy alixand"
pour fere soun message

Andeolus sentorne
li sest du roi partis
Vait sen grant aleure
defus son arrabis
Deuant la roine
descent sus·i· tapis
Biaus fis fait la roine molt venes escthieris
Que fait li mieudres rois qui onques fust escris

68   A Dominican preaching., c. 1344, MS Bodleian 264, fol. 79r. Courtesy of the Bodleian Library, Oxford University.

   In the second half of the thirteenth century, the mendicant piazza and pulpit became the site for the public condemnation of heretics. In 1245 the sentence condemning the Baroni and confiscating their possessions was read in the Piazza Vecchia of Santa Maria Novella.[81] The Franciscan Inquisition did the same at Orvieto and Viterbo.[82] In 1325 in Florence the sentence against the noble Altafronte was pronounced in the external pulpit of Santa Croce.[83] The infamous inquisitor Fra Mino in 1332 preached on the fate of seven accused heretics in this piazza.[84] On the other hand, the culmination of these terrible events – the execution (usually through burning) of heretics – took place in the communal piazzas. In this way, mendicant houses were geographically shielded from the ultimate consequences of accusations, and condemnations for, heresy. In Bologna, for example, the execution of two heretics in 1299 occurred in the central piazza, and although many in the crowd

69   Pola (Istria), San Francesco, the external flank of the nave.

were enraged against the Preachers who had pronounced the sentences, the convent itself was physically disassociated from the executions, if not the anger of the public (see below, Chapter Five).

For the friars' relations with the public, therefore, already existing "voids" of civic space were at least in the early decades of the thirteenth century, as important as the "solids" (the buildings) of churches (fig. 70). Friars established the place of the sacred in the open spaces of the city – in piazzas, markets, and streets, in short, *in the world* – by activating them as sites of salvation, both individual and collective. Public space acquired a valence that merged the practical and functional with the spiritual. Although by mid-century, piazzas for preaching came to be increasingly associated with each specific convent, friars also continued to preach in communal squares and markets.

Concepts from the marketplace, including competition for customers, became part of the mentality and language of preaching, a process that reflects marketplace thinking on the part of the friars. The connections between preaching and commercial activity had already been suggested by the assimilation of the spaces of social and commercial life with

70   Florence, Santa Maria Novella, aerial view, from Google Earth. Image copyright 2014 Digital Globe.

those of religion. But beyond the common use of urban space, the connections between mendicants and markets were made much more explicit in sermons. It was pointed out that Francis began as a merchant, and sermons in the thirteenth century not infrequently used the metaphor of Christ as a "merchant for souls." One notable example is Federico Visconti, the archbishop of Pisa, who spoke in these terms when preaching in San Francesco in Pisa.[85] It was also sometimes suggested that God instituted a relationship of exchange with mankind that could be described as a system of credit.[86]

The ease with which metaphors connected financial transactions with spiritual ones merged the association of personal salvation with the market economy. This is evident from descriptions of the friars: not only was Francis a "merchant for souls," but even the leaders of the orders themselves, such as Humbert of Romans, suggested that Preachers should emulate merchants "for the gain of souls" ("pro lucro animorum"). The Franciscan friar Guibert of Tournai (c. 1200–1284), a friend and supporter of Bonaventure, stated that "Christ comes like a merchant to do business . . . for in the manner of a merchant or one working for money he brought precious goods in worthless cloths, that is, a kingdom in poverty, consolation in grief, plenty in hunger."[87] In the fourteenth century Aldobrandino Cavalcanti, the distinguished Dominican theologian, continued to promote these concepts, describing Christ as the good merchant. And of course the concept of purgatory, so close to the concerns of the medieval lay public with regard to the afterlife, and a theme that lurks behind many of the arguments of this book, is in itself closely related to the concept of double-entry bookkeeping: the debits (sins) versus the credits (good deeds, prayers, etc.) set within an accounting system based on that of the numerate merchants in the marketplace.

Franciscans and Dominicans approached preaching in public spaces differently, however, and with considerable awareness of the other's practice. Humbert of Romans stated:

> not every place is suitable for solemn preaching, for one must not preach in secret assemblies as do the heretics, but in public places like our Lord. . . . Public places and crossroads where men carry on business and employ themselves in worldly affairs, and other places whose secular use makes them unfit for this ministry ought not to be used for preaching. One should choose more suitable places, as did St. Paul, who spoke in the synagogues, or as Our Lord, Who spoke in the temple, or sometimes in the country, apart from the bustle of the world.[88]

Quattrocento images of preachers in pulpits confirm these norms: Dominican preachers are almost always represented in a dignified open space in front of a church. In noting that not every place was suitable for preaching, Humbert seems to have been discretely remarking on the practices of the Friars Minor, who preached in markets, along streets, at crossroads, and even (if descriptions of Saint Anthony of Padua are reliable) in trees.

In creating their own exterior spaces for preaching, friars sited new or reconstructed convents so that outdoor preaching could be part of the spatial and structural concept of the whole. These spaces were conceived of as preaching theatres: we noted that in Parma, in 1233, enthusiastic townspeople helped the Preachers clear a space in front of their church for a piazza dedicated to outdoor sermons.[89] At Sant'Eustorgio in Milan, the space in front of the church was enclosed on two sides, with a permanent stone and brick pulpit inserted into the corner (see fig. 21). The acoustics would have been enhanced by the location of the pulpit in the angle between two buildings.

Piazzas were not neutral spaces, however: their positioning and "spatial framing" could be arranged to enhance or reinforce the messages of sermons. As noted above, at Santa Maria Novella the design of the west facade (see figs. 7, 63, and 70) included a row of tomb niches that folded around the right flank of the church to integrate with the cemetery (the Chiostro de' Morti). The preacher, in his pulpit in front of the church, would have been framed by tombs, thereby providing a vivid reminder of the fragility of life, the inevitability of death, and the need to prepare the soul through penitence and confession. Tomb niches were systematically integrated into the design of facades (see fig. 63) and the flanks of many churches (the Dominican churches in Prato and Florence, see figs. 55 and 56). To judge from the surviving evidence, Dominicans were more systematic in their integration of tomb memorials into spaces that served the purpose of preaching, and the systematic inclusion of tombs could also dominate interior space, as noted at the Dominican friary of Roscommon, Ireland (see fig. 57).

As was the case with many other aspects of mendicant planning, San Domenico in Bologna established the precedent. Here the external pulpit and piazza in front of the church were combined with tombs and burials; the pulpit (no longer extant) overlooked the western cemetery. Although the north and west flanks of the church had already been developed as a burial area starting c. 1220,[90] the Preachers continued to purchase land in front of the recently completed church in October 1240 in order to extend the piazza around the front.[91] This pulpit is mentioned in the sepultuary of 1291 as located on the north side of the facade,[92] presiding over the open space filled with a well-organized cemetery of parallel rows of tombs that included those of the city council.

Another, potentially more theatrical scenographic element is suggested by the 1291 sepultuary of the Dominicans in Bologna: a "gratam feream" under the pulpit. Could this have been used for the exposition of heretics? If this was the case, it could have functioned as a prop for the preacher, presenting a compelling visual reminder of the brevity of life and the need for repentance. Insofar as the work of the preacher was to bring the soul to contrition, persuasion could be enhanced by the powerful presentation of visual aids that illuminated the concepts of sin, penitence, death, and burial, themes I shall develop more fully in the next chapter. In the piazzas of the preachers, voice and the visual props functioned in symbiosis to enhance and emphasize the fundamental message of the preacher. Preacher, piazza, pulpit, and tombs (and perhaps iron grates) thus formed an integrated rhetorical whole.

Preaching outdoors had antecedents in the eleventh and twelfth centuries. These events are sometimes described as incorporating structures such as porches and windows. As Miller notes, Bruno of Segni's final sermons were preached from a window, and Innocent IV did the same in Ferrara.[93] The use of architectural forms as the setting for preaching was certainly not new. But the ubiquity of the friars and their construction of permanent pulpits transformed what seems to have been episodic practice into a common and systematized feature of urban life, and created dramatic stage settings for preaching from church facades. Occasional surviving examples of external pulpits indicate that this architectural feature was adopted by other institutions, as can be seen at Santo Stefano in Bologna and Santo Stefano (now the cathedral) of Prato, both of which added pulpits into their facades. But as often as not friars used temporary and moveable wooden pulpits in front of churches or in other spaces, as attested in illuminations of friars preaching from the thirteenth century and panel paintings from later periods. Visual evidence of portable wooden pulpits exists by the end of the thirteenth century and into the fourteenth (for an example, see fig. 68). Some may have had wheels, and could perhaps have been rolled along like wheelbarrows, tilted up, and put to use. The notorious Fra Mino used a portable pulpit created at great expense in 1332, both in the piazza of Santa Croce and within the church.[94] Pulpits on the flanks of churches, as at the Franciscan church of Pola (see fig. 69) and San Domenico in Arezzo, were accessible from the interior via the raised walkway of the choir screen.[95] At San Domenico in Naples, the external pulpit of 1546 was accessible from one of the lateral chapels (fig. 71) and became a feature of the church only after the creation of the new piazza in the fifteenth century.[96]

The integration of pulpits into urban spaces – whether moveable and wooden or the more dignified stone pulpits incorporated into facades – activated the public spheres of the city for religious purposes and charged urban space with the role of collective and individual salvation. In the following pages of this chapter, I suggest that, in the wake of the Gregorian reform, the pulpit also became the locus of clerical and ecclesiastical authority on the right to preach, a debate further stimulated by the mendicant propulsion into the

71   Naples, San Domenico, the external pulpit.

open spaces of cities. Yet in concluding this section we might also note that the mendicant activation of urban spaces went beyond pulpits and visiting homes: by the fourteenth century, urban networks of streets were enlisted for parading heretics on the backs of donkeys, a feature of urban spectacle prompted by the Inquisition, and therefore the friars. These phenomena, however, are part of a larger discourse on urban ritual that would require a case-by-case study in each city.

Preaching and Pulpits

"Nothing is more effective in bringing penitence than preaching," stated Humbert of Romans in his treatise.[97] This was the primary function of the new orders. Yet, well before the arrival of mendicants there had been much debate over who had authority to preach and where it should be done. By the twelfth century, canons regular and Benedictine monks were often in conflict with the secular clergy over the right to preach, especially in parishes where they claimed the right of "cura animarum."[98] Although Saint Jerome had stated that the central task of monks was prayer and penitence rather than preaching, by the central Middle Ages ordained monks had nonetheless acquired clerical duties, including the right to preach, and indeed public sermons played a central role in promoting and publicizing the aims of Gregorian reform. To achieve its reform goals, the papacy in the third quarter of the eleventh century allowed certain individuals to "preach anywhere" ("ubique predicare"), as Gregory VII did for Abbot William of Hirsau.[99] In pressing the goals of reform against obdurate bishops who resisted this perceived encroachment on their prerogatives, Gregory and some of his successors (Urban II and Gelasius II) enlarged the concept of who had a right to preach by enlisting itinerant preachers to drum up support.[100]

Many twelfth- and thirteenth-century reformers (or heretics, who are also in their own way reformers) promoted a reforming or "apostolic" vision through preaching, which became the central instrument for disseminating information and promoting new ideas.[101] In addition, some laity were given permission to preach (such as the Umiliati), although they were limited to offering moral exhortations and prohibited from touching upon matters of doctrine.[102]

In the context of these evolving practices, Gratian's *Decretals* of c. 1140 addressed fraught attempts to distinguish ordained clergy with the responsibility for the "cura animarum" from those given special authorization to preach and administer the sacraments. Nevertheless, a typical feature of medieval religion from the eleventh century onwards was the charismatic itinerant preacher, such as Robert d'Abrissel (c. 1060–1115) who, long before the friars came along, wandered from village to village in rough clothing in a clear and obvious imitation of Christ and the apostles.[103]

In order to swing public opinion against a conservative and resistant episcopacy, Innocent III exceeded the practices of his predecessors in the utilization of itinerant preachers. After the precedent of conceding the limited authority to preach to the Umilati in the late twelfth century, it is no surprise that in 1210 he allowed the Friars Minor and, five years later, the Dominicans to preach on the condition that they first acquire permission from the local bishop. The preaching of the new orders was in keeping with the tenth canon of the Fourth Lateran Council, which emphasized the importance of preaching for spreading the word of God, even as it recognized that many bishops were too busy, or not in adequate health, to be effective preachers.[104] By the thirteenth century there developed what D'Avray has described as a "feverish market for preaching," a sort of race for souls between the various institutions of the church and its heretical rivals.[105] This "feverish market" entailed an ongoing debate between the different orders and the secular clergy over the authority to preach.

Mendicant preaching became a central component of the conflict between friars and the secular clergy in the mid-thirteenth century.[106] Aggravating the situation were the rights that friars had acquired to hear confession (1221) and to administer the sacraments.[107] By the 1230s friars were conducting "full service" sacramental operations,[108] and as noted, at least in Italy these took place outside in the public and open spaces of the campo, piazza, and market (see fig. 20).

Preaching in combination with the sacraments had important financial implications: it meant that customary oblations offered to the clergy were now often deflected to friars.[109] Increasing conflict with the secular clergy meant that toward the fourth and fifth decades of the thirteenth century the new orders needed their own spaces (indoors in churches and outdoors in piazzas) for preaching and administering to the public. Growing crowds were a direct impetus for the monumentalization of mendicant churches and piazzas.[110]

It is interesting to reflect upon whether the invention of the monumental marble pulpits of mid-thirteenth-century Tuscany, such as Nicola Pisano's pulpits in Pisa, represented an ecclesiastical response to the ubiquitous preaching of mendicant friars in their sometimes flimsy wooden pulpits. Could the large historiated pulpit in noble and permanent materials have been a way for the secular clergy to reaffirm their rights to the "cura animarum" and administration of the sacraments? The fundamental themes of contrition, confession, penitence, redemption, and salvation are implicit in the New Testament scenes executed in prestigious "classic" marble surfaces of the Pisan pulpits of the thirteenth century.[111] The 1260 pulpit of the Pisa baptistery presented a powerful contrast to the (often) rustic and portable wooden pulpits of the friars, the former conveying the special aura of authority through apostolic succession to the sacrament of baptism as a ritual of membership in both church and commune.[112] It was entirely fitting that Nicola's pulpit was erected in the space dedicated to entry into the Christian community and to citizenship in the city.[113]

The emergence of historiated pulpits in the middle of the thirteenth century also suggests the possibility of new types of visual aids used by preachers, although this point is difficult to prove for the medieval period. There is some evidence that visual props or tools, such as paintings on linen, may have been part of preaching; perhaps the series of linen paintings produced in early trecento Naples that represent scenes from the Crucifixion, a seated Virgin, and Francis receiving the stigmata may be examples of these.[114] Fra Mino of Santa Croce had an image of the devil on the portable pulpit.[115] If the medieval evidence is tenuous, for later periods there are more secure examples of the use of images in preaching: in the fifteenth century Bernardino da Siena was famous for preaching outdoors with a plaque on which was inscribed the holy name of Christ,[116] and the illustrations of the *Rhetorica Christiana* by Valadés shows friars pointing to images during sermons.[117] This approach to effective communication is parallel to the mendicant practice of preaching in the vernacular, a departure from the tradition of the Latin sermon that was inaccessible to the broad range of the lay public.[118] The use of vivid everyday stories from the lives of saints, codified in the *Legenda aurea* and other treatises, brought preaching into a direct and accessible "story" mode for the laity.[119] We might imagine that the stories from the Bible or the lives of saints could have been illustrated by lightweight portable images in the form of scrolls like the *exultet* rolls or paintings on linen that could be rolled up.

Mendicant sermons in the vernacular as a tool for conversion and penitence transformed the art of preaching, and the Dominicans were in the forefront of developing an educational system aimed at the creation of effective and doctrinally correct preachers. A fundamental concept was "gratia," the gift of eloquence and grace as a prerequisite for effective preaching.[120] Archbishop Federico Visconti of Pisa, lamenting the woeful morals and education of his own clergy, urged his priests to emulate and take advantage of a free education with the friars, whose goal was to produce a "gratiosus praedicator." Dominican prayers for the community, for example, asked for "the ability to speak with grace."[121] But for their enemies, mendicant eloquence did not always posses a positive value: William of Saint-Amour in his treatise *De periculis novissimorum temporum* called effective and eloquent preaching into question, associating it with false prophecy and seduction.[122] Talent in argument and words could be a distortion of the word of God, and as Szittya noted, the use of logic or philosophy could be seen as constituting empty babbling contributing to impiety.[123]

In any event, for the secular clergy, the marble pulpits within sacred space could have represented an affirmation of the right to preach and administer the sacraments; the representation of New Testament scenes in the context of a permanent and monumental pulpit took on significance as part of the "voice" of the clergy in affirming its sacrosanct rights to the "cura animarum" in an apostolic succession embedded in the New Testament. It also affirmed the place of the cathedral at the center of sacred ritual. Nicola Pisano's citations of the classical style gave forceful visual eloquence to issues of ecclesiastical authority and provided a monumental form of illustration to sermons within the baptistery, in striking contrast with the flimsy pulpits and, possibly, the portable paintings of a friar. The images produced on the Tuscan cathedral pulpits were, moreover, executed in the majestic, dignified, and noble material of marble,[124] a material that conveyed venerable tradition as well as vague notions of antiquity and authority.

Domestic Space

The externalized mission of friars had another component: visiting parishioners in their homes, especially the homes of the sick and dying. William of Saint-Amour, whose tract was composed early in the 1250s, suggests that one of the friars' most offensive practices, visiting homes, was a novelty. His description of visiting homes as "penetrans domus" moves quickly from the simple act of entering domestic space to an invasion of conscience and secrets. Saint-Amour and his followers in the clergy argued that the duties of preaching and the care of souls were expressly reserved for bishops and their parochial clergy in the lineage of Christ and the apostles. These views were widely broadcast in Paris and in much of France through sermons, lectures, and large public meetings, and the potentially scurrilous implications of friars entering homes were expanded in stories, poems, and vernacular literature (such as the friar represented as Faux Semblant in the *Roman de la Rose*).[125] Although it can be no accident that the language William uses is one of sexual violation, a formulation that in part inspired the bosom-fondling friars in the narratives of Chaucer and Boccaccio, it is more important for our purposes to note that this activity brought friars into direct connection with the dying at the moment of preparation of a will. The connection between visiting homes and raising funds for construction was often explicit. The close links that friars developed with families and neighborhoods was so new and noteworthy that Saint-Amour in his tract of 1256 gave special emphasis to the dangers of this activity: friars "penetrate," "meddle," and "invade" homes, they "prod" and "pry" into secrets, and they "seduce," women especially.[126]

Because friars went into homes, they played an important role in the composition and execution of wills and testaments, an activity that naturally irritated local clergy because it provided friars with special access to the ill and dying at the moment when they were urgently concerned with the fate of their soul. Our primary sources for this are literary, including, first and foremost, the wills themselves. In a later tract composed in the 1260s, William of Saint-Amour specifically pointed to the relationship between the friars' activities and their buildings, reversing the biblical theme of turning stones into bread:

> By building the aforementioned buildings, men, too, of this sort seem to turn bread into stones, namely by turning the bread of the poor (that is, the alms obtained by begging, from which the bread of Christ ought to be distributed to the poor) into heaps of stones, that is, into expensive and excessive stone houses. And for this reason they seem to be crueler than the Devil and more merciless, although the Devil himself on the other hand asked that stones be turned into bread, saying to the Lord: *Command that those stones be made bread.*[127]

Thus, friars, in taking bread from the poor to turn into the stones of their churches, were worse than the devil himself.

The apostolic poverty professed by friars was widely believed to enhance the power of their prayers for the soul. The perceived efficacy of mendicant prayer was an active and ongoing stimulus for donations; at the moment of death, too much was at stake for the donor to risk less reliable or effective intercession. Chaucer's Friar John in "The Summoner's Tale" spoke of the prayers of the "charitable, chaste, and busy friars" that fly like a hawk "to God's two ears."[128]

Mendicant prayer was in this sense a form of "death insurance." Friar John expressed the situation in unambiguous terms. (This quotation consists of a series of excerpts from John's speech to the burgher Thomas, who is ill in bed):

> And so we mendicants, we simple friars
> Have wedded poverty and continence
> Charity, humbleness, and penitence
> And persecution too for righteousness;
> Pure, merciful, austere, but quick to bless
> Though weeping often. Therefore our desires –
> I'm speaking of ourselves, mendicant friars –
> Are more acceptable to God, more able
> Than yours, with all your feasts upon the table.
> . . .
> And as a hawk springs up into the lonely
> Regions of heaven, so the prayer . . . of
> Charitable, chaste and busy friars,
> Takes flight, and enters into God's two ears.
> . . .

> Do you suppose our convent, and I, too,
> Are insufficient, then, to pray for you?
> Thomas, that joke's not good. Your faith is brittle.
> You're ill because you've given us too little . . .[129]

If the prayers of friars were indeed to "take flight" through donations from lay patrons, the latter naturally requested that the physical setting for their memorials be as close as possible to the place of prayers as a stimulus and reminder: preferred positions for those of adequate means and status were under the feet of praying friars in the choir or in the cloister, especially at the doorway that gave access to the choir. Patrons desired the place of prayer to be suitable and dignified. The involvement of patrons and donors in negotiations for the duration of their time of purgation meant that it was *this* place of prayer, *this* choir, and *those* friars (or nuns) who weighed in the equation. And indeed, the promise of intercessory prayer as an incentive for donations was surely one of many factors in the completion of choirs long before naves, as we have seen in the Franciscan churches of Pistoia and Florence (see Chapter Three).

Donations for intercessory prayer in wills and testaments thus stipulated tangible verification through architectural space, and wills often specified donations for buildings in combination with requests for burial. As John Fleming observed,[130] the primary objective of the "poking and prying" friar's visit to the bedside of the ailing Thomas in "The Summoner's Tale" was precisely to raise funds for completion of the convent:

> Then give me of your gold to make our cloister . . .
> We've hardly finished the foundation.
> There's not a tile yet, or a tessellation
> Upon the pavement that we hope to own,
> And forty pound is owing still for stone.[131]

5

MONEY, SOCIAL PRACTICE,

AND MENDICANT BUILDINGS

On February 28, 1305, the Blessed Giordano da Rivalto, standing in the piazza (*in platea*) of Santa Maria Novella, concluded his sermon with these words: "And of this thing [death and purgatorial suffering] we should be in a state of perpetual fear, and therefore hold firmly in front of our eyes that we must not die in a state of mortal sin . . . but [rather] always be prepared so that wherever death finds us, at whatever moment, we will be secure."[1] We can imagine Fra Giordano preaching in front of the partially completed facade of Santa Maria Novella (see fig. 63), his figure set against the series of niche tombs (*avelli*) built into its structure: Giordano's audience would indeed have been staring death in the face.[2] What image could better enforce exhortations for penitence than the tombs of neighbors and fellow citizens presenting "in front of our eyes" the urgency of preparation for death through confession and absolution? Death could come at any place and at any moment, said Giordano, and death displayed in the row of tombs arrayed across the face of the church was visibly present. Tombs and the dead collaborated in enforcing a message of penitence and absolution.

The promotion of spiritual practices through the fear of eternal punishment was reflected not only in the positioning of tombs but also in the design of churches. Penitence and death deeply inflected mendicant economic practice and, through it, the construction and shaping of their churches and convents. Preaching, penitence, and the mendicant economy are, of course, vast topics; my purpose in this chapter is to develop the themes discussed previously in this book in order to suggest how some of the social and economic activities that connected laity to friars in an exchange of services affected the shaping of architectural space. The salvific action of mendicant prayer was in effect a medium of exchange, a commodity offered in return for contributions. The conspicuous instrument of exchange was the last will and testament, the document that solidified the connection of the laity to the convent.

Mendicant ideals of institutional and individual poverty bear the same relation to financial operations as architectural legislation bore to actual building practice. On the one hand, there was the theory and rhetoric of apostolic poverty; on the other, there was the reality of possessions and the daily economic transactions of mendicant communities, the latter poorly documented and, until recently, little studied. The gap between theory and

OPPOSITE PAGE 72   Prato, San Domenico, an avello. With kind permission of Alick McLean.

reality was evident to medieval critics and, when made highly visible in large buildings, became dry fuel for the fire of invective. It is no wonder that in many respects architecture exemplifies the heart of the mendicant dilemma.

Until recent decades the economic practices of friars remained elusive: prior to c. 2000, Giacomo Todeschini was one of the few scholars to analyze mendicant economic thinking from a theoretical and structural point of view.[3] Since then, however, several important collections of essays have emerged: the Società Internazionale di Studi Francescani in 2004 published a volume dedicated to the economy of the mendicants (see especially the essay by A. Bartoli Langeli and G. P. Bustreo). This volume was complemented in 2009 by another important contribution: *Économie et religion: L'expérience des ordres mendicants*, edited by Nicole Bériou and Jacques Chiffoleau. These studies have transformed our understanding of mendicant economic practice. In addition, the recent publication of the inquiry into Franciscan economic practices in Padua, edited by Elisabetta Bonato in 2002, with its remarkable introduction by Antonio Rigon (2002), and the accounts of the Servite church of Santa Maria della Scala of Verona, edited by Arturo Sandrini in 2006, cast new (and grim) light on mendicant financial activities in the late thirteenth and early fourteenth centuries. Because of its thorough examination of tombs in relation to wills and the construction of the church, Frithjof Schwartz's recent and thorough analysis of burial practice at Santa Maria Novella has added further illuminating insights.[4]

Unfortunately there are few surviving accounts from the first decades of the new orders. The earliest documents date from the late thirteenth century and after, by which time the original rigor of the founders had been transformed. Indeed, over the course of the thirteenth century, friars often adopted a series of strategies that concealed or obscured income-bearing properties or rights, efforts which hid financial transactions from their contemporaries as well as from the modern historian. The study of the early mendicant economy is thus something like entering a theatre in the second act of a play: the narrative unfolds without providing a full understanding of the characters and setting, dimly inferred only from the subsequent course of events.

The Economy of Mendicant Convents

Land and buildings are intimately tied to money, yet studies of mendicant architecture have rarely been concerned with the problem of financing construction. It has generally been assumed that questing for funds and donations in wills were sufficient to pay for buildings. But the evidence suggests otherwise: the constant injunctions within the orders against debt, which often closely followed instructions on restraint in architecture, indicate that as communities grew larger, questing mostly supported victualing and clothing rather than building. Construction imposed another level of urgency and creativity for raising funds.

The paucity of scholarship on how the Friars Minor paid for buildings is in part the result of their regulations against property ownership. As the order in which the concept of being *pauperes Christi* was particularly strong, they made a deliberate effort to distance themselves or to obscure financial and property transactions. Economic matters were systematically delegated to third parties, including tertiaries, "spiritual friends," Beguines, female convents (the Poor Clares), and, above all, procurators. In this matter communities of Franciscan women often proved useful, for by papal edict they were obliged to accept the ownership of property to support themselves. The Friars Minor, who performed the liturgy and heard confessions for their enclosed female counterparts, could thus often "fuse" the management of properties and possessions for their own benefit.

Conflicts over property and poverty were, of course, not unique to the mendicant orders. Property was an inevitable feature of monastic life, existing in a tense and complex relationship with a simultaneous commitment to some form of poverty, corporate or personal. But although monastic establishments usually, and in principle, rejected individual property, monks were sustained by the collective ownership of land usually worked by peasants or serfs. Monastic domains also came to include parishes and parish churches; income was derived from the sale of produce or from rents and tithes, as well as from donations from the faithful, patrons, and pilgrims. In addition, monasteries received income from tolls and taxes on roads and rivers, rights to forests and rivers, the administration of justice, and the fees from parishes within their jurisdiction. They also engaged in financial activities by lending money,[5] and, at least in southern Italy, they sometimes owned ships and participated in extensive international trade (at Cava de' Tirreni and some of the monasteries of Naples, for example). In the twelfth century, certain orders, such as the Cistercians, eliminated some elements of these economic structures (thus reducing, at least for a time, many obligations to laity).[6] This reform order also brought the monastic agrarian system into a state of great efficiency by using lay brothers, or *conversi*, to manage properties, eliminating the burdens and complexities of management and labor by peasants or serfs and their families.

To these material sources of monastic income could be added the intangible but immense value of donations of money and property for prayer on behalf of the souls of benefactors and patrons.[7] As early as the sixth century, Gregory the Great had emphasized the efficacy of monastic prayer for the dead – indeed, this was one of the primary duties of monks.[8] Through prayer, monks perpetuated the memory of the dead and mitigated their fate in the afterlife, as attested in donations *pro remedio animae* and *pro sepulture*. Burial near or around a convent also provided assurances that through their beneficent presence monks could assist the itinerary of the soul through purgatory and to eternal salvation: monastic prayer could guarantee immortality and eventual salvation. In addition, the good deeds of monks (charity, for example) reflected virtue back upon donors and patrons.

Long before the arrival of friars on the scene, therefore, the power and efficacy of commemorative prayer was intimately associated with monasticism, and especially the orders associated with religious reform.[9] This was an important feature of early tenth-century Cluny and later of the twelfth-century Cistercians. Friars benefited from this long tradition in many ways; their claims to both institutional and individual poverty meant that they were perceived as closer to Christ and their prayers, therefore, more effective. The mission to the cities, moreover, meant that friars engaged with the merchant and manufacturing class (conspicuous noble or royal patronage tended to come somewhat later, and was especially influenced by the example of Louis IX on his return from Crusade in the 1250s).

The urban setting of mendicant reform, its association with the extirpation of heresy, and its (at least initial) engagement with the poor and needy in squalid industrial areas of production differed profoundly from the monastic culture of reform in isolated rural settings. Mendicant reform renounced property in order to relive the ideal of absolute apostolic poverty based on the New Testament – to be poor and, initially, for Franciscans, homeless like the poor. Yet precisely because of the renunciation of clerical income, mendicant reform, perhaps more than any other, became intimately associated with donors and their bequests through wills and testaments, a social practice revived in the thirteenth century. I shall explore the implications of writing wills for the construction of buildings later in this chapter.

In addition to poverty, the early years of the mendicant orders were characterized by itinerancy, a feature that emphasized other differences between friars and monks. Itinerancy was not new: itinerant preaching had been practiced by heretical groups such as the Cathars, Waldesians, and Umiliati, as well as by eccentric wandering preachers such as Robert of Abrissel early in the twelfth century. While itinerancy eliminated or reduced the cares of property, it was contrary to the monastic concept of *stabilitas loci* (permanence in location) as articulated in the Benedictine rule. Benedict inveighed against wandering monks as gyrovagues, a practice also prohibited in the Council of Chalcedon (451) and the Second Council of Nicaea (787). For friars, the itinerancy of the early years eliminated, or at least reduced, the vulnerability of mendicant communities to local ties – family, friends, and neighborhood.[10] Francis and Dominic rejected the notion of providing funds for travel, and Francis severely prohibited his followers from touching coins.

Initially the Friars Minor engaged in physical labor, a practice that the Preachers, as priests, rejected. But even in the early years, when begging alone was the primary means of survival, donations imposed a series of management issues: every gift – with the possible exception of comestibles – presented the contingent consideration of distribution and the problem of accumulation and storage, both of which were contrary to poverty. Donations of houses and land were particularly complex: for the Friars Minor, these remained the property of the donor until a papal decree of 1245 established that all gifts to Franciscans were owned by the papacy.[11]

Recent scholarship now permits some understanding of how the mendicant economy functioned on a daily basis in the decades and centuries after the foundation of the new orders. As we have seen, circumstances both internal and external to the orders changed rapidly and profoundly over the course of the thirteenth century. While it had been possible for begging and questing to support the small missions of the early years, with the rapid expansion and success of the mendicants, they were inadequate by the middle of the thirteenth century.[12] The urgent need to engage in fund-raising for large communities that required housing, food, and clothing was exacerbated by the arrival of other, newer, begging orders beginning c. 1250 – the Friars of the Sack, Carmelites, Augustinians, Servites, to name only a few. There were also other types of religious institutions and good causes that required support, such as hospitals, orphanages, convents of enclosed women, and beguinages. All competed for the attention and donations of the faithful.

The new studies on the mendicant economy help answer some questions on how friars sustained their communities when begging no longer sufficed. More than any other religious organization, mendicants came to be associated with making wills and the role of executors; indeed, the connection is so strong that Bériou has suggested that friars had a direct hand in reviving the practice.[13] Over time, as the donations from wills aggregated to form a substantial patrimony for each community, friars were increasingly supported by income from annual rents from bequests that could be exchanged or sold, as well as the donations of funds that permitted the purchase of income-bearing properties. Friars were often reluctant to renounce the economic security guaranteed by the predictable and regular infusions of cash from these sources.[14] In the largest houses, such as Santa Croce in Florence (where it is estimated there were roughly 140 friars c. 1300), such sources of income were of vital importance for the daily operations of the community.[15] By the late thirteenth century, documents such as the *Liber depositionum, venditionum et aliorum variorum contractuum* of Santa Maria della Scala in Verona reveal the depth and extent of mendicant financial transactions and property ownership.[16]

Those properties could be rural as well as urban and they were exempt from episcopal taxation and control. In time, the ownership of property came to coincide with the profound reversal of the notion of itinerancy, so much so that by the mid-fourteenth century friars in some areas were not allowed to leave their houses without express permission.[17] Over time the accumulated donations of property resulted in large estates, causing conflict and resentment with neighbors and putting pressure on cities, as noted in the preceding chapter. By the mid-thirteenth century there were inquests into Franciscan landholdings in England; in 1279 Edward I had prohibited the sale or donation of land to the clergy. This was later extended by Edward III.[18]

The absence of accounts from the first decades of the new orders may be attributed in part to the existence of "spiritual friends" or other types of third-party intermediaries outside the convent who handled financial and property transactions.[19] This type of arrangement was legislated in the rules of the Franciscan order and allowed friars to acquire property without (literally) owning it. Sometimes such matters were handled by officially designated members of a pious confraternity associated with the friary. In other cases, as for the Franciscans in London, city officials managed their financial affairs.[20] The deliberate and obligatory "distancing" of financial documents to third parties in external locations obfuscated the economic bases of mendicant communities, preserving the appearance of poverty, vitally important for the perceived efficacy of mendicant prayer, one of the primary motivators of donations. In the north, associations of Beguines were particularly useful in this regard, as Bertrand has observed for Liège.[21] Within this type of arrangement, pious associations or convents could accept property on behalf of the friars who would receive the income; properties thus entailed to the friars generated funds while avoiding the problem of *mortmain*, thereby remaining within the economic structures of the city.[22] In this way, some of the problems noted in Chapter Four within cities such as Strasbourg could be avoided. These types of systems were used not only for the Friars Minor: fraternal institutions also benefited other mendicant institutions such as the Preachers.

As we shall see below in more detail, the Inquisition also played a role in the finances of some mendicant houses. Friars as inquisitors were often intimately associated with (and an instrument of) political factions, especially the anti-Ghibelline movement of the 1260s and 1270s.[23] In Padua, for example, vast properties belonging to pro-imperial families and their associates were transferred to agents of the Friars Minor. These transactions were recorded in the investigation of the commune and Bishop Ottobono of Padua, who requisitioned documents from the convent of Sant'Antonio, now published in the *Liber contractuum* and the *Liber possessionum*, as proof of the financial machinations of the Friars Minor.[24] The extent of the friars' financial operations is startling: they bought and sold properties received as bequests in perpetuity, expropriated donations left *pro remedio animae*, and lent money at usurious levels. The documents attest to these expropriations, the deviation of legacies (including those destined for underage orphans), and multiple other abuses. The level of abuse and misappropriation of funds is perhaps especially striking at Padua, a convent with a significant income from pilgrim donations, which was not the case with most other mendicant houses.

As almost any homeowner knows, property – and above all construction, enlargement, or major repairs – entails heavy expense and often debt. Dominic had been keenly concerned with this issue early in the history of the Order of Preachers, and Bonaventure inveighed against it in his encyclical letters. Both Dominican and Franciscan houses were plagued by debts to individuals, money-lenders, and other religious organizations. In Pistoia, for example, the Friars Minor owed an annual rent of 12 denari pisani to the Vallombrosans at Badia a Taona, which Innocent IV asked the monks to excuse.[25] This debt may have been caused by many factors, but we know from bequests of the 1230s that a Franciscan church in Pistoia was under construction in that period. Most importantly, the problem of endemic debt made friars particularly susceptible to pressures exerted by benefactors for special considerations, especially burial in church or choir.

Capillary Action in the City

FRIARS IN THE HOME

William of Saint-Amour, a secular master of theology at the cathedral school of Paris, described friars as the fulfillment of the eschatological themes in the first verse of 2 Timothy 3:1–6: "and there will be men who are self-lovers, greedy, elated, and so forth. . . . of this sort are those who penetrate homes [*qui penetrant domus*]."[26] The homes in question were not only literal and material houses, but also the spiritual "house" of the inner mind, or conscience, of parishioners. In either case, the *domus* was the rightful terrain of the parish priest, whose task as ordained by apostolic succession was to examine and understand the spiritual well-being of his flock.

It may also be inferred from Saint-Amour's invective that parochial visits in homes by members of the clergy may have been something of a novelty. The intensity of William's prose, and his emphasis on this point as a sign of the last times, suggests that mendicants were particularly innovative in their encounters with laity in private domestic spaces. In addition, of course, there was concern that homes were labile settings for the practice of religion, one in which familiarity and the presence of women presented not only a potentially powerful and receptive audience, but also temptations and risks.

In the matter of visiting homes friars adopted a practice characteristic of heretical groups. Cathars and other heretics propagated and practiced their faith within the domestic context;[27] the house as a private space offered a secluded but structured social outlet for the practice of religion. For heretical groups it was as suitable to pray in the house as in a church.[28] In addition, the Petrobrusians extended this notion to the barn, with a bale of hay as a substitute for the altar, as we have seen. In this manner, the home could become an explicit rejection of the spaces dominated by the structure and hierarchy of the church, from bishops down to the parish priest, and could help generate autochthonous religious practices.

Homes were thus a suspect, unmanaged, "unaligned" territory for religious thought and life. They were also the place where the friar could relate to his parishioners in an unmediated way (as with Friar John in "The Summoner's Tale"). In this context friars could also exert undue influence in the composition of wills and the cultivation of donations. In his fourteenth chapter, William of Saint-Amour emphasized that one of the signs of the last times was false apostles who preached for material gain rather than the welfare of parishioners, a criticism later reflected by Chaucer in the person of Friar John, who was seeking funds for the completion of the convent. Homes were the terrain of friars' capillary action in cities. In homes, as well as in piazzas and marketplaces, friars were able to involve the public in their new interpretation of appropriate spiritual engagement. Above all, the penetrating of homes circumvented the traditional role of the parochial clergy and aligned friars with the practices of the heretics. In *Montaillou*, Le Roy Ladurie suggests that the Inquisition was more an attack on the *domus* as the cradle of heretical thought than on the individual heretic; he describes the *domus* as a kind of conservatory, a "barricade limiting compromising contacts with houses which were not heretical."[29] In some instances the "penetration of homes" during the Inquisition could also entail their violation: in Toulouse, Preachers dragged heretics from their bedchambers. Perhaps by visiting parishioners in homes, friars had also appropriated to themselves the right to consider the home (as well as the physical person of the heretic) as a terrain of action.

WILLS AND TESTAMENTS

The patrimony of the church was constituted in large measure from the legacies and donations of the faithful that accumulated over centuries, sometimes into vast agricultural and urban holdings dispersed over large territories. Both ecclesiastical and monastic establishments as a result had become deeply enmeshed in the administration of farms and the sale of excess produce. Although friars initially renounced these types of possessions and economic engagements, by the mid-thirteenth century they nevertheless developed certain economic strategies to circumvent their own early legislation on property and the income derived therefrom. Procurators were immensely important for managing properties and conducting lawsuits to defend or protect bequests. Friars engaged other types of third parties (Beguines and nuns) to hold and manage property, as we shall see below in the example of Obizzo II's will of 1292, in which the Poor Clares of Rovigo were to buy property, but the income was to go to the local Franciscans.

The prospect of death, whether imminent or in an imagined future, meant a perpetual concern for the fate of the soul. The fourteenth-century merchant Paolo di Certaldo expressed it thus: salvation depended upon confession, contrition, and satisfaction (to restore things that belonged to others) through the composition of a will.[30] Death, after all, could come at any time, and to die intestate was to relinquish the possibility of mediating the tortures of purgatory.

The revival of will-making coincided almost exactly with the rise of the mendicant orders. This had been an ancient custom that had fallen into disuse until the late twelfth and early thirteenth centuries when it was first revived in Italy, possibly as a result of the strong notarial culture of the north. By the late thirteenth century, however, the practice of making a will was widespread, and included small-scale artisans and farmers.[31] After c. 1350, making a will was ubiquitous and equally distributed between genders and social classes. Wills were redacted in preparation for a journey, at outbreaks of infectious diseases, and above all during illnesses. For our purposes, it is important that this phenomenon became an instrument fundamental to the well-being of mendicant communities. Donations in wills were a central component of funding for friars, not only monetary (funeral and burial fees, offerings for intercessory prayers, donations for the fabric or the construction of private altars and chapels) but also, as noted, in land or houses that could provide a steady income through rentals. There were also gifts of candles, habits, and the other items of daily life needed by the communities.

A will could be composed in two ways, as an oral (*sine scriptis*) or as a written (*in scriptis*) document.[32] Normally a testator dictated his wishes (a nuncupative will) to a notary in front of witnesses. Wills contained instructions for the division of property, provisions for intercessory Masses, and, above all, donations *pro remedio* or *pro salute animae* to pious institutions and the poor (which included friars as the apostolic poor). Bequests to the poor might include clothing and meals in return for ritual participation in the funeral, a process in which the poor took on the role of symbolic intercessors. As Chiffoleau has noted, the ostentatious presence of poverty was "a demonstration of the power and compassion of the deceased."[33] Of course, the composition of a will was inflected by the presence of a notary who dictated a formula for its composition. The additional presence of a friar at the bedside of the testator, along with members of the family, could also condition its composition in important ways.

A thirteenth-century will usually contained the following clauses, more or less in this order:

1   The choice of place of burial (by the early thirteenth century, burial in the parish was no longer obligatory although this remained an area of contestation between parishes and the new orders).[34]
2   An offering for the service of burial.
3   Arrangements for the funeral, also normally associated with an offering.
4   Requests for intercessory prayers, the frequency and number of which were established in relation to a donation.
5   The recompense of those wronged or taken advantage of, and the payment of debts.
6   Pious donations *pro remedio animae* or *pro salute animae*.

7 At a somewhat later date, specific donations to be made to individuals: heirs, family members, and friends.

The most common source of sustained funding for mendicant communities came from outright donations in return for intercessory prayer and burial. Often these came in the form of perpetual rents given in return for eternal prayer.[35] This system avoided some of the problems of possession or dominion, thus preserving the principle of the rejection of goods. It was therefore in the interests of religious institutions to support the practice of preparing a last testament. And because the priest who administered confession often wrote the will or sat alongside the notary at the deathbed, this action was often associated with last rites. Pious legacies were such an integral part of a will that those who died without making them were assumed to have died unconfessed; the provincial Council of Narbonne of 1227 forbade them Christian burial unless their relatives prepared a will in their place.[36]

But who should the priest at the bedside be? This was clearly a matter of continued contestation from an early date. In Perugia in 1258 the bishop ordained that only a local parish priest could take last confession or, in the necessity of an alternative, that the parish priest had to give permission.[37] The priest was instructed to inquire about pious donations for the poor. Alexander IV, the former Cardinal Protector of the Franciscans, took this disposition to be directed specifically against the Franciscans and Dominicans and demanded that the edict be withdrawn. Later, in Clement VI's bull *Exivi qui seminat* of 1312, Franciscans were prohibited from acting as witnesses in wills, an edict that reflected both abuse as well as political pressures. Yet there is evidence as early as 1227, if not sooner, that Friars Minor had been acting as executors from the first decades of the new order;[38] one may reasonably imagine that in this matter, also, legislation and common practice diverged.

Alexander IV authorized the Friars Minor to receive cash legacies through third parties by reissuing *Ordinem vestrum* in 1257.[39] The original bull had been emitted in 1245 by Innocent IV, a measure resisted by John of Parma and later by Bonaventure. It is likely, though, that some form of the practice of third-party management of properties and legal affairs already existed. The agents, known as procurators or *dispensatores*, technically represented the donor, and the gift continued to be controlled by the giver.[40] There was a difficulty when the donor died, as was inevitably the case when a will was executed. The matter was complicated enough in relation to food and other supplies, but increasing numbers of bequests from legacies and wills meant growing problems with heirs over inheritances, as well as with the management of accumulated properties. It is, quite honestly, difficult to imagine that any mendicant house could do without lay agents of some kind as by the 1240s the funds, land, and supplies left to friars were indispensable for buildings.

A will could be either private or public, and this was often a matter of local legislation. In Bologna, for example, wills were regulated by ordinances issued by the commune.[41] They were to be registered with the public authorities within a day of their composition, and a list of them was kept in the commune's *Libri memorialium*. Copies were preserved in a cabinet of the communal palace and deposited with the Franciscans and Dominicans in order to remain valid.[42] The deposit of a will in a church or convent was made in the presence of two witnesses, and the document had to be locked in a cabinet in the sacristy in perpetuity or until the testator requested its return. The contents of wills were to be kept secret until the death of the testator.

Although provisions such as those of Bologna were local, they demonstrate the importance of religious institutions in the composition, recording, and protection of wills and testaments, as well as their secrecy until the death of the testator. The deposit of documents for safe keeping attests to the web of exchanges of services that took place between convents, individuals, and the commune, each one of which tightened the bonds of mutual dependency.

A Pisan will of 1273 provides a good index for the value of certain types of donations. The merchant Gerardo Alliata dictated his will on October 31, 1273 requesting burial in the church of San Francesco. Twenty lire were provided for the funeral. In the list of requests for commemorative prayers, five lire were designated for this purpose in the Franciscan church, and ten for construction.[43] Another will, cited by Étienne Hubert, is a donation by Simeone Malabranca in 1348 for the construction of a chapel dedicated to Saint John in return for thirty florins.[44] At the Franciscan church of the Aracoeli, Eduardo di Pietro Sassone left fifteen golden florins in 1296 for construction on the church ("pro opere ipsius ecclesie"), with the understanding that he would be buried in a private chapel – for which he left 100 florins – the location of which would be designated by the friars.[45] The most important donors might bequeath an entire church, and even stipulate its dimensions. By the mid-fourteenth century, many testators of high social status or with great wealth who chose burial at a mendicant convent requested burial in the church or cloister, and they often specified the location of their tomb: "in front of the west door," "beside the holy water font," "by the image of . . ."[46]

Donations for construction were particularly encouraged. Federico Visconti suggested this in his sermons: gifts for the work at the Dominican church of Santa Caterina in Pisa would release the living from death and give life. He cited the example of a certain Sismondello, well known for pious gifts to the friars that included funds for the construction of churches, liturgical objects, books, clothes, and work on the dormitory. Sismondello not only would receive eternal life himself, but his good works would radiate to family and friends by association, saving them from the dangers of the sea, from tribulations of all kinds, illness, and even death.[47] Donors might also bequeath materials, such as bricks and mortar. Bequests could be *pro fabrica*, *ad opus*, *in adiutorium*, or *pro reparatione*. A gift to decorate a chapel or an altar might be *pro ornamentis*. Votive paintings, only a small proportion of which survive, functioned as a commemoration of the donor, almost always representing them on their knees in front of or beside their patron saint(s) (fig. 73). Sometimes, as with Antonio Fissiraga or Guglielmo di Castelbarco, the donor carries a model of the church, and in these cases it may be safe to assume that their gifts were substantial indeed.

Donors, however, were careful to diversify requests for intercessory prayer. Testators gave donations to multiple mendicant foundations, sometimes (as in Bologna) to all the

OPPOSITE PAGE 73 Lodi, San Francesco, the tomb of Antonio Fissiraga, upper section. With kind permission of the Université de Lausanne, Department of History of Art.

churches within the walls. They often left equal sums for all male mendicant establishments, with lesser sums for convents for women.[48] At Rieti in 1311 Giovanni of Secinari left twenty soldi each to San Francesco and San Domenico, and then ten soldi each to seven other houses, mostly Benedictine, Augustinian, and Cistercian male houses and nuns of the same orders.[49] Preferences for one house or another can often only be identified through the choice of burial location, sometimes accompanied perhaps by larger gifts to that institution for construction. Donors could also change their plans for any aspect of a will or donation; the example of Guglielmo di Castelbarco in Verona suggests a volatile swing between the Friars Minor at San Fermo (where he is represented on the triumphal arch with a model of the church) and the Preachers of Sant'Anastasia, where his lavish tomb presides over the entrance to the cloister beside the facade. In some cases, as with Giovanni of Secinari mentioned above, the first request was for burial in the cathedral if an acceptable location could be found for the tomb; if not, it was to be placed with the Franciscans.[50] For the fifteenth century, Noël Coulet has demonstrated that the mendicant houses continued to be favored for burial rather than the cathedral or other churches: Coulet's statistics indicate that between 1400 and 1430, 36 percent of residents chose burial in a mendicant convent; between 1441 and 1450 requests for mendicant burial rose to 48 percent; and between 1450 and 1453 they rose to 57 percent.[51] The financial impact on the remainder of the clergy (parish priests and others) would have been significant.

The wealthiest donors might on occasion found an entirely new church, as we have seen. In 1292 Obizzo II d'Este, lord of Ferrara, bequeathed 10,000 Venetian pounds for a new Franciscan convent to be established outside the walls of Rovigo.[52] The house was to contain fifty friars, at least twelve of whom were to be priests. The donor stipulated that the church should be "great, long, wide, and spacious" and that construction should begin within two years of his death.[53] If the friars delayed work on the new complex, the donation would pass to the Preachers, along with the reimbursement of any funds already disbursed for the Franciscan project. In the same will, Obizzo II gave a yearly donation of 1,000 Venetian pounds to the Poor Clares of Rovigo with an additional 3,000 pounds to buy land, 90 percent of the income from which, however, was to go to the new Franciscan foundation.

In Naples Robert the Wise and Queen Sancia of Mallorca founded the vast convent of Corpus Domini (now Santa Chiara) in 1310, soon after their arrival as the newly crowned king and queen (see figs. 2 and 84).[54] In this case, the new foundation was meant to have a political and urban presence that affirmed the authority of the monarchy. The location of the convent, on the southwest side of the ancient city, shifted the focus of the city toward the royal palace (Castel Nuovo), and anchored its expansion into what had been a semi-rural area: both phenomena were emphasized by the construction of a massive new tower on the lower *decumanus* of the city.[55] The queen took a direct role in the foundation, legislation, and concept of the structure, repeatedly soliciting the papacy for special permissions and establishing the numbers of friars and nuns. By the death of Robert the Wise, the church had become a necropolis for the royal family and many members of the court, creating within the church a mirror of the court through tombs and memorials. Santa Chiara and its cloisters exemplify the new monumentality of mendicant architecture early in the fourteenth century, as described in the earlier chapters of this study.

There were customary and standardized (but unwritten) understandings of the amounts appropriate for requests for burials, funerals, altars, and chapels. The greater the donation and the more important the patron, the better the location of tomb or altar: in this way the Bardi and Peruzzi families acquired the prestigious locations for the chapels to the right of the apse of Santa Croce between the altar and the sacristy. According to Borsook, one of the Baroncelli chapels at Santa Croce cost the elevated sum of 1,008 lire, approximately 336 florins,[56] an amount related to its favored location. In 1339 a chapel in an angle near the friars' choir at Santa Maria Novella cost 500 florins.[57] Other chapels in the less splendid buildings of other cities tended to cost less, but this was contingent upon location and, no doubt, the ostentation of the building. In Florence, as Sylvain Piron has demonstrated, the mendicant houses came to represent and reflect the interests of distinct family groups, neighborhoods, confraternities, and business consortia in life and in death: the scale of Santa Maria Novella and Santa Croce attest to the competitive environment in which the friars played a full and largely unfettered role.[58]

Yet even if a will left money for construction, work was often postponed until enough legacies had accumulated to sustain a workshop. Although a will might specify funds for building, there might be (and often was) an extensive delay between the execution of the will and the initiation of construction of either church or chapel. Therefore, by the early fourteenth century funds were often given on the condition that work should begin within a certain number of years, often ten: Donato di Amideo Peruzzi stated in his will that work on the chapel must be initiated within ten years of his death.[59] A major donation from a prestigious donor was no doubt a convincing argument for undertaking construction, and burials must have occurred even within the early stages of a building project. For example, the earliest recorded burial at Santa Croce was in 1298, only four years after the inception of work.[60] It seems reasonable to suppose that mendicant churches were often initiated on the basis of projected future income – in the case of Santa Croce not only contributions from the commune, but also the donations of successfully executed wills and prospective further bequests from donors; the failure of these to materialize (often because of litigation from family members) could involve religious communities in substantial debt.[61]

The practice of cultivating wealthy and pious patrons in return for legacies to support construction was becoming notorious in the late thirteenth century, precisely in the period when friars were building their largest churches. Even if we discount the cranky voices of the antifraternal critics, the problem within the Franciscan order is attested as early as the 1250s and 1260s by the remonstrations of Bonaventure, as noted in chapter 1. In his encyclical letter of 1266, Bonaventure (then Minister General) deplored the "sepulturarum ac testamentorum litigiosa et avida quaedam invasio," and associated it with "murorum curiositas." In addition, Bonaventure noted and deplored the association of burial and wills with buildings. In his first encyclical letter of 1257, he insisted "that the constitution on burials be strictly observed."[62] In the Constitutions of Narbonne of 1260, written under his administration, article 22 pronounced: "The burial of the brothers is to be strictly reserved, so that no one whom they could refuse without notable scandal is to be admitted there." The previously mentioned second encyclical letter of 1266 expanded on burials and legacies that provoked the hatred of the clergy.[63]

Mendicant preachers sometimes addressed the potential dangers of associating bequests with commemorative Masses, attempting to address the possible implication that salvation was for sale and therefore more easily accessible to the rich. Giordano of Pisa early in the fourteenth century pronounced sermons in which he rejected the commodification of intercessory action:

> There are many who when they request masses do it above all for a certain reason: [they think that] so many masses are worth so much money and add up as though getting four or six for one, and reason as though they were in the market. Cursed be anyone who has this intention and whomever gives these funds or takes them away. . . . But if you want to request masses or other benefactions and wish to give what you have, you may do it in this way, that the money that you offer is not offered as a purchase but rather for the love of God, as to the poor in charity, in charity, I say, and in no other way.[64]

It is interesting to note that in statistical studies of bequests of wills, the largest donations tended to be made to the wealthiest of the mendicant orders, the Franciscans and Dominicans, and especially to the former. In Marseilles, for example, the poorer and newer mendicant orders received fewer donations. Several of these (such as the Friars of the Sack) were suppressed in the 1274 Council of Lyons.[65] How are we to interpret this? Did donations tend to be directed toward those orders that had already demonstrated success (by erecting large churches and convents), where the donor felt that strong institutional presence secured the continuity of prayers in perpetuity? Did the existence of large buildings attest to the greater efficacy of prayer, perhaps a greater visibility (to God?), and a sort of "guarantee" of greater success of salvation?

For the port city of Marseilles, Michaud demonstrated that women were much more favorable to the Friars Minor than to other religious institutions, including Preachers.[66] Women donated not only to convents, but also to individual confessors and executors. Yet donations by women to the Friars Minor of Marseilles ceased almost completely in the third decade of the fourteenth century after the execution (by burning) of four dissident Franciscans who were committed to the original ideal of apostolic poverty.

Brentano has observed that over the course of the fourteenth century wills became more voluble and more personal.[67] Donors increasingly used the will to reflect upon and express their preferences and desires; the formulation of these later documents became less controlled by legal formulas and evolved into a reflective consideration on the fragility of human life. Michele Bacci quotes the poetic and personalized introduction of a will from 1383 that admirably makes this point: "Because man, born of woman, is here for a brief interval filled with sorrow, only to soon disappear like a shadow, without ever remaining in a fixed state, he can never have faith in the [continued] prosperity of the moment."[68]

CONVENTS AS CEMETERIES

Friars played an important role in popularizing the burial of middle-class laity in churches and convents, in what some have called the "democratization" of death.[69] The proliferation of burials and tombs in mendicant establishments is indeed one of the central themes of

74 Lodi, San Francesco, tomb of Antonio Fissiraga, lower section. With kind permission of the Université de Lausanne, Department of History of Art.

this book, and architectural space came to resemble (and be designed as) "warehouses" or "hangars" for tombs and other kinds of interventions of the faithful: paintings, banners, coats of arms, and other paraphernalia. Lay patrons could ask to be buried in the habit of the order, *ad succurendum*, as can be seen below the tomb of Antonio Fissiraga (fig. 74).[70] The location of burial was determined largely by money and social rank: if this phenomenon was, indeed, "democratization," it was nonetheless intimately tied to property and cash. The poor continued to be buried outside city walls and, one suspects, in anonymity.

But what was the process through which religious communities attracted burials and tombs, and how did they "manage" their dead? Where did they put them? How did all this begin? From time immemorial the care and burial of the dead has been the concern of the living; those who had not received last rites and burial were lost souls and in antiquity condemned to wander the banks of the river Styx, while Christians were consigned to perdition.[71] Later in the Middle Ages the right to select the place of burial was codified in Gratian's *Decretals*,[72] but until the arrival of the mendicant orders this legislation presented few challenges to the established tradition of burial in the parish or cathedral churchyard. Fees from funerals and burials were an important form of income for the clergy. Most religious institutions reserved (or attempted to reserve) burial within churches for the upper clergy, nobles, or founders,[73] and provided burial for others in outdoor cemeteries and churchyards.

Roman practice had strictly legislated burial outside the city walls. By the sixth century CE, however, there is strong evidence from both archaeological and textual sources that burials were occurring not only within the walls but also within churches. As had occurred previously with extramural funerary basilicas, the more elaborate tombs of the wealthy tended to be located close to and sometimes within churches, while those of the poor were peripheral.[74] Gregory the Great in his *Dialogues* mentions the burial of important personages in churches as accepted practice, although he also noted the example of a dyer who was (in Gregory's view, inappropriately) able to obtain church burial.[75] Privileged graves also began to appear in public squares and around the periphery of churches and baptisteries.[76] The names of the dead are still visible along the lower exterior flanks of the cathedrals of Pisa and Florence (at the west end) as well as around San Frediano in Lucca and San Francesco in Prato (figs. 75 and 76). In late antiquity burials were already encroaching into residential areas (for example, the Campo Marzio in Rome); the evidence suggests that this phenomenon was promoted and regulated by the clergy.[77]

By the eighth and ninth centuries the systematic translation of saints' relics from extramural locations into churches *intra muros*, and the resulting multiplication of altars became an added incentive for the urban burial of laity. When the saints moved into town, the public followed. This created additional tension between traditional church legislation on burial and the desire of the faithful to be placed as close as possible to the burial of a holy body. When burial near the relics of a saint was not possible, a location adjacent to doorways and entrances was favored. Cathedral builders in France seem to have had the unique right to be interred under the drainpipes of the cathedral (*sub stillicidio*), so that the rainwater falling on sacred space would then drain onto them, as was the case of Robert de Luzarches at Amiens.[78]

The issue was exacerbated by the powerful economic interests of the religious institutions that benefited from accepting tombs. Dyggve has associated the transformation of burial practice in late antiquity with pious donations: inheritances, votive gifts, and landed property, and of course, as we have seen, at a much later period the mendicants were far from indifferent to these economic considerations.[79]

Urban expansion caused by the population explosion after c. 1100 meant that cities swelled beyond the girdle of late antique walls and often absorbed pre-existing extramural cemeteries. With new expanded walls, the *extra muros* cemetery became *intra muros* (see the location of Santa Maria Novella, fig. 66).[80] At the same time that cemeteries were absorbed within the walls, the new establishments of friars were often "planted" in cemetery chapels or churches on the margins. Friars were reluctant to disrupt the traditional role of a cemetery, and soon not only adopted but also expanded this activity with systematically placed tombs integrated into an overall plan: in Florence the Preachers created the Chiostro

75   Lucca, San Frediano, inscription on the church exterior.

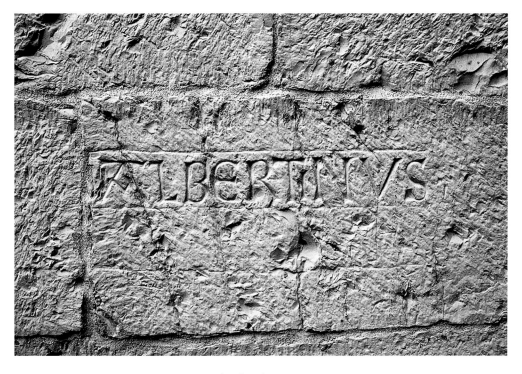

76   Prato, San Francesco, inscription on the church exterior.

dei Morti flanking the right side of Santa Maria Novella, with tomb niches that range along the side wall of the nave and across the facade (see figs. 7 and 63).[81] The friars' rights to cemeteries was affirmed in 1227, although as early as 1217 Honorius III had protected the rights of the Dominicans to cemeteries.[82] The cemetery at San Domenico in Bologna was integrated into the spatial concept of the north and west sides of the conventual complex by the mid-1220s, and at Toulouse the new chevet expanded over what was a cemetery to the east of the original church (see fig. 34). In the matter of attending to their patrons after death and in creating long-term associations with families and confraternities, the Preachers were prescient, organized, and systematic.

Friars thus played an important role in the "democratization" of death by burying the middle class in and around their churches and cloisters. Although this was not a new phenomenon, mendicants engaged in lay burial (and its associated accoutrements) so systematically that it became an important factor in the design and scale of buildings. Their success represented a direct threat to the income of parishes and cathedrals, and came to be one of the primary causes of contention between friars and the secular and monastic clergy. Strife emerged at a surprisingly early date: for example, in Bergen c. 1230 a community of local canons emptied their sewers into the adjacent cemetery of the Preachers.[83] As a result of friars' openness to lay burials, other religious organizations – even those like the Cistercians who as reform movements had strictly prohibited such practices – liberalized their legislation on lay burials to allow tombs within strictly reserved church spaces.

I have noted that one of the most powerful incentives for burial in a friary was the perceived power of mendicant prayer for the soul. In the thirteenth century the need for intercessory prayer seems to have rivaled the importance of *ad sanctos* burial: Chaucer's friar in "The Summoner's Tale" attests vividly to the value of mendicant prayer for the salvation of the soul: "so the prayer . . . of charitable, chaste, and busy friars, takes flight, and enters into God's two ears."[84] With a few exceptions (Santa Corona in Vicenza, San Domenico in Bologna, Sant'Eustorgio in Milan, Sant'Antonio in Padua, Santa Margherita in Cortona, and San Francesco in Assisi), mendicant churches are not known for conspicuous relics or as pilgrimage places: proximity to the chorus of perpetual prayer seems to have been more important. As far as possible, tombs were therefore clustered around the choir, a location generally reserved for patrons with high social or economic status. Local practice, and the rigor of a particular house in this matter, could also be strong determining factors, however. In Bologna, for example, burial within the church was for a long time stoutly resisted, except for the exceptional dead, at both the Franciscan and Dominican churches. Elsewhere, and in cities where church burial was more commonly accepted, locating a tomb at the head of the nave, or on either side of the door to the cloister (or "walking space" of English convents), was highly desired (see fig. 28). Many churches and cloisters were paved with tomb slabs (fig. 77 and see figs. 4).

Integrating tombs and cemeteries with new foundations began at an early date. As noted, some convents, like Santa Maria Novella, had been founded in cemeteries (1221). This was also the case of Sant'Eustorgio in Milan, where the late antique and early medieval tombs are now visible beneath the church. In any event, the association of mendicant houses with cemeteries was inevitable, as friars needed to bury their own dead, and if at

77 Venice, San Francesco della Vigna, cloister.

all possible within the precinct of the community. The first document in this regard refers to the Preachers at Saint-Jacques in Paris, who were granted the right of a cemetery in February 1220, only shortly after Réginald of Orléans had been interred at a parish cemetery.[85] Shortly afterwards, however, the cemetery at San Domenico in Bologna was in place (the early 1220s) along the north flank of the new church; it received formal authorization in 1227. At this site members of the community were interred north of the choir, followed to the west by a cemetery for students and finally the vast and highly systematized burial area for laity (see fig. 36). At Arles a donation for the foundation of the Dominican convent in 1231 specified the creation of the church, cloister, residential buildings, and cemetery;[86] in this city, however, the older tradition of burial in the Aliscamps cemetery (see below) remained strong. In some cases, as with the Jacobins at Toulouse, the friars' cemetery was blessed in 1229, the year of the foundation of the new convent; we have already seen that the creation of a new chevet sometime after 1234 expanded over it (see fig. 34). Although the Preachers in Toulouse acquired official authorization to bury laity

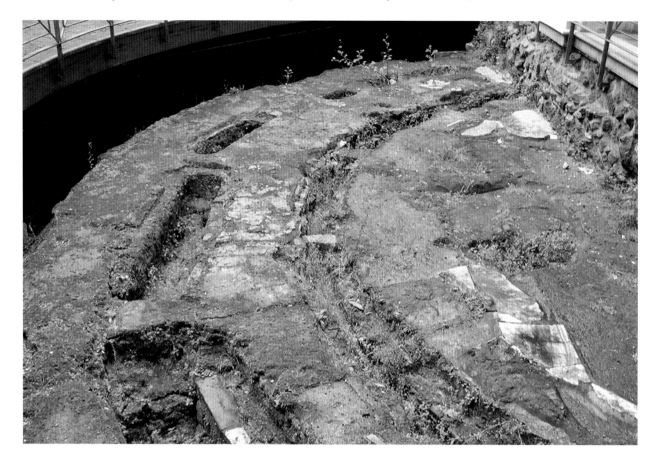

78   Naples, San Lorenzo cloister, view of the tombs carved into the foundations of the *macellum*.

in 1244, burials in the old cemetery had probably continued at the site from the time of the foundation of the new house in 1229. The official authorization exacerbated continuing conflicts over burials with the ancient church of La Daurade.[87] Here as elsewhere, families must have urged the friars to preserve and continue pre-existing cemeteries, and because Preachers were sometimes given cemetery chapels from the outset, it is likely that they played a pivotal role in launching the practice of lay burial. But the Friars Minor soon followed suit: at San Lorenzo in Naples, an early medieval cemetery in the area of the *macellum* was expanded into a systematic burial area to the west of the church outside the narthex (figs. 78 and 79).[88]

Research on wills and lists of burials in various cities (Bologna, Arles, Avignon) suggests that the choice of cemetery was often tied to proximity to the residence and family of the deceased. The neighborhood around a mendicant convent often provided its most loyal clientele. Burial location also was socially inflected: nobles and wealthy merchants tended to incline toward the friars, whereas workers and menial laborers tended to retain the tradition of burial in the parish.[89] In many places the Preachers from an early date attracted the highest levels of patrons: nobles and royalty.

The late thirteenth-century *Libellus funerum* of San Domenico in Bologna lists about 350 lay burials at the convent, mostly on the north and western sides of the church.[90]

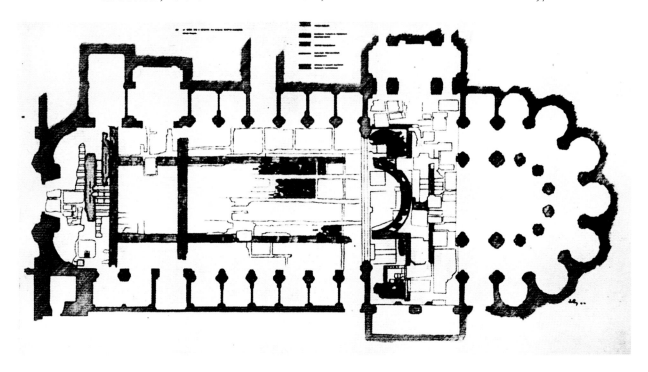

79   Naples, San Lorenzo, excavation plan from Fino, 1987, p. 17.

Although the cemetery was officially authorized by Gregory IX in 1227,[91] the earliest datable tombs (those with inscriptions) mentioned are those along the north flank of the church from the third quarter of the thirteenth century.[92] By this time, however, the cemetery had long been in place and, as the nave reached completion in c. 1234, the cemetery was expanded and developed into a carefully planned organizational system. The canonization of Dominic in July of the same year became added impetus for burial adjacent to the church. By 1291, there were three rows of tombs parallel to the front, and numerous rows of tombs set out in the shape of a "T" on either side of the path leading to the portal on the north flank (see fig. 36). Here, as in other cities, tombs clustered on the side of the convent that faced the city: at San Domenico they were mostly located on the north flank of the church and in front of the facade, whereas at San Francesco the cemetery was to the east and north of the nave and apse. At both, tombs were densely packed around doors and portals, so much so that at San Francesco they may have presented an obstacle to access to church and cloister.[93]

   Burials in or around convents multiplied everywhere toward the middle of the thirteenth century, and by this time patrons or donors in increasing numbers included such requests in their wills: at Ferrara, for example, the earliest surviving example of a will requesting burial with the Dominicans dates to 1252.[94] On the other hand, the Franciscan Order lagged in the matter of burials. Salimbene noted that in 1245 Count Raymond Berenguer had not been permitted burial within the Franciscan church "since at that time they almost always refused sepulture, both because they sought to avoid the labor and because they were at odds with the regular clergy."[95] The friar went on to note that this was why the Friars Minor had declined to bury Saint Elizabeth of Hungary after her death in 1231,[96] an error they must have greatly regretted over the course of time. Yet by c. 1294, the reconstruction of Santa Croce in Florence seems to have been predicated both economically and architecturally upon burials (see fig. 80).

In this as in every other matter there was, of course, considerable regional variation. Stouff has noted that at Arles the tradition of extramural burial in the Roman necropolis of the Aliscamps remained strong through the fourteenth century in spite of local friaries with cemeteries.[97] In Rome, on the other hand, the vast circumference of the Aurelian walls meant that burial *intra muros* offered ample available space: evidence suggests that already in the fifth century bodies were being buried in cemeteries and in or around churches within the walls.[98] Here the earlier practice of burying at extra-mural funerary basilicas such as San Lorenzo and Sant'Agnese fuori le Mura had probably "loosened up" the exclusion of tombs from sacred space, and because Rome so often provided a model for Christian practice elsewhere, other cities naturally followed suit where space within the walls permitted. The later translations of the sacred remains of martyrs and bishops into cities brought new pressures to associate the burial of prestigious individuals with the sacred numen of relics inside churches,[99] and by his death in 1216 Innocent III referred to burials within the church as an established custom that should not be denied to the faithful.[100]

What was particular to the thirteenth century and to friars was their direct agency in accepting and promoting middle-class burial within churches. In spite of periodic and sporadic efforts by the orders to eliminate, or at least to control, this practice, and notwithstanding the indecorous behavior in relation to wills and legacies deplored by Bonaventure, economic, social, and community pressures for burials were too powerful for most mendicant communities to resist. Bodies brought resources in the form of land, property, and funding that were essential for survival; charity no longer sufficed, especially when large-scale construction projects were under way. What resulted were symbiotic communities that linked the physical presence of the tomb to prayer, redemption, and salvation for the middle class, often merchant, soul.

Yet mendicant funerals and burials presented a severe threat to the traditional prerogatives of the parochial and cathedral clergy. Instances of street fights and battles over bodies at both funerals and burials were numerous. For example, just before Easter 1288, the canons of Salerno Cathedral stormed the funeral of a pious Florentine merchant who wished to be buried in San Francesco in the habit of the Friars Minor. The canons attacked the friars, kidnapped the corpse, and took it to the cathedral for the funeral and burial. Once the obsequies were over, the cathedral clergy returned to the Franciscan church, broke down the doors and windows, knocked over the reserved host, stoned the friars, and dragged some of them naked through the streets.[101] Within a few decades of the arrival of the Preachers in Pisa, an agreement was reached (February 1236) between them and the cathedral that nobody who rightfully belonged in the cathedral cemetery would be interred at Santa Caterina.[102] Yet in spite of this and further mediation, conflict continued in Pisa into the second half of the thirteenth century and well beyond: in 1260, for example, Cardinal Riccardo Annibaldi issued a decree that reaffirmed the right of *ius sepeliendi* for friars, permitting them to inter anyone who requested burial in their convent.[103]

Erickson mentions a similar situation between mendicants and the local clergy in Exeter. Here the burial of an English nobleman in the Dominican cemetery prompted a dispute with the canons of the cathedral, who insisted that the deceased be brought there for the funeral before burial; when the Preachers refused, the canons seized the body. After the funeral, it was returned, naked, to the Preachers. The friars washed their hands of the corpse, however, leaving it where it lay outside the convent until hygienic concerns impelled the canons to recover and bury it at the cathedral.[104]

Contestation over funerals and burials was not new and had existed for centuries between religious institutions long before the arrival of the friars.[105] "Laudable custom" established the emoluments offered for last rites, funerals, and burials in towns and regions, and are reflected in the amounts left to the clergy in wills and last testaments. These documents often differentiated between the sums left for the funeral, for the burial, and for the clergy.[106] Customary payments are explicitly mentioned in the provisions of the Fourth Lateran Council and were extended by Gregory IX to allow bishops to enforce payment. The difficulties arose when parishioners chose burial not in the parish cemetery but at an alternative site; although this was guaranteed in principle by ecclesiastical legislation, in practice it threatened the hegemony of parishes and bishops.

"Laudable custom," whether voluntary or imposed, however, could not easily absorb or adjust to new religious institutions or changing patterns in preferences for funerals and burials. When friars settled in a new town, they were required to request permission from the bishop or cathedral canons for the right to bury laity in their churches or cemeteries.[107] Depending on the town, friars often had to promise a third to a quarter (the canonical quarter) of their income from funerals and burials to the parish or cathedral. But with the bull *Pacem vestram* issued by Innocent IV in 1253, Franciscans were exempted from paying the quarter; Preachers also became exempt in 1257 in a bull issued by Alexander IV.[108] These exemptions were reversed by Boniface VIII in 1300 in *Super cathedram*, which attempted to impose once and for all the required payment of the canonical quarter to the secular clergy for all burials.[109] Even so, papal edicts did not quell the controversy or the bitter resentment: too much money was at stake and the well-being of ecclesiastical institutions was under threat. The rights of the friars against the parochial clergy bounced from papal court to papal court and often elicited local legislation. In some places (Metz, for example) the friars categorically refused to honor Boniface's injunction. In other cities, they attempted to avoid or subvert its conditions. In 1304 *Super cathedram* was rescinded by Benedict XV, only to be reinstated again by Clement V in 1311. The Council of Vienne in 1312 affirmed the rights of the friars to episcopal exemption, preaching in public squares, hearing confession, and burying anyone who desired to be interred in their convents.

There were repeated attempts within the Franciscan Order to come to grips with this complicated and contentious matter. Bonaventure's attempts to curb burials have been noted above. His successor, Jerome of Ascoli, announced in 1274 to the community of Friars Minor that, on the order of the pope, no one should be buried elsewhere than in the family tomb. The 1279 chapter of Assisi repeated this injunction, with the important addition that no one should be received for burial in a church of the order without just compensation to the parish according to local custom. This edict also forbade litigation over bodies.[110] The themes were vividly echoed by Peter John Olivi in 1279.[111] Yet only a few years later (1283), Olivi's position against burials was cited among the articles of condemnation, which stated that "burying the dead is a work of mercy, spiritual and in no way out of harmony with evangelical perfection."[112] If the dead found peace in the mendicant cemetery, the friars themselves found only money and trouble, and this trouble was particularly acute for Franciscans.

TOMBS

In the thirteenth century, friars thus played an important role in "moving" the tombs of the middle-class dead into sacred space.[113] In spite of the internationalism of the mendicant movement, there were strong regional, economic, and social preferences and variations. Although the evidence is exiguous for the thirteenth century, it appears that the wealthiest and most ostentatious family chapels often included tomb slabs outside the entrance to a chapel as a gesture of humility, even as the wealth and good taste of the family in question were prominently displayed in its decoration. In certain convents, perhaps particularly in those of special significance for the orders, such as San Domenico in Bologna, there may have been initial rigor with respect to allowing lay tombs in the church, reserved primarily as the shrine of Dominic. Farther afield, especially at convents where there was less institutional pressure to set an example, tombs crept into interiors by the middle of the thirteenth century, if not before. Sepultuaries, or lists of the locations of tombs and burials, begin to proliferate around the last decade of the thirteenth century, attesting to the accumulation of tombs in and around churches and cloisters. Indeed, the existence of sepultuaries as documents indicates that friars had a management problem in keeping track of the locations of tombs and the names of the dead, forgotten or effaced by foot traffic.

It is, of course, frustrating that the lists of tombs in the sepultuaries are so laconic. They rarely if ever include the date of death. It could also be that tomb slabs may not always have included the name of the deceased. In Italy this is not certain: the will published by Hubert in 1995 specifies the location for a new tomb near that of a supposed Ceco: by 1367 either the inscription had been effaced by pedestrians or it had never existed.[114] By the sixteenth century this situation had changed dramatically: a tomb slab for a woman buried at San Zaccaria in Venice even records the name of the notary and the date and number of the notarial act, and Hubert noted that a separate notarial act to guarantee the location of the tomb was attached to a will of 1353.[115]

The sepultuaries of Bologna have been the object of important research by Bruno Breveglieri. Frithjof Schwarz has recently thoroughly examined the tombs and documentation for Santa Maria Novella in Florence, including both the lists of burials as well as the archaeological evidence from the site. But elsewhere material of this kind often remains unpublished. Yet the sepultuaries in particular attest to the emergence of systematic planning for graves, as can be seen in Breveglieri's reconstructions of the tombs at San Domenico in Bologna (see fig. 36). The excavations at San Lorenzo in Naples reveal a similarly systematized allotment of burial slots outside the west doors of the narthex and adjacent to the old city market (see fig. 79).

The shortage of surviving inscribed tomb slabs before c. 1300 may suggest that many early tombs were anonymous.[116] At San Domenico in Bologna the earliest recorded inscribed tombs were those of 1315 and 1319.[117] Of the more than 200 wills examined by

Jean-Louis Gaulin for this site, only five mention a sepulchral monument.[118] This may have been a matter of the prestige of the deceased: one of those instances, a 1280 will, specified ten lire for a stone *archa*; in 1292 Petrus Capretus de Lambertinis, the famous canonist, offered 150 lire to Bologna for burial.[119]

Evidence from France suggests that by the fourteenth century testators often requested a named tombstone, however.[120] Early in the fifteenth century in Italy great sculptors such as Lorenzo Ghiberti were commissioned to design and sculpt highly personalized sepulchral monuments: at Santa Croce in Florence, four tomb slabs are attributed to him.[121] Burials and chapels were available for an entire family and generations of descendants: by the fourteenth century tombstones were often equipped with a resealable "plug" (*chiusino*) to permit the addition of successive generations of family members. These can be seen as squares in the 1784 plan of San Francesco at Bologna (see fig. 4). The permanent association of the dead with family, and the reinforcement of lineage (marked by the coats of arms on tombs), were important considerations in the choice of place of burial. Tombs and family chapels had become multigenerational repositories, "homes away from home" for families who thereby developed a deep and umbilical bond with the religious institution that hosted the physical remains and remembered the dead through prayer.

Until the fourteenth century the majority of graves seem to have been located outside a church, often on the north flank if space was open and available. In densely packed urban environments, however, this was not always possible, so that burial inside church and cloister became increasingly important. At Santa Croce in Florence tombs were placed in the two external lateral galleries (see fig. 22); on the north side of the church the gallery flanked the street. (Santa Croce also innovated with an eastern crypt entirely dedicated for burials, discussed below.) At San Lorenzo in Naples, as noted, the excavation report of the first (early Christian) church indicates a systematic layout of tombs outside the narthex of the old basilica, a structure that remained in place until c. 1325, when the church was extended to the west (see figs. 41 and 79). At this site, tightly packed into the grid of the ancient city, tombs of donors were placed outside the west front, but by the late thirteenth century at the latest they also invaded the church interior. By the time of its western extension, however, San Lorenzo had evolved into a royal necropolis with tombs of princes and nobles in the church and cloister. Although few of these survive, that of Catherine of Austria (d. 1323) indicates that high-prestige monuments had become lavish and multilevel structures, often associated with altars and placed against a wall in the transept or in the radiating chapels around the apse. They also often included wall paintings, as will be seen in more detail below. The systematized and practical arrangement of burials outside the old narthex gave way to ostentatious monuments that glorified the royal family.

The rigor of certain convents notwithstanding, by the mid-thirteenth century there is thus considerable evidence for tombs inside mendicant churches (though few if any thirteenth-century slabs survive). This is demonstrated by legislation that attempted to control the practice. The Preachers resisted pressure to place tombs in churches; by 1246 there were strictures against tombs, repeated in 1250: "Let burials not take place in our churches" ("in nostris ecclesiis sepulture non fiant"). There was particular opposition to elaborate memorials: the Dominican chapter of 1245 stipulated that tombs with prominent carved sculpture should not be permitted within churches: "Let tombs not be made in our churches with projecting carving, and those that have been made are to be removed" ("non fiant in ecclesiis nostris cum sculpturis prominentibus sepulture et quie facte sunt, auferantur").[122]

The necessity of creating a foundation above the flood plain for Santa Croce became the mother of invention in matters of burial: a long corridor for tombs and family memorials was inserted below the eastern chapels (fig. 80 and see fig. 9). This disposition was copied after c. 1309 at Santo Stefano in Prato, where a new east end was constructed over a burial crypt (fig. 81). When work at Santa Croce proceeded to the eastern bays of the nave after c. 1301, the two long external galleries for more tombs and commemorations were erected to flank the nave, as noted above (see fig. 22); the church foundation had therefore been conceived as wide enough to contain these second, external galleries. Only family coats of arms, some with short commemorative inscriptions, survive. We should therefore understand that Santa Croce was at least in part designed to absorb and include many of the Florentine dead: neighbors, patrons, donors, and members of affiliated confraternities. Indeed, one function of confraternities was to encourage friends and neighbors to request burial in the convent, as well as to leave legacies and bequests; there was a symbiotic relationship between these practices and the shape and scale of the church.[123] Furthermore, members of confraternities probably played a significant role in obtaining the commune's annual subvention of 1,200 pounds for construction.

We noted that tomb slabs inserted in floors were easily forgotten and inscriptions (if they existed) often effaced by pedestrian traffic (see fig. 77). As a result, starting in the late thirteenth century, a new type of document, list of burials, or the sepultuary, was created. Two early examples of such lists from Bologna suggest that not all tombs were marked with the name of the deceased or the slabs had already been effaced by the time of their composition in 1291. The tomb at Sant'Angelo in Pescheria in Rome, as noted above, was placed near another tomb, the inscription of which had been effaced: "quod dicitur esse sepulturam Ceconis."[124] An inscribed slab dated to 1310 at Santa Maria in Aracoeli survives against the west wall of the church, its preservation contingent upon its protected location.

Tomb niches placed in the wall, or *avelli*, may in part have developed as as a solution to this problem. The niches in the Chiostro de' Morti at Santa Maria Novella, Florence, date from c. 1300 (see figs. 7 and 55),[125] as do those along the flank of the Dominican church in Prato (fig. 72 and see fig. 56). At the Dominican friary in Roscommon, Ireland, as noted above, they were systematically incorporated into the interior and are an integral part of the construction of the church (see fig. 57). This systematic approach to the integration of niche or wall tombs into the architectural structure, a feature especially typical of the Preachers, is somewhat rarer in Franciscan churches, although the Friars Minor had many individual tomb niches or canopies attached like barnacles to their churches, as at San Francesco in Lucca (fig. 82). The back wall of the niche was usually decorated with a fresco.

Niche tombs, or tombs raised on bases or pedestals, had many advantages. They were protected from the wear and tear of pedestrians. They offered greater visibility and could be incorporated with an effigy or other sculpture, as well as commemorative images (see figs. 73 and 74). The wall tomb was a more conspicuous and prestigious intervention that could be located in a strategic position if the patron had been particularly generous or was especially prominent. Even when not integral to the construction of the lower walls, it

80   Florence, Santa Croce, crypt.

could be added to facades (San Francesco in Lucca), or cloisters (San Francesco in Lodi), and incorporated with secondary altars.

Until Napoleon's Civil Code of 1804, nothing could stop the flow of burials to churches. Nevertheless, certain conventions of restraint remained: in thirteenth- and early four-teenth-century Tuscany, tombs were often placed outside family chapels, not within them. The Santa Croce *sepultuario* of 1439 lists eleven tombs for men of the Alberti family at the base of the stairs below the main altar, whereas the women were interred outside the choir enclosure.[126] Other favored locations were the entrances to churches, especially the door from the cloister in the friars' choir, where tombs clustered in great profusion. A location near or beside a font was desirable.[127] The social topography of death reflected class, wealth, and gender.

The burial of the dead was, of course, not unique to the mendicant orders. But friars in the early decades were exceptional in their willingness to inter the middle class, the

81   Prato, Santo Stefano, view of the crypt of 1309.

merchants or the bankers, upon whose generosity they depended. The combination of the tomb with intercessory prayer provided an assurance of salvation even and especially for those whose income had derived from usury. Indeed, only the particular weight of mendicant prayer could erase the burden of sin from ill-gotten gains (*male ablata*).

The importance and proliferation of tombs are mentioned in *Piers the Plowman's Crede*, a text that highlights the decorative element of gilding on many monuments:

> Tombs in canopied niches set on high,
> Kept in corners and closely clustered
> Of alabaster with coats of arms, appropriately appointed,
> Made upon marble in many ways,
> Knights clad just so in their proper emblems,
> All, as it seemed, saints sanctified on the earth;
> Lovely ladies are wrought lying by their sides
> In many gay garments all of beaten gold.[128]

82   Lucca, San Francesco, facade. © Bildarchiv Foto Marburg/Paul Haag.

The same poem also associates burials with windows, altars, paintings, stained glass, and coats of arms, as will be seen below.

LATERAL CHAPELS

The practice of adding lateral chapels with secondary altars to pre-existing buildings was well established by the twelfth century, particularly in monastic churches.[129] In the early decades of the thirteenth century, these began to be inserted at some cathedrals (Chartres, Le Mans) and, after c. 1220, in a systematic arrangement along the flanks of Notre-Dame in Paris.[130] After mid-century chapels sometimes became an integral part of the plans of new churches, including cathedrals (Naples, Orvieto), and by the end of the century pre-existing chapels originally intended for liturgical purposes were often repurposed by individuals or families for burial and commemoration. New churches often included long rows of chapels specifically for the commemoration of prestigious donors: perhaps those off the transept at Santa Croce in Florence are the most conspicuous instances of this phenomenon, but in Naples, for example, they also characterize a great number of mendicant buildings such as Santa Maria del Carmine, San Domenico, and Santa Chiara (figs. 83 and 84). Donations for private commemorative chapels financed building projects, a practice not by any means restricted to the churches of friars: the vast unfinished chevet of Toulouse Cathedral, begun in 1272, was conceived with burial chapels for the canons as an integral part of the plan. Once these were in place, however, there was little incentive for funding the rest of the new cathedral, which remains incomplete.

By the late thirteenth century religious institutions thus instigated the construction of lateral chapels and imposed uniformity in their design.[131] Cathedrals were far more reticent to accept lay burials and private family chapels: the first known tomb associated with the construction of a chapel at Notre-Dame in Paris dates to 1279 (the fourth radiating chapel on the north side of the chevet).[132]

Chapels contained secondary altars to make space for the obligatory daily Mass of the ordained clergy. Initially these had been placed against the side walls or the piers and columns of a nave; however, the creation of separate spaces by demolishing the side walls and extending back between the buttresses of vaulted buildings provided greater privacy and reduced noise.[133] Gardner quotes a document from Arezzo that mentions the destruction of a church wall ("rompere il muro de la ghiesa") in order to insert a chapel.[134] When such chapels were later co-opted for family commemoration and burials with the usual provision of a prebend, a practice known as *ius patronatus* (the right of patronage in return for a benefice, or regular revenues, from property), the church could reward benefactors by long-term arrangements in return for an annual rent. This practice was often associated with construction or repair to churches. Heirs could inherit the grant, and, indeed, some chapels such as the Capella Minutolo at the cathedral of Naples, founded in 1301, still remain within the use and jurisdiction of the original family. In many instances, however, chapels passed from one family or patron to another, especially in moments of financial crisis or events such as wars and plague, which eliminated large numbers of benefactors in one sweep.[135] Although the religious institution maintained control of the allocated space,

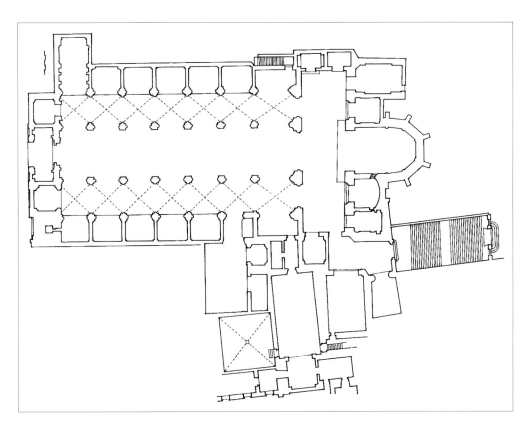

83   Naples, San Domenico, plan from Bruzelius, 2004, page 96.

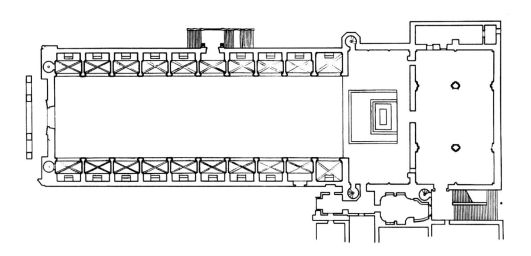

84   Naples, Santa Chiara, plan from Bruzelius, 2004, p. 135.

and usually required consistency, regularity, and control over appropriate decoration and design, family coats of arms, tombs, and painted decoration were clearly acceptable individualizing features. Structural consistency is evident, for example, in the chapels added in clusters of two to four along the nave flanks of San Lorenzo in Naples, although the internal decoration differed. The terms used in concessions of patronage to donors sometimes specified similarity and consistency (*nella maniera*) with already existing chapels.[136] This explains the regularity of clusters of chapels on the exteriors of naves, as at Sant'Eustorgio (the eastern four chapels on the south side of the nave, see fig. 37) and the 1740 plan of San Francesco a Folloni (see fig. 49). By insisting upon architectural uniformity, the religious institution visually asserted its rights over the space by embracing it into the spatial context of the building, while its (presumably more fleeting) use and decoration was granted to the donor or patron. Patrons, in turn, as was noted above, often insisted in their wills that funds left for construction of a chapel be put to use for the project within a certain period, often ten years: Donato di Amideo Peruzzi left 200 lire for the construction of a chapel to be built within ten years of his death ("infra decem annos post obitum suis").[137] In churches where only the fragmentary vestiges of votive paintings remain on columns, we can perhaps imagine that these were often associated with either tombs or altars, or both: chapels co-existed with freestanding altars within the open spaces of the nave (see fig. 85).

Lateral chapels *ad ius patronatus* partially financed the construction of many mendicant churches. Although the phenomenon may have originated with the need for secondary altars in large communities, by the second half of the thirteenth century it had evolved into a method of securing the long-term commitment and patronage from donors.[138] By the end of the same century, what had begun as a largely ad hoc arrangement had become the systematic incorporation of ancillary spaces into the design process that was integrated with the construction of adjacent cloisters, as visible in the nave walls of San Francesco Grande and Sant'Eustorgio in Milan. In these two buildings shallow chapels were built along the length of the nave in conjunction with the construction of the cloisters on the north (see figs. 37 and 45). At a later date, chapels became larger (see again San Francesco Grande, south side of the nave) and competed with each other for grandeur and complexity. The chapels once attached to San Domenico and San Francesco in Bologna attest to increasingly complex and prominent spaces (see fig. 4). Freigang has pointed out that there was greater freedom and variation in the scale and decoration of chapels along the nave compared with those around the apse or inside the preserve of the choir.[139]

We noted above that wills usually left bequests to multiple institutions as a form of "diversification of assets." This could also apply to chapels, although only the wealthiest families could normally afford more than one: the Baroncelli of Florence founded contemporary chapels – one at Santa Croce and one at San Pier Scheraggio.[140] In addition, this family founded two other chapels in Santa Croce, neither of which is extant: the chapels of San Martino and the Blessed Gherardo da Villamagna.[141] The former was attached to the choir screen and destroyed in the sixteenth century, whereas the latter may have been in the old church which remained partially in place at least until the mid-fourteenth century (for a schematic reconstruction of this process; see fig. 12). By 1338 it was relocated to the fifth bay from the west on the north side where it was described in an inventory of 1439.[142] The Blessed Gherardo was a popular saint in Florence, so that the location of the altar and tomb near the doorway on the north flank of the church accessible to the Via delle Pinzochere was a strategic choice.

FAMILIES

In his study of the convent of Santa Croce in Florence, Sylvain Piron highlighted the powerful ties between the friars and the city.[143] By the late thirteenth century, in a community of roughly 150 friars, about 88 percent were from Florence or its region:[144] the Franciscans of Florence were no longer "strangers and pilgrims" but rather neighbors and brothers, a community deeply inserted into the social fabric of urban life. At both Santa Croce and Santa Maria Novella élite families were well represented within friaries, which also had close ties to the communities of male and female confraternities that helped to provide financial support. Piron noted, that "around 1300, Santa Croce was more of a Florentine than a Franciscan institution."[145]

Close ties to local communities meant that mendicants were intimately involved in local political and social networks. It also meant, however, that the divisions and tensions between a city's families, social categories, and political alliances were also fully active and present within a convent. Furthermore, the desire to assert the prestige and importance of a particular house became enmeshed in a network of external associations. Santa Croce, as Piron notes, attests to precisely this kind of scenario in the vast scale of the church begun in 1294. The goal must have been to create a convent larger and more ostentatious in every way than any counterpart within the city, a monument to attract admiring and sympathetic patrons from within certain social and economic circles, and one which could provide majestic spaces for the work of the most important artists (such as Giotto) in the decoration of its most prestigious chapels.

Even before William of Saint-Amour noted the susceptibility of women to the friars in his treatise of 1256, female penitents and devotees had flocked to support the new orders, often inducing their husbands and families to become pious associates of convents. Umiliana de' Cerchi (d. 1246) of Florence is an early and well-attested example of the kind of devoted laywoman whose miracles after death did much to stimulate the renown of Santa Croce.[146] Saint Clare herself, of course, is another example, although in her case she founded an entirely new order for women inspired by Francis's evangelical poverty. By the late thirteenth century, the Friars Minor were particularly cultivated by noble and royal women, a phenomenon still evident in the massive convents of Santa Chiara in Naples (see fig. 2), and Pedralbes in Barcelona, for example.[147]

A DEMOGRAPHY OF PATRONS AND PATRONAGE

There were significant differences between the orders: the Preachers tended to attract a more elevated (noble) and more literate social sector from the start. In Arles, for example, they almost immediately acquired wealthy patrons and the educated classes who subsidized

Masses, constructed chapels, and installed monumental tombs.[148] This was also true in the rest of southern France, where the Preachers attracted the local élites, as demonstrated by Rigon, Chiffoleau, and Stouff.[149] By the second half of the thirteenth century, the Dominican and Franciscan convents of Padua were both highly favored for burial by the local nobility and urban patriciate.[150]

The new orders also benefited from the support of women, as noted above. There are examples of passionate devotees in Strasbourg defending the Preachers with wooden clogs and rolling pins when they were exiled by the commune. At San Domenico in Bologna a greater proportion of women from the urban patriciate chose to be buried in the cemetery of the convent, while their husbands often preferred the traditional location of the parish.[151] In Arles women seem to have favored the Franciscans for burial in greater numbers than men, as was also the case at Marseilles.[152] Often these were widows of considerable means. As Michaud points out, whereas men who chose burial with the mendicants were sometimes merchants or foreigners from another city, the sepultuary of San Domenico in Bologna of 1291 indicates that the majority of tombs were local, and we can safely assume that those who were buried in the church were also patrons.[153] There are many testaments that request burial in a mendicant convent should the testator die while away from home. Presumably the traveler carried with him a copy of his will in case of sudden death. Women, on the other hand, tended to be local, and therefore more deeply engaged with the communities around them.[154] Should we agree with Michaud's interpretation that men chose the friars as "une famille d'accueil" when they were traveling, whereas women were more directed toward "un repos plus salvateur"? William of Saint-Amour's diatribe and other (more pro-mendicant) sources often emphasize the particular receptivity of women to the mendicant message and mission.

The case of Bologna is particularly instructive because the sepultuaries of both the Dominican and Franciscans churches have been preserved and well studied by Breveglieri and Gaulin.[155] In this city there was clear resistance to burial inside churches before the fourteenth century and, as noted above, the cemetery of San Domenico was set out in systematized rows on the western and northern flanks of the church, with a path passing through the northern cemetery to a portal on the north side. The most important families were buried outside the western portal, near the pulpit, including a collective tomb for the *podestà* of the city who died in office, a monument decorated with the coats of arms of the commune.[156] The *Libellus funerum* of San Domenico lists only five burials within the church by 1291: King Enzo (son of Frederick II) in the left transept near the altar of Saint Catherine, the archbishop of Poland, and Teodorico, the Dominican archbishop of Faenza. Another, nameless tomb was located in front of the altar of the Virgin, and the last, the tomb of Enrico Fieschi, was placed before the altar of Saint Peter Martyr.[157] Only in the early fourteenth century was the cloister of San Domenico opened to lay burials, and it soon became the most prestigious area for tombs. At San Francesco, however, the Friars Minor initially resisted pressure to place lay burials in the cloister,[158] and were restrained in permitting tombs in the church interior. Conversely, the exterior east and north sides of the church were thickly packed with tombs, some of which were slabs raised from the ground on supports as tables: they clustered thickly around the doorway on the north flank of the church. The predilection for doorways is attested in England, where Shepherd's reconstruction of the tombs at the Greyfriars in London indicated strong preference for the "walking place," the corridor through the church from the street to the cloister. The choir was reserved for the tombs of nobles and royalty (see fig. 28).

INTERIOR DECORATION

The interiors of mendicant churches were full. They contained the furnishings of the liturgical choir with altars and memorials and a choir screen to which were attached more altars. Naves often pullulated with tombs and the commemorative paraphernalia of individuals, families, and confraternities as well as carved effigies, votive paintings, altars with panel paintings, coats of arms, flags, and dedicatory windows. On occasion manuscript illuminations attest to the richly decorated church interiors, though inevitably the genial clutter is often tidied up in these images (fig. 85). Fragments of votive paintings show the superimposed layers of images clustered with particular density around the altars and the choir screen.[159] More evocative still are the poems of antifraternal critics, such as *Piers the Plowman's Crede,* with a description of an unknown Franciscan convent and its decoration:

> For we construct a convent – a capacious one, and large –
> A church and a chapel with chambers on high,
> With wide wrought windows and walls soaring high,
> That might be portrait-covered and painted and polished to a shine
> With gay glittering glass glowing like the sun.
> And if you might help us with money of your own,
> You could kneel before Christ encompassed by gold
> In the wide west window, well nigh in the middle,
> And Saint Francis himself shall enfold you in his cloak,
> And present you to the Trinity and pray for your sins.
> Your name shall be nobly written and wrought just so,
> And in your remembrance, read there forever.[160]

Descriptions of decorative exuberance in the churches of the friars formed a powerful topos in English antifraternal literature. Wycliffe, for example, referred to "gaye windows and colours and peyntingis and bybwinrie."[161] Stained glass windows were a particularly effective (and ostentatious) form of commemoration for donors: the light that flowed through them set off coats of arms and donor portraits in radiant glow.

The importance of objects and other paraphernalia associated with especially venerated tombs is evident from a variety of sources. For example, the decrees that announced that the Blessed Armanno Pungilupo, buried in the cathedral of Ferrara, was a heretic instead of a saint state that not only his stone sarcophagus and altar but also the decoration around them were to be removed, including all ex-votos, sculpture, and other images that represented him in the cathedral and other city churches.[162]

The decorative intervention of the laity is a topic of particular importance for the architecture of the friars. As religious space increasingly became the setting for secular monu-

85　The Apparition
of the Virgin to a
group of Dominicans,
Northern Netherlands
(Utrecht?) 1500–25
(detail). Utrecht,
Museum Catharijne-
convent, ABM s71.
Photo: Ruben de
Heer.

ments that commemorated individuals, families, and associations, churches and convents were progressively "colonized," as the 1784 plan from Bologna attests (see fig. 4). Mendicant churches became the locus of the identity and multigenerational continuity of individuals and communities. The church was increasingly a place where ancestors were remembered, and where the longevity of a family line was commemorated in monument, coats of arms, and pictures. In the stripped and denuded interiors of churches as we perceive them today, these testaments to the importance of the private individual are long gone – instead they have become objects and artifacts in our museums.

CONFRATERNITIES

Laymen and women associated with the mendicant orders increasingly formed associations that played vital roles in the well-being of communities by providing networks of support closely tied to families, neighborhoods, civic groups, guilds, and communal governments. Fraternal groups received preferential treatment for burial and other spiritual transactions such as intercessory prayer. Confraternities made pious donations to the poor, organized and attended the funerals and burials of their members, and supported orphans and widows, in addition to organizing banquets to commemorate their deceased members, for which large sums were donated. Giovanni Falchi, a member of the confraternity of Santa Maria Novella, left four times more money for the commemorative feast (*pietanza*) on behalf of his brother than to the confraternity itself.[163] In Florence and elsewhere, the inquisitorial activities of Peter of Verona in the 1240s inspired new associations, such as the company of the Crocesegnati, knights who received a plenary remission for all their sins in return for assisting inquisitors in their sometimes violent work; they were also obliged by oath to provide material or financial support to the convent when called upon to do so by the inquisitor.[164]

Confraternities often seem to have urged the friars to build on a large scale.[165] Santa Croce and Santa Maria Novella in Florence had associations of *pinzocheri* and Laudesi by c. 1245;[166] members encouraged friends and relations to make donations, as has been noted. By the middle of the thirteenth century, they also served as supporters and informers in the work of the Inquisition: the statutes of many of these organizations included their role in the "revelation and destruction . . . of every error and every mortal sin."[167] In 1244 Peter of Verona (Peter Martyr) founded the Compagnia Maggiore della Vergine as well as the confraternity of the Laudesi. He organized "in quasi-military fashion, popular religious support behind the banner of the Inquisition,"[168] through an association of armed and strictly orthodox nobles who defended the Dominicans under the name of the Società de Capitani di Santa Maria.[169] A friar was present at all of the meetings of these associations. In most Italian cities the confraternities usually received a portion of the legacies left by a member in a will, and in time, especially after the Black Death of 1348, these became immensely wealthy with significant investments to support their activities and the religious community.[170]

Other practices that involved confraternities as well as individuals were important for the friars. Salimbene remarked on the custom of providing letters of fraternity to men and women who wished to be associated with the Friars Minor, a practice initiated in 1254 by Minister General John of Parma:

> In this marvelous way, many men and women have become devotees of God and of the Order of St. Francis. And this concession has perhaps been the efficient cause for these people to lay aside their sinning ways and be converted to God, both by reason of their own will and by the power of the prayers of the Brothers. For as Augustine says, "It is impossible that the prayers of the multitude will not be heard."[171]

Salimbene then quoted the wording of such a letter: "I here receive you into the universal and individual spiritual benefits of our Order both in life and in death. And I grant to you by virtue of this present letter full participation in all the spiritual benefits which the mercy of the Saviour through the prayers of our Brothers living throughout the world shall deign to concede."[172] In the fullness of time, such letters of fraternity became a commercial transaction between friars and laity.[173] They would be heavily criticized as symbols of decay and corruption. In the early years, however, they were remarkably effective in creating associations of intimate support between mendicants and their lay followers.

There was an explosion of other, and some more private, types of association with friars, especially in the form of recluses and female penitents (often widows and virgins) who lived in proximity and sometimes adjacent to convents in enclosed cells.[174] As Vauchez notes, the Franciscan movement itself started as a penitential group, "viri poenitentiales de Assisio,"[175] and the first cluster of primitive structures around the chapel of the Porziuncola (see fig. 15) was probably typical of the kind of simple and rustic structures that such groups often occupied. There were many other specifically penitential groups that formed mendicant orders: the Brothers of the Sack, founded in Provence in 1248; the Servites, founded by Florentine merchants; the Brothers of the Penitence of the Holy Martyrs; and several flagellant associations. Members were often middle-class tradesmen and manufacturers or their families. After c. 1300 this type of association was less frequent, and starting in the 1280s there were attempts to legislate and organize such groups under the direct supervision of friars.

Similarly, Clare and her followers, though strictly enclosed by c. 1219, were an example of the female equivalent. The architecture of enclosed female penitents was often appended to older churches like barnacles on a pier and the early arrangements for the choirs of female penitential groups, such as that of Clare at San Damiano, often followed the model of the hermetic cell.[176] These ad hoc arrangements for communities of women often placed the oratory near the altar area and through the separation of a grate the female religious penitent could meditate upon the consecrated host placed on the altar or in a special niche. Other women lived individually in cells constructed beside a convent church (Margaret of Cortona, for example), or at home with special arrangements that guaranteed isolation and seclusion, such as Umiliana de' Cerchi and Catherine of Siena.

*   *   *

THE INQUISITION

By the middle of the thirteenth century, inquisitorial activities brought revenues and access to properties that increased the wealth and power of friaries.[177] Accusations of heresy meant that a heretic's goods and properties were confiscated and sold; the income derived was distributed in thirds between the ecclesiastical authority (the bishop), the communes (or, in the case of France and the Kingdom of Sicily, royal authority), and the office of the Inquisition, usually located within a mendicant convent. Although inquisitors were exempt from the jurisdiction of the priors or the Minister General of the orders, convents that hosted inquisitors benefited from the income of outright confiscations or from bribes and extortion. A few notorious cases clearly demonstrate the link between the acquisition of wealth and property and inquisitorial activities, as we shall see below.

Franciscans and Dominicans had been entrusted with inquisitorial authority beginning in the second quarter of the thirteenth century, and because the orders had become increasingly well-organized institutions, both urban and international, they were immensely effective instruments of control and repression. In 1258 Alexander IV appointed the Friars Minor as inquisitors in the cities of Umbria where heresy was particularly strong, especially in Perugia, Spoleto, Orvieto, and Narni.[178] As has been noted, accusations of heresy were often associated with pro-imperial sympathies: the conquest of Charles of Anjou in 1266 affirmed the equation between Ghibellinism and heresy, with new energy invested in the systematic extirpation of both. Guelph–Ghibelline tensions were certainly in the background of the ill reception accorded the Franciscans in Ferentino. In some cases, the role of friars as inquisitors elicited revolts and resistance: for example, the communal government of Narni in 1260 violently opposed the election of the Dominican Rolando as bishop precisely because of his prior reputation as an inquisitor. This type of tension also existed in Orvieto,[179] and here the inquisitorial office, initially located at the Dominican convent, was attacked and burned by Ghibellines in 1239. By 1268–9 the office was transferred to the Franciscan friars Bartolomeo D'Amelia and Benvenuto d'Orvieto, who condemned eighty-seven persons.[180]

Is it a coincidence that mendicant convents with offices for the Inquisition often erected the largest and most prestigious churches (San Lorenzo in Vicenza, Sant'Antonio in Padua, Santa Maria Novella, and Santa Croce in Florence)? Although documentation for money passing directly from the Inquisition to the building fund is rare, the presence of the office in a convent had broad implications for its well-being, as well as for the communities in the larger sense. On the local level of the convent, space was required for notaries, meetings, and the juridical procedures. Convents entrusted with the Inquisition also had prisons (at Santa Croce in its damp basements, and these also existed in the convents of Prato, Siena, Arezzo, and Pisa).[181] Each tribunal was responsible for salaries and had to cover its own continuous and sometimes onerous administrative costs, which often included armed guards. The office staff was large and consisted of both friars and laymen. Lay personnel (notaries, spies, accountants, for example) were exempt from taxation.[182]

The expenses associated with maintaining an office meant that tribunals had an interest in continued activity even after local heresies had been largely extirpated by the last decades of the thirteenth century. Continuation of the office therefore required an ever-greater dependence upon posthumous trials, with egregious episodes of corruption and abuse.[183] Although the Inquisition in principle took place in collaboration with the bishop and communal government, in reality (as in Padua) this was not always the case. Bishops resented the encroachment on their rights and prerogatives, not to mention the loss of income and authority, especially as inquisitors were exempt from their legal jurisdiction.

Santa Croce in Florence is an example of the intricate involvement of a mendicant house with the Inquisition. The Franciscan Provincial Minister for Tuscany resided in this convent and supervised the Inquisition throughout the region. In October 1254 Clement IV permitted secret accusations against any sympathizer of the Ghibellines, who would thus de facto be considered a heretic.[184] (Indeed, from that moment onwards, anyone opposed to the mission and activities of the Inquisition could also be considered a heretic.) Within the orders, legislation issued by provincial chapters imposed on all friars fidelity to the Guelph cause; prisons were instituted in the Dominican convents of Pisa, Siena, Rome, Florence, and Orvieto for those members of the communities whose sympathies lay elsewhere.[185]

By the last decades of the thirteenth century heretics and Ghibellines had been largely exterminated, although in the north of Italy new waves of immigrant heretics fleeing from the Inquisition in France continued to be sought and persecuted; the phenomenon of renewed waves of heretics has been described by Biscaro as the "ripullulante idria dell'eresia" of northern Italy.[186] Elsewhere, inquisitors who ran short of bona fide heretics began to prosecute posthumously in order to confiscate property from the heirs of purported heretics in trials after their deaths.[187] Eventually this practice was limited to forty years after death. In the fourteenth century, abusive inquisitors such as Fra Mino of Santa Croce even began to prosecute, or at least blackmail, by threatening with prosecution fellow prelates and religious institutions, a practice prohibited only in 1311 by Clement V.[188]

Paolini has observed that aside from economic prerogatives, however, the role of friars as inquisitors played an important role in legitimizing the position of the new orders within the ecclesiastical system, especially at a time when they were under threat from the secular clergy.[189] The papacy and mendicants developed a mutually beneficial and symbiotic relationship in this matter, one not always welcomed by bishops, whose ecclesiastical authority in their diocese was on occasion usurped.[190] The Franciscan and Dominican role in the Inquisition helped to concretize the process of their institutionalization and probably had a role in the survival of these two orders in the 1274 Council of Lyons at a time when several other mendicant orders were eliminated.[191]

Fines and the confiscation of property and goods commenced early in the history of the Inquisition, and beginning sometime in the early 1230s they began to have a relation to the support of religious communities; for Franciscans this was especially important after 1258.[192] Sentences with fines and expropriations can be found as early as 1237 and 1245: inquisitor Pierre Cella of Toulouse imposed the fine of maintaining a priest or poor man for a period of several years, and in other cases for life, in addition to regular fines and penalties.[193] Penances were often entirely converted for money, with the proviso that such funds were to be designated for pious uses such as donations to friaries. (Starting as early as 1248, this also became a common form of support for the Crusades.) In 1244 the Council of Narbonne, attempting to maintain some vestige of apostolic poverty, instructed its inquisitors to abstain from penalties that involved fees, and Innocent IV intervened in 1249, rebuking inquisitors for the heavy exactions wrested from their victims. In 1251 he prohibited financial exactions if any other form of penance was possible. Previously (in 1245) this pope had instructed that all fines should be paid to two persons selected by the bishop and inquisitor, and that the funds be used for the construction of prisons and feeding indigent prisoners.

Fines were paid directly to the inquisitorial office located in the mendicant convent. Not long after Innocent's instructions, Alexander IV (in 1260) ordered the inquisitors of Rome and Spoleto to send the proceeds from the sale of confiscated estates directly to the papacy. Lea observed that, under Benedict XI, the custom of the division of income from the Inquisition became a tripartite division between the local community, the Inquisition, and the papacy,[194] but this appears to be contradicted by the more recent studies of Paolini (1998 and 1999). In any event, bishops risked being marginalized. Within the Kingdom of France, the third that would have gone to the commune was instead placed under the authority of the royal fisc. After the conquest of Charles of Anjou, the Inquisition in the Kingdom of Sicily was run by the royal administration, although Charles II restored the system of tripartite division, except in feudal domains.[195] Louis IX in France reserved the right to reassign confiscated properties to his vassals.[196]

I have noted that inquisitorial rapacity continued beyond the grave. The death of the accused did not end susceptibility to prosecution and punishment. In Florence a certain Gherardo, who died before 1250, was prosecuted in 1313 and his children and grandchildren were disinherited.[197] The confiscation of property and goods often meant that spouses and children became beggars and the houses of heretics destroyed. Even converts who were absolved were required to pay bail in case of possible relapse. In Albi the city in 1338 was forced to ransom a number of its citizens who had been accused of heresy. Benedict XII ordered his nuncio in Italy, the archbishop of Embrun, to investigate complaints from the entire peninsula that inquisitors were engaging in extortion, punishing the innocent and soliciting gifts. In 1346 the entire Florentine republic revolted against the inquisitor, but only after many decades of extortionate practices by Fra Mino and Pietro dall'Aquila. Fra Mino's accusations of heresy extended to priests, as well as to the abbots and priors of other religious houses, who were obliged to pay vast sums or "donate" horses and other items in order to avoid prosecution.[198]

Documents from the *Liber contractuum* of Padua, a compilation of documents produced in 1302 by communal notaries against the Friars Minor, supplied the evidence for an inquiry into their financial transactions and abuse of authority. The compilation, which includes recorded documents stretching from 1263 to c. 1302, was taken to Rome by a committee of representatives sent by the commune and bishop. It attests to extortion, the deflection of legacies away from rightful heirs, and numerous other crimes and doubtful practices.[199] It also confirms the infiltration of friars throughout the juridical and administrative structures of the city. Yet when the Inquisition was transferred instead to the Preachers in Padua, they soon engaged in these same practices.

In Florence inquisitors were allowed an armed retinue, and in time came to traffic in the right to bear arms in the city as defenders of the faith.[200] These became large retinues of armed supporters. At San Domenico in Naples the inquisitor was protected by a force of more than fifty armed men.[201] As a result, the numbers of citizens with the right to bear arms increased exponentially in many cities, and it is perhaps not surprising that this exacerbated the problems of factionalism, as in the 1346 battles at the Piazza dei Priori in Florence. Prior to his tenure in Florence, while Fra Mino was inquisitor in Siena, feeling against the Friars Minor became so intense in that city that the friars were instructed to remain within the convent.[202]

The list of accusations in the Paduan documents is long and harrowing. The entire proceeds from properties confiscated from heretics were absorbed by the Franciscans at Sant'Antonio instead of being divided into thirds. The friars also colluded with the parish priest to defraud the church of the quarter due to the parish from funerals and burials. The executors of wills diverted inheritances, including those of minors, and sold the goods for a profit.[203] Friars engaged in usurious loans. Franciscan executors required bribes in order to fulfill the bequests to private individuals as specified by the testator and sold or transferred properties illegally acquired to members of their own families. They engaged in transactions that favored certain political alliances, destabilizing the balance of power and family networks within the city. Family connections between the friars and the urban population were deeply implicated in many of these transactions.

The Inquisition thus had important economic implications for mendicant convents. Although the principle of dividing the income from confiscations into thirds varied from place to place and over time,[204] there were usually significant and lasting economic benefits for all parties. Yet the failure of the Friars Minor to honor the system of tripartite division in Padua and Florence was the reason for the complaints filed by bishop and communes against inquisitors.

Fines and confiscations designated for pious uses passed to the religious communities and building funds under the generic formula "for the necessities of the friars."[205] There was a precedent for using income from the Inquisition for construction: in Florence inquisitorial funds had already been used for construction by the commune, in 1231 for the maintenance of city fortifications, and after 1289 for the erection of additional walls on the south side of the Arno.[206] Although documentation of such practices is rare – as few records survive, and accounting for funds was often deliberately obfuscated by the inquisitors and their assistants – some evidence survives from diverse parts of Europe. Fines levied on the heretics of Lavaur were used to build the city cathedral.[207] The church of Najac was paid for in the same way. Bernard Gui allowed absolution and dispensation to be granted in return for donations to build bridges and churches, and "pious uses at our discretion."[208] From 1319 to 1329 the construction of Florence Cathedral was partially funded by the third designated for the commune from properties confiscated by the Florentine Inquisition.[209] Starting in 1324 two-thirds of these confiscated sums were designated for the construction and embellishment of Santa Croce and one-third for work on Santa Maria Novella.[210] In 1321 the penalty imposed upon the town government of Cordes for harboring heretics was used for the construction of a chapel decorated with images of Saints Peter Martyr, Cecilia, Louis, and Dominic over the altar, as well as statues of the bishop and the two inquisitors over the church portal. When, in 1348, the portal had still not received the prescribed decoration, the city was obliged to give pledges that it would be completed.[211] In other examples the refusal to honor the statues of saints was in itself a sign of heresy, as in the case of the two men who refused to venerate the images of saints while stopping by a church and were denounced by their friend, a local notary.[212] When seventy heretics were burned in Verona in 1278, the city was fined 4,000 lire as reparations for its heretical past and commanded to found a new Franciscan convent in Sermione.[213] Similarly, after the attack on the office of the Inquisition in the Dominican friary of Parma in 1279, and as a result of the agreement reached between the city and the Order, the city council voted to pay the Preachers 1,200 imperial lire, in six installments of 200 lire, for the construction of a church dedicated to Peter Martyr.[214] And in Naples Robert of Anjou directed a portion of the royal proceeds from an inquisitorial trial (50 *once*) to the prior of San Domenico to aid in the completion of the church.[215] In Vicenza the third due to the commune from the sale of lands confiscated from a heretic was deflected instead to be used "in constructione ed edificatione ecclesie beati Laurencii."[216] In Pavia Fra Lanfranco contributed in 1293 to the construction of the tower at the Dominican house of San Tommaso.[217]

The Inquisition was connected with the foundation and construction of churches in more general ways as well. After the death of Ezzelino da Romano (1259), the bishop of Vicenza returned to the city with relics of the crown of thorns and a piece of the true cross given by Louis IX. These became the chief ornaments of the newly founded Dominican church of Santa Corona, established on the site of the gathering place of an extirpated heretical sect.[218] According to reports, the new relics "healed" the city of its three primary sins: avarice, heresy, and discord. After his canonization in March 1253, numerous churches, chapels and altars were dedicated to Peter Martyr. Saint Dominic was retroactively described as an inquisitor, and the fact that Peter Martyr's new tomb of 1340 was modeled on that of the *arca* in Bologna seems to affirm to this posthumous association.[219] Sant'Eustorgio had been entrusted with the Inquisition in Milan since 1228, and the cult of Peter Martyr in the church, especially with the miracles performed at his tomb, exalted this activity. The cult of the saint became a central instrument of the Preachers: in one sermon of 1291 Peter Martyr's wounds were compared to Saint Francis's reception of the stigmata (subsequently Nicholas IV, a Franciscan pope, called the Dominican preacher to Rome for punishment).[220]

Income from the Inquisition also went toward clothing, shoes, food, and the hosting of the general chapters.[221] Inquisitorial offices occupied large sectors of convent space. In 1289 at Sant'Eustorgio in Milan a large vaulted hall was built over the *cellarium* for the Inquisition. It held a large cupboard for books, even a bed.[222] At Santa Croce, the offices of the Inquisition were in a wing of the complex to the right of the main entrance adjacent to the courtyard and refectory. When the office was finally abolished by Leopold of Habsburg, there were more than thirty rooms and a separate chapel associated with Inquisition activities.[223] In the flood of 1333, at least one prisoner (a priest) drowned in its prison. Paolini has noted that the inquisitor was independent of the prior, so that his part of the convent was, as it were, a separate "principality" with the potential to launch internal accusations and threats.[224] In the mendicant houses (often Franciscan) with an office of the Inquisition, there was, on occasion, dissent over its existence and the financial transactions that its activities necessarily entailed. We have echoes of this in the prosecution of Fra Mino, when other members of the community of Santa Croce asserted their innocence, ignorance, and repulsion at the activities he conducted within the walls of the convent.[225] Yet even if inquisitors did not have the support of some segments of the religious community, or that of the lay public outside, convents benefited materially from the their financial transactions.

The documents published for Padua are unusual in both their origin and the fact of their survival. They suggest that the exigencies of large-scale construction, even in places where relics brought in large numbers of pilgrims (as at Sant'Antonio in Padua), presented the temptation to divert funds toward institutional needs. André Vauchez, writing in response to the publication of the *Liber contractuum* of Padua, suggested that the financial transactions undertaken there by the Friars Minor were in part driven by a culture of architectural extravagance and an obsession with building.[226] The activities of Fra Mino in Siena published by Biscaro in 1933, as well as the investigation of the inquisition in Padua and Vicenza cited above, suggest that mendicants as inquisitors engaged in financial and property-related transactions of all kinds and sometimes of a scurrilous nature.

The Inquisition inspired cautious animosity from the lay public, and on rare occasions opposition led to attacks upon or the destruction of convents. It was widely perceived that inquisitors coveted properties and wealth.[227] In Parma townspeople sacked San Domenico in 1279 and destroyed the Inquisition records; as noted, the friars returned only in 1287, induced by a fine to be paid in installments to rebuild the church.[228] Some witnesses to the burning of heretics in Bologna in 1299 referred to the attack on the Dominicans in Parma and suggested that the same should occur in their own city.[229] Another effect was the falling off of pious legacies, as occurred in Limoges early in the fourteenth century after the executions of heretics. As noted above, some Friars Minor were conflicted by the Inquisition and its secondary effects, not the least of which was the funneling of large amounts of cash through convents; these friars were often members of the groups associated with what has come to be called the Spirituals. Rigorist Franciscans were repelled by the ostentation of big churches and by the type of funding acquired by inquisitors, and by the early years of the fourteenth century this faction was radically opposed to the Inquisition. The descent of Louis of Bavaria into central Italy in 1328–9 solicited pro-imperial uprisings in many cities and some mendicant convents: in the Franciscan convent of San Fortunato in Todi more than seventy friars were excommunicated as a result.[230] Issues of communal sympathy with the Spiritual Franciscans were not uncommon; Becker demonstrated that in Florence these friars preached against wealth and property.[231] Much later, in sixteenth-century Naples, the Franciscans at San Lorenzo supported the revolts against the Spanish viceroy; indeed, the historical mythology surrounding the reconstruction of this church (attributing the Gothic choir to the first Angevin king, Charles of Anjou) was generated by anti-Spanish sentiment.[232]

As noted in the previous chapter, the Bologna sepultuary of 1291 refers to an iron grate ("gratam feream") by the pulpit on the exterior of San Domenico. Could such devices have been used for condemned heretics? The sermons of Fra Mino proclaimed from an outdoor pulpit (before a public seated on benches) at the condemnation of a heretic suggest that they were exposed to the public.[233] As noted above, on at least one occasion Fra Mino seems to have preached with a painted depiction of the devil adjacent to (hanging from?) the pulpit. If we are to think of pulpits as presenting a scenography of penitence on the exteriors of churches for public preaching, we might then wish to expand that vision to include terrifying images of the devil and the trembling victims of the Inquisition.

CONCLUSION

This study has been about the "social lives of buildings." It is an attempt to describe how cultural and economic phenomena came to shape the spaces of mendicant convents and in turn what impact these structures had on the medieval city. Although, of course, human action always determines architectural form, the particularly close relationship between friars and the public meant that mendicant buildings responded with almost visceral elasticity to changes in the spiritual and economic systems of their times.

One of the radical aspects of the mendicant movement was the externalization of religion into the open spaces of cities as well as into the private spaces of homes. The action of friars was outside the friary and toward the public. At the same time, however, friars lived within religious institutions that were increasingly like the spaces of monasticism. Urban engagement was thus mated with the architectural structures of withdrawal and seclusion. By the 1220s the Preachers, and not long afterwards the Franciscans, were building large (and later multiple) cloisters, refectories, dormitories, and other spaces associated with monastic life. By the 1240s there is evidence that mendicant houses were often preceded or flanked by piazzas for preaching: convent space existed both indoors and out (see fig. 6). Convents were also open to sectors of the public in different ways: they were meeting places for communes or, in southern Italy, the *seggi*, as well as for associations and guilds; they served as repositories for archival documents; they interred within their walls generations of the dead. Mendicant schools taught theology to secular clerics. Archbishop Visconti recommended them for his cathedral clergy in Pisa. In the 1250s certain convents made space for the offices and prisons of the Inquisition, consisting of as many as thirty rooms at Santa Croce in Florence. Through all these activities friaries evolved into new urban centers closely tied to local governments, populations, and fraternal organizations.

The process of conventualization, however, presented challenges not only for the friars but also for their neighbors. Whereas monastic architecture had evolved mostly in rural settings to serve the needs of separation and self-sufficiency, friaries were located in cities. But finding space within a city to construct a full-scale convent often engaged friars in the acquisition and expense of property. It squeezed neighborhoods. It challenged the authority and economic well-being of the nearby parish. In some places the friars established new poles of influence that deflected attention away from the traditional religious institutions (parish and cathedral) that united townspeople within an ecclesiastical structure. The friars' pulpits projected out over streets and open spaces, as at Pola (see fig. 69): in some towns it was impossible to take chickens to market without overhearing a friar haranguing on sin and death.

Conventualization meant big buildings in urban space. As early as 1243, critics such as Matthew Paris noted the discrepancy between the friars' large houses and their claims to poverty: "In enlarging their sumptuous edifices and erecting lofty walls, the brothers in England transgress the limits of their original poverty and violate the basis of their religious profession."[1] This early attestation to the expansion of mendicant friaries exemplifies the contradiction between fidelity to the vow of poverty and the creation of adequate space for communities. On the one hand, the increasing size of convents simply reflected the vertiginous growth of the new orders and their need for liturgical, teaching, and communal spaces. On the other hand, the material response to these exigencies exposed friars to accusations of excessive ambition and wealth in buildings. Architecture was a highly visible and permanent reminder of a fugitive ideal.

Mendicants thus brought the spaces of monasticism into the city. At the same time, they renegotiated the concept of what we normally call "church," religious space for the laity. Friars' churches were often aggressively utilitarian and multipurpose. At least in the early years of the orders, church space for lay services was less important than the public spaces of markets and piazzas, or the private spaces of homes, for an encounter between friars and their lay parishioners.[2]

In this volume I have therefore been concerned not only with built space, but also with the "activated voids" of piazzas and other open spaces for the public performance of spirituality. Such spaces existed not only in the thriving communes and economic centers of central and northern Italy, but everywhere in the peninsula, through the Kingdom of Sicily, the Papal States, and north of the Alps. Architectural historians have tended to think of "the church" as a distinct and concrete entity, but this book proposes that for mendicant friars churches were, at least initially, secondary to the primary mission of outreach and conversion *outside*. To preach indoors was "to preach to the choir"; the friars reached out specifically to those who were *not* within.

At the same time, friars constructed their own liturgical choirs or oratories as part of the essential residential structures of their communities, often in the form of a long rectangular wing south of the choir. By the late 1230s the space that would (eventually) be occupied by the nave could be set out as an enclosed precinct or a low provisional structure, perhaps covered by a wooden roof. The area of the projected nave may have served as a cemetery for devoted lay patrons.[3] Friars reversed the tradition of reserving church and cloister burial as an honor for the upper clergy, royalty, and nobles, making sacred space available for the middle-class merchants and bankers. Burial was "democratized," though not perhaps for the poor.

The concept of church was fluid and multivalent for the mendicant orders. Some liturgical activities were moved outside as full service operations in the open space of the piazza, where preachers flanked by additional friars received confession and were offered absolution. At the same time, the sacred spaces the church itself came to serve as a cemetery and as a negotiable container (hangar) for the paraphernalia associated with the burial of the laity. Friars renegotiated the activities and purposes of the clerical ministry indoors and out.

The founders had been acutely aware of the problem of poverty and building. The Preachers introduced rules about property and poverty in their first General Chapter of 1221. Although Francis offered numerous injunctions against buildings, it should be noted that he himself repaired churches and put them back into use for his followers, as at the Porziuncola. The issue of poverty within the church played an important role in a period in which the growing monetization of the relationship between clergy and laity had become an urgent matter, as secular clergy increasingly insisted upon the payment of tithes and the systematic emoluments in return for the sacraments: what Jacques Chiffoleau called the "monétarisation et la fiscalisation . . . de tous les échanges paroissiaux."[4] Friars' renunciation of such payments in the early decades offered an immediate and pungent appeal to a resistant public, and on a certain level friars became allies of popular public resistance toward the financial obligations imposed by parish and cathedral clergy.[5] Though donations to friars were voluntary, there evolved many kinds of social and spiritual transactions related to absolution and the promise of salvation that had a powerful economic component, especially as these aggregated over time to form significant patrimonies.

Economic historians have noted that in time the orders that adopted the idea of evangelical poverty came to have an intimate acquaintance with wealth. Indeed, Franciscans were among the first economic theorists of the Middle Ages. They benefited in a variety of ways from the circulation of money, and the restitution of interest on usurious loans (*male ablata*) as a form of penance in wills often passed to friars (instead of the borrower). Time in purgatory was negotiable, and income-bearing donations from property (often held for the friars by a third party), offerings for intercessory prayer, burials, altars, and commemorative chapels all stimulated donations that funded mendicant communities and their buildings. Attendance at the bedsides of the ill and dying, as well as inquisitorial activities, brought both property and income to communities and to individual friars, as is well documented in descriptions of the inquisitor Fra Mino's luxurious lifestyle. Ironically, the renunciation of money, the rejection of property, and the commitment to poverty generated a wide array of engagements that brought land and wealth. In a cycle that has been repeated over the centuries, religious institutions that began as reform movements and a return to the apostolic church became enmeshed in a web of transactions and exchanges of a profoundly economic nature, often within a century of their foundation. Would it be fair to say religious reform is something like George Bernard Shaw's famous quip that second marriages represent the triumph of hope over experience?

To some extent the large scale of mendicant convents can be blamed on their supporters, the donors who requested prayers and burial rights in return for donations. Friars came to accept, even to welcome and encourage, the interventions of lay patrons within sacred space: altars and altarpieces, tombs, frescoes, sculpture in the form of family memorials, as well as crucifixes and votive paintings, coats of arms, and flags. Occasional manuscript illuminations convey the type of lavish ornament, much of it given by lay patrons, that filled mendicant churches (see fig. 85) This image shows us, albeit in tidy form, the multitude of altars, altarpieces, and votive paintings that decorated church interiors in front of the screen that separated the choir from the nave. Columns were painted with the figures of saints and donors. Flags with coats of arms hung from the upper walls and rafters. At the Franciscan church of Nicosia, a gigantic crocodile was suspended from the beams.[6]

The important point here is that architecture was created in relation to these lay interventions, and they in turn influenced the shaping of mendicant space. This suggests, as noted in the preceding chapters, an attitude toward planning and construction that was essentially organic and responsive to the desires of donors. With this in mind – with the idea that the buildings of the friars were conditioned by and responsive to the pressures imposed by lay communities – we may wish to revisit the analysis of mendicant space as consisting of ideal proportional systems, as exemplified, for example, in the work of De Angelis d'Ossat.[7]

The international character of the orders and mobility of the friars (as well as their patrons, often merchants and bankers) meant that new trends, styles, and social practices spread rapidly throughout Europe: friars were as much "missionaries" of social practices as they were of architectural or decorative ones. Aside from individual patrons, often in the form of tertiaries (third-order supporters), confraternities were also a major factor. Every convent of any significance had at least one group of laity associated with it.[8] Tertiaries were not only generous – they also persuaded friends and neighbors to make donations and request burial in the friars' cemeteries, or to appoint a friar as an executor.[9]

If friars' prayers were indeed to "take flight, and enter into God's two ears," donors had a right to insist that the physical setting for prayer, and the spaces for tombs and family memorials, should be appropriate and worthy. Benevolent lay patrons, either as individuals or as members of pious confraternities, took an acute interest in the physical setting of friars' communities. They became involved in decisions about buildings, often supporting a portion of construction costs. The small number of votive images of donors that survive represent them on their knees in front of the Virgin or Saint Francis with models of the church they helped to construct as a reminder for posterity. Within a few decades of their foundation, mendicant churches and convents became vast repositories for the art and monuments offered by lay donors, such as a stained glass window in the Franciscan church of Limoges showing Saint Francis with the stigmata,[10] tombs, altars, votive paintings, and the coats of arms of donors and patrons. So intimately did the friars come to depend upon the largesse of patrons that they designed and built their churches to accommodate the interventions that donors requested. Construction itself was a road to salvation, as we see in the image from Antonio Fissiraga's tomb in San Francesco, Lodi (see figs. 73 and 74).

Literary sources attest as well to the abundance of luxurious decoration, as noted in a quotation from *Piers the Plowman's Crede* in which a friar seeks to cultivate a donor by offering the following:

> And if you might help us with money of your own,
> You could kneel before Christ encompassed by gold
> In the wide west window, well nigh in the middle
> And Saint Francis himself shall enfold you in his cloak,
> And present you to the Trinity and pray for your sins.[11]

The text could almost be a description of the fresco above Fissiraga's tomb.

The generosity of donors to friars enraged some of the secular clergy, as did the friars' encroachment on the traditional prerogatives of the parish. As early as the 1220s the "climate" around Franciscan and Dominican settlements was becoming fraught with complexity. In 1220 Honorius III set up a commission to constrain the canons of Paris Cathedral to allow the Preachers to hold public services at Saint-Jacques.[12] In *Nimis iniqua* (1231), Gregory IX tried to protect the friars from the persecution of the secular clergy; the text includes a long summary of the complaints made against them.[13] Friaries were thus often founded, and then expanded, in contexts that entailed tension or conflict. Sometimes, as at Strasbourg, a convent may have been built or enlarged in defiance of civic or ecclesiastical authorities. Mendicant architecture is not, therefore, a neutral subject, nor for the most part was it erected in neutral environments.

As the thirteenth century progressed and the new orders were transformed from small and marginal groups to central players in the spiritual life of medieval cities, their relationship to other sectors of the clergy changed. Though often at first welcomed by ecclesiastical authorities and frequently offered provisional space in old churches or hospitals, their rapidly increasing popularity, their rights to the administration of the sacraments, and the growing size of their communities began to produce tension. As Dawson noted, "The new orders represented the most striking institutional discontinuity and the most direct challenge to the force of tradition [within the church] that had ever appeared."[14] The areas of conflict were many: friars increasingly seemed to usurp the traditional role of parishes in relation to laity, they competed with parishes for donations and bequests, and they attracted the best students and teachers. Their externalized mission and their higher level of education were appealing to a literate and numerate middle class that expected a more sophisticated level of clergy.

Because the secular clergy had made such a concerted effort to suppress them, the survival and success of the new orders were all the more a triumph. Yet conflict with the secular clergy represented a deep threat to the continued existence of the friars, one that intermittently provoked papal intervention. These episodes affected mendicant building projects in several ways: at the height of the struggle in the 1250s they may have discouraged or postponed new construction projects, but later, once survival and success were secure, they may have stimulated a new triumphalist monumentality in buildings that affirmed notions of permanence and authority, albeit within the constraints of architectural austerity.[15] This formed part of a more general process of institutionalization under the direction of Humbert of Romans and Bonaventure, prompted in part by the crisis; each Minister General attended to formalizing internal administrative structures and establishing consistency in habits, liturgy, and uniformity in buildings. It is therefore no coincidence that the Franciscan statutes on architecture, the Constitutions of Narbonne, date to 1260. There were new regulations and clearer, more carefully articulated governing principles that included architecture. This represented the culmination of a process that shifted the character of the new orders into institutional frameworks parallel to those of monasticism. For the Franciscans the need for structure and order was more acute, and Bonaventure in particular urged a wide range of reforms in his encyclical letters for the community. He also, however, acknowledged the need for tall and permanent stone buildings, rejecting the early ideal of simple mud and wattle structures promoted by Francis.[16] As David Burr has observed, for Bonaventure "true poverty need not be compromised by involvement in teaching and pastoral duties, for Franciscan poverty is not to be measured by any absolute standards, even by the example of Francis. It is defined by the role one is called upon to perform, and it requires taking only what is necessary for the fulfillment of that role."[17]

Because they were highly visible, and because they became very large, buildings (and their decoration) were the crux of controversy, dissension, and bitter invective from both within the orders (especially some Franciscans) and outside. To their clerical critics (as well as much later to clusters of rigorously minded friars within the orders such as Angelo Clareno), the large convents that emerged by the middle of the thirteenth century were a symbol of hypocrisy and of the downfall of the founding ideals. Franciscan communities in particular were riven with controversy over issues of poverty and property ownership, as well as over the construction of buildings, and after c. 1280 the rigorists within the order were viciously persecuted. By their very existence, large Franciscan churches and convents represented not only a victory over the secular clergy, but also the victory of the realists, those Franciscans who applied a practical and livable interpretation of Francis's example.

Many well-known Wycliffite treatises vividly attest to the role of buildings as symbols of hypocrisy. FitzRalph said that while the friaries had become larger than cathedrals, rain fell on the altars of parish churches.[18] Criticisms similar to those in England were echoed on the Continent. Many of the tensions with local communities, and with the secular clergy, had to do with the friars' settling near existing parishes (almost inevitable in tightly packed medieval cities) and acquiring large tracts of urban space.

As we have seen, the orders themselves were not neutral environments in relation to architecture. Within both orders some friars promoted larger, renewed buildings,[19] a departure from the founding ideals.[20] Saint Dominic himself expressed dismay at the excessively large scale of the works at San Nicolò delle Vigne in Bologna in 1221. By the 1240s claims to apostolic poverty seemed blatantly contradicted by the lavish size of the convents, as attested by Matthew Paris and confirmed in Bonaventure's encyclical letters to the order of the 1250s and 1260s. Angelo Clareno recounts that tensions over property and buildings among the Friars Minor were already present in the early 1220s during the lifetime of Francis, and this is confirmed by various episodes regarding buildings in biographies of the saint. Clareno maintained that the saint's withdrawal from leadership indicated his perplexity in the face of its growth and change, as well as a concern that his founding vision had been irretrievably transformed.[21] Within communities of Friars Minor, the rigorous factions remembered the austere early years and resisted the construction of monumental architecture;[22] much of the dissension within the Franciscan movement was driven by this issue, perhaps best expressed through the bitter invective of Angelo Clareno:

> When you will see the brothers minor . . . procuring temporal goods beyond the things needed for the day-to-day survival of their bodies, for themselves and their places, or when you will see the brothers asking for money and *denarii*, or seeking legacies and testamentary bequests for building churches in any manner or under any guise, then you should know that these brothers have been deceived and seduced. . . . When you will see the brothers leaving the impoverished, wretched, and small places that are situated away from the world and buying and exchanging places in the towns and fortified places, or when you will see the brothers building beautiful and sumptuous struc-

tures – using the excuse that these buildings will serve the popular good by enhancing preaching – or when you will see the brothers omitting holy prayer and devotion and instead giving themselves to the reading and acquisition of books, possessing sepulchres, wanting and procuring affluent use of all things, and, in order to obtain and acquire all these things, seeking privileges from the Roman curia, and bringing lawsuits to protect these privileges, then open your eyes and pay attention and do not follow them nor hear them, because such friars are only brothers minor in name. By works and by their words they will destroy and battle against the poverty and humility that they promised to the Lord. They will be the source of many evils in the religious and in the church.[23]

How seriously should we take the criticisms of Angelo Clareno, Ubertino da Casale, and other critics of the orders, either internal or external? Quite seriously, I think. In the *Declaratio* Ubertino named specific provincial ministers as particularly culpable in the matter of excessive building: Giacomo del Tondo, Manfredo Banfi, Giovanni da Siena (Custodian of Siena in 1297),[24] Andrea de' Tolomei, and Illuminato de' Caponsacchi.[25] Convents were no longer for pilgrims and strangers but for locals, whose ancient rivalries and affiliations began to express themselves through buildings, in what André Vauchez called "une maladie de la pierre."[26] And indeed Ubertino observed that friars in Florence wanted their convent to exceed all the other convents in the city.[27]

Ubertino attributed the problem of local ties to the *appropriatio locorum* – that friars by the late thirteenth and early fourteenth centuries were native to the location of their convent, and that local friars refused to live elsewhere.[28] The truth of his words has been demonstrated in the recent research of Piron on Santa Croce in Florence. Minister John of Murrovalle attempted to inhibit intimate ties to place by ordaining that no more than a third of any convent should be *nativi de terries*, but this instruction was solidly rejected by most of the order.[29] In his work on Santa Croce, Piron noted that the friars were mostly from the city or its *contado*. According to his statistics, 64 percent of the community at Santa Croce was local, and the rest from the *contado* and nearby regions; by the end of the thirteenth century, of the 103 friars at Santa Croce, only three were not Italian.[30]

How closely was the Inquisition tied to the construction of convents? It is difficult to be precise, but the evidence points in the direction of a strong connection at some sites. Fra Mino had been in the Franciscan convent of Siena prior to moving to Florence; the reconstruction of Santa Croce began after his arrival there as inquisitor. Although this notorious friar spent large sums from his extortionary activities on himself in food and drink as well as elegant means of transportation,[31] it seems evident that at least some members of the communities were complicit with his activities and appreciated the benefits that accrued to the convent.[32] The Franciscan friaries of Prato, Pistoia, Siena, and San Quirico were all implicated in the scandal of the inquest into Fra Mino's activities.

In addition to conflict with the secular clergy and the strife within the Franciscan order, there was intense rivalry between the orders. This started early and led to competition for recruits and patrons. In architectural terms this rivalry is nowhere more evident than in Venice, where the two major churches of the new orders, Santi Giovanni e Paolo (Dominican) and Santa Maria Gloriosa dei Frari (Franciscan), rose like great ships over the jagged profile of rooftops, rivaling each other so intensely that they became similar in appearance.

Each architectural intervention at one site stimulated a corresponding response in the other, creating a polyphony of additions and responses across the breadth of the city in between (see fig. 3).

The expansion of convents with larger churches, choirs, dormitories, and refectories was expensive. The Preachers were worried about the potential debt almost from the beginning, a concern affirmed by Humbert of Romans, Minister General between 1254 and 1263. In their Constitutions of 1260, Franciscan guardians also warned against the debts incurred in construction. In the mid-thirteenth century, Bonaventure and Humbert both mentioned excessive building as the cause of indebtedness, an especially delicate matter for orders dedicated to apostolic poverty. The discomfort of debt drove home the criticisms of the antifraternal enemies.

In practical terms, however, indebtedness meant that the friars became more dependent upon their patrons, with a concomitant lack of autonomy or ability to resist external pressures. Until about 1300, the order of Preachers attempted to restrain the ineluctable drive toward larger buildings and resulting debt. But as Minister General, Niccolò Boccasini, the future Pope Benedict XI (elected in 1303), eliminated all earlier regulations on architecture; he himself may have had a role in the reconstruction of San Nicolò in Treviso, the splendor of which in many ways exemplifies the triumphant new scale and internal coherence of mendicant buildings by c. 1300 (see fig. 23).

This volume has not addressed the architecture of mendicant women for the obvious reason that strict enclosure dictated an entirely different approach to space and the construction of buildings. But women nonetheless played a fundamentally important role in the success and development of the new orders. According to William of Saint-Amour, they were the primary vehicles for spreading devotion to the friars through families. In cities like Strasbourg they defended the friars from the agents of the commune with their clogs and rolling pins. Women's communities, obliged by papal legislation to own property, sometimes functioned as holding institutions for their male counterparts. They created clusters of devout and devoted supporters in their religious and neighborhood associations, and affiliated women such as the Blessed Umiliana de' Cerchi and Catherine of Siena became important local saints. The voices of Catherine and other devout recluses propagated ideas about the reform of the papacy, and there is some thought that Sancia of Mallorca, Queen of Naples, may also have been influenced by these ideas in her foundation of the vast convent of Corpus Domini in Naples. Above all, women in their donations in wills and testaments helped to build the churches we see today. William of Saint-Amour inveighed against them precisely because they were so powerful and unmanageable a force. His stark choice of the word "penetration" cast a distinctly sexual tone into his complaint, one which stimulated a vast and bumptious literature in thirteenth- and fourteenth-century satires. However, as a social and spiritual tool for the friars themselves, "penetrating homes" in the neutral and correct sense was an immensely effective strategy.

In their own way, heretics have also been important in this narrative: their example of preaching and poverty inspired some aspects of friars' engagement with the public. Friars' adoption of visiting the laity in their homes was an effective strategy for creating the intimate and long-term bonds between patrons and friaries.

The mendicant movement cast itself as a reform of the church, one that sought a return to apostolic origins. In this connection, it is interesting to consider the early Christian basilicas assigned to the mendicants, such as Santa Sabina in Rome and San Lorenzo in Naples. The preservation of these churches (at San Lorenzo only until c. 1324) may have been not only a practical solution for providing ready-made liturgical space, but also may have had some level of ideological association with the apostolic church, with an aesthetic of the early Christian basilica that could convey in a vague associative way the values of the New Testament. It is striking, for example, that in some instances such as the Franciscan church of Santa Maria in Aracoeli in Rome, the late thirteenth-century nave was created with columns and round arches in order to mimic the appearance of an early Christian basilica. The wooden-roofed naves that can still be seen in San Giovanni a Canale in Piacenza (see fig. 16) attest to the persistence of the basilican model as a powerful ideological statement, as well as a practical solution, to mendicant church design.

On the other hand, new apses looked distinctly Gothic, with rib vaults, tracery windows, and often gables on the outside, an architectural language that could not be more different from the wooden-roofed spaces that prevail in the rest of the building (Santa Croce in Florence, Santa Maria in Aracoeli in Rome, San Fermo in Verona). The choice of rib-vaulting for apses and choirs was not coincidental and not simply acoustical: rib-vaulted architecture had acquired the connotation of spirituality, as a kind of marker of divinity on earth. As the "guardians of contemporary spirituality,"[33] friars needed to distinguish themselves from local Romanesque traditions. Rib vaults represented a highly effective etherealization of architecture, markers that salvation could be attained through the spaces and the sacraments offered below. Rib vaults, gables, and tracery were spatial indicators that friars in their choir were the mediators between the earthly and the divine, and that magnificence, as Aquinas noted, was inherent in sacrality.

The first decades of the mendicant movement revolutionized Christian practice, in effect recalibrating and reversing the introversion of sacred ritual that began in the early Christian period. In contrast to pagan religions, in which cultic ritual was largely performed outside temples, the early Christian basilica "encouraged collective worship within the body of the building, through the complex metaphor of the church as the body of Christ."[34] In the early Christian period, decoration was concentrated on interior spaces with lavish ornament in mosaic, fresco, and colored marble; for the most part, the exteriors of churches were plain and largely undecorated. Christians withdrew religious practice away from the public spheres of city centers into the interiors of churches, and because these were often associated with the burial of saints, their churches were usually on the periphery.[35] It was with mendicant friars, and with the inspired (but perhaps anxious) authority placed upon them by Innocent III, that the church moved toward an aggressive externalized mode with the goal of a capillary presence throughout both public and domestic spaces of the city.

It is within the context of the externalized mission that we can understand the episodic construction of mendicant churches (and convents more generally). The focus, especially in the early years, was on an ubiquitous presence in the city; churches for the laity were at first superfluous. To the modern mind a culture of incompletion may seem improbable and illogical, but in the premodern world of architectural procedure this approach was practical and represented a viable solution to financial exigency. And conspicuous incompletion, especially of a large building, was in its own way a testimony to poverty. Above all, the reader needs to recall that when we look at the architecture of the mendicants today, we see buildings at a terminal point of their long life, buildings that often were furnished with facades only in the nineteenth century (Santa Croce in Florence) or "completed" with vaults.

Is there a mendicant architecture? Was there something particular and identifiable about the buildings of the friars, something shared between churches such as the Frari and Santi Giovanni e Paolo in Venice, Santa Chiara in Naples, and Santa Maria in Aracoeli in Rome? I would suggest that their recognition as mendicant churches has more to do with their difference from other buildings than in identifiable common characteristics. But we can say this: the churches of the friars became vast in scale, strategically positioned, and conspicuous in their massive austerity.

NOTES

INTRODUCTION

1 Murray, 1981, p. 61.

2 Ibid., n. 162: "wherever laymen may sleep, or lie awake, or walk, or stand, or work on the land, or sail on the sea, may they be kept safe from adversity by the prayers of friars and may their business ventures be guided to prosperity, for many times they are kept safe from great disagreements and distress on behalf of their benefactors, although laymen themselves are ignorant [of the aid of friars]" (translation by Mackenzie Zalin). "unde sive dormiant seculares, sive vigilent sive ambulant, sive stent sive laborent in terra, sive navigent in mari, fratrum orationibus ab adversitatibus et defendantur et eorum negotia in prosperum dirigantur multoties enim a magnis diversitatibus et tribulationibus defenduntur pro benefactoribus suis quod ipsi seculares ignorant."

3 Vauchez, 2011, pp. 370–1.

4 Christians, of course, had for centuries engaged in public ritual after the Edict of Milan; in the fourth century there developed the practice of utilizing cities as theaters of stational processions that involved the clergy from numerous churches in ritual movement through a city (Constantinople, Rome, Jerusalem). Each parish also had litany processions within its area: see Baldovin, 1987. This, however, was the externalization of public, communal practice, whereas mendicants appealed to the personal conscience of the individual. It was not so much a matter of corporate action but rather one of outreach for private conversion. I thank Byron Stuhlman for this observation.

5 An excellent historical overview can be found in Lawrence, 1994. The intellectual, social, and spiritual activities of the other mendicant orders (the Celestinians, Augustinians, and Friars of the Sack) were also profoundly important in the late Middle Ages: see Andrews, 2006. Their buildings, however, were in most respects similar to those of the Dominicans and Franciscans, as were also issues relating to their physical presence in the city; all the orders competed for patrons and resources. Although multiple mendicant communities added to the congestion of religious foundations within cities, their presence did not substantially change the issues and problems presented by the Friars Minor and Preachers.

6 Showalter, 1973, pp. 556–74, especially p. 573. See also Vauchez, 2011, p. 368, who notes that Réginald of Orléans was also a strong candidate as founder. Gregory IX was, however, a strong proponent for Dominic's primacy as founder and supported the translation of his relics; Vauchez, 2011, p. 369, notes that the translation occurred prior to the canonization.

7 A. Thompson, 2005, p. 420.

8 From Coghill's translation of *The Canterbury Tales* (Chaucer, 1977, p. 310).

9 Republished in numerous subsequent editions and translations.

10 For a recent survey of the bibliography on mendicant architecture since c. 2000, see Bruzelius, 2012.

11 See the brilliant observations by Bonelli, 1990, pp. 15–26. His approach and line of reasoning is echoed in the work of G. Villetti, 1990 and 2003. See also Gilardi, 2004, pp. 436–9, who emphasizes the "inseparable" nature of church and conventual buildings (p. 436).

12 A recent study that demonstrates this phenomenon is Bourdua, 2004, pp. 64–9.

13 Trachtenberg, 2010, pp. 103–43.

14 Volti, 2003, p. 105.

15 For a summary of the excavations, see Rocchi Coopmans de Yoldi, 2004a, pp. 11–112, and more recently Giorgi and Matracchi, 2011, pp. 15–34.

16 De Marchi and Piraz, 2011, especially pp. 33–71.

17 Bruzelius, 2004, pp. 47–73.

18 See, for example, De Angelis d'Ossat, 1982a, pp. 150–61.

19 Menestò, 2004; Bériou and Chiffoleau, 2009; Todeschini, 1976.

20 Clareno, 2005, pp. xvii–xxii.

CHAPTER 1

1 The anecdote appears twice in *De conformitate vitae beati Francisci ad vitam Domini Jesu Christi*, composed between 1385 and 1390, published in the *Analecta Franciscana* (Bartolomeo da Pisa, 1906, IV, p. 440, and 1912, V, p. 108): "Multum Deo de beato Francisco displicent aedificia sumptuosa, quae fiunt in ordine. – Frater Iuvenalis de Aliis, de Florentia, qui fuit unus de principalioribus fratibus ad fundandum ecclesiam Sanctae Crucis de Florentia, habet pro purgatorio istam poenam, sicut ipse rescravit cuidam fratri, quod usque ad diem indicii semper sunt duo mallei, qui eius caput percutiunt." On Fra Giovinale, see Piron, 2009, p. 331.

2 Santa Croce, begun in 1294, was consecrated in 1444 (the neat 150-year interval is perhaps more symbolic than a reflection of the actual state of completion – the facade was erected only in the nineteenth century). See now Giorgi and Mattracchi, 2011, pp. 15–3.

3 For a synthetic study of the mendicant orders, see Lawrence, 1994.

4 Hinnebusch, 1966, p. 91.

5 "Devotionis vestrae" and "Quia populares" in Eubel, 1908, no. 9, p. 2, and no. 16, p. 3.

6 Rigon, 1997, p. 264.

7 Alce, 1972a, p. 145.

8 Barclay Lloyd, 2004, pp. 251–4, suggests that the screen at Santa Sabina may date to as early as 1222. For an important demonstration of this principle, see recently De Marchi, 2008, and fig. 11. See Gilardi, 2004, pp. 413–25, on internal and external churches.

9 Edgerton, 2001, pp. 73–106.

10 Sundt, 1987, p. 396.

11 Chiffoleau, 1995, p. 72.

12 In c. 1224. Sundt, 1987, p. 397.

13 Meersseman, 1946, p. 142–89, divided Dominican building into three phases that roughly coincide with what is described here: an early period, c. 1216–40, when priories existed to prepare friars for preaching; a second phase, c. 1240–63, when the first churches were enlarged;

and a third period, c. 1264–1300, at the end of which regulations on scale were eliminated.

14 Luigi Pellegrini, 1974, pp. 198–9. Dominic rarely confronted the issue of building entirely new churches, as the foundations during his lifetime were older buildings: Santa Sabina, San Nicolò (later San Domenico) in Bologna, Saint-Jacques in Paris, and Saint-Romain in Toulouse.

15 Meersseman, 1946, pp. 140–1, gives special emphasis to this point. See also Bonelli, 1990, pp. 23–5, who suggests that the stabilization of the orders into existing sites, either by borrowing or being given "the use of," occurred after an initial phase of preaching outdoors or in existing buildings (parish churches, cathedrals). See also Bonelli, 1982, "Introduzione," p. 7.

16 See Barclay Lloyd, 2004, p. 243.

17 Rigon, 1997, p. 270.

18 Ibid., p. 264.

19 Barclay Lloyd, 2004, pp. 259–64.

20 Alce, 1972b, p. 16.

21 Meersseman, 1946, p. 143.

22 Quoted from Sundt, 1987, p. 396. On Dominican architectural legislation, see also Meersseman, 1946, Montagnes, 1974, and Gilardi, 2004.

23 "Ita quod nec ipsi expensis graventur nec alii seculares vel religiosi in nostris sumptuosis edificiis scandalizentur" (Denifle, 1885, p. 225).

24 Hinnebusch, 1966, pp. 85–6.

25 See the important introductory essay by Burr and Daniel in the translation of Clareno's *A Chronicle of the Seven Tribulations* (Clareno, 2005, pp. i–xxx). Burr, 1989, p. 17, questions Clareno's account of conflict within the order in the early years. For a more complete, and negative, assessment of his reliability as a historical source, see Burr, 2009, pp. 119–38.

26 See the letters of Jacques de Vitry in Armstrong et al., 1999, pp. 578–88; also their contextualization in Little, 1978, pp. 150–1.

27 Rigon, 1997, p. 270.

28 A papal bull of Gregory IX confirmed their permanent presence there in 1228. Davidsohn, 1960–78, II, p. 172.

29 On the transition from itinerancy and rural hermitages to more permanent and settled communities in towns, see now Röhrkasten, 2012, pp. 178–92.

30 Rigon, 1997, p. 262.

31 MGH *Scriptores* (Paris, 1888, p. 397).

32 The Cerchi chapel is controversial as the first urban chapel of the Franciscans: see Busignani and Bencini, 1974, p. 23, versus Rocchi Coopmans de Yoldi, 2004, p. 243.

33 Rigon, 1988, pp. 264–5.

34 Ibid., pp. 183–94.

35 Luigi Pellegrini, 2000, pp. 66–7.

36 The bibliography on Assisi is vast, but for starters see Schenkluhn, 1994.

37 Tugwell, 1982, p. 25.

38 On the other hand, in writing in favor of Dominic's canonization, Jordan described Dominic as "first founder, master and brother." Hinnebusch, 1966, p. 14.

39 Alce, 1972b, p. 5.

40 This is an example of the "institutional thinking" that characterizes the order of Preachers.

41 This was confirmed in the narrative panels of the *arca* in which the saint is buried.

42 See Cooper, 2005, and J. Robson, 2005.

43 Schenkluhn, 2000, pp. 56–63.

44 Ibid.

45 This was the case at Saint-Jacques in Paris.

46 Barclay Lloyd, 2004, p. 243.

47 Ronzani, 2003, pp. 31–48, and Ronzani, 1977a, pp. 672–3.

48 As Villetti, 2003, p. 33, notes, in this second phase the Preachers often converted their original chapel into a chapter house or sacristy (as at Santa Caterina in Pisa, or San Domenico in Pistoia). Not all sources would agree that the Cistercian connection should be emphasized; for example, Meersseman, 1946, p. 142, argues that the Preachers did not have the concept of an "architectural identity" until after the order's "gestational phase," which he dates up to c. 1240.

49 This is what Villetti, 2003, p. 33, called the "fase di stabilizzazione."

50 Rigon, 1997, p. 266. For a broad overview, see now Peterson, 2012.

51 See, for example, Vauchez, 1990, pp. 151–4.

52 The foundation documents of the Dominican house in Sigtuna, Sweden: Meersseman, 1946, pp. 140–1.

53 Bonelli, 1990, pp. 23–5.

54 For Santa Sabina, perhaps as early as 1222: Barclay Lloyd, 2004, pp. 251–4. Galvano Fiamma dated the choir screen of Sant'Eustorgio to 1239: Meersseman, 1946, p. 152, and Galvano Fiamma, 1940, p. 326.

55 Vicaire, 1974, p. 210.

56 Sundt, 1987, pp. 398–400.

57 Manselli, 1974, pp. 192–4.

58 For a summary of the archaeological evidence, see Carbonai, Gaggio, and Salmi, 2004, pp. 243–72, and more recently on the cloister Giorgi and Matracchi, 2011, pp. 21–2.

59 O'Carroll, 1995, p. 197.

60 Baird, Baglovi, and Kane, 1986, p. 301.

61 Sundt, 1987, pp. 400–1 and 406; Meersseman, 1946, pp. 171–3; Gilardi, 2004, pp. 379–443.

62 Sundt, 1987, p. 406; see also Montagnes, 1974, p. 89.

63 Montagnes, 1974, p. 90.

64 Between 1244 and 1257 over 100 communities were authorized to move to more central sites: Monti, 1994, p. 60.

65 For the mendicant–secular conflict, see Geltner's 2008 translation of William of Saint-Amour's *De periculis novissimorum temporum*. See also Dossat, 1973; Geltner, 2012.

66 There had been bitter rivalry between the two orders as early as the 1220s. See Tugwell, 1982, p. viii.

67 Burr, 1989, p. 149.

68 Ibid., p. 46.

69 D'Alatri, 1987, pp. 32–3.

70 Cacciarini, 1968, pp. 55–61, and most recently Giorgi and Matracchi, 2011, pp. 13–31.

71 Bonaventure's first encyclical letter and the other decrees issued under his administration quoted here are taken from Monti, 1994, pp. 59–60.

72 Ibid., pp. 59–60.

73 Ibid., pp. 226–9.

74 Ibid., pp. 81–5.

75 Ibid., p. 86.

76 Ibid., p. 140.

77 Ibid., p. 86.

78 Ibid., p. 87.

79 Ibid., p. 87, n. 69.

80 Ibid., p. 227.

81 Ibid., p. 60.

82 In 1277 the public mission was substantially aided by the election of the powerfully pro-Franciscan pope, Nicholas III.

83 Paolini, 1998, pp. 198–200.

84 Monti, 1994b, pp. 192–3. See also Emery, 1953, pp. 259–60, on the role of the Franciscans and Dominicans in suppressing the more recent begging orders, who were perceived as rivals.

85 For example, Humbert of Romans initiated a rigorous attempt to impose liturgical uniformity in all matters concerning the Dominican order. See Brett, 1979, pp. 97–100. For the Constitutions of Narbonne, see Burr's interesting insights, 1989, pp. 8–9.

86 Humbert of Romans, *Opera de vita regulari*, 1956, p. 5. It may be important to note that this concern for clear and distinct institution identity may also have been stimulated by the rise of numerous other mendicant groups toward the middle of the thirteenth century.

87 Franciscan legislation prior to 1260 does not survive. See Sundt, 1987, p. 402.

88 Ibid., pp. 394 and 401–2. This was also the period (c. 1279–83) in which the controversy on *usus pauper* heated up with new intensity within the Franciscan order: see Burr, 1989, pp. 49–51.

89 For a summary of the controversy within the order over evangelical poverty, see M. Lambert, 1961, pp. 157–95.

90 See Angelo Clareno, the Fifth Tribulation, in Clareno, 2005, pp. 129–78.

91 The rigorists were primarily in the Ancona region. See Clareno, 2005, pp. 148–89; also Burr, 1989, pp. 28–9, on the polarization of the order after 1274, and especially after 1278. Burr describes this as "essentially an Anconan problem."

92 "Praefectus operum circa opera quae fiunt debet attendere diligenter ne fiat aliquid quod super-fluitatem aut superbiam praetendat, et ad hoc operam dare quod fiant opera durabilia et humilia, et quae paupertati et religioni consona videantur" (Meersseman, 1946, p. 168). See also Goldthwaite, 1993, p. 75, Dimock, 2000, p. 21–2, and Sundt, 1987, p. 401.

93 Sundt, 1987, p. 401.

94 Ibid.

95 Ibid.

96 Erickson suggests that responsibility for large and lavish buildings was prompted by the desires and donations of lay patrons (1975, p. 120).

97 "Let barriers which are in our churches be established between laymen and friars everywhere by the priors in such a way that the friars cannot be seen by the laymen exiting and entering from the choir, and so that the friars cannot see them [laymen]. Some windows, however, will be able to be fitted there, so that they can be opened during the time of the elevation of the Lord's body. Likewise, in the aisles that are in churches next to the friars' choir on the right and the left, let women not be permitted to enter" (translation by Mackenzie Zalin). "Intermedia que sunt in ecclesiis nostris inter seculares et fratres, sic disponantur ubique per priores. Quod fratres egredientes et ingredientes de choro non possint videri a secularibus, vel videre eosdem. Poterunt tamen alique fenestre ibidem aptari, ut tempore elevacionis corporis dominici possint aperiri. Item. In alis que sunt in ecclesiis iuxta chorum fratrum a dextris et a sinistris, mulieres ingredi non permittantur." Sundt, 1987, p. 406.

98 Humbert of Romans, in Tugwell, 1982, p. 250.

99 For example, the paintings by the Degli Erri workshop at the National Gallery in Washington, D.C., and in the museum of Modena.

100 See Cadei, 1980, p. 349.

101 Ibid.

102 See Dellwing, 1970 and 1990.

103 On the development of mathematical or "accounting" thinking and the friars as "the pioneers of calculation," see Chiffoleau, 1995; also Murray, 1986, p. 182.

104 Chiffoleau, 1995, p. 98.

105 It is not our concern to discuss the dissent over property represented by the Fraticelli, or Spirituals, though this issue must have lurked in the background of many building projects and no doubt elicited internal dissent within those houses engaged in monumental construction projects, as at Santa Croce in Florence.

106 See Mäkinen, 2001, pp. 65–76. These concepts were affirmed by Nicolas III (1277–80) in *Exiit qui seminat*, which accepted the papal ownership of Franciscan property.

107 In Pisa, for example, Archbishop Federico Visconti in 1261 placed the first stone of the new Franciscan church that would replace the old small structure acquired earlier in the century.

108 Montagnes, 1974, pp. 90–1.

109 Vauchez, 2003, p. 566.

110 Ahlquist and Cook, 2005, pp. 211–56.

111 Dominic's tomb inspired, for example, that of Saint Peter Martyr in Milan, just as the fresco cycle of Assisi spawned many imitations in fresco. For the architectural repetitions, see Schenkluhn, 2000.

112 Bourdua, 2004, p. 92.

113 Murray, 1981, pp. 59–61. Indeed, as the author notes, the alms given the friars were to be considered a "fair wage for work done."

114 "Divites quippe et raptores et usurarios publicos circumeundo visitabant, et si qua invenirent ambitione secularium vel rapto et denique fenore ab illis acquisita, ad monasteria sua, que permaxima edificare coeperant, efficiebant ut donarentur, et ita per interpretes, illas res in edificiorum suorum vel victualium usus convertebant, licet non ignorarent rapinas vel usuras nisi eis a quibus extorte sunt, reddi debere." Quoted by Vauchez, 2003, p. 566. The English translation is by Mackenzie Zalin.

115 Piron, 2009, pp. 327–8.

116 Ibid.

117 Ibid., p. 328.

118 Ibid., p. 329.

119 Burr, 1989, pp. 97–8.

120 Ibid., pp. 98–101.

121 Piron, 2009, p. 325.

122 Ibid., p. 329; Burr 1989, pp. 98–101.

123 Sundt, 1987, p. 404.

124 Erickson, 1976, p. 138.

125 Erickson, 1975, pp. 130–1.

126 Bonaventure's first encyclical letter and the other decrees issued under his administration quoted here are taken from Monti, 1994, p. 60. In the same letter of 1257 he noted: "The construction of buildings on a lavish and extravagant scale is upsetting many brothers, becoming a burden to friendly benefactors, and leaving us prey to hostile critics."

127 Burr, 2001, p. 206.

128 Ronzani, 1985b, "Il francescanesimo," p. 5, on Pisa, Boncllli, 1990, pp. 15–26, and Villctti, 2003, are among the few scholars to have addressed problems of simplistic dating in mendicant buildings.

129 At Pistoia, for example, there were indulgences issued in 1250 for the construction of the church and convent, but the buildings we have now date only to 1289 and afterwards: Gai, 1993, pp. 36–8. As we shall see in Chapter Five, clauses to wills often stipulated that construction should begin within five or ten years of the donation.

CHAPTER 2

1 For a broad survey of the orders in English, see Lawrence, 1994.

2 Jordan of Saxony, 1982, pp. 5–6. The apostolic mission was given great emphasis in Dominican imagery, which illustrated Dominic's vision of Saints Peter and Paul, an image included in the *Arca di San Domenico* as well as in fresco cycles. See Cannon, 1998, p. 31; and Cooper, 2011, p. 98.

3 On the relation between Cistercian and Dominican architecture, see Schenkluhn, 1985, p. 98; also H. W. Hubert, 2000, p. 17.

4 See Barclay Lloyd, 2004, pp. 254–5. Meersseman, 1946, pp. 139–40, notes, however, that the obligation of celebrating public Mass was essential to new foundations.

5 Sundt, 1987, p. 396.

6 Ibid., p. 405.

7 "Vultis tam cito paupertatem relinquere et magna palatia edificare?" The canonization testimony of Brother Stephen of Spain, August 1233, from Tugwell, 1982, p. 80; quoted in Barclay Lloyd, 2004, p. 250, n. 79.

8 These are the words attributed to Dominic in the testimonies for his canonization by Brother Amizio and Stephen of Spain. See Meersseman, 1946, p. 145.

9 Sundt, 1987, pp. 398–9. According to Meersseman, 1946, pp. 146–7, a *pedes* was between 35 and 38 cm. in Italy; north of the Alps it would equal c. 31.5 cm.

10 Initially the lay public was prohibited from access to the interior of Cistercian churches, and lay altars were located instead in western porches. A radical Dominican innovation for lay participation, however, was the addition of a designated exterior piazza for preaching. Improta, 2011, p. 107, notes that the body of Peter Martyr was exposed in the piazza of Sant'Eustorgio for public veneration in the summer of 1253.

11 Alce, 1972b, p. 9.

12 Ibid., pp. 12–45, for transcriptions of the documents. We may therefore be able to propose a date of c. 1238 for a choir screen at San Nicolò. As Meersseman, 1946, p. 156, suggests, the west wall of the old church of San Nicolò could have served as a temporary screen depending on its location in relation to the new church.

13 Barclay Lloyd, 2004, p. 252.

14 For the issue of access and the role of choir screens, see most recently Cooper, 2011, pp. 95–100.

15 See Schmid, 2002, pp. 27–30 and 157–60.

16 The reader might wish to consider whether the increasing importance of noble and royal burials in mendicant choirs had an impact upon the reconfiguration of tombs and burial space in the churches of other institutions, as, for example, in the choir of the Benedictine abbey of Saint-Denis, where Louis IX promoted the creation of a monumental set of ancestral tombs celebrating the Merovingian and Carolingian dynasties. If this had been the case, the royal tombs program at the abbey would have been a reaffirmation of Saint-Denis as the royal burial church.

17 On this issue see Benvenuti-Papi, 1977, pp. 598–602.

18 "In the aforesaid church of Saint Romanus, straightaway a cloister was built with cells above rather suitable for studying and sleeping" (translation by Mackenzie Zalin). "In predicta ecclesia Sancti Romani protinus edificatum est claustrum, cellas habens ad studendum et dormiendum desuper satis aptas." Jordan of Saxony 1935, p. 46.

19 Meersseman, 1946, p. 144.

20 Barclay Lloyd, 2004, pp. 259–87.

21 Here the example of the Blackfriars in Oxford is instructive. See Hassall et al., 1989, pp. 184–6.

22 Tugwell, 1982, p. 141. On Humbert and uniformity within the order, see Gilardi, 2004, pp. 380–2.

23 Vicaire, 1974, p. 210.

24 See, for example, Smith, 2010, on the piazza of Santa Maria Novella.

25 Meersseman, 1946, pp.164–5.

26 "Then, with the growth of the number of friars, it was necessary that the houses and the church be expanded; when the new buildings followed, the old ones were torn down" (translation by Mackenzie Zalin). "Crescente denique fratrum numero. . . . Necesse erat domos et ecclesiam dilatari; novis succedentibus, vetera diruntur." Jordan of Saxony, 1935, p. 84.

27 Meersseman, 1946, p. 155.

28 For the canonization of Dominic, see Vicaire, 1965, pp. 31–2.

29 Moskowitz, 1992, pp. 271–90.

30 Vauchez, 2011.

31 Vicaire, 1974, pp. 222–4.

32 Ibid., p. 227.

33 Ibid., p. 240.

34 Sundt, 1989, pp. 204–5, makes a convincing argument that this solution was the least costly and the most efficient in relation to the dimensions of the terrain available.

35 Vicaire, 1974, pp. 217–20.

36 See ibid., pp. 225–6, on the sources of these funds, mostly from the revenues of the order obtained from questing in Toulouse itself.

37 Ibid., p. 226.

38 Ibid., p. 230.

39 Few of these tombs survive, and some must have already been destroyed in the reconstructions of the thirteenth and fourteenth centuries.

40 Sundt, 1989, p. 205.

41 For symbolic interpretations, see Schenkluhn, 1985, pp. 71–6; for a summary of other theories, see Sundt, 1989, pp. 188–97.

42 Sundt, 1989, p. 203 and n. 49; and Schenkluhn, 1985, pp. 55–62.

43 Schenkluhn, 1985, p. 61, proposes that this was the old hospice of Saint-Jacques, built in 1209 by the royal chaplain Jean le Barastre.

44 Sundt, 1989, p. 203.

45 It is thought that San Nicolò delle Vigne dated to the twelfth century. See Rinaldi, 1987, p. 78.

46 Alce, 1972a, p. 146.

47 Rinaldi, 1987, pp. 75 and esp. p. 80.

48 He is cited in numerous documents for the acquisition of the surrounding land and houses. See Alce, 1972a, pp. 140–42 and 146–9.

49 During one of Dominic's absences the ceilings of the cells were raised by Rudolph of Faenza. When Dominic returned, he reproached Rudolph and the other friars: "Do you want so quickly to give up poverty and to put up great

palaces?" (Hinnebusch, 1966, p. 151). At a later date, anonymous sources state that Dominic's tomb was exposed to rain and snow. Jordan of Saxony, 1982, p. 93.

50 Alce, 1972a, pp. 127–39.

51 Ibid., p. 152.

52 Gelichi, Merlo, and Nepoti, 1987, p. 110; Alce, 1972a. See also Gilardi, 2004, pp. 392–4.

53 Rinaldi, 1987, p. 84.

54 On the tombs, see Breveglieri, 1995, pp. 166–88.

55 Rinaldi, 1987, p. 86.

56 Ibid., p. 84.

57 Breveglieri, 1995, pp. 204–24.

58 Alce, 1972a, p. 154. The chronology is still debated, however: see Gelichi, Merlo and Nepoti, 1987a, p. 109.

59 Alce, 1972a, p. 157.

60 Alce, 1972a, p. 169, has pointed out the consistency of the brickwork where it can be seen, from the facade through the east end of the church. Nonetheless, although the nave was erected with great rapidity, work on the choir was slower, and completed only sometime after the translation of Dominic's remains in 1233. The choir could have been in use with a provisional ceiling, for example, while the vaults were completed.

61 Alce, 1972b, pp. 9 and 23.

62 Ibid., pp. 9 and 39–40.

63 Translation by Mackenzie Zalin. Quoted in Alce, 1972a, p. 164.

64 Ibid.

65 Meersseman, 1946, p. 156.

66 Hindin, 2008, p. 381, has also noted that when the Dominicans settled into a pre-existing church in Prague in 1226–7 they reconstructed the chevet with a flat termination.

67 Hinnebusch, 1966, p. 90.

68 Barclay Lloyd, 2004, p. 242.

69 Palmerio and Villetti, 1989, p. 46. The reconstruction of Santa Maria sopra Minerva was begun only in the early 1280s.

70 Barclay-Lloyd, 2004, p. 243. By 1320, however, the Preachers seem to have taken over the fees: ibid., pp. 257–8.

71 Ibid., pp. 284–7. Barclay Lloyd has written an exemplary study of the chronology of these buildings.

72 Odetto, 1940, p. 322.

73 For a summary of the chronology of Sant'Eustorgio, see Romanini 1964, pp. 85–9.

74 Odetto, 1940, p. 323.

75 Righetti Tosti-Croce, 1984, p. 59.

76 Galvano Fiamma, 1897, pp. 337–8.

77 Romanini, 1964, p. 85: "la basilica extra murana presenta oggi un'ossatura romanica . . . inglobata, per cosi dire, incastonata come nocciolo primitivo entro tutta una serie di amplicazioni e traformazioni e aggiunte; non compiute tutte nel corso del solo Duecento, peraltro, ma via via susseguitesi dalla prima metà di questo secolo sino al tarde Quattrocento."

78 Armstrong et al., 1999, p. 103.

79 *Scripta Leonis, Rufini et Angeli Sociorum S. Francisci* in Brooke, 1970, pp. 113–15.

80 Armstrong et al., 1999, p. 126.

81 Röhrkasten, 2012, pp. 180–1.

82 The great basilica of San Francesco at Assisi is an exceptional monument in large part funded by the papacy and therefore not central to the discussion here.

83 On itinerancy, see now Röhrkasten, 2012, especially pp. 178–9.

84 San Francesco at Assisi, begun in 1228 at the instigation of the papacy and designated as *ecclesia specialis*, was funded by pilgrim donations, the papacy, and the commune, and therefore does not conform to the usual nexus of external and social considerations that influenced mendicant building elsewhere.

85 See Bruzelius, 1992, pp. 84–5.

86 See ibid., pp. 84–6, and Bruzelius, 1996, pp. 53–74.

87 See now the excellent publication and analysis by De Marchi and Piraz, 2011.

88 For a possible chronology of construction at San Lorenzo, see Bruzelius, 2004, pp. 57–70.

89 For the chronology of the chapels and important consideration on the chronology, see Krüger, 1986, pp. 35–6, and 2004; also Berger-Dittscheid, 1990, pp. 41–64.

90 On San Lorenzo and the Seggio di Montagna, see Di Meglio, 2003, pp. xxxi–xli.

91 For the chronology of San Fermo, see Bourdua, 2004, pp. 33–4.

92 Romanini, 1964, pp. 80–5.

93 Ibid., p. 81 and n. 35.

94 The following analysis is largely derived from Ronzani, 1985.

95 Ibid., p. 35, n. 92; Ronzani, 2003, pp. 38–42. *Incerta* are the funds of uncertain origin (the interest paid by persons unknown) offered by repetent usurers.

96 Sbaralea, I, 361, pp. 560–1; Andreini, Cerrato, and Feola, 1993a, p. 36.

97 Andreini, Cerrato, and Feola, 1993a, p. 40.

98 Gai, 1993, pp. 27–80.

99 Andreini, Cerrato, and Feola, 1993, p. 40.

CHAPTER 3

1 A number of the strategies I describe here were deduced by James, 1989: see especially "Construction Strategies," pp. 39–62. His important work on this topic suggests that these opportunistic building strategies were common in the monumental churches in the Île-de-France in the twelfth century.

2 On this phenomenon in general, see Freigang and Gardner, both 2002.

3 Odetto, 1940, pp. 324–36; Romanini, 1964, pp. 85–7.

4 Improta, 2011, p. 107. Another example is the Franciscan church in Cairo (Liguria): see Rossini, 1981, pp. 93–4.

5 Romanini, 1964, pp. 80–5.

6 On the tombs and the construction of the church, see now Schwartz, 2009, pp. 56–66.

7 See Smith, 2010. Also Trachtenberg, 2010, pp. 205–22. The completion of the nave may have occurred only toward the middle of the fourteenth century.

8 Most recently Edgerton, 2001, pp. 73–106.

9 Cooper, 2011, pp. 96–7.

10 Bruzelius, 2004, pp. 68–9.

11 Krüger, 1986, p. 130; Bruzelius, 2004, pp. 68–9.

12 The interior reconfiguration of San Lorenzo, which occurred after 1324, might in part have been inspired by the construction of Santa Chiara as one vast interior volume flanked by chapels. Bruzelius, 2004, pp. 68–9.

13 And the burials were for the most part those of Roman senators. See Romano, 1998a, p. 206; for the chronology of construction, ibid., pp. 195–208, especially p. 199. See also E. Hubert, 1995a, p. 211.

14 E. Hubert, 1995a, p. 211: "centum florenos auri, in qua michi eligo sepulturam, de quibus fiat una cappella in qua me iubeo sepelliri, item relinquo dicte ecclesie Sancte Marie de Capitolio XV florenos auri pro opere ipsius ecclesie, dummodo fratres ipsius ecclesie dent et assignent locum pro dicta cappella facienda. Et aliter dictos XV nec dictos centrum florenos auri petere dicta ecclesie non possit."

15 Bruzelius, 2004, pp. 80–1.

16 Moretti, 2001, p. 68.

17 Nelli, 2001, p. 119. This early church of the Franciscans dedicated to "Sancte Crucis in Pistoia" for which the funds were given is no longer extant.

18 Ibid.

19 Trachtenberg, 2010, pp. 63–101 and 357–76.

20   The reader might wish to consider these comments in relation to Trachtenberg, 2010, passim, but particularly the Introduction, pp. 1–23.

21   Bruzelius, 2007, p. 209.

22   It may also be useful to consider that life expectancy through much of the medieval period ranged between twenty-seven and thirty-three years. William of Sens's short tenure at Canterbury was probably the norm rather than the exception. Other types of vicissitudes, such as famines, foul weather, tempests, crusading taxes, and bankruptcy, could intervene as conditions affecting the construction of large-scale projects. Incompletion was perhaps an inevitable component of human existence in the Middle Ages, as well as intrinsic to the lives of medieval buildings.

CHAPTER 4

1   Chiffoleau, 1980, p. 61.

2   This phenomenon began in full vigor in the last decade of the twelfth century with the communal palaces of Modena (1194), Brescia (1198), and Bologna (1200). On the typological dependence of the communal palace on episcopal models, see Miller, 2000, pp. 137–45.

3   The process began with the translation of saintly bishops into the cathedrals of urban centers: see ibid., pp. 126–33. Santo Stefano in Bologna was reconfigured with a marble tomb for the fifth-century bishop of the city, San Petronio. At the same time, the interior of the rotunda was covered with a dome, work that seems to have been completed by c. 1255. This coincides with the composition of heroic narratives on the life of San Petronio that cast him as the patron saint of the city: H. W. Hubert, 2000, p. 14.

4   Fundamental to this study is the challenge presented by Le Goff, 1968, pp. 335–52. Although many of the ideas rapidly sketched in his article are now controversial (for example, see Coomans, 2001, p. 11), it was one of the first studies to present some of the social considerations that form this chapter.

5   Evans, 1949, pp. 206–7, is one of the few scholars to have applied the descriptions of mendicant churches from sources such as *Piers the Ploughman's Crede* to the analysis of mendicant churches.

6   In some ways this reflected the locations of early Christian communities in the pagan cities of the Roman Empire: see Canniffe, 2008, p. 39.

7   The new walls of Florence were erected between 1172 and 1174. In 1299 a larger ring of city walls was initiated. For the recentering of the city in the twelfth century: Miller, 2000, pp. 137–45.

8   Lesnick, 1989, pp. 82–92.

9   Cohn, 1992, p. 5.

10   On poverty and wages, Jones, 1997, pp. 234–7, 242–3, and 252–3; also Little, 1978, pp. 28–9.

11   See Caby, 2004, p. 312.

12   Smith, 2010, pp. 486–91.

13   Le Goff, 1970, p. 930, poses the question of a possible "déchristianization urbaine."

14   This is what D'Avray, 1985, p. 26, has called the "unstable piety of the towns."

15   Ibid., p. 19, on the education of parish clergy.

16   See Benvenuti-Papi, 1977, p. 600 and n. 8.

17   Recorded by Jordan of Saxony in his life of Dominic: 1982, p. 6. Some of these debates continued for as many as fifteen days: see Hinnebusch, 1966, pp. 24–5. The type of language stuck: Anthony of Padua was described as the "hammer" against the heretics: D'Alatri, 1952, p. 225.

18   Le Goff, 1970, p. 936, n. 3.

19   Humbert of Romans, 1956, pp. 7–9: "In civitatibus sunt plures quam in aliis locis, et ideo melius est ibi predicare quam alibi." See Carozzi, 2001, pp. 249–61.

20   Quoted in Luigi Pellegrini, 1974, p. 173. These translations are by Mackenzie Zalin.

21   Ibid.

22   Hinnebusch, 1966, pp. 260ff.

23   Francis's *Rule for Hermitages* (1217–21), in Armstrong et al., 1999, pp. 61–2.

24   Röhrkasten, 2012, pp. 178–9.

25   *Later Admonition*, c. 1220, in Armstrong et al., 1999, pp. 45–51. Le Goff, 1970, p. 926, speaks of the Friars Minor as "oscillating" between the city and the desert in the early years.

26   Le Goff, 1970, pp. 927–8.

27   See on this Benvenuti-Papi, 1977, p. 599.

28   In Naples the site of the market was moved from the center to the port by Charles of Anjou after 1266.

29   Inga, 1978, p. 44.

30   Ronzani, 2003, pp. 33–5.

31   Ibid.

32   Zannela, 1978, pp. 40–1.

33   Delorme, 1939, pp. 201–59.

34   Ibid., pp. 207 and 232–3.

35   Ibid.

36   See Coomans, 2001, p. 12, for Belgium.

37   See the forthcoming book by Claudia Bolgia on this church.

38   Coomans, 2001, p. 12.

39   Spada, 1932, pp. 71–6.

40 Lombardi, 1993, p. 206.

41 Gai, 2001, p. 75, n. 16.

42 Coomans, 2001, p. 14.

43 For this issue in Umbria, see Da Campagnola, 1971, pp. 469–532.

44 See in particular the example of Foligno mentioned by Guidoni, 1977, pp. 73–4, where the friars became what he calls the "condizionatori politici di una vera e propria 'repubblica ecclesiastica'," with reciprocal responsibilities of support and service for the commune established in 1314. On mendicants as civic administrators, see also Jones, 1997, p. 437, and Cannon, 2004, p. 256.

45 Rigon, 1997, p. 273.

46 Da Campanola, 1971, p. 506.

47 Rigon, 1997, pp. 270–1.

48 Bourdua, 2004, p. 92.

49 Salvatori, 1981, p. 71.

50 Rubiani's heavy-handed restoration has made analysis of this church very difficult, but its importance in relation to subsequent structures (Piacenza, Naples, Padua) would seem to confirm a date in the 1250s or 1260s. See Schenkluhn, 1985, pp. 122–36.

51 Farina, 1978, pp. 56–61.

52 Piron, 2009, p. 330.

53 Da Campagnola, 1971, pp. 469–532, especially pp. 501–5.

54 Ibid.

55 D'Avray, 1985, p. 33.

56 Di Meglio, 2003, pp. xxvii–xli.

57 Moretti, 2001, pp. 66–7.

58 Ibid., p. 67.

59 Piron, 2009, p. 333.

60 Ibid., pp. 334–8.

61 Romanini, 1964, p. 78.

62 Spigarolli, 1983, p. 152.

63 Stanford, 2005, p. 188.

64 Ibid., p. 189.

65 Ibid., p. 187.

66 See Bourdua, 2004, pp. 65–6.

67 Guidoni, 1977, pp. 69–106, developed this into a triangular geometry applied to medieval cities, a system that seems improbable given the real difficulties of finding available land for mendicant houses in most cities.

68 Green Labunski, 2010, pp. 99–105.

69 Could the numerous painted cycles of the lives of Saint Benedict and the exaltation of his cult in various Roman churches in the thirteenth century have been a response to the threat presented by the Franciscans?

70 Guidoni, 1977, p. 84. A *canna* varies in length but is usually slightly more than 2 meters.

71 Trevisan, 2003, pp. 143–51.

72 Gai, 2000, p. 101, especially n. 108.

73 Hinnebusch, 1966, p. 260.

74 Miller, 2000, p. 168.

75 H. W. Hubert, 2000, pp. 3–9.

76 Canniffe, 2008, p. 39.

77 Delcorno, 2000, p. 456.

78 Lea, 1888, II, p. 211; Smith, 2010, p. 480.

79 See Guidoni, 1977, p. 75, n. 7. Translation by Mackenzie Zalin.

80 Inga, 1978, p. 44.

81 Lea, 1888, II, p. 212.

82 Lansing, 1998, pp. 137–8.

83 Davidsohn, 1929, pp. 168–9 – see also below in Chapter Five on the Inquisition.

84 Biscaro, 1933, p. 166.

85 Bériou and Chiffoleau, 2009, pp. 165–7, as well as the essays in Quaglioni, 2005; for a nuanced discussion of analogies between salvation and commerce, see also D'Avray, 1985, pp. 235–7.

86 Bériou and Chiffoleau, 2009, p. 164, n. 23; D'Avray, 1985, p. 235.

87 D'Avray, 1985, pp. 208–9.

88 Humbert of Romans, 1951, p. 56.

89 Hinnebusch, 1966, p. 260.

90 Preachers received papal authorization to bury laity in 1220: ibid., p. 63.

91 Alce, 1972b, p. 9. The document is published ibid., pp. 39–41.

92 See Breveglieri, 1995, on the tombs at San Domenico.

93 Miller, 2000, pp. 180–1.

94 Biscaro, 1933, pp. 166–7. See also Giraldi, 2004, pp. 428–31 and plate II, on moveable wooden pulpits.

95 Cooper, 2011, p. 97, has recently noted this type of arrangement at San Domenico in Arezzo.

96 De Divitis, 2011, p. 196.

97 Humbert of Romans, 1956, p. 376: "nihil autem tam valet ad huiusmodi poenitentiae consummationis accelerationem, sicut praedicatio." The translation is by Mackenzie Zalin.

98 Rénard, 1977, pp. 37–44.

99 Ibid., p. 42.

100 Ibid., pp. 43–4.

101 Ibid., pp. 34–60.

102 See Mulchahey, 1998, p. 9.

103 Rénard, 1977, pp. 41–2.

104 On mendicant preaching in general, see Menestò, 1995.

105 D'Avray, 1985, pp. 25–8.

106 Rénard, 1977, pp. 59–71.

107 Mulchahey, 1998, p. 53. On the role of the friars as confessors, see Menestò, 1996; also Rusconi, 1981b, pp. 251–309, especially pp. 261–7.

108 Though as Rusconi, 1981b, pp. 260–2, notes, there was considerable regional variation.

109 There is a great deal of literature on the controversy; see, among other sources, ibid., pp. 279–89. The classic study is Dufeil, 1972.

110 Built, as Rénard, 1977, p. 71, noted, "ad capiendos homines in praedicationibus."

111 Angiola, 1977, pp. 9–18, and Seidel, 1993, p. 34. See most recently on this, Dent, 2011, p. 40.

112 On this issue see Gilbert, 2000, pp. 9–30.

113 A. Thompson, 2005, pp. 309–20 and 326–35; and Longhi, 2003, especially pp. 105–27. See also Angiola, 1977.

114 First published by Bologna, 1969, pp. 235–45.

115 Biscaro, 1933, p. 167.

116 See Mallory and Freuler, 1991.

117 See Lara, 2004, pp. 51–2.

118 On this point see, for example, the remarks in Moskowitz, 2001, p. 287.

119 As is well known, narratives on the lives of saints, such as the *Legenda aurea* and the concordances to the Bible, were developed by the mendicant orders as aids in preaching.

120 See Rénard, 1977, pp. 159–63, on "gratia" as fundamental to preaching; he quotes Humbert of Romans, who remarks that those who have "grace" in preaching ought to do more of it: "Those who have grace in this receive grace from those who have it" ("illi qui in hoc habent gratiam, ab habentibus gratiam in hoc") and should devote themselves to "the grace of preaching and keeping company with men" ("gratia praedicandi et inter homines conversandi").

121 Rénard, 1977, p. 163, quotes a Dominican prayer: "Accord to your servants, Lord, the ability to speak with grace" (or eloquence), "verbum tribue graciosum." Humbert of Romans stated that each convent should have several "praedicatores gratiosi." General chapters instructed that preaching should be done by gifted friars ("de bene dotatus") and preachers full of grace ("praedicatores gratiosi").

122 Szittya, 1986, p. 53.

123 Ibid.

124 Angiola, 1977, p. 26, notes that the Pisa pulpit is "self-consciously retrospective."

125 And for antifraternalism in southwest France, see Dossat, 1973, pp. 263–306.

126 I have used the translation by Geltner, 2008; see for example pp. 49–51 and 67.

127 Fleming, 1966, pp. 696–7: "Huius modi etiam homines praedicta fabricantes aedificia, videntur convertere panes in lapideas; videlicet panes Pauporum (id est eleemosynas mendicatas, de quibus deberent panes Christi Pauperibus erogari) in congeries lapidum, id est in domos lapideas sumptuosas et superfluas, convertentes. Et ideo videntur esse Diabolo crudeliores et magis immisericordes; cum ipse Diabolus e contrario petierit lapides converti in panes, dicens Domino. *Dic, et lapides isti panes fiant.* Matth. 4 [3]." I thank Mackenzie Zalin for the translation.

128 For the background on Chaucer's views, see A. Williams, 1953.

129 Chaucer, 1951, extracts from pp. 310–11.

130 Fleming, 1966, pp. 688–700.

131 Chaucher, 1977, p. 315.

CHAPTER 5

1 Giordano da Pisa, 1867, p. 314. On Giordano (d. 1310) see the introduction by Delcorno to Giordano da Pisa, 1999, pp. 7–16.

2 For the dating of the *avelli* on the facade to c. 1300: Schwartz, 2009, pp. 112–14. Delcorno, in Giordano da Pisa, 1999, p. 10, states that Giordano began preaching at Santa Maria Novella in 1303. It is interesting to note that in his sermon on the Virgin Martyrs of Cologne, Fra Giordano describes the church as "tutto pieno di bellisime arche di marmoro grande, che sono piene de' chorpi" – as though he were describing the new tombs on the facade of Santa Maria Novella. Delcorno, 1975, p. 211.

3 Todeschini, 1976, 1994, 2003, 2004.

4 Schwartz, 2000, pp. 201–29, emphasizes the extent to which the *avello* of Aldobrandino Cavalcanti (d. 1270) in the transept of Santa Maria Novella in Florence established the prototype for the tombs on its east exterior walls (the Chiostro dei Morti), as well as at San Domenico in Prato. This would be consistent with Humbert of Romans's emphasis a few decades earlier on uniformity and consistency within the order, as noted above.

5 See in general Génestal, 1901.

6 For an example of monastic finance, see Bouchard, 1991.

7 See Paxton, 1993.

8 On the tradition and background of monastic burials, see Wollasch, 1990, pp. 47–54.

9 Ibid., pp. 47–9.

10 Piron, 2009, pp. 321–55, demonstrates how completely this practice was abandoned by the late thirteenth century.

11 M. D. Lambert, 1961, pp. 101–2.

12 Chiffoleau, 1987, pp. 135–49.

13 Bériou and Chiffoleau, 2009, p. 19.

14 Röhrkasten, 2009, p. 212.

15 Piron, 2009, p. 327.

16 Bonato, 2002.

17 Erickson, 1975, p. 130, although in this instance it was to guarantee the safety of the friars.

18 Erickson, 1976, p. 112.

19 M. D. Lambert, 1961, pp. 89–90, is useful on these questions.

20 Röhrkasten, 2009, p. 215.

21 Bertrand, 2009, p. 109.

22 Ibid., pp. 108–9.

23 Vauchez, 2003, p. 562.

24 See the introduction to the documents by Rigon, 2002, pp. v–xxxvi, for a survey of the materials, as well as the illuminating comments on this publication by Vauchez, 2003, and Paolini, 2003.

25 Nelli, 2001, p. 123.

26 William of Saint-Amour, 2008, p. 49. Italics not in original.

27 Le Roy Ladurie, 1978, pp. 25–52.

28 Ibid., pp. 26–8.

29 Ibid., p. 27.

30 Bacci, 2003, p. 53.

31 Stouff, 1998, p. 200.

32 See Chiodi, 1997, pp. 516–56.

33 Chiffoleau, 1980, pp. 126–35.

34 Bruzelius, 2007, p. 211, on the right to choose the site of burial.

35 Bertrand, 2009, pp. 106–7.

36 Timbal, 1977, p. 24.

37 Nicolini, 1985, p. 32. This article is fundamental for the role of Franciscans as witnesses to and executors of wills.

38 Luigi Pellegrini, 2000, pp. 66–7.

39 Manselli, 1974, p. 205; Burr, 1989, p. 100.

40 Burr, 1989, pp. 99–101.

41 Bertram, 1990, pp. 151–233.

42 Gaulin, 2000, p. 286.

43 Ronzani, 1985, p. 34.

44 E. Hubert, 1995a, p. 210.

45 Ibid., p. 211.

46 Stouff, 1998, pp. 209–10.

47 Bériou and le Masne de Chermont, 2001, sermon XLV, pp. 682–3.

48 Stouff, 1998, p. 218.

49 Brentano, 1994, pp. 277–8.

50 Ibid., p. 276.

51 Coulet, 1972, p. 255–6.

52 Burr, 1989, pp. 13–14 and p. 34, n. 53.

53 This donation is discussed in detail ibid. For the document, see Giordani, 1927, pp. 256–62.

54 Bruzelius, 2004, pp. 133–54. Important for Santa Chiara are the many publications of Mario Gaglione between 1996 and 2010.

55 See Bruzelius, 2006a, pp. 234–5, on the importance of this tower and a possible dynamic relationship between the construction of Santa Chiara and the reconfiguration of the nave of San Lorenzo after 1324.

56 Borsook, 1961–2, pp. 90–8 and 103–5.

57 Ibid., p. 98, n. 45.

58 Piron, 2009, pp. 335 and 345–7. Though, as he notes, there were also many critics, among them Ubertino da Casale and Fra Bartholomeo of Pisa.

59 Borsook, 1961–2, p. 99, n. 49, and p. 105.

60 Paatz, 1952, I, pp. 499–500.

61 As noted, the commune of Florence subsidized the construction of Santa Croce with 1,200 florins a year. Piron, 2009, p. 330.

62 Monti, 1994, p. 60.

63 Ibid., p. 61. For the long history of the division of legacies, see Trexler, 1972, pp. 397–450.

64 Iannella, 1997, pp. 111–12. "Sono molti che quando vogliono fare dire messe, si fanno innanzi la ragione: cotante messe vo'far dire cotanti danari; montano a denari quattor l'una o a sei, e fanno raggione come fossero al mercato. Maladetto chiunque hae questa intenzione, e quigli, che gli dà questi danari, et quegli, che gli toglie. . . . Ma se tu vogli far dire messe, o altri beni, e vuoli dare del tuo avere, puoi tenere questo modo, d'avere questa intenzione, che idanari, che tu dai, non gli dare per modo di compera, no, ma daglile solo per amore di Dio, come a povero in limosina, in limosina dico, e non in altro modo."

65 Michaud, 1992, p. 12.

66 Ibid., pp. 7–18.

67 Brentano, 1994, p. 293.

68 Bacci, 2003, p. 52.

69 Chiffoleau, 1982, pp. 456–7; Stouff, 1998, p. 212.

70 Giebben, 1981, p. 178.

71 On this general topic as an anthropological phenomenon, see Van Gennep, 1960, pp. 146–65.

72 A. Bernard, 1933, p. 85.

73 Infractions to this preference are known to have existed since the early Christian period, however: see ibid., pp. 2–5. As this author points out, burial in churches in some places had become so common that the word for cemetery often designated the church (pp. 4, 13, and 30), and Theodulph of Orléans complained that churches had been transformed into cemeteries. Honorius of Autun considered the church as the normal place of burial (ibid., p. 23), but in Arles

the ancient cemetery of the Aliscamps continued to be the preferred place of burial through the Middle Ages.

74 Meneghini and Santangeli Valenzani, 1995, pp. 286–7.

75 Ibid.

76 Dyggve, 1952, p. 149.

77 Meneghini and Santangeli Valenzani, 1995, pp. 284–5 and 289.

78 A. Bernard, 1933, p. 35.

79 Dyggve, 1952, pp. 147–58.

80 For Santa Maria Novella as a cemetery, see Schwartz, 2009.

81 Ibid., pp.62–6; Schwartz emphasizes the extent to which the tombs are integral to the construction of the east nave wall of Santa Maria Novella.

82 Luigi Pellegrini, 1981, p. 146.

83 A. Bernard, 1933, p. 75, n. 4.

84 Chaucer, 1977, pp. 310–13.

85 Hinnebusch, 1966, p. 63.

86 Stouff, 1999, p. 148.

87 Catalo, Cazès, et al., 2010, p. 132.

88 The date of the burials was not discussed in the laconic reports of the excavations.

89 Stouff, 1998, p. 215.

90 Gaulin, 2000, p. 288.

91 Ripoll, *Bullarium Ordinis FF. praedicatorum*, I, pp. 24–5.

92 Gaulin, 2000, p. 293.

93 Breveglieri, 1993b, p. 191.

94 Samaritani, 1982, p. 107.

95 Baird, Baglivi, and Kane, 1986, pp. 294–5.

96 Ibid.

97 Stouff, 1998, p. 213.

98 One stimulus may have been the siege of the city during the invasions of the fifth century. See Meneghini and Santangeli Valenzani, 1992, pp. 90–1. Also Meneghini and Santangeli Valenzani, 1995, p. 288.

99 P. Brown, 1981, p. 4, describes how the cult of relics broke down the repulsion towards the dead of pre-Christian times, including "the touching and kissing of the bones of the dead, and, frequently, the placing of these in areas from which the dead had once been excluded."

100 Bride, 1941, col. 1889.

101 Sbaraleae, 1768, IV, p. 38. See also De Blasiis, 1892, pp. 82–3.

102 Ronzani, 1980, p. 61.

103 Ronzani, 1977a, pp. 668–70.

104 Erickson, 1976, p. 129.

105 A. Bernard, 1933, pp. 137–50.

106 Ibid., p. 153.

107 Ibid., p. 182.

108 Ibid., p. 183.

109 Trexler, 1971, pp. 29–74, and 1972, pp. 397–450.

110 Burr, 1989, p. 104, n. 30.

111 Piron, 2009, p. 329.

112 Burr, 1989, p. 97.

113 On the history of *intra muros* burial, see Dyggve, 1953.

114 E. Hubert, 1995a, pp. 214 and 226–7.

115 Ibid., p. 213.

116 For this important topic, see above all the work of Garms, Juffinger, and Ward-Perkins, 1981, and Garms and Romanini, 1990.

117 Breveglieri, 1993a, pp. 14–15.

118 Gaulin, 2000, p. 294.

119 Ibid., n. 52.

120 Stouff, 1998, p. 212.

121 Pines, 1985, p. 2.

122 Meersseman, 1946, p. 171. In 1251, Humbert of Romans added language on decoration, confirmed in the General Chapters of 1261, 1262, 1263.

123 Piron, 2009, p. 329.

124 E. Hubert, 1995a, pp. 213–14 and 226.

125 Schwartz, 2009, pp. 56–62.

126 Pines, 1985, p. 16.

127 Ibid., p. 20.

128 Translated by Fiona Somerset and William Revere. My thanks to the authors for permission to include their translation in this volume.

129 For example at Vézélay, Saint-Germain des Près, Pontigny: see Freigang, 2002, p. 527.

130 Ibid., pp. 525–35.

131 Ibid., p. 520.

132 Ibid., p. 532.

133 Freigang notes two ordinances from the cathedral of Paris in 1209 and 1245 that concerned the problem of noise within the cathedral from altars and the movement of priests "de stallo ad stallum" within the church: 2002, p. 531.

134 Gardner 2002, p. 548.

135 Ibid., p. 547.

136 Borsook, 1961–2, p. 92.

137 Ibid., p. 99, n. 49, and p. 105.

138 Although preachers were exempt from some of their obligations in order to focus on learning and preaching, the private Mass remained an important element of personal and institutional piety. As the Franciscans became almost completely clericalized by 1239, they soon followed suit. On the clericalization of Franciscans, see for example Manselli, 1974, and Landini, 1969.

139 Freigang, 2002, pp. 527–8.

140 Borsook, 1961–2, p. 90.

141 Ibid., pp. 92–3.

142 Ibid., pp. 93–4.

143 Piron, 2009, pp. 321–55, especially 344–55.

144 Ibid., p. 335.

145 Ibid., p. 353.

146 Benvenuti-Papi, 1980, pp. 87–117.

147 For example, the royal family of France: see Field, 2012, pp. 213–18.

148 Stouff, 1999, p. 152. Also, Manselli, 1974, p. 189, who described the attraction of the new orders for different social classes in this way: "i Domenicani, ma non bastavano per la loro specifica caratteristica di Ordine colto, per sua natura destinato ad incidere in determinate strati e realtà sociali, a livello, diremmo oggi, di cultura universitaria e di classi dirigenti, mentre si rivelarono meno capaci e meno abili nell'affrontare il rapporto con le popolazioni, le quali avvertirono verso di loro una diffidenza, se non un'ostilità assai netta, decisa e, qualche volta, violenta. Fu invece caratteristica del francescanesimo la sua capacità di penetrazione e diffusione proprio fra i gruppi socialmente ed economicamente più modesti: ciò risulta dalla loro tendenza ad insediarsi in localià cittadine dove più fitta era la popolazione e quindi più modesta la sua condizione economica" ("the educated and cultivated character of the Dominican order naturally led them to have an impact on social strata analogous to what we would today call the university or managing classes; they revealed themselves to be less adept at connecting with more socially modest circles, who were often either diffident or actually hostile, sometimes even violent, in their reaction to these friars. Franciscans, on the other hand, had the capacity to penetrate and mingle within the more socially and economically modest communities, and this resulted in their tendency of settling in poorer and more densely inhabited areas of the city").

149 Rigon, 1985, p. 46; Chiffoleau, 1980, pp. 258–66; Stouff, 1999, pp. 145–58. See also Gaulin, 2000, p. 295, n. 54.

150 Rigon, 1985, p. 46.

151 Gaulin, 2000, p. 297.

152 Stouff, 1999, p. 151; Michaud, 1992, p. 10.

153 Gaulin, 2000, p. 288.

154 Michaud, 1992, p. 11.

155 Gaulin, 2000, pp. 283–99; Breveglieri, 1995, pp. 165–234.

156 Gaulin, 2000, p. 297.

157 Breveglieri, 1995, p. 186.

158 Breveglieri, 1993, p. 184.

159 See the important work of Michele Bacci on this topic.

160 Somerset and Revere as per n. 126.

161 Erickson, 1975, p. 114.

162 Guiraud, 1938, p. 590.

163 Davidsohn, 1929, pp. 180–1, n. 1; see also Benvenuti-Papi, 1977, pp. 606–8.

164 Davidsohn, 1929, p. 217.

165 Erickson, 1975, I, p. 120.

166 Davidsohn, 1960–78, II, pp. 177–9 and 408–9.

167 Davidsohn, 1929, p. 169.

168 Stephens, 1972, p. 29.

169 Lea, 1887–8, II, p. 211.

170 Davidsohn, 1929, p. 173.

171 Baird, Baglivi, and Kane, 1986, p. 298.

172 Ibid.

173 Giebben, 1981, p. 177, on this phenomenon.

174 The classic study is Grundmann, 1970, English ed. 1995. Also Vauchez, 1990, especially pp. 206–20. Giebben, 1981, p. 179, notes that the *pinzochiere* of Florence were buried at Santa Croce.

175 Vauchez 1990, p. 209.

176 Bruzelius, 1992, p. 84.

177 For many years the literature on the Inquisition was dominated by the studies of Lea and D'Alatri; more recently the publication of the investigations on Padua, Vicenza, and Florence have vastly expanded our knowledge of the practices of inquisitors. See in particular the work of Rigon, Paolini and Bonato.

178 Da Campagnola, 1971, pp. 509–32.

179 Lansing, 1998, pp. 57–9.

180 Ibid., pp. 137–9.

181 The priest Bernardo da Prato, jailed because he could not pay a fine of fifteen florins, was drowned in the prison of Santa Croce, in the flood of November 1333. Biscaro, 1933, p. 192.

182 Vauchez, 1990, p. 166. Benedetti, 2004, p. 373, notes that Fra Lanfranco of Pavia paid for his quarters out of income from the inquisitorial office.

183 A 1295 will listed in the *Liber contractuum* (Bonato, 2002, p. 33) makes a substantial donation specifically to the inquisitorial office in the Franciscan house. Vauchez, 2003, p. 564, suggests that this type of donation sometimes reflected extortion by friars from laity susceptible to accusations of heresy, who risked possible confiscation of property.

184 Davidsohn, 1960–78, II, pp. 794–6. On the merging of accusations of heresy with political affiliation, see also Biscaro, 1933, pp. 165–6 and 198–9.

185 Biscano, 1933, pp. 165–6 and 198–9.

186 Biscaro, 1921, p. 449.

187 Stephens, 1972, p. 54; D'Alatri, 1953, p. 97.

188 Paolini, 1999, p. 464.

189 Paolini, 1998, pp. 192–3.

190 Ibid., p. 193.

191 Ibid.
192 Ibid., p. 197.
193 Lea, 1887–8, I, p. 472.
194 Ibid., p. 510.
195 Paolini, 1999, pp. 471–2.
196 Lea, 1887–8, pp. 504–5 and 513–14.
197 Ibid., p. 523.
198 Biscaro, 1933, pp. 162, 178, and 192.
199 Rigon, 2002, pp. xv–xvi.
200 Davidsohn, 1929, p. 165.
201 Amabile, 1987, p. 66.
202 Also Biscaro, 1933, p. 186. The friars at Siena were apparently at risk of expulsion from the city.
203 Rigon, 2002, p. xvi.
204 Paolini, 1999, pp. 450–65 and 471.
205 Amabile, 1987, p. 63.
206 Davidsohn, 1929, p. 169.
207 Lea, 1887–8, I, p. 473.
208 Ibid., p. 474.
209 Ibid., p. 510.
210 Davidsohn, 1929, p. 169. See also Murray, 1986, p. 177.
211 Lea, 1887–8, I, pp. 483–4.
212 A. Thompson, 2005, p. 122.
213 Lea, 1887–8, II, pp. 235–6; Guiraud, 1938, p. 573.
214 Guiraud, 1938, p. 578.
215 Lea, 1887–8, I, p. 506. In vol. II, p. 246, Lea states that an equal sum was used for the church of San Pietro Martire in Naples.
216 Rigon, 2002, p. xxxv, n. 168.
217 Benedetti, 2004, p. 373. Later, Inquisition funds are used to contribute towards the expenses of the *arca* for Saint Peter Martyr: ibid., p. 394.
218 Lea, 1887–8, II, p. 234.
219 See Improta, 2011, pp. 106–19.
220 Lea, 1887–8, II, p. 216.
221 Paolini, 1998, p. 203.
222 Biscottini and Ambrosiani, 1998, p. 140.
223 Davidsohn, 1929, p. 163.
224 Paolini, 1998, p. 200.
225 See Biscaro, 1933, pp. 182–3. One of these is the infamous Fra Giovinale degli Agli mentioned by Bartolomeo da Pisa (see Chapter One).
226 Vauchez, 2003, p. 566: "une politique somptuaire en matière de construction . . . une 'maladie de la pierre'."
227 Lansing, 1998, p. 155.
228 Lea, 1887–8, II, pp. 237–8.
229 Lansing, 1998, p. 153.
230 Da Campagnola, 1971, p. 512.
231 Becker, 1959, pp. 60–75.
232 Bruzelius, 2004, p. 56.
233 Biscaro, 1933, pp. 165–7.

CONCLUSION

1 Giles and Rishanger, 1852–4, I, p. 475.
2 Ubertino da Casale, in his last *Declaratio* of 1311, put it this way (citing the authority of Brother Leo): "St. Francis wished that [preaching, confession, and prayer] should take place in parish churches established for the purpose, and that the little oratories of the brothers should be for the brothers themselves to pray in quietly and celebrate mass, not for the racket of a large congregation; and that the brothers should so hold themselves to Godward that they were drawn to God by Christ's mighty works, not by the distracting craftsmanship of their buildings." Brooke, 1970, p. 55.
3 As discussed in earlier chapters, in 1227 Gregory IX authorized the mendicants to permit lay burial at their convents, but it is difficult to find indicators of consistency in this practice, and indeed the evidence for early burials is largely anecdotal and episodic.
4 Chiffoleau, 1995, p. 85.
5 Within the radical faction of the Franciscan order, those who maintained a rigorous interpretation of evangelical poverty thus had some areas in common with the guiding principles ofthe Cathars and Waldesians. See Volpe, 1961, pp. 155–62. The nonpayment of tithes was often associated with and persecuted as heresy.
6 Olympios, 2012, p. 35.
7 De Angelis d'Ossat, 1982a, pp. 150–61.
8 Callaey, 1921, p. 372.
9 Erickson, 1976, p. 126.
10 Delorme, 1939, vol. 32, pp. 222–3.
11 Translated by Fiona Somerset and Will Revere.
12 Hinnebush, 1966, p. 63.
13 The bibliography on antifraternal literature is vast, but see, for example, Angelo Clareno's words about buildings in the Fifth Tribulation (as well as elsewhere in the text): Clareno, 2005, p. 150; now also Geltner, 2012.
14 Dawson, 1978, pp. 223–38.
15 This was the result of the conflict with the secular masters.
16 M. D. Lambert, 1961, p. 27, with regard to Francis's intentions for his Testament. "According to the *Intentio*, Francis intended to command his followers to build their churches and houses of mud and wattle. He altered his draft version into a general injunction to poverty in deference to the plea of the ministers that in many provinces, wood was more expensive than stone."
17 Burr, 1989, p. 25.

18 Gwynn, 1937, p. 59.

19 See Bourdua, 2004, pp. 67–8.

20 See Angelo Clareno's words about buildings in the Fifth Tribulation (as well as elsewhere in the text): Clareno, 2005, p. 150.

21 Ibid., p. 38, for example.

22 Again, Angelo Clareno is compelling here on issues of property, legacies, and burials. See the Third Tribulation ibid., pp. 87–8.

23 Ibid., pp. 38–9.

24 Is it a coincidence that Giovanni da Siena was a notorious inquisitor after 1301?

25 Piron, 2009, p. 331, n. 44.

26 Vauchez, 2003, p. 566.

27 Piron, 2009, p. 333, n. 52.

28 Ibid., p. 342, n. 47. He notes that Ubertino had complained about this in "Sanctitas Vestra."

29 Ibid., p. 333.

30 Ibid., p. 335.

31 Biscaro, 1933, pp. 166–207.

32 Ibid., pp. 182–8.

33 Romanini, 1964, p. 80.

34 Canniffe, 2008, p. 39.

35 Thus leaving the old cult centers in the urban centers as cow pastures and fields of ruins, as in Rome. See Elsner, 1998, p. 141.

BIBLIOGRAPHY

Abate, Giuseppe. "Memoriali, statuti e atti di capitoli generali dei frati minori dei secoli XIII e XIV." *Miscellanea francescana* 33 (1933): 15–45, 320–36; 34 (1934): 248–53; 35 (1935): 10–106, 232–9.

Aceto, Francesco. "Spazio ecclesiale e pale di 'primitivi' in San Lorenzo Maggiore a Napoli: Dal 'San Ludovico' di Simone Martini al 'San Girolamo' di Colantonio, I." *Prospettiva: Rivista di storia dell'arte antica e moderna* 137 (2010): 2–50.

Adhémar, Jean, and Gertrude Dordor. *Les Tombeaux de la collection Gagnières.* Paris, 1974.

Ahlquist, Gregory W., and William R. Cook. "The Representation of the Posthumous Miracles of St Francis of Assisi in Thirteenth-Century Italian Painting." In *The Art of the Franciscan Order in Italy*, ed. W. R. Cook. Leiden, 2005, 211–56.

Alberti, Giovanni, Chiara Leardini, and Gina Rossi. *L'azienda convento nei registri contabili di Santa Maria della Scala a Verona 1345–1355.* Padova, 2008.

Alberzoni, Maria Pia et al. *Francesco d'Assisi e il primo secolo di storia francescana.* Turin, 1997.

Alce, Venturino. "Il convento di San Domenico in Bologna nel secolo XIII." *Culta Bononia: Rivista di studi bolognesi* 4, no. 2 (1972a): 127–74.

——. "Documenti sul convento di San Domenico in Bologna del 1221 al 1251." *Archivum Fratrum Praedicatorum* 42 (1972b): 5–45.

——. *I Domenicani nell'Emilia Romagna dal 1218 ad oggi.* Bologna, 1983.

Amabile, Luigi. *Il santo officio della inquisizione in Napoli.* Naples, 1987.

Ames, Christine Caldwell. *Righteous Persecution: Inquisition, Dominicans and Christianity in the Middle Ages.* Philadelphia, 2009.

Andenmatten, Bernard. "Les Frères prêcheurs et les revenus des anniversaires. Le témoignage de l'obituaire du couvent dominicain de Lausanne." In *Économie et religion: L'Expérience des ordres mendiants (XIIIè–XVè siècle)*, ed. N. Bériou and J. Chiffoleau. Lyon, 2009, 153–69.

Andreini, Alessandro, Cristina Cerrato, and Giuliano Feola. "Dalla chiesa alto-medievale di S. Maria al Prato alla fondazione del complesso conventuale di S. Francesco: Origine e trasformazioni urbane del prato di Piunte." In *San Francesco: La chiesa e il convent in Pistoia*, ed. L. Gai et al. Pisa, 1993a, 27–46.

——. "I cicli costruttivi della chiesa e del convent di S. Francesco dal XIII al XV secolo." In *San Francesco: La chiesa e il convent in Pistoia*, ed. L. Gai et al. Pisa, 1993b, 47–80.

Andrews, Frances. *The Other Friars: The Carmelite, Augustinian, Sack and Pied Friars in the Middle Ages.* Woodbridge, 2006.

——, ed. *Ritual and Space in the Middle Ages: Proceedings of the 2009 Harlaxton Symposium.* Donington, Lincolnshire, 2011.

Angiola, Eloise M. "Nicola Pisano, Federigo Visconti, and the Classical Style in Pisa." *Art Bulletin* 59, no. 1 (1977): 1–27.

Apolloni, Michela. "Testamenti a favore dei frati minori di San Lorenzo a Vicenza tra 1280 e 1348." *Il Santo: Rivista antoniana di storia dottrina arte* 30 (1990): 181–237.

Archetti, Paola, and Andrea Francesco Fiore. *San Francesco del Prato in Parma.* Parma, 1998.

Abate, Giuseppe. "Memoriali, statuti e atti di capitoli generali dei frati minori dei secoli XIII e XIV." *Miscellanea francescana* 33 (1933): 15–45, 320–36; 34 (1934): 248–53; 35 (1935): 10–106, 232–9.

Aceto, Francesco. "Spazio ecclesiale e pale di 'primitivi' in San Lorenzo Maggiore a Napoli: Dal 'San Ludovico' di Simone Martini al 'San Girolamo' di Colantonio, I." *Prospettiva: Rivista di storia dell'arte antica e moderna* 137 (2010): 2–50.

Adhémar, Jean, and Gertrude Dordor. *Les Tombeaux de la collection Gagnières.* Paris, 1974.

Ahlquist, Gregory W., and William R. Cook. "The Representation of the Posthumous Miracles of St Francis of Assisi in Thirteenth-century Italian

Painting." In *The Art of the Franciscan Order in Italy*, ed. W. R. Cook. Leiden, 2005, 211–56.

Alberti, Giovanni, Chiara Leardini, and Gina Rossi. *L'azienda convento nei registri contabili di Santa Maria della Scala a Verona 1345–1355*. Padova, 2008.

Alberzoni, Maria Pia et al. *Francesco d'Assisi e il primo secolo di storia francescana*. Turin, 1997.

Alce, Venturino. "Il convento di San Domenico in Bologna nel secolo XIII." *Culta Bononia: Rivista di studi bolognesi* 4, no. 2 (1972a): 127–74.

—. "Documenti sul convento di San Domenico in Bologna del 1221 al 1251." *Archivum Fratrum Praedicatorum* 42 (1972b): 5–45.

—. *I Domenicani nell'Emilia Romagna dal 1218 ad oggi*. Bologna, 1983.

Amabile, Luigi. *Il santo officio della inquisizione in Napoli*. Naples, 1987.

Ames, Christine Caldwell. *Righteous Persecution: Inquisition, Dominicans and Christianity in the Middle Ages*. Philadelphia, 2009.

Andenmatten, Bernard. "Les Frères prêcheurs et les revenus des anniversaries. Le témoignage de l'obituaire du couvent dominicain de Lausanne." In *Économie et religion: L'Expérience des ordres mendiants (XIIIè–XVè siècle)*, ed. N. Bériou and J. Chiffoleau. Lyon, 2009, 153–69.

Andreini, Alessandro, Cristina Cerrato, and Giuliano Feola. "Dalla chiesa alto-medievale di S. Maria al Prato alla fondazione del complesso conventuale di S. Francesco: Origine e trasformazioni urbane del prato di Piunte." In *San Francesco: La chiesa e il convent in Pistoia*, ed. L. Gai et al. Pisa, 1993a, 27–46.

—. "I cicli costruttivi della chiesa e del convent di S. Francesco dal XIII al XV secolo." In *San Francesco: La chiesa e il convent in Pistoia*, ed. L. Gai et al. Pisa, 1993b, 47–87.

Andrews, Frances. *The Other Friars: The Carmelite, Augustinian, Sack and Pied Friars in the Middle Ages*. Woodbridge, 2006.

—, ed. *Ritual and Space in the Middle Ages: Proceedings of the 2009 Harlaxton Symposium*. Donington, Lincolnshire, 2011.

Angiola, Eloise M. "Nicola Pisano, Federigo Visconti, and the Classical Style in Pisa." *Art Bulletin* 59, no. 1 (1977): 1–27.

Apolloni, Michela. "Testamenti a favore dei frati minori di San Lorenzo a Vicenza tra 1280 e 1348." *Il Santo: Rivista antoniana di storia dottrina arte* 30 (1990): 181–237.

Archetti, Paola, and Andrea Francesco Fiore. *San Francesco del Prato in Parma*. Parma, 1998.

Arias, Paolo E., E. Cristiani, and E. Gabba, eds. *Il camposanto monumentale di Pisa: Le antichità*. Pisa, 1977.

Ariès, Philippe. *The Hour of Our Death*, trans. H. Weaver. New York, 1981.

Armstrong, Regis J., J. A. Wayne Hellmann, and William J. Short. *Francis of Assisi: Early Documents*, vol. 1, New York, 1999.

Arthur, Kathleen Giles. "The Strozzi Chapel: Notes on the Building History of Santa Maria Novella." *Art Bulletin* 65, no. 3 (1983): 367–86.

Artifoni, Enrico. "Gli uomini dell'assemblea: L'oratoria civile, i concionatori e i predicatori nella società comunale." In *La predicazione dei frati dalla metà del '200 alla fine del '300: Atti del XXII Convegno internazionale, Assisi, 13–15 ottobre 1994*, ed. E. Menestò. Spoleto, 1995, 141–88.

Ascani, Valerio. "Giovanni di Simone." In *Enciclopedia dell'arte medievale*, vol. 6. Rome, 1995, 757–8.

—. "Pisa: Architettura." In *Enciclopedia dell'arte medievale*, vol. 9. Rome, 1998a, 417–29.

—. "Prato." In *Enciclopedia dell'arte medievale*, vol. 9. Rome, 1998b, 728–33.

Ascher, Yoni. "The Church and the Piazza: Reflections on the South Side of the Church of San Domenico Maggiore in Naples." *Architectural History* 45 (2002): 92–112.

Aubert, M. "Les Tombeaux de l'Abbaye de Longpont." *Congrès archéologique de France* 78, no. 2 (1911), 305–16.

—. *L'Architecture cistercienne en France, avec la collaboration de la Marquise de Maillé*, ed. G. Aliette de Rohan-Chabot Maillè. Paris, 1947.

Bacchi, Giuseppe, and G. Gianni. *La Certosa di Firenze*. Florence, 1956.

Bacci, Michele. "Le antiche lapidi della chiesa del Carmine." *L'Aldilà: Rivista di Storia della Tanatologia* 3, no. 1 (1997): 19–53.

—. *"Pro remedio animae": Immagini sacre e pratiche devozionali in Italia centrale (secoli XIII e XIV)*. Pisa, 2000.

—. *Investimenti per l'aldilà: Arte e raccomandazione dell'anima nel medioevo*. Rome, 2003.

—. *Lo spazio dell'anima: Vita di una chiesa medievale*. Rome, 2005.

—. "Les Frères, les legs et l'art: Les Investissements pour l'augmentation du culte divin." In *Économie et religion: L'Expérience des ordres mendiants (XIIIè–XVè siècle)*, ed. N. Bériou and J. Chiffoleau. Lyon, 2009, 563–90.

—. "Side Altars and 'pro anima' Chapels in the Medieval Mediterranean: Evidence from Cyprus." In *The Altar and its Environment*, ed. J. E. A. Kroesen and V. M. Schmidt. Turnhout, 2010, 11–30.

Badstübner, Ernst. "Kirchen und Klöster der Bettelorden im sozialen und gestalterischen Gefüge der mittelalterlichen Stadt." *Wissenschaftliche*

Zeitschrift der Friedrich-Schiller-Universität Jena 30 (1981): 323–35.

Baird, Joseph L., Giuseppe Baglivi, and John Robert Kane. *The Chronicle of Salimbene de Adam.* Binghamton, N.Y., 1986.

Baldini, Umberto, Lando Bartoli, and Massimo Listri. *Santa Maria Novella: La basilica, il convento, i chiostri monumentali.* Florence, 1981.

Baldovin, John. *The Urban Character of Christian Worship: The Origins, Development, and Meaning of Stational Liturgy.* Rome, 1987.

Banker, James. *Death in the Community: Memorialization and Confraternities in an Italian Commune in the Late Middle Ages.* Athens, Ga., 1988.

Banti, Ottavio, ed. *Cronaca di Pisa di Ranieri Sardo.* Rome, 1963.

—. *La chiesa di San Francesco: Come luogo di aggregazione civile culturale e religiosa della società pisana nel medioevo e nell'età moderna.* Pisa, 1984 (unpaginated pamphlet).

—, ed. *Amalfi, Genova, Pisa, Venezia: La cattedrale e la città nel medioevo; Aspetti religiosi istituzionale e urbanistici; Atti della Giornata di Studio, Pisa, 1 giugno 1991.* Vol. 42, *Biblioteca del Bollettino storico pisano.* Pisa, 1993.

—, ed. *Le iscrizioni delle tombe terragne del Campo Santo di Pisa, secoli XIV–XVIII.* Pontedera, 1998.

Banti, Ottavio, and M. Soriani Innocenti, eds. *Il francescanesimo a Pisa (secc. XIII–XIV) e la missione del Beato Agnello in Inghilterra a Canterbury e Cambridge (1224–1236): Atti del convegno di studi, Pisa, Chiesa di San Francesco 10–11 marzo 2001.* Pisa, 2003.

Baracchini, Clara, and E. Castelnuovo, eds. *Il Camposanto di Pisa.* Vol. 27: *Biblioteca di storia dell'arte.* Turin, 1996.

Barclay Lloyd, Joan. "Medieval Dominican Architecture at Santa Sabina in Rome, c. 1219–c. 1320." *Papers of the British School at Rome* 72 (2004): 231–92.

Baron, H. "Franciscan Poverty and Civic Wealth as Factors in the Rise of Humanistic Thought." *Speculum* 13 (1938): 1–37.

Barone, Giulia. "L'ordine dei predicatori e le città: Teologia e politica nel pensiero e nell'azione dei predicatori." *Mélanges de l'École française de Rome, Moyen Âge/Temps Modernes* 89 (1977): 609–18.

—. "I Francescani a Roma." *Storia della città* 9 (1978): 33–5.

Barraud, M. L'abbé. "Notice sur les chaires a prêcher." *Bulletin monumental,* ser. 4, 6 (1870): 5–43, 113–47.

Barret, Sébastian. "À propos des documents d'archives du couvent Saint-Jacques de Paris (XIIIè–XIVè siècle)." In *Économie et religion: L'expérience des ordres mendiants (XIIIè–XVè siècle),* ed. N. Bériou and J. Chiffoleau. Lyon, 2009, 129–52.

Bartalani, Roberto. " '*Et in carne mea videbo Deum meum*': Maso di Banco, la cappella dei Confessori e la committenza dei Bardi; A proposito di un libro recente." *Prospettiva* 98–9 (2000): 58–103.

—. " 'Monumenta laicorum': I sepolori della cappella Bardi in Santa Croce a Firenze." In *Scultura gotica in Toscana: Maestri, monumenti, cantieri del Due e Trecento,* ed. R. Bartalani and C. Balsamo. Milan, 2005, 178–203.

Bartalani, Roberto, and C. Balsamo, eds. *Scultura gotica in Toscana: Maestri, monumenti, cantieri del Due e Trecento.* Milan, 2005.

Bartlett, R. *The Making of Europe: Conquest, Colonization and Cultural Change, 950–1350.* Princeton, N.J., 1993.

—. "Medieval and Modern Concepts of Race and Identity." *Journal of Medieval and Early Modern Studies* 31, no. 1 (2001): 39–56.

Bartoli Langeli, Attilio, ed. '*Nolens intestatus decedere*': *Il testamento come fonte della storia religiosa e sociale.* Perugia, 1985a.

—. "Nota introduttiva." In '*Nolens intestatus decedere*': *Il testamento come fonte della storia religiosa e sociale.* Perugia, 1985b, ix–xvii.

Bartoli Langeli, Attilio, and Gian Paolo Bustreo. "I documenti di contenuto economico negli achivi conventuali dei Minori e dei Predicatori nel XIII e XIV secolo." In *L'economia dei conventi dei frati minori e predicatori fino alla metà del Trecento: Atti del XXXI convegno internazionale, Assisi, 9–11 ottobre 2003,* ed. E. Menestò. Spoleto, 2004, 119–50.

Bartoli Langeli, Attilio, and Nicolangelo D'Acunto. "I documenti degli ordini mendicanti." In *Libro, scrittura, documento della civiltà monastica e conventuale nel basso medioevo (secoli XIII–XV): Atti del convegno di studio, Fermo, 17–19 settembre 1997,* ed. G. Avarucci, R. M. Borraccini Verducci, and G. Borri. Spoleto, 1999, 381–3.

Bartolini Salimbene, Lorenzo. *L'architettura francescana in Abruzzo dal XIII al XVIII secolo.* Chieti, 1993.

Bartolomeo de Pisa, Fr. *De conformitate: vitae beati Francisci ad vitam Domini Iesu.* Analecta Franciscana, vol. 4: Liber 1; vol. 5: Liber 2, 3. Florence, 1906, 1912.

Bataillon, Louis-Jacques. "La predicazione dei religiosi mencicanti del secolo XIII nell'Italia centrale." *Mélanges de l'École française de Rome, Moyen Âge/Temps Modernes* 89 (1977): 691–4.

—. *La Prédication au XIIIe siècle en France et en Italie: Études et Documents.* Aldershot, 1994.

Bauch, Kurt. *Das mittelalterliche Grabbild: Figürliche Grabmäler des 11. bis 15. Jahrhunderts in Europa.* Berlin, 1976.

Baud, Anne. "La Place des morts dans l'abbaye de Cluny: État de la question." *Archéologie médiévale* 29 (2000): 99–114.

Bayley, T. D. S. "The Grey Friar Church, Chichester: The Problem of the Nave." *Sussex Archaeological Association* 105 (1967): 70–5.

Beaumont-Maillé, Laure. *Le Grand Couvent des Cordeliers de Paris: Étude historique et archéologique du XIIIè siècle à nos jours.* Vol. 325: *Bibliothèque de l'École des hautes études.* Paris, 1975.

Becker, Marvin. "Florentine Politics and the Diffusion of Heresy in the Trecento: A Socioeconomic Inquiry." *Speculum* 34, no. 1 (1959): 60–75.

—. "Florentine Popular Government (1343–1348)." *Proceedings of the American Philosophical Society* 106, no. 4 (1962): 360–82.

—. "Economic Change and the Emerging Florentine Territorial State." *Studies in the Renaissance* 13 (1966): 7–39.

Bellinati, Claudio, and Lionello Puppi, eds. *Padova: Basiliche e chiese.* Vicenza, 1975.

Bellosi, Luciano. *Buffamalco e il Trionfo della Morte.* Turin, 1974.

—. "I capitelli figurati del transetto di Santa Maria Novella." In *Santa Maria del Fiore e le chiese fiorentine del Duecento e del Trecento nella città delle fabbriche arnolfiane,* ed. G. Rocchi Coopmans de Yoldi. Florence, 2004, 113–32.

Beltramo, Silvia. "The Construction Sites of the Mendicant Orders in Northwestern Italy (13th–15th centuries): 'Civitas,' Masters and Architecture." In *Kirche als Baustelle: Große Sakralbauten des Mittelalters,* ed. K. Schröck, B. Klein, and S. Bürger. Cologne, 2013, 88–103.

Benadusi, Giovanna. "Investing the Riches of the Poor: Servant Women and their Last Wills." *American Historical Review* 109, no. 3 (2004): 805–26.

Benedetti, Marina. "Le finanze dell'inquisitore." In *L'economia dei conventi dei frati minori e predicatori fino alla metà del Trecento: Atti del XXXI convegno internazionale, Assisi, 9–11 ottobre 2003,* ed. E. Menestò. Spoleto, 2004, 363–401.

Benevole, Leonardo. "La chiesa e l'oratorio della SS. Annunziata a Ravello." *Quaderni dell'Istituto di Storia dell'Architettura (saggi in onore di G. De Angelis d'Ossat)* 12 (1955): 9–16.

Bennett, R. F. *The Early Dominicans: Studies in Thirteenth Century Dominican History.* Cambridge, 1937.

Benocci, C. "Niccolò III: I Domenicani e la committenza di Santa Maria sopra Minerva a Roma." In *Roma anno 1300: Atti del Congresso internazionale di storia dell'arte medievale, Roma, 19–24 maggio 1980.* Rome, 1980, 585–90.

Benson, R. L., G. Constable, et al., eds. *Renaissance and Renewal in the Twelfth Century.* Cambridge, Mass., 1982.

Benvenuti-Papi, Anna. "L'Impianto mendicante in Firenze: Un problema aperto." *Mélanges de l'École française de Rome, Moyen Âge/Temps Moderne* 89 (1977): 595–608.

—. "Umiliana dei Cerchi: Nascita di un culto nella Firenze del Dugento." *Studi francescani* 77 (1980): 87–117.

—. *Pastori di popolo: Storie e leggende di vescovi e di città nell'Italia medievale.* Florence, 1988.

—. *"In castro poenitentiae": Santità e società femminile nell'Italia medievale.* Rome, 1990.

Benz, E. *Ecclesia spiritualis: Kirchenidee und Geschichtstheologie der franziskanischen Reformation.* Stuttgart, 1964.

Berg, Dieter. *Armut und Wissenschaft: Beiträge zur Geschichte des Studienwesens der Bettelorden im 13. Jahrhundert.* Düsseldorf, 1977.

—, ed. *Bettelorden und Stadt: Bettelorden und städtisches Leben im Mittelalter und in der Neuzeit.* Werl, 1992.

Berger-Dittscheid, C. "S. Lorenzo Maggiore in Neapel: Das gotische 'Ideal-Projekt' Karls I. und seine 'franziskanischen' Modifikationen." In *Festschrift für Hartmut Biermann.* Weinheim, 1990, 41–64.

Berghoef, J. F. "Les Origines de la place ducale de Vigevano." *Palladio: Rivista di storia dell'architettura* 4 (1964): 165–78.

Bériou, Nicole. *L'Avènement des maîtres de la Parole: La Prédication à Paris au XIIIè siècle.* Vol. 2: *Collection des Études Augustiniennes: Moyen Âge et Temps Modernes.* Paris, 1998.

—. "Le Vocabulaire de la vie économique dans les textes pastoraux des frères mendiants au XIIIè siècle." In *L'economia dei conventi dei frati minori e predicatori fino alla metà del Trecento: Atti del XXXI convegno internazionale, Assisi, 9–11 ottobre 2003,* ed. E. Menestò. Spoleto, 2004, 153–86.

Bériou, Nicole, and Jacques Chiffoleau, eds. *Économie et religion: L'Expérience des ordres mendiants (XIIIè–XVe siècle).* Lyon, 2009.

Bériou, Nicole, and David L. D'Avray, eds. *Modern Questions About Medieval Sermons: Essays on Marriage, Death, History and Sanctity.* Vol. 11: *Biblioteca di medioevo Latino.* Spoleto, 1994.

Bériou, Nicole, and Isabelle le Masne de Chermont. *Les Sermons et la visite pastorale de Federico Visconti, Archevêque de Pise (1253–1277).* Sources et documents d'histoire du Moyen Âge, vol. 3. Rome, 2001.

Berlioz, Jacques, and Polo de Beaulieu, Marie-Anne Polo de. "Les Prologues des recueils d'*exempla* (XIIIe–XIVè siècles). Une grille d'analyse." In *La Predicazione dei frati dalla metà del '200 alla fine del '300: Atti del XXII convegno internazionale, Assisi, 13–15 ottobre 1994*, ed. E. Menestò. Spoleto, 1995, 268–300.

Bernacchi, Gastone Alberto. "Il Pensiero tanatologico nel Pellegrino medioevale." *L'Adilà: Rivista di Storia della Tanatologia* 3, no. 1 (1997): 55–60.

Bernard, Antoine. *La Sépulture en droit canonique du décret de Gratien au Concile de Trente*. Paris, 1933.

Bernard, Eugène. *Les Dominicains dans l'Université de Paris ou le grand Couvent des Jacobins de la Rue Saint-Jacques*. Paris, 1883.

Bernardus Guidonis. *De fundatione et prioribus conventuum provinciarum Tolosanae et Provinciae Ordinis Praedicatorum*, ed. P. A. Amargier. Vol. 24: *Monumenta Ordinis Fratrum Praedicatorum Historica*. Rome, 1961.

Bertram, Martin. "Mittelalterliche Testamente: Zur Entdeckung einer Quellengattung in Italien." *Quellen und Forschungen aus italienschen Archiven und Bibliotheken* 68 (1988): 509–45.

—. "Hundert Bologneser Testamente aus einer Novemberwoche des Jahres 1265." *Quellen und Forschungen aus italienschen Archiven und Biblioteken* 69 (1989): 80–110.

—. "Bologneser Testamente. Erster Teil: Die Urkundliche Überlieferung." *Quellen und Forschungen aus italienschen Archiven und Biblioteken* 70 (1990): 151–233.

—. "Bologneser Testamente. Zweiter Teil: Sondierungen in den Libri Memoriali." *Quellen und Forschungen aus italienschen Archiven und Biblioteken* 71 (1991): 195–240.

—. "Testamenti medievali Bolognesi: Una miniera documentaria tutta da esplorare." *Rassegna degli Archivi di Stato* 52 (1992): 307–23.

—. " 'Renaissance Mentality' in Italian Testaments?" *Journal of Modern History* 67 (1995): 358–69.

Bertrand, Paul. "Économie conventuelle, gestion de l'écrit et spiritualité des ordres mendiants: Autour de l'example liégeois (XIIIè–XVè siècle)." In *Économie et religion: L'Expérience des ordres mendiants (XIIIè–XVè siècle)*, ed. N. Bériou and J. Chiffoleau. Lyon, 2009, 101–28.

Bevere, R. "Suffragi, espiazioni postume, riti e cerimonie funebri dei secoli XII, XIII e XIV nelle provincie napoletane." *Archivio Storico per le province napoletane* 21 (1896): 119–32.

Bianchi, R. *Il San Domenico e i Domenicani di Torino*. Torino, 1932.

Bianchini, N. *La chiesa e il convento di S. Giovanni in Canale a Piacenza*. Piacenza, 2000.

Biddick, Kathleen. "Becoming Collection: The Spatial Afterlife of Medieval Universal Histories." In *Medieval Practices of Space*, ed. B. A. Hannawalt and M. Kobialka. Minneapolis, 2000, 223–41.

Biebrach, K. *Die holzgedeckten Franziskaner- und Dominikanerkirchen in Umbrien und Toskana*. Berlin, 1908.

Bigaroni, M., E. Lunghi, and H.-R. Meier. *La Basilica di S. Chiara in Assisi*. Perugia, 1994.

Bihl, M. "E sermonibus Friderici de Vicecomitibus, archiep. Pisani de San Francisco (1263–1267)." *Archivum Franciscanum Historicum* 1 (1908): 652–5.

—. "Constitutiones generales editae in Capitulis Generalibus Caturci an. 1337 et Lugduni an. 1351 celebratis." *Archivum Franciscanum Historicum* 30 (1937): 69–169.

Binding, Günther, et al. *Baubetrieb im Mittelalter*. Darmstadt, 1993.

Binski, Paul. *Medieval Death: Ritual and Representation*. London, 1996.

Biscaro, Gerolamo. "Inquisitori ed eretici Lombardi (1292–1318)." *Miscellanea di storia italiana* 18 (1921): 445–57.

—. "Inquisitori ed eretici a Firenze (1319–1334)." *Studi Medievali* 6 (1933): 161–207.

Biscottini, P., and Annamaria Ambrosioni. *I chiostri di Sant'Eustorgio in Milano*. Milan, 1998.

Blatchly, J., and K. Wade. "Excavations at Ipswich Blackfriars in 1898 and 1976." *Proceedings of the Suffolk Institute of Architecture* 34 (1977): 25–34.

Blough, Karen. "The Abbatial Effigies at Quedlinburg: A Convent's Identity Reconfigured." *Gesta* 47, no. 2 (2008): 147–69.

Blume, Dieter. *Wandmalerei als Ordenspropaganda: Bildprogramme im Chorbereich franziskanischer Konvente Italiens bis zur Mitte des 14. Jahrhunderts*. Worms, 1983.

—. "Ordenskonkurrenz und Bildpolitik: franziskanishe Programme nach dem theoretischen Armutsstreit." In *Malerei und Stadtkultur in der Dantezei*, ed. Dieter Blume and Hans Belting. Munich, 1989, 149–70.

Boase, T. S. R. "Fontevrault and the Plantagenets." *Journal of the British Archaeological Association*, ser. 3, 34 (1971): 6–9.

—. *Death in the Middle Ages: Mortality, Judgement, and Remembrance*. London, 1972.

Boccaccio, Giovanni. *The Decameron*, trans. M. Musa and P. Bondanella. New York, 1982.

Boccazzi, F. Z. *La Basilica dei Santi Giovanni e Paolo in Venezia*. Venice, 1965.

Bock, Nicolas, Peter Kurmann, Serena Romano, and Jean-Michel Spieser, eds. *Art, cérémonial et liturgie au Moyen Âge: Actes du colloque de 3è Cycle Romand de Lettres Lausanne-Fribourg, 24–25 mars, 14–15 avril, 12–13 mai 2000.* Études lausannoises d'histoire de l'art, vol. 1. Rome, 2002.

Bock, Nicolas, and Serena Romano, eds. *Le chiese di San Lorenzo e San Domenico: Gli ordini mendicanti a Napoli.* Naples, 2005.

Bolgia, Claudia. "Il coro medievale della chiesa di S. Maria in Aracoeli a Roma." In *Arte d'Occidente: Temi e metodi; Studi in onore di Angiola Maria Romanini*, vol. 1. Rome, 1999, 233–42.

—. "An Engraved Architectural Drawing at Santa Maria in Aracoeli, Rome." *Journal of the Society of Architectural Historians* 62, no. 4 (2003): 436–47.

—. "The So-Called Tribunal of Arnolfo di Cambio at S. Maria in Aracoeli, Rome." *Burlington Magazine*, 68 (2005): 753–5.

Bologna, Ferdinando. *I pittori alla corte angioina di Napoli, 1266–1414 e un riesame dell'arte nell'età fridericiana.* Rome, 1969.

Bonaini, Francesco, ed. *Statuti inediti della città di Pisa dal XII al XIV secolo.* Florence, 1854.

Bonato, Elisabetta, ed. *Il "Liber contractuum" dei frati minori di Padova e di Vicenza (1263–1302).* Rome, 2002.

Bonaventure of Bagnoregio. *Opera Omnia*, ed. A. Lauer. 10 vols. Florence, 1882–1902.

—. *The Works of Bonaventure, Cardinal, Seraphic Doctor and Saint*, ed. and trans. J. de Vinck. Paterson, N.J., 1960–70.

—. *St. Bonaventure's Writings Concerning the Franciscan Order*, trans. D. Monti. New York, 1994.

Bonelli, R. "La chiesa di S. Domenico in Orvieto." *Palladio* 7 (1943): 139–51.

—, ed. *Francesco d'Assisi: Chiese e conventi.* Milan, 1982.

—. "Nuovi sviluppi di ricerca sull'edilizia mendicante." In *Gli ordini mendicanti e la città: Aspetti architettonici, sociali e politici*, ed. J. Raspi Serra. Milan, 1990, 15–26.

Boner, G. "Das Predigerkloster in Basel von der Gründung bis zur Klosterreform 1233–1429." *Basler Zeitschrift für Geschichte und Altertumskunde* 33 and 34 (1934–5): 195–303 and 107–295.

Bonniwell, W. R. *A History of the Dominican Liturgy.* New York, 1944.

Bonsanti, G., ed. *La basilica di San Francesco ad Assisi.* Modena, 2002.

Borsook, Eve. "Notizie su due cappelle in Santa Croce a Firenze." *Rivista d'arte* 36 (1961–2): 89–107.

Bossaglia, R. "Per un profilo del gotico piemontese: Le chiese degli ordini mendicanti nei secoli XIII e XIV." *Palladio* n.s. 4 (1954): 27–43.

Bouchard, Constance. *Holy Entrepreneurs: Cistercians, Knights, and Economic Exchange in Twelfth-century Burgundy.* Ithaca, N.Y., 1991.

Bouchot, Henri, ed. *Inventaire des dessins exécutés pour Roger de Gaignières et conservés aux départements des estampes et des manuscrits.* Paris, 1891.

Bougerol, Jacques Guy. *Introduction to the Works of Bonaventure.* Paterson, N.J., 1964.

Bourdua, Louise. "Friars, Patrons, and Workshops at the Basilica del Santo, Padua." In *The Church and the Arts: Papers Read at the 1990 Summer Meeting and the 1991 Winter Meeting of the Eccesiastical History Society*, ed. D. Wood. Studies in Church History, 28 (1992): 131–41.

—. " 'De origine et progressu ordinis fratrum heremitarum': Guariento and the Eremitani in Padua." *Papers of the British School at Rome* 66 (1998): 177–92.

—. "I frati minori al Santo nel Trecento: consulenti, committenti o artisti?" *Il Santo* 42 (2002): 17–28.

—. *The Franciscans and Art Patronage in Late Medieval Italy.* Cambridge, 2004.

Bove, Gennaro. "Gli insediamenti minoritici della Campania nei secoli XIII–XIV." *Miscellanea francescana* 102 (2002): 337–62.

Bowsky, William. "The Medieval Commune and Internal Violence: Police Power and Public Safety in Siena, 1287–1355." *American Historical Review* 73, no. 1 (1967): 1–17.

Boyd, Catherine Evangeline. *Tithes and Parishes in Medieval Italy: The Historical Roots of a Modern Problem.* Ithaca, N.Y., 1952.

Boyer, Jean-Paul. "Les Baux et le modèle royal: Une oraison funèbre de Jean Regina de Naples (1334)." *Provence historique: Revue trimestrielle* 181 (1995): 427–52.

—. "La Noblesse dans les sermons des dominicains de Naples (première moitié du XIVè siècle)." In *La Noblesse dans les territoires angevins à la fin du Moyen Âge: Actes du colloque international organisé par l'Université d'Angers*, ed. N. Coulet and J.-M. Matz. Rome, 2000.

Bozzoni, C. "Architettura degli ordini mendicanti in Umbria: Le tipologie." In *Lo Spazio dell'Umiltà: Atti del Convegno di studi sull'edilizia dell'ordine dei minori, Fara Sabina, 3–6 novembre 1982*, ed. M. B. Mistretta. Fara Sabina, 1984a, 275–326.

—. "L'edilizia degli ordini mendicanti in Europa e nel bacino del Mediterraneo." In *Lo Spazio dell'Umiltà: Atti del Convegno di studi sull'edilizia dell'ordine dei minori, Fara Sabina, 3–6 novembre 1982*, ed. M. B. Mistretta. Fara Sabina, 1984b, 275–326.

—. "Osservazioni sui procedimenti costruttivi e su alcune soluzioni tecniche in edifici mendicanti dell'Umbria." In *Gli ordini mendicanti e la città: Aspetti architettonici, sociali e politici*, ed. J. Raspi Serra. Milan, 1990, 133–50.

—. "Il 'cantiere mendicante': Osservazioni su chiese francescane dell'Umbria." In *Saggi in onore di Renato Bonelli*, vol. 1, ed. C. Bozzoni, G. Carbonara, and G. Villetti. Rome, 1992, 143–52.

Braca, Antonio. *Il duomo di Salerno: Architettura e culture artistiche del medioevo e dell'Età Moderna*. Salerno, 2003.

Branca, Vittore, Paolo di Certaldo, et al. *Mercanti scrittori: Ricordi nella Firenze tra medioevo e Rinascimento*. Milan, 1986.

Brancia di Apricena, Marianna. *Il complesso dell'Aracoeli sul Colle capitolino (IX–XIX secolo)*. Rome, 2000.

Bräuer, Uta Maria, Emanuel S. Klinkenberg, and Jeroen Westerman, eds. *Kunst & Religion: Architektur und Kunst im Mittelalter. Beiträge einer Forschungsgruppe, Clavis kunsthistorische monografien* 20. Utrecht, 2005.

Breckenridge, J. "Christian Funerary Portraits in Mosaic." *Gesta* 13 (1974): 29–43.

Brentano, Robert. "The Archepiscopal Archives at Amalfi." *Manuscripta* 4 (1960): 98–105.

—. "Sealed Documents and the Medieval Archbishops at Amalfi." *Medieval Studies* 23 (1961): 21–46.

—. *Two Churches: England and Italy in the Thirteenth Century*. Princeton, N.J., 1968.

—. *Rome Before Avignon: A Social History of Thirteenth Century Rome*. New York, 1974.

—. "Considerazioni di un lettore di testamenti." *Nolens intestatus decedere: Il testamento come fonte della storia religiosa e sociale*, ed. A. Bartoli Langeli. Perugia, 1985, 3–9.

—. "Burial Preferences at Rieti around 1300." In *Skulptur und Grabmal des Spätmittelalters in Rom und Italien*, ed. J. Garms and A. M. Romanini. Vienna, 1990.

—. *A New World in a Small Place: Church and Religion in the Diocese of Rieti, 1188–1378*. Berkeley, 1994.

Bresc, Henri. "1282: Classes sociales et révolution nationale." In *La società mediterranea all'epoca del Vespro*, ed. F. Giunta and P. Corrao. Palermo, 1983, 241–58.

Bresciani Alvarez, Giulio, and Giovanni Lorenzoni, eds. *L'edificio del Santo di Padova*. Vicenza, 1981.

Brett, Edward T. "The Life and Works of Humbert of Romans: Fifth Master General of the Dominican Order (1254–1263)." Ph.D. thesis, Rutgers University, 1979.

—. *Humbert of Romans: His Life and Views of Thirteenth-century Society*. Vol. 67: *Studies and Texts*. Toronto, 1984.

Breveglieri, Bruno. *Scrittura e immagine: Le lastre terragne del medioevo bolognese*. Vol. 7: *Testi, Studi, Strumenti*. Spoleto, 1993a.

—. "Tentavito di ricostruzione topografica del cimitero di San Francesco in Bologna." In *Atti e memorie: Deputazione di storia patria per le province di Romagna* 44 (1993b): 179–223.

—. "Le aree cimiteriali di San Domenico a Bologna nel medioevo (ricostruzioni topografiche)." In *Atti e memorie della Deputazione di storia patria per le province di Romagna* 45 (1995): 165–234.

Bride, A. "Sépulture." In *Dictionnaire de théologie catholique*, vol. 14, pt. 2, ed. A. Vacant, E. Mangenot, and Mgr. E. Amann. Paris, 1941, cols. 1884–1905.

Brink, J. "Saints Martin and Francis: Sources and Meaning in Simone Martini's Montefiore Chapel." In *Renaissance Studies in Honor of Craig Hugh Smith*, ed. A. Morrogh. Florence, 1985, 79–96.

Brogiolo, Gian Pietro, and Bryan Ward-Perkins, eds. *The Idea and Ideal of the Town between Late Antiquity and the Early Middle Ages*. Leiden, 1999.

Brooke, Rosalind B. *Early Franciscan Government: Elias to Bonaventure. Cambridge Studies in Medieval Life and Thought*, vol. 7. Cambridge, 1959.

—. *Scripta Leonis, Rufini et Angeli, sociorum S. Francisci. The Writings of Leo, Rufino and Angelo Companions of St. Francis*. Oxford, 1970.

—. *The Coming of the Friars. Historical Problems: Studies and Documents*, vol. 24. London, 1975.

Brown, Elizabeth A. R., ed. *The Oxford Collection of the Drawings of Roger de Gaignières and the Royal Tombs of Saint-Denis. Transactions of the American Philosophical Society*, vol. 78, pt. 5. Philadephia, 1988.

—. "Authority, the Family, and the Dead in Late Medieval France." *French Historical Studies* 16, no. 4 (1990): 803–32.

—. *The Monarchy of Capetian France and Royal Ceremonial*. London, 1991.

Brown, James Wood. *The Dominican Church of Santa Maria Novella at Florence: A Historical, Architectural and Artistic Study*. Edinburgh, 1902.

Brown, Peter. *The Cult of the Saints: Its Rise and Function in Latin Christianity*. Chicago, 1981.

Bruni, S. "Piazza dei Miracoli: Aspetti e problemi dell'insediamento antico in Piazza del Duomo." In *Storia e arte nella Piazza del Duomo: Conferenze 1992–1993*. Pisa, 1995, 163–85.

Bruzelius, Caroline. "Hearing is Believing: Clarissan Architecture 1212–1340." *Gesta* 31 (1992): 83–92.

—. "L'Abbaye de Longpont." *Congrès archéologique de France: Aisne méridionale, 1990*, 148 (1994): 431–43.

—. "Queen Sancia of Mallorca and the Church of Sta. Chiara in Naples." In *Memoirs of the American Academy in Rome* 40 (1995): 41–72.

—. "Nuns in Space: Strict Enclosure and the Architecture of the Clarissa in the Thirteenth Century."

In *Clare of Assisi: A Medieval and Modern Woman*, ed. I. Peterson. New York, 1996, 53–74.

—. *The Stones of Naples: Church Building in Angevin Italy 1266–1343*. New Haven and London, 2004.

—. "Relazione." In *Il francescanesimo in Calabria: Atti del I convegno internazionale di studi, Siderno Gerace, 26–28 maggio 2006*. Soveria Mannelli (Catanzaro), 2006a, 81–4.

—. "A Note on the 1233 Tower of Archbishop Peter of Sorrento and the Topography of Naples." In *Architektur und Monumentalskulptur des 12.–14. Jahrhunders*, ed. S. Gasser, C. Freigang, and B. Boener. Bern, 2006b, 225–35.

—. "The Dead Come to Town: Preaching, Burying and Building in the Mendicant Orders." In *The Year 1300 and the Creation of a New European Architecture*, ed. A. Gajewski and Z. Opačić. Turnhout, 2007, 203–24.

—. "From Empire to Commune to Kingdom: Notes on the Revival of Monumental Sculpture in Italy." In *Gothic Art and Thought in the Later Medieval Period*, ed. C. Hourihane. Princeton, N.J., 2011, 134–55.

—. "The Architecture of the Mendicant Orders in the Middle Ages: An Overview of Recent Literature." *Perspective: Le Journal de l'INHA* 2 (2012): 95–116.

Bullough, Donald A. "Urban Change in Early Medieval Italy: The Example of Pavia." *Papers of the British School at Rome* 34 (1966): 82–130.

—. "Burial, Community and Belief in the Early Medieval West." In *Ideal and Reality in Frankish and Anglo-Saxon Society*, ed. J. M. Wallace-Hadrill, P. Wormald, D. Bullough, and R. Collins. Oxford, 1983, 177–201.

Burns, Howard. "Building against Time: Renaissance Strategies to Secure Large Churches against Changes to their Design." In *L'Église dans l'architecture de la Renaissance*, ed. J. Guillaume. Paris, 1995, 107–31.

Burr, David. *Olivi and Franciscan Poverty: The Origins of the "Usus Pauper" Controversy*. Philadelphia, 1989.

—. *The Spiritual Franciscans: From Protest to Persecution in the Century after Saint Francis*. University Park, Penn., 2001.

—. "History as Prophecy: Angelo Clareno's *Chronicle* as a Spiritual Franciscan Apocalypse." In *Defenders and Critics of Franciscan Life: Essays in Honor of John V. Fleming*, ed. M. F. Cusato and G. Geltner. Boston, 2009, 119–38.

Burr, David, and David Flood. "Peter Olivi: On Poverty and Revenue." *Franciscan Studies* 40 (1980): 18–58.

Burresi, Mariagiulia, and Antonino Caleca, eds. *Cimabue a Pisa: La pittura pisana del Duecento da Giunta a Giotto; Museo Nazionale di San Matteo*, exh. cat. Pisa, 2005.

Burroughs, Charles. "Spaces of Arbitration and the Organization of Space in Late Medieval Italian Cities." In *Medieval Practices of Space*, ed. B. A. Hanawalt and M. Kobialka. Minneapolis, 2000, 64–100.

Buscaroli, Beatrice, and Roberto Sernicola, eds. *Petronio e Bologna: Il volto di una storia; Arte storia e culto del Santo Patrono*, Bologna, Palazzo di Re Enzo e del Podestà, exh. cat. Bologna, 2001.

Busignani, Alberto, and Raffaello Bencini. *Le chiese di Firenze 2: Quartiere di Santa Maria Novella*. Florence, 1979, 23–76.

—. *Le chiese di Firenze 3: Quartiere di Santa Croce*. Florence, 1982.

Butler, L. "The Houses of the Mendicant Orders in Britain: Recent Archaeological Work." In *Archaeological Papers from York presented to M. W. Barley*. York, 1984, 123–36.

Butterfield, Andrew. "Social Structure and Typology of Funerary Monuments in Early Renaissance Florence." *RES: Anthropology and Aesthetics* 26 (1994): 47–67.

—. "Monument and Memory in Early Renaissance Florence." In *Art, Memory and Family in Renaissance Florence*. ed. G. Ciappelli and P. L. Rubin. Cambridge, 2000, 135–62.

Bynum, Caroline. "Why All the Fuss about the Body? A Medievalist's Perspective." *Critical Inquiry* 22 (1995): 1–33.

Cabrol, F., and E. Leclercq, eds. *Dictionnaire d'archéologie chrétienne et de liturgie*, 15 vols. Paris, 1903–53.

Caby, Cécile. "Il costo dell'inurbamento: Monaci e frati a confronto." In *L'economia dei conventi dei frati minori e predicatori fino alla metà del Trecento: Atti del XXXI Convegno internazionale, Assisi, 9–11 ottobre 2003*, ed. E. Menestò. Spoleto, 2004, 295–337.

Cacciarini, G. "In S. Croce la chiesa del 1250." *Città di vita* 23 (1968): 55–61.

Caccin, Angelo Maria. *La basilica di S. Maria Gloriosa dei Frari in Venezia*. Venice, 1968.

Cadei, Antonio. "La chiesa di S. Francesco a Cortona." *Storia della città* 9 (1978): 16–23.

—. "Si può scrivere una storia dell'architettura mendicante? Appunti per l'area padano-veneta." In *Tomaso da Modena e il suo tempo: Atti del convegno internazionale di studi per il VI centenario della morte, Treviso, 1979*, ed. Comitato manifestazione Tomaso da Modena. Treviso, 1980, 337–62.

—. "Architettura mendicante: Il problema di una definizione tipologica." *Storia della città* 8 (1983a): 21–32.

—. "Assisi, San Francesco: L'architettura e la prima fase della decorazione." In *Roma anno 1300: Atti del congresso internazionale di storia dell'arte medievale, Roma, 19–24 maggio 1980*, ed. A. M. Romanini. Rome, 1983b, 141–74.

—. "Cori francescani ad ambulacro e cappelle radiali." *Storia e cultura a Padova nell'età di Sant'Antonio. Fonti e ricerche di storia padovana* 16 (1985): 467–500.

—. "Scultura e monumento sepolcrale del tardo medioevo a Roma e in Italia." *Arte medievale*, ser. 2, no. 2 (1988): 243–60.

—. "Studi sulla basilica di S. Francesco ad Assisi: Architettura (seconda parte)." *Arte medievale* 3 (1989): 117–136.

—. "Architettura e scultura." In *Enciclopedia dell'arte medievale*, vol. 2. Rome, 1991, 629–36.

—. "Secundum loci conditionem et morem patriae." In *Saggi in onore di Renato Bonelli*, vol. 1, ed. C. Bozzoni, G. Carbonara, and G. Villetti. Rome, 1992, 135–42.

Calabi, Donatella, and Jacques Bottin, eds. *Les Étrangers dans la ville: Minorités et espace urbain du bas Moyen Âge à l'époque moderne.* Paris, 1999.

Caleca, Antonio. "Il Camposanto: Profilo di una storia edilizia." In *Pisa: Museo delle Sinopie del Camposanto Monumentale*, ed. A. Caleca, G. Nencini, G. Piancastelli, et al. Pisa, 1979, 43–4.

—. "Un documento per la piazza del Duomo." In *Il Duomo e la civiltà pisana del suo tempo.* Pisa, ed. F. Gabrieli. 1986, 83–6.

Caleca, Antonino, Gaetano Nencini, and Giovanna Piancastelli, eds. *Pisa: Museo delle Sinopie del Camposanto Monumentale.* Pisa, 1979.

Callaey, Frédégand. "Le Tiers Ordre de Saint François d'Assise." *Études franciscaines* 33 (1921): 360–82.

Callebaut, P. A. "Essai sur l'origine du premier couvent sur des Mineurs à Paris et sur l'influence du frère Grégoire de Naples." *La France franciscaine: Mélanges d'archéologie, d'histoire, et de littérature* 11 (1928): 1–26.

Calzolai, Carlo C. "Il 'Libro dei morti' di Santa Maria Novella (1290–1436)." In *Santa Maria Novella: Un convento nella città; Studi e fonti. Memorie Domenicane* n.s., 11. Pistoia, 1980, 15–218.

Calzona, A. "I francescani a Mantova." *Storia della città* (1983): 26–7, 161–76.

Cammarosano, Paolo. "Aspetti delle strutture familiari nelle città dell'Italia comunale (secoli XII–XIV)." *Studi medievali* 16 (1975): 417–35.

Canale, C. G., and P. La Spina. *Cosenza: Sintesi compositiva e geometrica progettuale nell'architettura mendicante.* Messina, 1990.

Canniffe, Eamonn. *The Politics of the Piazza: The History and Meaning of the Italian Square.* Aldershot, 2008.

Cannon, Joanna. "Dating the Frescoes by the Maestro di S. Francesco at Assisi." *Burlington Magazine* 124, no. 947 (1982): 65–9.

—. "The Creation, Meaning, and Audience of the Early Sienese Polyptych: Evidence from the Friars." In *Italian Altarpieces 1250–1550: Function and Design*, ed. E. Borsook and F. Gioffredi Suberbi. Oxford, 1994, 41–79.

—. "Dominic 'Alter Christus?' Representations of the Founder in and after the 'Arca di San Domenico.'" In *Christ among the Medieval Dominicans*, ed. K. Emery Jr. and J. Wawrykow. Notre Dame, Ind., 1998, 26–48.

—. "Popular Saints and Private Chantries: The Sienese Tomb-Altar of Margherita of Cortona and Questions of Liturgical Use." In *Kunst und Liturgie im Mittelalter: Akten des internationalen Kongresses der Bibliotheca Hertziana und des Nederlands Instituut te Rome, Rom 28–30 September 1997*, ed. N. Bock, S. De Blauuw, H. Kessler, and C. Frommel. Munich, 2000, 149–62.

—. "Sources for the Study of the Role of Art and Architecture within the Economy of the Mendicant Convents of Central Italy: A Preliminary Survey." In *L'economia dei conventi dei frati minori e predicatori fino alla metà del Trecento: Atti del XXXI Convegno internazionale, Assisi, 9–11 ottobre 2003*, ed. E. Menestò. Spoleto, 2004, 215–62.

—. "'Panem petant in signum paupertatis': L'Image de la quête des aumônes chez les frères d'Italie centrale." In *Économie et religion: L'Expérience des ordres mendiants (XIIIè–XVè siècle)*, ed. N. Bériou and J. Chiffoleau. Lyon, 2009, 501–33.

Capeluti, G. *L'ordine domenicano in Puglia.* Teramo, 1965.

Capitani, Ovidio, et al., eds. *Da Gregorio VII a Bernardino da Siena: Saggi di storia medievale. Con scritti in ricordo di Zelina Zafarana.* Quaderni del Centro per il Collegamento degli Studi Medievale e Umanistici. Spoleto, 1987.

Caponeri, Marilena Rossi. "Nota su alcuni testamenti della fine del secolo XIV relativi alla zona di Orvieto." In *Nolens intestatus decedere: Il testamento come fonte della storia religiosa e sociale*, ed. A. Bartoli Langeli. Perugia, 1985, 105–11.

Caponeri, M. R., and L. Riccetti, eds. *Chiese e conventi degli ordini mendicanti in Umbria nei secoli XIII–XIV.* Perugia, 1987.

Carbonai, Franco, Gianni Gaggio, and Mario Salmi. "Nuove acquisizioni sulla cripta e sul transetto di S. Croce in Firenze." *Città di vita* 38 (1983): 32–59.

—. "Santa Croce: Interpretazione attraverso le indagini metriche e documentaire." In *Santa Maria del Fiore e le chiese fiorentine del Duecento e del Trecento nella città delle fabbriche arnofiane*, ed. G. Rocchi Coopmans de Yoldi. Florence, 2004, 243–62.

Carbonara, G. "Gli insediamenti degli ordini mendicanti in Sabina." In *Lo Spazio dell'Umiltà: Atti del convegno di studi sull'edilizia dell'ordine dei minori, Fara Sabina, 3–6 novembre 1982*, ed. M. B. Mistretta. Fara Sabina, 1984, 123–224.

Carbonell-Lamothe, Y. "Les Établissements franciscains de Gascogne vers 1300." *La Naissance et l'essor du gothique méridional du XIIIè siècle, Cahiers de Fanjeaux* 9 (1974): 165–84.

—. "Les Églises des Ordres mendiants du Puy." *Congrès archéologique de France* 133 (1975): 354–72.

Carli, Enzo. *L'arte nella basilica di San Francesco a Siena*. Siena, 1971.

Carli, Enzo, and Paolo E. Arias. *Il Camposanto di Pisa*. Rome, 1937.

Carlini, A. "Constitutiones generales ordinis Fratrum Minorum anno 1316 Assisii conditae." *Archivum Franciscanum Historicum* 6 (1911): 276–302, 508–26.

Carmassi, Massimo. *Camposanto di Pisa*. Rome, 1993.

Carozzi, Claude. "Le Ministère de la confession chez les prêcheurs de la province de Provence." *Les Mendiants en Pays d'Oc au XIIIè siècle, Cahiers de Fanjeaux* 8 (1973): 321–53.

—. "Humbert de Romans et la prédication." *L'Ordre des Prêcheurs et son histoire en France méridionale, Cahiers de Fanjeaux* 36 (2001): 249–61.

Carta, Marina, and Laura Russo. *S. Maria in Aracoeli. Le Chiese di Roma illustrate* n.s., 22. Rome, 1988.

Caseau, Béatrice. "Sacred Landscapes." In *Late Antiquity: A Guide to the Postclassical World*, ed. G. W. Bowersock, P. Brown, and O. Grabar. Cambridge, Mass., 1999, 21–59.

Caskey, Jill. *Art and Patronage in the Medieval Mediterranean: Merchant Culture in the Region of Amalfi*. Cambridge, 2004.

Castillo Utrilla, M. J. "Tipología de la arquitectura franciscana española desde la Edad Media hasta el Renacimiento." In *Actas del XXIII Congreso de Historia del Arte*, ed. Universtaad de Granada. Granada, 1973, 323–7.

Catalo, Jean, Quittere Cazès, et al. *Toulouse au Moyen Âge: 1000 Ans d'histoire urbaine (400–1480)*. Paris, 2010.

Ceccarelli Lemut, Maria Luisa. "Economia e società: Le attività commerciali e produttive e i protagonisti dell'economia cittadina." In *Cimabue a Pisa: La pittura pisana del Duecento da Giunta a Giotto*, Museo Nazionale di San Matteo, exh. cat., ed. M. Burresi and A. Caleca. Pisa, 2005, 21–4.

Celano, Thomas of. "The Life of St. Francis." In *Francis of Assisi: Early Documents*, vol. 1, ed. R. J. Armstrong, J. A. W. Hellmann, and W. J. Short. New York, 1999, 171–310.

Cenci, Cesare. "Le Clarisse a Mantova (sec. XIII–XV) e il primo secolo dei frati minori." *Le venezie francescane* 31 (1967): 3–92.

—. "Costituzioni della provincia Toscana tra i secoli XIII e XIV." *Studi francescani* 79 (1982): 369–409.

—. "De Fratrum Minorum Constitutionibus Praenarbonensibus." *Archivum Franciscanum Historicum* 83 (1990): 50–95.

Cervini, Fulvio, and Andrea De Marchi. *Santa Croce: Origini. Firenze 1300, frammenti di un discorso sugli ornati e sugli spazi. Ricerche di Storia dell'arte*, 102. Rome, 2010.

Chapotin, Marie-Dominique. *Histoire des Dominicains de la Province de France: Le Siècle des fondations*. Rouen, 1898.

Chaucer, Geoffrey. *The Canterbury Tales*, trans. N. Coghill. London, 1977.

Chiffoleau, Jacques. *La Comptabilité de l'au-delà: Les Hommes, la mort et la religion dans la région d'Avignon à la fin du Moyen Âge (vers 1320–vers 1480). Collection de l'École française de Rome*, 47. Rome, 1980.

—. "Perché cambia la morte nella regione di Avignone alla fine del medioevo." *Quaderni storici* 50, no. 2 (1982): 449–65.

—. "*Usus pauper?* Les franciscains, la règle et l'argent en Avignon (vers 1360–1430)." In *Horizons marins, itinéraires spirituels (Vè–XVIIIè siècle)*. Vol. 1: *Mentalités et sociétés*, ed. H. Dubois, J. C. Hoquet, and A. Vauchez. Paris, 1987, 135–49.

—. "Les Transformations de l'économie paroissiale en Provence (XIIIè–XVè siècles)." In *La parrocchia nel Medio Evo: Economia, scambi, solidarietà*, ed. A. Paravicini Bagliani and V. Pasche. *Italia Sacra*, vol. 53. Rome, 1995, 61–117.

Chiodi, G. *L'interpretazione del testamento nel pensiero dei glossatori*. Milan, 1997.

Chittolini, Giorgio, and Giovanni Miccoli, eds. *La chiesa e il potere politico dal medioevo all'età contemporanea*. Vol. 9: *Storia d'Italia*. Turin, 1986.

Christie, Neil, and S. T. Loseby, eds. *Towns in Transition: Urban Evolution in Late Antiquity and the Early Middle Ages*. Aldershot, 1996.

Ciampoltrini, G. "La trasformazione urbana a Lucca fra XI e XIII secolo." *Archeologia Medievale* 19 (1992): 701–28.

Ciardi, R. P. "Quest'insigne dormentorio de' morti: Chiesa, cimitero, museo." In *Il Camposanto di Pisa*, ed. C. Baracchini and E. Castelnuovo. Turin, 1996, 57–68.

Ciccuto, Marcello. "Figures et culture des images dans les récits exemplaires du XIVè siècle." In *Les Exempla médiévaux: Nouvelles perspectives*, ed. J. Berlioz and M. A. Polo de Beaulieu. Paris, 1998, 371–84.

Cipolla, C. "Ricerche storiche intorno all chiesa di Santa Anastasia in Verona." *Archivio Veneto* 18 (1879): 274–314.

Clapham, A. W. "On the Topography of the Dominican Priory of London." *Archeologia* 63 (1912): 57–84.

Clareno, Angelo. *A Chronicle or History of the Seven Tribulations of the Order of Brothers Minor*, trans. D. Burr and E. R. Daniel. New York, 2005.

Coakley, John. "Gender and the Authority of Friars: The Significance of Holy Women for the Thirteenth-century Franciscans and Dominicans." *Church History* 60 (1991): 445–60.

Cobianchi, Roberto. "Fashioning the Imagery of the Franciscan Observant Preacher: Early Renaissance Portraiture of Bernardino da Siena in Northern Italy." Vol. 12: *I Tatti Studies in the Italian Renaissance*. Chicago (2009): 55–83.

Cohen, Jeremy. *The Friars and the Jews: The Evolution of Medieval Anti-Judaism*. Ithaca, N.Y., 1982.

Cohn, Samuel K., Jr. *Death and Property in Siena, 1205–1800: Strategies for the Afterlife*. Baltimore and London, 1988.

—. *The Cult of Remembrance and the Black Death: Six Renaissance Cities in Central Italy*. Baltimore and London, 1992.

—. "The Place of the Dead in Flanders and Tuscany: Towards a Comparative History of the Black Death." In *The Place of the Dead: Death and Remembrance in Late Medieval and Early Modern Europe*, ed. B. Gordon and P. Marshall. Cambridge, 2000, 17–43.

Colardelle, M., and M. de Boüard. *Sépulture et traditions funéraires du Vè au XIIIè siècle ap. J. C. dans les campagnes des Alpes françaises du Nord: Drôme, Isère, Savoie, Haute-Savoie*. Grenoble, 1983.

Coleman, Edward. "Sense of Community and Civic Identity in the Italian Communes." In *The Community, the Family and the Saint: Patterns of Power in Early Medieval Europe. Selected Proceedings of the International Medieval Congress*, ed. J. Hill and M. Swan. Turnhout, 1998, 45–60.

Coleman, J. "Property and Poverty." In *The Cambridge History of Medieval Political Thought c. 350–c. 1450*, ed. J. H. Burns. Cambridge, 1991, 607–52.

Colvin, Howard. *Architecture and the Afterlife*. New Haven and London, 1991.

Coniglione, M. A. *La provincia domenicana in Sicilia*. Catania, 1937.

Conti, Alessandro. "Pittori in Santa Croce: 1295–1341." *Annali della Scuola Normale Superiore di Pisa*, ser. 3, 2, no. 1 (1972): 247–63.

Conti, Martino. "Lo sviluppo degli studi e la clericalizzazione dell'ordine." In *San Francesco e la Chiesa: Studi e testi pubblicati nell'ottavo centenario della nascita di Francesco d'Assisi 1182–1982*. Rome, 1982, 321–46.

Cook, William R. *The Art of the Franciscan Order in Italy*. Leiden and Boston, 2005.

Coomans, Thomas. *L'Architecture médiévale des ordres mendiants (Franciscains, Dominicains, Carmes et Augustins) en Belgique et aux Pays-Bas*. Vol. 70: *Revue Belge d'archéologie et d'histoire de l'art*. Brussels, 2001.

—. "Les églises des Dominicains et du Grand Béguinage à Louvain: Comparaisons typologiques." In *Mulieres religiosae et leur univers: Aspects des établissements Béguinaux au Moyen Age tardif*, ed. P. Volti. Paris, 2003, 25–41.

—. "Assisi and Cologne on the Banks of the Meuse: The Two Medieval Franciscan Churches at Maastricht." In *Kunst & Religion: Architektur und Kunst im Mittelalter; Beiträge einer Forschungsgruppe*, ed. U. M. Bräuer, E. S. Klinkenbert, and J. Westerman. Utrecht, 2005, 96–117.

—. "Cistercian Nuns and Princely Memorials: Dynastic Burial Churches in the Cistercian Abbeys of the Medieval Low Countries." In *Sépulture, mort et symbolique du pouvoir au Moyen Âge*, ed. M. Margue. Luxembourg, 2006a, 683–734, 776–98.

—. "De oudste dakconstructie in de Leuvense binnenstad: bouwhistorisch onderzoek in de predikherenkerk (prov. Vlaams-Brabant.)" *Relicta: Archeologie, Monumenten- en Landschapsonderzoek in Vlaanderen/Relicta: Heritage Research in Flanders*, vol. 1 (2006b): 183–212.

—. "Architectural Competition in a University Town: The Mendicant Friaries in Late Medieval Louvain." In *Architecture, Liturgy and Identity: Liber Amicorum Paul Crossley*, ed. Z. Opačić and A. Timmermann. Turnhout, 2011, 207–20.

Coomans, Thomas, and Anna Bergmans. "L'église Notre-Dame des Dominicains à Louvain (1251–1276): Le Mémorial d'Henri III, Duc de Brabant, et d'Alix de Bourgogne." *Bulletin monumental* 167, no. 2 (2009): 99–125.

Cooper, Donal. "The Painted Cross in the Thirteenth Century and the Liturgical Layout of Early Mendicant Churches." *Papers of the British School at Rome* 67 (1999): 407–8.

—. "Franciscan Choir Enclosures and the Function of Double-Sided Altarpieces in Pre-Tridentine Umbria." *Journal of the Warburg and the Courtauld Institutes* 64 (2001a): 1–54.

—. " 'Qui Perusii in arca saxea tumulatus': The Shrine of Beato Egidio in San Francesco al Prato, Perugia." *Papers of the British School at Rome* 69 (2001b): 223–44.

—. " 'In loco tutissimo et firmissimo': The Tomb of St. Francis in History, Legend and Art." In *The Art of the Franciscan Order in Italy*, ed. W. R. Cook. Leiden, 2005, 1–37.

—. "Gothic Art and the Friars in Late Medieval Croatia." In *Croatia: Aspects of Art, Architecture and Cultural Heritage*, ed. J. J. Norwich et al. London, 2009a, 76–97.

—. "'A great sumptuousness of paintings': Frescoes and Franciscan Poverty at Assisi in 1288 and 1312." *Burlington Magazine* 151 (2009b): 656–62.

—. "Access All Areas? Spatial Divides in the Mendicant Churches of Late Medieval Tuscany." In *Ritual and Space in the Middle Ages: Proceedings of the Harlaxton Symposium 2009*, ed. F. Andrews. Donington, 2011, 90–107.

—. "The Franciscan Context." In *The Caporali Missal: A Masterpiece of Renaissance Illumination*, ed. S. N. Fliegel. Cleveland, Ohio, 2013, 51–67.

Cooper, Donal, and James Banker. "The Church of Borgo San Sepolcro in the Late Middle Ages and the Renaissance." In *Sassetta: The Borgo San Sepolcro Altarpiece*, vol. 1, ed. M. Israels. Leiden and Florence, 2009, 53–105.

Corallini, Guido. *La chiesa di S. Caterina in Pisa dalle origini ad oggi*. Pisa, 1965.

Coulet, Noël. "Jalons pour une histoire religieuse d'Aix au Bas-Moyen Âge (1350–1450)." *Provence historique: Revue trimestrielle* 22 (1972): 203–60.

—. "Un couvent royal: Les Dominicaines de Notre-Dame-de-Nazareth d'Aix au XIIIè siècle." *Les Mendiants en Pays d'Oc au XIIIè siècle, Cahiers de Fanjeaux* 8 (1973): 233–61.

Creytens, R. "Les Constitutions des Frères Prêcheurs dans la rédaction de San Raymond de Peñafort." *Archivum Fratrum Praedicatorum* 18 (1948): 5–68.

Criscito, Angelo. "Sepoltura ecclesiastica." In *Enciclopedia cattolica*, vol. 11, ed. P. Paschini and G. Pizzardo. Vatican City, 1953, 363–6.

Crossley, Paul. "Medieval Architecture and Meaning: The Limits of Iconography." *Burlington Magazine* 130, no. 1019 (1988): 116–21.

Crouzil, Lucien. "Cimitière." In *Dictionnaire de droit canonique*, vol. 3, ed. R. Naz. Paris, 1942, 729–45.

Cullen, B. "Property in the Writings of St. Bonaventure." In *L'Homme et son univers au Moyen Âge*, ed. C. Wenin. Louvain-la-Neuve, 1986, 827–34.

Curuni, A. "Architettura degli Ordini Mendicanti in Umbria: Problemi di rilievo." In *Francesco d'Assisi: Chiese e conventi*, ed. R. Bonelli. Milan, 1982, 83–4.

Cusato, M. F., and G. Geltner, eds. *Defenders and Critics of Franciscan Life: Essays in Honor of John V. Fleming*. Boston, 2009.

Da Campagnola, Stanislao. "Gli ordini religiosi et la civiltà comunale in Umbria." In *Storia e arte in Umbria nell'età comunale: Atti del VI convegno di Studi Umbri, Gubbio, 1968*, ed. F. Ugolini. Perugia, 1971, 469–532.

—, ed. *I frati minori e il terzo ordine: Problemi e discussioni storiografiche; Atti del XXIII Convegno del Centro di studi sull spiritualità medievale, Todi, 17–20 ottobre 1982*. Vol. 23, Convegni del Centro di studi sulla spiritualità medievale. Todi, 1985.

D'Achille, P. "Camposanto." In *Enciclopedia dell'arte medievale*, vol. 4, ed. A. M. Romanini et al. Rome, 1993, 117–18.

Dalarun, Jacques. "Francesco nei sermoni: Agiografia e predicazione." In *La predicazione dei frati dalla metà del '200 alla fine del '300: Atti del XXII convegno internazionale, Assisi, 13–15 ottobre 1994*, ed. E. Menestò. Spoleto, 1995, 338–404.

D'Alatri, Mariano. "L'inquisizione francescana nell'Italia centrale nel secolo XIII." *Collectanea francescana* 22 (1952): 225–50; 23 (1953): 51–165.

—. "I più antichi insediamenti dei mendicanti nella Provincia di Campagna." *Mélanges de l'École française de Rome, Moyen Âge/Temps Modernes* 89 (1977): 575–618.

—. "I minori e la 'cura animarum' di fraternite e congregazioni." In *I frati minori e il terzo ordine: Problemi e discussioni storiografiche; Atti del XXIII convegno del centro di studi sulla spiritualità medievale, Todi, 17–20 ottobre 1982*, ed. S. da Campagnola. Todi, 1985, 145–70.

—. "A proposito di più antichi insediamenti francescani in Sicilia." *Francescanesimo e cultura in Sicilia (secc. XIII–XVI). Schede medievali* 12–13 (1987): 25–35.

—. *Eretici e inquisitori in Italia: studi e documenti. Bibliotheca Seraphica Capuccina*, vols. 31 and 32, Rome, 1986–7.

—. "Pulpito e navata." In *Dal pulpito alla navata: La predicazione medievale nella sua recezione da parte degli ascoltatori (sec. XIII–XV); Atti del convegno internazionale di storia religiosa in memoria di Zelina Zafarana, Firenze, 5–7 giugno 1986*. Vol. 3: *Medioevo e rinascimento*. Florence, 1989a, 181–99.

—. "Pulpito e navata nella cronaca di Fra Salimbene." *Collectanea Franciscana* 59 (1989b): 5–21.

D'Alessandro, Vincenzo. "Il ruolo economico e sociale della Chiesa in Sicilia dalla rinascita normanna all'età aragonese." In *Gli spazi economici della chiesa nell'occidente mediterraneo (secoli XII–metà XIXV): Sedicesimo convegno internazionale di studi, Pistoia, 16–19 maggio 1997*, ed. Centro italiano di studi di storia e d'arte. Pistoia, 1999, 259–312.

Dal pulpito alla navata: La predicazione medievale nella sua recezione da parte degli ascoltatori (sec. XIII–XV): Atti del convegno internazionale di storia religiosa in memoria di Zelina Zafarana, Firenze, 5–7 giugno 1986. Medioevo e Rinascimento: Annuario del Dipartimento di stud i sul medioevo e il Rinascimento dell'università di Firenze, 3. Florence, 1989.

D'Amato, A. "I Domenicani a Bologna nel '200." In *Archeologia medievale a Bologna: Gli scavi nel Convento di San Domenico; Bologna, Museo Civico Archeologico, 31 maggio–4 aprile 1987*, exh. cat., ed. S. Gelichi and R. Merlo. Bologna, 1987, 91–7.

Daniell, Christopher. *Death and Burial in Medieval England 1066–1550*. London and New York, 1997.

Davidsohn, Roberto. *Firenze ai tempi di Dante*, trans. E. Duprè Theseider. Florence, 1929.

—. *Storia di Firenze*, vols. 1–5, ed. and trans. G. B. Klein, R. Palmarocchi, and E. Sestan. Florence, 1960–78.

Davis, Michael. "Splendor and Peril: The Cathedral of Paris, 1290–1350." *Art Bulletin* 80, no. 1 (1998): 34–66.

—. "Sic et Non: Recent Trends in the Study of Gothic Ecclesiastical Architecture." *Journal of the Society of Architectural Historians* 58 (1999): 414–23.

—. "Fitting to the Requirements of the Place": The Franciscan Church of Saint-Marie-Madeleine in Paris." In *Architecture, Liturgy and Identity*, ed. Z. Opačić and A. Timmermann. Turnhout, 2011, 247–61.

D'Avray, David L. *The Preaching of the Friars: Sermons Diffused from Paris before 1300*. Oxford and New York, 1985.

—. "Philosophy in Preaching: The Case of a Franciscan Based in Thirteenth-century Florence (Servasanto da Faenza)." In *Literature and Religion in the Later Middle Ages: Philological Studies in Honor of Siegfried Wenzel*, ed. R. G. Newhauser and J. A. Alford. Binghamton, N.Y., 1994, 263–74.

Dawson, James Doyne. "William of Saint-Amour and the Apostolic Tradition." *Medieval Studies* 40 (1978): 223–38.

De Angelis d'Ossat, Guglielmo. "Proporzioni e accorgimenti visuali negli interni." In *Francesco d'Assisi: Chiese e conventi*, ed. R. Bonelli. Milan, 1982a, 150–61.

—, ed. *Il Tempio di San Fortunato a Todi*. Milan, 1982b.

Debby, Nirit Ben-Aryeh. "Patrons, Artists, Preachers: The Pulpit of Santa Mara Novella (1443–1448)." *Arte Cristiana* 90 (2002): 261–72.

—. "The Santa Croce Pulpit in Context: Sermons, Art and Space." *Artibus et historiae* 57 (2008): 75–93.

De Blasiis, G. "La dimora di Giovanni Boccaccio a Napoli." *Archivio Storico per le province napoletane* 17 (1892): 71–102.

Dectot, X. *Pierres tombales médiévales: Sculptures de l'au delà*. Paris, 2006.

Dedieu, H. "Les Sépultures de quelques églises franciscaines du nord de la Loire d'après les dessins de la collection Gaignières: Répetoire géographico-chronologique (XIIIè–XVIIè siècle)." *Archivum Franciscanum Historicum* 71 (1978): 3–36.

De Divitiis, Bianca. *Architettura e committenza nella Napoli del Quattrocento*. Venice, 2007.

—. "Un caso di rinnovamento urbano nella Napoli aragonese. La *regio nilensis* e il largo di San Domenico Maggiore." In *I grandi cantieri del rinnovamento urbano*, ed. P. Boucheron and M. Folin. École française de Rome, Rome, 2011, 181–97.

Delamaire, Bernard. "Liturgie, sacrements et ressources des curés dans le Nord de la France (XIè–XIVè siècles)." In *La parrocchia nel Medio Evo: Economia, scambi, solidarietà*, ed. A. Paravicini Bagliani and V. Pasche. *Italia Sacra*, vol. 53. Rome, 1995, 27–41.

De la Roncière, Charles M. "Présence et prédication des dominicains dans le *contado* florentin (1280–1350)." In *La Parole du prédicateur 5è–15è siècle*, ed. R. M. Dessì and M. Lauwers. Nice, 1997, 261–393.

Delcorno, Carlo. *La predicazione dell'età comunale*. Florence, 1974.

—. *Giordano da Pisa e l'antica predicazione volgare*. Florence, 1975.

—. "Predicazione volgare e volgarizzamenti." *Mélanges de l'École française de Rome, Moyen Âge/Temps Modernes* 89 (1977): 679–89.

—. "La predicazione volgare in Italia (sec. XIII–XIV): Teoria, produzione, ricezione." *Revue Mabillon* 4 (1993): 83–107.

—. "La lingua dei predicatori: Tra latino e volgare." In *La predicazione dei frati dalla metà del '200 alla fine del '300: Atti del XXII Convegno internazionale, Assisi, 13–15 ottobre 1994*, ed. E. Menestò. Spoleto, 1995, 19–46.

—. "Medieval Preaching in Italy." In *The Sermon*, ed. B. M. Kienzle. Louvain, 2000, 449–78.

Deliyannis, Deborah Mauskopf. "Church Burial in Anglo-Saxon England: The Prerogative of Kings." *Frühmittelalterliche Studien: Jahrbuch des Instituts für Frühmitterlaterforschung der Universität Münster* 29 (1995): 96–119.

Dell'Acqua, Gian Alberto, and Giulio Bora, eds. *La basilica di Sant'Eustorgio in Milano*. Milan, 1984.

Delle Rose, M. "Cimitero." In *Enciclopedia dell'arte medievale*, vol. 4. Rome, 1993, 770–85.

Dellwing, Herbert. *Studien zur Baukunst der Bettelorden im Veneto: Die Gotik der monumentalen Gewölbebasiliken*. Munich, 1970.

—. "Der Santo in Padua: Eine baugeschichtliche Untersuchung." *Mitteilungen des Kunsthistorischen Institutes in Florenz* 19 (1975): 197–240.

—. *Die Kirchenbaukunst des späten Mittelalters in Venetien*. Worms, 1990.

Delmaire, Bernard. "Liturgie, sacrements et ressources des curés dans le Nord de la France (XIè–XIVè siècles)." In *La parrochia nel Medio Evo: Economia, scambi, solidarietà*, ed. A. Paravicini Bagliani and V. Pasche. *Italia Sacra*, vol. 53. Rome, 1995, 27–41.

Delogu, R. *L'architettura del medioevo in Sardegna*. Rome, 1953.

Delorme, F.-M. "Les Cordeliers dans le Limousin aux XIIIè–XVè siècles." *Archivum Franciscanum Historicum* 32 (1939): 201–59; 33 (1940): 114–60.

De Marchi, Andrea. "Due fregi misconosciuti e il problema del tramezzo in San Fermo Maggiore a Verona." In *Arredi liturgici e architettura*, ed. A. C. Quintavalle. Milan, 2007, 129–42.

—. "Il 'podiolus' e il 'pergulum' di Santa Caterina a Treviso: Cronologia e funzione delle pitture murali in rapporto allo sviluppo della fabbrica architettonica." In *Medioevo: Arte e storia; Atti del convegno internazionale di studi, Parma 18–22 settembre 2007*, ed. A. C. Quintavalle. Milan, 2008, 385–407.

—. "Relitti di un naufragio; affreschi di Giotto, Taddeo Gaddi e Maso di Banco nelle navate di Santa Croce." In *Quaderni di Santa Croce*, vol. 4, Pistoia, 2011, 33–71.

De Marchi, Andrea, and Giacomo Piraz, eds. *Santa Croce: Oltre le apparenze*. Quaderni di Santa Croce, vol. 4. Pistoia, 2011.

Denifle, H. "Die Constitutionen des Prediger-Ordens vom Jahre 1228." *Archiv für Literatur- und Kirchengeschichte des Mittlealters* 1 (1885): 165–227.

Dent, Peter. " 'Laude dei trini': Observations towards a Reconstruction of Giovanni Pisano's Pistoia Pulpit." *Journal of the Warburg and Courtauld Institutes* 71 (2008): 121–38.

—. " '[P]er concorrenza d'uno [. . .] da un Tedesco': Giovanni Pisano, Vasari, and the Competitive Motive at Pistoia, c. 1301." *Zeitschrift für Kunstgeschichte* 74 (2011): 29–44.

Derégnaucort, J. P. "L'Élection de sépulture d'après les testaments douaisiens (1295–1500)." *Revue du Nord* 65 (1983): 343–52.

Dérens, J.-A. "La Prédication et la ville: Pratiques de la parole et religion civique à Montpellier aux XIVè et XVè siècles." *La Prédication en Pays d'Oc (XIIè–début XVè siècle), Cahiers de Fanjeaux* 32 (1997): 335–62.

De Roover, Raymond. "The Scholastic Attitude toward Trade and Enterprenuership." In *Business, Banking, and Economic Thought in Late Medieval and Early Modern Europe*, ed. Raymond De Roover and J. Kirschner. Chicago, 1974, 336–45.

De Sceaux, R., and E. Houth. "Le Couvent des Cordeliers de Mantes dans la diffusion géographique des maisons des Frères Mineurs." *Le Mantois* 21 (1971): 3–18.

Dickson, Gary. "Encounters in Medieval Revivalism: Monks, Friars, and Popular Enthusiasts." *Church History* 68 (1999): 265–93.

Di Meglio, Rosalba. *Il convento francescano di S. Lorenzo di Napoli: Regesti dei documenti dei secoli XIII–XV: Documenti per la storia degli ordini mendicanti nel mezzogiorno*, 2, ed. G. Vitolo. Salerno, 2003.

—. "Ordres mendiants et économie urbaine à Naples entre Moyen Âge et époque moderne: L'Exemple de Sant'Agostino." In *Économie et religion: L'Expérience des ordres mendiants (XIIIè–XVè siècle)*, ed. N. Bériou and J. Chiffoleau. Lyon, 2009, 591–636.

Dimock, Giles R. "St. Thomas Aquinas and Church Architecture." *Sacred Architecture* 3, (2000): 21–2.

Dipple, Geoffrey. " 'Sie sind alle glichsner': Antifraternalism in Medieval and Renaissance German Literature." In *Defenders and Critics of Franciscan Life: Essays in Honor of John V. Fleming*, ed. M. F. Cusato and G. Geltner. Boston, 2009, 177–94.

Donato, Maria Monica. " 'Constructa civibus suis': Un itinerario dentro ed intorno alla cattedrale di Pisa." In *Alla riscoperta di piazza del Duomo di Firenze. Vol. 7: Santa Maria del Fiore nell'Europa delle cattedrali*, ed. T. Verdon and E. Brivio. Florence, 1998, 67–95.

Dondarini, Ronaldo. "Una basilica civica nel nome di San Petronio." In *Petronio e Bologna: Il volto di una storia; Arte storia e culto del Santo Patrono*. Bologna, Palazzo di Re Enzo e del Podestà, exh. cat., ed. B. Buscaroli and R. Sernicola. Bologna, 2001, 93–102.

Dossat, Yves. "Opposition des anciens ordres à l'installation des mendiants." *Les Mendiants en pays d'Oc au XIIIè siècle, Cahiers de Fanjeaux* 8 (1973): 263–306.

—. "Le Couvent des Jacobins de Toulouse et son endettement en 1278." *La Naissance et l'essor du gothique méridional au XIIIè siècle, Cahiers de Fanjeaux* 9 (1974): 255–72.

Douie, Decima. *The Conflict between the Seculars and the Mendicants at the University of Paris in the Thirteenth Century*. London, 1954.

Dufeil, M.-M. *Guillame de Saint-Amour et la polémique universitaire parisienne, 1250–1259*. Paris, 1972.

Dupré dal Poggetto, Maria Grazia Ciardi, Antonella Chiti, and Rita Jacopino. "Un 'corpus' delle lastre tombali della basilica di Santa Croce a Firenze." In *Skulptur und Grabmal des Spätmittelalters in Rom und Italien: Akten des Kongresses "Scultura e monumento sepolcrale del tardo medioevo a Roma e in Italia" (Rom, 4–6 Juli 1985)*, ed. J. Garms and A. M. Romanini. Vienna, 1990, 331–44.

Durliat, M. "Le Rôle des ordres mendiants dans la création de l'architecture gothique méridionale." *La Naissance et l'essor du gothique méridional du XIIIè siècle, Cahiers de Fanjeaux* 9 (1974): 71–85.

Durliat, M., G. Costa, et al. *Les Jacobins, 1385–1985: Sixième Centenaire de la dédicace de l'église des Jacobins. Toulouse, 19 septembre–27 octobre, 1985, exh. cat.* Toulouse, 1985.

Duval, Noël. "L'Afrique dans l'Antiquité tardive e la période byzantine: L'Évolution de l'architecture et de l'art dans leur environnement." *Antiquité tardive* 14 (2006): 119–64.

Duval, Yvette. *Loca sanctorum Africae: Le Culte des martyres en Afrique du IVè au VIIè siècles.* Rome, 1982.

—. *Auprès des saints corps et âme: L'Inhumation "ad sanctos" dans la chrétienité d'Orient et d'Occident du IIIè au VIIè siècle.* Paris, 1988.

Duval, Yvette, and J.-Ch. Picard, eds. *L'Inhumation privilégiée du IVè au VIIIè siècle en Occident: Actes du colloque tenu à Créteil les 16–18 mars 1984.* Paris, 1986.

Dyggve, Ejnar. "The Origin of the Urban Churchyard." *Classica et medievalia: Revue danoise de philologie et d'histoire* 13 (1952): 147–58.

—. "L'origine del cimitero entro la cinta della città." *Atti dell VIII congresso internazionale di Studi Bizantini e Neoellenici* 8 (1953): 137–41.

Dykmans, M. "Les Obituaires romains: Une Définition suivie d'une vue d'ensemble." *Studi medievali,* ser. 3, 19 (1978): 591–652.

Eccleston, Thomas of. *The Friars and How They Came to England,* trans. Father Cuthbert. London, 1903.

Edgerton, Samuel. *Theaters of Conversion: Religious Architecture and Indian Artisans in Colonial Mexico.* Albuquerque, N.Mex., 2001.

Ehrle, Franz. "Die ältesten Redaktionen der Generalconstitutionen des Franziskanerordens." *Archiv für Literatur und Kirchengeschichte des Mittelalters* 6 (1892): 1–138.

Eldin, Grégoire. "Les Chapellenies à Notre-Dame de Paris (XIIè–XVIè siècle)." In *Positions des thèses soutenues par les élèves de la promotion de 1994.* Paris, 1994.

Elm, Kaspar, ed. *Stellung und Wirksamkeit der Bettelorden in der städtischen Gesellschaft. Berliner Historische Studien,* vol. 3. Berlin, 1981.

Elsner, Jaś. *Imperial Rome and Christian Triumph: The Art of the Roman Empire AD 100–450.* Oxford and New York, 1998.

Emery, Kent, Jr., and Joseph Wawrykow, eds. *Christ among the Medieval Dominicans: Representations of Christ in the Texts and Images of the Order of Preachers.* Notre Dame, Ind., 1998.

Emery, Richard W. "The Second Council of Lyons and the Mendicant Orders." *Catholic Historical Review* 39 (1953): 257–71.

—. *The Friars in Medieval France: A Catalogue of French Mendicant Convents 1200–1550.* New York, 1962.

Epstein, Steven. *Wills and Wealth in Medieval Genoa, 1150–1250.* Cambridge, Mass., 1984.

Erickson, Carolly. "The Fourteenth-century Franciscans and Their Critics." Pt. 1, "The Order's Growth and Character." *Franciscan Studies* 35 (1975): 107–35.

—. "The Fourteenth-century Franciscans and Their Critics." Pt. 2, "Poverty, Jurisdiction, and Internal Change." *Franciscan Studies* 36 (1976): 108–47.

Erlande Brandenburg, A. "La Priorale Saint-Louis de Poissy." *Bulletin monumental* 129 (1971): 85–113.

—. *Le Roi est mort: Étude sur les funérailles, les sépultures et les tombeaux des rois de France jusqu'à la fin du XIIIè siècle.* Geneva, 1975.

Eubel, Conrad, ed. *Bullarii Franciscani Epitome.* Florence, 1908.

Evangelisti, Paolo. *I francescani e la costruzione di uno stato: Linguaggi politici, valori identitari, progetti di governo in area catalano-aragonese. Fonti e ricerche di storia ecclesiastica padovana* 20. Padua, 2006.

Evans, Joan. "English Art, 1307–1461." In *The Oxford History of English Art,* vol. 5. Oxford, 1949.

Fanelli, Giovanni. *Firenze.* Bari, 1980.

Fanti, Mario. *La fabbrica di S. Petronio in Bologna dal XIV al XX secolo: Storia di una istituzione. Italia Sacra,* vol. 32. Rome, 1980.

Fanti, Mario, G. Lorenzoni, A. M. Matteucci, and R. Roli, eds. *La Basilica di San Petronio in Bologna.* Milan, 1984.

Farina, Sandra. "I conventi mendicanti nell tessuto urbanistico di Bologna." *Storia della città* 9 (1978): 56–61.

Faron, Olivier, and E. Hubert, eds. *Le Sol e l'immeuble: Les Forms dissociées de propriété immobilière dans les villes de France et d'Italie (XIIè–XIXè siècle). Collection de l'École française de Rome,* 206. Lyon, 1995.

Fentress, Elizabeth, et al. *Walls and Memory: The Abbey of San Sebastiano at Alatri (Lazio) from Late Roman Monastery to Renaissance Villa and Beyond.* Turnhout, 2005.

Ferruolo, Stephen C. *The Origins of the University: The Schools of Paris and their Critics, 1100–1215.* Palo Alto, Calif., 1985.

Fiamminghi, S. "Santa Maria Novella: Indagine sulle murature del nucleo originario." In *Santa Maria del Fiore e le chiese fiorentine del Duecento e del Trecento nella città delle fabbriche arnolfiane,* ed. G. Rocchi Coopmans de Yoldi. Florence, 2004, 233–42.

Field, Sean L. "Franciscan Ideals and the Royal Family of France (1226–1328)." In *The Cambridge Companion to Francis of Assisi*, ed. M. J. P. Robson. Cambridge, 2012, 208–23.

Fiengo, Giuseppe, and Maria Russo. "Il chiostro del Paradiso di Amalfi." *Apollo* 12 (1996): 105–23.

Filipiak, Mary Angelina. "The Plans of the Poor Clares' Convents in Central Italy from the Thirteenth through the Fifteenth Century." Ph.D. thesis, University of Michigan, 1957.

Fineschi, Vincenzio. *Il forestiero istruito in S. Maria Novella di Firenze*. Florence, 1790.

—. *S. Maria Novella: Memorie sull'antico cimitero della chiesa*. Rome, 1977.

Fino, Lucio. *Arte e storia in S. Lorenzo Maggiore a Napoli*. Naples, 1987.

Firpo, Marina. "Primordi della presenza a Genova dei frati minori: Prospettive per una futura ricerca." *Arte medievale* 10, no. 1 (1996): 109–19.

Fiumi, Enrico. *Demografia, movimento urbanistico e classi sociali in Prato dall'età comunale ai tempi moderni*. Florence, 1968.

Fleming, John V. "The Antifraternalism of the 'Summoner's Tale'." *Journal of English and Germanic Philology* 65, no. 4 (1966): 688–700.

—. *An Introduction to the Franciscan Literature of the Middle Ages*. Chicago, 1977.

Flood, D. "Franciscan Poverty: A Brief Survey (Introduction)." *Chronica* (1996): 1–53.

Flora, Holly, and Arianna Pecorini Cignoni. "Requirements of Devout Contemplation: Text and Image for the Poor Clares in Trecento Pisa." *Gesta* 45, no. 1 (2006): 61–76.

Fohlen, C. "Connaissance et utilisation des tombes antiques pendant le haut Moyen Âge." *Mélanges de la Société toulousaine d'études classiques* 2 (1946): 179–83.

Fonseca, Cosimo Damiano. " 'Ordines' istituzionalli e ruoli sociali." In *Condizione umana e ruoli sociali nel Mezzogiorno normanno-svevo: Atti delle IX Giornate normanno-sveve, Bari, 17–20 ottobre 1989*, ed. G. Musca. Bari, 1991, 9–18.

Francescanesimo e cultura in Sicilia (secc. XIII–XIV). Vols. 12–13: *Schede medievali*. Palermo, 1987.

Francescanesimo e la vita religiosa dei laici nel '200: Atti dell'VIII Convegno Internazionale, Assisi, 16–18 ottobre 1980. Assisi, 1981.

Franco, Tiziana. "Appunti sulla decorazione dei tramezzi nelle chiese mendicanti: La chiesa dei Domenicani a Bolzano." In *Arredi liturgici e architettura*, ed. A. C. Quintavalle. Milan, 2007, 115–28.

Franco, Tiziana, and Giovanna Valenzano, eds. *De Lapidibus Sententie: Scritti di storia dell'arte per Giovanni Lorenzoni*. Padua, 2002.

Frank, Thomas. "Exploring the Boundaries of Law in the Middle Ages: Franciscan Debates on Poverty, Property, and Inheritance." *Law and Literature* 20, no. 2 (2008): 243–60.

Fraschetti, Stanislao. "I sarcofagi dei reali angioini in Santa Chiara di Napoli." *L'Arte* 1 (1898): 385–438.

Freed, J. B. *The Friars and German Society in the Thirteenth Century*. Cambridge, Mass., 1977.

Freigang, Christian. "Chapelles latérales privées: Origines, fonctions, financement; Le Cas de Notre-Dame de Paris." In *Art, cérémonial et liturgie au Moyen Âge: Actes du colloque de 3è Cycle Romand de Lettres Lausanne-Fribourg, 24–25 mars, 14–15 avril, 12–13 mai 2000*, ed. N. Bock, P. Kurmann, S. Romano, and J.-M. Spieser. Rome, 2002, 525–44.

Frommel, Sabine, Laurent Lecomte, et al., eds. *La Place du choeur*. Paris, 2012.

Frugoni, Chiara. "Altri luoghi, cercando il paradiso: Il ciclo di Buffalmacco nel Camposanto di Pisa e la committenza domenicana." *Annali della Scuola Normale Superiore di Pisa* 18 (1988): 1557–1643.

—. "The City and 'New' Saints." In *City States in Classical Antiquity and Medieval Italy: Athens and Rome*, ed. A. Molho, K. Raaflaub, and J. Emlen. Stuttgart, 1991, 71–91.

—. *Francesco e le l'invenzione delle stimmate: Una storia per parole e immagini fino a Bonaventura e Giotto*. Turin, 1993.

—. *L'affare migliore di Enrico: Giotto e la Cappella Scrovegni*. Turin, 2008.

Gaffuri, Laura. "Nell' 'Officina' del predicatore: Gli strumenti per la composizione dei sermoni latini." In *La predicazione dei frati dalla metà del '200 alla fine del '300: Atti del XXII convegno internazionale, Assisi, 13–15 ottobre 1994*, ed. E. Menestò. Spoleto, 1995, 81–111.

Gaglione, Mario. *Nuovi studi sulla Basilica di Santa Chiara in Napoli*. Naples, 1996.

—. "Il Campanile di Santa Chiara in Napoli." *Quaderni di antichità napoletane* 1 (1998): 5–23.

—. "Qualche ipotesi e molti dubbi su due fondazioni angioine a Napoli: S. Chiara e S. Croce di Palazzo." *Campania Sacra* 33 (2002): 61–108.

—. "Quattro documenti per la storia di Santa Chiara in Napoli." *Archivio Storico per le province napoletane* 121 (2003): 399–431.

—. "Sancia d'Aragona-Majorca: Da regina di Sicilia e Gerusalemme a monaca di Santa Croce." In *Archivio per la storia delle donne*. Naples, 2004, 28–54.

—. "Sancia d'Aragona-Maiorca tra impegno di governo e 'attivismo' francescano." *Studi Storici* 4 (2008): 931–85.

—. "Sancia di Maiorca e la dotazione del monastero di S. Chiara in Napoli nel 1342." *Rassegna storica salernitana* 27 (2010): 149–87.

Gai, Lucia, et al., eds. *San Francesco: La chiesa e il convento in Pistoia.* Pisa, 1993.

—, ed. *Il complesso monumentale di San Francesco in Pistoia.* Pistoia, 1994.

—. "Vie di pellegrinaggio e configurazione dei centri abitati nell'Italia centro-settentrionale." In *Le vie e la civiltà dei pellegrinaggi nell'Italia Centrale.* Atti del Premio internazionale Ascoli Piceno, n.s. 10, ed. E. Menestò. Spoleto, 2000, 75–110.

—. "Insediamento e prima diffusione degli ordini mendicanti a Pistoia." In *Gli ordini mendicanti a Pistoia (secc. XIII–XV): Atti del convegno di studi, Pistoia, 12–13 maggio 2000,* ed. R. Nelli. Pistoia, 2001, 74–99.

Galbraith, Georgina R. *The Constitution of the Dominican Order, 1216 to 1360.* London, 1925.

Galletti, A. "L'insediamento e primo sviluppo dei frati minori a Perugia." In *Francescanesimo e società cittadina: L'esempio di Perugia; Studi storici per il VII centenario del Convento Francescani di Monteripido in Perugia (1276–1976),* ed. U. Nicolini. Perugia, 1992, 1–32.

Galvano Fiamma. *Cronica Ordinis Praedicatorum ab Anno 1170 usque ad 1333,* ed. B. M. Reichert. Vol. 2, no. 1, *Monumenta Ordinis Fratrum Praedicatorum Historica.* Rome, 1897.

Gardner, Julian. "The Early Decoration of Santa Croce in Florence." *Burlington Magazine* 113 (1971): 391–3.

—. "Arnolfo di Cambio and Roman Tomb Design." *Burlington Magazine* 115 (1973): 420–39.

—. "Some Franciscan Altars of the Thirteenth and Fourteenth Centuries." In *The Vanishing Past: Studies of Medieval Art, Liturgy and Metrology Presented to Chirstopher Hohler,* ed. A. Borg and A. Martindale. Oxford, 1981, 29–38.

—. "A Princess among Prelates: A Fourteenth-century Neapolitan Tomb and Some Northern Relations." *Römisches Jahrbuch für Kunstgeschichte* 23/24 (1988): 31–60.

—. "The French Connection: Thoughts about French Patrons and Italian Art, c. 1250–1300." In *Art and Politics in Late Medieval and Early Renaissance Italy, 1250–1300,* ed. C. M. Rosenberg. Notre Dame, Ind., 1990, 82–102.

—. *The Tomb and the Tiara: Curial Tomb Sculpture in Rome and Avignon in the Later Middle Ages.* Oxford, 1992.

—. "L'introduzione della tomba figurativa in Italia centrale." In *Il Gotico europeo in Italia,* ed. V. Pace and M. Bagnoli. Naples, 1994, 207–19.

—. "Il patrocinio curiale e l'introduzione del gotico, 1260–1305." In *Il Gotico europeo in Italia,* ed. V. Pace and M. Bagnoli. Naples, 1995, 85–8.

—. "Seated Kings, Sea-faring Saints and Heraldry: Some Themes in Angevin Iconography." In *L'État Angevin: Pouvoir, culture, et société entre XIIIè et XIVè siècles; Actes du colloque international organisé par l'American Academy in Rome, l'École française de Rome, l'Istituto storico italiano per il medioevo, l'U. M. R. Telemme et l'Université de Provence, e l'Università degli Studi di Napoli, 1995,* ed. École française de Rome. Rome, 1998, 115–26.

—. "The Family Chapel: Artistic Patronage and Architectural Transformation in Italy circa 1275–1325." In *Art, Cérémonial et Liturgie au Moyen Âge: Actes du colloque de 3è Cycle Romand de Lettres Lausanne–Fribourg, 24–25 mars, 14–15 avril, 12–13 mai 2000,* ed. N. Bock, P. Kurmann, S. Romano, and J.-M. Spieser. Rome, 2002, 545–64.

—. "Stone Saints: Commemoration and Likeness in Thirteenth-century Italy, France, and Spain." *Gesta* 46, no. 2 (2007): 121–34.

Garini, L. *Il bel San Francesco di Bologna: La sua storia.* Bologna, 1948.

Garms, Jörg. "Lastre." In *Enciclopedia dell'arte medievale* 7 (1999): 543–7.

Garms, Jörg, R. Juffinger, J. B. Ward-Perkins, et al. *Die Mittelalterlichen Grabmäler in Rom und Latium, vom 13. bis zum 15. Jahrhundert.* 5 vols. Rome, 1981–94.

Garms, Jörg, and Angiola Maria Romanini, eds. *Skulptur und Grabmal des Spätmittelalters in Rom und Italien: Akten des Kongresses "Scultura e monumento sepolcrale del tardo medioevo a Roma e in Italia," Rom, 4–6 Juli 1985.* Vienna, 1990.

Garzella, Gabriella. *Pisa com'era: Topografia e insediamento; Dall'impianto tardoantico; Alla città murata del secolo XII.* Naples, 1990.

—. "La forma della città tra persistenze e rinnovamento." In *Cimabue a Pisa: La pittura pisana del Duecento da Giunta a Giotto; Museo Nazionale di San Matteo,* exh. cat., ed. M. Burresi and A. Caleca. Pisa, 2005, 17–19.

Gasparini, Giuseppina de Sandre. "Movimento dei disciplinati confraternite e ordini mendicanti." In *I frati minori e il terzo ordine: Problemi e discussioni storiografiche; Atti del XXIII convegno del centro di studi sulla spiritualità medievale, Todi, 17–20 ottobre 1982,* ed. S. da Campagnola. Todi, 1985, 79–114.

Gasparotto, Cesira. *Il convento e la chiesa di S. Agostino dei Domenicani in Padova.* Florence, 1967.

Gaulin, Jean-Louis. "Le Cimetière du couvent Saint-Dominique de Bologne au XIIIè siècle." In *Religion et société urbaine au Moyen Âge: Études offertes* à Jean-Louis Biget par ses anciens élèves, ed. P. Boucheron and J. Chiffoleau. Paris, 2000, 283–99.

Geary, Patrick. *Phantoms of Remembrance: Memory and Oblivion at the End of the First Millennium.* Princeton, N.J., 1994.

Geddes, Helen. "Altarpieces and Contracts: The Marble High Altarpiece for San Francesco, Bologna (1388–1392)." *Zeitschrift für Kunstgeschichte* 67, no. 2 (2004): 153–82.

Gelichi, Sauro, and Riccardo Merlo, eds. *Archeologia medievale a Bologna: Gli scavi nel Convento di San Domenico. Bologna, Museo Civico Archeologico, 31 maggio–4 aprile 1987.* Bologna, 1987.

Gelichi, Sauro, and Riccardo Merlo. "Le vicende storico-architettoniche di un settore del convento di San Domenico." In *Archeologia medievale a Bologna: gli scavi nel Convento di San Domenico. Bologna, Museo Civico Archeologico, 31 maggio–4 aprile 1987,* ed. Sauro Gelichi and Riccardo Merlo Bologna, 1987, 113–18.

Gelichi, Sauro, Riccardo Merlo, and Sergio Nepoti. "La chiesa di San Domenico nel XIII secolo." In *Archeologia medievale a Bologna: gli scavi nel Convento di San Domenico. Bologna, Museo Civico Archeologico, 31 maggio–4 aprile 1987,* ed. Sauro Gelichi and Riccardo Merlo. Bologna, 1987, 109–11.

Gelichi, Sauro, and Rosella Rinaldi. "Il Sepoltuario del 1291." In *Archeologia medievale a Bologna: gli scavi nel Convento di San Domenico. Bologna, Museo Civico Arch-eologico, 31 maggio–4 aprile 1987,* Sauro Gelichi and Riccardo Merlo. Bologna, 1987, 99–107.

Geltner, Guy. *The Medieval Prison: A Social History.* Princeton, N.J., 2008.

—. "Mendicants as Victims: Scale, Scope and the Idiom of Violence." *Journal of Medieval History* 36 (2010): 126–41.

—. *The Making of Medieval Antifraternalism: Polemic, Violence, Deviance, and Remembrance.* Oxford, 2012.

Génestal, R. "Rôle des monastères comme établissements de credit etudié en Normandie du XIè à la fin du XIIIè." Ph.D. thesis, University of Paris, 1901.

Gennep, Arnold Van. *The Rites of Passage.* Chicago, 1960.

Gibert, P. *Recherches sur l'architecture des ordres mendiants dans le diocèse de Bayonne, de Dax et d'Aire (XIIIè–XIVè siècles).* Bordeaux, 1978.

Giebben, Servus. "Confraternite e penitenti dell'area francescana." In *Francescanesimo e la vita religiosa dei laici nel '200: Atti dell'VIII convegno internazionale, Assisi, 16–18 ottobre 1980,* ed. Società internazionale di Studi francescani. Università degli Studi di Perugia. Perugia, 1981, 171–201.

Gilardi, Costantino. " 'Ecclesia laicorum' e 'ecclesia fratrum': Luoghi e oggetti per il culto e la predicazione secondo 'l'ecclesiasticum officium' dei fratri predicatori." In *Aux Origins de la liturgie dominicaine: Le Manuscript Santa Sabina XIV L1,* ed. L. Boyle and P.-M. Gy. Collection de l'École française de Rome, 327. Rome, 2004, 379–443.

Gilbert, Chreighton. "The Pisa Baptistery Pulpit Addresses its Public." *Artibus et Historiae* 21 (2000): 9–30.

Gilchrist, Roberta. "Medieval Bodies in the Material World: Gender, Stigma and the Body." In *Framing Medieval Bodies,* ed. S. Kay and M. Rubin. Manchester, 1994, 43–61.

—. "Magic for the Dead? The Archaeology of Magic in Later Medieval Burials." *Medieval Archaeology* 52 (2008): 119–59.

Gilchrist, Roberta, and Barney Sloane. *Requiem: The Medieval Monastic Cemetery in Britain.* London, 2005.

Giles, J. A., and William Rishanger, eds. *Matthew Paris's English History: From the Year 1235 to 1273.* 3 vols. London, 1852–4.

Gillerman, David. "San Fortunato in Todi: Why the Hall Church?" *Journal of the Society of Architectural Historians* 48 (1989): 158–71.

Gillet, Louis. *Histoire artistique des ordres mendiants: Essai sur l'art religieux du XIIIè au XVIIè siècle.* Paris, 1939.

Gilyard Beer, R. "Ipswich Blackfriars." *Proceedings of the Suffolk Institute of Architecture* 34 (1977): 15–23.

Ginatempo, M., and Lucia Sandri. *L'Italia delle città: Il popolamento urbano tra medioevo e Rinascimento (secoli XIII–XVI).* Florence, 1990.

Giné Torres, Anna Maria. "Establiments franciscans a Catalunya: Arquitectura franciscana." *Acta historica et archaeologica medievalia* 10 (1989): 125–43.

Giordani, Bonaventura, ed. *Acta franciscana e Tabulariis Bononiensibus deprompta: Analecta Franciscana, sive chronica aliaque varia documenta ad historiam Fratrum Minorum spectantia* 9. Florence, 1927.

Giordano da Pisa. *Prediche inedite del B. Giordano da Rivalto dell'ordine de predicatori, recitate in Firenze dal 1302 al 1305,* ed. E. Narducci. Bologna, 1867.

—. *Prediche sul secondo capitolo del Genesi,* ed. S. Grattarola. Vol. 28: *Monumenta Ordinis Fratrum Praedicatorum Historica.* Rome, 1999.

Giorgi, Luca, and Pietro Matracchi. "La chiesa di Santa Croce e i precedenti insediamenti francescani: Architettura e resti archeologici." In *Santa Croce: Oltre le apparenze,* ed. A. De Marchi and G. Piraz. Florence, 2011, 13–31.

Giurescu, Ena. "Trecento Family Chapels in Santa Maria Novella and Santa Croce: Architecture,

Patronage, and Competition." Ph.D. thesis, New York University, 1997.

Giusti, Paola. "I resti di una sepoltura reale angioina." In *Scritti di storia dell'arte in onore di Raffaelo Causa*, ed. P. Leone di Castris. Naples, 1988, 39–45.

Gli spazi economici della chiesa nell'occidente mediterraneo (secoli XII–metà XIV): Sedicesimo convegno internazionale di studi, Pistoia, 16–19 maggio 1997, ed. Centro italiano di storia e d'arte. Pistoia, 1999.

Goffen, Rona. *Piety and Patronage in Renaissance Venice*. New Haven and London, 1986.

—. *Spirituality in Conflict: Saint Francis and Giotto's Bardi Chapel*. University Park, Penn., 1988.

Goldthwaite, Richard. *The Building of Renaissance Florence*. Baltimore, 1980.

—. "An Empire of Things: Consumer Demand in Renaissance Italy." In *Patronage, Art, and Society in Renaissance Italy*, ed. F. Kent and P. Simons. Oxford, 1987, 153–75.

—. *Wealth and the Demand for Art in Italy, 1300–1600*. Baltimore, 1993.

Golinelli, Paolo, and C. G. Brenzoni, ed. *I santi Fermo e Rustico: Un culto e una chiesa in Verona*. Verona, 2004.

Gollob, Hedwig. "L'Abbaye de Saint-Denis et les problèmes de l'architecture de la fin de l'antiquité jusqu'à l'époque carolingienne." *Palladio: Rivista di storia dell'architettura* 4 (1964): 139–46.

Gordon, Bruce, and Peter Marshall. *The Place of the Dead: Death and Remembrance in Late Medieval and Early Modern Europe*. Cambridge, 2000.

Grand, Roger. "Les Chaires à prêcher au dehors des églises." *Bulletin monumental* 83 (1924): 305–25.

Grandi, Renzo. *I monumenti dei dottori e la scultura a Bologna (1267–1348)*. Bologna, 1982.

Gratien, P. *Histoire de la fondation et de l'évolution de l'ordre des frères mineurs au XIIIè siècle*. Paris, 1928.

Green Labunski, Meagan. "Friars in the City: Mendicant Architecture and Pious Practice in Medieval Verona, c. 1220–c. 1375." Ph.D. thesis, Duke University, 2010.

Grevet, René. "L'Élection de sépulture d'après les testaments audomarois de la fin du XVè siècle." *Revue du Nord* 65 (1983): 353–60.

Grundmann, H. *Religiöse Bewegungen im Mittelalter: Untersuchungen über die geschichtlichen Zusammenhänge zwischen der Ketzerei, den Bettelorden und der religiösen Frauenbewegung um 12. und 13. Jahrhundert und über die geschichtlichen Grundlagen der deutschen Mystik*. Darmstad, 1970. (English ed.: *Religious Movements in the Middle Ages*, trans. S. Rowan, Notre Dame, Ind., 1995.)

Grzybkowski, Andrzej. "Das Problem der Langchöre in Bettelordenskirchen im östlichen Mitteleuropa

des 13. Jahrhunderts." *Architettura* 13, no. 2 (1983a): 152–68.

—. "Early Mendicant Architecture in Central-Eastern Europe: The Present State of Research." *Arte medievale* 1 (1983b): 135–56.

—. "An Early Gothic Franciscan Church in Cracow." *Arte medievale* 2 (1993): 81–6.

Guenée, Bernard. "Histoire, mémoire, écriture: Contribution à une étude des lieux communs." *Comptes rendus de l'Académie des Inscriptions et Belles-lettres* 127 (1983): 441–56.

Guidoni, Enrico, ed. *Storia della Città 9: Architettura e urbanistica degli ordini mendicanti*. Milan, 1976.

—. "Città e ordini mendicanti: Il ruolo dei conventi nella crescita e nella progettazione urbana del XIII e XIV secolo." *Quaderni medievali* IV (1977): 69–106.

Guiraud, Jean. *Cartulaire de Notre-Dame de Prouille: Précédé d'une étude sur l'albigéisme languedocien aux XIIè et XIIIè siècles*. Paris, 1907.

—. *Histoire de l'inquisition au Moyen Âge, 2: L'Inquisition au XIIIè siècle en France, en Espagne et en Italie*. Paris, 1938.

Gurney Salter, E. *The Coming of the Friars Minor to England and Germany: Being the Chronicles of Brother Thomas of Eccleston and Brother Jordan of Giano*. Toronto, 1926.

Gurrieri, Francesco. *La fabbrica di San Francesco in Prato*. Prato, 1968.

Gwynn, Aubrey. "Richard FitzRalph, Archbishop of Armagh." *Studies: An Irish Quarterly Review* 22, no. 87 (1933): 389–405.

—. "Archbishop FitzRalph and the Friars." *Studies: An Irish Quarterly Review* 26, no. 101 (1937): 50–67.

Gy, Pierre-Marie. "Liturgies occidentales: De Grégoire VII au Concile de Trente." In *Dictionnaire de spiritualité ascétique et mystique: Doctrine et histoire*. Paris, 1976, 906–7.

Haensch, Rudolf. "Le Financement de la construction des églises pendant l'antiquité tardive e l'évergétisme antique." *Antiquité tardive* 14 (2006): 47–58.

Haines, M. "The Sacristy of Santa Maria Novella in Florence: The History of Its Functions and Furnishings." *Memorie Dominicane* n.s. 11 (1980): 576–626; n.s. 12 (1981): 269–86.

Haines, M., and Lucio Riccetti, eds. *Opera: Carattere e ruolo delle fabbriche cittadine fino all'inizio dell'età moderna: Atti della Tavola rotonda, Villa i Tatti, Firenze, 3 aprile 1991*. Florence, 1996.

Hall, Marcia. "The 'Ponte' in Santa Maria Novella: The Problem of the Rood Screen in Italy." *Journal of the Warburg and the Courtauld Institutes* 37 (1974a): 157–73.

—. "The Tramezzo in Santa Croce, Florence, Reconstructed." *Art Bulletin* 56 (1974b): 325–41.

—. "The Italian Rood Screen: Some Implications for Liturgy and Function." In *Essays Presented to Myron P. Gilmore*, ed. S. Bertelli and G. Ramakus. Florence, 1978, 213–18.

Hallam, E. M. "Royal Burial and the Cult of Kingship in France and England, 1066–1330." *Journal of Medieval History* 8, no. 4 (1982): 359–80.

Hamesse, Jaqueline. "La Prédication universitaire." In *La predicazione dei frati dalla metà del '200 alla fine del '300: Atti del XXII convegno internazionale, Assisi, 13–15 ottobre 1994*, ed. E. Menestò. Spoleto, 1995, 49–79.

Hanawalt, Barbara A., and Michal Kobialka, eds. *Medieval Practices of Space*. Minneapolis, 2000.

Hassall, T. G., C. E. Hapin, and M. Mellor. "Excavations in St. Ebbe's, Oxford, 1967–1976: Part 1: Late Saxon and Medieval Domestic Occupation and Tenements, and the Medieval Greyfriars." *Oxoniensia* 54 (1989): 72–277.

Hecker, Norbert. *Bettelorden und Bürgerturm: Konflikt und Kooperation in deutschen Städten des Spätmittelalters*. Frankfurt am Main, 1981.

Héliot, P. "La Filiation de l'église haute à Saint François d'Assise." *Bulletin monumental* 126 (1968): 127–40.

—. "Sur Les Églises gothiques des ordres mendiants en Italie Centrale." *Bulletin monumental* 130 (1972): 231–5.

Herde, Peter. "Matteo d'Acquasparta cardinale." In *Matteo d'Acquasparta: Francescano, filosofo, politico; Atti del XXIX convegno storico internazionale, Todi, 11–14 ottobre 1992*, ed. Centro Italiano di Studi sul Basso medioevo. Spoleto, 1993, 79–108.

Herklotz, Ingo. *Sepulcra e monumenta del medioevo: Studi sull'arte sepolcrale in Italia*. Rome, 1985.

Herman, Emil. " 'Chiese private' e diritto di fondazione negli ultimi secoli dell'impero bizantino." *Orientalia christiana periodica* 12 (1946): 302–21.

Hertlein, Edgar. *Die Basilica San Francesco in Assisi*. Florence, 1964.

Hiestand, R. "L'arcivescovo Ubaldo e i pisani alla terza crociata alla luce di una nuova testimonianza." *Bollettino storico pisano* 58 (1989): 37–51.

Hill, Joyce, and Mary Swan, eds. *The Community, the Family and the Saint: Patterns of Power in Early Medieval Europe; Selected Proceedings of the International Medieval Congress, University of Leeds, 4–7 July 1994 and 10–13 July 1995*. Turnhout, 1998.

Hindin, Seth Adam. "Gothic Goes East: Mendicant Architecture in Bohemia and Moravia, 1226–1278." In *Bettelorden in Mitteleuropa: Geschichte, Kunst, Spiritualität*, ed. H. Specht and R. Andraschek-Holzer. St. Polten, 2008, 370–405.

Hinnebusch, William A. "The Pre-Reformation Sites of the Oxford Blackfriars." *Oxonensia* 3 (1938): 57–84.

—. *The Early English Friars Preachers*. Rome, 1951.

—. "Poverty in the Order of Preachers." *Catholic Historical Review* 45 (1959–60): 439–53.

—. *The History of the Dominican Order*. Vol. 1: *Origins and Growth to 1500*. New York, 1966.

—. *The History of the Dominican Order*. Vol. 2: *Intellectual and Cultural Life to 1500*. New York, 1973.

Holmes, George. "The Emergence of an Urban Ideology at Florence c. 1250–1450." *Transactions of the Royal Historical Society*, ser. 5, 23 (1973): 111–34.

—. *Florence, Rome and the Origins of the Renaissance*. Oxford, 1988.

Hood, William. "Saint Dominic's Manners of Praying: Gestures in Fra Angelico's Cell Frescoes at San Marco." *Art Bulletin* 68, no. 2 (1986): 195–206.

Howard, Peter Francis. *Beyond the Written Word: Preaching and Theology in the Florence of Archbishop Antoninus, 1427–1459*. Florence, 1995.

Huber, Raphael M. *A Documented History of the Franciscan Order (1182–1517)*. Washington, D.C., 1944.

Hubert, Étienne. "Élection de sépulture et fondation de chapelle funéraire à Rome au XIVè siècle: Donation et concession de l'espace sacré." In *La parrocchia nel Medio Evo: Economia, scambi, solidarietà*, ed. A. Paravicini Bagliani and V. Pasche. *Italia Sacra*, vol. 53. Rome, 1995a, 209–27.

—. "Gestion immobilière, propriété dissociée et seigneuries foncières à Rome aux XIIIè et XIVè siècles." In *Le Sol et l'immeuble: Les Formes dissociées de propriété immobilière dans les villes de France et d'Italie (XIIè–XIXè siècle)*, ed. O. Faron and É. Hubert. Rome, 1995b, 185–205.

—. "Propriété ecclésiastique et croissance urbaine (à propos de l'Italie centro-septentrionale, XIIè–début du XIVè siècle)." In *Gli spazi economici della chiesa nell'occidente mediterraneo (secoli XII–metà XIV), Sedicesimo convegno internazionale di studi, Pistoia, 16–19 maggio 1997*, ed. Centro italiano di studi di storia e d'arte. Pistoia, 1999, 125–55.

Hubert, Hans W. "Architettura e urbanistica nel Duecento a Bologna." In *Duecento: Forme e colori del medioevo a Bologna; Bologna, Museo Civico Archeologico*, exh. cat., ed. M. Medica and S. Tumidei. Venice, 2000, 3–24.

Hueck, Irene. "Stifter und Patronatsrecht: Dokumente zu zwei Kapellen der Bardi." *Mitteilungen des Kunsthistorischen Institutes in Florenz* 20 (1976): 263–70.

—. "Der Lettner der Unterkirche von San Francesco in Assisi." *Mitteilungen des Kunst-historisches Institutes in Florenz* 28 (1984): 173–202.

Hughes, Diane Owen. "Sumptuary Laws and Human Relations in Renaissance Italy." In *Disputes and Settlements: Law and Human Relations in the West*, ed. J. Bossy. Cambridge, 1983, 69–94.

Humbert of Romans. *Treatise on Preaching*, ed. W. M. Conlon, trans. Dominican students of the Province of St. Joseph. Westminster, Md., 1951.

——. *Treatise on Preaching*, ed. W. M. Conlon. London, 1955.

——. *Opera de vita regulari, 2: Expositio in constitutiones. Instructiones de officiis ordinis. De eruditione praedicatorum. Epistolae encyclicae*, ed. J. J. Berthier. Rome, 1888–9, repr. Turin, 1956.

Humphreys, S. C., and H. King, eds. *Mortality and Immortality: The Anthropology and Archaeology of Death*. London, 1981.

Iacobini, Antonio. "L'architettura religiosa." In *Storia di Venezia*, ed. R. Pallucchini. Rome, 1994, 185–235.

Ianella, Cecilia. *Prediche inedite (dal ms. Laurenziano, Acquisti e Doni 290)*. Pisa, 1997.

Iannelli, Pio. *Lo studio teologico OFMConv nel San Lorenzo Maggiore di Napoli: Cenni storici e serie dei reggenti, lettori e studenti (1482–1990)*. Rome, 1994.

Imperato, Alberto. "Il Francescanesimo nel territorio di Principato nel sec. XIII." *Archivum Franciscanum Historicum* 63 (1970): 241–7.

Improta, Andrea. "Dal pulpito al sepolcro. Contributo per l'iconografia di San Pietro Martire da Verona tra XIII e XIV secolo." *Porticum. Revista d'Estudis Medievals*, vol. 1 (2011): 105–19.

Inga, G. "Gli insediamenti mendicanti a Cortona." *Storia della città* 9 (1978): 44–55.

Ingold, T. "The Temporality of the Landscape." *World Archaeology* 25, no. 2 (1993): 152–74.

Innocenti, Marina Soriani. "San Francesco e i francescani nella predicazione dell'Arcivescovo di Pisa Federico Visconti (1253–1277)." In *Il francescanesimo a Pisa (secc. XIII–XIV) e la missione del beato Agnello in Inghilterra a Canterbury e Cambridge (1224–1236): Atti del convegno di studi, Pisa, Chiesa di San Francesco 10–11 marzo 2001*, ed. O. Banti and M. Soriani Innocenti. Pisa, 2003, 73–88.

Jacquet, L. "Les Cordeliers à Beaune, 1239–1503." *Mémoires de la Société d'histoire et d'archéologie de Beaune* 75 (1994): 57–109.

Jäggi, Carola. *Frauenklöster im Spätmittelalter: Die Kirchen der Klarissen und Dominikanerinnen im 13. und 14. Jahrhundert*. Petersberg, 2006.

James, John. *The Template Makers of the Paris Basin: Toichological Techniques for Identifying the Pioneers of the Gothic Movement with an Examination of Art-Historical Methodology*. Leura, Australia, 1989.

Jaton, Philippe. "Un Sujet de réflexion: La Notion 'd'original' en architecture, à l'image de trois églises des Ordres Mendiants." In *Das Denkmal und die Zeit: Festschrift für Alfred A. Schmid*, ed. B. Anderes. Luzerne, 1990, 158–65.

Johnson, Allan Chester, Paul Robinson Coleman-Norton, Clyde Pharr, and Frank Card Bourne, eds. *Ancient Roman Statutes: A Translation*. Austin, Tex., 1961.

Jones, Phillip J. *The Italian City State: From Commune to Signoria*. Oxford, 1997.

Jordan of Saxony. *Libellus de Principiis Ordinis Praedicatorum*, ed. H. C. Scheeben. Vol. 16: *Monumenta Ordinis Fratrum Praedicatorum Historica*. Rome, 1935, 1–88.

——. *On the Beginnings of the Order of Preachers*, ed. and trans. S. Tugwell. Chicago, 1982.

Joubert, Fabienne. "Parigi: Secolo 14°." In *Enciclopedia dell'arte medievale*, vol. 9, ed. A. M. Romanini et al. Rome, 1998, 203–16.

Kaeppeli, T. *Acta Capitulorum Provincialium Provinciae Romanae*. Vol. 20: *Monumenta Ordinis Fratrum Praedicatorum*. Rome, 1941.

Kaeppeli, T., and Emilio Panella, eds. *Scriptores Ordinis Praedicatorum Medii Aevi*. Rome, 1970–93.

Kalina, Pavel. "Giovanni Pisano, the Dominicans, and the Origins of the 'Crucifixi Dolorosi.'" *Artibus et Historiae* 24, no. 47 (2003): 81–101.

Karkov, Catherine E., Kelley M. Wickham-Crowley, and Bailey K. Young, eds. *Spaces of the Living and the Dead: An Archaeological Dialogue*. Exeter, 1999.

Kent, F. W. *Household and Lineage in Renaissance Florence*. Princeton, N.J., 1977.

Kent, F. W., J. C. Eade, and P. Simons. *Patronage, Art and Society in Renaissance Italy*. Oxford, 1987.

Kienzle, Beverly Mayne. "The Sermon." *Typologie des sources du Moyen Âge occidental* (2000): 81–3.

Kingsford, C. L. *The Archaeology of Medieval London*. Aberdeen, 1915.

Kirschner, Julius, and Raymond De Roover, eds. *Business, Banking, and Economic Thought in Late Medieval and Early Modern Europe*. Chicago, 1974.

Klebanoff, Randi. "Sacred Magnificence: Civic Intervention and the Arca of San Domenico in Bologna." *Renaissance Studies* 13, no. 4 (1999): 412–29.

Kleefisch-Jobst, U. *Die römische Dominikanerkirche Santa Maria sopra Minerva: Ein Beitrag zur Architektur der Bettelorden in Mittelitalien*. Munster, 1991.

Kleinschmidt, B. *Die Basilica San Francesco in Assisi*. Berlin, 1915.

Kölmel, W. "Apologia Pauperum: Die Armutslehre Bonaventuras da Bagnoregio als soziale Theorie." *Historisches Jahrbuch* 94 (1974): 46–68.

Koudelka, Vladimir J. "Le 'Monasterium Tempuli' et la fondation dominicaine de San Sisto." *Archivum Fratrum Praedicatorum* 31 (1961): 5–61.

——. *Monumenta Diplomatica S. Dominici*. Vol. 25: *Monumenta Ordinis Fratrum Praedicatorum Historica*. Rome, 1966.

—. "Il fondo 'libri' nell'archivo generale dell'ordine domenicano." Pts. 1 and 2. *Archivum Fratrum Praedicatorum* 38–9 (1968): 99–147; (1969): 173–217.

Kraus, Henry. "Notre-Dame's Vanished Medieval Glass." Pts. 1 and 2. *Gazette des Beaux-Arts* 68–9 (1966): 131–48; (1967): 65–78.

—. "New Documents for Notre-Dame's Early Chapels." *Gazette des Beaux-Arts* 74 (1969): 121–34.

—. "Plan of the Early Chapels of Notre-Dame de Paris." *Gazette des Beaux-Arts* 76 (1970): 271.

Krautheimer, R. *Die Kirchen der Bettelorden in Deutschland*. Cologne, 1925.

Kreytenberg, Gerd. "L'Enfer d'Orcagna: La Première Peinture monumentale après les Chants de Dante." *Gazette des Beaux-Arts* 114, no. 131 (1989): 243–62.

—. *Andrea di Cione: Ein universeller Künstler der Gotik in Florenz*. Mainz, 2000.

Krönig, Wolfgang. "Hallenkirchen in Mittelitalien." *Römisches Jahrbuch für Kunstgeschichte* 2 (1938): 1–139.

—. "Caratteri dell'architettura degli ordini mendicanti in Umbria." In *Storia e arte in Umbria nell'età communale: Atti del VI convengo di studi Umbri*, ed. F. Ugolini. Perugia, 1971, 165–98.

Krüger, Jürgen. *San Lorenzo Maggiore in Neapel: Eine Franziskanerkirche zwischen Ordensideal und Herrschaftsarchitektur; Studien und Materialen zur Baukunst der ersten Anjou-Zeit*. Werl, 1986.

—. "San Lorenzo Maggiore, gli Angiò e Bartolomeo da Capua: appunti per una storia della construczione." *Le chiese di San Lorenzo e San Domenico*, ed. S. Romano and N. Bock. Naples, 2004, 51–60.

Kurmann-Schwarz, Brigitte. "Das 10000-Ritter-Fenster im Berner Münster und seine Auftraggeber: Überlegungen zu den Schrift- und Bildquellen sowie zum Kult der Heiligen in Bern." *Zeitschrift für Schweizerische Archäologie und Kunstgeschichte* 49 (1992): 40–54.

—. "Die Sorge um die Memoria: Das Habsburger Grab in Königsfelden im Lichte seinter Bildausstattung." *Kunst & Architektur in der Schweiz* 50 (1999): 12–23.

La coscienza cittadina nei comuni italiani del Duecento: Convegno del Centro di studi sulla spiritualità medievale dell'Università degli studi di Perugia, Todi, 11–14 ottobre 1970. Vol. 11. Todi, 1972.

Ladis, Andrew. "The Velluti Chapel in Santa Croce, Florence." *Apollo* 120 (1984): 238–44.

Lambert, Chiara. "L'Entrée des morts dans les villes d'Italie du Nord." In *Archéologie du cimitière chrétien: Actes du 2e colloque A.R.C.H.E.A., Orléans, 29 septembre–1 octobre 1994*, ed. H. Galinié and E. Zadora-Rio. Tours, 1996, 31–5.

Lambert, Élie. "L'Église et le couvent des Jacobins de Toulouse et l'architecture dominicaine en France." *Bulletin monumental* 104 (1946): 141–86.

Lambert, Malcolm D. *Franciscan Poverty: The Doctrine of the Absolute Poverty of Christ and the Apostles in the Franciscan Order, 1210–1323*. London, 1961.

Lambertini, Roberto. *Apologia e crescita dell'identità francescana (1255–1279)*. Rome, 1990.

—. " 'Pecunia, possessio, proprietas' alle origini di minori e predicatori: Osservazioni sul filo della terminologia." In *L'economia dei conventi dei frati minori e predicatori fino alla metà del Trecento: Atti del XXXI convegno internazionale, Assisi, 9–11 ottobre 2003*, ed. E. Menestò. Spoleto, 2004, 3–42.

Lambrick, George, and Humphrey Woods. "Excavations on the Second Site of the Dominican Priory, Oxford." *Oxoniensia* 41 (1976): 168–231.

—. "Further Excavations on the Second Site of the Dominican Priory, Oxford." *Oxoniensia* 50 (1985): 131–208.

Lanaro, Paola. "Guild Statutes in the Early Modern Age: Norms and Practices; Preliminary Results in the Veneto Area." In *Guilds, Markets and Work Regulations in Italy, 16th–19th Centuries*, ed. A. Guenzi, P. Massa, and F. Piola Caselli. Aldershot, 1998, 191–207.

—. "Workshops and the Town: Artisans and Places of Work in Verona (15th Century)." In *Shaping Urban Identity in Late Medieval Europe*, ed. M. Boone and P. Stabel. Louvain-Apeldoorn, 2000, 137–69.

—. "Economic Space and Urban Policies: Fairs and Markets in the Italy of the Early Modern Age." *Journal of Urban History* 30, no. 1 (2003): 37–49.

—. "Corporations et confréries: Les Étrangers et le marché du travail à Venise (XVè–XVIIIè siècles)." *Histoire urbaine* 21 (2008): 31–48.

Lanaro, Paola, and Gian Maria Varanini. "Funzioni economiche della dote nell'Italia centro-settentrionale (tardo medioevo/inzi età moderna)." In *La famiglia nell'economia europea secc. XIII–XVIII: The Economic Role of the Family in the European Economy from the 13th to 18th centuries; Atti della "Quarantesima Settimana di Studi," Prato, 6–10 aprile 2008*, ed. S. Cavaciocchi, Florence, 2009, 81–102.

Landini, Lawrence C. *The Causes of the Clericalization of the Order of Friars Minor, 1209–1260, in the Light of Early Franciscan Sources*. Chicago, 1968.

Langholm, Odd. *Economics in the Medieval Schools: Wealth, Exchange, Value, Money and Usury according to the Paris Theological Tradition, 1200–1350*. Leiden, N.Y. and Cologne, 1992.

Lansing, Carol. *Power & Purity: Cathar Heresy in Medieval Italy*. Oxford, 1998.

Lara, Jaime. *City, Temple, Stage: Eschatological Archi-tecture and Liturgical Theatrics in New Spain.* Notre Dame, Ind., 2004.

Larner, John. *Culture and Society in Italy 1290–1420.* London, 1971.

Laughlin, M. F., G. Marcil, and D. Monti, eds. *Works of Saint Bonaventure 5: St. Bonaventure's Writings Concerning the Franciscan Order.* New York, 1994.

Laurent, M.-Hyacinthus. *Monumenta Historica S. P. N. Dominici.* Vol. 15: *Monumenta Ordinis Fratrum Praedicatorum Historica.* Rome, 1933.

Lauwers, Michel. *La Mémoire des ancêtres, le souci des morts: Morts, rites et société au Moyen Âge, Diocèse de Liège, XIè–XIIIè siècles.* Paris, 1997.

Lawrence, C. H. *The Friars: The Impact of the Early Mendicant Movement on Western Society.* London and New York, 1994.

Lea, Henry Charles. *A History of the Inquisition of the Middle Ages,* 2nd ed. 3 vols. New York, 1887–8.

——. *The Inquisition of the Middle Ages: Its Organization and Operation.* New York, 1954.

Leclercq, Jean. "Experience and Interpretation of Time in the Early Middle Ages." *Studies in Medi-eval Culture* 5 (1975): 9–19.

——. "I 'sermones' Antoniani nella storia della confessione." *Il Santo: Rivista antoniana di storia dottrina arte* 29 (1989): 333–42.

Leclercq, Henri, and F. Cabrol, eds. "Autel: Nombre d'autels." In *Dictionnaire d'arch-éologie chrétienne et de liturgie,* vol. 1, pt. 2. Paris, 1924, cols. 3185–9.

——. "Cimitière." In *Dictionnaire d'archéologie chréti-enne et de liturgie,* vol. 3, pt. 2. Paris, 1914, cols. 1625–66.

——. "La Messe." In *Dictionnaire d'archéologie chréti-enne et de liturgie,* vol. 2, pt. 1. Paris, 1933, 763–74.

——. "Liturgies neo-gallicanes. VII: Brevarium: Le mot et la chose." In *Dictionnaire d'archéologie chréti-enne et de liturgie,* vol. 9, pt. 2. Paris, 1930, cols. 1654–8.

——. "Sépulture." In *Dictionnaire d'archéologie chréti-enne et de liturgie,* vol. 15, pt. 1. Paris, 1950, cols. 1266–94.

Le Goff, Jacques. *Marchands et banquiers au Moyen Âge.* Paris, 1956.

——. "Métier et profession d'après les manuels de con-fesseurs du Moyen Âge." *Beiträge zum Berufsbe-wusstsein des mittelalter-lichen Menschen,* ed. P. Willpert and W. P. Eckert. *Miscellanea Medievalia* 3 (1964): 44–60.

——. "Apostolat mendiant et fait urbain dans la France médiévale: L'Implantation des ordres mendiants." *Annales économies-sociétés-civilisations* 23 (1968): 335–52.

——. "Ordres mendiants et urbanisation dans la France médiévale: État de l'enquête." *Annales économies-sociétés-civilisations* 25 (1970): 37–40, 924–46.

——. "Les Paysans et le monde rural dans la littérature du haut Moyen Âge." In *Pour un autre Moyen Âge,* ed. J. Le Goff. Paris, 1977, 131–44.

——. "The Usurer and Purgatory." In *The Dawn of Modern Banking,* ed. R. S. Lopez. New Haven and London, 1979, 25–52.

——. "Franciscanisme et modèles culturels du XIIIè siècle." In *Francescanesimo e la vita religiosa dei laici nel '200: Atti dell'VIII convegno internazionale, Assisi, 16–18 ottobre 1980,* ed. Società internazionale di studi francescani. Perugia, 1981, 85–128.

——. *The Birth of Purgatory,* trans. A. Goldhammer. Chicago, 1984.

——. *Your Money or Your Life: Economy and Religion in the Middle Ages,* trans. P. Ranum. New York, 1989.

——. *Le Moyen Âge et l'argent: Essai d'anthropologie his-torique.* Paris, 2010.

Le Goff, Jacques, and Nicolas Truong. *Une Histoire du corps au Moyen Âge.* Paris, 2003.

Leineweber, Rosemarie. "Die 'Mönchskirche' in Sal-zwedel: Erkenntnisse zur Baugeschichte von 13–15. Jahrhundert." *Archäologische Informationen aus der Altmark* 3 (1992), 68–75.

Lemaître, Jean-Loup, ed. *L'Église et la mémoire des morts dans la France médiévale.* Paris, 1986.

——. "Mort et sépulture des prieurs de la première province de Provence d'après Bernard Gui." *L'Ordre des Prêcheurs et son histoire en France mérid-ionale, Cahiers de Fanjeaux* 36 (2001): 123–97.

Lemaître, Jean-Loup, and Lemaître, N. "Un Test des solidarités paroissiales: La Prière pour les morts dans les obituaires." In *La parrocchia nel Medio Evo: Economia, scambi, solidarietà,* ed. A. Paravicini Bagliani and V. Pasche. *Italia Sacra,* vol. 53. Rome, 1995, 255–78.

Leonardi, C. "Il francescanesimo nasce all'insegna della Santa Croce." In *Santa Croce nel solco della storia,* ed. M. Rosito. Florence, 1996, 17–26.

Leoncini, Giovanni, and James Hogg. *La certosa di Firenze nei suoi rapporti con l'architettura certosina.* Salzburg, 1980.

Leone, Alfonso, and G. Capone, eds. *Ricerche sul medioevo napoletano: Aspetti e momenti della vita economica e sociale a Napoli tra decimo e quin-dicesimo secolo.* Naples, 1996.

Leone, Anna. "L'inumazione in 'spazio urbano' a Cartagine tra V e VII secolo D. C." *Antiquité tardive* 10 (2002): 233–48.

Lepelley, Claude, ed. *La Fin de la cité antique et le début de la cité médiévale.* Bari, 1996.

Le Roy Ladurie, Emmanuel. *Montaillou: The Prom-ised Land of Error,* trans. B. Bray. New York, 1978.

Lesnick, Daniel R. *Preaching in Medieval Florence: The Social World of Franciscan and Dominican Spirituality.* Athens, Ga., 1989.

Liberati, Alfredo. "Chiese, monasteri, oratori e spedali senesi." *Bollettino senese di storia patria* 64 (1957): 86–201.

Lilley, Keith. "Colonialism and Urbanism in High Medieval Europe: Identifying Morphologies of Urban Change." In *Urbanism in Medieval Europe*, ed. G. de Boe and F. Verhaeghe. Zellik, 1997, 189–204.

Little, Lester. "St. Louis' Involvement with the Friars." *Church History* 33 (1964): 125–48.

—. "Pride Goes Before Avarice: Social Change and the Vices in Latin Christendom." *American Historical Review* 76 (1971): 16–49.

—. *Religious Poverty and the Profit Economy in Medieval Europe*. Ithaca, N.Y., 1978.

—. "Les Techniques de la confession et la confession comme technique." In *Faire Croire: Modalités de la diffusion et de la réception des messages religieux du XIIè au XVè siècle*, ed. J. Boutier. Collection de l'École française de Rome, 51. Rome, 1981, 87–99.

—. " 'Imitatio Francisci': The Influence of Francis of Assisi on Late Medieval Religious Life." In *Defenders and Critics of Franciscan Life: Essays in Honor of John V. Fleming*, ed. M. F. Cusato and G. Geltner. Boston, 2009, 195–218.

Lombardi, Ferrucio. *Roma: Chiese, Conventi, Chiostri – Progetto per un inventario, 313–1925*. Rome, 1993.

Long, Jane C. "Bardi Patronage at Santa Croce in Firenze 1320–1343." Ph.D. thesis, Columbia University, 1988.

—. "Salvation Through Meditation: The Tomb Frescoes of the Holy Confessors Chapel at Santa Croce in Florence." *Gesta* 34 (1995): 77–88.

Longère, Jean. *La Prédication médiévale*. Paris, 1983.

Longhi, Andrea. *L'architettura del battistero: Storia e progetto*. Milan, 2003.

Lopez, Robert Sabatino. "Économie et architecture médiévales: Cela aurait-il tué ceci?" *Annales, économies, sociétés, civilisations* 7 (1952): 433–8.

—. *The Commercial Revolution of the Middle Ages, 950–1350*. Cambridge, 1976.

—. "The Culture of the Medieval Merchant." In *Medieval and Renaissance Studies: Proceedings of the Southeastern Institute of Medieval and Renaissance Studies, Summer 1976*, ed. D. Randall. Durham, N.C., 1979, 52–73.

Lorcin, Marie-Thérèse. "Les Clauses religieuses dans les testaments du plat pays lyonnais aux XIVè et XVè siècles." *Le Moyen Âge* 78 (1972): 287–323.

—. *Vivre et mourir en Lyonnais à la fin du Moyen Âge*. Paris, 1981.

Lorenzoni, Giovanni, and G. Alvarez Bresciani, eds. *L'edificio del Santo di Padova (Fonti e studi per la storia del Santo a Padova), 3*. Vicenza, 1981.

—. "La basilica del Santo di Padova: La struttura architettonica." In *Ordini religiosi e produzione artistica*, ed. M. T. Mazzilli Savini. Pavia, 1998, 67–75.

—. "Le chiese degli ordini mendicanti." In *L'architettura gotica veneziana*, ed. F. Valcanover and W. Wolters. Venice, 2000a, 105–8.

—. "Una possibile conclusione con particolare riferimento ai pontili." In *Il Duomo di Modena e la basilica di San Zeno a Verona*, ed. G. Lorenzoni and G. Valenzano. Verona, 2000b, 237–76.

Luisetto, Giovanni, and Antonio Sartori, eds. *Archivio Sartori: Documenti di storia e arte francescana*. Padua, 1983.

Lupi, C. "Sulle origini del Camposanto." *Notizie d'arte* 2 (1910): 10–20.

Luzzati, Michele. "Le origini di una famiglia nobile pisana: Roncioni nei secoli XII e XIII." *Bolletino senese di storia patria* 73–5 (1966–8): 60–118.

—. "I registri notarili pisani dal XIII al XV secolo." In *Sources of Social History: Private Acts of the Late Middle Ages*, ed. P. Brezzi and E. Lee. Toronto, 1984, 7–22.

—. "Simone Saltarelli Arcivescovo di Pisa (1323–1342) e gli affreschi del maestro del Trionfo della Morte." *Annali della Scuola Normale Superiore di Pisa* n.s. 3, 18 (1988): 1645–64.

Magro, Pasquale M. *La basilica sepolcrale di San Francesco in Assisi: Percorsi storico-artistici, quadri concettuali*. Assisi, 1991.

Mäkinen, Virpi. *Property Rights in the Late Medieval Discussion on Franciscan Poverty*. Leuven, 2001.

Mallory, Michael, and Gaudenz Freuler. "Sano di Pietro's Bernardino Altar-Piece for the Compagnia della Vergine in Siena." *Burlington Magazine* 133 (1991): 186–92.

Mancini, F. F., and A. Scotti, eds. *La basilica di Santa Maria degli Angeli*. Perugia, 1989.

Mancini, P. "L'insediamento dei mendicanti a Firenze." *Storia della città* 23 (1982): 75–82.

Mandonnet, Pierre, and H.-M. Vicaire, eds. *Saint Dominique, l'idée, l'homme, et l'oeuvre*. 2 vols. Paris, 1937–8.

Manselli, Raoul. "Divergences parmi les mineurs d'Italie et de France méridionale." *Les Mendiants en Pays d'Oc au XIIIè siècle, Cahiers de Fanjeaux* 8 (1973): 355–74.

—. "La clericalizzazione dei Minori e San Bonaventura." In *San Bonaventura francescano: Atti del XIV convegno del centro di studi sulla spiritualità medievale, 14–17 ottobre, 1973*, ed. Centro di studi sulla spiritualità medivale. Todi, 1974, 183–208.

Marani, Giuseppe, and Luigi Marioli. *San Francesco al Prato: Dall'abbandono al ripristino*. Perugia, 1977.

Marantonio Sguerzo, E. *Evoluzione storico-giuridica dell'istituzione della sepoltura ecclesiastica.* Milano, 1976.

—. "Sepultura." In *Dizionario degli istituti di perfezione,* vol. 8, ed. G. Pelliccia and G. Rocca. Rome, 1988, 1281–6.

Martin, Alan R. *Franciscan Architecture in England.* Manchester, 1937.

Martin, Hervé. "Deux Predicateurs du XVè siècle parlent de la Mort." In *La Mort au Moyen Âge: Actes de 6è congrès de la Société des historiens médiévistes de l'enseignement supérieur publique,* ed. B. Guillermain, P. Chaunu, and F. Thiriet. Strasbourg, 1975a, 103–24.

—. *Les Ordres mendiants en Bretagne (vers 1230–vers 1530).* Paris, 1975b.

—. *Le Métier de prédicateur en France septentrionale à la fin du Moyen Âge, 1350–1520.* Paris, 1988.

Martindale, Andrew. "Patrons and Minders: The Intrusion of the Secular into Sacred Spaces in the Late Middle Ages." *The Church and the Arts: Papers read at the 1990 Summer Meeting and the 1991 Winter Meeting of the Ecclesiastical History Society,* ed. D. Wood. Studies in Church History, 28 (1992): 143–78.

Martines, Ruggero. *La Cattedrale di Ravello e i suoi pulpiti.* Viterbo, 2001.

Mathis, B. *Die Privilegien des Franziskanerordens bis zum Konzil von Vienne (1311).* Paderborn, 1927.

Matsuda, Takami. *Death and Purgatory in Middle English Didactic Poetry.* Cambridge, 1997.

Mazzilli Savini, Maria Teresa, ed. *Ordini religiosi e produzione artistica.* Pavia, 1998.

McGovern, J. F. "The Rise of New Economic Attitudes – Economic Humanism, Economic Nationalism – During the Later Middle Ages and the Renaissance, A.D. 1200–1550." *Traditio* 26 (1970): 217–53.

McLaughlin, R. Emmet. "The Word Eclipsed? Preaching in the Early Middle Ages." *Traditio* 46 (1991): 77–122.

Meersseman, Gilles Gérard. "L'Architecture dominicaine au XIIIè siècle: Législation et pratique." *Archivum Fratrum Praedicatorum* 16 (1946): 136–90.

—. "Les Débuts de l'ordre des Frères Prêcheurs dans le comté de Flandre (1224–1280)." *Archivum Fratrum Praedicatorum* 17 (1947): 5–40.

—. "Le origini del tipo di chiesa umbro-toscano degli ordini mendicanti." In *Il gotico a Pistoia nei suoi rapporti con l'arte gotica italiana: Atti del II convegno internazionale di studi, Pistoia, 24–30 aprile 1966,* ed. Centro Italiano di studi di storia e d'arte. Rome, 1972, 63–77.

Meier, H.-R. "Santa Chiara in Assisi: Architektur und Funktion im Schatten von San Francesco." *Arte medievale* 2 (1990): 151–78.

Melkinas, Anthony. *The Corpus of the Miniatures in the Manuscripts of the Decretum Gratiani.* Columbus, Ohio, 1975.

Menache, Sophia. "Réflexions sur quelques papes français du bas moyen âge: Un Problème d'origine." *Revue d'Histoire Ecclésiastique* 81, nos. 1–2 (1986): 117–31.

Mencherini, S. "Constitutiones generales Ordinis Fratrum Minorum a Capitolo Perpiniani anno 1331 celebrato, editae." *Archivum Franciscanum Historicum* 2 (1909): 276–92, 412–30, and 575–98.

Meneghini, Roberto, and Riccardo Santangeli Valenzani. "Sepolture intramuranee e paesaggio urbano a Roma tra V e VII secolo." In *La storia economica di Roma nell'Alto medioevo alla luce dei recenti scavi archeologici,* ed. L. Paroli and P. Delogu. Florence, 1992, 89–111.

—. "Sepolture intramuranee a Roma tra V e VII secolo d.C.: Aggiornamenti e considerazioni." *Archeologia medievale* 22 (1995): 283–90.

Menestò, Enrico, ed. *La predicazione dei frati dalla metà del '200 alla fine del '300: Atti del XXII convegno internazionale, Assisi, 13–15 ottobre 1994.* Spoleto, 1995.

—. *Dalla penitenza all'ascolto delle confessioni: Il ruolo dei frati mendicanti; Atti del XXIII convegno internazionale, Assisi 12–14 ottobre, 1995.* Spoleto, 1996.

—. *Il papato duecentesco e gli ordini mendicanti: Atti del XXV convegno internazionale, Assisi 13–14 febbraio, 1998.* Spoleto, 1998.

—, ed. *L'economia dei conventi dei frati minori e predicatori fino alla metà del Trecento: Atti del XXXI convegno internazionale, Assisi, 9–11 novembre 2003.* Spoleto, 2004.

—, ed. *Frati minori e l'inquisizione: Atti del XXXIII conuegno internazionale, Assisi 6–8 ottobre, 2005.* Spoleto, 2006.

—, ed. *Angelo Clareno Francescano: Atti del XXXIV convegno internazionale Assisi 5–7 ottobre, 2006.* Spoleto, 2007.

Merlo, Riccardo. "La piazza San Domenico: Le vicende dopo il 1600." In *Archeologia medievale a Bologna: Gli scavi nel Convento di San Domenico; Bologna, Museo Civico Archeologico,* exh. cat., ed. S. Gelichi and R. Merlo. Bologna, 1987, 133–40.

Merotto Ghedini, Monica. *La chiesa di Sant'Agostino in Padova: Storia e ricostruzione di un monumento scomparso.* Padua, 1995.

—. "Santi Giovanni e Paolo." In *L'architettura gotica veneziana,* ed. F. Valcanover and W. Wolters. Venice, 2000, 115–22.

—. "Il tramezzo nella chiesa dei santi Giovanni e Paolo a Venezia." In *De lapidibus sententiae: Scritti di storia dell'arte per Giovanni Lorenzoni*, ed. G. Lorenzoni, G. Valenzano, and T. Franco. Padua, 2002, 257–62.

Mesini, C. "San Francesco d'Assisi a Bologna." *Studi francescani* 80 (1983): 207–19.

Michaud, Francine. "Liaisons particulières? Franciscains et testatrices à Marseille (1248–1320)." *Annales du Midi* 104, no. 197 (1992): 7–18.

Middledorf Kosegarten, Antje. "Beiträge zur sienesischen Reliefkunst des Trecento." *Mitteilungen des Kunsthistorischen Institutes in Florenz* 12 (1966): 207–24.

—. "Die erste Marmorstatue des heiligen Franziskus." *Wiener Jahrbuch für Kunstgeschichte* 46–7 (1993–4): 495–506.

—. "The Origins of Artistic Competition in Italy." In *Lorenzo Ghiberti nel suo tempo: Atti del convegno internazionale di studi (Firenze 1978)* ed. Istituto nazionale di studi sul Rinascimento. Florence, 1980.

—. "Situazioni conflittuali nei rapporti tra artisti, committenti e operai intorno al 1300." In *Opera: Carattere e ruolo delle fabbriche cittadine fino all'inizio dell'età moderna*, ed. M. Haines and L. Riccetti. Florence, 1991, 371–95.

Miele, M. "Appunti sui Domenicani in Puglia e nel Mezzogiorno." *Nicolaus studi storici* 3 (1992): 145–51.

Milanesi, Gaetano. *Nuovi documenti per la storia dell'arte toscana dal XII al XV secolo*. Soest, 1973.

Miller, Maureen. *The Bishop's Palace: Architecture and Authority in Medieval Italy*. Ithaca, N.Y., 2000.

Mistretta, Maria Beatrice, ed. *Lo spazio dell'Umiltà: Atti del convegno di studi sull'edilizia dell'ordine dei minori, Fara Sabina 3–6 novembre 1982*. Fara Sabina, 1984.

Moisè, F. *Santa Croce di Firenze: Illustrazione storico-artistica*. Florence, 1845.

Mollat, Michel. *The Poor in the Middle Ages: An Essay in Social History*. New Haven and London, 1986.

Montagnes, Benoît. "L'Attitude des Prêcheurs à l'égard des oeuvres d'art." *La Naissance et l'essor du gothique méridional du XIIIe siècle, Cahiers de Fanjeaux* 9 (1974): 87–99.

—. "Les Prêcheurs d'Arles." *Congrès archéologique de France* 134 (1976): 480–501.

—. *L'Architecture dominicaine en Provence*. Paris, 1979.

Monti, Dominic, ed. *St. Bonaventure's Writings Concerning the Franciscan Order*. New York, 1994.

Moorman, John R. H. *A History of the Franciscan Order from its Origins to the Year 1517*. Oxford, 1968.

—. *Medieval Franciscan Houses*. New York, 1983.

Moretti, Italo. "Ordini mendicanti e organizzazione dello spazio urbano nelle città toscane." In *Gli ordini mendicanti a Pistoia (secc. XIII–XV): Atti del convegno di studi, Pistoia 12–13 maggio 2000*, ed. R. Nelli. Pistoia, 2001, 55–68.

Morris, Ian. "Cemeteries." In *The Oxford Classical Dictionary*, ed. S. Hornblower and A. Spawforth. Oxford, 1996, 307.

Morrisson, Cécile. "Coin Usage and Exchange Rates in Badoer's 'Libro dei Conti'." *Dumbarton Oaks Papers* 55 (2001): 217–40.

Moskowitz, Anita. "Giovanni di Balduccio's Arca di San Pietro Martire: Form and Function." *Arte lombarda* 96–7 (1991): 7–18.

—. "On the Sources and Meaning of Nicola Pisano's Arca di San Domenico in Bologna." In *Verrochio and Late Quattrocento Italian Sculpture*, ed. S. Bule, A. P. Darr, and F. Gioffredi Superbi. Florence, 1992: 271–90.

—. *Italian Gothic Sculpture: c. 1250–c. 1400*. Cambridge, 2001.

Motta, Luigi, and Armando Novasconi. *Il tempio di San Francesco in Lodi*. Milan, 1958.

Muessig, Carolyn. *Preacher, Sermon and Audience in the Middle Ages*. Leiden and Boston, 2002.

Mulchahey, Marian Michèle. *"First the Bow is Bent in Study": Dominican Education Before 1350*. Toronto, 1998.

Mundy, John Hine. *Liberty and Political Power in Toulouse, 1050–1230*. New York, 1954.

Murray, A. "Archbishop and Mendicants in Thirteenth-century Pisa." In *Stellung und Wirksamkeit der Bettelorden in der städtischen Gesellschaft*, ed. K. Elm. Berlin, 1981, 19–75.

—. "The Medieval Inquisition: An Instrument of Secular Politics?" *Peritia: Journal of the Medieval Academy of Ireland* 5 (1986): 161–200.

Murray, Alan V. "Ethnic Identity in the Crusader States: The Frankish Race and the Settlement of Outremer." In *Concepts of National Identity in the Middle Ages*, ed. S. Forde. Leeds, 1995, 59–73.

Nannini Berti, P. "Il complesso del convento e chiesa di San Francesco in Prato." *Bollettino del Centro di studi per la storia dell'architettura* 28 (1982): 9–98.

Nathan, Johannes. "Neue Literatur zu Orsanmichele in Florenz." *Zeitschrift für Kunstgeschichte* 62, no. 4 (1999): 541–70.

Naz, R. "Sépulcre." In *Dictionnaire de droit canonique*, ed. R. Naz. Vol. 7 (1965): 971–3.

Neff, Amy. "Lesser Brothers: Franciscan Mission and Identity at Assisi." *Art Bulletin* 88 (2006): 676–706.

Neidiger, Bernhard. "The Basle Dominicans Between Town and Province." *Mendicants, Military Orders, and Regionalism in Medieval Europe*, ed. J. Sarnowsky. Aldershot and Brookfield, Vt., 1999, 131–41.

Nelli, R. "Clero secolare e ordini mendicanti a Pistoia nei secoli XIII–XIV." *Gli ordini mendicanti a Pistoia (secc. XIII–XV): Atti del convegno di studi, Pistoia, 12–13 maggio 2000.* Pistoia, 2001, 115–40.

Nelson, Benjamin. "The Usurer and the Merchant Prince: Italian Businessmen and the Ecclesiastical Law of Restitution, 1100–1550." *Journal of Economic History* 7 (1947): 104–22.

Neri Lusanna, Enrica. "Maso di Banco e la cappella Bardi di San Silvestro." In *Maso di Banco: La cappella di San Silvestro*, ed. Acidini Luchinat and E. Neri Lusanna. Milan, 1998, 17–51.

—. "La pittura del Trecento in Santa Croce." In *Alla riscoperta delle chiese di Firenze*. Vol. 3: *Santa Croce*, ed. T. Verdon et al. Florence, 2004, 33–63.

Nicholas, D. *The Growth of the Medieval City*. New York, 1997.

Nicolini, Ugolino. "I frati minori da eredi a esecutori testamentari." In *Nolens intestatus decedere: Il testamento come fonte della storia religiosa e sociale*, ed. A. Bartoli Langeli. Perugia, 1985, 31–3.

Nimmo, Duncan. *Reform and Division in the Medieval Franciscan Order from Saint Francis to the Foundation of the Capuchins*. Rome, 1987.

Noisette, Patrice. "Usages et représentations de l'espace dans la regula benedicti: Une nouvelle approche des significations historiques de la règle." In *Regulae Benedicti Studia: Annuarium internationale*. Erzabtei St. Ottilien, 1988, 69–80.

Noonan, John T. *The Scholastic Use of Usury*. Cambridge, Mass., 1957.

Nova, Alessandro. "I tramezzi in Lombardia fra XV e XVI secolo: Scene della Passione e devozione francescana." In *Il Francescanesimo in Lombardia: Storia e arte*, ed. M. D. Aberzoni et al. Milan, 1983, 197–214.

Nuti, Gian Carlo. "Pisa: 'Il Campo dei Miracoli.'" *Palladio: Rivista di storia dell'architettura* 4 (1964): 147–56.

Oberst, Johannes. *Die mittelalterliche Architektur der Dominikaner und Franziskaner in der Schweiz*. Zurich, 1927.

O'Carroll, Maura. "The Friars and the Liturgy in the Thirteenth Century." In *La predicazione dei frati dalla metà del '200 alla fine del '300: Atti del XXII convegno internazionale, Assisi, 13–15 ottobre 1994*, ed. E. Menestò. Spoleto, 1995, 189–227.

Ó Clabaigh, Colmán. *The Friars in Ireland*. Dublin, 2012.

Odetto, Gundisalvo. "La cronaca maggiore dell'ordine domenicano di Galvano Fiamma." *Archivum Fratrum Praedicatorium* 10 (1940): 297–373.

Olivieri, Achille. "Gli spazi mentali ed urbani della morte in occidente: Alcune tipologie mediterranee." *Ricerche di storia sociale e religiosa* 14 (1978): 119–34.

Olympios, Michalis. "Change of Orders: A Reassessment of the Excavated Church of Beaulieu Abbey, Nicosia." *Architectural History* 55 (2012): 22–55.

O'Malley, Michelle. *The Business of Art: Contracts and the Commissioning Process in Renaissance Italy*. New Haven and London, 2005.

Onians, John. "Santa Maria Novella and the Meaning of Gothic." In *Scritti di storia dell'arte in onore di Roberto Salvini*, ed. C. De Benedictis. Florence, 1984, 143–7.

Orlandi, Stefano, ed. *Necrologio di S. Maria Novella: Testo integrale dall'inizio (MCCXXXV) al MDIV corredato di note biografiche tratte da documenti coevi*. Florence, 1955.

Orme, Nicholas. "Church and Chapel in Medieval England." *Transactions of the Royal Historical Society* 6 (1996): 75–102.

Orsi, B. *Il S. Domenico di Prato: Notizie e documenti*. Prato, 1977.

Osborne, J. "The Tomb of Alfanus in S. Maria in Cosmedin, Rome." *Papers of the British School at Rome* 51 (1983): 240–7.

—. "The Roman Catacombs in the Middle Ages." *Papers of the British School at Rome* 53 (1985): 278–328.

Paatz, Walter and Elizabeth. *Die Kirchen von Florenz*. 6 vols. Frankfurt am Main, 1952–5.

Pace, Valentino. "Morte a Napoli: Sepolture nobiliare del Trecento." In *Regionale Aspekte der Grabmalforschung*, ed. W. Schmid. Trier, 2000, 41–62.

Palmerio, Giancarlo, and Gabriela Villetti. *Storia edilizia di S. Maria sopra Minerva in Roma, 1275–1870*. Rome, 1989.

Panella, Emilio. "Libri di ricordanze di S. Maria Novella in Firenze (XIV–XV sec.)." *Memorie Domenicane* 26 (1995): 319–67.

—. "Cronica fratrum dei conventi domenicani Umbro-Toscani (secoli XIII–XV)." *Archivum Fratrum Praedicatorium* 68 (1998): 223–94.

Paoli, Marco. *Arte e committenza privata a Lucca nel Trecento e nel Quattrocento: Produzione artistica e cultura libraria*. Lucca, 1986.

Paolini, Lorenzo. "Gli ordini mendicanti e l'inquisizione: Il 'comportamento' degli eretici e il giudizio sui frati." *Mélanges de l'École française de Rome, Moyen Âge/Temps Modernes* 89 (1977): 695–709.

——. "Domus e zone degli eretici: L'esempio di Bologna nel XIII secolo." *Rivista di storia della chiesa in Italia* 35 (1981): 371–87.

——. "Papato, inquisizione, frati." *Il papato duecentesco e gli ordini mendicanti: Atti del XXV convegno internazionale, Assisi, 13–14 febbraio 1998*, ed. E. Menestò. Spoleto, 1998, 179–204.

——. "Le finanze dell'inquisizione in Italia (XIII–XIV)." In *Gli spazi economici della chiesa nell'occidente mediterraneo (secoli XII–metà XIV)*, ed. Centro italiano di studi di storia e d'arte. Pistoia, 1999, 441–81.

——. "In merito a una fonte sugli 'Excessus' dell'inquisizione medievale, 2." *Rivista di Storia e letteratura* 39 (2003): 567–78.

Paravicini Bagliani, Antonio. *I testamenti dei cardinali del Duecento*. Rome, 1980.

Paravicini Bagliani, Antonio, and V. Pasche, eds. *La parrocchia nel medioevo: Economia, scambi, solidarietà*. Rome, 1995.

Paris, Matthew. *Historia Anglorum. Monumenta Germaniae Historica inde ab anno Christi quigentesimo usque ad annum millesimum et quingentensimum: Scriptores*, ed. Societas Aperiendis Fontibus rerum Germanicarum Medii Aevi, 28. Hannover, 1888, 390–434 (abbreviated as MGH *Scriptores*).

Pásztor, Edith. "La chiesa dei frati minori tra ideale di San Francesco ed esigenze della cura delle anime." In *Lo Spazio dell'Umiltà: Atti del convegno di studi sull'edilizia dell'ordine dei minori, Fara Sabina, 3–6 novembre 1982*, ed. M. B. Mistretta. Fara Sabina, 1984, 59–75.

——. "Ricordo di Raoul Manselli." In *La predicazione dei frati dalla metà del '200 alla fine del '300: Atti del XXII convegno internazionale, Assisi, 13–15 ottobre 1994*, ed. E. Menestò. Spoleto, 1995, 5–18.

Paton, Bernadette. " 'Una città faticosa': Dominican Preaching and the Defence of the Republic in Late Medieval Siena." In *City and Countryside in Late Medieval and Renaissance Italy: Essays Presented to Philip Jones*, ed. T. Dean and C. Wickham. Ronceverte, W.Va., 1990, 109–24.

Paul, Jacques. "Évangélisme et franciscanisme chez Louis d'Anjou." *Les Mendiants en Pays d'Oc au XIIIè siècle, Cahiers de Fanjeaux* 8 (1973): 376–401.

——. "Le Commentaire de Hughes de Digne sur la règle franciscaine." *Revue de l'histoire de l'église de France* 61 (1975): 231–41.

Pavoni, Romeo. "Il mercante." In *Condizione umana e ruoli sociali nel mezzogiorno normanno-svevo: Atti delle IX giornate normanno-sveve, Bari, 17–20 ottobre 1989*, ed. G. Musca. Bari, 1991, 215–50.

Paxton, Frederick S. *Christianizing Death: The Creation of a Ritual Process in Early Medieval Europe*. Ithaca, N.Y., 1990.

——. *Liturgy and Anthropology: A Monastic Death Ritual of the Eleventh Century*. Missoula, Mont., 1993.

——. "Communities of the Living and the Dead in Late Antiquity and the Early Medieval West." In *The Making of Christian Communities in Late Antiquity and the Middle Ages*, ed. M. Williams. London, 2002, 49–92.

——. "Death by Customary at Eleventh-century Cluny." In *From Dead of Night to End of Day: The Medieval Customs of Cluny*, ed. S. Boynton and I. Cochelin. Turnhout, 2005, 297–317.

——. "Performing Death and Dying at Cluny in the High Middle Ages." *Practicing Catholic: Ritual, Body and Contestation in Catholic Faith*, ed. B. T. Morrill, J. Ziegler, and S. Rodgers. New York, 2006, 13–56.

Pelhisson, Guillaume. *Chronique de Guillaume Pelhisson*, trans. J. Duvernoy. Toulouse, 1958.

Pellegri, M. "San Francesco del Prato (Parma)." *Parma nell'arte* 3 (1971): 129–49.

Pellegrini, Letizia. "I predicatori e i loro manoscritti." In *La predicazione dei frati dalla metà del '200 alla fine del '300: Atti del XXII convegno internazionale, Assisi, 13–15 ottobre 1994*, ed. E. Menestò. Spoleto, 1995, 113–39.

Pellegrini, Luigi. *Storia francescana: Momenti e problemi di storia francescana dalle origini al secolo 16.* Rome, 1973.

——. "L'ordine francescano e la società cittadina in epoca bonaventuriana." *Laurentianum* 15, nos. 1–2 (1974): 154–200.

——. "Gli insediamenti degli ordini mendicanti e la loro tipologia: Considerazioni metodologiche e piste di ricerca." In *Les Ordres mendiants et la ville en Italie centrale (v. 1220–v. 1350), Mélanges de l'École française de Rome, Moyen Âge/Temps Modernes* 89 (1977): 563–6.

——, ed. *Chiesa e società dal secolo IV ai nostri giorni: Studi storici in onore del P. Ilarino da Milano. Italia Sacra*, vol. 30, Rome, 1979a.

——. "Gli insediamenti francescani nella evoluzione storica degli agglomerati umani e delle circoscrizioni territoriali dell'Italia del secoli XIII." *Chiesa e società dal secolo IV ai nostri giorni*, ed. L. Pellegrini et al. *Italia Sacra*, vol. 30. Rome, 1979b, 195–237.

——. "Mendicanti e parroci: Coesistenze e conflitti di due strutture organizative della 'cura animarum'." In *Francescanesimo e la vita religiosa dei laici nel '200: Atti dell'VIII convegno internazionale, Assisi, 16–18 ottobre 1980*, ed. Società internazionale di Studi francescani. Università degli Studi di Perugia. Perugia, 1981, 129–67.

——. *Insediamenti francescani nell'Italia del Duecento.* Rome, 1984a.

—. "La prima fraternità minoritica ed i problemi dell'insediamento." In *Lo Spazio dell'Umiltà: Atti del convegno di studi sull'edilizia dell'ordine dei minori, Fara Sabina, 3–6 novembre 1982*, ed. M. B. Mistretta. Fara Sabina, 1984b, 17–57.

—. "Modalità insediative e organizzazione territoriale dei francescani in territorio Veneto nel secolo XIII." In *Storia e cultura a Padova nell'età di Sant'Antonio: Atti del convegno internazionle di studi, Padova, 1–4 ottobre 1981*, ed. Istituto per la storia ecclesiastica Padovana. Padua, 1985a, 152–81.

—. "A proposito di eremiti laici d'ispirazione francescana." In *I frati minori e il terzo ordine: Problemi e discussioni storiografiche; Atti del XXIII convegno del centro di studi sull spiritualità medievale, Todi, 17–20 ottobre 1982*, ed. S. da Campagnola. Todi, 1985b, 117–42.

—. "Territorio e città nella dinamica insediativa degli ordini mendicanti in Campania." In *Gli ordini mendicanti e la città: Aspetti architettonici, sociali e politici*, ed. J. Raspi Serra. Milan, 1990, 27–59.

—. "I francescani in Lombardia nel secolo XIII." In *Ordini religiosi e produzione artistica*. ed. M. T. Mazzilli Savini. Pavia, 1998, 27–42.

—. *Che sono queste novità: Le "religiones novae" in Italia meridionale (secoli XII e XIV)*. Naples, 2000.

Pelligrini, Luigi, and Stanislao da Campagnola, eds. *Il francescanesimo della Valle Reatina*. Rieti, 1993.

Pellegrini, P. Lodovico. *Alessandro IV e i Francescani (1254–1261)*. Rome, 1966.

Perdereau, M. "Les Cordeliers à Soissons de 1228 a 1587." *Mémoires de la fédération des sociétés d'histoire et d'archéologie de l'Aisne* 75 (1993): 57–109.

Perriaux, Lucien. *Histoire de Beaune et du pays beaunois: Des Origines préhistoriques au XIIIè siècle*. Paris, 1974.

Peterson, Ingrid. "The Third Order of Francis." In *The Cambridge Companion to Francis of Assisi*, ed. M. J. P. Robson. Cambridge, 2012, 193–207.

Petrucci, Armando. "Note su il testamento come documento." In *Nolens intestatus decedere: Il testamento come fonte della storia religiosa e sociale*, ed. A. Bartoli Langeli. Perugia, 1985, 11–15.

—. *Le scritture ultime: Ideologia della morte e strategie dello scrivere nella tradizione occidentale*. Turin, 1995.

Piastra, William. *Storia della chiesa e del convento di San Domenico in Genova*. Genoa, 1970.

Picou, F. "Églises et couvents de Frères Mineurs en France: Recuil de plans." *Bulletin archéologique du Comité des Travaux historiques et scientifiques* 17–18 (1984): 115–76.

Pietramellara, Carla T., ed. *Il sacro Convento di Assisi*. Rome, 1988.

Pines, Doralynn Schlossman. "The Tomb Slabs of Santa Croce: A New Sepoltuario." Ph.D. thesis, Columbia University, 1985.

Pirenne, Henri. "L'Instruction des marchands au Moyen Âge." *Annales d'histoire économique et sociale* 1 (1929): 13–28.

Piron, Sylvain. "Le Poète et le théologien: Une Recontre dans le studium de Santa Croce." *Picenum Seraphicum* 19 (2000): 87–134.

—. "Censures et condamnation de Pierre de Jean Olivi: Enquête dans les marges du Vatican." *Mélanges de l'École française de Rome* 118, no. 2 (2006a): 313–73.

—. "Franciscan 'Quodlibeta' in Southern 'Studia' and at Paris, 1280–1300." In *Theological Quodlibeta in the Middle Ages: The Thirteenth Century*, ed. C. D. Schabel. Leiden, 2006b, 403–38.

—. "Un Couvent sous influence: Santa Croce autour de 1300." In *Économie et religion: L'Expérience des ordres mendiants (XIIIè–XVè siècle)*, ed. N. Bériou and J. Chiffoleau. Lyon, 2009, 321–55.

Pirri, Pietro. *Il Duomo di Amalfi e il Chiostro del Paradiso*. Rome, 1941.

Poeck, Dietrich. "Laienbegräbnis in Cluny." *Frühmittelalterliche Studien* 15 (1981): 68–179.

Poloni, Alma. "Società e politica a Pisa nel Duecento: Un secolo di trasformazioni." In *Cimabue a Pisa: La pittura pisana del Duecento da Giunta a Giotto; Museo Nazionale di San Matteo*, exh. cat., ed. M. Burresi and A. Caleca. Pisa, 2005, 25–7.

Pranzataro, Umberto. *Diritto di sepolcro: nella sua evoluzione storica e nella speciali attinenze col diritto moderno*. Turin, 1895.

Prin, M. "La Première église des Frères Prêcheurs de Toulouse, d'après les fouilles." *Annales du Midi* 67 (1955): 5–18.

—. "L'Église des Jacobins de Toulouse: Les Étapes de la construction." *La Naissance et l'essor du gothique méridional du XIIIe siècle, Cahiers de Fanjeaux* 9 (1974): 185–208.

Quaglioni, Diego, Giacomo Todeschini, and Gian Maria Varanini, eds. *Credito e usura fra teologia, diritto e amministrazione: Linguaggi a confronto (sec. XII–XVI)*. Collection de l'École française de Rome, 346. Rome, 2005.

Quintavalle, Arturo Carlo, Andrea De Marchi, et al., eds. *Arredi liturgici e architettura*. Milan, 2007.

Ragni, C. "La povertà francescana e i tasti cittadini: Una ricerca a Perugia." *Annali della Facoltà di Lettere e Filosofia dell'Università di Perugia* 18 (1980–1): 51–74.

Rahtz, P. "Artefacts of Christian Death." In *Mortality and Immortality: The Anthropology and Archaeology of Death*, ed. S. C. Humphreys and H. King. London, 1981, 117–36.

Raspi Serra, J. "Esempi e diffusione della tipologia architettonica Minorita nell'Alto Lazio." *Bollettino d'Arte* 58 (1973): 207–12.

—. "Architettura francescana a Viterbo." *Storia della città* 9 (1978): 36–8.

—. "L'architettura degli ordini mendicanti nel principato salernitano." *Mélanges de l'École française de Rome, Moyen Âge/Temps Modernes* 93 (1981): 605–81.

—. "Le grandi chiese mendicanti di Rieti." In *Lo Spazio dell'Umiltà: Atti del convegno di studi sull'edilizia dell'ordine dei minori, Fara Sabina, 3–6 novembre 1982*, ed. M. B. Misttretta. Fara Sabina, 1984, 107–22.

—, ed. *Gli ordini mendicanti e la città: Aspetti architettonici, sociali e politici.* Milan, 1990.

Ravaglioli, A. "I santuari della Valle Santa di Rieti." *Lunario Romano* 21 (1992): 371–92.

Rebillard, É., and C. Sotinel, eds. *Économie et religion dans l'antiquité tardive.* Turnhout, 2006.

Recht, R. "L'Ancienne église des Dominicains de Colmar." *Congrès archéologique de France* 136 (1982): 9–24.

Redi, Fabio. *Pisa com'era: Archeologia, urbanistica e strutture materiali (secoli V–XIV).* Naples, 1991.

—. "Pisa." In *Enciclopedia dell'arte medievale*, vol. 9, ed. A. M. Romanini. Milan, 1998, 412–17.

Reichert, Benedictus Maria, ed. "Acta Capitulorum Generalium Ordinis Praedicatorum, I: Ab Anno 1220 usque ad Annum 1303." Vol. 3: *Monumenta Ordinis Fratrum Praedicatorum Historica*. Rome, 1898.

—. "Acta Capitulorum Generalium Ordinis Praedicatorum II: Ab Anno 1304 usque ad Annum 1378." Vol. 4: *Monumenta Ordinis Fratrum Praedicatorum Historica*. Rome, 1899.

Renard, Jean-Pierre. *La Formation et la désignation des prédicateurs au début de l'Ordre des Precheurs.* Fribourg, 1977.

Renouard, Yves. *Les Hommes d'affaires italiens du Moyen Âge.* Paris, 1968.

Reynaud, Jean-Francois. "Les Morts dans les cités épiscopales de Gaule du IVè au XIè siècle." In *Archéologie du cimitière chrétien: Actes du 2è colloque A.R.C.H.E.A., Orléans, 29 septembre–1 octobre 1994*, ed. H. Galinié and E. Zadora-Rio. Tours, 1996, 23–31.

Reynolds, Susan. *Kingdoms and Communities in Western Europe, 900–1300.* Oxford, 1984.

Riccetti, Lucio. "Orvieto: I testamenti del 'Liber donationem' (1221–1281)." In *Nolens intestatus decedere: Il testamento come fonte della storia religiosa e sociale*, ed. A. Bartoli Langeli. Perugia, 1985, 95–103.

—. "La facciata del Duomo di Orvieto: Cronologia, cantieri, committenza (1290–1310). *Nuova Rivista Storica* 91 (2007): 1–64.

Rich, J., ed. *The City in Late Antiquity.* London, 1992.

Richter, M. "Urbanitas-Rusticitas: Linguistic Aspects of a Medieval Dichotomy." In *The Church in the Town and Countryside*, ed. D. Baker. Oxford, 1979, 149–57.

Ricozzi, Paolo. "Necrologio di S. Maria Novella (1505–1666)." *Santa Maria Novella: Un convento nella città; Studi e fonti. Memorie Domenicane* n.s., 11. Pistoia, 1980, 219–324.

Riedl, P. A., and M. Seidel, eds. *Die Kirchen von Siena.* Munich, 1985.

Righetti Tosti-Croce, Marina. "Gli esordi dell'architettura francescana a Roma." *Storia della città* 9 (1978a): 28–32.

—. "Roma e la cultura Federiciana." *Storia dell'Arte* 34 (1978b): 289–98.

—."Architettura e scultura medievale." In *La basilica di Sant'Eustorgio in Milano*, ed. G. A. Dell'Acqua. Milan, 1984, 45–71.

—. "L'architettura tra il 1254 e il 1308." In *Roma nel Duecento*, ed. A. M. Romanini. Turin, 1991, 73–143.

—. "Domenicani." In *Enciclopedia dell'arte medievale*, vol. 5, ed. A. M. Romanini et al. Rome, 1994, 677–91.

—. "Francescani: Architettura." In *Enciclopedia dell'arte medievale*, vol. 6, ed. A. M. Romanini et al. Rome, 1995, 337–57.

Rigon, Antonio. "Orientamenti religiosi e pratica testamentaria a Padova nei secoli XII–XIV (prime ricerche)." In *Nolens intestatus decedere: Il testamento come fonte della storia religiosa e sociale*, ed. A. Bartoli Langeli. Perugia, 1985, 41–63.

—. *Clero e città: "Fratalea cappellanorum," parroci, cura d'anime in Padova dal XII al XV secolo.* Fonti e ricerche di storia ecclesiastica Padovana, 22. Padua, 1988.

—. "Frati Minori e società locali." In *Francesco d'Assisi e il primo secolo di storia francescana*, ed. A. Bartoli Langeli and E. Prinzivalli. Turin, 1997, 259–81.

—. "Frati minori, inquisizione e comune a Padova nel secondo Duecento." In *Il "Liber contractuum" dei frati minori di Padova e di Vicenza (1263–1302)*, ed. E. Bonato and E. Bacciaga. Rome, 2002, v–xxxvi.

—. "Conflitti tra comuni e ordini mendicanti sulle realtà economiche." In *L'economia dei conventi dei frati minori e predicatori fino alla metà del Trecento: Atti del XXXI convegno internazionale, Assisi 9–11 ottobre 2003*, ed. E. Menestò. Spoleto, 2004, 339–62.

Rinaldi, Rossella. "Dalla chiesa di San Nicolò delle Vigne al convento di San Domenico: Strutture sociali, topografia urbana, edilizia conventuale." In *Archeologia medievale a Bologna: Gli scavi nel Convento di San Domenico; Bologna, Museo Civico Archeologico*, exh. cat., ed. S. Gelichi and R. Merlo. Bologna, 1987, 75–90.

Ripoll, Thomas. *Bullarium Ordinis Praedicatorum. Rome, 1729–1740.*

Rippmann, D., B. Kaufmann, J. Schibler, and B. Stopp, eds. *Basel Barfüsserkirche: Grabungen 1975–1977; Ein Beitrag zur Archäologie und Geschichte der mittelalterlichen Stadt.* Olten, 1987.

Rizzi, A. "Le chiese degli ordini mendicanti a Treviso nel Due e Trecento in rapporto coltesto storico-ambientale." *Ateneo Veneto* 17 (1979): 3–18.

Robson, Janet. "The Pilgrim's Progress: Reinterpreting the Trecento Fresco Programme in the Lower Church at Assisi." In *The Art of the Franciscan Order in Italy*, ed. W. R. Cook. Leiden and Boston, 2005, 39–70.

Robson, Michael J. P. "Agnellus of Pisa, Minister Provincial of England (1224–1236)." In *Il francescanesimo a Pisa (secc. XIII–XIV) e la missione del Beato Agnello in Inghilterra a Canterbury e Cambridge (1224–1236): Atti del convegno di studi, Pisa, Chiesa di San Francesco 10–11 marzo 2001*, ed. O. Banti and M. Soriani Innocenti. Pisa, 2003, 1–30.

—. *The Franciscans in the Middle Ages.* Woodbridge, 2006.

—, ed. *The Cambridge Companion to Francis of Assisi.* Cambridge, 2012.

Robson, Michael J. P., and Jens Röhrkasten, eds. *Franciscan Organization in the Mendicant Context: Formal and Informal Structures of the Friars' Lives and Ministry in the Middle Ages.* Berlin and London, 2010.

Roccaro, Cataldo. "La 'scrittura' dei sermoni latini: Struttura e tecnica compositiva fra enunciazioni teoriche ed applicazione practica." In *La predicazione dei frati dalla metà del '200 alla fine del '300: Atti del XXII convegno internazionale, Assisi, 13–15 ottobre 1994*, ed. E. Menestò. Spoleto, 1995, 229–65.

Rocchi Coopmans de Yoldi, Giuseppe. *La basilica di San Francesco ad Assisi: Interpretazione e rilievo.* Florence, 1982.

—. "L'architettura della basilica di San Francesco in Assisi." In *La basilica di San Francesco ad Assisi*, ed. G. Bonsanti. Modena, 2002, 57–9.

—, ed. *S. Maria del Fiore e le chiese fiorentine del Duecento e del Trecento nella città delle fabbriche arnolfiane.* Florence, 2004.

—, ed. *La basilica di San Domenico di Perugia.* Perugia, 2006a.

—, ed. *S. Maria del Fiore: Teorie e storie dell'archeologia e del restauro nella città delle fabbriche arnolfiane.* Florence, 2006b.

Rohault de Fleury, G. *Gallia Dominicana: Les Couvents de St. Dominique au Moyen Âge.* Paris, 1903.

Röhrkasten, Jens. "Local Ties and International Connections of the London Mendicants." In *Mendicants, Military Orders, and Regionalism in Medieval Europe*, ed. J. Sarnowsky. Aldershot and Brookfield, Vt., 1999, 145–83.

—. "Regionalism and Locality as Factors in the Study of Religious Orders." In *Mittelalterlichen Orden und Klöster im Vergleich: Methodischen Ansätze und Perpektiven*, ed. G. Melville and A. Müller. Berlin, 2007, 243–68.

—. "L'Économie des couvents mendiants de Londres à la fin du Moyen Âge, d'après l'étude des documents d'archives et des testaments." In *Économie et religion: L'Expérience des ordres mendiants (XIIIè–XVè siècle)*, ed. N. Bériou and J. Chiffoleau. Lyon, 2009, 211–45.

—. "The Early Franciscans in the Towns and Cities." In *The Cambridge Companion to Francis of Assisi*, ed. M. J. P. Robson. Cambridge, 2012, 178–92.

Romanini, Angiola Maria. *L'architettura gotica in Lombardia.* Milan, 1964.

—. *Arnolfo di Cambio e lo "stil novo" del gotico italiano.* Milan, 1969.

—. "L'architettura degli ordini mendicanti: Nuove prospetive di interpretazione." *Storia della città* 9 (1978a), 5–15.

—, ed. *Architettura e urbanistica degli ordini mendicanti.* Milan, 1978b.

—. "Die Architektur der ersten franziskanischen Niederlassungen." In *800 Jahre Franz von Assisi: franziskanische Kunst und Kultur des Mittelalters: Katalog der Niederösterreichische Landesausstellung, Krems-Stein, Minoritenkirche, 15 Mai–17 Oktober 1982*, exh. cat., ed. H. Kühnel, H. Egger, and G. Winkler. Vienna, 1982, 404–11.

—, ed. *Roma anno 1300: Atti del congresso internazionale di storia dell'arte medievale, Roma, 19–24 maggio 1980.* Rome, 1983.

Romano, Serena. "Gli affreschi di San Pietro in Vineis." In *Il collegio Principe di Piemonte e la chiesa di San Pietro in Vineis di Anagni*, ed. M. Rak. Rome, 1997, 101–16.

—. "L'Aracoeli, il Campidoglio, e le famiglie romane nel Duecento." In *Roma Medievale: Aggiornamenti*, ed. P. Delogu. Florence, 1998a, 193–209.

—. "La Morte di Francesco: Fonti francescane e storia dell'Ordine nella basilica di San Francesco ad Assisi." *Zeitschrift für Kunstgeschichte* 61, no. 3 (1998b): 339–68.

—. "L'Arca di San Domenico." In *Memory and Oblivion: Proceedings of the 29th International Congress of* the History of Art held in Amsterdam, 1–7 September, 1996, ed. W. Reinink and J. Stumpel. Dordrecht, 1999, 499–513.

—. La basilica di San Francesco ad Assisi: Pittori, botteghe, strategie narrative. Rome, 2001.

—. La O di Giotto. Milan, 2008.

Ronan, Helen Ann. "The Tuscan Wall Tomb 1250–1400." Ph.D. thesis, Indiana University, 1982.

Ronzani, Mauro. "Gli ordini mendicanti e le istituzioni ecclesiastiche preesistenti a Pisa nel Duecento." Mélanges de l'École française de Rome, Moyen Âge/Temps Modernes 89 (1977a): 667–77.

—. "Penitenti e ordini mendicanti a Pisa sino all'inizio del Trecento." Mélanges de l'École française de Rome: Moyen Âge/Temps Modernes 89 (1977b): 733–41.

—. "L'organizzazione della cura d'anime nella città di Pisa (secoli XII–XIII)." In Istituzioni ecclesiastiche della Toscana medioevale, ed. C. Wickham et al. Galatina, 1980, 35–85.

—. "La 'chiesa del Comune' nelle città dell' Italia centro-settentrionale (secoli XII–XIV)." Società e storia 21 (1983a): 499–534.

—. "Gli ordini mendicanti e la 'cura animarum' cittadina fino all'inizio del Trecento: Due esempi." In Nolens intestatus decedere: Il testamento come fonte della storia religiosa e sociale, ed. A. Bartoli Langeli. Perugia, 1983b, 115–30.

—. "Il francescanesimo a Pisa fino alla metà del Trecento." Bollettino storico pisano 54 (1985): 1–55.

—. "Arcivescovi, chiesa cittadina e comune di Pisa nella prima metà del Trecento." Bollettino storico pisano 57 (1988a): 11.

—. "Il 'cimitero della chiesa maggiore Pisana': Gli aspetti istituzionali prima e dopo la nascita del Camposanto." Annali della Scuola Normale Superiore di Pisa, ser. 3, 18 (1988b): 1665–90.

—. "Da aula cultuale del vescovato a 'ecclesia maior' della città: Note sulla fisionomia istituzionale e la rilevanza pubblica del Duomo di Pisa." In Amalfi, Genova, Pisa, Venezia: La cattedrale e la città nel medioevo; Aspetti religiosi istituzionale e urbanistici, ed. O. Banti. Pisa, 1993, 71–102.

—. "Dal cimietro della chiesa maggiore di Santa Maria al Camposanto: Aspetti giuridici e istituzionali." In Il Camposanto di Pisa, ed. C. Baracchini and E. Castelnuovo. Turin, 1995, 49–56.

—. "Dall' 'edificatio ecclesiae' all'Opera di Santa Maria: Nascita e primi sviluppi di un'istituzione nella Pisa dei secoli XI e XII." In Opera: Carattere e ruolo delle fabbriche cittadine fino all'inizio dell'età moderna, ed. M. Haines and L. Riccetti. Florence, 1996, 1–70.

—. Chiesa e Civitas di Pisa nella seconda metà del secolo XI: Dall'avvento del vescovo Guido all'elevazione di Daiberto a metropolita di Corsica (1060–1092). Pisa, 1997a.

—. "La formazione della Piazza del Duomo di Pisa (secoli XI–XIV)." In La piazza del Duomo nella città medievale: Italia settentrionale, secoli XII–XV, ed. L. Riccetti. Orvieto, 1997b, 19–129.

—. "La chiesa e il convento di S. Francesco nella Pisa del Duecento." In Il francescanesimo a Pisa (secc. XIII–XIV) e la missione del beato Agnello in Inghilterra a Canterbury e Cambridge (1224–1236): Atti del convegno di studi, Pisa, Chiesa di San Francesco, 10–11 marzo 2001, ed. O. Banti and M. Soriani Innocenti. Pisa, 2003, 31–48.

—. "La chiesa pisana nel Duecento." In Cimabue a Pisa: La pittura pisana del Duecento da Giunta a Giotto; Museo Nazionale di San Matteo, exh. cat., ed. M. Burresi and A. Caleca. Pisa, 2005a, 29–32.

—. Un'idea trecentesca di cimitero: La costruzione e l'uso del Camposanto nella Pisa del secolo XIV. Pisa, 2005b, 29–32.

Rosenthal, J. T. The Purchase of Paradise: Gift Giving and the Aristocracy, 1307–1485. London, 1972.

Rosito, Massimiliano, ed. Santa Croce nel solco della storia. Florence, 1996.

Rossi, P. "Modena." In Enciclopedia dell'arte medievale, vol. 8, ed. A. M. Romanini. Rome, 1997, 496–505.

Rossini, G. L'architettura degli ordini mendicanti in Liguria nel Due e Trecento. Collana storico-architettura della Liguria occidentale, 22. Bordighera, 1981.

Rowell, Geoffrey. The Liturgy of Christian Burial: An Introductory Survey of the Historical Development of Christian Burial Rites. London, 1977.

Rubbiani, Alfonso. La chiesa di San Francesco in Bologna. Bologna, 1886.

—. La chiesa di San Francesco e le tombe dei glossatori in Bologna: Note storiche ed illustrative. Bologna, 1900.

Ruiz, Damien. "La Législation provinciale de l'ordre des frères mineurs et la vie économique des couvents en France et en Italie (fin XIIIè–milieu XIVè siècle)." In Économie et religion: L'Expérience des ordres mendiants (XIIIè–XVè siècle), ed. N. Bériou and J. Chiffoleau. Lyon, 2009, 357–86.

Rullo, Alessandra. "L'incontro di Boccaccio e Fiammetta in San Lorenzo Maggiore a Napoli: Un'ipotesi di ricostruzione del coro dei frati nel XIV secolo." In Boccaccio angioino, ed. G. Allano, T. D'Urso, and A. Perriccioli Saggese. Brussels, 2012, 303–16.

—. "Patronato laico e chiese mendicanti a Napoli: I casi di Santa Chiara e San Lorenzo Maggiore." In Committenza artistica, vita religiosa e progettualità politica nella Napoli di Roberto d'Angiò e Sancia di

Maiorca, ed. F. Aceto. Convengo internazionale di studi, 28–30 April 2011. Naples, 2014, in press.

Rusconi, Roberto. "De la Prédication à la confession: Transmission et contrôle de modèles de comportement au XIIIè siècle." In *Faire croire: Modalités de la diffusion et de la réception des messages religieux du XIIè au XVè siècle*, ed. J. Boutier. Collection de l'École française de Rome, 51. Rome, 1981a, 67–85.

———. "I francescani e la confessione nel secolo XIII." In *Francescanesimo e la vita religiosa dei laici nel '200: Atti dell'VIII convegno internazionale, Assisi, 16–18 ottobre 1980,* ed. Società internazionale di studi francescani. Assisi, 1981b, 251–309.

———. "La predicazione: Parole in chiesa, parole in piazza." In *Lo spazio letterario del medioevo II: La circolazione del testo.* Salerno, 1992, 571–603.

———. " 'Trasse la storia per farne la tavola': Immagini di predicatori degli ordini mendicanti nei secoli XIII e XIV." In *La predicazione dei frati dalla metà del '200 alla fine del '300: Atti del XXII convegno internazionale, Assisi, 13–15 ottobre 1994*, ed. E. Menestò. Spoleto, 1995, 405–50.

———, "Immagini della confessione sacramentale (secoli XII–XVI)." *Dalla penitenza all'ascolto delle confessioni: Il nuolo dei frati mendicanti. Atti del XXIII convegno internazionale, Assisi 12–14 ottobre 1995,* ed. E. Menestò. Spoleto, 1996, 263–85.

———, ed. *Francesco d'Assisi nelle fonti e negli scritti.* Bergamo, 2002.

Rush, Alfred. *Death and Burial in Christian Antiquity.* Washington, D.C., 1941.

Russell, J. C. *Late Ancient and Medieval Population.* Philadelphia, 1958.

Saalman, Howard. "Carrara Burials in the Baptistery of Padua." *Art Bulletin* 69, no. 3 (1987): 376–94.

Saffioti, T. *I giullari in Italia: Lo spettacolo, il pubblico, i testi.* Milan, 1990.

Salvatori, Marcello. "Costruzione della basilica dall'origine al secolo XIV." In *L'edificio del Santo a Padova*, ed. G. Lorenzoni. Vicenza, 1981, 31–81.

———. "Conventi e città: Rapporto tra conventi e città nell'evoluzione del fenomeno francescano." In *Francesco d'Assisi: Chiese e conventi*, ed. R. Bonelli. Milan, 1982a, 32–3.

———. "Le prime sedi francescane." In *Lo Spazio dell'Umiltà: Atti del convegno di studi sull'edilizia dell'ordine dei minori, Fara Sabina, 3–6 novembre 1982*, ed. M. B. Mistretta. Fara Sabina, 1982b, 77–106.

———. "Quadro storico geografico." In *Francesco d'Assisi: Chiese e conventi*, ed. R. Bonelli. Milan, 1982c, 13–22.

Samaritani, Antonio. "Mentalità religiosa nell'ora del testamento in una città italiana: Ferrara, durante le temperie degli ordini mendicanti (sec. XIII–XIV)."

Analecta pomposiana: Studi di storia religiosa delle diocese di Ferrara e Comacchio 7 (1982): 59–129.

Sandrini, Arturo, et al., eds. *Santa Maria della Scala: La grande "fabrica" dei Servi di Maria in Verona.* Verona, 2006.

Sanfilippo, Mario. "Il convento e la città: Nuova definizione di un tema." In *Lo Spazio dell'Umiltà: Atti del convegno di studi sull'edilizia dell'ordine dei minori, Fara Sabina, 3–6 novembre 1982*, ed. M. B. Mistretta. Fara Sabina, 1984, 327–41.

Santoro, E. *La basilica di San Domenico: Storia della sua demolizione (1859–1879).* Cremona, 1968.

Sapin, Christian. "Architecture and Funerary Space in the Early Middle Ages." *American Early Medieval Studies* (1999): 39–60.

Sapori, Armando. "La beneficenza delle compagnie mercantili del Trecento." *Archivio Storico Italiano* 4, no. 83 (1925): 251–72.

———. *Studi di storia economica medievale: secoli XIII, XIV, XV.* Florence, 1946.

Sartori, A. *Archivio Sartori: Documenti di storia e arte francescana.* Vol. 1: *Basilica e convento*, ed. G. Luisetto. Padua, 1983.

Savonni, D. "Il complesso architettonico di San Francesco in Brescia." *Arte Cristiana* 64 (1976): 189–98.

Saxer, Victor. *Morts, martyrs, reliques en Afrique chrétienne au premiers siècles.* Paris, 1980.

Sbaralea, Joannis Hyacinthi, ed. *Bullarium franciscanum romanorum pontificum . . .* Rome, 1768.

Scalia, G. "Ancora intorno all'epigrafe sulla fondazione del duomo pisano." *Studi medievali* 10 (1970): 483–519.

———. " 'Romanitas' pisana tra XI e XII secolo: Le iscrizioni romane del duomo e la statua del console Rodolfo." *Studi medievali* 13, no. 2 (1972): 791–843.

Scarlato, M. "Il monastero domenicano di Altomonte e Covella Ruffo." *Calabria Letteraria* 38 (1990): 68–70.

Schätti, Nicolas. "Chapelles funéraires de quelque églises de l'ancienne Savoie du Nord au XVè siècle: Organisation de l'espace sacré, décors et aménagement." In *Art, cérémonial et liturgie au Moyen Âge: Actes du colloque de 3ème cycle Romand de Lettres Lausanne-Fribourg, 24–25 mars, 14–15 avril, 12–13 mai 2000*, ed. Nicolas Bock. Rome, 2002, 595–610.

Schenkluhn, Wolfgang. *Ordines studentes: Aspekte zur Kirchenarchitektur der Dominikaner und Franziskaner im 13. Jahrhundert.* Berlin, 1985.

———. *La basilica di San Francesco in Assisi: ecclesia specialis; La visione di papa Gregorio IX di un rinnovamento della chiesa*, trans. G. L. Podestà. Milan, 1994.

—. *Architektur der Bettelorden: die Baukunst der Dominikaner und Franziskaner in Europa.* Darmstadt, 2000. Italian ed.: *Arch-itettura degli Ordini Mendicanti: Lo stile architettonico dei domenicani e dei francescani in Europa*, trans. A. M. Sbeveglieri. Padua, 2003.

—. "Regionale und Überregionale Prägung der Bettelordensarchitektur." In *Kunst & Region: Architektur und Kunst im Mittelalter.* Vol. 20: *Beiträge einer Forschungsgruppe (Clavis kunsthistorische Monografien)*, ed. U. M. Bräuer, E. S. Klinkenberg, and J. Westerman. Utrecht, 2005, 34–44.

Schmid, Josef. *"Et pro remedio animae et pro memoria": Bürgerliche Repräsentation in der Cappella Tornabuoni in S. Maria Novella.* Munich, 2002.

Schmid, Karl, and Joachim Wallasch. *Memoria: Der geschichtliche Zeugniswert des liturgischen Gedenkens im Mittelalter.* Vol. 48: *Münstersche Mittelalter-Schriften.* Munich, 1984.

Schmidt, Charles. *Notice sur le Couvent et l'église des Dominicains à Strasbourg.* Strasbourg, 1876.

Schröck, Katia, Bruno Klein, and Stefan Bürger, eds. *Kirche als Baustelle: Große Sakralbauten des Mittelalters.* Cologne, 2012.

Schwartz, Frithjof. "Die Memoria bei den Fratres: Das Grabmal des Fra Aldobrandino Cavalcanti und ein dominikanischer Typus für Bischofsgrabmäler." In *Grabmäler: Tendenzen der Forschung an Beispielen aus Mittelalter und früher Neuzeit*, ed. W. Maier, W. Schmid, and M. V. Schwarz. Berlin, 2000, 201–29.

—. *Il bel cimitero: Santa Maria Novella in Florenz 1279–1348. Grabmäler: Architektur und Gesellschaft.* Berlin and Munich, 2009.

Segagni Malacart, A. "L'Architettura." In *Storia di Piacenza.* Vol. 2: *Dal Vescovo Conte alla Signoria (966–1313)*, ed. P. Castignoli and M. A. Romanini. Piacenza, 1984, 435–601.

—. "Piacenza." In *Enciclopedia dell'arte medievale*, vol. 9, ed. A. M. Romanini. Rome, 1998, 347–63.

Seidel, Max. "Die Kanzel als Bühne: Zur Funktion der Pisani-Kanzeln." In *Begegnugen: Festschrift für Peter Anselm Riedl zum 60. Geburtstag*, ed. K. Güthlein and F. Matsche. Worms, 1993, 28–34.

Senocak, Neslihan. *The Poor and the Perfect: The Rise of Learning in the Franciscan Order, 1209–1310.* Ithaca and London, 2012.

Settis, Salvatore, ed. *Il Camposanto monumentale di Pisa: Le antichità.* Modena, 1984.

Shepherd, R. B. S. "The Church of the Friars Minor in London." *Archaeological Journal* 59 (1902): 238–87.

Showalter, Dennis E. "The Business of Salvation: Authority and Representation in the Thirteenth-century Dominican Order." *Catholic Historical Review* 58, no. 4 (1973): 556–74.

Sicard, Damien. *La Liturgie de la mort dans l'église des origines à la réforme carolingienne.* Liturgiewissenschaftlichen Quellen und Forschungen, vol. 63. Münster, 1978.

Sickert, R. *Wenn Klosterbrüder zu Jahrmarktsbrüdern werden: Studien zur sozialen Wahrnehmung der Franziskaner und Dominikaner im 13. Jahrhundert.* Berlin, 2006.

Silber, Ilana. "Gift-Giving in the Great Traditions: The Case of Donations to Monasteries in the Medieval West." *Archives européenes de sociologie* 36 (1995): 209–43.

Simi Varanelli, E. "La tipologia delle chiese a sala e la sua diffusione nelle Marche ad opera degli ordini mendicanti nei secoli XIII c XIV." *Annali della Facoltà di Lettere e Filosofia dell'Università di Macerata* 2 (1978): 131–85.

Simon, Robin. "Towards a Relative Chronology of the Frescoes in the Lower Church of San Francesco at Assisi." *Burlington Magazine* 158, no. 879 (1976): 361–6.

Sisi, Carolo. "Le tombe di Santa Croce." *Alla riscoperta delle chiese di Firenze.* Vol. 3: *Santa Croce*, ed. Timothy Verdon. Florence, 2004, 93–117.

Smith, Elizabeth Bradford. "Santa Maria Novella and the Problem of Historicism/Modernism/Eclecticism in Italian Gothic Architecture." In *Medioevo: Il tempo degli antichi; Atti del convegno internazionale di studi, Parma, 24–28 settembre 2003*, ed. A. C. Quintavalle. Milan, 2006, 621–30.

—. "Santa Maria Novella e lo sviluppo di un sistema gotico fiorentino." In *Arnolfo di Cambio e la sua epoca: Costruire, scolpire, dipingere, decorare; Convegno Internazionale di Studi, Firenze, Colle di Val d'Elsa, 7–10 marzo 2006*, ed. V. Franchetti Pardo. Rome, 2007, 289–98.

—. "City Planning in the Florentine Commune: Santa Maria Novella, its Piazza and its Neighborhood." In *Construir la ciudad en la Edad media*, ed. B. Arízaga Bolumburu and J. A. Solórzano Telechea. Logroño, 2010, 477–96.

Smith, Elizabeth Bradford, Ece Erdogmus, and Thomas E. Boothby. "Structural Appraisal of the Florentine Gothic Construction System." *Journal of Architectural Engineering* 13, no. 1 (2007): 9–17.

Spada, N. "I Frati Minori a Venezia nel terzo decennio del Duecento." *Le Venezie Francescane* 1, no. 2 (1932a): 71–6.

—. "Le origini del convento dei Frari." *Le Venezie Francescane* 1, no. 3 (1932b): 163–71.

Spigarolli, M. "Tempio francescano, palazzo publico, piazza della città: Piacenza alla fine del XIII secolo." *Storia della città*, 26/27 (1983): 149–54.

Stanford, Charlotte A. "Architectural Rivalry as Civic Mirror: The Dominican Church and the Cathedral in Fourteenth-Century Strasbourg." *Journal of the Society of Architectural Historians* 64, no. 2 (2005): 186–203.

—. "The Body at the Funeral: Imagery and Commemoration at Notre-Dame, Paris, about 1304–1318." *Art Bulletin* 89, no. 1 (2007a): 657–73.

—. "From Bishop's Grave to Holy Grave: The Construction of Strasbourg Cathedral's St. Catherine Chapel." *Gesta* 46, no. 1 (2007b): 59–80.

Stephens, John N. "Heresy in Medieval and Renaissance Florence." *Past & Present* 54 (1972): 25–60.

Stocker, A. D. "The Remains of the Franciscan Friary in Lincoln: A Reassessment." In *Archaeological Papers from York presented to M. W. Barley*, ed. P. V. Addyman and V. E. Black. York, 1984, 137–44.

Stouff, Louis. "Les Provençaux et la mort dans les testaments (XIIIè–XVè siècle)." *La Mort et l'au-delà en France méridionale (XIIè–XVè siècles), Cahiers de Fanjeaux* 33 (1998): 199–222.

—. "Ordres mendiants et société urbaine: L'Exemple d'Arles (XIIIè–XVè siècle)." In *La Ville au Moyen Âge: Actes du 120è congrès national des sociétés historiques et scientifiques, Aix-en-Provence, 23–29 octobre 1995*. Vol. 1: *Ville et espace au Moyen Âge*, ed. N. Coulet. Paris, 1999, 145–58.

Strazzullo, Franco. *Il complesso monumentale di San Francesco a Folloni in Montella*. Naples, 2000.

Strocchia, Sharon T. "In Hallowed Ground: The Social Meaning of Burial Revenues at Santa Maria del Carmine, Florence (1350–1380)." *Michigan Academician* 14 (1982): 445–52.

Stüdeli, B. E. J. *Minoritenniederlassungen und mittelalterliche Stadt: Beiträge zur Bedeutung von Minoriten- und anderen Mendikantenanlagen im öffentlichen Leben der mittelalterlichen Stadtgemeinde, insbesondere der deutschen Schweiz*. Franziskanische Forschungen 21. Werl, 1969.

Suitner Nicoloni, Gianna. "L'architettura religiosa medievale nel Veneto di terraferma." In *Il Veneto nel medioevo: Dai communi cittadini al predominio scaligero nella Marca*, ed. A. Castagnetti and G. M. Varanini, Verona, 1991, 493–591.

Sundt, Richard A. "The Churches of the Dominican Order in Languedoc, 1216 to ca. 1550." Ph.D. thesis, University of Wisconsin-Madison, 1981.

—. "*Mediocres domos et humiles habeant fratres nostri*: Dominican Legislation on Architecture and Architectural Decoration in the 13th Century." *Journal of the Society of Architectural Historians* 46 (1987): 394–407.

—. "The Jacobin Church at Toulouse and the Origin of its Double-Nave Plan." *Art Bulletin* 71 (1989): 185–207.

—. "From Half to Full 'Palmier': Factors Contributing to the Final Chevet Design of Toulouse's Jacobin Church." *AVISTA Forum* 9, no. 2 (1995–6): 7–15.

—. "Text as Visual Document: The Case of the Dominican Church at Nîmes." *Visual Resources* 9 (2010): 223–36.

Supino, Igino Benvenuto. *Il Camposanto di Pisa*. Florence, 1896.

—. *La basilica di San Francesco in Assisi*. Bologna, 1924.

Szittya, Penn. *The Antifraternal Tradition in Medieval Literature*. Princeton, N.J., 1986.

—. "Kicking the Habit: The Campaign Against the Friars in a Fourteenth-century Encyclopedia." In *Defenders and Critics of Franciscan Life: Essays in Honor of John V. Fleming*, ed. M. F. Cusato and G. Geltner. Boston, 2009, 159–76.

Sznura, Franek. *L'espansione urbana di Firenze nel Dugento*. Florence, 1975.

Tangheroni, Marco. "La piazza del Duomo come espressione di una civiltà mediterranea." In *Storia ed arte nella Piazza del Duomo: Conferenze 1992–1993*, ed. Opera della Primaziale Pisana. Pisa, 1996, 277–94.

Thode, Henry. *Franz von Assisi und die Anfänge der Kunst der Renaissance in Italien*. Berlin, 1885.

Thomas, Antoninus Hendrik. *De oudste constituties van de Dominicanen: Voorgeschiedenis tekst. Bronnel, onstaat en ontwikkeling (1215–1237)*. Leuven, 1965.

Thompson, Augustine. *Revival Preachers and Politics in Thirteenth-century Italy: The Great Devotion of 1233*. Oxford, 1992.

—. *Cities of God: The Religion of the Italian Communes 1125–1325*. University Park, Penn., 2005.

Thompson, Nancy M. "The Fourteenth-century Stained Glass of Santa Croce." Ph.D. thesis, University of Indiana, 1999.

Thomson, Williell R. *Friars in the Cathedral: The First Franciscan Bishops 1226–1261. Studies and Texts* 33. Toronto, 1975.

Tigler, Guido. "Tipologie di monumenti funebri." *Storia delle arti in Toscana*. Vol. 2: *Il Trecento*, ed. M. Seidel. Florence, 2004, 45–74.

Timbal, P. C. "Les Legs pieux au Moyen Âge." In *La Mort au Moyen Âge: Colloque de l'Association des historiens médiévistes français réunis à Strasbourg en juin 1975 au Palais Universitaire*, ed. B. Guillemain. Strasbourg, 1977, 23–6.

Tirelli, Vito, and Matilde Tirelli Carli, eds. *Le pergamene del convento di S. Francesco in Lucca (secc. XII–XIX)*. Rome, 1993.

Tocci, M. "Problemi di architettura minorita: Esemplificazioni in Puglia." *Bollettino d'Arte* 60 (1975): 201–8.

——. "Architettura mendicante in Puglia." *Storia della città* 9 (1978): 24–7.

Todenhöfer, Achim. "Apostolisches Ideal im sozialen Kontext: zur Genese der Bettelordensarchitektur im 13. Jahrhundert." *Marburger Jahrbuch für Kunstwissenschaft* 34 (2007): 43–75.

——. *Kirchen der Bettelorden: die Baukunst der Dominikaner und Franziskaner in Sachsen-Anhalt.* Berlin, 2010.

Todeschini, Giacomo. "Oeconomica franciscana: Proposte di una nuova lettura delle fonti dell'etica economica medievale." *Rivista di storia e letteratura religiosa* 12 (1976): 15–77.

——. *Il prezzo della salvezza: Lessici medievali del pensiero economico.* Rome, 1994.

——. *I mercanti e il tempo: La società cristiana e il circolo virtuoso della ricchezza fra medioevo ed età moderna.* Bologna, 2003.

——. *Richezza francescana: Dalla povertà volontaria alla società del mercato.* Bologna, 2004.

Tolaini, Emilio. "Campo Santo di Pisa: Progetto e cantiere." *Rivista dell'Istituto Italiano d'archeologia e storia dell'arte*, ser. 3, 17 (1994): 101–45.

——. "I muriccioli e i sarcofagi del Duomo di Pisa." *Bollettino storico pisano* 67 (1998): 129–41.

Tomei, Alessandro. "Un frammento ritrovato dal mosaico del monumento di Bonifacio VIII in San Pietro." *Arte medievale* 10 (1996): 123–31.

——. "Dal documento al monumento: Le lettere di Niccolò IV per Santa Maria Maggiore." *Studi medievali e Moderni* 1 (1997): 73–92.

Trachtenberg, Marvin. "Gothic/Italian Gothic: Towards a Redefinition." *Journal of the Society of Architectural Historians* 50 (1991): 22–37.

——. "Desedimenting Time: Gothic Column/Paradigm Shifter." *Res* 40 (2001): 5–27.

——. *Building-in-Time: From Giotto to Alberti and Modern Oblivion.* New Haven and London, 2010.

Treglia, Giovanna. "I beni immobili del Convento di San Francesco attraverso la documentazione archivistica." In *Il francescanesimo a Pisa (secc. XIII–XIV) e la missione del beato Agnello in Inghilterra a Canterbury e Cambridge (1224–1236): Atti del convegno di studi, Pisa, Chiesa di San Francesco 10–11 marzo 2001*, ed. O. Banti and M. Soriani Innocenti. Pisa, 2003, 105–16.

Trevisan, G. " 'Cum squadra et cordula et aliis edificiis ingeniosis': La facciata della chiesa di San Fermo Maggiore a Verona e la misurazione della distanza da Santa Maria della Scala nel 1327." In *Arredi ligurgici e architettura*, ed. C. Quintavalle, Milan, 2003, 143–51.

Trexler, Richard C. "Death and Testament in the Episcopal Constitutions of Renaissance Florence (1327)." In *Renaissance Studies in Honor of Hans Baron*, ed. A. Molho and J. A. Tedeschi. DeKalb, Ill., 1971, 29–74.

——. "The Bishop's Portion: Generic Pious Legacies in the Late Middle Ages in Italy." *Traditio* 28 (1972): 397–450.

Tugwell, Simon, ed. *Early Dominicans: Selected Writings.* New York, 1982.

——, ed. *Miracula Sancti Dominici Mandato Magistri Berengarii Collecta: Petri Calo Legendae Sancti Dominici.* Vol. 26: *Monumenta Ordinis Fratrum Praedicatorum Historica.* Rome, 1997.

——. "L'Évolution des 'vitae fratrum': Resumé des conclusions provisoires." *L'Ordre des Prêcheurs et son histoire en France méridionale, Cahiers de Fanjeaux* 36 (2001): 415–18.

Ulpts, I. "Stadt und Bettelorden im Mittelalter." *Wissenschaft und Weisheit: Franziskanische Studien zu Theologie, Philosophie und Geschichte* 58 (1995): 223–60.

Urban, G. "Die Kirchenbaukunst des Quattrocento in Rome." *Römisches Jarhbuch für Kunstgeschichte* 9–10 (1961–2): 73–289.

Urbani, Elena. "Santa Maria dei Servi." In *L'architettura gotica veneziana: Atti del convegno internazionale di studio; Venezia 27–29 novembre 1996*, ed. F. Valcanover and W. Wolters. Venice, 2000, 109–13.

Valenzano, Giovanna. "Santa Maria Gloriosa dei Frari." In *L'architettura gotica veneziana: Atti del convegno internazionale di studio; Venezia 27–29 novembre 1996*, ed. F. Valcanover and W. Wolters. Venice, 2000, 123–30.

——. "Le prime chiese degli ordini mendicanti." In *Ezzelini: Signori della Marca nel cuore dell'Impero di Federico II; Bassano del Grappa, Palazzo Bonaguro, 16 settembre 2001–6 gennaio 2002*, exh. cat., ed. C. Bertelli and G. Marcadella. Milan, 2001, 120–1.

——. "La suddivisione dello spazio nelle chiese mendicanti: Sulle tracce dei tramezzi delle Venezie." In *Arredi liturgici e architettura*, ed. A. C. Quintavalle. Milan, 2007, 99–114.

——. "Gli insediamenti degli ordini mendicanti," *Storia di Piacenza*: Vol. III: *Dalla signoria viscontea al principato Farnesiano (1313–1545)*, ed. P. Castignoli, Piacenza, 2007, 558–68.

Van Gennep, Arnold. *The Rites of Passage.* Chicago, 1960.

Varanini, Giorgio, and Guido Baldassarri, eds. *Racconti esemplari di predicatori del Due e Trecento.* Rome, 1993.

Vasoli, C. "Lo studio generale dell'ordine, crocevia di idee." In *Santa Croce nel solco della storia*, ed. M. Rosito, Florence, 1996, 46–64.

Vauchez, André, ed. *Les Ordres mendiants et la ville en Italie centrale (v. 1220–v. 1350): Mélanges de*

l'École française de Rome, Moyen Âge/Temps Mod-
ernes 89, no. 2, Rome, 1977.

——. *Ordini mendicanti e società italiana XIII–XV*
secolo. Milan, 1990.

——. "In merito a una fonte sugli *Excessus*
dell'inquisizione medievale, I." *Rivista di Storia e*
letteratura 39 (2003): 561–7.

——. "Grégoire IX et la politique de la sainteté." *Gre-*
gorio IX e gli ordini mendicanti: Atti del XXXVIII
convegno internazionale, Assisi, 7–8 ottobre 2010, ed.
Società Internazionale di studi Francescani, 38
(2011): 353–77.

——. *Francis of Assisi: The Life and Afterlife of a Medi-*
eval Saint. New Haven and London, 2012.

Vecchio, Silvana. "Le prediche e l'istruzione religiosa." In *La predicazione dei frati dalla metà del '200*
alla fine del '300: Atti del XXII convegno internazi-
onale, Assisi, 13–15 ottobre 1994, ed. E. Menestò.
Spoleto, 1995, 302–36.

Verde, A. F., ed. *Convento domenicano di S. Romano*
a Lucca. Pistoia, 1991.

Verdon, Timothy. "La più grande chiesa francescana." In *Alla riscoperta delle chiese di Firenze.*
Vol. 3: *Santa Croce,* ed. T. Verdon. Florence,
2004a, 9–32.

——. "Santa Croce nel contesto dell'arte dei secoli XIII–
XIV." In *Alla riscoperta delle chiese di Firenze.*
Vol. 3: *Santa Croce,* ed. T. Verdon. Florence,
2004b, 119–49.

Vergnolle, Élaine. "L'Ancienne collégiale Notre-
Dame de Beaune: Les Campagnes des XIIè et XIIIè
siècles." *Congrès archéologique de France* 152 (1997):
179–201.

Verhaeghe, F. "L'Espace civil et la ville: Rapport
introductif." *Archéologie des villes dans le Nord-*
Ouest de l'Europe, VIIè–XIIIè siècle: Actes du IVè
Congrès International d'Archéologie Médiévale
(1994): 145–90.

Vestri, Pietro, and Silvestro Bardazzi. *Prato: Nascita e*
sviluppo di una città di mercanti. Turin, 1983.

Viallet, Ludovic. "Procureurs et 'personnes interpo-
sées' chez les Franciscains." In *Économie et religion:*
L'Expérience des ordres mendiants (XIIIè–XVè siècle),
ed. N. Bériou and J. Chiffoleau. Lyon, 2009,
661–705.

Vicaire, M.-H. "De la règle de S. Augustin à la règle
de S. Dominique." In *Saint Dominique, l'idée,*
l'homme, et l'oeuvre, vol. 2, ed. P. Mandonnet and
M.-H. Vicaire. Paris, 1938, 203–30.

——. *Saint Dominique: La Vie apostolique.* Paris, 1965.

——. "Le Financement des Jacobins de Toulouse: Conditions spirituelles et sociales de construction
(1229–ca. 1340)." *La Naissance et l'essor du gothique*
méridional au XIIIè siècle, Cahiers de Fanjeaux 9
(1974): 208–53.

——. "Les Origines de la pauvreté mendiante des prêcheurs." *Vie dominicaine* 34 (1975): 59–79, 195–206,
and 259–79. (Republished in *Dominique et ses prê-*
cheurs. Fribourg, 1977, 222–65.)

——. *Dominique et ses prêcheurs.* Studia Friburgensia,
n.s. 55. Fribourg, 1977.

——. "Sacerdoce et prédication aux origines de l'ordre
des prêcheurs." *Revue des sciences philosophiques et*
théologiques 64 (1980): 241–54.

——. "Prêcheurs et paroisse." *La Paroisse en Languedoc*
(XIIIè–XIVè siècles), Cahiers de Fanjeaux 25 (1990):
261–83.

Villetti, Gabriela. "L'Edilizia degli ordini mendicanti:
Prospettive di ricerca." In *Gli ordini mendicanti e*
la città: Aspetti architettonici, sociali e politici, ed. J.
Raspi Serra. Milan, 1990, 179–93.

——. *Studi sull'ediliza degli ordini mendicanti.* Rome,
2003.

Vitale, Giuliana. "Nobiltà napoletana della prima età
angioina: Élite burocratica e famiglia." In *Ricerche*
sul medioevo napoletano: Aspetti e momenti della vita
economica e sociale a Napoli tra decimo e quin-
dicesimo secolo, ed. A. Leone. Naples, 1996,
187–223.

Vitolo, Giovanni. *Città e coscienza cittadina nel Mez-*
zogiorno medievale. Salerno, 1990.

——. " 'Vecchio' e 'nuovo' monachesimo nel regno
svevo di Sicilia." In *Friedrich II: Tagung des*
Deutschen Historischen Instituts in Rom im Geden-
kjahr 1994, ed. A. Esch and N. Kamp. Tübingen,
1996, 182–200.

——. "Il monachesimo benedittino nel Mezzogiorno
angioino: Tra crisi e nuove esperienze religiose." In
L'État Angevin: Pouvoir, culture, et société entre
XIIIè et XIVè siècles; Actes du colloque international
organisé par l'American Academy in Rome, l'École
française de Rome, l'Istituto storico italiano per il
medioevo, l'U. M. R. Telemme et l'Université de
Provence, e l'Università degli Studi di Napoli, 1995,
ed. École française de Rome. Rome, 1998, 205–20.

——. "La Noblesse, les ordres mendiants et les mouve-
ments de réforme dans le royaume de Sicile." In
La Noblesse dans les territoires angevins à la fin du
Moyen Âge: Actes du colloque international organisé
par l'Université d'Angers, ed. N. Coulet and J.-M.
Matz. Rome, 2000, 553–66.

——. *Tra Napoli e Salerno: La costruzione dell'identità*
cittadina nel Mezzogiorno medievale. Salerno, 2001.

Vogel, Cyrille. "Une Mutation cultuelle inexpliqué:
Le Passage de l'eucharistie communautaire à la
messe privée." *Revue des sciences religieuses* 54
(1980): 231–50.

——. "La Multiplication des messes solitaires au Moyen
Âge: Essai de statistique." *Revue des sciences reli-*
gieuses 55 (1981): 206–13.

Volpe, Gioacchino. *Movimenti religiosi e sette ereticali nella società medieval italiana, secoli XI–XIV.* Biblioteca storica Sansoni, 27. Florence, 1961.

Volti, Panayota. *Les Couvents des ordres mendiants et leur environnement à la fin du Moyen Âge: Le Nord de la France et les anciens Pays-Bas méridionaux.* Paris, 2003.

—. "L'Explicite et l'implicite dans les sources normatives de l'architecture mendiante." *Bibliothèque de l'École des Chartes* 16 (2004): 51–73.

Vovelle, Michel. *La Mort et l'occident de 1300 à nos jours.* Paris, 1983.

Wagner-Rieger, Renata. "Zur Typologie italienischer Bettelordenskirchen." *Römisches historisches Mitteilungen* 2 (1957–8): 266–98.

—. "San Lorenzo Maggiore in Neapel und die süditalienische Architektur unter den ersten Königen aus dem Hause Anjou." *Miscellanea Bibliotecae Hertzianae* 16 (1961): 131–43.

Walz, Angelus. *Beati Jordani de Saxonia Epistulae. Monumenta Ordinis Fratrum Praedicatorum,* 23, 1951.

Ward-Perkins, J. B. "Memoria, Martyr's Tomb and Martyr's Church." *Journal of Theological Studies* 17 (1966): 20–7.

Wickham, Chris, M. Ronzani, Y. Milo, and A. Spicciani, eds. *Istituzioni ecclesiastiche della Toscana medioevale.* Galatina, 1980.

Will, R. "Le Couvent des Cordeliers de Strasbourg et les origines de la place Kléber." *Cahiers alsaciens d'architecture et d'histoire* 12 (1968): 55–68.

Willesme, Jean.-Pierre. *Les Ordres mendiants à Paris.* Paris, 1992.

William of Saint-Amour. *De Periculis Novissimorum Temporum,* ed. and trans. G. Geltner. Dudley, Mass., 2008.

Williams, Arnold. "Chaucer and the Friars." *Speculum* 28 (1953): 499–513.

Williams, Howard. "Remembering and Forgetting the Medieval Dead: Exploring Death, Memory, and Material Culture in Monastic Archaeology." In *Archaeologies of Remembrance: Death and Memory in Past Societies,* ed. H. Williams. New York, 2003, 227–54.

Wolff, Charles. "Église Saint-Matthieu de Colmar." *Congrès archéologique de France* 136 (1982): 25–32.

Wollasch, Joachim. "Les Moines et la mémoire des morts." In *Religion et culture autour de l'an mil: Royaume capétien et Lotharingie,* ed. D. Iogna-Prat and J.-C. Picard. Paris, 1990, 47–54.

Wright, Georgia Sommers. "A Royal Tomb Program in the Reign of St. Louis." *Art Bulletin* 56 (1974): 224–43.

Yasin, Ann Marie. "Funerary Monuments and Collective Identity: From Roman Family to Christian Community." *Art Bulletin* 87 (2005): 433–57.

Zafarana, Zelina. "Predicazione francescana ai laici." In *I frati minori e il terzo ordine: Problemi e discussioni storiografiche; Atti del XXIII convegno del Centro di Studi sulla Spiritualità Medievale, Todi, 17–20 ottobre 1982,* ed. S. da Campagnola. Todi, 1985, 173–86.

Zannella, Caterina. "L'inserimento dei francescani a Ferentino." *Storia della città* 9 (1978): 39–43.

Zanotti, Gino. *La basilica di San Francesco in Bologna.* Bologna, 1973.

Ziche, Hartmut G. "Administrer la propriété de l'église: L'Évêque comme clerc et comme entrepreneur." *Antiquité tardive* 14 (2006): 69–78.

INDEX